MATRIARCH

BOOKS BY ANNE EDWARDS

Biography

A Remarkable Woman: A Biography of Katharine Hepburn
Matriarch: Queen Mary and the House of Windsor
Road to Tara: The Life of Margaret Mitchell
Sonya: The Life of Countess Tolstoy
Viven Leigh: A Biography
Judy Garland: A Biography

Autobiography

The Inn and Us with Stephen Citron

Novels

The Survivors
Miklos Alexandrovich Is Missing
Haunted Summer
Shadow of a Lion
The Hesitant Heart
Child of Night

Children's Books

The Great Houdini
Barnum
A Child's Bible

MATRIARCH

Queen Mary and the House of Windsor

Reprint Edition of the Classic

ANNE EDWARDS

ROWMAN & LITTLEFIELD
Lanham • Boulder • New York • London

The author would like to thank the Radio Hulton Picture Library, *Illustrated London News,* and British Museum for permission to reprint the following photographs: Princess Mary Adelaide; Duke of Teck; Prince Franz, Duke of Teck, with children; Princess May at 7; the Teck family in 1891: Radio Hulton Picture Library; The Prince of Wales: *Illustrated London News;* Page from *North London Press,* November 30, 1889: British Museum; Duke of Clarence in hunting outfit; Duke of Clarence in uniform; Balmoral, c. 1891; Queen Victoria in cart with dog and Tsar and Tsarina, c. 1896: Radio Hulton Picture Library; Princess May, c. 1891: *Illustrated London News;* wedding picture; Prince George and the future Nicholas II, 1892; York Cottage, Sandringham; Sandringham; Princess May with Edward, Prince of Wales; Queen Victoria and her family, 1895; Princess May, Duchess of York, with two infant sons; Two future Kings of England; Prince George and Prince John, 1909; The four oldest York children; Princess May as Duchess of York; Interior York House; The drawing room at Sandringham; Edward VII with Caesar; Princess May in dress worn at Coronation of Edward VII; King Edward VII and Queen Alexandra on Royal Yacht; Mr. and Mrs. George Keppel: Radio Hulton Picture Library; Mrs. George Keppel: *Illustrated London News;* Nine kings; Funeral procession, King Edward VII; The new Prince of Wales: Radio Hulton Picture Library; Coronation, interior Westminster Abbey: *Illustrated London News;* Queen Mary, Coronation procession; Queen Mary in Coronation robes; Entering Delhi; Leaving the train; The Durbar Coronation: Radio Hulton Picture Library; King George as big-game hunter: *Illustrated London News;* Under pavilion, Indian Durbar; King George and Queen Mary: Radio Hulton Picture Library; Princess Victoria Louise and Prince Ernest Augustus; Kaiser Wilhelm and King George: *Illustrated London News;* Queen Mary wearing the Durbar Emeralds; Queen Mary and King George with President and Mrs. Wilson: Radio Hulton Picture Library; Prince of Wales with King George in France: *Illustrated London News;* Queen Mary reviewing arsenal; Review of American troops; King George and his four sons: Radio Hulton Picture Library; Queen Mary in car; Royal brothers; Royal guests; Wedding of Lord Mountbatten and Miss Edwina Ashley: Radio Hulton Picture Library; Prince of Wales at the Derby, 1926: *Illustrated London News;* Queen Mary smiling; The Prince of Wales and Mrs. Simpson; Freda Dudley Ward with Sir P. Sassoon: Radio Hulton Picture Library; Gloria Vanderbilt and Lady Thelma Furness; Royal group on balcony: *Illustrated London News;* Queen Mart with granddaughter Elizabeth II: Radio Hulton

Picture Library; State funeral: *Illustrated London News*; Queen Mary and King Edward VIII; Queen Elizabeth and Osbert Sitwell; Eleanor Roosevelt and King George VI; Three Queens; The Royal Family at Royal Lodge; Four Generations: Radio Hulton Picture Library; Queen Mary at the Festival of Britain; Queen Mary with grandson (Duke of Kent); Queen Mary's last photograph; a Royal Matriarch's funeral: Radio Hulton Picture Library.

Published by Rowman & Littlefield
A wholly owned subsidiary of The Rowman & Littlefield Publishing Group, Inc.
4501 Forbes Boulevard, Suite 200, Lanham, Maryland 20706
www.rowman.com

Unit A, Whitacre Mews, 26-34 Stannery Street, London SE11 4AB, United Kingdom

Distributed by NATIONAL BOOK NETWORK

British Library Cataloguing in Publication Information Available

The first edition of this book was previously cataloged by the Library of Congress as follows:

Edwards, Anne, 1927–
   Matriarch : Queen Mary and the House of Windsor
   Bibliography: p.
   Includes index.
   1. Mary, Queen, consort of George V, King of Great Britain, 1867–1953. 2. Windsor, House of. 3. Great Britain—Queens—Biography. I. Title.
   DA574.A2E38   1986
   941.083'092'4   [B]   85-24462

ISBN 978-1-4422-3655-4 (pbk. : alk. paper)
ISBN 978-1-4422-3656-1 (electronic)

♾™ The paper used in this publication meets the minimum requirements of American National Standard for Information Sciences—Permanence of Paper for Printed Library Materials, ANSI/NISO Z39.48-1992.

Printed in the United States of America

For Hilary
who helped me to span an ocean

CONTENTS

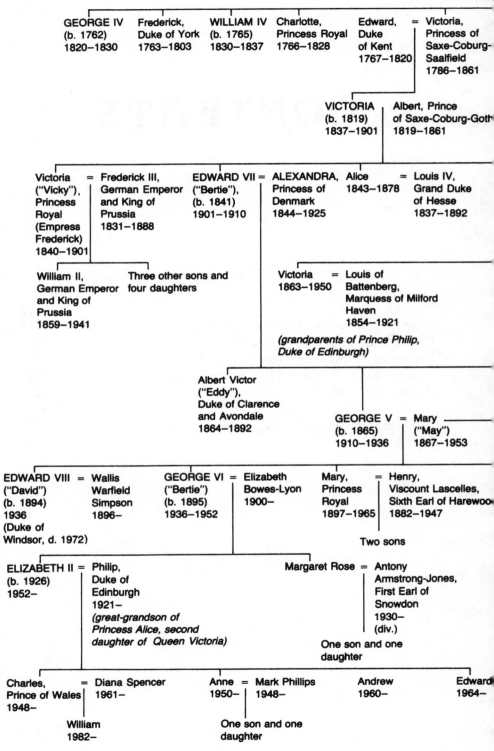

GEORGE
(b. 1738)
1760–1820

GEORGE IV
(b. 1762)
1820–1830

Frederick,
Duke of York
1763–1803

WILLIAM IV
(b. 1765)
1830–1837

Charlotte,
Princess Royal
1766–1828

Edward,
Duke
of Kent
1767–1820

= Victoria,
Princess of
Saxe-Coburg-
Saalfield
1786–1861

VICTORIA
(b. 1819)
1837–1901

Albert, Prince
of Saxe-Coburg-Gotha
1819–1861

Victoria
("Vicky"),
Princess
Royal
(Empress
Frederick)
1840–1901

= Frederick III,
German Emperor
and King of
Prussia
1831–1888

EDWARD VII =
("Bertie"),
(b. 1841)
1901–1910

ALEXANDRA,
Princess of
Denmark
1844–1925

Alice
1843–1878

= Louis IV,
Grand Duke
of Hesse
1837–1892

William II,
German Emperor
and King of
Prussia
1859–1941

Three other sons and
four daughters

Victoria
1863–1950

= Louis of
Battenberg,
Marquess of Milford
Haven
1854–1921

*(grandparents of Prince Philip,
Duke of Edinburgh)*

Albert Victor
("Eddy"),
Duke of Clarence
and Avondale
1864–1892

GEORGE V = Mary
(b. 1865)   ("May")
1910–1936   1867–1953

EDWARD VIII =
("David")
(b. 1894)
1936
(Duke of
Windsor, d. 1972)

Wallis
Warfield
Simpson
1896–

GEORGE VI =
("Bertie")
(b. 1895)
1936–1952

Elizabeth
Bowes-Lyon
1900–

Mary,
Princess
Royal
1897–1965

= Henry,
Viscount Lascelles,
Sixth Earl of Harewood
1882–1947

Two sons

ELIZABETH II =
(b. 1926)
1952–

Philip,
Duke of
Edinburgh
1921–
*(great-grandson of
Princess Alice, second
daughter of Queen Victoria)*

Margaret Rose =

Antony
Armstrong-Jones,
First Earl of
Snowdon
1930–
(div.)

One son and one
daughter

Charles,
Prince of Wales
1948–

= Diana Spencer
1961–

Anne =
1950–

Mark Phillips
1948–

Andrew
1960–

Edward
1964–

William
1982–

One son and one
daughter

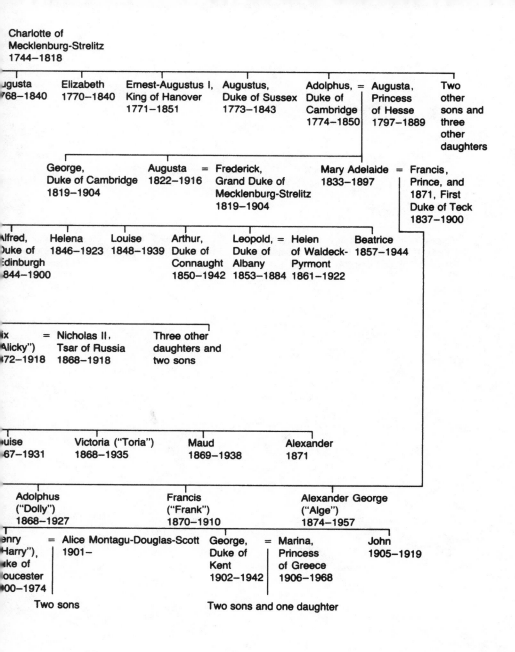

Charlotte of
Mecklenburg-Strelitz
1744–1818

ugusta
768–1840

Elizabeth
1770–1840

Ernest-Augustus I,
King of Hanover
1771–1851

Augustus,
Duke of Sussex
1773–1843

Adolphus, = Augusta,
Duke of   Princess
Cambridge of Hesse
1774–1850 | 1797–1889

Two
other
sons and
three
other
daughters

George,
Duke of Cambridge
1819–1904

Augusta   = Frederick,
1822–1916   Grand Duke of
            Mecklenburg-Strelitz
            1819–1904

Mary Adelaide = Francis,
1833–1897   Prince, and
                1871, First
                Duke of Teck
                1837–1900

Alfred,
Duke of
Edinburgh
1844–1900

Helena
1846–1923

Louise
1848–1939

Arthur,
Duke of
Connaught
1850–1942

Leopold, = Helen
Duke of   of Waldeck-
Albany   Pyrmont
1853–1884 1861–1922

Beatrice
1857–1944

ix   = Nicholas II,
Alicky")   Tsar of Russia
872–1918   1868–1918

Three other
daughters and
two sons

uise
67–1931

Victoria ("Toria")
1868–1935

Maud
1869–1938

Alexander
1871

Adolphus
("Dolly")
1868–1927

Francis
("Frank")
1870–1910

Alexander George
("Alge")
1874–1957

enry   = Alice Montagu-Douglas-Scott
Harry"), | 1901–
ke of |
oucester |
00–1974 |

George,   = Marina,
Duke of   Princess
Kent   of Greece
1902–1942 1906–1968

John
1905–1919

Two sons

Two sons and one daughter

PREFACE

In the first half of this century, wars came and went, foreign powers fell, countries disappeared in alarming numbers from the maps of the world, but the English monarchy and Queen Mary remained to provide an element of continuity. Although consort and not part of the direct line, her maternal grandfather was the son of George III and had been fourth in line to the throne after Victoria. Queen Mary was the daughter-in-law of Edward VII, wife of George V, mother of Edward VIII and George VI, and grandmother of Elizabeth II. Close examination of her character, her dedication to the cause of monarchy, the influence she had on lives inextricably linked with hers solves a great many mysteries on how Great Britain survived the eclipse of other European monarchies and maintained its strength and stability even—and perhaps especially—during the trying days of the Abdication of King Edward VIII, Queen Mary's eldest son and the future Duke of Windsor.

On a clear winter night in 1936, King Edward VIII publicly renounced the throne "for the woman I love." After his famous broadcast, made from Windsor Castle, he returned to nearby Royal Lodge where his mother, sister, and three brothers (the oldest of whom was now King) had listened to his radio speech.* His youngest brother could not contain his emotion. He shook his head and cried almost fiercely, "It isn't possible! It isn't happening!" Tall and elegant, her silver hair piled high, ropes of pearls swirling down the front of her grey chiffon gown, Queen Mary showed no outward signs of emotion. She asked for her coat, and her daughter prepared to leave with her for London and her home at Marlborough House. Her four sons followed her out into the hallway.

"Goodbye David, God go with you," she said to the son who for ten months had been Great Britain's uncrowned King. Then she turned to her second son, the lean, nervous, stuttering young man, with the slightly bulging rabbity eyes, to whom she knew this unexpected happening in his life was a severe blow, and she curtsied. "God save the King," she said clearly and then departed, leaving her eldest son with the distinct feeling that with her words one King had been unthroned and another created. For him, his mother, Queen Mary, had always been the very essence of monarchy.

*His sister was Princess Mary, his three brothers Prince Albert (soon to be crowned George VI), Prince Henry (Duke of Gloucester), and Prince George (Duke of Kent).

I live with bread like you, feel want
Taste grief, need friends; subjected thus,
How can you say I am a king?

SHAKESPEARE
King Richard II, Act III, Scene III

Abergeldie

Balmoral Castle

Braemar

Glamis

Wood Farm

Sandringham
York Cottage

Buckingham Palace
Kensington Palace
St. James's Palace
Clarence House
Marlborough House
York House
White Lodge, Richmond

Badminton

Windsor Castle
Frogmore

Bognor Regis

Osborne House
Isle of Wight

Eastbourne

PART ONE

WHEN GRANDMAMA WAS QUEEN

ONE

The rumours were correct. The summons to Balmoral Castle by Her Majesty, Queen Victoria, could be interpreted only one way. Princess May of Teck was being considered as a suitable wife for Prince Albert Victor, Duke of Clarence and Avondale, known as Prince Eddy and second heir to the British Throne. Even to contemplate the possibility of one day becoming Queen Consort of England was a heady experience for the twenty-four-year-old woman. The fact that Prince Eddy was one of her less endearing Wales cousins and that he had never taken the slightest interest in her was no deterrent. Royalty was a profession, and she was being given a chance to audition for its most highly coveted role.

November 4, 1891, was blustery cold and London a hard, metallic grey. Princess May's parents, the Duke and Duchess of Teck, drove with her and the eldest of her three brothers, Prince Adolphus ("Dolly") from their home, White Lodge, Richmond, to see her safely aboard the train at Euston Station for Aberdeen. At first glimpse, the young woman would not have been called beautiful. A touch of merriment gleamed in her deeply set, clear China-blue eyes, and when amused, her softly curved mouth twitched into a fleeting smile. Yet, little diminished the gravity of Princess May's expression. ("I always have to be so careful not to laugh," she once confided to a friend,* "because, you see, I have such a *vulgar* laugh.")

Princess May's natural beauty was easy to overlook for she combed her shiny wheat-coloured hair into an unflattering style, too high and tight at the sides and with a frizzled, low fringe in front that had prompted the Queen to remark that Princess May resembled nothing so much as a poodle with her hair so low on her forehead. Nonetheless, the style was distinctive, adding inches to her height (she was five foot, six inches tall) and giving her a statuesque elegance, an impression she much enjoyed and was to nurture throughout her life.

The young woman sat between her slim, moustached brother and her aristocratic, if foppish-looking, father in the front seat. The entire rear seat of the luxurious carriage was occupied by her flamboyant mother, Princess Mary Adelaide, Duchess of Teck, who—though handsome of face and possessing a charismatic personality—was a woman of extraordinary girth, the most conservative estimate of her weight having been put at seventeen stone.† Fortunately, Princess Mary Adelaide was tall and carried herself well. She also dressed in exquisite taste and had the same startling blue eyes that she had bequeathed to her daughter. "Fat Mary," the people called her affectionately. She had always been popular because of her irrepressible high spirits and her accessibility at a time when the widowed Queen so seldom appeared in public (and on those rare occasions was to be seen swathed in black mourning clothes). Even now as she stifled her injured pride at not being invited by her cousin, the Queen,‡ to accompany Princess May and Prince Dolly to Bal-

---

*Mabell, Countess of Airlie (1866–1956), Queen Mary's Lady-in-Waiting for over fifty years.

†238 pounds.

‡Princess Mary Adelaide replied to Queen Victoria's summons: "Only a line not to keep the messenger too long waiting to thank you for your very kind letter and to say with what joy my Children will obey your gracious and more than kind summons. Though I must add that I feel inclined to be rather envious! and not a little jealous at being left out in the cold & not invited to accompany them! albeit *very much gratified* at your most kind wish to have them with you for a little while."

moral, Princess Mary Adelaide smiled broadly; chatted merrily away; leaned out a window, exposing her face to the raw winter day, and enthusiastically raised a pudgy hand to people on the streets who had recognised and waved at her, craning their heads to get a good look at her stylish hat and new furs. Princess Mary Adelaide had a passion for beautiful clothes and, as the superlative quality and lavish detail of her daughter's travelling outfit revealed, had passed on this extravagance to Princess May. Otherwise more conservative than her mother, Princess May did enjoy being well dressed.

The price of Princess Mary Adelaide's hat would have been a fortune to the countless men who had lost their jobs in the tottering economy. Yet, ironically, the majority of London's masses of poor did not begrudge the aristocracy their finery. Anarchists and revolutionaries existed, but the greater segment of the poor looked to the Royal Family for the colour and pagentry missing from their own drab lives. Princess Mary Adelaide with her ornate jewels and her fine feathers and opulent furs had become a pet of the public, a substitute perhaps for the mourning Queen.

Until the invitation had come from Balmoral, Princess May had not expected more than marriage to a sensible man of mediocre means and acceptable rank. She had been only too aware that among the royal houses of Europe a marriage between herself and one of their princes would have been deemed a misalliance because her own father, Prince Franz, Duke of Teck, was the son of a morganatic marriage.* To add to this difficult situation, the Duke of Teck was penniless, his wife impossibly extravagant, and the family had more than once barely sidestepped the bailiffs. In fact, Princess May's parents had often been the butt of sharp comment among royalty and the aristocracy.

*The Duke of Teck's father had been heir-apparent to the throne of Württemberg, a state in Southwest Germany with Stuttgart as its capital. His rights to the succession were forfeited in 1835 when he married the Hungarian Countess Rhedey; the marriage, because of the Countess's lower rank, was unconstitutional in Württemberg. Prince Franz thus had no claim in the succession. Countess Rhedey was trampled to death by a squadron of cavalry led by her husband, her mount having bolted while she watched manoeuvres, when Prince Franz was four years old.

19

Before their marriage, the Duke of Teck, who loved the good
life, had been living on his meagre military pay and an occasional handout from the Austrian Emperor. Though oversized,
as well as being four years older than he, Princess Mary Adelaide
was the impoverished Duke's greatest hope come true. Not until
after the wedding did he learn that his bride was as penniless
as he.

Queen Victoria had arranged for the Tecks to live in the South
Wing of Kensington Palace where she had been brought up as
a girl. On the stroke of midnight, on May 26, 1867, in the same
room and bed where the Queen had been born, Princess Mary
Adelaide gave birth to a daughter, christened Victoria Mary
Augusta Louisa Olga Pauline Claudine Agnes, but always called
"May" by her parents and family because of the month in which
she was born. When the new baby was one month old, Queen
Victoria made a rare expedition to London to see her son's—the
Prince of Wales's—firstborn daughter, Princess Louise, whom
she found "puny and pigeon breasted." After leaving Marlborough House, the Prince of Wales's home, the Queen headed
westward in an open carriage-and-four through "the densely
crowded Park to see dear Mary Teck. It seemed strange," she
wrote in her journal, "to drive into the old Courtyard and to get
out at the door, the very knockers of which were very old friends.
My dear old home, how many memories it evoked walking
through the well-known rooms!" At the top of the house, in the
room that had heard her own first lusty cries, the Queen saw
Princess May and deemed her "a very fine child, with quantities
of hair—brushed up into a curl on top of its head!"

In the next seven years, Princess May was to have three brothers, the eldest being Prince Adolphus. The Tecks were always
in humiliating debt. In 1883, when Princess May was sixteen,
they were in such "short street," with bailiffs set to seize their
possessions, that to escape their creditors they had run off to
Florence. There they fell upon the charity of relations and
friends. Only the Queen's grace permitted them to return to
England two years later to live modestly at White Lodge in
Richmond Park. Though not one of the Crown's most luxurious
houses, White Lodge had an historic past. On a table in the
study of this house, Lord Nelson "had dipped his finger in a

glass of port and sketched his plan for the Battle of Trafalgar." Edward, Prince of Wales, had been established at White Lodge when he was seventeen "under conditions of strict security so that he might be away from the world and lose himself entirely to study." The Prince of Wales was always to think of the house as a prison, and his time spent there—a sentence. But the Tecks had found it a prestigious home, and Princess Mary Adelaide, with her great flair for decoration, had added much to its charm, pretentious and overly elaborate though her additions might have been.

What saved the Teck family from ruin during Princess May's youth was her mother's keen ability to wheedle the Queen into advancing her large sums of money. But the importuning on the Crown had not made the family popular with their royal relations.

Princess May was never to forget the circumstances of her forced exile in Florence, and she was determined to turn this embarrassing period to her own advantage, learning German and studying art. At nineteen, she had made an unsuccessful London debut, for no beau appeared on the scene. Aware that her marriage prospects were grim and being a practical young woman, Princess May had lived quietly with her family at the understaffed White Lodge, assisting her mother with her household accounts and correspondence, giving much time to the London Needlework Guild, and reading six hours daily under the tutelage of Madame Bricka, "a tactless Alsatian woman with radical good brains." Yet, here she was on her way to Balmoral Castle with the possibility of becoming betrothed to the second heir to the British Throne.

The long ride to Euston Station could well have afforded Princess May time to think of how she, the most unlikely of all Princesses, was being considered. She knew Prince Eddy had become a serious problem to his parents, the Prince and Princess of Wales, and to his grandmother, the Queen. He had always been slow and immature, unable to grasp most situations, awkward in all sports except shooting, and frail in health. And, however steadfastly Princess May refused to consider it true, scandal was attached to his name.

In 1889, a police raid on a male brothel at 19 Cleveland

Street, not far from Euston Station, had spawned much private speculation about Prince Eddy's proclivities. The establishment catered to titled and wealthy homosexuals, and during that raid it was alleged that Prince Eddy's close friend, Lord Arthur Somerset, had been found with a young man. A warrant was issued in connection with these offences, but Lord Arthur (known in Court circles as "Podge") was able to flee the country before it could be served.

No proof was ever presented that Prince Eddy had been with "Podge" at the brothel. However, there was never any official denial to allay public suspicions that the police had concealed evidence (an accusation broadly hinted at in the press).

The Prince was a natural candidate for public conjecture because of the gossip and rumour that had steadily grown since his youth. Even his devoted mother, Alexandra, Princess of Wales, was aware of her elder son's shortcomings and did nothing to hide them. In 1883, when he was nineteen, the Princess had written to her son's childhood tutor, the Reverend John Dalton: "We are neither of us blind to his faults." And to her mother-in-law, the Queen, she wrote a short time later, "Eddy is a very good boy at heart though perhaps he is a little slow and dawdly which I always attribute to his having grown so fast."

Princess May had known Prince Eddy since childhood, and her memory of her cousin was not pleasant. In childhood, he had bullied her, and she had thought him dull-witted and had far preferred the company of his younger brother, Georgie. Boorish though he had been and still might be, Prince Eddy would one day be King, and if her stay at Balmoral proved successful, she would be Queen.

She had accepted the idea quite easily. The power, glory, and riches that came with the title could have been one reason, but the status such a marriage would bring her family was a great consideration. The Tecks had always been the poor royal relations, and her mother, whom she loved dearly, had been made to feel this all too frequently. Even she had been treated shabbily by her English relations at times. Under such circumstances, it would have been difficult for Princess May to refuse the most brilliant position in the realm; to become successively Duchess of Clarence and Avondale, Princess of Wales, and ultimately Queen Consort of England.

Her mother stepped down from the carriage with surprising grace and led the way through the harsh wind to the platform where she rendered her last-minute instructions ("Remember, Aunt Queen can't abide people who sleep late"). Princess Mary Adelaide then kissed her daughter on the cheek and hurried her two children into the carriage bearing the Royal Crest. Once they were situated, she stood implanted upon the platform dwarfing all else about her, one hand holding her boldly feathered hat, the other waving in the sharp wind as her daughter's train steamed out of the station and into the cold, grey distance.

At what moment in his childhood Prince Eddy realised that one day he was going to be King is hard to know. Years later his future great grand-nephew, Charles, Prince of Wales, Heir-Apparent to the Throne,* was to say the knowledge was "something that dawns on you in the most ghastly inexorable sense. Slowly you get the idea that you have a certain duty and responsibility." Prince Eddy, at twenty-six, was aware of his future, but either he could not or did not want to grasp what he had to live up to in order to fulfil it.

Prince Eddy had been born January 8, 1864, two months premature and without preparations or a nurse in attendance. This had caused a furore, since the duty of the Home Secretary was to be present at the birth of those in direct succession to the Throne. From infancy the Prince had been blighted with poor health. As he matured, his lack of character and his inordinate slowness were causes for greater concern. From birth he bore a hearing deficiency, a problem which accounted for his learning disability. Since his mother was extraordinarily sensitive about it, suffering this same handicap, she was not told, and the condition was never medically treated. Prince Eddy was inclined to dark moods, and though his manners were correct, he was aloof and awkward, suffered a nervous tic, and possessed a piercing, unpleasant, high-pitched voice.

*Charles, Prince of Wales (1948-   ), Queen Mary's great-grandson.

His younger brother, Prince George, had quite another personality. Though only seventeen months separated them, Prince George was full of high spirits and eminently more attractive and adept at most things. The Princes were to be seen side by side throughout their youth. Their parents apparently believed that with their close association the older brother might eventually take on the younger's characteristics and hoped that the public would associate Prince Eddy with Prince George's bright affability.

The Royal brothers were schooled together until their mid-teens. Then, in a move that drew strongly adverse comment in Parliament, at fourteen and fifteen respectively, they were sent as cadets on a three-year world cruise aboard both H.M.S. *Britannia* and H.M.S. *Bacchante,* chaperoned by the Reverend John Dalton, whose duty was to report their activities to their parents. By the end of the cruise, expectations were that Prince Eddy might have matured into a more personable and knowledgeable young man. Instead, while Prince George learned the sea and navigation, his elder brother absorbed little except (according to Mr. Dalton) things of "a dissolute nature," referring to the young man's liking for alcohol and his penchant for escaping Mr. Dalton's careful guard to frequent seaside dives while in port with young ruffians of poor reputation.

On returning from their world travels, and after being away from the family for a painfully long time, the brothers were once again sent abroad—this time to Switzerland for six months to learn French. Such long separations in a family whose mother was almost incestuously close to her sons and to whom partings had invariably brought on the most terrible scenes of despair must have been difficult for the young Princes. An unusually close relationship existed between them. On Prince George's part, the responsibility for his brother and attendant lack of privacy had a sobering and maturing influence. When they were finally forced to go their independent ways—Prince Eddy to Cambridge to further his education and Prince George to pursue his naval career on H.M.S. *Canada* in the Royal Navy's West Indian and North American squadron—the older brother wrote:

24

My dear George. So we are at last separated for the first time and I can't tell you *how* strange it seems to be without you and how much I miss you in everything *all day long*.

While at Cambridge, Prince Eddy's tutor was James Kenneth Stephen,* a young man (twelve years his student's senior), who, according to his colleagues, was a scholar "with cultivated taste and a natural bent towards dainty and exquisite language." The relationship between tutor and pupil was extremely close, hardly surprising given Prince Eddy's lifelong dependence upon his brother and his position, which disallowed the usual friendships of university life. After two years at Cambridge, he was gazetted to the 10th Hussars, but the relationship with Stephen did not end, and they continued a frequent and intimate correspondence.

From the time Prince Eddy left Cambridge in 1885, he became the subject of intense family concern and public censure. There were persistent and worried exchanges that touched upon Eddy's "dissipations." What these might be was never spelled out. If, indeed, they were homosexual indiscretions, the Prince at least seemed to be attracted to women. To his parents' displeasure and the Queen's disapproval, he was reported in and out of love with a series of unsuitable ladies with alarming speed.

Alix of Hesse,† his first cousin, the daughter of his father's sister Princess Alice and of her husband, Louis IV, Grand Duke of Hesse, was his first acceptable Royal attachment. The Queen, anxious to see her problem grandson married and settled, was most agreeable to the idea of "Alicky" (her family name), as both a granddaughter and granddaughter-in-law. To her disappointment, Princess Alix refused the proposal.

"It's a real sorrow to us," the Queen wrote to her daughter, the Empress Frederick, in 1880, "she [Princess Alix] says that if she is *forced* she will do it—but that she would be unhappy & he

*James Kenneth Stephen (1852–1892), a cousin of Virginia Woolf (1882–1941).

†Alix of Hesse (1872–1918), later Empress Alexandra Fyodorovna of Russia. See Relationships.

—too. This shows gt strength of character as all her family & all of us wish it, & she refuses the greatest position there is."

Princess Alix had refused Prince Eddy's proposal on the grounds that she did not love her cousin in the way a woman should love her husband. The Queen, who had adored Prince Albert, could understand this rationale, even though love matches at that time were relatively rare among the Royal families of Europe. In fact, the Princess not only felt no passion for Prince Eddy, she found his lethargy and his immature appearance disagreeable. Even his mother had been alarmed by the last. "What I do not understand," she wrote Prince George upon receiving a photograph of her younger son with a full beard, "is why, you little mite, should have so much hair about you, whereas he [Prince Eddy], the biggest, has none yet?"

Prince Eddy finally had grown a small, blond cavalry moustache which was waxed and turned up at the ends, but his neck and arms were freakishly long and out of proportion to the rest of his body. Self-conscious about his awkward appearance, he wore high starched collars and extraordinarily wide cuffs, making him look more ridiculous and prompting his father to tease him unmercifully. "Don't call him Uncle Eddy," the sartorially splendid Prince of Wales would advise younger members of the Royal Family. "Call him 'Uncle-Eddy-Collars-and-Cuffs.' " This curious manner of dress and his father's often indiscreetly voiced nickname, "Collars-and-Cuffs," which soon became public knowledge, was to make Prince Eddy a whispered suspect for "Jack the Ripper."

On August 31, 1888, an aging prostitute named Mary Ann Nicholls was strangled to death and then fiendishly disemboweled in London's East End. Within the next nine weeks, four more women were murdered in the same bizarre, clinical, ritualistic, and horrifying fashion and in the same area—Whitechapel. Terror spread throughout London as the murderer, named by the press "Jack the Ripper," remained at large. The last victim, Mary Kelly, was pregnant; the final act of butchery the bloodiest. "Ripper" headlines circled the globe. The glare of publicity brought the terrible conditions that flourished in London's East End to the shocked attention of people all over the world. Sixty brothels were revealed to be operating at the time in White-

26

chapel. More than two hundred lodging houses were brothels in all but name. Prostitutes were so plentiful, their lives so futile, that they were indifferent to the dangers of dark alleys and deserted yards.

With the exposure of such squalid and appalling conditions, the incensed public demanded immediate action in the apprehension of the Ripper. The Queen took an active interest in the case; supposedly consulted with a psychic, a man named Lees; and made suggestions to the authorities on how the murderer might be caught. Eyewitness descriptions of the man suspected to be the Ripper and seen leaving the scene of one murder described him as being of medium height, possessing a small, fair moustache, and wearing a deer-stalker's hat and "collars and cuffs."

This last item of information gave rise to the theory espoused behind closed doors, and in the offices of the police station in the precinct of the "Jack the Ripper" atrocities, that Prince Eddy was the fiendish murderer. The accusation was never proved, but the Duke of Clarence's name remained linked with the horrendous crimes. People spoke of the fact that he hunted deer and had been taught how to dissect venison to remove their vital organs. A published photograph showed him wearing a deer-stalker's hat such as was described by the witnesses. And the *Court Circular*, which reported the whereabouts of the members of the Royal Family on a daily basis, had not included Prince Eddy's name on the dates and at the times of the murders. In effect, he had no alibi.

Other rumours proliferated, claiming that Prince Eddy was suffering from brain decay caused by syphilis. If true, the actions of his parents and the Queen gave no indication that they had this knowledge. They were concerned with his instability and were agreed that marriage to an attractive and solid young woman would greatly improve his public image.

After Prince Eddy's rejection by Princess Alix, he appeared to fall legitimately in love with the beautiful Princess Hélène of Orléans, second daughter of the Comte de Paris, head of the House of Bourbon (who had recently been banished from France and taken refuge in England). For over a year Prince Eddy and Princess Hélène gave every evidence of a young couple very much in love. But Princess Hélène was a Catholic. In order for them to marry, the Pope would have had to grant a dispensation.* The young people, with the Prince of Wales's prodding, enlisted the Queen's help. The idea of Prince Eddy forfeiting his rights to succession in order to marry Princess Hélène was discussed. The Pope refused to ordain such a marriage. Even if he had, Parliament would have intervened and the Queen could not have overridden its decision. If this had been a ploy on the part of the Crown to force Prince Eddy out of the line of succession in an honourable fashion, the scheme did not work.

The end of the relationship came in July 1891.† A month later Prince Eddy's erratic behaviour and his worsening appearance (waxy skin, sunken eyes, dark circles beneath them, and a careless disregard for his grooming and dress) gave his parents great anxiety. His love for Princess Hélène cannot be held responsible for his condition. Documentary evidence exists in the form of letters that he was simultaneously wooing another beautiful woman, Lady Sybil St. Clair-Erskine.‡

"I thought it was impossible a short time ago to love more than one person at the same time," he wrote Lady St. Clair-Erskine on June 21, 1891. "I only hope and trust that this charming creature which has so fascinated me is not merely playing with my feelings. I can't believe she would after what she has already said, and asked me to say." He closed with: "I am writing in an odd way and have no doubt you will think so but I do it for a particular reason and want you to promise me to cut out the crest and signature . . . for . . . supposing some one got hold of the letter by any chance? You understand why I say this?"

---

*It would have also required an Act of Parliament to enable Prince Eddy to retain his rights of succession in order to circumvent the English Constitution, where a King may neither be Catholic nor be married to a Catholic.

†Princess Hélène (b. 1871) married the Duke of Aosta in 1895, d. Naples January 20, 1951, daughter of Louis Philippe Albert d'Orléans, Comte de Paris (1838–94). (See footnote, page 57)

‡Lady Sybil St. Clair-Erskine (b. 1871) was the second daughter of the 4th Earl of Rosslyn; married the 13th Earl of Westmorland May 28, 1892; died 1910, leaving two sons and two daughters.

Lady St. Clair-Erskine did not cut out the crest and signature. Indeed, she preserved, intact, this and several other letters from her Royal admirer.

"I wonder if you really love me?" he wrote a week later. And, when he learned of Lady St. Clair-Erskine's engagement: "Don't be surprised if you hear before long that I am engaged also [a reference to Princess May], for I expect it will come off soon. But it will be a very different thing to what it might have once been [perhaps a reference to Princess Hélène] but it can't be helped."

This last letter was written just a few days after he had been given an ultimatum that if Princess May agreed, they were to be married. For Prince Eddy's drinking and carousing had become so public and his health so frail that the Prince of Wales had had his Private Secretary, Sir Francis Knollys, speak to the Princess of Wales to convince her that some drastic action must be taken. Sir Francis met with the Princess in her private sitting room at Marlborough House. "I told her," Knollys reported later to Sir Henry Ponsonby, the Queen's Private Secretary, "that the Prince [of Wales] would agree to:

"1. The Colonial Expedition [a plan the Prince of Wales endorsed and which would ensure Prince Eddy's absence from the public eye for a reasonably long time].

"2. The European *cum* Colonial Plan [to keep him away even longer].

"3. To be married to the Princess May in the Spring.

"She [the Princess of Wales]," Knollys continues, "came to the conclusion that she would prefer No. 3 and that he should marry Princess May in the Spring. I think the preliminaries are now pretty well settled, but do you suppose Princess May will make any resistance?"

The die was cast, and yet no one could be sure that the young woman who was even now en route to a rendezvous with the Queen would sacrifice her own future happiness for her "duty." Queen Victoria could not command her to marry Prince Eddy, and if the Queen's influence should fail, then what was to be done with the awkward problem of the Prince?

The choice of Princess May had been a careful, cautious process of elimination. Prince Eddy's wife not only had to be of

Blood Royal; to compensate for his failings she must be totally trustworthy and absolute in her sense of duty. Not many young women would have cared to fill the position. Queen Victoria was well aware of Princess May's bleak future and of her mother's ambitious nature. No other Princess of the Realm was as indebted to the Crown as was Princess Mary Adelaide's daughter. Princess Mary Adelaide would know how to apply the proper pressure to win over the young woman's cooperation, of that the Queen could be certain.

TWO

The next day Princess May wrote her mother: "Reached Aberdeen at 8, red carpet & the station master to meet us, felt rather shy, he took us to the hotel close by where we washed & breakfasted. Miss Cochrane [a member of the Queen's Household] joined us for breakfast & we left again by the 9:30 train (we kept our saloon carriage for Ballater)."

Princess May and her party were met by a royal carriage for the last leg of the journey, a ten-mile drive to Balmoral. The young woman's first view of the castle (designed for Queen Victoria by Prince Albert) was breathtaking. Set in the valley of the Dee in Aberdeenshire, and surrounded by the wild mountains of Cairngorms, it emerged in a light, snowy mist with a fanfare of turrets and towers, round and square, and rippling crenellations.

The Queen's life at Balmoral was deliberately isolated. There were fewer servants than at any of the other Royal residences, and the Queen was attended by the controversial John Brown, a Scotsman who had been with her since Prince Albert's death. Except for her daughter, Princess Beatrice, and her daughter's husband, Prince Henry of Battenberg, and their nursery full of children—three boys and a girl all under the age of five—who lived with the Queen, few guests were ever invited. The Castle of Abergeldie, which was several miles along the Dee, was occupied during early autumn by the Prince and Princess of Wales. The Queen's eldest granddaughter (and Prince Eddy's eldest sister), Princess Louise, spent the season with her much older husband, the Duke of Fife,* at Mar Lodge, beyond Braemar, a half hour's ride in good weather. The Queen remained at Balmoral from August until late November, relishing and protecting her privacy, making it difficult for her Prime Minister, Lord Salisbury,† whom she was obliged to see, to manage an audience. Since she passionately disliked the Liberal Party leader who had fought long and hard for Home Rule for Ireland, she was not terribly concerned about his comfort.

The proud, imperious old lady who would rule England longer than any other monarch remained in her heart as sentimental as the young girl she had been at the start of her reign in 1837. She was not an intellectual. She never thought of inviting to her table any of the galaxy of brilliant thinkers and writers who flourished during her reign—Macaulay, Carlyle, Ruskin, Tennyson, Browning, Darwin, Livingstone, Thackeray, Dickens, Trollope, Charlotte Brontë, George Eliot, and Robert Louis Stevenson, to name a few.

Still, the Queen was a fiery English patriot and in English politics a fierce partisan. She was indefatigably industrious and carried a unique authority to her judgement, which perhaps only Elizabeth I, and then in her later years, possessed. The Oxford movement, the socialist movement, the rationalist movement, and the feminist movement were all abhorrent to her plain and steadfast Conservatism. Yet, her Teutonic simplicity, her maternal qualities, her capacity for entering into the common griefs and joys of her ordinary subjects evoked the people's loyalty. Her Court (unlike that of her son, the Prince of Wales) was dull. So far as the public knew, no personal profligacy or scandal touched it. Ironically, the Prince of Wales's excesses and the censurable behaviour of the Duke of Clarence and Avondale brought her the esteem of the nation for her majestic forebearance.

*Duke of Fife (1849–1912). Created Duke of Fife 1889.

†Robert Arthur Salisbury (1830–1903), 3rd Marquess of, Prime Minister 1885–1886, 1887–1892, and 1895–1902. In each of his three ministries he acted as his own foreign minister.

The Queen possessed a strong mind and a stubborn nature. Her loyal servant, John Brown, might have been a bone of contention with her Cabinet, but she refused to dismiss him. Balmoral was a most difficult and far-removed location from which to rule a nation that in turn ruled about one-quarter of the world, but she still came there five months of the year to refresh the memories of her beloved Albert. A disgruntled Gladstone came as well, and her dispatch boxes containing all new matters of state business arrived. She often sat up late in the night to go through their contents to make up for the lost time of the long journey they must make back to London. She ruled her family with dedication and unswerving attention, and overlooked their faults with the same devoted blindness that kept her from seeing the faults of her nation.

As Princess May stepped down from the carriage before the front door of Balmoral, she could well have considered the importance of her visit for the Queen to have interrupted her much cherished privacy. Scotland was bitterly cold in November and the Queen would move shortly to Windsor, which would have made a meeting much easier. Quite obviously the woman Princess May called Aunt Queen felt their discussion could not be delayed.

None of what was happening came as a complete surprise to Princess May. There had been "rumblings" that had reached her ears. Her name *had* been linked with Prince Eddy's. They had seen each other once, recently, at a large family gathering, but her cousin had been almost unaware of her presence. At the time she had been concerned that she had not tried sufficiently hard to draw him out. Conversation of the purely social kind had never been easy for her, partly because her mother's loquaciousness gave her little opportunity to slip in a word, and partly because she was not one for small talk.

The next ten days were to be a "test," and she held up admirably in face of it. She possessed a great sense of the special circumstances of being born a royal personage, understanding that this gave her certain privileges, yet she was conscious that it also carried with it the weight of dedication and duty. Sir Francis Knollys need not have worried. No matter what Princess May's personal feelings about Prince Eddy (and she entertained

33

no romantic thoughts about her Wales cousin as had Princess Hélène), if Queen Victoria decided she should marry the Duke of Clarence, Princess May would do so.

The visit to Balmoral then was a call to duty, and Princess May entered the great house with majesty, her brother a few steps, almost deferentially, behind her. Outside, the beautiful pale-coloured stone of the façade had given the castle a softness, but the interior was formidably dark and dismal, Prince Albert's heavy Germanic tastes dominating everything. Woodwork and panelling were painted a murky amber. Rugs were a deep green tartan, as were many of the upholstery fabrics and the window drapes. There was a masculine odour in the hall, "a smell of wood fire, stags' heads [three of them shot by Prince Albert], rugs and leather . . . "

Upon her arrival at noon, Princess May was met by stout, fluttery Princess Beatrice, who, despite her matronly appearance, was at thirty-four the youngest of the Queen's nine children. A nervous woman of good nature, Princess Beatrice often functioned as secretary-companion to her mother, and the relationship between them bore some similarity to that of Princess May and the Duchess of Teck. Princess May had last seen Princess Beatrice and the Queen in the Spring of 1889 at the funeral of her grandmother (the ninety-one-year-old Duchess of Cambridge).* A short time later she was escorted through the winding corridors for her first audience at Balmoral with the Queen.

Upon being presented to Queen Victoria when she had been a small child, Princess May had burst into tears from fear. Through the years she had visited Windsor Castle quite often with her mother. The Queen had always enjoyed the company of children and, though she had numerous grandchildren of her own, frequently entertained the small Royal cousins. The quiet, serious Princess May had made a good impression.

Recollections of her previous royal visits were mainly as a

---

*The very elderly Duchess of Cambridge was Princess Mary Adelaide's mother and Queen Victoria's aunt. The Queen went to very few other funerals in the years after Prince Albert's death—her son Leopold's, and those of Lady Augusta Stanley and one of her maids (who died in the South of France). Later she was to attend Princess Mary Adelaide's funeral.

child, and then always in the company of her Wales cousins or her brothers. Never alone. After tea, at which—according to one of the Queen's grandchildren—"the children would squabble over a particular curly biscuit amongst all other biscuits," they could go to Grandmama's or Aunt Queen's (whichever the case might have been) room to play while she sat writing at a diminutive table. As in Balmoral and all of the Queen's homes, the Queen's boudoir was crowded with commemorative statuettes, miniatures, gold lockets containing strands of hair, and letter weights of bronze and marble hands modelled after death, for the Queen liked to surround herself with countless memorials to her beloved dead.

Princess May's tremendous awe towards her Aunt Queen continued throughout her childhood. "Mind you curtsy at the door," the children's nanny would admonish before they were allowed to enter. "Kiss Aunt Queen's hand, and don't make a noise, and mind you are good."

Now, in the cluttered sitting room at Balmoral with its clashing tartans and heavy furniture, she kissed her Aunt Queen's chubby hand and was rewarded with a fond, maternal smile.

Despite certain criticisms from her advisors, the Queen refused to abandon her mourning attire. Such a mark of respect to the dear departed was *de rigeur* at that time. But Albert, the Prince Consort, had been dead thirty years. The Queen was dressed as usual in black silk, with a very full skirt, the bodice buttoned down the front, and a square *décolletage* which was filled in with a dainty *chemisette* of white *lisse* (similar to tulle). The sleeves were wide, reaching to just below the elbow, and to them were attached full sleeves of white *lisse*—much like those of a bishop—fastened at the wrists with small buttons and loops. On her feet she wore flat-heeled silk-satin sandals with ribbons crossed over the instep. Her black stockings, the soles of which were white, were of the finest silk.

Over her wispy grey hair, which was caught back in a tiny bun, she wore a crisp, tulle cap with streamers.* When she withdrew her hand, her bracelets—which were gold chains hung with a

---

*Several diamond stars were added to the widow's cap in the dress she adopted for a dinner party or a formal function.

jumble of lockets containing strands of hair from her children and grandchildren—jangled. About her neck was a larger gold locket holding miniatures of two of her children. The Queen was at least seven inches shorter than Princess May, and, though not as fat as Princess Mary Adelaide, a considerable woman with several chins. At seventy-two years of age, her posture was as correct as that of the young woman whom she faced, and her eyes were quick to take in every detail of her visitor's appearance. Princess May regarded her Aunt Queen with no less awe than she had had for her as a child. She managed a few comments on her journey and then was relieved when, after a few minutes, lunch was announced. Dolly was seated to the left and she to the right of the Queen at the round mahogany table in the dining room. Stationed behind them, ready to serve the Queen, were two of her famous Indian servants in their crimson costumes and winding turbans. A rare glint of winter sun shone through the huge arched windows of the otherwise dark wood-panelled room.

To Princess May's surprise (and moderate disapproval), the Battenbergs' two eldest children, Prince Alexander and Princess Ena, five and four years old respectively, joined the luncheon group, little Ena, her long blond hair held back by a starched bow, perched on two pillows to reach the table.

"Your dear children arrived safely after 12, looking very well," the Queen telegraphed to Princess Mary Adelaide. "Fine day. Very pleased to see them here."

In answer to which the Duchess of Teck wrote her daughter: "Most dear & kind & thoughtful of her! I feel *sure* you are already quite *sous son charme* & becoming very devoted to 'Aunt Queen.'"

Balmoral was a mystical experience for Princess May. In early morning the winter hoarfrost was so thick one could not see beyond the great arched windows. By noon visibility returned, but Balmoral remained a world unto itself since the castle was so isolated.

Never before had Princess May been in daily contact with monarchial power. The Queen's unrelenting majesty greatly impressed her. Upon hearing the rustle of her voluminous black silk skirts in the dim corridors of the castle, footmen and maids instantly drew to attention. Not even with Princess Beatrice did the Queen abandon Royal protocol; only with the children did she relax her stiff household laws.

Despite her age and weight, and in the face of the bracing and often bitter Scottish weather, the Queen went out daily. The satin slippers would be replaced by sturdy boots, her black silk dress hidden beneath heavy woollen outer garments. Snow fell during much of Princess May's stay at Balmoral. Nonetheless, she accompanied the Queen on her daily outings, often walking long distances around the grounds where every turn of a path brought one face to face with a statue, erect or recumbent; an inscribed granite drinking fountain; or a seat dedicated to the memory of a relation or a faithful retainer, or even a pet dog. During these country walks, the Queen came to know Princess May as a grown woman, and Princess May came to understand the heavy duties, the total dedication that were required of a monarch. The Queen was surprised by Princess May's maturity, her superior intelligence, and—most of all—her intuitive grasp of situations. Educated far better than her Wales cousins, including Prince Eddy, Princess May was also fluent in French and German, the latter ability—because it recalled Albert's Teutonic cadences—greatly pleasing to the Queen.

By the time Princess May left Balmoral, the Queen's tacit approval to the plan for her and Prince Eddy to marry was certain. In fact, on November 18, just a few days after Princess May's departure, the Queen wrote the Empress Frederick: "You speak of May Teck. I think & hope that Eddy will try & marry her for I think she is a superior girl. Quiet & reserved *till* you know her well, but she is the reverse of *oberflächlich.* She has no frivolous tastes, has been very carefully brought up & is well informed & always occupied."

Princess Mary Adelaide had never had too many loyal admirers in the Royal circle. Members of the aristocracy were sometimes as critical. One of these Court detractors was Lady Geraldine Somerset ("Podge's" mother),* a woman of violent temper and great charm in combination. On her part, Princess

*Lady Geraldine Somerset (1832–1915). Well known for her Journal. She was closely related to the Sitwell family.

Mary Adelaide had always admired Lady Geraldine's ability to speak French, Italian, and German correctly and fluently, and to write in a fine hand. In fact, Lady Geraldine had been a model for the kind of daughter Princess Mary Adelaide wanted to bring up. Neither mother nor daughter ever realised what a false friend Lady Geraldine was, and yet, in a curious way, Princess May might well have owed her education to her.

The day of Princess May's return from Balmoral, the Teck family, all except Princess May, called upon Lady Geraldine. After they had departed, Lady Geraldine recorded in her Journal, "Presently the rest of the party came P[rincess] M[ary Adelaide], P[rince] T[eck] and Dolly just returned (this morning only) from Balmoral!—Evidentally that is to be!!! P[rincess] M[ary Adelaide] informed me 'the Queen has fallen in love with my children! specially May!!!' She thinks her . . . *so amusing* (the very last thing in the world I should say she is!!!) . . . The Duke talking of May's prospects!! enchanted at them!!"

The betrothal was almost certain when the Prince of Wales wrote to his mother, the Queen: "You may, I think, make your mind quite easy about Eddy—& that he has made up his mind to propose to May but we thought it best *'de pas brusque les choses'* & as she is coming to us with her Parents after Xmas to Sandringham everything will I am sure be satisfactorily settled then."

The day this was written, however, the plans were suddenly changed. The Wales family decided not to wait until Christmas. Princess May was that day leaving for a visit to Luton Hoo, the Bedfordshire home of the Tecks' good friends, Mr. Christian de Falbe, the Danish Minister at the Court of St. James, and his rich English wife, Eleanor; and, since the Princess of Wales was Danish, their home was the ideal place for the two young people to come together and for Prince Eddy, if so inclined, to propose.

The young man whom Princess May knew could soon be her husband and about whom she had heard the most terrible of rumours looked thin and stiff, somewhat like a tailor's dummy in his clothes. His brown wavy hair had already begun to recede, and his fair moustache was so heavily waxed and so sharply turned up at the ends that it looked artificial. Though oddly doe-shaped, his eyes were a soft brown and his profile aquiline.

He was, indeed, awkward in appearance, a fact emphasised more by his astonishingly long neck, the high white starched collar he still insisted upon wearing, his almost simian arms cuffed at his knobby wrists, and his stiff gait caused by gout—a most unusual complaint for one so young. Despite these distractions, his slow, languid manner and the way he had of smiling slyly and glancing out of the sides of his eyes gave Prince Eddy a sensual quality. Yet it is hard to imagine that Princess May, who had found him disagreeable as a child, could suddenly have fallen in love with him, dismissing all gossip, his far inferior mind, immaturity, and strangeness.

The sun was shining when on December 2, 1891, Princess May left for Luton Hoo in a large party of over twenty invited guests which included Prince Eddy and Lord Arthur Somerset —the same infamous "Podge" who had been involved in the Cleveland Street scandal. Two years had passed since "Podge" had gone abroad to avoid prosecution, and he had only recently returned and reestablished his close association with Prince Eddy. The conversation while en route centered on the recently published and heatedly discussed *The Picture of Dorian Gray* by Oscar Wilde. Prince Eddy had not read it, unlike "Podge," who described its shocking contents in colourful detail.

Luton Hoo was a luxurious country house and the de Falbes were superb hosts. Little free time was afforded their guests. During the day they played tennis, went boating on the estate's small, gemlike lake, took drives through the surrounding woods, visited the church in the neighbouring town of Hatfield, and did some shooting. The Danish minister and his wife loved tropical plants, and card games of whist, halma, and bezique were played in the conservatory (a large glass-domed room filled with potted palms, exotic climbing plants, camellias, begonias, sweet geraniums spilling out of wicker wheelbarrows, and brilliantly feathered birds flapping about in ornate cages). The one difficulty about all this tropical splendour was that, as Princess May had written on a previous visit, " . . . the heat was so terrific that we nearly all died of it, it was like being shut up in a hot house."

Thursday, December 3, the day following her arrival at Luton Hoo, Princess May lunched with the shooting party (including Prince Eddy) and took a walk with them in the afternoon through the thick, dark woods behind the estate. The sport of shooting had always distressed her, and the constant report of the guns and the sight of the day's bag, bloodied feathered creatures piled high, left her feeling depressed. Her spirits were, however, lifted that evening, for the de Falbes were the patrons of a county ball held in their gaily decorated ballroom. Princess May loved dancing, and she dressed for the gala affair with great relish in a mauve-and-deep-rose, lavishly beaded ball gown, one of her mother's most extravagant purchases, which had shocked the more conservative members of her circle (" . . . over 40 pounds for *one* gown! most probably torn to shreds the very first night she wears it!—it is monstrous!" the capricious Lady Geraldine Somerset commented).

Prince Eddy stood on the sidelines and watched the dancers whirling about in the gilt and mirrored ballroom. When Princess May, flushed and laughing and looking quite lovely, stepped off the dance floor with Arthur Somerset, he asked her to come with him. He then led her away from the sound of the Viennese waltz music and through the winding upstairs corridors of the large house, coming to a stiff halt at the door of Mme. de Falbe's boudoir, which he opened and then stepped back for his flustered cousin to enter first. Obviously the moment had been prearranged, for the door was unlocked, the stuffy, overdecorated room deserted, and a fire burned in the grate.

Prince Eddy closed the door and faced Princess May. For the first time the two of them were alone. He stood staring at her for a long time in the flickering light from the fire, and her shyness returned. Nervously, she began to edge back to the door, but he took her hand and began what sounded like a short, memorised speech. "To my surprise, Eddy proposed to me during the evening in Mme. de Falbe's boudoir—of course I said yes," adding to her observations in her diary that she and Prince Eddy "flitted about in suppressed excitement," and that later, when she told the other young ladies in her party about the engagement, she had picked up her skirts and "waltzed round and round" her bedroom. No comment exists in her diary of any fond feelings for Prince Eddy or mention of her own happiness. Instead, there is a sense of gloating, of a competition won.

The ten days at Balmoral had reached their final outcome.

The Queen had approved the match, Prince Eddy had accepted the Royal dictum and Princess May his proposal. The news of the engagement did not heighten the gaiety of the weekend. Prince Eddy occupied himself with shooting most of the next day. That evening he and Princess May played bezique together, but not alone. The following morning they were photographed standing in the garden at Luton Hoo, a winter sun casting a harsh light that pointed up the reserved expressions on both their faces. Prince Eddy departed for London and Windsor immediately after the picture was taken, to tell his parents of the engagement and to seek the final approval of Queen Victoria, a necessary bit of protocol. The newly engaged couple could hardly have come to know one another well, for they were alone only once.

By that evening, when the newspapers all carried the engagement picture and were filled with romantic stories about the Royal couple, Lady Geraldine Somerset recorded in her diary: "The newspapers are twaddling and *asinine* over this desperate love match and the attachment of years triumphing over all obstacles! Columns of *rot*. How Princess Hélène must laugh in her sleeve as she reads of this long devotion! And P. Alix of Hesse, too!"

On that same day Princess May returned to London by train and was greeted at Euston Station by a lustily cheering crowd. Radiant, dressed elegantly in a blue velvet suit trimmed in the finest lace,* and accompanied by a protective Prince Dolly, Princess May waved to the public as confidently and exuberantly as her mother had done in the past. The Tecks—mother, father, Princess May and her three brothers—lunched at Marlborough House with the Prince and Princess of Wales and Prince Eddy. Later, the Queen, making one of her infrequent journeys into London, was ushered in to congratulate the affianced couple. As Princess May curtsied and kissed Queen Victoria's hand, she could easily have had a moment of speculation as to how it might one day feel to receive such obeisance and to wear the Crown.

*Throughout most of her life Queen Mary was to keep a record of the clothes and jewels she wore on special occasions.

THREE

The morning following the luncheon at Marlborough House, a silent, brooding Prince Eddy accompanied Princess May and her parents down to Windsor Castle to spend a week as guests of the Queen. The engaged couple sat at the front of Prince Eddy's private coach with Prince Franz, who kept up a lively conversation with his wife, seated—as was her habit—in the rear. Always the optimist, Princess Mary Adelaide attributed the sulky behaviour of her son-in-law-to-be to his irritation at not being able to be alone with his fiancée. In fact, Prince Eddy had just learned that his former teacher and close friend, James Kenneth Stephen, had been committed to a mental institution and suspected his engagement to Princess May could have been the cause.

In forty-eight hours Princess May's life had taken a dramatic and swift change. Though her disposition was inclined to the pragmatic and she had resignedly accepted her future, the now-altered attitudes of her parents and even the servants at White Lodge toward her were difficult for her to assimilate. She was not sure what to expect during her week at Windsor, but she had a suspicion she was to receive a short, intense course in the special requirements of her new status.

The massive gates of Windsor swung open, and Prince Eddy's carriage, emblazoned with his royal arms, moved toward the

Sovereign's entrance. Princess May sat stiffly, a fixed smile on her face, and when the door of the carriage was opened and the royal footmen stood on each side to assist her down, she looked every bit a Queen-to-be. Once inside, she was greeted with the special Windsor Castle smell—ancient furniture heavily polished and musk-scented flowers. An *aura* pervaded Windsor Castle that extended to the dignified pages, the housekeeper in black silk and lace cap, and the elegant equerry-in-waiting. The Queen's private apartments were rich with gilded woodwork and plaster, elaborate carved doors, and sumptuous crimson and shimmering green silk brocaded walls. The wide, endless corridor, which connected one part of the castle to another, had been built by George IV to accommodate a vast and magnificent collection of paintings. As a child, Princess May had played hide-and-seek with her Wales cousins in this corridor, running in and out among the marble statuary that lined it.

Windsor Castle held many childhood memories for Princess May. In the vast, dark-panelled library (William IV's contribution) the visiting children had called to one another with shrieks of joy, up and down the austere Gothic corridors lined with bookshelves. Through the windows to one side were the gently sloping green lawns which spread away to the horizon and to the small hill that led down to Frogmore, the house that the Wales family occupied when at Windsor. Princess May had often had tea with the Wales sisters at Frogmore, while their brothers, Georgie and Eddy, played tag on the lawns. Bucolic as those activities were, Windsor was an ancient construction fraught with inconveniences and health hazards (Prince Albert's premature death from typhoid could well have been caused by the antiquated drainage system at the castle). Food was impossible to keep hot because of the distance servants had to travel from basement kitchens to upstairs dining rooms. Spillage en route caused them many burns, and poor lighting resulted in frequent nasty falls.

On this stay, Princess May would not visit the subterranean kitchens of Windsor which had been a wonderland to her when she was a child. The Queen never entered these rooms and, in fact, had no contact with the kitchen staff except for the Royal Chef, M. Menager, a tall, volatile Frenchman with a bushy grey moustache. The kitchens of Windsor were large, high-domed

43

rooms with white-tiled walls reflecting the giant, well-scrubbed, and polished copper pots which, when not in use, hung on hooks in a vast half-circle about each of the two huge black coal stoves that were warm on the coldest days and fragrant with the products of pastry chefs, roast cooks, bakers, confectioners, and *sauciers*. The kitchens had been a natural lure to the Royal children, who would sneak away from their nannies in small groups and, after a great deal of melodramatic cloak-and-dagger activity, wend their way through the castle's circuitous corridors to end up giggling in the kitchens, where they would be given fresh sweets and asked to leave in mock reproof by M. Menager.

The Royal Household for many years had had a permanent staff of three hundred; a kitchen staff of forty-five. In addition, the Queen employed four pages, the Scottish servants who rode on the box of her carriage, and the Indian servants whose sole duty was to prepare the curry that was served each day at luncheon whether the guests partook of it or not. The Indians were greatly resented by M. Menager and his kitchen staff, so that angry flurries of temper below stairs were frequent.

Whereas the Queen began her day with a Spartan boiled egg, served, however, in a gold egg cup and eaten with a gold spoon and with an Indian servant in full regalia at each Royal elbow in the lavishly decorated private dining room, Princess May, the Tecks, and everyone else, including the staff at Windsor, were served a five-course breakfast. Luncheon never had fewer than ten courses, dinner a minimum of twelve. There were no parties during the Tecks' stay at Windsor, but the intimate family, the Royal Entourage, and Princess May and her parents put the count at about twenty-four at every meal.

The engaged couple was never left alone. Repeating the pattern formed at Balmoral, the Queen demanded a good portion of Princess May's time. If family secrets involving Prince Eddy were discussed, the Princess gave no outward sign that she had been disturbed by them.

The Queen's approval of the match was obvious to all. The morning of her departure, Princess May and Prince Eddy accompanied her to the mausoleum, where she asked the posthumous blessing of her "dearly departed husband," Albert, for the engaged couple. To the Queen, this was as binding a ceremony as the exchange of vows, and henceforth she regarded Princess May as her "Darling Child," and as "My Granddaughter."

A letter bearing the Royal Seal awaited Princess May upon her return to White Lodge later that day (December 13, 1891). The Queen wrote that she rejoiced at Princess May becoming "My Grandchild" and assured her of "how much confidence I have in you to fill worthily the important position to which you are called by your marriage with Eddy.

"Marriage is the *most* important step which can be taken & should not be looked upon lightly or as *all roses*. The trials of life in fact *begin* with marriage, & no one should forget that it is only by mutually giving to one another, & by mutual respect & confidence as well as love—that true happiness can be obtained. Dear Eddy is a dear, good boy . . . "

Princess May was now getting to know the "dear, good boy" a great deal better, and her enthusiasm and courage began to flag. Her fiancé was slow and dull-witted at times. "Keep Eddy up to the mark," his father, the Prince of Wales, constantly reminded her. "See that Eddy does this, May," or "May, please see that Eddy does that." She soon found that she was answering a good portion of his correspondence and functioning—much as she had once done for her mother—as his private secretary.

Prince Eddy spent two days at White Lodge as the guest of the Tecks after their return from Windsor, and during that time Princess May cried to her mother: "Do you think I can *really* take this on, Mama?" Her mother assured her she could, and in no uncertain language that she *must*.

"Mary [Princess Mary Adelaide] is indeed a lucky person," the Empress Frederick wrote her mother, the Queen, "the *one wish* of her heart has been fulfilled for her child."

Princess Mary Adelaide's sister, the Grand Duchess Augusta of Mecklenburg-Strelitz, an autocratic woman who—though resident in her husband's country for over thirty years—retained her matriarchal control of the Teck family, corroborates this: "It is an immense position and has ever been your heart's desire, but it is a serious, great undertaking for poor May," she wrote the day that Princess May returned from Luton Hoo. Aunt Augusta, who was the Queen's contemporary, knew very well the limitations of Prince Eddy and had heard most of the rumours of his poor character. Yet, to her, "poor May" had no other recourse but to marry the future heir.

In the week before Christmas, the young couple drove about London incognito in the Prince of Wales's hansom, attended performances of *Cavalleria Rusticana* and the *Pantomime Rehearsal,* and glided in a gondola down a replica of the Grand Canal at an exhibition of "modern Venice" at Olympia. The Queen had given them rooms at St. James's Palace (recently occupied by Princess May's deceased grandmother, the Duchess of Cambridge), and Princess May and Prince Eddy selected new wallpapers. Their wedding day, February 27, was set so that the marriage could take place before Lent, and because, the Queen emphasised, "long engagements were very trying & not very good." Quite possibly the Queen feared that given more time to think about it, Princess May would change her mind.

On December 26, she and her betrothed attended a dance given by Prince Eddy's eldest sister, Princess Louise, who was a childhood friend. The occasion was a happy one for Princess May. "We danced to a most lovely Viennese band which played several things out of the lovely *Cavalleria Rusticana,*" she wrote to her Aunt Augusta, to whom she had been devoted since childhood. "It was a charming little fête & we all thoroughly enjoyed ourselves."

The holidays were the gayest she had ever spent, and her head was filled with plans. They were to marry "at Windsor & afterwards we are to drive thro' the principal streets of London on our way to St. Pancras to Sandringham for the honeymoon."

"Goodbye to 1891, a most eventful year to me," wrote Princess May on the last day of her 1891 diary.

Few unpleasantries had marred the excitement of the engagement. However, Prince George, recuperating from a serious case of typhoid (possibly ill-gotten at Windsor, for he had been a recent guest), had not been able to attend the festivities. At the funeral of Queen Victoria's half-sister's son (Prince Victor of Hohenlohe-Langenburg),* Prince Eddy had caught a slight

*Queen Victoria's half-sister was Princess Feodora of Leiningen, the Queen's mother having been the widow of Emich-Charles, Prince of Leiningen, before marrying the Queen's father, Edward, Duke of Kent.

cold, and a delicate situation had occurred the day of the Tecks' luncheon at Marlborough House when Princess Helena, the Prince of Wales's middle sister, had been "positively rude to Mary [Adelaide] & May . . . "

A family crisis now arose. Princess Helena, with her amber eyes and slim waist, was thought to be the most attractive of the Queen's daughters. She was also a fine pianist and a talented artist, and was married to Prince Christian of Schleswig-Holstein. Nonetheless, she had always been jealous of Princess Mary Adelaide's great public popularity. She also had an unmarried daughter, known to the family as "Tora," whom she thought should have been selected as Prince Eddy's fiancée.* Princess Helena obviously chose to disregard the risks her daughter might encounter should she marry her cousin and bear his children, and, even after his engagement to Princess May, she pressed on in anger at her daughter's rebuff.

A suspicion arises that the Queen would not have wanted her granddaughter to marry Prince Eddy. Much of his unstable character had come to light since she had approached her other granddaughter, Princess Alix of Hesse, on his behalf. The prospect of Prince Eddy as a future King of England was a bleak one. Intimate members of the Court were aware of his irrational behaviour. Some thought a plan was being hatched that Princess May must be party to—that perhaps Prince Eddy would be "committed" sometime in the future. Princess Helena, nonetheless, thought her daughter should have the dubious honour of becoming fiancée to the second heir. After much heated family correspondence, she withdrew her objections. On December 30, the Queen wrote to Princess Mary Adelaide:

"I am glad to say H[elena] speaks most affectionately of dear May, & Eddy—& that the little cloud at M[arlborough] House— was a little inexplicable *moment d'humeur*, wh. I hope you will quite dismiss from mind & forget."

Princess Mary Adelaide did not forget, but the matter paled when an invitation was received to spend ten days with the Prince and Princess of Wales at Sandringham to celebrate Prince Eddy's twenty-eighth birthday on January 8. For the first time,

---

*"Tora," Princess Helena Victoria (1870–1948) never married.

Princess May was to be an intimate part of the Wales household, quite different from being a luncheon guest at Marlborough House.

The Royal Family, including distant relatives, knew all was not well between the Prince and Princess of Wales. In fact, the Prince of Wales's transgressions were constantly being reported in English and foreign newspapers. While the Prince of Wales —in the long wait for his reign to begin—indulged himself with food, gambling, and beautiful women, Princess Alexandra had been majestically forebearing. The daughter of an impoverished Danish Prince (now Christian IX of Denmark), she had risen from obscurity to marry the Prince of Wales when she was just eighteen. Years of an unhappy marriage in a foreign land, where her lack of education and difficulty with the language and customs had made her feel the outsider, had turned what was originally a natural charm into a defensive façade.

At forty-seven, Princess Alexandra remained a great beauty. Her colouring was spectacular—deep blue eyes, soft brown hair, and skin that was like fine ivory. The one thing she and the Prince of Wales did share was a love of fashion, and each was an innovator in this sphere. A small scar on her neck caused by a childhood injury had impelled her to design a wide jewelled collar, somewhat like a dog collar, to hide the unsightly mark. These dog collars became the rage, and for over fifty years or more every fashionable woman wore one when in evening dress. She had a slim, exquisite figure, and her clothes were cut to emphasise the narrowness of her waist, a fact that caused women around the world to suffer beneath cruel whalebone stays.

As a young bride, Princess Alexandra revelled in the gaiety of the Prince of Wales's set. Then, no more than five years after their marriage, his affairs had become the subject of scandal. The situation was not helped when she became ill with rheumatic fever, which caused her not only years of pain, but for the rest of her life a stiffness in her hip and leg that produced a noticeable limp. She had suffered a hereditary form of deafness known as ostosclerosis, and after the birth of her first two children, this condition grew worse. Never much of a conversationalist, years would pass before she would be able to lip-read, and she was always to speak English crudely and with a thick Danish accent. She had never understood why her husband was so blatantly unfaithful to her when her beauty far outshone any of his mistresses. Her many problems and her insecurity had turned Princess Alexandra into an overly possessive mother and a willful woman. She was one of those women who won hordes of admirers on first meeting, but who, despite being dazzlingly beautiful, disappointed on further acquaintance.

In the course of their nearly twenty-nine years together, Princess Alexandra had more or less shut her eyes to the Prince of Wales's flagrant affairs. He had been fascinated by, among others, an American debutante, a Miss Chamberlayne (whom the Princess renamed "Miss Chamberpots"), by the great actress Sarah Bernhardt (some claimed he was the father of the Divine Sarah's son, Maurice), by the scintillating Lillie Langtry, the socially prominent Lady Aylesford, and by Lady Brooke (later the Countess of Warwick). Princess Alexandra had been forebearing with the beautiful Lillie and had looked at Lady Aylesford with disdain, but she truly loathed Lady Brooke who still had some hold on the Prince of Wales's affections.

Shortly after the announcement of their elder son's engagement, a wide rift became evident between the Prince and Princess of Wales. Whatever its cause, the Princess left for Livadia in the Crimea, very much in a pique, to celebrate the silver wedding of Tsar Alexander III and her sister, the Empress Maria Fyodorovna,* on October 13, just after approving the liaison of Prince Eddy and Princess May. So acrimonious was the Princess of Wales's relationship with her husband at this time that she preferred to attend her sister's anniversary than to be present at the festivities planned for his fiftieth birthday on November 9, 1891.

The great misfortune of the Prince of Wales's life was that his mother refused to take him into partnership. He claimed that he knew less than the secretaries of the ministers about the contents of the boxes that were piled upon Queen Victoria's desk. The knowledge within them was out of his reach, and a minis-

---

*The Empress Maria Fyodorovna (1847–1928) was formerly the Princess Dagmar of Denmark.

ter's occasional confidence only made his predicament all the more frustrating.

But in 1891, Britain was involved in a political crisis that would grow steadily over the next two years, and the Prince of Wales, perhaps satiated with his useless life, turned his energies toward it. In 1886, Gladstone had surprisingly converted his former stand in favour of Home Rule.* The Liberal faction in Parliament, angry at what it considered a betrayal, broke with its elderly leader. Turning for support to the back streets of Glasgow and Cardiff, Gladstone provided one of the few instances in history of a statesman becoming progressively more radical with the passing years. The Queen called him "a dangerous old fanatic" and was to add, "The idea of a deluded excited man of 82 trying to govern England and her vast Empire with the miserable democrats under him is quite ludicrous. It is like a bad joke!"

This crisis was to be a turning point in the life of the Prince of Wales. There were to be no more public scandals, but on November 12, 1891, when Prince George fell desperately ill with typhoid and his "Motherdear" (as he always called Princess Alexandra) rushed back to his bedside from the Crimea, Lady Brooke still cast a shapely shadow. In early January 1892, when the Tecks arrived at Sandringham House, the atmosphere between husband and wife was markedly strained.

The country estate of Sandringham in Norfolk, overlooking the Wash, is a little more than a hundred miles north of London, or close to three hours by train; this was the Prince of Wales's country home. Bought for him by his father in the hope that it would keep his son away from the gaming tables, the original house burned to the ground in 1867. With his wife's help, the Prince built, furnished, and landscaped the new rambling orange-brick mansion, and work was completed in 1870. Situated in a park of about two hundred acres, it is approached by a broad drive that sweeps northward to the front entrance and continues on to the stables and to the other houses on the estate. On the east front, a wide lawn separated the house from an immense walled garden and a congeries of buildings which com-

*Irish self-government.

prised the stud-farm, stables, kennels, and Princess Alexandra's model dairy.

Money had been lavished to make Sandringham one of the best shooting estates in the country. The weeks around Christmas were called the Sandringham Season and were a notable social event each year. Platoons of servants would arrive first to prepare the house for its Royal occupants and their guests. Fires would be lit and clocks set forward one half-hour, for the Prince, wishing to make the most of the short winter day for the shooting, was a pioneer in the use of daylight saving time. On December 1, the Princess's birthday, carriages and *fourgons* overladen with baggage and shooting equipment would begin to arrive, their passengers cheered in the gloom of the grey December by the bright gaslights that shone from the windows of most of the rooms.

For a week the shooting party decimated the clouds of pheasants that had been raised the previous summer. Lunch, which was a "veritable feast," was served in a tent in the field. With the best of the shooting season over, the first group of guests, the sportsmen and their ladies, departed. Then the Prince's international friends—the actresses and writers and social scions—arrived. "Beauty, wit, wealth, sophistication" were the valid passports to the Prince and Princess of Wales's close circle.

The Christmas season cast a different spell over Sandringham as members of the Royal Family gathered. The big pond was the scene of skating parties, "the lake and island illuminated with coloured lamps and torches, the skating chairs with glow-worm lights, and the skaters flitting past and disappearing in the darkness." The ballroom was in constant use as the Prince and Princess of Wales gave county, farmers', and servants' balls.

The fourth of January, when the Tecks set out for Sandringham, was a bleak day with such thick fog that the house, although brightly lit, could only be seen dimly until the carriage was a stone's throw from the front door. When they arrived, the men were out shooting and Prince Eddy's two unmarried sisters, the Princesses Victoria ("Toria") and Maud, were both in bed with flu.

Sandringham possessed no grand entrance hall, no circular staircase down which ladies could sweep majestically, no rooms of state. In fact, one walked from the front door into a small drawing room overcrowded with furniture and separated from the open hall by a partial screen painted with country scenes. Elsewhere, a larger drawing room more formally decorated in gold, white, and blue was used mainly for the gathering of guests before dinner and led into a pleasant—but surprisingly compact —dining room; a billiards room hung with Leech cartoons; a newly converted, well-stocked library (which had originally been a large bowling alley); and the ballroom.

A strong Russian flavour pervaded Princess Alexandra's sitting room and the main drawing room, with displays of a remarkable collection of Fabergé objects in each. An over-furnished, cluttered appearance prevailed here as it did at Marlborough House, giving both houses a look of long-established domesticity. The reception rooms notwithstanding, Sandringham was vast, containing enough small rooms to accommodate the multitudes of guests and servants. At dinner, the Royal ladies wore their diamonds and tiaras, the men their uniforms and Orders. Still, the portly Prince of Wales, who was responsible for setting the men's fashions, would often take his nine-course meals (of which he was extremely fond) in his apartments, since he did not like to wear formal attire at dinner —one reason being that he could not eat comfortably restricted by such dress.

The atmosphere at Sandringham was quite foreign to the Tecks, who were a harmonious and uncomplicated family. The Wales family maintained an appearance of loving devotion, but on closer observation, the acrimony among them surfaced. "Motherdear" was overly possessive of her sons and dominated her daughters. The Prince of Wales teased his sons unmercifully and was fond of playing childish and often mean-tempered practical jokes on them as well as his guests, supervising the making of beds so that the covers did not turn down, stuffing the pockets of a guest's dinner jacket with sticky sweets, or squirting another with a bicycle pump filled with water. Princess Mary Adelaide had always found her host's "odious chaffing moods" unsettling and stalwartly disapproved the "fast ladies and gamblers" of his "Marlborough House Set." Still, they had had in their youth an amiable, cousinly relationship, and he had once sent her feathers from his game-catch to decorate her stylish hats. Princess May was no more at ease with "Uncle Wales" than her mother and stayed out of his way as much as possible.

For that matter, she was only a bit more comfortable with the Princess of Wales. To Princess May, who was inclined to be snobbish in her disdain of ignorance, Princess Alexandra's mediocre mind, always flitting butterflylike from superficial subject to inconsequential chatter, made friendship difficult.

Coal fires burned in every room, yet Sandringham was damp and cold. Within twenty-fours hours May and her mother were suffering from heavy colds, and Toria and Maud's influenza had spread to other members of the household. The dismal weather did not deter the Prince of Wales and Prince Eddy (who shared his father's enthusiasm for the sport) from joining the shooting party each morning.

Lunch on January 7 was served at the Sandringham cottage of Sir Dighton Probyn, since 1877 the Prince of Wales's equerry, and formerly a dashing young officer and recipient during the Indian Mutiny of the Victoria Cross. Probyn was a talented raconteur, and the ladies braved the inclement weather to be his guest. Prince George, still recuperating from his bout with typhoid, had not gone shooting but did escort his future sister-in-law to lunch, where his brother later joined them.

Directly after lunch, Prince Eddy was taken suddenly ill with abdominal pains and dizziness, and was driven back to the house and put to bed. During the afternoon, Princess May sat in his small, cramped bedroom by the side of his narrow bed reading to him, while Prince George answered his brother's congratulatory birthday telegrams in the adjoining study. By evening the pain had lessened, and Prince Eddy's fever dropped. The next morning, a Friday, his birthday, he felt well enough to insist on going downstairs to open his presents. Freezing snow had fallen during the night, and Sandringham's corridors were mostly unheated. By the time he returned to his room, his breathing had become laboured, his fever up. Quinine, the standard treatment for influenza, which had plagued the Court that winter, was administered to family and guests as well, as a precautionary measure.

Though unable that night to join in his birthday celebration,

53

Prince Eddy sat up in his bed and bantered with the relay of friends and family who came to congratulate him. Downstairs, a gala dinner was served in his honour, followed by the entertainments of a banjo player and a ventriloquist. There were high spirits among the celebrants. No one had any suspicion of impending tragedy. Even the protective Princess Alexandra telegraphed the Queen that evening after dinner with some annoyance, "Poor Eddy got influenza, cannot dine, so tiresome."

The next morning, January 9, Prince Eddy's fever soared, and he had a rattling cough. The Prince of Wales's physician, Dr. Francis Laking,* was sent for. He diagnosed incipient pneumonia and telegraphed Dr. W. H. Broadbent,† who had treated Prince George for typhoid fever a few weeks earlier. Dr. Broadbent arrived the next day to find the patient coherent and in good spirits. No one at Sandringham thought his condition was of a serious nature, although precautions were taken to protect the other guests. A screen surrounded his bed, and only close family members and Princess May were permitted in the room. She would peer at him on tiptoes over the top of the barrier separating them, but even then the nurse or doctor obscured her view. The morning after Dr. Broadbent's arrival, Prince Eddy's condition worsened. His mind shifted in and out of consciousness, his cough was worse, and his breathing short and painful enough to elicit cries and moans from him. That night he grew delirious, and by the early hours of January 14, the weather bitter-cold and the sun not yet risen, he was heard shouting in fury at Lord Randolph Churchill and Lord Salisbury (neither of whom was present). Suddenly the invective dissolved into sobs as he cried out for his grandmother, the Queen.

Princess Alexandra sat by his bed, her delicate profile etched

*Dr. Francis Laking (1847–1914), afterwards made a Baronet, was Physician-in-Ordinary and Surgeon-Apothecary to Edward, Prince of Wales, and to Queen Victoria. He was knighted by Edward VII. In London the doctor lived at Pall Mall, practically across the street from Marlborough House. He also had a home at Broadstairs. Dr. Laking enjoyed a close relationship with the Royal Family.

†Dr. W. H. Broadbent was subsequently knighted. His medical affiliation with the Royal Family, however, ended after Prince Eddy's illness and death.

into the greyness of the room as she leaned over her dying son, tenderly stroking his damp hair back from his feverish forehead, while the Prince of Wales—a look of hopeless distraction on his heavy-jowled face—wandered restlessly in and out. Prince Eddy called out wildly "with great difficulty and effort and with [a] terrible rattle in his throat . . . 'Hélène! Hélène!' "* Pain overcame him and he lapsed into unconsciousness, only to return to consciousness moments later to cry out again.

Family members and guests crowded into the small, overheated sickroom, after being informed the end might be near. No one spoke. The eyes of those present were riveted to the terrifying spectacle of the young man struggling against an agonising death, his body writhing, his head rising stiffly from his pillows and falling back with piercing, unintelligible cries that were not usually symptomatic of pneumonia. Princess Alexandra, muffling her own sobs, sat in the straight wooden chair beside the bed. Standing beside her was Princess Victoria and next to her—sharing a chair—Princess Maud and Princess May, the latter dazed by the horror of what was happening in the room. Positioned behind them were Princess Louise and the Duke of Fife. On the other side of the bed, Dr. Laking kneeled while he continually took Prince Eddy's pulse, Prince George on his knees beside him. Dr. Broadbent, a nurse, and the Duke and Duchess of Teck were lined up at the foot of the bed, while the Rector of Sandringham, Reverend Frederick Hervey, stood next to the bay window reading the prayers for the dying in the dim grey light. The Prince of Wales kept demanding the latest medical report from the doctors, peering down at the glassy eyes of his dying son and then stalking from the overheated and increasingly foul-smelling room in a state of great distraction.

The vigil lasted for six hours. Princess Alexandra was wiping the sweat from Prince Eddy's face when—with a sudden and

---

*Princess Hélène married the Duke of Aosta (1869–1931) a few years later. She became an arrogant, imperious woman. Her husband was a cousin of Victor Emmanuel III of Italy and an Italian general and close to the King. Princess Hélène, who believed herself to be heiress to the grandeur of the Bourbons of France, proudly signed her name *Hélène de France*, was affected, and thought *she* was the rightful sovereign, which did not endear her to Queen Elena.

unexpected strength—he called out, "Something too awful has happened! My darling brother George is dead!" His mother leaned in close across the bed. "Can you do anything to save him?" she asked Dr. Laking. He shook his head, and the Princess of Wales placed her hand over her mouth to suppress a cry. A few moments later Prince Eddy muttered, "Who is that?" As he repeated the question, his voice grew weaker and then was silenced. At 9:35 on the leaden morning of January 14, 1892, Prince Albert Victor, Duke of Clarence and Avondale—second in line to the Throne of England, newly engaged, and just twenty-eight years of age—was dead.

His fiancée rose slowly from her chair, came around the side of the Princess of Wales, leaned over and kissed Prince Eddy's brow, and then left the death room with her parents.

Many unanswered questions surrounded Prince Eddy's death. Was it just coincidence that the young man took a dramatic turn for the worse directly after the arrival of the Queen's physician? Why was he in such agonising pain? Was pneumonia the true cause of his death? To this day, there are those who are convinced that poison was administered to Prince Eddy under the very eyes of his family and without their knowledge. There can be no doubt that Prince Eddy would never have been capable of reigning, and those at Court knew this. Could he have been deposed on the grounds of insanity when the Crown was finally placed on his head? Was there another way to remove him from the succession other than his death? And would not public knowledge of his instability reflect dangerously upon the Royal Family's ability to reign?

The Queen remained cloistered at Windsor. Princess May was the immediate recipient of everyone's sympathy. No one thought of offering condolences to the mother of "the poor young Bride," but Princess Mary Adelaide was also in a state of shock. Her life-long dream had come so close to being realised. Now her daughter was once again without prospects and the Tecks' future more precarious than ever, for Princess Mary Adelaide had spent lavishly and had been extended credit on the strength that Princess May would soon be the Duchess of Clarence and Avondale. How were they to pay these bills? In compensation, Princess May had received only two rings without nearly enough value to satisfy the creditors, who were certain to waste no time with Prince Eddy dead in trying to collect their money.

"*I clung to hope* even through the terrible watch of that awful *never* to be forgotten night of agony," Princess Mary Adelaide wrote the Queen. "It wrung one's heart to hear Him, & to see Alix's wretched, imploring face, Bertie's bowed head, & May's *dazed misery*. It seemed *too much, too hard* to bear! . . . All today telegrams have been *pouring in* & I have been much with darling Alix & the dearest girls *angelic* George who is the *tower* of strength to us all! in His room (where he lies amid flowers, chiefly Maiblumen—*Her* flower *now* being woven for the wedding train!) . . . his adoring Mother & poor May could not tear themselves away—they have just 11 o'clock borne him to the church . . . Bertie & Alix kindly wished to keep us on, united as we all are in common sorrow—Our presence seems a comfort to them!—Of their kindness to our May, I cannot say enough. They have quite adopted her as their daughter and she called Alix 'Motherdear'—& hopes you will allow her to call you 'Grandmama'? These privileges & *two rings* are all that remain to her, poor child! of her bright dream of happiness."*

Princess Mary Adelaide firmly believed her daughter was owed some recompense. But for the present the mother of the widowed fiancée said nothing.

The body remained for five days in the chancel of the small parish church adjoining the grounds of Sandringham House. The great unpolished oak coffin rested upon its bier, covered with exotic flowers and with the silken Union Jack for its pall. The weather was dull, the lowering skies threatened snow on the morning of January 20, when the coffin was transferred from Sandringham to Windsor. As the funeral procession made its way through the Royal borough of Windsor, blinds were drawn and townspeople in sombre dress lined the streets, their heads bowed. The only colour in the gloomy scene was provided by the troopers of the Horse Artillery and by the scarlet uniforms of the Foot Guards as they did sentry duty round the castle. The coffin was flanked by Prince Eddy's own Tenth Royal Hussars,

*Italicised words were underscored in the original letter.

and the procession was led by the Prince of Wales. Prince George was still in a weakened condition and joined the procession only when it reached St. George's Chapel at Windsor.

No hymns were to be sung, but the whole of the music used in the service (Purcell, Croft, Chopin, and Arthur Sullivan) had been selected by Princess Alexandra, who, defying both custom and the Queen's wish, attended the funeral service (Queen Victoria was not present). "I shall hide upon the staircase, in a corner, unknown to the world," Princess Alexandra told her mother-in-law. She remained behind the curtains of the Edward IV Chantry on the left hand side from where Queen Victoria had witnessed the Prince of Wales's wedding in 1863, accompanied by her three daughters as well as by Princess May, Princess Mary Adelaide, and three of her husband's sisters—the Princesses Louise, Helena, and Beatrice. The other royal ladies were seated nearby. Representatives of almost all the royal families of Europe (most of whom were related in some way to the deceased) attended.

The day was one of national mourning. Businesses were closed, as were theatres and music halls. The entire country was profoundly moved by the death of Prince Eddy, who—in his engagement to Princess May—had suddenly emerged from a position of ridicule to a romantic figure. The saddest and most moving moment of the funeral came when the Prince of Wales placed Princess May's bridal bouquet of orange blossoms on her dead fiancé's coffin.

After the service the pall was borne from St. George's Chapel to the adjoining Albert Memorial Chapel, where Prince Albert Victor, Duke of Clarence and Avondale, would come to final rest in a grandiose tomb (that had not yet been erected) between the memorial to his grandfather, the Prince Consort, and his uncle, the Queen's son Leopold, Duke of Albany (who had died in 1884, aged thirty-one). Princess Alexandra, noted the Queen in her journal, looked " . . . the picture of grief . . . " adding, and " . . . lovelier than ever in her deep mourning." She was taken by her husband and surviving children to the strict seclusion of Compton Place, the Duke of Devonshire's palatial seaside estate in Eastbourne, where on February 3 she was forced to bear the news of a potential scandal. James Kenneth Stephen, Prince

Eddy's Cambridge don and close friend, had died as the result of a fast begun the day of his Royal student's death. Stephen had been committed to St. Andrew's Hospital, a lunatic asylum in Northampton, ten weeks earlier, and a question was posed: exactly how crazy was Stephen when he had carried on a perfectly lucid correspondence with his former pupil until the day Prince Eddy died? Rumours of a homosexual nature began to circulate at Court, linking Stephen with Prince Eddy and to the Jack-the-Ripper murders, with suggestions that Stephen had been confined to a mental home against his will to get rid of his possible disruptive presence.

Two days after the funeral, Princess May wrote to her old friend, Miss Emily Alcock, "It is so difficult to begin one's old life again after such a shock. Even reading, of which I am so fond, is a trouble to me & I cannot settle down to anything—As for writing I simply *cannot* write . . . for it is so dreadful to have to open the wound afresh . . . "

All hope had vanished for her as she prepared to return to the life she had left so willingly that windy morning only three months earlier when she and her brother had boarded the train for Balmoral.

No one commented that Prince George, that "tower of strength," was infinitely more equipped for the position of heir presumptive than his brother, brighter, more attractive, with no rumours or scandal attached to his name, or that he was also of a marriageable age.

FOUR

Most eligible and acceptable young Royal ladies would have been only too pleased to marry Prince George. Therefore, Princess May's present close ties to the Queen and to the Prince and Princess of Wales had to be preserved and dignified reminders repeatedly made by Princess Mary Adelaide of her daughter's sacrifice, loyalty, and the manner in which she had endeared herself to the public during her short engagement to Prince Eddy. Princess Mary Adelaide was aware—as was most of the Royal Family—that the Queen favoured announcing a bride-to-be for Prince George as soon as a respectable period of mourning had passed. However remarkable the Queen's stamina, she was a woman in her seventies. And though robust in appearance, the Prince of Wales was now past fifty and, having led a life of excess, did not engender a sense of security in the strength of the succession in the minds of the British people.

Pale and gaunt from his recent illness, still shocked by the suddenness of his brother's death, Prince George's appearance fed the public's fears for the Monarchy. If another tragedy should strike the Royal Family and Prince George die before he was to marry and father a child, his eldest sister, Princess Louise, flighty and not terribly bright and wed to a commoner,* would become Queen Regnant, not an eventuality that the country would welcome. An immediate marriage was therefore imperative. The Queen and her ministers were considering prospects within weeks of Prince Eddy's death. No one could blame Princess Mary Adelaide for hoping that her daughter would be chosen a second time round.

Though Princess May was aware of her current popularity and knew that the Queen and the Prince and Princess of Wales were fond of her, her mother's ambitions placed her in an extraordinarily difficult position. Prince George had always shown her great kindness, but he had never given her any indication of a deeper emotion. There was also his long-standing and deep affection for Julia Stonor,† although she had married the previous July.

Directly after Prince Eddy's death, to Princess May's further distress, her father had been overheard by most members of the bereaved family at Sandringham, chanting repeatedly in a deranged manner: "It must be a Tsarevitch, it must be a Tsarevitch!" This was a pointed reference to Princess Alexandra's sister, Empress Maria Fyodorovna, who had been engaged to the young Tsarevitch Nicholas at the time of his death and had expediently married his younger brother, the future Tsar Alexander III. The fact that this royal union had been successful did not ease Princess May's embarrassment over her father's insensitivity.

The Duke of Teck had always been enveloped by his wife's enormous shadow. The marriage that he had thought would save him from his own impecunity and shaky royal footing had instead formed him into a totally dependent and useless man.

---

*Before his marriage to the Princess Louise, the Duke of Fife had been a wealthy landowner near the Castle Abergeldie, a home of the Prince and Princess of Wales.

†The Honourable Julia Caroline Stonor (1861–1950), a commoner and a Roman Catholic. Her mother had been lady-in-waiting to Alexandra, Princess of Wales. After her mother's death in 1883, Julia Stonor remained close to Alexandra. She and Prince George were childhood friends, and for a time he was devotedly in love with her. She married the Marquis d'Hautpoul Seyre on July 17, 1891.

Having married the burdensome Princess Mary Adelaide, he had not been rewarded with work commensurate with his position. In fact, since coming to England, he had never had any specified occupation. To compensate, he gardened when he could and took an interest in his home, but most times he simply remained at his wife's considerable elbow or walked her small pet dog named, incongruously, "Yes." But Princess Mary Adelaide was the one who had to deal with creditors and who was forced to importune on the kindness and loyalty of friends and family. In short, the Duke of Teck was a weak man without his wife's charm, in his daughter's eyes a social climber and an embarrassment, and whose ineptitude was a major cause of the Teck family's constant financial crises.

Two months after the death of Prince Eddy, Princess May had written to Helene Bricka, "I must say I do like Men & here I see nothing but women, women, women, except Papa & he don't [sic] count to talk to—I am indeed a funny person!" A few days later she confided to Mlle. Bricka, "Mama is quite happy here. Papa is as usual rather trying but we are accustomed to this, wherever we are *c'est toujours la meme histoire!*"

Most of the men in Princess May's intimate circle were either weak or irresponsible. She identified most strongly with the women in her world: her resourceful mother, the indomitable Queen, and the strong-willed, high-principled Princess of Wales. In her own family, her mother was the dominating force, and even with three brothers, Princess May would not have considered turning to any one of the men in her house for advice. Her eldest brother, Dolly, had always had a peppery temper and an immature attitude and had looked to *her* for guidance; Alge, who was equally immature, she had mothered through their childhood; and Francis, whom they all called Frank, had been a great trial since he was a boy, constantly in trouble over money and women. Since a sense of duty of what was expected of one in her position was so deeply ingrained, Princess May had, therefore, not concerned herself with the poor character of Prince Eddy. Nor did she now think less of Prince George for the nurserylike attitude he still maintained towards his "Darling Motherdear."

"Motherdear" was a most theatrical woman who, though lacking artistic taste, possessed an inimitable sense of style. Her tremendous dignity in the face of her husband's flagrant infideli- ties added to her aura. Women, parties, and gambling filled the Prince of Wales's empty hours, whereas the Princess of Wales spent her time stage-managing her awkward, flighty daughters, set-decorating her homes with a clutter of memorabilia, attend- ing diligently to her vast circle of friends and her small depen- dent family, visiting the ill in hospital, and supporting numerous charities. All comparison between husband and wife had to be to the Princess's best advantage.

Shortly after Prince Eddy's funeral, his family took Princess May with them to Queen Victoria's Isle of Wight home, Osborne House. From there she returned to White Lodge for a little over a fortnight before her father escorted her to Eastbourne to rejoin the Prince and Princess of Wales at Compton Place. This last invitation was at the instigation of Princess Mary Adelaide. "May has become the child of the Waleses," the Duke of Teck wrote to his sister, Amelia, as soon as he returned to White Lodge. "I foresee she will be very much taken up with them."

On February 27, which would have been her wedding day, "Uncle Wales and Motherdear" gave her a magnificent *revière* of diamonds which they had intended as a wedding present, as well as a handsome dressing bag, fitted in gold and precious jewels, which their elder son had ordered as a gift for his bride. At Compton Place, drawn together by their grief, Prince George and Princess May for the first time were placed in a situation where they could assess each other as man and woman, and not —as had been previously the case—as future in-laws. Except for Julia Stonor and his mother, and perhaps because of his years in the Navy, Prince George had always preferred masculine com- pany to feminine. He also cared little for social life.

Although he was the most conservative of dressers, he had a kind of dapper air and a jaunty walk typical of sailors, and was never as comfortable in civilian clothes as in a uniform. He had his mother's clear blue eyes, smiled easily, and possessed a good sense of humour, but he suffered great insecurity because of knock-knees and a slight lisp.

From the very start of their friendship, Princess May was de- termined to overcome the intellectual chasm between them. She

63

read to him for hours and helped him to perfect his French. She took time to look at his beloved stamp collection, and while he told her about particular stamps, she explained some of the background of the country and period of their origin. They were about the same height, although her curious hairdo made her appear taller. They could be seen walking round the grounds of Compton Place, for Princess May had never trusted horses and only mounted one when forced.

Whatever reservations she had about Princess Alexandra's possessive attitude toward Prince George, she kept to herself. And when with Princess Alexandra, she remained loving and respectful. With Princess Mary Adelaide prodding her from behind the scenes, and with her own sense of ambition to encourage her efforts, before long Princess May had managed to attract Prince George's full attention. His bereavement was intense, and Princess May had the sensitivity to understand why. The two brothers had been raised as if they were twins, obsessively close, their relationship reversed (the older following the younger's lead), and they had shared the experience of being at a great distance from the family.

Terrified of his father, Prince George also had difficulty relating to the witty young men and beautiful women who were a part of the Prince of Wales's circle, or with the effete companions of his brother. He loved the Navy life, yet the protection he was given at sea had kept him immature. He still signed his letters to Princess Alexandra, "Darling Motherdear! Your loving little Georgie."

Mother and son had a common bond. Neither shared the Prince of Wales's artistic tastes or intellectual curiosity. To add to this, Prince George had not been well educated. He was, one could say, a very ordinary fellow, better suited for the life of a country squire than that of a future King of England. According to Sir Harold Nicolson, he "preferred recognition to surprise, the familiar to the strange." That could have accounted for his attraction to Princess May. And she would always be the tie to his dead brother that guilt and love demanded.

Another candidate for Prince George's hand in marriage was Marie, the eldest daughter of his father's brother, Alfred, Duke of Edinburgh. Marie was both clever and comely, and the previous year when Prince George's ship had put into port in Malta where the Edinburghs had a home, the two had seen each other. However, Marie had intensely disliked Prince Eddy, a fact that created an uncomfortable situation, whereas "Dear Miss May" had deep understanding in her clear blue eyes when he spoke tearfully of his brother as "my darling boy."

Shortly after Princess May returned to White Lodge from Compton Place, Princess Mary Adelaide set upon a scheme that she hoped would further the young couple's affection for each other. Upon hearing that the Prince and Princess of Wales were about to depart for the South of France, she decided that the Tecks would also visit France and stay nearby. Since the Tecks could hardly afford such a journey, someone had to be found to finance it. Princess Mary Adelaide had a clique of wealthy friends desirous of remaining in the good graces of the Royal circle and to whom she often turned when in financial need. Lady Wolverton was one of this select group,* and "dear Lady Wolverton" wished for nothing more than the flowers and sunshine of the South of France and the chance to be near the Prince and Princess of Wales. So while the Prince and Princess of Wales settled into an elegant, quiet hotel at Cap Martin (a promontory that juts out into the Mediterranean between Monte Carlo and the Italian border), Princess Mary Adelaide and Lady Wolverton's party arranged to take a villa at Mentone, only two miles away.

When word of this reached the Prince of Wales, he was appalled. Although quite in favour of Princess May as a future daughter-in-law, he found Princess Mary Adelaide's plan to thrust her daughter into his house indecent. The Duke of Cambridge, Princess Mary Adelaide's brother and known to Princess May as Uncle George, was duly notified of the Prince of Wales's displeasure and asked to arrange for the Wolverton-Teck contingent to look for another villa at a more discreet distance—say Cannes, which was ninety-six miles away.

After several prodding reminders by the Prince of Wales, the Duke of Cambridge convinced his sister that Cannes would be more convivial for her party, and he personally put Lady Wolv-

---

*Georgiana Maria (d. 1894), wife of the 2nd Lord Wolverton, founder of the Needlework Guild, and a good friend of Princess Mary Adelaide.

erton on a train in London for that city to locate a villa. By March 9 a suitable villa had been found, and Uncle George escorted the Tecks, Princess May and two of her young friends, Lady Katy Coke and Lady Eva Greville,* to Victoria Station on the first lap of their journey. Uncle George was a handsome, dashing man who had made the Army his career and beautiful women his passion. In his youth he had turned down the opportunity to be Prince Consort, reportedly saying, "What? Marry ugly little Victoria? Never!" Subsequently he had married an actress, Louisa Fairbrother, and they had three perfectly legitimate sons; but as the wedding had been secret and the Duke had not obtained Victoria's Royal Consent as required by law, the Queen refused to believe that a wedding had taken place or grant Louisa or her children the use of the family name of Cambridge. They were thus given the name of Fitz-George.

Although the Queen thought her cousin George Cambridge morally unstable and was shocked by his "scandalous behaviour," she was personally fond of him, and Princess May, always a bit prim in her opinions, felt much the same way. Her departure for Cannes was a happy one as Uncle George was more amusing and charming than ever, and he had brought her a basket of sweets and scents to enjoy on the journey to the commodious Villa Clementine in Cannes.

An anxious three weeks was to pass after they reached the South of France before the Prince and Princess of Wales contacted the Tecks. A note from Prince George to Princess May finally arrived on March 29. "Papa & I are coming over to Cannes towards the end of the week for a few days (incog.). I hope I shall see you then, we hope one day you will give us a little dinner, we are going to stay at a quiet hotel, only don't say anything about it. The others will remain here . . . Goodbye dear 'Miss May' . . . ever your very loving old cousin Georgie."

Prince George spent every possible moment of his five-day stay with Princess May. The young woman, though still dressed in severe black mourning attire, showed a renewed enthusiasm

*Later to be Lady Eva Dugdale (d. 1940). She was the only daughter of the 4th Earl of Warwick. Married Colonel F. Dugdale in 1895. She was Princess May's first lady-in-waiting.

for life. The colour returned to her face, the gleam to her eyes. The local paper predicted an engagement was imminent, and these reports were repeated in the English press.

During April, the Tecks visited Cap Martin for three days. Then the Prince and Princess of Wales, accompanied by Prince George and his sisters, Maud and Toria, journeyed to Cannes for a short stay, before leaving for Hyères. With no further reason for the Tecks to remain in the South of France, Princess Mary Adelaide shepherded her party to Stuttgart to visit the Duke of Teck's relatives, and there they remained until late June.*

"The reason why we are always putting off the return to England is the rumour of a new engagement for May," the Duke of Teck wrote his sister, Amelia, on May 15. "We have not spoken to her about it, but it seems she feels frightened by an early return home."

Princess May's hesitancy to face a new engagement had nothing to do with any part of the recent past. Nor was she fearful that talk of a new engagement was too premature or that her cousin might decide upon someone else. She was quite confident, in fact, that this was not the case—for Princess Marie had just announced her engagement to the Crown Prince of Rumania, and there was no pressure from the Queen for any other Royal alliance.

As unlikely is the idea that Princess May had learned anything not already known to her about Prince George. She might not have been head over heels in love with him, and during their last meeting she had become aware of his immaturity and his depen-

---

*A curious incident occurred while the Tecks were on this trip to Stuttgart. A fire ignited in the small niche of the bedroom of the guest room which Princess Mary Adelaide was occupying in the home of the Princess Catherine of Würtemberg. The only damage was to the desk where Princess Mary Adelaide had left assorted letters and photographs. Supposedly, while the fire brigade was being called, Princess May salvaged all she could from her mother's desk. The fire was put out before any great damage was done. And the only loss seems to have been the desk, three signed photographs of Prince Eddy, and his correspondence to Princess May during their short engagement. What these mementoes were doing on Princess Mary Adelaide's desk while on holiday was never explained.

dent nature. But Prince George was dutiful, conservative, and straightforward, all traits she admired. If she married him, she could be certain that he would not philander as his father did, nor lead a life of dissipation as his brother most assuredly would have continued to do. He might well be dull, but she was somewhat stiff and private and not particularly demonstrative. The answer to the riddle then is not Prince George. It is Princess Alexandra.

The Princess of Wales had become overtly more possessive of her only surviving son, and she had suddenly realised in Cannes that she was in danger of losing him to Princess May, for she suspected that he was truly in love. Her fondness for Princess May remained in evidence, but she now became intensely competitive. Shortly after leaving Cannes, Prince George, recently removed from the Royal Navy, was sent to Germany to continue his studies. His first letters to his mother mentioned Princess May. Princess Alexandra replied with frequent underscoring to emphasise her points, "The bond of love between us—that of Mother and child—which *nothing can* ever diminish or render less binding—and *nothing* and *nobody* can or shall come between me and my darling Georgie boy."

She followed this letter with another: "You know my Georgie that you are everything to me now—you must give us *double* affection for the one that has gone before us!"

If Princess May was to marry Prince George, quite clearly she must fight desperately hard to win him away from his mother or share him unequally. Neither prospect was too encouraging in the face of the long years under her own mother's domination.

FIVE

B y the time the Tecks returned to London in the first week in July, the Queen had made up her mind that Prince George should marry Princess May. She minced no words with the Duke of Cambridge, who found the idea "unseemly and unfeeling and horrible," since he did not believe his niece loved Prince George. The Queen glanced at him disdainfully. "Well," she said, "you know May never was in love with poor Eddy!" The Prince and Princess of Wales, after the close association with the Tecks in the South of France, were less enthusiastic than Uncle George over the match. "The Prince of Wales must not prevent the marriage," the Queen wrote to her private secretary, Sir Henry Ponsonby. "Something dreadful will happen if he does not marry."

Having thus made up her mind about Princess May's future, she suggested a financial advisor take over the Tecks' money affairs. Princess Mary Adelaide was grossly offended, but to no avail. The Queen was determined that if Princess May married Prince George, the Tecks' reputation for financial crises would have to be improved. And not only was a comptroller installed at White Lodge, but a young steward as well. The idea was to stop Princess Mary Adelaide's extravagances and to relieve Princess May of her former unsavoury task of putting off their creditors. With the arrival of these two men, the household was at once in a terrible "fluster," Princess Mary Adelaide insisting that the family needed three carriages and the harrassed comptroller, Alexander Nelson Hood,* countering that the small family could easily go about in one.

The Tecks were heavily in arrears in paying their bills of the local tradespeople. Now that Princess May was not to marry Prince Eddy, they feared they might never be paid, and these rumours came back to the steward (a Mr. Hough), and consequently to Princess Mary Adelaide, who declared at luncheon one day, "Since it seems the tradespeople are so fond of talking about me I shall stop the beer, bread, and cheese!" These inducements had been dispersed to delivery boys in lieu of tips and therefore were actually financed by their own employers.

With Prince George in Germany, the summer and autumn of 1892 was an anxious time for the Tecks. Nervously but patiently they awaited a sign, and on November 29 it finally came. The Tecks were invited to Sandringham to observe both the birthday of the Princess of Wales and the one-year anniversary of Princess May's engagement to Prince Eddy. Always optimistic, Princess Mary Adelaide was hopeful that with Prince George at Sandringham, a proposal was in the offing. But the visit to Sandringham proved to be disappointing.

The Princess of Wales, still dressed poignantly in heavy mourning, fell into a terrible depression. She wept as she opened her birthday gifts and insisted the Tecks visit Prince Eddy's bedroom. A fire burned in the little grate; flowers stood about in vases; the room was as he had left it; even his soap had been religiously preserved in a soapdish. From this shrine, the Tecks were escorted on a family pilgrimage to Sandringham Church, where a stained-glass window representing an idealised Prince Eddy as Saint George in shining armour, with a halo, had been newly installed. The incongruity of this memorial was enough to prompt Princess Mary Adelaide to write to her sister that she supposed "the cruel battle with death" had created "a noble young knight."

It rained hard for most of the visit. Still, Princess May trudged

*The Honourable Alexander Nelson Hood (1854–1927), private secretary to Queen Mary 1901–1910, treasurer to Queen Mary 1910–1919.

through the mud to meet Prince George and the rest of the shooting party for lunch. In the evenings, they would play cards, particularly bezique. The emotional climate at Sandringham this December 1892 was certainly not conducive to romance. Unsure but hopeful that their inclusion at this memorial "celebration" was the sign they had anticipated, the Tecks returned to White Lodge.

Then, at Christmas, Prince George sent Princess May a handsome brooch, an encouraging sign. The first anniversary of Prince Eddy's death, January 14, found Princess May at the chapel at Windsor. " . . . How beautiful it is," she wrote Prince George directly after, " . . . and how calmly and peacefully our beloved Loved One lies there at rest from all the cares of this world. God be with you and help us bear our cross is the fervent prayer of your very loving cousin—May."

The year of respectful mourning had passed. If Prince George was so inclined, now was the time he would make his intentions known.

Once out of mourning, Princess May was able to enjoy the fruits of her current popularity. To her mother's delight, the Tecks were tendered more invitations than they could accept. This season Princess Mary Adelaide would not have to inveigle fashionable country holidays for her family. She could pick and choose. The most prestigious offer came from the Duke and Duchess of Newcastle at their celebrated hunting estate at Clumber, a favourite of the Prince of Wales. The Tecks—father, mother, daughter, and son Alexander (Alge)—were most pleased to be given the Prince of Wales's usual suite of rooms. Other guests included Lord Randolph Churchill,* as well as his American wife, Jenny, once a mistress of the Prince of Wales and at thirty-nine still one of London's most celebrated beauties.

Lord Randolph was not well and remained in his room. The

---

*Lord Randolph Churchill (1849–95) was the son of the 7th Duke of Marlborough and the father of Sir Winston Churchill. He was Chancellor of the Exchequer and leader of the House of Commons, Chairman of the National Union of Conservative Associations, and (1885–86) Secretary of State for India. His wife was Jenny Jerome (1854–1921), an American who became a leader in English society.

71

rumour was that he was losing his mental capacities. A short time later his wife was to claim, "He is quite unfit for society . . . one never knows what he may do." Still, this gloomy prediction did not preclude the spirited Lady Randolph from joining the dancing and festivities along with Princess Mary Adelaide, who loved to dance. One evening when the young people were dancing the new *pas de quatre,* she remarked how "stupid" the girls were in the execution of it. There and then she began dancing the intricate steps down the long hall from the ballroom with one of the elderly male guests, much to the great delight of all present. In spite of her tremendous girth, Princess Mary Adelaide was exceptionally nimble on her feet. Before long she had a great deal to kick up her heels about.

On April 29, Prince George, who had recently been gazetted Duke of York upon his father's request to the Queen, returned to England from Athens, where he had been visiting with his mother.* Arriving alone, he went immediately to Sheen, the home of his sister, Princess Louise. Since Sheen was near White Lodge, the newspapers were filled with speculation of an imminent Royal engagement. The evening of May 2, Prince George dined with the Tecks. The next afternoon, Princess May was a guest for tea at Sheen, after which Prince George and Princess May sat awkwardly among the formal gathering, not quite knowing what was expected of them. "Now, Georgie," his sister finally said, "don't you think you ought to take May into the garden to look at the frogs in the pond?" Hardly a romantic suggestion; still, the young couple seized upon it. "We walked together . . . in the garden and he proposed to me, & I accepted him," Princess May confided to her diary. "I drove home to announce the news to Mama and Papa & Georgie followed. He went back to Sheen after dinner. We telegraphed to all the relations."

Princess Mary Adelaide, in fact, telegraphed everyone she

*In the Birthday Honours of May 24, 1892, Prince George became the Duke of York, Earl of Inverness, and Baron Killarney. "I am afraid I do not [like the title Duke of York] and wish you had remained as you are," Queen Victoria wrote her grandson. "A prince *no one* else can be, whereas a Duke any nobleman can be and many are. I am not very fond of that of York which has not very agreeable associations."

could think of to proclaim: "May engaged to Duke of York," completing her list late at night before being struck by the terrifying thought that the Queen's consent had not yet been given. Her rush to announce the news could, at the very least, raise the Royal wrath. Working through the night, she sent out second telegrams to cover her *faux pas*, which read: "Unless announced in papers keep engagement secret." To her great relief, the Queen gave her consent. The next day the newspapers reported the engagement. Princess Alexandra, still in deep mourning, remained in Athens. On May 13, she wrote to Princess May from Venice: "*God bless* you *both* & let me welcome you back once more as my dear daughter, & grant you all the happiness here on earth—which *you* so fully deserve with my Georgie & which was alas denied you with my darling Eddy. I am sure . . . his spirit is watching over you now & rejoicing with us & that the clouds have been lifted once more from your saddened young life & that you may yet look forward to a bright & happy future with the brother he loved so well . . . I know we two will always understand each other & I hope my sweet May will always come straight to me for everything . . . Ever yr most loving & devoted old Motherdear."

Princess Alexandra did not hurry home from Venice, however, and the young couple discussed the arrangements for their wedding with the Queen. Princess Alexandra returned only days before the wedding and just in time to greet her own family's arrival from Denmark. To the Queen's chagrin, she remained in deep mourning until her first public appearance before the wedding. At no time did she oppose the wedding or the arrangements, but she had become considerably cooler in her attitude toward Princess May. There were no further references to "my darling May" in her letters, no special gifts. Nor did she include Princess May in any of her social activities or dinners where her son was included. To Princess Alexandra, Princess May's new engagement made a travesty of the first.

The wedding date had been set for July 6. The newlyweds would have the use of the homely, aptly named York Cottage at Sandringham. But during their two-month engagement, they had no time alone together, for Princess Mary Adelaide was never far away from her daughter's side. Prince George wrote his fiancée of his grievances toward his mother-in-law-to-be, and Princess May, after some cross words to Princess Mary Adelaide, confessed to Prince George that her mother was "*so* obstinate" and that the harsh words they had exchanged made her feel "like a little devil," but that she had not "forgiven her yet." She adds, "This is a simply *horrid* time we are going through and I am only looking forward to the time when you and I shall be alone at Sandringham."

Nevertheless, mother and daughter gave the impression of being warm and close as they scurried about to purchase the bride's trousseau. A generous "contribution" by "dear Aunt Augusta," the Grand Duchess of Mecklenburg-Strelitz, allowed the two women an opportunity to be wildly extravagant. Forty outdoor suits, fifteen ball dresses, five tea gowns, and a vast number of bonnets, shoes, and gloves were ordered along with matinée gowns, travelling capes, travelling wraps, and driving capes. The *Lady's Pictorial* in its Royal Wedding Number gave a full description of each gown made exclusively by English dressmakers but did not include the lavish selection of undergarments made in part of "some beautiful flounces of black lace."

"I am determined," Princess Mary Adelaide told the press, "that all the silk [in the trousseau] shall come from England, all the flannel from Wales, all the tweeds from Scotland, and every yard of lace and poplin from Ireland." The bridal dress with *Maiblumen* and the extravagant trousseau that had been ordered (and only recently paid for by the Prince and Princess of Wales) during her engagement to Prince Eddy were packed away, eventually to be misplaced and lost. Silver and white brocade from the Spitalfield looms was ordered for a new wedding gown.

The affianced couple's social commitments escalated alarmingly. Almost everyone in position at Court rushed to honour them with a lunch, garden party, tea, dinner, or ball, and protocol made it difficult to refuse. Gala performances at the opera, theatre invitations, and a constant flow of Royal wedding guests to be met filled the daily calendar. And time still had to be found to receive deputations from cities and organisations from all over England. Wedding gifts (nearly fifteen hundred of them in the first weeks) had to be opened, sorted, and acknowledged. Amongst the presents was a dazzling display of brooches, tiaras, pins, bracelets, and necklaces studded with diamonds and gemstones for Princess May, and a boudoir grand pianoforte (she could play tolerably well), as well as rare antique furniture, crystal, paintings, silver, books, magnificent porcelain, and all manner of clocks for the bridal couple. Each day the newspapers would list the latest gifts, and each day Princess May would show visitors round the ever-growing displays at White Lodge. She was also sitting for two portraits, which led her concerned fiancé to write: "I must say that it is a great shame making you sit to all these artists at this time."

Along with all her new responsibilities and Lady Geraldine Somerset's vitriolic comments ("It is clear there is not even a *pretense* at lovemaking. May is radiant at her *position* . . . but placid and cold as always"), Princess May, who had never had youthful crushes like other girls, was embarrassed by her own timidity. In early June, she wrote her fiancé: "I am sorry that I am still so shy with you, I tried not to be the other day, but alas failed. I was angry with myself! It is so stupid to be so stiff together and really there is nothing I would not tell you, except that I *love* you more than anybody in the world, and this I cannot tell you myself so I write it to relieve my feelings."

To which he replied: "Thank God we both understand each other, and I think it really unnecessary for me to tell you how deep my love for you my darling is and I feel it growing stronger and stronger every time I see you; although I may appear shy and cold. But this worry [Princess Mary Adelaide's constant presence] and busy time [the acceleration of their social life] is most annoying and when we do meet it is only [to] talk business."

The couple complemented each other physically as well as emotionally. Prince George, who was about the same height as Princess May, gained stature from her imperious carriage, and her unyielding smile was softened by his easier smile that exposed his flashing white teeth. Though somewhat prissy and possessing a slight lisp, Prince George was still attractive; he had even features, startling blue eyes, and an intelligent, sensitive look about him.

Three weeks before the wedding, a popular newspaper, the *Star,* printed the salacious gossip that claimed Prince George had been wed to the daughter of an English admiral and had fathered three children with her while he had been stationed in Malta. His more abrasive qualities—a coarse laugh, loud voice, and bluff manner—were unrestrained when he brought this story to his fiancée's attention. He is reported to have told her at the time, "I say, May, we can't get married after all! I hear I have got a wife and three children!"

The rumour was otherwise ignored, and the prenuptial festivities culminated just a few days before the wedding in a huge garden party given by the Tecks at White Lodge. Afterwards an exhausted Princess Mary Adelaide took to her bed but revived sufficiently the next day, July 4, to accompany Princess May to Buckingham Palace, where they were to stay until the wedding two days later.

On a "thunderous, drowsy afternoon," Princess May and her parents left White Lodge for Buckingham Palace. "Inside," reported the *Daily Telegraph*, "the Lodge presented a complete contrast to its usual aspect. In the entrance hall the flowers were in gay profusion, but all along the walls were chests and trunks, filled or being filled with wedding presents while in the picturesque corridor . . . dismantled tables and two or three huge packing cases gave proof that the remarkable array of wedding gifts . . . was at an end." The bulk of the wedding gifts had been moved the day before to the Imperial Institute,* where they would be open to the inspection of visitors. The presents had filled twenty vans and did not include the horses, ponies, carriages, sleighs, and boats, also gifts, to be exhibited in the Institute stables.

Shortly before 4:00 P.M., a squadron of the Middlesex Yeomanry, seated on their massive bay chargers and dressed in bright blue uniforms and busbies with brilliant green and crimson plumes, lined up smartly in front of the lodge. A large crowd of well-wishers had gathered at the gates. They cheered loudly as Princess May, dressed in mauve, a soft brown cape over her shoulders, a small flowered bonnet of deep blue forget-me-nots

---

*The Imperial Institute is now the Commonwealth Institute and is no longer in its original location in South Kensington behind Royal Albert Hall, but in a new building in Holland Park.

and purple auricula tied beneath her chin with purple velvet, circumvented the heap of luggage still stacked in the doorway and with her parents stepped briskly into one of the two waiting carriages. Alexander Nelson Hood and Mary Thesiger, Lady-in-Waiting to Princess Mary Adelaide, entered the second carriage.

The Household Cavalry now surrounded the vehicles, and as the spectators shouted and waved handkerchiefs, the cortege moved forward amid whirling dust. No rain had fallen for over a fortnight and most of June had been unbearably hot. The procession made its way through a circuitous decorated route lined with crowds and at twenty minutes past five turned the corner from Constitution Hill. "There was a quick movement among the crowds, a craning of necks, lifting up of children, raising of hats and a waving of kerchiefs." A great cheer went up as Princess May, bowing graciously inside her carriage, entered through the south central gates of Buckingham Palace, at the same time as the skies opened up to pour rain in a sudden cloudburst.

In the forty-eight hours at Buckingham Palace before the wedding, Princess May and the Tecks joyously anticipated the fulfillment of all their dreams. They were given a magnificent suite, usually reserved for foreign sovereigns. The first evening, amid a torrential downpour, they were driven to an elegant dinner honouring the bride at nearby Marlborough House (two hundred guests), followed by a command performance at the Royal Opera, Covent Garden. "Fairyland," reported the *Daily Telegraph*, "is no longer a myth, but a reality." Roses were festooned over every box from tier to tier. The proscenium of the stage was traced with roses, the architectural columns covered entirely with them. Into the arm of every other stall was tucked a small bouquet of pink, white, and crimson roses bound with crimson and white satin ribbons, so that each lady present had a bouquet of flowers in her hand, as well as a white-and-gold-satin libretto to consult and a white-satin programme lettered in gold and illustrated with portraits of the principal members of the Royal Family.

Princess May's portrait was not in the programme, but as she entered—elegantly dressed in ice-blue brocade, the bodice

77

studded with several of her newly acquired, glittering diamond wedding pins, a double strand of perfectly matched pearls around her neck, and wearing a diamond-and-pearl tiara and matching earrings—she was given a rousing cheer by the three thousand people present and was escorted by the Duke of York to the centre of the Royal box, the Prince and Princess of Wales taking side seats. The opera was Gounod's *Roméo et Juliette* (sung by Mme. Nellie Melba and M. Jean de Reszke); in order to make it "more appropriate" the tragic denouement had been deleted, so that for perhaps the only time in theatre history the lovers survived the tomb scene.

The next morning the rain continued, and in the state apartments of Buckingham Palace from eleven-thirty until one o'clock, at half-hour intervals, Princess May and the Duke of York received deputations of ladies (representing various townships) who had not already presented their wedding gifts. "In every case offerings of jewels were made and the Princess received them with evident pleasure," the *Times* reported. "Shortly after the last donor departed, Princess May met with the Queen who had just arrived from Windsor and, it is understood, received from the Royal hands a personal present of great value."

The Royal gift was a spectacular diamond fleur-de-lys-and-collet fringe (smaller diamonds forming the fringe) necklace. Princess May was only now coming to realise the tremendous wealth she was about to possess. Her personal wedding gifts were worth upwards of a million pounds and included fabulous jewels given to her by Tsar Alexander and the Empress Maria Fyodorovna, Queen Isabella of Spain, and all the many members of Queen Victoria's family at home and abroad. Her new jewel collection would have filled almost every jewelry display case at Asprey's, and these gem gifts were in addition to the jewel-studded objects presented to the bridal pair.

By afternoon the rain had stopped, but the sky remained grey and threatening. Still, this did not obscure the beauty or liveliness of the grand garden party given at Marlborough House in honour of the bridal couple and attended by two thousand people. Each lady guest was given a cream-coloured Rose of York to carry, whereas Princess May wore a satin dress of that shade

trimmed in crimson-silk Lancaster Roses, her straw hat bedecked with them as well; in her arms she carried a bouquet of
real crimson roses. The Tsarevitch (who in one year was to
become Nicholas II) was on his first trip to England and was
lodged at Marlborough House, as were his grandparents (Princess Alexandra's parents), King Christian IX and Queen Louise
of Denmark. The Tsarevitch Nicholas and the Duke of York,
who were first cousins, shared an uncanny resemblance; during
the afternoon Nicholas was taken for George and warmly congratulated, while George was asked whether he had come to
London only to attend the wedding or whether he had other
business to transact. In a letter to his mother, Nicholas wrote,
"Uncle Bertie, of course, sent me at once to a tailor, a boot-
maker and a hatter." Since this was the same tailor employed by
the Duke of York, they were even dressed in similar suits. The
likeness did not stop there, for their Vandyke beards were simi-
larly trimmed and their hair parted in the same way—in the
middle. Photographs were taken of the two young men to point
up this resemblance.

No one appeared happier than the Queen at this gathering.
A tent with a carpeted approach had been specially erected for
her, and she sat under the tent curtain, her Court in a wide circle
around her chair. She gave a festive dinner at Buckingham Palace that night, followed by a spectacular ball in honour of the
wedding couple. Princess May had never looked as radiantly
beautiful, nor had she known such popularity both from the
Court and the people who stood singing and chanting outside
the gates.

Her engagement to Prince Eddy had been brief and had
stopped tragically short of the prenuptial Court festivities. Her
youthful grief had touched both the Court and the nation, and
made her appear vulnerable, more human. The public was able
to relate to her private suffering in a way it could not with any
other members of the Royal Family. She was the daughter of
Princess Mary Adelaide, "the people's princess," whom they
loved, as well as a poor relation—a position that commanded
much sympathy. Being chosen as a bride for Prince Eddy had
transported her overnight from the plain, poor, unendowed
princess into a celebrity. Then his sudden death only weeks

before her marriage had brought her new supporters. Princess May was now a national heroine, and even the Queen was aware of it and used this newfound Royal popularity intelligently to the Crown's best advantage.

No wonder then that the Prince and Princess of Wales took side seats in the Royal Box at the opera so that all eyes were on Princess May and Prince George. The Prince of Wales's scandals were gratefully overshadowed by Princess May's romantic triumph. And Queen Victoria could well hold a smiling Court at the garden party at Marlborough House, assured that her Crown would eventually rest in capable hands. For the Queen, though she gave her devotion to even the most wayward of her offspring and their children, was always cognizant of their inadequacies. Her grandson George was no exception. An improvement over Prince Eddy, he was still not terribly clever or well educated. He was also weak and dominated by a willful mother who could have destroyed any sense of leadership he might naturally possess. From their close association at Balmoral before the young woman's engagement to Prince Eddy, the Queen was confident that Princess May would change this.

Princess May's life-long conception of what her future was to be had so greatly altered that she no longer had any guidelines. But the inequities of the past—being a princess who survived on the bounty of others, the strongest child in a family where she was the only girl among three brothers, and the daughter who too often was forced to reverse roles with a flighty, irresponsible mother—had honed her into the kind of woman who was curiously impervious to change. None of the crowd's adulation, the Court's approbation, or her sudden acquisition of worldly treasures went to her head. Still, she was now, as the *Lady's Pictorial* pointed out, " . . . the third greatest Royal Lady of Great Britain."

That was true, but in addition she was marrying a man whom she loved perhaps more than she thought she would. And not because he had swept her off her feet, but rather because he allowed her to dig her toes firmly into the ground.

80

SIX

July 6, 1893, the morning of the wedding, vast crowds assembled before the gates of Buckingham Palace as early as eight o'clock. The wedding day had not been decreed a national holiday, but the people declared it one themselves. Anyone who could take leave from his work did so. People stood on rooftops, clinging to statues that overlooked the Palace balustrades. The forecourt of the Palace was a mosaic of brilliant scarlet uniforms, bright tartan kilts, the sharp green of the 15th Middlesex, and the deep blue of the Yeomanry.

A grandstand had been erected in the courtyard of Buckingham Palace, which by 10:00 A.M. was filled with a full complement of Life Guards, Australian Horse Artillerymen, and Indian Horseguards armed with lance and saber and resplendent in their vivid attire. As each of the Royal Guests arrived to form the wedding procession, he or she was greeted with wild cheering. The Duchess of Edinburgh and her children were the earliest arrivals. Then Princess Louise and the Duke of Fife, the Prince and Princess of Wales, the King and Queen of Denmark, Prince Albert of Belgium, the Tsarevitch, and finally the bridegroom in his naval uniform. Yet, no matter how exciting the events outside the Palace, they could not compare to those occurring inside, as the Palace staff prepared for the afternoon's wedding festivities and the bridegroom chatted nervously to his Royal guests.

The bride was still sequestered in her suite. Earlier that morning, she had written Prince George a pencilled note:

> I should much like to give you a wedding ring if you will wear it for my sake—I therefore send you herewith one or two to try on for size—Let me have the one you choose at once and I will give it to you in the Chapel. What a memorable day in our lives this will be. God grant it may bring us much happiness. I love you with all my heart. Yrs. for ever and ever—May.

Prince George had brought the ring with him and had given it to a courier to dispatch immediately to his bride. As the door to her apartments opened, the bridegroom, standing at the end of the majestic, long, red-carpeted corridor, caught sight of Princess May. He swept her a low and courtly bow; she returned the handsome gesture with a deep curtsy and then quickly withdrew.

Although the Chapel Royal is only a few hundred yards from Buckingham Palace, the procession was routed the long way round. The first thirteen open state landaus, gleaming with scarlet and gold, left Buckingham Palace at 11:30, following a route up Constitution Hill, along Piccadilly, and then on to the destination. The Prince of Wales's landau led this procession. Seated beside him was his brother Arthur, Duke of Connaught. They were followed by Princess Louise and her family, and then by Toria and Maud. In the last carriage rode the King and Queen of Denmark, the Tsarevitch, and the Princess of Wales, "ethereal in white satin and shimmering with diamonds in the sunlight." The Tsarevitch was mistaken by the crowds for the bridegroom, and great shouts and strident cheering greeted him all along the way. The crowds were so dense that there was no room to bring in a stretcher for anyone who might faint. Men and boys perched insecurely in the branches of trees. Small children were given precedent and sat in a line on the edge of the kerbstones.

*　　*　　*

At 11:45 the Queen's procession left the palace with the Queen—wearing a diamond crown, the bright ribbon of the Garter across her black bodice—and a radiant, triumphant Princess Mary Adelaide riding with her in the glass coach drawn by "four of the Creams." Queen Victoria was to have made her entry into the chapel from St. James's Street, which was a shorter route from the palace than the earlier-departing processions had taken, but she arrived at the chapel door first, instead of last (the correct official position for the Sovereign at all times). Only a gentleman usher was present to receive her. Instantly assessing the situation, Princess Mary Adelaide suggested she should proceed in her place and that the Queen remain in an anteroom that had been prepared for her use. Scarcely had Princess Mary Adelaide taken a few steps up the corridor when her lady-in-waiting, Miss Thesiger, felt a little pull at her dress and at the same time heard a voice saying, "I am going first." Looking back, she saw the Queen on the arm of her grandson, the Grand Duke Ernest Louis of Hesse,* on her way to wait in the anteroom until she was to enter the chapel. A wedding guest recalled that "some minutes later the Lord Chamberlain and the great officers of the Household arrived in breathless haste; but Her Majesty was not at all perturbed by the incident, only saying that she was glad it had happened so, for it was very amusing to see everyone come in."

Members of the Royal Family and Royal guests now streamed into the interior of what the Queen called "this ugly chapel." Whatever the chapel lacked in eccesiastical splendour was more than made up by the assemblage gathered there. "Scarlet was lent to the pageant," reported the *Daily Telegraph*, "by the appearance of Her Majesty's Royal Body Guard in their red and gold uniforms, their gauntlets, and white plumed casques, and bearing their gleaming parisaus adorned with tassels of crimson silk and gold buillion." The jewels worn by the lady guests at the Royal Wedding were given a full column in the same newspaper,

---

*Grand Duke Ernest Louis V of Hesse-Darmstadt (1868–1937), eldest son of Queen Victoria's second daughter, Alice, and also Princess Alix of Hesse's brother.

83

with those worn by Lady Rothschild described as arousing particular admiration and being valued at an estimated £250,000.

At 12:15 a distant cheering could be heard inside the chapel as the bridegroom's cortege arrived. The Queen's State Trumpeters played a ringing fanfare from their silver clarions, and the Gentlemen-at-Arms entered, followed by the Lord Chamberlain, who, walking backwards, conducted the Queen, still supported by the Grand Duke, to her appointed place. Another flourish of trumpets was sounded, and Princess May, flanked by her father and her brother Prince Dolly, entered—her train being borne by her ten bridesmaids.

Queen Victoria noted in her journal that day, "Dear May looked so pretty & quiet and dignified. She was vy. simply & prettily dressed—& wore her mother's veil lace. The bridesmaids looked vy. sweet in white satin, with a little pink & red rose on the shoulder & some small bows of the same on the shoes . . . Georgie gave his answers distinctly . . . while May, though quite self-possessed, spoke vy. low."

But it is Lady Geraldine Somerset's journal for July 6, 1893, that reveals the true spirit of the day:

"May's Wedding Day! The greatest success ever seen or heard of! not a hitch from first to last, nor an if or a but!! everything went *absolutely a souhait!* first of all it was the most *heavenly* day ever could be—such a summer's day as you get solely and only in England—not the heavy oppressive atmosphere of yesterday, but the *most brilliant* glorious *really* tropical sunshine with tropical heat,—yet with it, mercifully, [breezes] from time to time refreshed one and recovered one! quite perfection . . . The town was alive!! swarms everywhere! . . . Piccadilly was beautifully decorated; but anything to equal the loveliness of St. James's Street I never saw—it was like a bower from end to end . . . garlands of green across and between the Venetians masts with bracelets of flowers suspended from them, *too* pretty.

"I went to the Household Pew in the Chapel Royal . . . It was all so admirably arranged I think everybody in the Chapel could see well! The first to enter the Chapel was the Queen followed by P[rincess] M[ary Adelaide] who drove *in* the Queen's carriage from Buckingham Palace!! will her head be still on her shoulder tomorrow! I believe it will have expanded and blown

84

to the moon! The Princess of Wales looked *more lovely*—than ever! none can approach her! but I was sorry for her today. May with the Duke of York standing at the Altar!! and for the Princess *what pain.*"

After the ceremonies the Royal guests returned to Buckingham Palace, where the newlyweds signed the register in the Bow Saloon overlooking the gardens.* Princess May signed first, "Victoria Mary of Teck"; the Duke next, "George"; and then the Queen's signature, followed by those of over a hundred Royalties, Court officers, ministers, clergy, peers; and for the Government Mr. Gladstone and Mr. Asquith; filling four pages of the Queen's special volume reserved by her for Royal marriages and christenings.

At luncheon in the state dining room amid the portraits of former monarchs of Great Britain, the bride and bridegroom sat on one side of the Queen, with the Danish King and Queen on the other. The royalties were seated according to rank, which meant that the Tecks were at another table. Princess Mary Adelaide's finest moment had come and gone.

At 5:00 P.M., the bridal couple left Buckingham Palace for the "Royal Transit" through London to Liverpool Street Station, where they were then to embark for their honeymoon at Sandringham, a curious choice in light of Prince Eddy's death there such a short time before. "Rather *unlucky* and sad," even the Queen commented. But the newly married couple were radiant as they waved to the crowds lining their route. The Duke of York had changed from his uniform to a frock coat and top hat, and

---

*The Royal signatures on the register were preceded by Edward Cantuar, Archbishop of Canterbury. Then came Victoria Mary of Teck (Princess May, Duchess of York), George (Duke of York), Victoria R.I. (the Queen), Albert Edward P. (Prince of Wales), Alexandra (Princess of Wales), Teck (Duke of Teck), Mary Adelaide (Duchess of Teck), Christian R. (King of Denmark), Louise (Queen of Denmark), Nicholas (Tsarevitch of Russia), Ernest Louis (Grand Duke of Hesse), Frederick (Grand Duke of Mecklenburg-Strelitz), Alfred (Duke of Edinburgh), Marie (Duchess of Edinburgh), Arthur (Duke of Connaught), Louise Margaret (Duchess of Connaught), Helena (Princess of Schleswig-Holstein), Louise (Princess, Duchess of Argyll), Beatrice (Princess of Battenberg), Henry (Prince of Battenberg), Henry (Prince of Prussia), Irene (Princess of Prussia), Louise (Duchess of Fife), Fife (Duke of Fife), George (Prince of Denmark), Philip (Prince of Saxe-Coburg).

the new Duchess of York wore a soft white Irish poplin gown trimmed with gold braid, a cape and bonnet to match.

Describing the departure of the newlyweds from the palace, Lady Geraldine Somerset wrote: " . . . We saw her [the bride] and the Duke of York get into the carriage, receive the shower of slippers and drive *au pas* round the Quadrangle amid cheers and as they passed under the portico we rushed into the bedroom and from the balcony saw the Prince [of Wales], the Duke of Edinbro [Edinburgh], the Duke of Cambridge and all the Princes standing round the *grandes grilles* of the outer railing and as the Duke and Duchess of York drove into the Mall shower them with rice! Then they drove along the Mall with the magnificent Blues amid ringing cheers."

Standing with the Queen on the central balcony to see them off, Princess Mary Adelaide and the Duke of Teck both dissolved into tears and "sobbed bitterly" when Auld Lang Syne was played ". . . a horrid moment," the Queen records.

The Royal train steamed into Wolferton (the station for Sandringham) at 7:55, three minutes early. After an official greeting, the newlyweds, in a victoria drawn by two of the Prince of Wales's finest Hungarian horses, drove through the gates of Sandringham, where Princess May would honeymoon as the Duchess of York, wife of the second heir to the Throne.

Before long, Princess May realised that the family she had married into was a closely guarded clique that excluded newcomers. This was particularly true of her mother-in-law and her three sisters-in-law. Nor were they interested in music, literature, or science as she was, or curious about foreign courts where none of their family reigned. Not only was Princess May on a higher plane intellectually than her in-laws, but she enjoyed an entirely different manner of life. She had far more serious notions of woman's place in society and very strong ideas of the responsibilities of the women in the Royal Family. To have to "follow the shooters, watch the killing, however faultless, to take always a cheerful appreciative part in man-made, man-valued amusements" greatly nettled her. She did so, but at a high cost in the sacrifice of her liberal ambitions and in her relationship with her mother-in-law.

Since she was living in cramped quarters almost in Princess Alexandra's garden and with a total lack of privacy, everything she did was duly reported, discussed, and most times discouraged or censored by the Princess of Wales. A crisis occurred when she rearranged the furniture in her sitting room, another when she planted a small garden without permission. Everything had to be referred to the Big House. She realised that she was being treated with an element of distrust, which made it impossible for her to follow her natural inclinations. Such worthwhile desires as helping to increase the well-being of Sandringham's poor families had to be put aside to wait until the Princess of Wales found time to extend her own benevolent hand.

Princess May's new home had begun life as a cottage to accommodate male guests who came to shoot at Sandringham, which had always been too small to use as a Royal residence. Located a hundred yards from the main house, "Bachelor's Cottage" was conceived as a strictly masculine dwelling. Princess Alexandra contributed little to its design or decor, but she did make sure that it was hidden from the view of the main house. This was achieved by concealing it behind laurels and rhododendrons, which soon became dense thicket. Bachelor's Cottage, thus camouflaged and shadowed, was dreary and dark. The exterior was built of local brown stone and ludicrously adorned with imitation Tudor beams, which gave the façade the look of a toy gingerbread house. Fumed oak, Doulton tiles, and stained-glass fanlights were profusely used in the interior. The Prince of Wales changed its name to York Cottage on presentation as a wedding gift to his son, who he knew loved Sandringham—but he never considered Princess May's wishes in this gesture.

Not only dark and ill heated, York Cottage had exceedingly primitive plumbing and a sparsity of bathrooms. Except for the Yorks' bedrooms and dressing rooms, all other bedrooms were almost cubical. The Duke of York was once to comment that the accommodations were so spare that he supposed "the servants must sleep in the trees." The house's most imposing feature was a handsome fireplace with a dark wood overmantel in the entry hall. The narrow winding staircase ascended from this reception area. Close to this was "a tiny snuggery" that was to serve as Prince George's smoking room, library, and gun room. The windows in here were blocked by heavy shrubberies, and the walls, rendering the room even darker, were covered by coarse red cloth, the kind used at the time for French Army trousers. Across the entry hall and curtained by gold-velvet portieres was the "still tinier" drawing room, which had a patent coal grate for a fireplace. The whole ambiance was homely, dark, and crowded, and none of the furnishings—an upright piano, a few cosy chairs, a pretty table or two, numerous potted palms, and far too many knick-knacks—gave the room even an illusion of style. The dining room which adjoined the drawing room was the largest downstairs room, but Princess May had brought with her from White Lodge her considerable collection of pet birds, and so a section of the room had been made into a large aviary.

Not even a hall separated the dining room from the kitchen. "This too, is absurdly small," the *Lady's Pictorial* reported after being given a tour of the cottage, "the ranges, gas-stove, and table almost entirely filling it before the cook and his assistant enter." A new wing had been built to accommodate the male servants, extending from the kitchen and over the old outer buildings which had been storerooms. The upstairs contained accommodations for the women servants,* two guest rooms "very plainly furnished with light-wood articles and flowered chintzes," and at the head of the narrow front staircase the Yorks' suite consisting of a pleasant bedroom with a dressing room of the most limited dimensions on either side. In each of these was a bath, no elaborate marbled silver-fitted arrangement, but a very plain affair, without, indeed, a "shower" attached. Two narrow brass bedsteads placed together beneath a gauzy canopy, wardrobes of satin-wood, and a pair of small chairs furnished the bedroom. Its prettiest feature was a bay window from which the sea was visible.

Princess May had as her own staff dresser Tatry, a French woman who had worked at White Lodge, and Lady Eva Greville, her lady-in-waiting. Lady Eva slept in one of the rabbit-warren

*These rooms were later converted to the nursery, schoolroom, and boys' room.

of tiny rooms over the kitchen, where all the sounds and smells came up through the thin floors. Close to mealtimes the house always had the odour of cooking throughout it. On one occasion, Lady Eva sent down word that "if the footmen cleaning the silver did not object to her overhearing their conversation, she for her part, had no objection to overhearing it."

York Cottage's proximity to her in-laws, not its many inconveniences and irredeemable ugliness, created the most difficulty for Princess May. Less than a year after she arrived there as a bride, she wrote in her journal, "I sometimes think that just after we were married we were not left alone enough and this led to many little rubs which might have been avoided."

Life at Sandringham revolved around the Princess of Wales. Her three daughters had been so eclipsed by their mother's strong personality that they were deadly dull, lethargic, and childlike. Worse, they resented their sister-in-law's intellect, position, and accessibility to their mother. Princess Louise was Prince George's only married sister. The other two lived at home and spent much of their time at Sandringham. The elder, Princess Victoria (Toria), was "delicate, hypochondriacal, and already slightly embittered." Her childhood friendship toward Princess May had disappeared now that the girl was a married woman while she remained a spinster and, in the words of a close member of the family, little more than "a glorified maid to her mother." In fact, Princess Alexandra kept a bell by her side and rang it when she wanted to summon Toria to fetch something for her or to help wind some knitting wool. Princess Maud, the youngest of the daughters, was less sharp-tongued toward her new sister-in-law, but she was a "grumbler," always bewailing her grievances, her paramount complaint being that her mother was doing nothing to find her a husband. Princess Maud, who was then aged twenty-four, was quite right. The Princess of Wales showed no desire that her younger daughters should marry and dismissed all suitors on what was at times quite insubstantial grounds. "It really is *not* wise to leave the fate of these dear girls *dan[s] la vague* for much longer," the Empress Frederick wrote to her sister-in-law, Princess Alexandra, in early 1894.

Had the Duke of York not been second heir to the Throne,

his mother might not have encouraged him to marry either. She had always turned to her children for the attention she felt she had been deprived of by their father's philandering. Princess May was not as malleable as her daughters, or her son, for that matter. Thus, for the new bride, her early months of marriage were a painful time.

For a start, the Duke of York (with his mother's help and without Princess May's knowledge) had furnished York Cottage entirely before his bride's arrival at Sandringham, and the finished rooms jarred Princess May's own good taste. She insisted on redoing the sitting room in yellow and white—colours more pleasing to her than its original browns and tans—and though this request was granted, her mother-in-law was most indignant about it. Without announcing herself, Princess Alexandra would drop by at breakfast or teatime whenever she wished, her two daughters at her elbows and her many dogs cavorting at her heels. Resentment began to mount from these insensitive beginnings.

There was another disturbing element in Princess May's new life: her realisation of the limitations of the man she had married. Nothing in the Duke of York's past had prepared him for his new responsibilities. One of his biographers, John Gore, wrote, "His planned education ended just where and when it should seriously have begun. He was . . . below the educational and perhaps intellectual standard of the ordinary public school-educated country squire." Princess May, who had been better educated in English, English history, and constitutional history, believed that she had to do something to repair these gaps.

Her husband was not terribly keen on books, and so Princess May began a lifelong habit of reading to him, pausing often to comment or to explain. This last was observed by several close members of the family, one of whom snidely commented that "May appears to be educating Georgie." But though she could help her husband broaden his interests, keep somewhat abreast of political happenings, and learn to speak German and French better, she could not supercede his mother's place in his life or overcome the habits of a pampered lifetime.

If the problems of her marriage were great, at least the power and position it brought to Princess May more than compensated. Her first taste of her new glory came only a few weeks after her wedding when, on July 31, she and the Duke of York joined his parents and sisters for a two-week holiday at Cowes on the Isle of Wight, perhaps the most famous of all yachting centres, as the guests of the Queen at Osborne House.

The bitterness of the past could at last be packed away. The two years of exile in Florence could be forgotten, along with all the unpleasant creditors and the Royal critics who had treated the Tecks in a condescending manner. Princess May was now her own person. Her new identity, Duchess of York, was an open sesame to the same world that had once closed its portals to her, and the holiday at Osborne was her grand entrance into the Royal corridors of power.

SEVEN

Osborne was magnificent in summertime with its great magnolias and fragrant jasmine dappling the Italianate terrace. Long soft shadows of oak and chestnut flowed like cool water across the lawns that stretched to the turquoise sea, dotted with the white sails of the fishing boats on the Solent. The grounds were rich with contrasts: the fresh green fields and turf, the masses of evergreens, the beach and the verdant woods, the rolling lawns and scented shrubs and the startling blue of the surf.

Although the Queen and the newlyweds remained at Osborne House, most of the Royal Family lived aboard their yachts while at Cowes: the Prince and Princess of Wales, with Toria and Maud, on their yacht *Osborne;* Kaiser Wilhelm and his suite housed on the imperial German yacht *Hohenzollern.*

The Kaiser's presence posed difficulties, for the Prince of Wales could barely tolerate his nephew and the Princess found him insufferably arrogant. The Kaiser, however, was devoted to his grandmother, the Queen. Princess May liked "William" and was flattered by his attention to her the first night at Osborne when all the Royal guests were dining in the new and splendid Indian Room. "I sat next to William, who made himself most agreeable," she wrote in her diary. "Fancy me, *little me,* sitting

next to William, the place of honour!!! It seemed so strange
. . . I talked my *best* German.''

And with girlish enthusiasm, she wrote her mother that she
wore her ''white *broche* satin low with the Iveagh's tiara,
Gdmama's necklace, the Kennington bow in front of the bodice
& the Warwicks' sun on the side. I wish you had seen me.''

Wilhelm was the son of Empress Frederick, the Queen's eldest and most imperious daughter. Injured in a difficult breech
birth, he had a withered arm twelve inches shorter than the
other. He also had the habit of slipping the hand of his crippled
arm into the pocket of his uniform, which meant his elbow would
protrude at a curious angle. His deformity had warped his personality. He identified strongly with Napoleon, and with his
pocketed hand and strutting gait a certain resemblance could be
detected. The Queen felt great pity for her deformed grandson,
and even when he was most irritating, arrogant, and quarrelsome, she never forgot the circumstances of his birth. Princess
May was apparently not distressed by his difficult personality.
He was the Kaiser and the power of a leading nation, which was
enough for him to gain and hold her respect.

A month after the visit to Cowes, Princess May learned she
could expect her first child that following June. Suddenly she
was the recipient of ''all sort of fuss and precautions of all kinds
& sorts,'' attention she did not enjoy. Nor did she find any sense
of satisfaction or pride in her swollen body, which kept her from
all her exciting new activities.

Besides the cottage at Sandringham, the Yorks had been given
a wing of St. James's Palace. They named their new quarters
York House, an uncomfortable accommodation consisting of
seventy-five small, virtually sunless rooms without architectural
interest.

By spring, Princess May was more or less confined to their
new home (which Prince George was now calling an ''unhealthy
and beastly'' place). In the afternoons, she would have tea on a
satin sofa in the Red Drawing Room, ''a coverlet of white satin,
embroidered with May blossoms, over her legs.'' The room was
panelled in crimson brocade, and through the windows one
could see ''nothing but grimy London walls.'' Much depressed

by her confinement, her inactivity, and the old red brick and gloom of York House itself, she convinced her husband and the Queen that it would be better if she could have the baby at White Lodge. She moved back into her old room and converted several others for her husband's convenience, but unfortunately these last weeks of her confinement proved a tremendous strain on the already tenuous relationship between the Duke of York and his mother-in-law—he did not appreciate her flamboyant nature —and tempers flared.

The waiting amidst such tense conditions came to an end at ten o'clock in the evening of June 23, 1894, when a son, eventually christened Edward Albert Christian George Andrew Patrick David,* but called David by his family and intimate friends throughout his life, was born. A tent was quickly set up on the lawn of White Lodge, and in this a book was placed in which callers were made to sign their names. The first day fifteen hundred people came to pay their respects. Princess May was never more exhilarated, and from Aunt Augusta came the excited acknowledgement of this "great Historical Event."

"Are *you* not beside yourself? I am! and long to *squeeze* everybody who comes in my way. Bruere [her dresser] was the first, who got a *hug,* such as she never had before, then followed old Hueber, *howling . . . in* Church people *winked* at me and loudly congratulated me; on Parade I was received with 'God Save the Queen' when, of course, I *howled.* Oh, it is so delightful! . . . I came to my room yesterday morning, saw a telegram laying, but thinking it came from Fritz first read my Prayers quietly, then opened it, read 'George' good Heavens! I could hardly read on and there it was 'a son, both doing well!' Down I went—mentally —on my knees, tears of gratitude and happiness flowing, streaming, and the hugging *followed . . .* oh, I longed to telegraph all over the world!!"

Aunt Augusta, at the age of seventy-one, was full of vigour— both of mind and body—and as sharp-tongued as ever. Only three years younger than her cousin, the Queen, they had both lived in the first half of the nineteenth century and from those

---

*Named for Prince Eddy, although Queen Victoria was to say that his name was *Albert,* not Edward.

decades had taken her philosophy. Though she had been Grand Duchess of Mecklenburg-Strelitz for many years, she never let the people forget that she was first and before all else an English Princess. The social leader of the Grand Duchy, she liked giving dinner parties and attending the opera in state. Her household was modelled on stern Victorian lines, and members of her family later claimed "she was such an old skin-flint that even at a thoroughly advanced age—[fifteen years hence]—she refused to have rubber tyres fitted to the wheels of her carriage and rattled along over the cobblestones on iron rims." She came to London several months each year and spent much of the time with Princess May, whom she had helped to dress and educate as a young woman. To her niece's horror, the Grand Duchess would go shopping alone, stopping her carriage some distance from a shop and walking to it, giving as alias the name of one of her servants when making a purchase, certain that she would not be recognised and would thereby obtain things much more cheaply. Not one to mince her words, she had always been critical of the marriage of the Prince and Princess of Wales, and only her more compelling displeasure with Princess Alexandra, whom she considered unpleasantly strong-willed, kept her from being outspoken against the escapades of the Prince of Wales.

On June 27, the Queen, with a huge entourage which included the Tsarevitch Nicholas and his bride-to-be, the Queen's grand-daughter, Princess Alix of Hesse,* arrived at White Lodge to see the new Prince and was welcomed by a beaming, "twittering" Princess Mary Adelaide. The Queen concurred that "the Baby, who is a vy fine strong Boy," was "a pretty Child." Four weeks later, the Queen returned for the christening of the infant Prince.

The family might have been overwhelmed with happiness at the birth of her son, but from the outset Princess May found motherhood and infants more than she could tolerate. Nursing

*The Tsarevitch Nicholas and Princess Alix were soon to become Tsar and Tsarina (Empress) Alexandra of Russia. Princess Alix was to be one of Queen Victoria's granddaughters who were carriers of haemophilia, and had she married into the British Royal line could have jeopardized its future. Princess Ena, future Queen of Spain, was another haemophilia carrier. Three of her four sons were afflicted with the dread disease, and one was mute.

the child was repugnant to her, the child's cries terrifying, the odours distressing. But at this time, the English nanny reigned supreme in all upper-class households, and their charges saw their parents perhaps once, seldom twice, a day in circumstances that were stiff and formal.

Mary Peters had been hired as a nanny before the baby's birth. Her excellent references stated that she had worked for a member of Princess May's Lady-in-Waiting Lady Eva Dugdale's family. She had been an orphan and, at twenty-seven, was approaching spinsterhood. With great relief, Princess May consigned the child into the care of this incredibly autocratic personality (a trait not undesirable in a nanny of that time). Mary Peters devoted herself entirely to her small charge, and though some indication of her growing instability might have been gleaned when she refused to take a day off and became unnaturally possessive of the baby in her care, staff problems were never brought to Princess May's attention.

Shortly after the christening, Princess May moved back to York House, but to the Duke of York's irritation, his mother-in-law came with her and the child. Princess May now had to contend with a serious situation that was growing worse between her husband and her mother.

The rooms of York House were strung together by narrow ill-lit passages interrupted by unexpected flights of steps. At night, these passages were treacherous. After returning from York House one evening, Princess Mary Adelaide wrote her daughter, "I know how distressed you will be when you learn that I fell down that horridly dangerous step from the night nursery into the passage, *tout de mon long* arriving on my hands and knees (I fear *mon ecriture se'en resent!*)"

"She might have been killed, and Peters, who heard the fall, nearly died of fright as when she ran up to Mama she found her lying quite still and thought she was dead," Princess May wrote her husband in a curt note and to which he replied, "There is a very good electric light at the top of the stairs and it ought to have been turned on."

Several cliques comprised London Society. The Marlborough House Set was one; then there were the "Incorruptibles," those reactionary, ancient families who looked upon the Prince of

Wales's circle as vulgar; and the "Intellectuals" (or "Souls"), who spun in orbit around their sun, Arthur Balfour, Lord Salisbury's nephew. No matter which group one belonged to, the daily routine was much the same. At ten one would parade in St. James's Park: if part of the Marlborough Set, on horseback and at a gallop; the "Incorruptibles" in an open carriage; while the "Intellectuals" strolled on foot. This same fixed outing occurred between tea and dinner. A witness of the period recalled that unless dying, no one remained home. "Splendid equipage filled the streets. Ladies driving in their victorias drawn by smart, high-stepping cobs with a 'tiger' sitting very straight with folded arms beside the coachman on the box, excited approving masculine gazes as they passed under club windows. Gentlemen sighed and told each other, 'What a pretty thing it was to see a lovely woman drive in London behind a well-matched pair.' " Down another street came trotting the Royal Horse Guards in blue tunics and white breeches on black horses with bridles and halter-chains shining and jingling. Tall silhouettes of hansom cabs carried the well-known profiles of statesmen and clubmen on their round of visits to the great houses and to the clubs in Pall Mall and St. James's.

If one could stand the pace a gala dinner could be attended every night, followed by the opera, reigned over that season by Mme. Melba, and balls that seldom ended before 3:00 A.M. The women, led by the style-setters of the day—Lady Warwick and Lady de Grey—shimmered with diamonds and floated from dinner to opera to ball in a diaphanous cloud of tulle escorted by the gentlemen in white tie and tails. Footmen wore their finest livery. Everyone wanted to be on the guest lists for the dances given by the Duchess of Devonshire or Lady Londonderry, the two arbiters of society. Lillie Langtry, as beautiful as she had been during her early glory as the mistress of the Prince of Wales, was back in the Marlborough House Set. Conversation invariably returned to the unsuccessful libel action Oscar Wilde had brought against the Marquess of Queensberry and the sensational trial that spring, which found the scandalous Wilde—whose play, *The Importance of Being Earnest,* was the success of the season—guilty of homosexual charges and committed to serve time at Reading Gaol.

Princess May was greatly admired, but the Yorks were never a part of any of these circles. The Duke of York did not approve of his father's set, and he was hardly inclined toward the Intellectuals. He preferred to dine with Princess May and their Household or to join his mother and sisters for tea than to attend any gala occasion. Not a good conversationalist, he did possess an amazing memory. He did not have a particularly inquiring mind, and his two consuming hobbies were shooting and stamp collecting.

Still, the Duke of York was not unhappy with his life but was content with the dullness of duties that did not draw too harshly upon his energies. He was also far more accustomed to the uncritical praise and effusive endearments showered upon him by his mother and sisters than by society. He soon grew to admire the candor possessed by his wife and to trust her opinions and decisions. Increasingly, his great dependency upon his mother transferred to Princess May, a fact that did not help the relationship between the two women.

The London social season of 1895 was especially brilliant, but as Princess May was carrying her second child at the time, she entered into few of the frivolities. Though the Yorks attended Ascot, Princess May was highly intolerant of racing and gambling. Not so her mother, who wrote to her son Alge, in India, "Tuesday we had a delightful day at the races [Ascot]! Glorious weather! A very fine procession up the course! 12 Psses and in all 20 *royalties* filling 5 carriages . . . Uncle Wales won 2 races and we all *won* our *money!* I cried with excitement at his first victory with *Persimmon,* and cheered when *Florizel 2* won him Her My's *Gold Vase.*"

Princess May admitted to her brother, "There have been a good many foreign royalties over in England this summer which has given *éclat* to the season." Still, she was not inclined either to write or indulge in gossip, as did the ladies surrounding Princess Alexandra and the smart set who were part of the Prince of Wales's social circle. She was aware of her father-in-law's strong liaison with Mrs. George Keppel, and that Alice Keppel had joined the Prince of Wales openly at Cowes that year, an act that "could not be easy for Motherdear," she wrote Aunt Augusta, without further comment than that. "Before her scandal sits dumb," a contemporary of Princess May wrote of her perceptively, adding, "she has a quiet but inflexible power of silencing everything which seems likely to approach ill-natured gossip. I am filled with admiration for the dignified simplicity & singlemindedness, & the high sense of duty . . . which will be the very salvation of England some day."

The business of government and empire was carried on during the season, but scant attention was paid to it by the Prince of Wales set. The Kaiser arrived with his mother, the Empress Frederick, early in August for the Royal Regatta at Cowes and at this social event crossed swords in conversations with Lord Salisbury (then in the second month of his new term of office).

The Queen remained an outsider to all the cliques of society. Amazingly alert for her years and in good health, she still refused to include the Prince of Wales in governmental matters or to give him some responsible post. This same exclusion was exercised toward the Duke of York. Except for the business of being on show, neither father nor son had much to do, other than attending a "function every few weeks at Lancaster or at Liverpool or at Halifax or at Brighton," and attendance at Royal funerals and weddings. Neither man was accorded access to official documents or Cabinet papers. Except for an occasional social meeting with leading politicians, the Duke of York's knowledge of the government would not have been more extensive than that of any man who read the *Times* each morning. The Prince of Wales, though exercising some small initiative in state matters, continued to stave off boredom with society galas, gambling, and the company of Alice Keppel; the Duke of York in gardening, his stamp collection, and shooting.

In November 1895, with Princess May in her ninth month, the Duke of York accompanied his parents to Russia to attend the funeral in Saint Petersburg of Tsar Alexander III (Princess Alexandra's brother-in-law) and the wedding of the new Tsar Nicholas II to Princess Alix of Hesse. To the Princess of Wales, the first meeting with her widowed sister was "unspeakable agony." She remained by the Empress's side throughout the nineteen days of funeral ceremonies, even sleeping by night in her bedroom. For years, her sister, the Empress Maria, and her brother-in-law, Tsar Alexander III, had been her closest confidants, the ones to whom she would run when life in England became too difficult. The death of the powerful Tsar, only forty-nine, had been a shock to her as well as to all of Europe's Royalties, sixty-one of whom—each with an entourage—were housed in the magnificent marble palaces of the Tsar's city.

Looking pale and bereaved, Princess Alexandra stood by her sister's side at midnight on the first night of her arrival in the light of flickering torches. Both women wept as the Tsar's coffin was carried over the threshold of his own home by his relatives and then borne on the shoulders of his faithful Cossacks to the little church on top of a neighbouring hill. Since the Tsar had died in Livadia, the coffin had first to go by ship to Moscow and then overland to Saint Petersburg.

"Every day, after lunch, we had another service at the Church,"* the Duke of York wrote Princess May from Saint Petersburg. "After the service, we all went up to [the] coffin which was open and kissed the Holy Picture which he holds in his hand. It gave me a shock when I saw his dear face so close to mine when I stooped down."

The wedding of Princess Alix, now Alexandra Fyodorovna, Empress of all the Russias, took place on November 26, one week after the funeral. The new Tsarina wrote her sister:† "One day in deepest mourning lamenting a beloved one, the next in smartest clothes being married. There cannot be a greater contrast, but it drew us more together, if possible."

Victoria's granddaughter Alix, the young woman who had refused to marry Prince Eddy, "looked too wonderfully lovely," the Duke of York wrote Princess May. "I must say I never saw two people more in love with each other or happier than they are. I told them both that I could not wish them more than that they should be as happy as you and I are together. Was that right?"

*   *   *

*The fortress church of Saint Peter and Saint Paul.

†The Grand Duchess Elizabeth (Ella) (1864–1918), wife of Grand Duke Serge, granddaughter of Queen Victoria. Kaiser Wilhelm had always been in love with Ella, and when her life was in danger in 1918, he begged her to leave Russia and join him. She refused and was brutally murdered by the Bolsheviks.

"A boy!!! What a joy!!!" Princess Mary Adelaide wrote to her son Prince Alge, who was still in India. On December 14, 1895 (unfortunately the anniversary of the deaths of the Prince Consort in 1861 and of the Queen's second daughter Alice, Tsarina Alexandra's mother, in 1878), the Yorks' second son, Prince Albert Frederick Arthur George (known ever after to his family as "Bertie") was born at York Cottage. "Dear Grandmama we propose with your permission to call him Albert after dear Grandpapa," the Duke of York wrote the Queen, hoping to appease her distress at the baby's inadvertent and sad choice of a day to enter this world. "He could hardly have been called by any other name," she commented. However, Princess Mary Adelaide, who had not been fond of the Prince Consort, had the final prophetic word. "George will be his *last* name and we hope some day may supplant the less favoured one!" she wrote to her second son, Frank, who was on his way to India to join his brother Alge's regiment.

The new baby was given over to Mary Peters and an additional nurse. Princess May was no more maternal toward her second child than toward her first, seeing her sons perhaps twice a day. Although quite happy to give Nanny Peters full authority, she was distressed that David, the older, cried when handed over to her. She seldom ever ventured into the nursery. Had she, she could not have helped but been alarmed at the Dickensian atmosphere that prevailed. Mary Peters was suffering severe mental problems, and no one in the nursery dared to touch or talk to David for fear of her reprisals towards the child or them. Nor was anyone courageous enough to tell Princess May that her second son was being underfed and neglected because Peters resented his presence.

Then, in autumn of 1896, Princess May became pregnant for the third time. A gentle Cockney woman, Lala Bill,* was engaged as a second nanny. She discovered to her horror that three-year-old David was covered with bruises and learned that Peters would pinch him or twist his arm nastily before handing him over to his mother, so that he would cry loudly and be handed directly back to her. The same bruising treatment was

---

*Charlotte Bill (1867–1963).

applied to the child whenever he approached a nursemaid. Little Bertie was being dealt with in a cold, brusque manner and was terrified of everything. Peters, she was told, had not had a day away from David in all the time she had been caring for him. Lala Bill gathered up her courage and told Lady Eva Dugdale, who in turn immediately reported the situation to Princess May. Peters was fired that very day. At first she refused to leave but was gone by nightfall. A week later, she was in hospital, having suffered a complete nervous breakdown from which she would never recover.

The possible effect those three years of Mary Peters's obsessive care had on small David's future relationships with women, as well as whether the little Prince was ever sexually abused, has been the subject of much public discussion. Whatever the extent of Mary Peters's abuse of the child, that it continued for almost three years without the Yorks' knowledge is shocking. For everyone in the Household appears to have had doubts about Mary Peters's stability and her treatment of little David.

Yet all the blame cannot be placed on Princess May. The Duke of York did not like babies and little boys any more than his wife did. York Cottage was small and cramped, and sound carried, and the Prince was often heard calling out in irritation to Lala Bill, "Can't you stop that child from crying?"

A girl, Princess Victoria Alexandra Alice Mary (Mary to her family) was born to Princess May on April 25, 1897, only seventeen months after Bertie's birth. Princess May was pleased to have a daughter—but she had no more to do with this new baby than with her sons. Helene Bricka was enlisted to join the Household to supervise the boys, and Lala Bill took on the care of the infant Princess. By the time of the Queen's Diamond Jubilee, which was only two months after the birth of her third child, Princess May was slim and ready to step back into the public limelight.

EIGHT

The day of the Queen's Diamond Jubilee, June 22, 1897,* was dazzlingly bright. "Queen's weather," the English called it, and no one was surprised that the sun, after an overcast morning, finally blazed high in the heavens. After all, were not the English now God's Chosen People destined to go forth in the world to do His will? And how symbolic that the young heir of York was called David!

> England! What shall men say of thee,
> Before whose feet the worlds divide?
> The Earth, a brittle globe of glass,
> Lies in the hollow of thy hand,

said Oscar Wilde, who had just been released from Reading Gaol.

In a sense, the English *had* been chosen. They had reached their apogee. Imperialism had become habit. Forty million strong, they had overflowed their shores and sailed across the world to plant their ideas, culture, and language. Having escaped the social upheavals that now shook Europe, having pro-

*Queen Victoria came to the Throne in 1837; the Diamond Jubilee was to celebrate the sixtieth year of her reign.

duced an imperial elite whose true vocation was Empire, and possessing a monarchy of semidivine nature, they believed they were as well fitted as any nation to govern one quarter of the world.

No other period of British history had been so theatrical as the last half of the nineteenth century, set-piece after set-piece appearing with wonderful precision, triumph and tragedy alternating to the greatest effect. And through the years the Empire grew mightier. To England and the world the indomitable old Queen symbolised the true might of that empire, unchanging, unwavering, bowing to no man.

The Queen's route had been thronged with celebrants since the previous night, when Big Ben sounded the last stroke of twelve and a peal of bells throughout London had proclaimed Diamond Jubilee Day. The crowds that filled the miles of streets and squares along the route answered with ringing cheers, and cries of "God Save the Queen" could be heard above blaring horns and cornets. On the streets, buskers entertained with mouth organs and concertinas. Inside the music halls, which were kept open specially until 2:00 A.M., every popular ditty was greeted by vociferous shouts and cheers. Everywhere hawkers vended fruit. The illuminations that decorated public buildings and store fronts remained lighted until dawn. And street stalls, where coffee, hot potatoes, and confections were on sale, did a brisk trade throughout the night.

Shortly before 6:00 A.M., the vestry carts arrived to gravel the roadways freshly, a custom, according to the *Daily Telegraph,* ". . . which prevailed [since] the good old days of Sam Pepys." By ten o'clock, the sun pierced sharply through the clouds. Less than an hour later, when the Royal procession formed in front of the Palace, uniforms, carriages, medals, and sabres filled the streets with a mass of blazing colours.

The procession was headed by a cavalcade of officers, military attachés, and representatives of all the Courts of Europe, followed by the Kaiser's regiments and a deputation from the First Prussian Dragoon Guards. The most brilliant group of all the soldiery were the officers of the Imperial Service troops from India, swarthy, mostly bearded men wearing a rare collection of wondrously twisted turbans in bright colours trimmed in gold.

Their tunics (or "Kirtas") were scarlet and peacock blue and jade green, laced and interlaced with gold or silver, broadly and vividly sashed. Many also wore massive gold earrings with enormous stones. The Fijians, their hair trained upward and dyed a bright red, followed. And after them came all the regiments of Britain and her Empire: Canadians, Australians, New Zealanders, Africans, the Zaptiehs from Cyprus, the Dyaks from Borneo. The crowds shouted its enthusiasm as each exotic regiment filed past. Their cheers rose to thunderous proportion and made even the saluting guns in St. James's Park barely audible as the Queen's carriage followed the troops.

Though nearing her eightieth year and exposed to uncommon heat and great strain, Queen Victoria still projected an animated figure to her cheering admirers. Her customary black-silk moiré dress was embroidered for the occasion with silver emblems of her reign. A wreath of white acacia and an aigrette of diamonds trimmed her black-lace bonnet. Attended by her marshals, clerics, and statesmen, she sat in her ornate, opened, gilded carriage drawn by eight of the Royal stable's finest cream-coloured horses ridden by elaborately uniformed postillions with scarlet-coated footmen walking at their sides. Her white-lace parasol, which she used to protect herself from the hot sun, bobbed up and down as the carriage made its way slowly along the Jubilee route. Beside her sat the Princess of Wales, elegantly costumed in mauve from her flower-bedecked bonnet to her satin shoes. The Prince of Wales, astride a magnificent black horse and resplendent in his field marshal's uniform, rode by their side. Princess May, in a dress of sky-blue, feathery clouds piled high on her hat, rode with Prince George. The rest of the Royal Family, including the children (David became so nauseous from sun and motion that he had to be transferred to an ambulance to relieve himself surreptitiously of his breakfast), rode in carriages behind the Queen's. The journey was a tedious three-hour procession through London and its outskirts, and most members of the Royal Family were exhausted at its end. Yet the Queen looked more radiant than she had in years.

For the Princess of Wales, the Jubilee celebrations were overshadowed by anxiety for her brother, the King of Greece, George I. Hostilities had erupted between Turkey and Greece on April 17, after Turkey had been urged on by Kaiser Wilhelm II. King George of Greece had sent frenzied telegrams to his sister begging her to enlist the Queen's aid, but Princess Alexandra was powerless. A week before the Jubilee, the Queen's Lady-in-Waiting, Marie Mallet, wrote her husband, "The Princess of Wales came down last night in an awful stew about Greece, imploring the Queen to do something to stop the war and stay the hand of the triumphant Turks . . . We live for nothing but the Jubilee and seem to ignore the doings of the world in general, and we snort at the Greek question."

Princess May also suffered from anxiety during the Jubilee. Her mother had been seriously ill and was operated upon for the removal of kidney stones on April 27. Nonetheless, Princess Mary Adelaide insisted upon being present in the Jubilee procession. A few days earlier, she had been wheeled about the grounds of Buckingham Palace in a chair for the Queen's garden party and the next night had attended the famous *bal costume* given by the Duchess of Devonshire, appearing in the character of the Electress Sophia. Lord Esher, slim and debonair in a costume from 1628—black velvet trimmed with beads and a ruff —his balding head exposed and his moustache waxed and curled, did what he could to bring guests to her so that she would not overexert herself. But the heat and the strain of Jubilee Week were too much for Princess Mary Adelaide to bear in her weakened condition. She spent a fortnight at York Cottage immediately following. A clergyman came to call upon her. Her grandson David was seated on her lap. "You will pray for him, won't you?" she asked with concern, adding, "He will indeed need your prayers." Then, kissing the small child who one day would be a troubled King, she said, "This kind gentleman will pray for you, dear."

On Saturday, October 23, Princess May spent a week at White Lodge with her failing mother. The doctors now concurred that Princess Mary Adelaide was suffering from a malignancy. A second operation was performed only two days after the first, but she was too weak to rally. After forty-eight hours she died without ever regaining full consciousness.

At the Duke of Teck's urgent request, the Princess of Wales was summoned and arrived at White Lodge to find ". . . everyone plunged in the most terrible grief—[Duke of Teck] poor man heart-broken utterly crushed," she wrote the Grand Duchess Augusta, Princess Mary Adelaide's sister, "poor darling May & her two brothers,* calm but in perfect despair—Uncle George [Duke of Cambridge] very much upset—Bertie [Prince of Wales] was also there having come up from Newmarket with the former —Sister Louise [Princess Louise, Duchess of Argyll] also there . . . & poor dear Geraldine [Somerset] was there—& so nice & feeling—We had a long talk together. Darling May who so far bears up wonderfully well took me upstairs at once into Mary's room! Where she was lying in her *last* long sleep. She looked *so* beautiful calm & peaceful with such a happy expression on her dear face." Lady Geraldine Somerset had remained the constant hypocrite to the end.

Lord Esher was asked to make the funeral arrangements. He found the vault where Princess Mary Adelaide, as a descendant of George III, was to be buried in a deplorable state.

"The partition between this vault and that in which Henry VIII, Charles I and Jane Seymour were buried is bricked up," he recorded. "But I saw an old man who was present as a boy when George IV opened the vault and the coffin of Charles I. This man told me that when the lid was removed, King Charles's face seemed that of a living man, absolutely perfect. In a few minutes, exposed to the air, it fell to pieces. There was a piece of black ribbon to hide the severance of the head from the body."

Lord Esher did what he could to have the vault made respectable, and at noon on Wednesday, November 3, wind and rain thrashing mournfully against the stained-glass windows, Princess Mary Adelaide, Duchess of Teck, was buried in the Royal Vault at St. George's Chapel, Windsor, with the Queen present and the Prince of Wales standing beside her bier. Princess May maintained her composure throughout the long service, bearing it with control. Princess Alexandra's loud sobbing was prompted as much by memories of Prince Eddy as by the death of Princess Mary Adelaide.

Within a few days of his wife's funeral, the Duke of Teck's once-erect form was bowed with grief, and the handsome face

*Prince Dolly and Prince Frank. Prince Alge was not in England at the time.

107

bore visible traces of mental anguish. Having leaned upon Princess Mary Adelaide during all the years of their marriage, he was never able to recover from her death. "I dread to think how we can live without her," Princess May wrote Aunt Augusta. "For Papa it is cruel & his sad state makes it so much worse. He was so dependent on Mama for everything & God knows what he will do."

The Duke of Teck's mental condition caused his daughter great alarm. He was, for the two years until his own death, to live in seclusion at White Lodge, looked after by a resident doctor and a series of male nurses. Princess May's first few visits so unbalanced him that she did not return.

Her parents' deaths fortified—rather than depleted—Princess May's strength. She also reached the zenith of her attractiveness during this period. "She was quite superb in white and many diamonds on Monday night and made quite a little sensation coming down into the dimly lighted Concert room by the staircase at the side of the stage [at Windsor] with the footlights shining upon her brightly as she followed the Queen into the room," the Empress Frederick wrote her daughter, Crown Princess Sophie of Greece. However, Princess May still wore a "towsel & fringe like a thick sponge over [her] forehead" (a wig front was attached to her own hair for this fashion).

Princess May was fast displaying the grandeur and majesty that were to be synonymous with her name when she became Queen Consort. This premature queenliness did not help her already strained relations with her mother-in-law, but it did please the Queen and assured her that she had been right in her choice of a wife for Prince George. Frequent invitations from the Queen (to her mother-in-law's extreme irritation) were more forthcoming to Princess May than to Princess Alexandra. In 1896, she spent a month with Queen Victoria at Osborne, eight days at Windsor Castle, six days at Balmoral, made four visits to Buckingham Palace and another four visits to Balmoral, during which she stayed at nearby Mar Lodge. The following year she joined the Queen (who travelled "incognito" as the Comtesse de Balmoral) on her last yearly migration to the Hotel Excelsior Regina at Cimiez near Nice. The Royal Entourage of over thirty people rode in the Queen's *Train Special,* its interior elegantly upholstered and tasselled in dove blue, soft rose, and pearl grey. Both of the Queen's ladies-in-waiting took ill with fevers and colds during the trip, and Princess May accompanied the Queen on daily excursions.

"I drove with Gdmama to Villefranche," she wrote to her husband who had remained in England. "You would have laughed at me sitting with Gdmama's purse in my hand giving one franc pieces to throw to the beggars, some such awful sights too, with horrible disfigurements!" And the next day she wrote him, "At 4 I drove with Gdmama . . . & she talked very kindly of you & said she was so glad we got on so well together as in these days it was such an example to others!"

These drives were never simple because the Queen's *Chasseurs d'Afrique* thundered behind the Royal carriage and people crowded the streets. A side entrance of the hotel had been set apart exclusively for the Queen's use. Her sitting-room walls of red brocade were hung with pictures lent during her stay by Nice's top art dealer. Picnics were held on the high slopes of the Corniche above Cimiez—a relief only for the Queen's Scottish gillie who trailed the Royal carriage on foot up the steep hills. Despite being served by the Indians on fine china and eating at comfortable tables and in comfortable chairs, luncheon alfresco in the South of France in the month of April was a chilly affair.

Impeccable care was given to each small detail of the installation of the Court at the Hotel Excelsior Regina. The Queen's writing paper was identical to that used at Windsor and Balmoral, except that beneath the embossed Crown was printed, "Hotel Regina, Cimiez." At half-past eight, she would come into the drawing room of her suite leaning on the arm of one of her Indian servants (who wore native costume and a gold-striped turban) and greet her dinner guests as they stood lined up uneasily. Dinner—as at Windsor—was served punctually at 9:15 in a room containing full-length coronation portraits of George III and Queen Charlotte. After dinner, the guests were shepherded back into the drawing room, where each in turn would be permitted a short conversation with the Queen. No one was allowed to sit until the Queen, as was her custom, retired precisely at eleven o'clock.

Now past eighty, Queen Victoria's failing eyesight created grave constitutional problems, for she could no longer keep abreast of affairs that were the Sovereign's prerogative. To further complicate this difficulty, she refused to take Sir Frederick (Fritz) Ponsonby,* her Assistant Private Secretary, into her confidence. All communiqués to the Queen were read to her by her daughter, Princess Beatrice. "The result is that the most absurd mistakes occur and the Queen is not even *au courant* with the ordinary topics of the present day," Sir Frederick wrote his mother in August 1898. "There is [also] the danger of the Q[ueen]'s letting go almost entirely the control of things which should be kept under the immediate supervision of the sovereign." Though nearly blind, the Queen's faculties remained sharp, ". . . Her memory . . . wonderful, her shrewdness of discrimination as strong as ever . . ." and her power to move her people obdurate.

The Queen had just returned from a visit to Ireland. On the way home, her yacht was caught in a particularly rough sea and the boat was harshly buffeted. Never a good sailor, she became violently seasick and summoned her private physician, who was in attendance. "Go up at once," she ordered, "and give the Admiral my compliments and tell him the thing must not occur again." Obviously her autocratic personality had not been humbled by age.

The long reign of Queen Victoria, which had given the British such a sense of "organic permanence," was nearing its close, and with the end in sight came a need for the Empire to bolster its strength to confront the inevitable changeover. In the beginning, the South African war, declared on October 11, 1899, had been expected to strengthen the Empire and to be over by Christmas. Instead, it lasted 33 months, cost over £100 million and at least 50,000 lives, and was the most humiliating war the British had fought in a hundred years.

"Every Englishman is born with [that] miraculous power," wrote George Bernard Shaw, "that made him master of the world. When he wants a thing he never tells himself he wants it.

---

*Upon the death of Sir Henry Ponsonby, his son, Sir Frederick Ponsonby, became Assistant Private Secretary to Queen Victoria.

He waits patiently until there comes into his mind, no one knows how, a burning conviction that it is his moral and religious duty to conquer those who possess the thing he wants."

The British and the Boers (the people of Dutch descent in the South African Republic known as Transvaal) had been enemies since the end of the Napoleonic Wars. The acquisition by Britain of the Cape of Good Hope had brought about periodic skirmishes. Through the years Great Britain had increased its territorial possessions in South Africa. Natal, Basutoland, Swaziland, Rhodesia, Bechuanaland, and other Bantu lands were theirs. The Transvaal, with great resentment, was finally annexed to Great Britain in 1877. Further anti-British feelings were inflamed when in 1886 gold was discovered in Witwatersrand and British prospectors began to flood the Transvaal. Great Britain soon controlled almost all the newly established mines. To protect itself, the Boer government heavily taxed the British and refused them citizenship. On December 29, 1895, Starr Jameson,* a British colonial administrator in the Transvaal, led a band of volunteers on the famous, supposedly unauthorized Jameson Raid to put down the resisters to a United (British) South Africa. Jameson was captured within a few days, returned to London for trial, and imprisoned. The Transvaalers considered Jameson's Raid an officially sponsored plot to seize their country and built up their military might by forming an alliance with the Orange Free State, a province bordering the Transvaal. To defend its position, Britain dispatched troops.

Germany, however, had supplied the Boers with arms, and to the dismay of the British, the Boer forces were not only larger than their own, but better equipped. After a succession of defeats in October 1899, known as Black Week, the British Commander-in-Chief, Sir Redvers Henry Buller,† was replaced by the well-loved but aged Lord Roberts of Kandahar, who brought with him as Chief-of-Staff Lord Kitchener of Khartoum,‡ former

*Sir Leander Starr Jameson (1853–1917). Colonial administrator and statesman in South Africa.

†Sir Redvers Buller (1839–1908).

‡Horatio Herbert Kitchener (1850–1916). 1st Earl, 1914. Secretary of State at outbreak of World War I.

Governor General of the Sudan and "the most imperial of all the imperial soldiers."

At home in Britain, officers prepared to leave for the Transvaal in a patriotic fury. "Imperial troops must curb the insolence of the Boers . . . For the sake of our Empire, for the sake of our honour, for the sake of the race, we must fight the Boers," the young Winston Churchill declared.* Officers arrived on the bloody, rugged front carrying packs of their favourite foods from Fortnum and Mason, vintage liquors, and ". . . dressing cases, with silver or gold fittings; they brought their splendid shotguns by Purdy or Westley-Richards; their magnificent hunters saddled by such masters as Gordon of Curzon Street, they brought their valets, coachmen, grooms and hunt-servants." They expected a gentlemanly war, and they walked into a massacre. Ten weeks after the war's outbreak, the British knew it would take more than gentleman officers and patriotic duty to win.

The second phase of the war began with the start of the twentieth century. "Of the new century," wrote poet and critic Wilfred Blunt, "I prophecy nothing except that it will be the decline of the British Empire." But for those to whom the Empire was the family business, no such fears existed. The war cast a shadow over the brilliance of their fashionable world. Because of the strong criticism in Germany, France, and Belgium concerning the morality of Britain's aggression, travelling abroad was dangerous for members of the Royal Family. Yet for the Duke and Duchess of York, the first year of the war was a period of great satisfaction, despite the fact that her father died on January 21, 1900, and all three of her brothers were dispatched to the front. Prince George had finally been given a greater share of responsibility and had begun to make contacts with some of the leading figures in public life. Both husband and wife were kept busy inspecting hospitals and hospital ships filled with returned casualties, presiding over meetings of the War Fund, reviewing troops and decorating heroes.

On April 4, 1900, the Prince and Princess of Wales were en route to Copenhagen (to visit Princess Alexandra's family) when

*Sir Winston Spencer Churchill (1874–1965).

112

they were the near-victims of an assassination attempt. They were seated in their private railway carriage at the Gare du Nord in Brussels, where the train had stopped to pick up passengers, when a sixteen-year-old youth ran toward the open carriage window and fired his revolver. "Thank God for his mercy, who saved us both," the Princess telegraphed her mother the following morning. "The ball was found in the carriage today having passed between our two heads. I felt it whizzing across my eyes and saw him coming straight at us." Charlotte Knollys, who was also in the carriage, wrote her brother, Sir Francis Knollys, "There was no time for anyone to be frightened, except the Princess's little Chinese dog, who was terrified by the explosion."

This assassination attempt was an example of anti-British hysteria that had infected young revolutionaries throughout Europe. By May 30, Lord Roberts had won a small, stunning victory and had taken the city of Johannesburg.* In a serious strategic error, he gave the Boers twenty-four hours to withdraw their army intact. Roberts thought he was bringing the war to a speedy and humane conclusion. But the Boer War was a guerrilla war. And because of Roberts's peaceful armistice, the Boers were able to extricate their best men and all their heavy artillery from Johannesburg. The same thing happened six days later when Roberts triumphantly entered the town of Pretoria, certain that he had once again brought about the end of hostilities.

The British had won the battle but lost the victory. The *Morning Post*'s war correspondent, Prevost Battersby, wrote that his fellow correspondents had been "cheated of their Armageddon." Instead of seeing "the last great flight of a free people brought to bay, Pretoria had merely exchanged one mayor for another, and Roberts's men had had to tramp on through choking dust and in unfamiliar harsh, rocky mountainous terrain."

The anxiety over the war was hardest on the Queen, who would often sob audibly when her weak eyes scanned the long lists of casualties. Roberts had never been one of her favourites.

*Frederick Sleigh Roberts (1832–1914). 1st Earl Roberts of Kandahar (1900), Commander-in-Chief of the Indian Forces in 1885, Commander-in-Chief of the British Army in the Boer War.

He did not help his cause by cabling her after capturing Pretoria to ask if she would like to have a statue of herself placed in the centre of town, where a huge bronze likeness of Transvaal's President Kruger stood.* Her Majesty was not in the least amused at the suggestion that she step into Kruger's shoes.

She was very much pleased, however, when a fourth child and third son, Prince Henry of York, was born to Princess May on March 31, 1900. No longer could the succession be feared. The second heir to the Throne had three sons who could, if required, become King (David, Bertie, and now Henry—known almost immediately as "Harry").

By the year 1900, Alice Keppel and the Prince of Wales had formed a liaison of sincere depth and durability. Everyone in Edward's Court adored Mrs. Keppel and felt she had brought dignity and stability into his life. Even his relations with his wife were more harmonious once Alice Keppel had become his mistress, and he was to remain true to her until the end of his life.

When the Prince of Wales first met Alice at the Portman Place home of his friends Lord and Lady Arlington, she was gracefully slender with masses of lovely chestnut hair, creamy white skin, and the most startling turquoise-coloured eyes. She was married to George Keppel, a tall man—six foot four inches tall, and with his Gordon Highlander bearskin (hat) which he often wore, nearly eight feet. The Keppels had one daughter, much charm and good looks, respectable family connections, and almost no money or prospects. The Prince of Wales and Mrs. Keppel fell immediately in love. George Keppel had no objections to his wife becoming the Prince of Wales's mistress and was to be unswervingly loyal to both of them.

In 1900, a fortnight after she had rather daringly sat astride a lion in Trafalgar Square to celebrate the Relief of Mafeking,†

---

*Paul Kruger (1825–1904), President of the Transvaal, 1883–1899. He died in exile in Switzerland.

†At the town of Mafeking in South Africa a British garrison under (later Lord) Baden-Powell (1857–1941) withstood a Boer siege for 217 days. The fort is now a national monument, and Mafeking, in 1965, became independent as Botswana.

Alice gave birth to a second daughter, Sonia.* On the day of Sonia's birth, the road outside the Keppel house was smothered in straw to deaden the sound of the traffic. After the child's birth, orchids, malmaisons, and lilies—great beribboned baskets of them—were delivered by a coachman and attendant in the Prince of Wales's livery. With Alice Keppel's devotion to her Royal lover, rumours that the child was Prince Edward's illegitimate daughter spread. No one was ever certain of the truth, but after Sonia's birth, the Prince of Wales and Alice Keppel were more devoted than ever.

Princess Alexandra was not blind to the strong bond between her husband and his lover. Nor was she untouched by it. She successfully involved the Prince of Wales in trips and ceremonies that would place them both on public display and show the world a united, happy family.

Throughout the autumn of 1900, all those close to Queen Victoria were aware of her failing health. She continued to attend to all the affairs of State. Councils were held at Balmoral and Windsor, ministers were received, diplomats appointed to fresh offices, representatives from foreign courts were presented, and visitors to the castle came and went as always. But her anxieties over the war; her concern over the grave illness of her daughter, the Empress Frederick; the malarial death of a grandson, Prince Christian Victor (oldest son of her daughter Helena); had taken their toll. On Christmas Day, her good friend, the Dowager Lady Churchill, collapsed and died at Osborne House. For the next week, she omitted her usual practise of coming down to dinner and rarely availed herself of the services of the Court officials whose duty it was to act as readers and to assist in her correspondence. Her doctors, fearing for her life, strongly urged total bed rest and complete cessation from her duties as head of State. The Queen refused. Lord Roberts returned to England from South Africa on January 15, and, at the Queen's request, he came to Osborne to speak to her about the progress of the war. After a lengthy visit of an hour, he left. The Queen was confused in her

*Sonia Keppel Cubitt (b. 1900), married 1920 the Honourable Roland Cubitt, divorced 1947 shortly before he succeeded to the Barony of Ashcombe. Mrs. Cubitt refuses either to affirm or deny that her father was the Prince of Wales.

conversation when the audience ended, but she insisted on going out for a drive as usual. The following day, this confusion became more marked. By Friday she was confined to bed. On Sunday, the Duke and Duchess of York arrived from London, where they had gone for a grand reception for Lord Roberts. On Monday, an official announcement was given to the press. The Queen was ill —but not gravely so.

Queen Victoria, however, was dying, and with the exception of the Empress Frederick—whose ill health forbade her leaving her German home—all her surviving sons and daughters gathered at Osborne. She lay in her great canopied bed, a small, wasted figure in white. The sound of an angry winter sea could be heard outside her window. The Queen turned weakly to Dr. Reid. "The Prince of Wales will be sorry to hear how ill I am," she whispered. "Do you think he should be told?" He was, in fact, already at Osborne and had not made his presence known for fear of alarming her. Accompanied by Kaiser Wilhelm (who came unasked and whose attendance was greatly resented by the Royal Family), he now entered the sick room. The Queen "gained consciousness for a moment and recognized him [her son]," wrote Sir Frederick Ponsonby, who was standing at the foot of her bed. "She put out her arms and said 'Berty,' whereupon he embraced her and broke down completely." A short time later, she sent for her favourite small white dog, Turi, and called it by name.

Then she sank into unconsciousness. The following evening (January 22, 1901), the end was near. Kaiser Wilhelm stood silently at the head of her bed, the Prince of Wales knelt at the side, and Dr. Reid "passed his arm round her and supported her." The Queen opened her eyes and acknowledged the Prince of Wales and the Kaiser by inclining her head in their direction. Then her eyes closed. She had died peacefully, having reigned nearly sixty-four years—longer than any of her predecessors on the British Throne.

Not only her family but the whole of the Empire had come to regard the Queen as permanent and indestructible. Britain's ministers now worried about the effect on the nation of the scandal that had always surrounded Edward—the women, the gambling, the wild extravagances.

Princess Alexandra's ability to make her marriage appear solid to the people was of equal concern. Edward, the uncrowned King, was asked to return immediately to his wife's side in London. Kaiser Wilhelm, to his uncle's annoyance, took charge of the first burial preparations. "His tenderness and firmness were extraordinary, so unlike what was expected of him," Ponsonby reports. He refused to allow the undertaker's assistants to measure the Queen for her coffin, angrily turning them out of the room. He ordered Dr. Reid to take all the measurements himself, but when the time came, Edward and his younger brother—Arthur, the Duke of Connaught—not the Kaiser, lifted the Queen into her coffin.

"Now she lies in her coffin in the dining room," Princess May wrote her Aunt Augusta, "which is beautifully arranged as a chapel, the coffin is covered with the coronation robes & her little diamond crown and the garter lie on a cushion above her head—4 large Grenadiers watch there day and night, it is so impressive & fine & yet so simple . . . "* Beneath the coronation robes lay a drape of white satin, for the Queen had forbidden black, believing her death reunited her with Albert.

"I don't want to die yet. There are several things I want to arrange," the Queen had said to her daughter Princess Louise the day before her death. She had indeed given certain instructions for her funeral. No black—no hearse—only a gun carriage. A military funeral was fixed for February 2. On this bitter-cold day she was conveyed across the channel to Gosport "to the doleful sound of minute guns and the sullen roar of saluting cannon of the fleet . . ." wrote Princess Alice,† one of the Queen's granddaughters and seventeen at the time. "The cortege went in solemn procession across London . . . through streets lined with silent mourning crowds . . . Uncle Bertie rode

---

*Actually, there were Parliamentary robes, and the "little diamond crown" was the same crown that many years later, at the end of her husband's reign, Queen Alexandra refused to return.

†Princess Alice (1883–1981) was the daughter of Queen Victoria's youngest son, Leopold. She was later to marry Princess May's brother Prince Alexander (Alge) of Teck, later Earl of Athlone.

behind the gun carriage on a bay charger wearing the uniform of a Field Marshal . . . On arrival at Windsor Station the coffin was transferred to another gun carriage drawn by the Royal Horse Artillery . . . they reared and plunged in such a dangerous manner that the whole team had to be unharnessed. It was as though they resented having any part in the separation of the Great Queen from her realm."

And writer Shane Leslie remembered,* " . . . a very small coffin, surmounted by sceptre and crown, and slowly hauled by blue jackets in their straw hats at the slope. A bunch of Kings and Emperors followed . . . Lord Roberts passed in tears, looking tiny in his big boots and cocked hat. And the Kaiser was obviously suffering from nerves, for compared to the solemnity of the others, he was chafing and twisting round. . . ."

The Duke of York was noticeably absent from the cortege. All four of the York children had been quarantined with German measles at York Cottage at the time of their great-grandmother's death, and their father had contracted the disease from them. The three older children had recuperated well enough by the following Sunday to be taken to see the Queen, who still lay in state in Saint George's Chapel before interment at Frogmore, and they were there for the memorial service. "The procession from the Sovereign's entrance, the Princess of Wales leading Prince Edward of York [David], the other children walking [behind] was very touching and beautiful," Lord Esher observed. "The sweet and sickly air [from the masses of flowers] smelt like laughing gas, and the soldiers toppled over, from time to time under the fumes." Lord Esher had arranged the memorial and the funeral according to the Queen's personal instructions to him. A marble likeness of her, made in 1861, was placed upon her bier, and she was entombed by the side of her beloved Albert in the mausoleum she had had built in 1862 beneath the largest single block of flawless granite ever quarried.

"London," Shane Leslie recalls of the next few days, "was plunged in fog and crepe. Every shop window was streaked by a mourning shutter. The women, old and young, were draped

*Sir Shane Leslie Bt. (1885–1971), Irish writer and cousin of Sir Winston Churchill. Father of Anita Leslie, the social historian.

with veils, and most touching was the mourning worn by the prostitutes, in whose existence the old Queen had always refused to believe . . . It seemed as though the keystone had fallen out of the arch of heaven."

But no matter how bitter, the truth had to be faced. Queen Victoria was dead. The Prince of Wales, as he approached his sixtieth year, was, at last, King Edward VII. And Princess May had moved up a notch to become the second most important woman in the Realm, for she was now the wife of the Heir-Apparent to the Throne.

PART TWO

UNCLE WALES BECOMES KING

NINE

On becoming Heir-Apparent, the Duke of York also became the Duke of Cornwall. The title was an irrelevancy; what mattered were its vast estates which produced substantial income. Princess May was now a rich woman. She was also much disgruntled.

Only a few days after Queen Victoria's death, she wrote her old friend, Mlle. Bricka, "We are to be called D. & Dss of Cornwall & York & I don't think the King intends to create G[eorge] Pce of Wales." To her Aunt Augusta on February 3, 1901, she added, "I believe this is the first time that the Heir-Apparent has not been created Prince of Wales!" Such an unprecedented oversight cut Princess May deeply. She felt that her mother-in-law was working against her, but without Prince George's support, she was helpless. Unfortunately, her husband was forever timid about supporting his wife's position in any matter in which his mother had taken a stand.

Her thirty-three years rested handsomely on Princess May, and her popularity was as high as ever. Still, at home she had to compete with her husband's mother for his affections.

Queen Alexandra was most reluctant to have another woman wear the title with which she had been personally identified for nearly forty years, and she convinced the King that much confusion might occur if the new Heir-Apparent and his wife assumed the titles of Prince and Princess of Wales too abruptly. Princess May was never to forgive her mother-in-law for her humiliating action, and though she thoroughly enjoyed her higher position (albeit without the title she coveted), her relations with the new Queen were considerably cooler than they had been with Victoria.

Yet (and perhaps due to her harsh feelings toward Queen Alexandra), Princess May overcame most of her timidity to her father-in-law, who included her in almost all social events during the first months of his reign as King Edward VII. King Edward respected her intelligence and admired her strength of character. He also took it upon himself to "loosen" her up a bit and was fond of telling her slightly risqué stories that, despite her general primness, set her to laughing. And when Princess May laughed, she lost much of her self-control and dissolved into loud guffaws.

Princess May suffered a great loss at Queen Victoria's death, her devotion to her mother having been transferred to the aging Queen. She now wrote with greater frequency to Aunt Augusta, her correspondence taking on a more confidential tone. Many letters were critical of King Edward's Court, which in her opinion fell far short of what she expected it should be.

Lord Esher apparently agreed with her, for less than a fortnight after the Queen's funeral, he complained that, "The sanctity of the Throne has disappeared. The King is kind and debonnair, and not undignified—but too human!" And, in fact, the austerity and rigidity that had characterised Queen Victoria's Court disappeared as soon as Edward became King. Windsor Castle and Buckingham Palace were quietly transformed into light-hearted cosmopolitan courts as beauty, wit, and charm swept out the old, musty regime.

To the despair of his ministers, who liked to have an opportunity alone with him after a palace dinner, the King had abolished at Windsor the time-honoured British custom by which the ladies, dinner over, left the gentlemen to their port. Instead, both sexes would proceed out of the dining room together, in continental fashion. King Edward loved society, especially the society of women.

The Monarchy had taken on a new shape better suited to the

twentieth century, and although Princess May was not entirely comfortable with the changes, the King's naturalness and his panache won her over. Never a hypocrite, and unable to adopt a façade of mock morality, King Edward left to Queen Alexandra the difficult task of easing the transition from the old world to the new. Within a year, a newly gay atmosphere pervaded London's upper-middle-class homes. Gone were the ottomans and antimacassars, the solid maple furniture and the turkey pile. In their places were little gilt "papier-mâché" chairs, "chaises-longues" smothered with lace cushions, "Lady Teazle" screens covered with machine-made Beauvais, and masses of "maddeningly midget" tables. Taste had taken a light-hearted feminine turn. The colour mauve (Queen Alexandra's favourite) dominated most decors. Pink shades shut out the sunlight at an early hour each day. Begonias were replaced by orchids, and petunias by malmaisons. The heavy Teutonic taste of Prince Albert, which Queen Victoria had preserved, disappeared almost entirely, and the deification of the feminine was re-established.

Still, a growing section of the population was unsympathetic to the King's attitude toward life, his open relationship with Alice Keppel, and his nouveau riche friends. The transition from being Prince of Wales to Monarch was not easy. At fifty-nine and after empty years of waiting, he had to learn, and learn quickly, the difficult trade of Kingship. He was not to be a great King, but his immense style and gusto, the force with which he propelled the nation from an old-fashioned stuffy monarchy into the twentieth century, made him a memorable one. And perhaps he could not have achieved this distinction without the woman he had married.

Queen Alexandra possessed an air of dignity and respectability that, combined with her remarkable beauty and good works, endeared her to the people. She had the ability to be stately and human at the same time, and quickly became Great Britain's ideal of womanhood. Considered to her credit was her mediocre mind, for it made her more typical of the accepted stereotype of her generation of upper-class English women. But there was another side to Queen Alexandra that Princess May knew too well. In private, the Queen was obstinate, overpossessive, domineering, and more than a little spoiled, traits that made her

125

children weak, her husband philander, and her daughter-in-law bristle. And though little has been said of it through the years, she and her own mother-in-law, Queen Victoria, had not been on intimate terms either. Lord Esher, who managed the Royal Household, wrote his son on March 7, 1901, "I was tired to death yesterday after two hours *alone* with the King and Queen at Buckingham Palace. They were fussing over domestic plans. *She* had never before been into Queen Victoria's rooms. Queer was it not? She examined every detail; and made all her own little domestic arrangements."

According to Lord Esher, "a smart difference of opinion" occurred between husband and wife during this tour of their new residence. The King insisted that they should occupy these private apartments, where he intended to renovate the memorial his father's room had become so that it was habitable for himself. Queen Alexandra was to take his mother's bedroom. The Queen, however, at first preferred the grander, airier, and more convenient rooms that had previously been reserved for visiting royalty and state officials. Finally, at the end of the tour, and under duress, she agreed to look at Victoria's chambers. By March 12, less than a week later, she made up her mind; she had Lord Esher take her through them privately and was "in tearing good spirits."

King Edward was never to like Buckingham Palace, which he called "the Sepulchre," but he put his stamp upon it nonetheless. Prince Albert's former dressing room was soon known as the Indian Room, the floor covered in a richly patterned Indian rug with tiger skins scattered on it. Gifts from Princes and Rajas were lavishly displayed, and the walls held glass cases filled with jewelled scabbards. His bedroom was unconventionally simple. Racks holding his hats (twelve daytime hats and six top hats) and canes (five or six dozen) were openly displayed right beside the doorway. No great canopy stretched over his low-backed, average-width bed. A screen, rather than the usual velvet drapes, gave a measure of privacy to the bed's occupant. The walls were covered with a severe blue-and-silver brocade stripe and hung with a dazzling collection of portraits of England's most beautiful Royal ladies. Nearest his bed, however, was a portrait of his father, Prince Albert (the only male portrait in the room), and another of Queen Victoria holding the infant Prince of Wales.

The state rooms were redecorated, but Queen Alexandra's cluttered hand was everywhere. Few of the many great treasures piled into the rooms could be seen to their best advantage. Abundant electric-light bulbs were installed instead of the sparse gas-lighting and sparser electricity which Queen Victoria had grudgingly allowed. Bathrooms were provided more generously, and in the zest for modern comfort many of the dressing rooms were fitted with three basins in a row, one for the hands, one for the face, and one for the teeth.

The grounds and the approach to Buckingham Palace breathed a sense of "new life." The forty-five acres of parkland surrounding the palace received much attention. Summerhouses and cupolas were added. Bronze storks were placed by the private lake, and boatmen in brilliant scarlet livery had been added to the staff to man the dozen new luxurious paddleboats with their elegant throne seats and colourful canopies.

Evening Courts, where elaborately gowned and bejewelled debutantes were presented to the King and Queen, were substituted for the less gala afternoon drawing rooms held for this purpose by Queen Victoria. With the sight of the equipages of the great families and their footmen and coachmen in their cocked hats and rich liveries driving up the Mall to Buckingham Palace, the final fusty Victorian years were banished to the past. The mere fact that the King had chosen to call himself Edward and not Albert promised the people a new epoch.

The King took a more lively interest in revitalising Windsor Castle than in the renovation of Buckingham Palace. He had almost everything rearranged and repainted, but he felt compelled to leave the heavy carpets and curtains untouched, for they were, although quite ugly, as good as new.* All the art

---

*Christopher Hibbert in *The Court at Windsor* (fn p. 240) writes that "some of them [the rugs] *were* new for Queen Victoria, unable to part with anything that she and Prince Albert had shared, had had the furnishings accurately copied when it became necessary to replace them." Still, she hated the replacements. A servant wrote that on one occasion while the Queen was away from Windsor "an armchair in her private sitting room was restuffed and recovered. Her Majesty at once ordered it out of her sight on her return, saying it was 'too smart.' " The Queen also passed the same verdict on the gates and railing that

works were rehung. "I do not know much about A*rr*t," he told Frederick Gibbs,* rolling his r's, "but I think I know something about A*rr-r*-angement."

By April 1, King Edward and Queen Alexandra were installed in the castle, and Esher describes the new atmosphere. "The King plays bridge after dinner, and keeps people up till nearly one, which is very tiring. He insists on having all his letters brought to him unopened, almost 400 a day, and sorts them by the envelopes. He tried at first to open them all, but found that impossible." A week later the King and Queen gave their first large dinner. The atmosphere of the castle had changed drastically. Victoria's Indian servants wandered about "like uneasy spirits, no longer immobile and statuesque," their places now filled by footmen vividly attired.

"The oak dining room," Esher noted, "is no longer used, and the quiet impressive entrance of the Queen into the corridor is as obsolete as Queen Elizabeth. We assembled in the Green drawing-room, and the King came in unannounced with his daughters and his sister. He took the Duchess of Fife in to dinner.† We dined in the White dining room, which looked very well. He retains the Indian servants.‡ The dinner was like an ordinary party. None of the 'hush' of the Queen's dinners. Afterwards we left 'arm-in-arm' as we entered.

"Then the party remained in the Green room, and he took me into the White drawing-room. It had been furnished with the famous Couttière Cabinet that belonged to the Compte d'Artois and with tapestry chairs, and other fine French things. The King began with the Queen's memorial, going back upon his approval of the scheme [to place it at the top of the Mall] persuaded by

---

divide Castle Hill from the South Terrace when the tops were gilded in her absence. An army of painters was summoned, and by the time the Queen left the castle for her afternoon drive, all traces of the garish display had been removed.

*Frederick Waymouth Gibbs, a Fellow of Trinity and a barrister. He was King Edward VII's tutor 1849–1858, but they never got on.

†Princess Louise was now the Duchess of Fife. Her husband, formerly the Earl of Duff, became the Duke of Fife in 1899.

‡The Indian servants were dismissed six months later.

X [Alexandra], who was angry because she had not been consulted, that there was danger 'of mobs in front of the Palace'—a tissue of rubbish.* I said what I thought, but I would not argue . . . Later he sat down to bridge; the Princesses slipped away, and I made my bow.

"I regret the mystery and awe of the old Court. However, the change was inevitable."†

Certainly the Court was a good deal more glittering, as the King insisted that his women guests should wear tiaras at dinner every night at Windsor (a command that greatly pleased Princess May) and that the men should wear Court costume and their decorations.

The King would take long walks with Lord Esher through the gardens at Windsor and Buckingham, and across the fields at Balmoral. Esher was younger by eleven years, but the King thought of him much like the tutors with whom the King had lived at White Lodge when he was a young man. Whatever the reasons, he felt relaxed with Esher and enjoyed their long tête-à-têtes. One day the King, with his dog Caesar at their heels, and Lord Esher wandered around Windsor Castle for over two

---

*It was installed as planned but was not completed until after King Edward's death.

†Reginald Brett (1852–1930). 2nd Viscount Esher (1899), served in Parliament 1880–85 as a Liberal, Governor of Windsor Castle 1901–1930; he managed the Royal Household for 30 years. He also edited *The Correspondence of Queen Victoria* (1907) with A. C. Benson. His influence was exercised behind the scenes, and he was at least partway responsible for many reforms, especially in the Army. Secretary to H. M. Office of Works and as such enjoyed a close relationship with the Crown. He was a sensitive, talented man of letters and a former M.P., having stood for Penryn and Falmouth from 1880 to 1885, and was much respected by all members of the Royal Family. At various times, Queen Victoria had offered him, and he had refused, the Under-Secretaryship for the Colonies, the Under-Secretaryship for War, and the Governorship of Cape Colony. King Edward later offered him the Viceroyship of India, which he likewise refused. He considered himself first a historian, and his observations of the Royal Family made in his Journals are marvellously incisive and revealing. He was more than a historian, having great interest in things artistic, for at the time he began his long work on Queen Victoria's letters, he was not only the Director of the Opera at Covent Garden, but Royal Trustee of the British Museum. He was also Lieutenant and Deputy Governor of Windsor Castle.

129

hours, presumably ransacking bookcases and picture cupboards while he reminisced with Esher about his youth. Lord Esher had greatly admired Queen Victoria, and he was not yet used to the familiarity with the Throne that had so quickly been thrust upon him following her death.

The new Queen's obdurate nature had surprised Lord Esher, but he quickly learned to take her at her word. "I sent a list of queries to the King tonight about the throne of the Queen," he wrote in his Journal during the planning of the Coronation.* "She objects to being called Queen *Consort*. She means to be Queen." For thirty-eight years as Princess of Wales, Alexandra had been obliged to defer to Victoria's tastes, wishes, and prejudices. Now she was steadfast in her resolve to have other people give way to her. This willfulness surfaced in her very first ceremonies as Queen. On February 16, she was expected to appear with the King for the opening of Parliament, and the correct dress for a Queen Consort and her Ladies at this ceremonial, and later at the Coronation (planned for a year from that June), became a major issue of the Court. The last Queen Consort had been the wife of William IV, Queen Adelaide, and no one remained who had a clear memory of what she wore on these occasions. Historians were consulted, but Queen Alexandra dismissed their findings. "I know better than all the milliners & antiquaries," she wrote to her husband's equerry, Sir Arthur Ellis. "I shall wear exactly what I like and so will all my ladies—*Basta!*"

"The Opening of Parliament went off without a hitch," Lord Esher reported. "The Queen looked beautiful, with all her jewels and the Koh-i-noor upon a black dress.† The contrast between the red robes of the peers, and the black dresses of the women, was very effective." Her decision had been to establish her own personality, while at the same time displaying her respect for the dead Queen. Yet for the Queen to have worn a

---

*Lord Esher, who had so successfully taken charge of Queen Victoria's Jubilee, was also responsible for the Coronation plans.

†For many centuries the Koh-i-noor diamond was the largest diamond in the world, a "title" lost in 1907 when King Edward was presented a tremendous stone from which two stones were cut that exceeded the Koh-i-noor in size. The Koh-i-noor is now in the Crown Jewels.

stone as vulgar in its opulence as the Koh-i-noor diamond at a time of national mourning not only was daring but would have been conceived as a major breech of etiquette by anyone other than Alexandra. For in 1901, the wearing of mourning had progressed to such utter severity that propriety obliged a second wife to don heavy black upon the death of her husband's first wife's mother or father. When the old Queen had died, most women in the nation wore mourning, and even small girls had black ribbons threaded in their petticoats. (Queen Victoria's death had come on the eve of the annual January white sales, and in the department stores of London and the provincial cities, hundreds of assistants worked throughout the night to pack away every white item on display and to drape their interiors and windows in black.) For months any woman who considered herself a lady wrote notes on black-edged paper, stuffed them inside black-edged envelopes, and sealed them with black wax. Thousands upon thousands of black-edged handkerchiefs —coarse cambric for daily use, finer cambric for formal occasions—were sold in the many stores specialising in general mourning that had been flourishing for years.

For the first time in over six decades the people had a King. "Saw the King again after lunch—sitting in his room upstairs with his after-luncheon cigar. Looking wonderfully like Henry VIII, only better-tempered," Lord Esher wrote.

The comparison was not untoward, for King Edward, always of ample frame, was now quite portly—a fact that did not at all diminish the fame he had as the "uncontested *arbiter elegantiarum*" in the matter of style. His considerable size had influenced him to adopt the fashion of open, or cutaway, singlebreasted jackets fastened usually with a jeweled link. He introduced the crease into men's trousers and the low-cut white waist-coat for wear with a dress coat, exposing for the first time a substantial expanse of shirt-front. "Stiff as a breastplate across the manly chest," his grandson David was to recall many years later, "this shirt-front was nevertheless vulnerable. My grandmother found it so one evening when my mother and father were dining with him and my grandmother at Buckingham Palace before going on to the opera. The menu included a purée of spinach, and the King was unfortunate enough to

131

spill a goblet of this vegetable on his wide and spotless shirt.

"Queen Alexandra took a knife and tried to scrape it off. My mother also did her best to repair the damage. But the tell-tale mark remained . . . He laughed boisterously, dipped his napkin in the spinach, and drew a picture with it all over his shirt-front —an abstract painting in spinach, in the style which on the Left Bank in Paris today [1951] is, I believe, called Tachiste. Then he went to change and this royal work of art was lost forever."

King Edward did indeed cut as memorable a figure with his top hat and formal attire as King Henry ever had with his massive scarlet robes. He wore a top hat for almost all occasions in London and for church on Sundays in the country. Hats were, in fact, the King's passion, and he championed the bowler and introduced the homburg to England.

None of this did Queen Alexandra approve, for she preferred men to wear uniforms. She could do little about persuading the King, but butlers, footmen, coachmen, and members of the Palace staff soon sported handsome new uniforms resplendent with gold braid and shiny brass buttons. She was also not too keen about Princess May, younger and extremely popular, having a share in her long-awaited glory.

One is therefore able to understand the easy approval she gave to a plan suggested by the King's ministers less than a month after the old Queen's death for the Duke and Duchess of York to embark on an ambitious colonial tour to include Gibraltar, Melbourne, Malta, Egypt, Ceylon, Singapore, Australia, then New Zealand and South Africa (with the hope that the war might then be over) and Canada. The trip would mean that Princess May and Prince George would be away from England and their four young children for eight months. No members of the Royal Family had ever undertaken such an extended tour of the Empire. But the death of Queen Victoria and the prolongation of the Boer War made personal contact with the colonies by members of the Royal Family a politic move. The King was not in favour of the tour because it left him with no one except for his brother Arthur, the Duke of Connaught, with whom he might share his greatly increased ceremonial burdens. Still, the ministers and the Queen convinced him of its rightness.

The cruise on the *Ophir,* an Orient liner chartered by the

Admiralty, was Prince George's first important independent constitutional command. The Yorks set sail on the afternoon of March 16. The King came aboard, inspected the crew, and lunched with his son and daughter-in-law. Tears were shed when they returned with him to the Royal yacht *Victoria & Albert* to say goodbye to the Queen. The two women exchanged final words about the children's special habits, and when Princess May returned to her suite aboard the *Ophir* she broke down and sobbed. But within a few minutes she had regained control, and, taking her husband's arm, went back up on deck. With the light just beginning to fade, the *Ophir* cast off and moved slowly out across Plymouth Sound, preceded first by the *Trinity House Yacht* and next by H.M.S. *Alberta.* Immense crowds lined the shores on both the Devon and Cornish sides, and "one could see handkerchiefs waving as far as the eye could reach." Several bands could be heard playing above the cheers of the people on the shore and on the many small boats that had accompanied the *Ophir.*

By nightfall they were well on their way, steaming south en route for Gibraltar. "I *detest* the sea," Princess May wrote Mlle. Bricka. From the first night she suffered seasickness, and unfortunately the *malaise* was to remain for most of the journey.*

Nothing could have pleased the Queen more than to have small boys to entertain once again. She was in her element with most children but enjoyed small boys more than little girls. Quite promptly their parents' strict regime for them at York Cottage was set aside, and Helena Bricka, plump and rather elderly now, could do little about it. The children were moved close to their grandparents and allowed free run of whichever

---

*The full list of the Royal suite on the *Ophir* cruise was: Lord Wenlock, Head of Household; Sir Arthur Bigge, Private Secretary; Sir Donald MacKenzie Wallace, Assistant Secretary; Sir Charles Cust, Equerry; Major Derek Keppel, Equerry; Commander Godfrey-Fausett, A.D.C.; Major Bor, A.D.C.; Lord Crichton, A.D.C.; Duke of Roxburghe, A.D.C.; Colonel Byron of the Australian Artillery, A.D.C.; Sir John Anderson of the Colonial Office; Canon Dalton (Prince George's former tutor), Chaplain; Chevalier de Martino, Marine Artist; Mr. Sidney Hall, Artist; Dr. A. Manby, Doctor-in-Attendance; Lady Mary Lygon, Lady-in-Waiting; Lady Katherine Coke, Lady-in-Waiting; Mrs. Derek Keppel, Lady-in-Waiting; Prince Alexander of Teck; Sir Arthur Lawley, Governor of Western Australia.

home or castle they happened to be visiting. Lessons were at a minimum, being thought rather inconsequential by Alexandra. So unconcerned were the grandparents over the lapses from schoolroom routine that on taking the children to Sandringham for a two-week stay, they left poor Mlle. Bricka behind in London, according to their eldest grandson, "lest she spoil the fun."

When the *Ophir* reached Gibraltar, there was a letter waiting for the Yorks from their second-eldest son—who was six at the time:

> MY DARLING MAMA AND PAPA
> We hope you are quite well and not seasick. Did you have a big wave when you went through the Bay of Biscay? We send you love and a lot of kisses,
>
> > From your loving
> > Bertie

No mention was made by the Queen to Princess May of the change in the children's lives. In fact, their studies were grossly neglected because King Edward, with his jovial bonhomie and enjoyment of life, and with formidable recollections of his own early strict instruction, discouraged lessons as constituting an unnecessary inhibition of fun.

Bertie was his grandfather's favourite, and the King would dash off short notes to him when he was gone for only an afternoon or evening. In the Royal Archives at Windsor, several of these survive, of which the following is an example:

> My Dearest Little Bertie
> You have written me a very nice little letter. How fortunate that Bland [a footman] caught Papa's parrot that had flown away or else he might have been shot! . . . Now that the weather is fine again you might have to play golf!
>
> > Ever your devoted Grandpapa,
> > EDWARD R.

Mlle. Bricka wrote Princess May that the children were being kept away from her classroom, and that David, being the eldest, would suffer the greatest loss in his studies and that she found this terribly upsetting, but as the Queen had sanctioned his absence, she did not know what to do. Princess May wrote immediately to her mother-in-law, who replied in a flurry of underscores and exclamations that she thought it "the *only* thing that *could* be done as *we all* noticed how precocious and *old-fashioned* he [David] was getting—and quite the way of *a single child!*—which would make him ultimately 'a tiresome child.' "

In lieu of the schoolroom, the Queen took the children to every special exhibition and tournament that was presented. She was delighted on an excursion to Virginia Water when "little David caught his first fish and danced about with joy," and was exceedingly proud—feeling it showed a good heart—when he turned around to the sailor helping him and said, "You must *not* kill him; throw him back into the water again!" Disappointed in all but one of her adult children [George], Alexandra was taking advantage of what she surely thought was a second chance at contributing to children's formative years.

At each colony visited, Princess May successfully coped with official receptions on landing, addresses received and replied to, deputations met, Durbars and meetings with native rulers and chiefs, receptions of local officials and their wives, visits to new works and famous buildings and beauty spots, the laying of foundation stones, inspections of hospitals, reviews of troops, investitures, presentations of colours and medals, openings of trade and other exhibitions, and banquets—always at her husband's side and always without any trace of impatience or fatigue (which he often displayed).

On board the *Ophir,* and except for Princess May's *malaise de mer,* the Yorks had a relaxed and happy time with old and tried friends; her brother, Prince Alexander of Teck (Alge), was aboard, as well as her husband's former tutor, Canon Dalton. For Prince George, memories were revived with each coastline they neared. From his days as a young midshipman he knew the Mediterranean intimately from Gibraltar to Suez. And whenever he fell in with ships of the fleet, he would welcome old shipmates aboard.

The tour vastly changed the Yorks' formerly vague notions of life in Australia, New Zealand, and Canada. They were surprised to see these countries' admirably disciplined armies. The same was true of the civil services and industry. In Australia, they

135

found the educational system producing results that England might envy. In whatever colony they visited, they were conscious of the great loyalty to the Crown possessed by all classes, creeds, and races. The Empire was still mighty, and Queen Victoria was firmly believed wholly responsible for it. She was a legend, thought to be invested with divine qualities by some. Few of her subjects had been old enough at her death to recall another monarch. Her reign had seen the development of many of the colonies from settlements to modern nations. On this tour the Yorks came to realise how widespread Grandmama's influence had been, and learned to attach a new importance to the private lives and examples of those called on—as Princess May defined it—"to assume the power and symbolism of her great office." The impression went deep and remained indelible in her mind. She would never again be quite the same person, at least in her outward behaviour, and she no longer could abide a lapse from any of her family in what she considered "the proper Royal attitude."

Princess May's confidence had been severely undermined by her mother-in-law's domineering attitude. But the wild reception she received wherever they went (and she was far more popular with the people than her husband), the obeisance that she had previously seen given only to the Queen, gave her a sense of her own power that she had not had before. Prince George disliked speechmaking and was dreadfully nervous when surrounded by huge crowds of people. As the tour progressed, he leaned more and more on his wife, later confiding to her that "I could never have got through it without you," and that it was she whom the people had loved and come to see, not he. At home, Alexandra might well have strengthened the ties to her grandchildren, but she was further losing her grasp on her son.

The tour ended on November 1, when the *Ophir* dropped anchor in a choppy sea just off the Isle of Wight. The Royal yacht, *Victoria & Albert,* its standard flying smartly to show Their Majesties were on board, came within a hundred feet and also dropped anchor. The King and Queen, with the four children and their nannies, then got into a steam barge from which they were to have boarded the *Ophir.* But the sea was too rough.

David came scrambling between the King's legs to have a first look at his parents, who had just appeared at the top of the ladder. The wind was blowing hard and they could not descend, but they were close enough for the children to see them. The three eldest appeared instantly relieved. The King, still the practical joker, had warned them to be prepared for a shock. Their parents, he had reminded them in a perfectly believable way, had been exposed a long time to the fierce tropical sun, and in all probability their skins had turned black. The children were horrified, and the excitement of being reunited with their parents had been mixed with apprehension. David, years later, was to recall his terror at "the drastically altered state in which he would doubtless find them."

Both ships then headed toward Portsmouth. They steamed slowly up the Solent and before long were "surrounded by pleasure boats and steamers crowded with enthusiastic people who cheered themselves hoars[e]." As the *Ophir* drew closer to shore, both sides of the harbour were thick with people, and despite a strong wind the cheering was "simply deafening with the bands ashore, and our band playing 'Home Sweet Home' it made a homecoming never to be forgotten."

The Yorks soon joined the King and Queen and the children aboard the *Victoria & Albert* for a tearful reunion. The baby, little Harry, who was not yet walking or talking when his parents had left, was doing both. He did not recognise his parents and set up a squall when his mother went to lift him. Princess Mary clung to her grandmother's skirts. Princess May fought back her injured pride at this rejection by her own children. David, however, stepped forward, and then Bertie followed him, and they were warmly embraced by both their parents. By the time they had reached London most of the first awkwardness was gone; but from that point on, the children, because of their long stay with their grandparents, had some means of comparison and found something missing in their home life. To Bertie especially, who feared his father and was so awkward with his mother, the change was the most disastrous. Only a short time after his parents' return, he began to have trouble with his speech, and within six months he was stuttering quite noticeably.

On the King's sixtieth birthday, November 9, 1901—just nine

days after the Yorks had returned from their eight-month journey—Prince George was at last created Prince of Wales, and Princess May was finally Princess of Wales. On January 16, 1902, they came up to London for the opening of Parliament. Prince George records the change in their status simply in his journal: "May and I went in our Glass Coach and we had an escort"; but Princess May took time to sit for her first portrait as Princess of Wales and proudly wore all her decorations. Inside Parliament, they ceremoniously took their places in the chairs of state placed for them below the dais of the Throne and facing the members of the House. Afterward, they both attended the King's reception at Windsor. Lord Salisbury, whose lengthy premiership was now drawing to a close, took Prince George aside, and the two had an extended private talk. King Edward was making sure that his son would not suffer the inactivity and sense of uselessness he had felt as King-in-waiting. From this day forward, Prince George was sent the Royal boxes and kept apprised of all the key issues in the nation.

Glass coaches and Royal boxes were not the only changes that took place in the York-cum-Wales household. Their staff was greatly increased, and they were given Marlborough House (which required much renovation) and the use of Frogmore at Windsor. Prince George was forever moaning that "the Windsor climate" was never very beneficial to him. With each notch up the Royal line of succession came new residences owned by the Crown. Most were old and antiquated, with draughts, bad heating, endless corridors, and hopeless plumbing. Kensington Palace and St. James's Palace provided London homes for numerous Royalties at the same time—each family having a wing or section for itself, and yet with cousins and aunts and uncles and in-laws within a courtyard's distance. Privacy was difficult to obtain, particularly since servants intermingled. The shadow of the last occupant (who had either gone up in line to the Throne or had died) hovered over each new resident. Princess May was first obliged to occupy her grandmother's apartments at St. James's. Now she was moving her family into Marlborough House, a home strongly identified with the former Princess of Wales. The two women's tastes were quite disparate. Whatever changes Princess May made could be found not only offensive but insulting to her mother-in-law.

His own awareness of how close he stood to the Throne also changed Prince George's ideas about his sons' education. A major upheaval took place in the nursery. "The feminine suzerainty that had ruled there was suddenly terminated when one evening Bertie and I were told that a man named Frederick Finch would wake us up next morning and thenceforth we should be under his care," David later wrote. Prince George's plans were for his sons to be raised along precisely the same lines that had been laid down some thirty years earlier for himself and Prince Eddy; they were to be taught at home by tutors until old enough to join the Royal Navy as cadets. So, along with the introduction of Finch, a tall, gaunt, solemn stranger with a large moustache named Henry Peter Hansell entered their lives as a tutor.

David had the least inhibitions at the time and had to be constantly reprimanded for small infractions of the rules set down by Finch and Hansell and the strict study and dress standards set by his father. The new Prince of Wales believed young boys should wear only kilts or sailor suits. "I hope your kilts fit well," he wrote David at Balmoral. "Take care and don't spoil them at once as they are new. Wear the Balmoral Kilt and grey jacket on weekdays and green Kilt and black jacket on Sunday. Do not wear the red Kilt until I come."

The two older boys saw their father every morning when the family was together. These meetings generally took place when Prince George would lead a military march—often twice—around the grounds of Sandringham and with little regard to weather. At their other homes, they would walk an equal distance. Upon learning that Princess May was once again pregnant, Prince George was overheard to say, "Well, soon I shall have a regiment."

They also expanded their staff on the female side at this time. Princess May brought in as Lady-in-Waiting an old friend from her childhood, Mabell, Countess of Airlie, whose husband had just been killed in the Boer War. The position was prestigious, but it also carried with it great dedication and sacrifice, which

139

might not in all cases have made up for the prestige of the title. A Lady-in-Waiting served for three months in the year. Princess May was now to have four ladies (she had had two),* as well as a private secretary. The duties of a Lady-in-Waiting were partially secretarial (personal correspondence only), and she was also expected to accompany the Princess of Wales wherever she went, and to keep her company when her husband might be engaged and no social event scheduled. In Princess May's case, the Lady-in-Waiting would read to her, or they would simply chat. She also ate meals with the Royal Household. Yet honour though the appointment might be, it also demanded the lady (who held a position in the aristocracy) desert her own comfortable home and her family (in some cases a husband and children) for the often austere and damp accommodations of the Royal residences. Lady Airlie had to sleep in that cubical room over the kitchen in York Cottage, as did the other ladies when in waiting at York Cottage—a matter of duty, of course, but it represented a great sacrifice.

After much persuasion, Lady Airlie finally entered the Princess of Wales's Household on March 1, 1902, feeling very new to her surroundings but "comforted by the fact that it was St. David's day, which seemed a good omen." Princess May received her in her sitting room at York House, "formally—almost coldly." Lady Airlie did not know what to make of Princess May's attitude. A short time later, when all the servants had gone and they were alone together, Princess May, however, put her arms around her childhood friend and kissed her on both cheeks, eyes full of tears. "Dearest, dearest Mabell, I can't tell you how much I have felt for you [because of her husband's death] and how glad I am that you have come to me. I will try to make you happy."

Lady Airlie observed that the new Princess of Wales had to cope with the drastic changes in Court life that had taken place during the eight months she had been away. Now, with the period of deep mourning over, the Edwardian Court appeared to her vulgar and flamboyant, and according to Lady Airlie,

---

*Princess May's four Ladies-in-Waiting were Lady Katharine Coke; Mabell, Countess Airlie; Lady Mary Lygon; and Lady Eva Dugdale.

"Money was the passport to society. Almost anyone who had enough of it could procure, sooner or later, an invitation to the splendid Court Balls at Windsor and the evening receptions at Buckingham Palace. Princess May's appreciation of restraint and dignity made her recoil from this 'surfeit of gold plate and orchids' as she once called it to me. Although she was the wife of the heir to the throne, the tact which always veiled her force of character enabled her to keep aloof and to lead within the framework of her public role a private life of quiet domesticity . . . Queen Alexandra, temperamentally cast in a lighter mould, had the faculty of skimming easily over the surface of life and ignoring things which she disliked. Nothing seriously perturbed her. Princess May would have been deeply distressed if she had annoyed her husband; Queen Alexandra serenely pursued her own way."

The private differences between the Queen and Princess May were never to be dissolved, but as the summer of 1902 approached, the younger woman was able to push them aside for the time being. She was three months pregnant with her fifth child and could still appear in public. June 26 had now been set as the date of the Coronation, and she would attend it as Princess of Wales.

TEN

The Edwardian age began in the wake of tremendous change. The British had lost their supremacy in foreign commerce. Unemployment was at a shocking high, bringing with it hunger and discontent. After a decade out of office, the Liberals now could look forward to their chance to satisfy the needs of the people. Upper-class life was far more cosmopolitan. But rich or poor, Tory or Liberal, all looked toward King Edward's reign with great optimism, and the vital and progressive part of the nation heaved a sigh of relief. Many believed it had been England's misfortune that Edward had not succeeded to the Throne ten years earlier. His greatest supporters were the youth of the country. Even his discarding of the name Albert gave assurance that he would do away with what the young regarded as the false morality, false behaviour, and false ideals of the Victorian era.

King Edward loved pomp, and Great Britain longed for pomp. The Boer War—the worst war England had suffered, with over a hundred thousand casualties and an army that was half-starved most of the time—ended on May 31, 1902. The nation wanted to forget, and the new King, attractive, displaying all that was impressive in British royalty, was about to give the people their first taste of coronation splendour in over sixty years.

The date was set for June 26. Wooden stands, barricades, flagpoles, and Venetian masts appeared on the main streets where the procession would pass, and as June approached, the city took on the atmosphere of a grand theatrical dress-rehearsal. With each new day, the Court Circular would print additional names of foreign royalties and deputations from the Empire arriving for the event. For Princess May, the daily rehearsals and unending amount of detail were tedious. As early as June 4, Lord Esher took the older children—David, Bertie, and Mary—to Westminster Abbey. The boys had been worked into a frenzy of excitement by Finch and their tutor, Mr. Hansell, and soon were very grubby from clambering over the dusty tombs. Mr. Hansell had been boning them up on English history, and David, quite zealously, told Lord Esher that the Duke of Buckingham had been a "wicked man."

"Why?" Lord Esher inquired.

"Because he gave bad advice to Charles I," the child replied.

Lord Esher wrote his son—who was to have charge of the two elder Royal Princes at the Coronation—"I think he [Prince David] must have been reading Dumas!" With some amusement, he also noted that the young boy possessed a slight trace of a cockney accent, picked up (and to remain with him his entire life) through his close association as a child with Lala Bill.

The rehearsals and preparations were extremely trying for the King, who was looking increasingly unwell. On June 23, he was found to be suffering from acute appendicitis. An operation was ordered by the Royal physician for the following day. The Coronation was indefinitely postponed. Fear spread throughout England that the King was critically ill, not surprisingly, for at this time such an operation was dangerous, and in the King's case complicated by his age and girth. The day of the operation, June 24, the rumour was that the King was "sinking fast."

Lady Mary Lygon, Lady-in-Waiting to Princess May at the time, wrote to a friend: "I have never felt anything like the physical and mental oppression of the day in London. It was hot and airless and muggy—the decorations flapped about in an ominous manner—gloom and consternation were in every face. The King's age etc. is much against him—but he has a wonderful constitution which may carry him through . . . I was very sorry for the Prince of Wales, for everything had to be decided by him; and besides his *great* devotion to his father—the feeling that at any moment he might find himself King of England must have hung like a horrible nightmare on him. He does not like responsibility and though he has aged much in the last eighteen months —one could wish for him another two or three years of respite and preparation."

On that same day, Princess May wrote in her diary that she had broken down in tears with Helena Bricka and told her: "Oh I do *pray* that Uncle Wales may get well. George says he isn't ready yet to reign."

But the day following the King's operation, Prince George found him "smoking a cigar & reading a paper. The doctors and nurses say they never saw such a wonderful man." By June 28, the King was declared out of danger, and the coronation was rearranged for August 9.

Lord Esher recorded a curious incident that occurred on July 27, just twelve days before the coronation. As he tells it, he sat next to Prince George at dinner that night and the Prince mentioned a queer prophecy which he made Esher promise he would not repeat to the King, who was terribly superstitious. A clairvoyant had told Victoria, about forty years earlier, that she would have a long and glorious reign, the longest and most glorious of all the English sovereigns; that she would be succeeded by *two* kings who would have short reigns; and by a third whose name would be David, and whose reign would be as glorious as hers. "One of Prince Edward's names is David!" Esher exclaimed, and then went on to say, "When Lady Waterford was dying (she was a dear thing who died of cancer about 8 years ago) she sent for the Prince of Wales and implored him to call his then unborn child David, as she had some fad about restoring the Jews to the Holy City. To humour her, he consented, and his newborn son was given the names of the four patron saints of England, Scotland, Ireland and Wales—i.e. George Andrew Patrick David!

"I don't think the Prince of Wales is altogether free from superstition himself, but he is reconciled to a short reign. He

144

would not, however, for worlds let the King hear the story," Esher exclaimed.

At the same dinner Lord Esher notes, "One source of amusement was the fascination which the Queen exercised over the Bishop of Winchester, when she led him away so far from the paths of virtue, as to make him smoke a cigarette with her."

The following day Lord Esher entertained Princess May and the old Grand Duchess of Mecklenburg-Strelitz (Princess May's Aunt Augusta) for tea. "She is a funny old woman—full of rather spiteful wit—who remembers William IV better than Edward VII. The Princess was gentle and homely in a rather stately way, as she always is. Probably the effect of living with such a *garçon eternel* as the P of Wales."

Lord Esher was entirely right. Prince George was a small boy where both his wife and mother were concerned, but there was another side to the Heir-Apparent which was seen most frequently by his children. At home Prince George was a strict father. According to his eldest son, "He had the Victorian's sense of probity, moral responsibility, and love of domesticity. He believed in God, in the invincibility of the Royal Navy, and the essential rightness of whatever was British . . . If through my family's position my childhood was spared the mundane struggle that is the common lot, I nevertheless had my full share of discipline. For the concept of duty was drilled into me, and I never had the sense that the days belonged to me alone."

Combined with his stern sense of duty, Prince George possessed "an almost fanatical sense of punctuality." His days were organised with "railroad precision—even to the habit of a post-luncheon nap, a carryover from his watch-keeping days in the Navy." He allotted himself exactly fifteen minutes, and without benefit of clock or alarm, he would awake at precisely the right moment.

Prince George treated his sons in a harsh, disciplinarian manner that suggested Naval duty, with the six- and eight-year-old boys in the position of Naval cadets and their father as their captain. In letters they called him *Papa,* but in private confrontation he was always *Sir.* David, in later years, could recall only one time in his childhood when his father ever embraced him—upon his return from the eight-month trip on the *Ophir*. Generally, the boys and their father shook hands; at most he gave the boys a perfunctory kiss on the cheek. No words were as disconcerting to the youngsters as a command that "His Royal Highness wishes to see you in the library." And nothing could have been farther from the easy, happy confrontations with their grandfather only a few months before.

The library was "the seat of parental authority, the place of admonition and reproof." The small, cheerless room with two windows opening upon the driveway was furnished sparingly with few books and a most conspicuous glass cabinet that housed just part of Prince George's vast collection of shotguns. The two boys would file into the room, the elder first, and stand before their father's desk in an "at ease" position. If during an interview they were so unfortunate as to stuff their hands into their pockets, Lala Bill was immediately summoned and ordered to sew up all the pockets on their suits, "a royal command which despite some inward reservations she did not dare to disobey."

The greater part of paternal reprimands the boys received concerned their classes. Bertie, being a slow child, unable to concentrate, was most often brought to task. Highly strung, excitable, fidgety, sensitive, easily rebuffed, and prone to take his weaknesses and mistakes too seriously, he did not have the charm of his older brother. During his parents' absence on the world tour, he had become quite attached to his grandfather, whom he truly adored. And, as the coronation approached, he felt rejected when the King had less and less time for his grandchildren. Bertie had been naturally left-handed, but in the fashion of the time, he was forced to write with his right hand. Psychiatry claims that this can affect a child's speech. Whatever the cause, his stammer grew worse, and nothing was done to correct it. Therefore, his oral work was backward and he was in a state of near-panic before a French or German conversation class. Mr. Hansell would then report the boy, who—as his biographer, Sir John Wheeler-Bennett, says—"had difficulty enough in expressing himself in his own tongue let alone in a foreign language—to his father. There followed one of those summonses to the Library, where Bertie, his knees knocking together as he stood tongue-tied before his father, suffered bitter humiliation, anguish of spirit, self-pity, exhaustion and pure frustration."

To make matters worse, there *was* the matter of Bertie's knees. He did indeed suffer knock-knees, as did his father, who insisted that the doctors devise some method of correction for the boy's legs so they would not be a source of embarrassment to him later in Naval uniform, as his had been to him. Dr. Laking devised a set of splints that Bertie had to wear for several hours during the day, and then sleep in at night. Wheeler-Bennett reports an occasion when the child pleaded so hard not to have the splints put on at night and wept so bitterly that Finch, whose duty it was to see that they were properly adjusted, relented and allowed him to sleep without them. "On this being reported to the Prince of Wales by Sir Francis Laking, Finch was sent for to the Library where, having heard his explanation, the Prince of Wales stood up and drawing his trousers tight against his legs, displayed his own knock-knees and said in a loud voice: 'Look at me. If that boy grows up to look like this, it will be your fault.' "

With their mother, life was less severe, although she backed up her husband in all matters of discipline. Lady Airlie recalled Princess May saying: "I must always remember their father will one day be their King." Both parents were constant in one theme—the idea that they and their children were not different from, or better than, other people—*other* people, of course, meaning the well-born. But this was difficult for the children to understand because in all relationships they could very well see that they were being *treated* differently—not only from other children, but from adults as well.

Princess May awoke early the morning of the coronation. Her gown was ready for her, and she was the first member of the Wales household dressed for the awesome occasion. Princess Mary Adelaide would have approved her daughter's magnificent coronation gown made entirely by English workers of English goods. It was of ivory-white satin, richly embroidered in four shades of gold and lavishly trimmed in pearls. On the bodice was fastened a corsage of diamonds and pearls. Over this she wore robes of richest purple velvet, a superb ermine cape being attached to the gown with large bows of gold and pearls.

147

London had been unseasonably cold until that morning, when the sun miraculously came out. David and Bertie stood in their kilts, their hair slicked down, their sister giggling nervously in her sweet white frock beside them, when their mother, looking grander than they had ever imagined she could, issued them last instructions.

The Prince of Wales's procession consisted of three carriages, preceded and followed by escorts of the Royal Horse Guards. The children had gone ahead in their own procession fifteen minutes earlier. The Abbey had been transformed into a great theatre. Galleries were built into almost every part of it; tiers of seats ascended on each side from the floor of the nave; vast platforms stood in the transepts over the statues of statesmen and the monuments to poets; and even near the altar there were pews and boxes for members of the Royal Family and visiting Royalties. The two young Princes stood with their mother in the Royal Box reserved for Princesses of the Blood Royal, their sister Mary with them. The spectacle was extraordinary for the children to see, but they were still so dazed from the sight of the vividly decorated stands in the streets, the large troop encampments in the parks, and the overwhelming cheering crowds that it was almost too much for them to take in.

At five minutes to twelve, the great officers of state took up their positions near the Throne. The Prime Minister,* the Duke of Devonshire,† and their attendants entered first. Then came the Queen, her diamond tiara dazzling. The splendour of her attire brought small, muffled gasps. Her gown was of shimmering gold, veiled with tulle and encrusted with *cabochon* embroidery. The neckline was framed by a wide, upstanding Medici collar in silver and gold and diamonds. Despite the King's request that her gown be British, the Queen had chosen a Parisian couturiere. Her voluminous purple robe with its long, sweeping train, all exquisitely embroidered, had been commissioned by Lady Curzon from some of India's finest seamstresses.‡

*Arthur James, first Earl of Balfour (1848–1930). Prime Minister (1902–05).

†Spencer Cavendish, Marquis of Hartington, 8th Duke of Devonshire (1833–1908).

‡Mary Lady Curzon (1870–1906).

To add to her grandeur, the Queen wore ropes of pearls and so many diamonds that she was reported as being "ablaze with light." She gave her hand to the bishop on her left and advanced to the cries of the boys of Westminster School up in the south triforium, *"Vivat Regina Alexandra!"*

Then all eyes were riveted on King Edward as he entered with his brilliant procession to louder cries of *"Vivat Rex Eduardus! Vivat! Vivat! Vivat!"* He walked slowly and with some difficulty. At one point he paused and faltered, his hesitation due more to the weight and the dragging of his train than his weakened condition. His face was pale, his expression solemn. The service had been shortened in consideration of his recent illness. Two moving moments stood out in the ceremony. First, when the eighty-one-year-old Archbishop of Canterbury knelt in homage and remained, unable to rise. The King held out both his hands and helped him steady himself. The old man walked away with the aid of his fellow bishops. Second, when the Prince of Wales took off his coronet and, kneeling at the feet of his father and King, vowed, "I, George, Prince of Wales, do become your liege man of life and limb, and of earthly worship and faith and truth I will bear unto you, to live and die, against all manner of folks. So help me God." Prince George then rose to his feet, touched the King's Crown, and kissed the King's left cheek as tradition demanded. To his surprise, the King drew his son back for an affectionate embrace, then broke away and shook his hands.

The Royal children were much taken with this incident. Moments earlier Princess Beatrice of Battenberg—to everyone's horror—had dropped her heavily embossed Order of the Service over the edge of the box with a deafening clatter. The boys were unable to restrain their nervous laughter until their mother, with a stern look, took hold of each of their arms.

The King was finally crowned at 12:40, the Queen a short time later. The King wore the historic Crown of Saint Edward. The Queen had commissioned the Carringtons to make a crown for her with the Koh-i-noor diamond at its centre and pavé diamonds so closely covering the frame that it was like one spectacular stone.

For fully a half-hour after the end of the service, the King rested in Saint Edward's Chapel. When he finally reappeared he walked with firm, though slow step to his coach. The Coronation had been exhausting; still, the King was more resilient than those around him had supposed, and by the next morning he was back at work.

"Very good reception from the crowds in the streets," Princess May commented on the coronation. But her Lady-in-Waiting, Mary Lygon, had the last word. "My Princess May attracted a great deal of admiration, as she walked down the Abbey, with Eva Dugdale and I staggering under her heavy purple velvet and ermine train." And she added that the Princess of Wales's ladies wore dresses of white satin with a design of feathers in *diamante* "all up the front and round the skirt," which she thought were "prettier than the gold and silver of the Queen's ladies."

ELEVEN

As early as the spring of 1894, Princess May, realising how limited her husband's schooling had been, set to work to better educate him. She read to him and had him read to her various histories and works of literature. She helped him to compose speeches and rehearsed him in his delivery. His grandmother, the Queen, was most pleased and suggested that the young man also be tutored by an authority on constitutional history. Mr. J. R. Tanner of St. John's College was engaged, and with him Prince George read and analysed Walter Bagehot's definitive volume, *The English Constitution.* * At the end of the course, the Prince was asked to put forth his definition of monarchy. What follows is Prince George's summary in its entirety, as he first wrote it in a school notebook that remains in the archives at Windsor Castle (italicised words were underscored by him).

Monarchy

(1) The value of the Crown in its *dignified* capacity
    (a) It makes Government *intelligible* to the masses.
    (b) It makes Government *interesting* to the masses.

*Walter B. Bagehot (1826–77), economist and author of *The English Constitution,* (1867).

   (c)   It *strengthens* Government with the religious tradition connected with the Crown.

        After the accession of George III the Hanoverian line inherited the traditional reverence of Stuart times.

   (d)   The *social* value of the Crown.

        Great for good or evil.

        Compare the Courts of Charles II and George III in their influence on the nation.

   (e)   .The *moral* value of the Crown.

   (f)   The existence of the Crown serves to *disguise* change & therefore to deprive it of the evil consequences of revolution. e.g. The Reform Bill of 1832.

(2)   The value of the Crown in its *business* capacity. The Crown is no longer an "Estate of the Realm" of itself the executive, but the [Monarch] nevertheless retains an immense unexhausted *influence* which goes some way to compensate for the formal *powers* which have been lost; this influence can be exercised in various ways:

   (a)   In the *formation* of Ministries; especially in choosing between the Statesmen who have a claim to lead a party.

   (b)   During the *continuance* of Ministries. The Crown possesses *first* the right to be consulted, *second* the right to encourage & *third* the right to warn. And these rights may lead to a very important influence on the course of politics, especially as under a system of party government, The Monarch alone possesses a *continuous political experience.*

   (c)   At the *break up* of a Ministry (but this can be treated best in connection with the House of Lords).

Thus, though it would be possible to construct a system of political machinery in which there was no monarchy, yet in a State where a monarchy of the English type already exists, it is still a great political force & offers a splendid career to an able monarch; he is independent of parties and therefore impartial, his position ensures that his advice would be received with respect; & he is the only statesman in the country whose political experience is continuous.

The British monarchy was and is a symbol with certain constitutional functions: mainly, the right to be consulted by the Government; and to encourage and to warn the Ministers of State.

152

The ruling monarch symbolised the nation in the same way a flag of another country might do for that nation, only, of course, this symbol was not an abstract piece of bunting but a person of flesh and blood.

In his book, Bagehot also said, "A *family* on the throne is an interesting idea . . . The women—one-half of the human race at least—care fifty times more for a marriage than a ministry . . . a princely marriage is the brilliant edition of a universal fact, and as such, it rivets mankind." England is very much a domestic country, where—as Disraeli said—"the home is revered and the hearth sacred," and the King and Queen and their family having been known by the people all their lives become a source of great security. But this kind of blind familial devotion meant that Royal marriages had to be ideal for British subjects to use as a measure of proper morality. Portraits of the Royal Family idealised them and showed them to be united, loving, unblemished; a "pool without a ripple." And all marriages within the Royal Family were presented as passionate courtships which culminated in fairy-tale endings of eternal harmony.

With King Edward and Queen Alexandra, this, of course, was not the case. Her Majesty's Ladies-in-Waiting were aware that the King and Queen had not shared a bed in years and that since the King's liaison with Alice Keppel had begun, he no longer even shared his anxieties and plans with his wife or sought her counsel for decisions. The Queen was helpless to alter the situation. Originally, she had been sharply disapproving of Mrs. Keppel. Time had tempered her feelings, and she now accepted the relationship. Alice Keppel did not flaunt herself or take advantage of her position as the King's mistress. Most of the King's former mistresses had been great beauties as well as intelligent and ingenious women, and the Queen had hated them all. Mrs. Keppel was well informed and a good conversationalist. To her credit, where the Queen was concerned, were her plain looks and simple dress. Her clothes were in exquisite taste; still, they were in no way showy. She wore few (though elegant) jewels, and she was no longer slim.

The King's dependence upon Mrs. Keppel grew. Occasionally, a ripple of Court censure could be discerned, as when the King named one of his horses "Ecila," which, of course, was

Alice in reverse. Yet the King's love for Alice Keppel had deepened with the years and those close to the Throne respected the liaison, for they had never seen the King so personally content.

Because Edward had brought such life back to the Throne, and because of his near-escape from death before his coronation, his subjects were as prepared to forgive and forget his former indiscretions as they were certain Alexandra was. In truth, the King and Queen were brought closer by their new responsibilities, but it was the King's mistress, Alice Keppel (called "Favorita" out of the King's hearing), to whom the King turned for companionship and advice, as well as love. Mrs. Keppel, besides her charm and great intelligence, was a reliable and discreet woman. All the King's Ministers liked and trusted her, and discussed His Majesty and problems of state freely in her presence.

Wherever the King went, Alice was invited, along with her husband George, a brother to the Earl of Albermarle and a great-nephew to Sir Henry Keppel, "the little Admiral" who had commanded the *Bacchante* when Prince George and Prince Eddy had been aboard.* By the time Edward became King, he and Mrs. Keppel had been inseparable companions for seven years. One close observer wrote that Edward "had found the most perfect mistress in the history of royal infidelity." By the same token, George Keppel had to be the most agreeable cuckold in the history of royal infidelity. Attractive, of a socially acceptable family, Keppel still did not have the charm or charisma or the talent for personal success that—without Alice—would have included him in the brilliant social circles in which he loved to travel. His easy acceptance of seignorial rights was downright feudal. By the time Edward was King, Alice Keppel was regarded in Court circles in England and abroad as a second wife to him, and treated as Royalty whenever she travelled. Only three bastions of English morality "let down the portcullis and would not let her pass: The Duke of Norfolk at Arundel, the Duke of Portland at Welbeck, and Lord Salisbury at Hatfield."

Becoming King did not end Edward's devotion to Alice's daughters, most especially little Sonia, who called him "Kingy." He continued to come to tea at the Keppel house on a regular

*Sir Henry Keppel (1809–1904), Admiral of the Fleet.

basis so that he could play with Sonia. Sonia Keppel remembers a plump man, bearded, with a "kind, deep voice, and beringed hands and cigars." She also recalls "a fascinating game" that she and Kingy devised. He would set her on his knee, holding two bits of bread and butter, butter-side down. "Then bets of a penny each were made (my bet provided by Mamma) and the winning piece of bread and butter depended, of course, on which was the more buttery." The fact that his Royal trousers would end up each time with butter stains did not bother the King.

At Easter, the year of his Coronation, he gave Sonia an exquisite blue-enamelled Fabergé egg "embossed with a diamond E, and topped by a tiny crown in gold and rubies."* Sonia was to travel with Kingy and Mamma each year to Biarritz, where roadside picnics were one of the King's favourite divertissements. Sonia was later to say, "In my life, Kingy filled the place of an accepted, kind uncle, of whom I was much less in awe than I was of my Uncle Harry . . . Kingy's advent always meant fun to me."

The King was occupied with affairs of state, as well as with Alice Keppel and familial entertainments. The Queen was tireless in her charity work, pious without being stuffy, and far and away the most beautiful Queen that England had seen in centuries. Whatever ripples existed in the pond were blamed on the imponderables of nature; though accepted at home and abroad, the public knew little of Alice Keppel.

Within three years of King Edward's accession, his diligence was such that the country began to brush aside memories of his dilettante past. His long princehood, when his close friends had all been Liberals, gave him new Royal insight. He had better understanding, thanks to his long period as a king-in-waiting and to Alice Keppel's more recent and intelligent counsel. The Victorian's stiffness, false gentility, and inhospitality to foreigners were dispersed. Yet he could still be criticised for going sailing with his "very rich grocer" friend, Sir Thomas Lipton.

---

*Carl Fabergé was the favourite jeweler of the Russian Imperial family. Queen Alexandra was the sister of the Empress Maria Fyodorovna and introduced Fabergé's work to her husband. Because of this the Royal Family owns a huge collection of this great jeweler's masterwork.

Edward was loud in his condemnation of such "snobs."

Breaking precedent, the King even accepted invitations to private dinner parties. These parties were often as gala as any full-fledged ball, for at that time Dorchester House, Grosvenor House, Lansdowne House, Derby House, Stafford House—all the beautiful homes that were to become official ministries, consulates, hotels, and clubs—were still inhabited by their owners. The Queen did not attend too many of the private parties; she was by the King's side at almost every public function, albeit arriving late. Princess Marie Louise (Princess Helena's daughter and the King's cousin) wrote that the Queen was "quite unmoved, and I might add, quite unrepentant at having kept the King and his guests waiting for at least a quarter of an hour. The darling Queen was a law unto herself."

On another occasion, having arrived for a Court at Buckingham Palace even later than usual, the Queen appeared wearing the Star of the Garter incorrectly positioned opposite the heart. She merely smiled when the King chastised her and replied "that to wear it on the left side interfered with the arrangement of her jewels." The King was adamant that she return to her dressing room and position the Star of the Garter correctly. The Queen obeyed, "absolutely unruffled." Then, after a more protracted wait by the King and Court, arrived with the position of the Star of the Garter correct but, in a bold display of recompense, the Koh-i-noor diamond worn over her right breast.

The Royal Family was well aware of the difficulties in their Monarch's marriage. During the night of December 10, 1903, Charlotte Knollys, the Queen's bedchamber woman,* awoke to find her room at Sandringham filled with smoke. She rushed downstairs and entered the Queen's bedroom, which was also smoke-filled. She shook the Queen to wake her, wrapped a dressing gown around her shoulders, and shepherded her to safety just before the fire consumed and nearly destroyed the Queen's bedroom. The Grand Duchess Augusta's comment to Princess May reveals the family's attitude. "I was horrified hearing of dear Alix's danger, too awful to think of! We must give

---

*Hon. (Elizabeth) Charlotte Knollys (1835–1930). Woman of the Bedchamber to Queen Alexandra (1870–1925).

credit to old Charlotte for *really* saving her life. What order will the King decorate Charlotte with to reward such readiness of thought and action? Though *he* was in no hurry to hasten to see Alix after her merciful escape."

After sitting next to the Queen at dinner one evening at Buckingham Palace, Lord Esher remarked, "It is queer, her determination to have her way. As Princess of Wales she was never, so she says, allowed to do as she chose. 'Now I do as I like' is the sort of attitude. And among her likes is a fixed resolve to go to India and 'see the natives.' I wonder if she will ever succeed?"

Lord Esher did not know the history behind the Queen's determination to go to India. Thirty years before, her husband had secretly planned such a trip without her. When she had learned of his scheme, she personally petitioned Disraeli, then the Prime Minister. The Prince of Wales, however, had already obtained his mother's consent to go alone. Princess Alexandra was thus forced to admit defeat, but she had not forgotten.

In the months following the Coronation, Princess May was in seclusion with her children, awaiting the birth of her fifth child. A fourth boy, Prince George Edward Alexander Edmund, was born on December 20, 1902. Five Princes were now in immediate line to the Throne of England.

Marlborough House, their new home in London overlooking the Mall, was redecorated and ready for occupancy by spring of 1903. Princess May had drastically altered the interior, and from the day she moved in—April 4—until May 10—when she and Prince George gave their first family dinner to the musical accompaniment of Gottlieb's Vienna Orchestra—she was in a tizzy as to whether the Queen would approve of the alterations. After the party, Princess May wrote in her diary: "The house looked lovely & the dinner went well." Slipped between the pages was a gold-trimmed menu card signed in the Queen's bold hand: "Motherdear Alix—the first dinner in our beloved old home," with no mention of the new decor or the evening's festivities.

The Queen was still reluctant to give up the past, despite the grand and glorious present. Marlborough House and the title of Princess of Wales were part of this. She also had to think of the future: What would happen if the King should predecease her?

She therefore viewed her daughter-in-law as an aging star might view her understudy. Princess May's popularity and the King's fondness for her did not ameliorate the strained relationship between the two women. Princess May, who was the soul of punctuality, found her mother-in-law's inability to be on time for any engagement a constant source of irritation. She was too respectful of the Monarchy—and consequently of the Queen Consort—to reveal the smallest trace of annoyance. On the other hand, Queen Alexandra never attempted to conceal her jealousy of her son's wife.

As Mabell, Countess of Airlie, illustrates, prior to one Court day, the King, Charlotte Knollys, and Lord Ormathwaite (H. M. Master of the Ceremonies) were in a terrible dilemma; the Queen had a bad cold, and the doctors insisted on her remaining in bed that day *and* the next. The Queen was determined that if she could not be at Court, a Court should not be held. The King protested and decided that the Princess of Wales would stand in for the Queen. Lord Ormathwaite was dispatched to convey this decision to the Queen, whose anger was so fierce it "rang through the corridors."

As Lord Ormathwaite was leaving, Charlotte Knollys ran after him with a message. "Her Majesty says that none of her ladies are to attend the Princess tomorrow and that the Mistress of the Robes is not to go to the Court. The Princess can take her own ladies."

"How can I tell the King this?" Lord Ormathwaite said helplessly.

Charlotte Knollys offered to do it for him. And the next day Princess May held the Court, but she did so with her own inexperienced ladies and without the Mistress of the Robes, which was previously unheard of.

Not only was the King fond of Princess May, he had a high opinion of her intelligence and "used to talk freely to her about political and foreign affairs which he would never have dreamed of discussing with his own daughters. In fact, the King's trust in Princess May was so great that he gave her his express permission to see the King's boxes along with the Prince of Wales."

"But Mamma doesn't see them," the Prince of Wales had replied, aghast.

"No, but that's a very different thing," the King had answered.

The truth was that Princess May understood their content better than did Prince George, and, as had always been her habit, she would discuss things with him in a manner that increased his perception. The King's respect for Princess May's intelligence did not help the relationship between the Queen and her daughter-in-law. Nothing could be kept secret in the Court, and Queen Alexandra learned quickly that Princess May had been accorded this special privilege. Her animosity toward her daughter-in-law increased, even though she herself was not the least bit interested in seeing the contents of the King's boxes.

Princess May had become a threat to the vain Queen Alexandra since the day she had become the Princess of Wales. Also, the younger woman had matured, narrowing the generation gap between them and placing Princess May in a more competitive position with her mother-in-law. Harshly critical of Queen Alexandra to those close to her, she doubled her own efforts in presenting herself as the most dedicated, intelligent, and industrious of the female members of the Royal Family. Had she been less of her own person, she might have enjoyed a better relationship with her mother-in-law. Princess May displayed a rigid nature that was unwilling to bend.

Few nations were without conflicts—ambitious leaders, dynastic squabbles, severe economic problems—that could easily explode into violence. The most direct threat was Kaiser Wilhelm of the German Empire, whose military power was growing at a startling pace. Britain had to look for allies, and she quickly made agreements and alliances with Japan, France, and finally—in 1907—with Russia. Meantime, the military potential of the dominions was enlisted. An Imperial General Staff was established, and Winston Churchill devised a scheme "for an Imperial Squadron of warships from all the major colonies, to be based upon Gibraltar and sent wherever it was needed."

The King had suddenly taken on his sovereignty with great drive and urgency. He spent hours each day over the dispatches and communiqués in his leather boxes, in meetings with his Ministers, and in consultation with his secretaries. Prince

George did not share the burden of the nation's problems. Despite being allowed access to the dispatches, he and his father never discussed state problems. Not that Prince George appeared concerned, being content to spend his days working with his collection of stamps or in shooting.

In 1903, Princess May's youngest brother, Alge, married Princess Alice, the King's niece and Prince George's first cousin. Nothing could have pleased Princess May more. Alge was her favourite brother, and as Princess Alice was the King's favourite niece, the alliance further bound her own relationship to the Wales family. Princess Alice, slight and delicate with wonderfully soft-curling dark hair and shining brown eyes, was a bright young woman, and her "Uncle Bertie" enjoyed having her at shooting parties at Sandringham. At one party, Princess Alice confessed to Mrs. Keppel: "Much as I love him I find it difficult when sitting next to him at a table not to be distracted by his habit of fiddling with his cutlery and I also find it almost impossible to keep up a consecutive conversation with him."

"Don't worry about that," Mrs. Keppel replied. "We all experience that trouble. He likes to join in general conversation injecting remarks at intervals, but he prefers to listen to others rather than talk himself. Often he starts a discussion, but as soon as he can get others involved in it he is content to listen and make occasional comments."

Alge's marriage to Princess Alice greatly helped Princess May's self-esteem. Since her mother's death, she had set herself up as matriarch of the Teck family. Her older brother, Dolly, after acquitting himself well in the Boer War, returned to England, married Lady Margaret Grosvenor, and had recently been appointed Military Secretary at the War Office. But Princess May's third brother, the good-looking and irresponsible Frank whom Princess Maud had once loved,* had never ceased being a humiliation to his sister. Princess Alice recalled that "from boyhood Frank had been a family problem. He had been expelled from Wellington College for throwing his housemaster over a hedge to win a bet. All through his life he was an incorrigi-

*Princess Maud married Prince Charles of Denmark in 1896. Later he became King Haakon of Norway and Princess Maud his Queen Consort.

TOP LEFT: The people's princess, rotund Princess Mary Adelaide, Duchess of Teck, mother of Princess May, 1868.

TOP RIGHT: The Duke of Teck.

ABOVE: The dapper and impecunious Prince Franz, Duke of Teck, with two of his children, Prince "Dolly" (standing) and Princess May, 1868.

RIGHT: Princess May at 7 and already mature for her age, 1873.

The Teck family in 1891. Creditors were pressing and Princess May's future was not bright. L to R, Prince Alexander of Teck (Alge), Princess Mary Adelaide, Prince Francis (Frank), Princess May, and Prince Adolphus (Dolly) who travelled with his sister to Balmoral. Prince Franz seated in front.

Edward, Prince of Wales, and his family. L to R standing—Albert Victor, Duke of Clarence, the dissolute second heir to the Throne; Princess Louise; Alexandra, Princess of Wales; Princess Victoria. Seated—Prince George and Princess Maud, who was to become Queen of Norway.

The North London Press's account of the Cleveland Street Trial

THE WEST-END SCANDALS.

COMMITTAL OF THE EDITOR OF THE "PRESS" FOR TRIAL.

A DEFENCE FUND OPENED.

Lord Euston emphatically denies the libellous statement, and explains the circumstances under which he once visited the house in Cleveland-street.

The editor of this paper has been committed to take his trial at the sessions of the Central Criminal Court, which open on Monday, 16 December. The proceedings were initiated last Saturday morning, when on the application of Mr. Lionel Hart, instructed by Messrs. Lewis & Lewis, Justice Field granted his fiat for the commencement of criminal proceedings against Mr. Ernest Parke, whose solicitor, Mr. Minton Slater, offered no opposition. At Bow-street Police Court the same afternoon, Mr. George Lewis obtained from Mr. Vaughan a warrant for

LORD EUSTON.

Mr. Parke's arrest, the Earl of Euston supporting the application by testifying to the truth of the affidavit he had made denying the libellous statements complained of. Sergeant Partridge was sent with the warrant to the *Star* office, but being by inadvertence informed that Mr. Parke had left, went to his place of residence at Clapham. Meanwhile, however, Mr. Parke heard of the issue of the warrant, and at once went to Bow-street

TO SURRENDER HIMSELF,

regarded as the disgrace and opprobrium of modern civilisation." The paragraph concluded by warning Mr. Matthews, the Home Secretary, that if he did not take action before Parliament met he would have a heavy reckoning to settle. Mr. Lewis continued that the accusation was a very atrocious one, and he should ask that the defendant be committed for trial. The circumstances, so far as Lord Euston were concerned, were these. He had never committed any crime of any sort or kind. That statement was

ABSOLUTELY WITHOUT ANY FOUNDATION

so far as he was concerned. He had never left the country, and there had been no warrant issued so far as he knew for his apprehension. If there was any warrant out, Lord Euston was present that day to be apprehended : but it was perfectly untrue that such a warrant had issued. All that he knew about the case was simply this. One evening at the end of May or the beginning of June Lord Euston was walking in Piccadilly at about 12 o'clock at night when a man put into his hand a card on which were the words " Poses Plas-

HAMMOND.

tiques.—Hammond, 19, Cleveland-street." About a week later

LORD EUSTON WENT TO THE HOUSE,

between 10.30 and 11 at night. A man opened the door to him and asked him for a sovereign, which Lord Euston gave him. Lord Euston asked about the poses plastiques, when the man made an indecent proposal to him, on which Lord Euston called him an infernal scoundrel, and threatened to knock him down if he did not at once allow him to leave the house. The door was then opened and Lord Euston at once left the house. That was all he knew of the matter.

Formal evidence was then given of the publication of the libel and of the connection of Mr. Parke with the paper, but Mr. Lockwood observed that the evidence was hardly necessary as the responsibility of the defendant was not disputed.

The Earl of Euston was then examined by Mr. Lewis. He said—My name is Henry James, Earl of Euston. When in London I reside at

4, GROSVENOR-PLACE.

When not in London, I reside at Euston Lodge, Thetford, or Wakefield Lodge, Stoney Stratford, my father's place.

You have seen the copy of the paper of the 16th of November, *The North London Press*.—I have. I at once gave instructions for a criminal prosecution for libel in respect of the matter contained in that paper.

Is there any truth Lord Euston, in the statement that you have been guilty of the crime alleged in that newspaper ?—Certainly not.

Is there any truth, so far as you know, that any warrant has been issued for your apprehension ?—No. There is no truth whatever in the statement that in order to abscond from arrest I went to Peru. I have not been out of England since I came from Australia in 1881.

Will you state to the court

WHAT YOU KNEW OF THIS HOUSE.

All I know is that one night I was walking in Piccadilly. I cannot quite say the date. It was either the end of May or the beginning of June. A card was put into my hand, which, on reading afterwards, I saw was headed, " Poses Plastiques, Hammond, 19, Cleveland-street." I do not remember whether Tottenham Court-road was on the card. About a week afterwards I went there. It was about half-past ten or eleven o'clock at night. The door was opened to me by a man. He asked me to come in, and then asked me for a sovereign. I gave it to him. I then asked him when these poses plastiques were going to take place. He then said, " There's nothing of the sort."

Mr. Lockwood here objected to the conversation being given, and the objection was upheld.

Mr. Lewis—Did he say something to you ?—He did.

Did you express anger ?

You say the statement was first made in the month of October :—Yes.

Have you made a statement at the Home Office about it :—No.

Or at the Treasury :—No.

You made no statement to any official :—None whatever.

Just wait and hear my question. You made no statement to any official at all either at the Treasury or the Home Office :—I have had no communication of any sort or kind either with the Treasury or the Home Office.

That you swear :—That I swear.

You said you first made your statement in October. That I take it meant to some friends :—Yes, privately.

IS LORD ARTHUR SOMERSET

a friend of yours :—I know him.

When did you see him ' last '—Last summer some time during the season. That is as near as I can remember. I was in London during May, June, and July. I saw him in society. I was in the habit of meeting him constantly.

Did you meet him in society :—Yes.

You have not seen him since :—No.

Do you know where he is :—No.

Now just tell me with regard to this occurrence in May or June, you say you afterwards read the card. How long afterwards :—When I got home I think. I don't remember particularly. I think when I got home and took my coat off. I did not read it in the street. I just shoved it in my pocket and looked at it when I got home.

Just tell me what it was that was on the card ; was it a printed or a lithographed card :—It was a lithographed card, but the words *poses plastiques* at the top were in writing.

Was the gentleman giving out these cards promiscuously, or

WERE YOU PARTICULARLY FAVOURED ?

—Witness (laughing) : I cannot tell you. He shoved one into my hand, and I put it in my pocket.

Was he giving them away to other people ?—I really cannot tell you. I was walking along pretty smart home. I do not walk slowly as a rule.

Did you see him give a card to anyone else :—No. It was near 12 o'clock as I was walking home.

I suggest to you that you had not time to stop and read it :—Well (laughing), I did not stop to read it under a lamppost.

Mr. Lockwood—I do not know what there is to laugh at.

Mr. Lewis—Well, it was a comical question.

Mr. Lockwood—Well, how long was it between your reading it and your going to see whether the promises in the card would be carried out :—Oh, at least a week.

Then you kept the card during the whole of that time :—Yes.

YOU WENT ALONE :—YES.

Did you bring the card back with you :—I brought it home.

What did you do with it :—I destroyed it. I was disgusted at having been found in such a place, and I did not want to have anything more to do with it.

You say you destroyed it. Did you burn it or tear it up :—Well, I think I tore it up. I should not have a fire in my room at that time of year.

You tore it up in disgust :—Yes.

In indignation :—Yes. I was very angry with myself for having been brought there.

Lord Euston, from what passed in that house you had no doubt what the character of the house was :—Not the smallest.

It is a house, as I understand you to say, of your own knowledge, where crimes such as those alluded to in the libel were probably committed :—I should think they might be, and probably were, from what was said to me.

Mr. Lockwood—That, sir, is at present all I have.

ABOVE: Press coverage of the famous Cleveland Street scandals involving Lord Arthur Somerset and his good friend, the Duke of Clarence, in an exposé of a male brothel in London.

LEFT: Prince Eddy—collar-and-cuffs (the Duke of Clarence) in the deer-hunting hat that also spawned rumours that he might be Jack the Ripper.

LEFT: The Duke of Clarence in the uniform of the Tenth Hussars. Circa 1891.

BELOW: Balmoral—the enchanted castle.

BOTTOM: At Balmoral—Queen Victoria with her favourite dog. Her granddaughter, the future Empress Alexandra, stands holding her pet dog. "Alixy," as she was called, chose to marry the future Tsar Nicholas II (far left in rakish hat) rather than the Duke of Clarence. Queen Victoria's daughter, the Empress Victoria, mother of Kaiser Wilhelm, stands between them.

OPPOSITE PAGE: Princess May—"the most unlikely princess in the realm." Circa 1891.

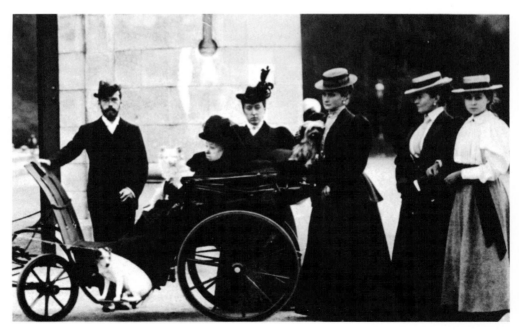

BELOW: Prince George (seated) with his cousin Nicholas at the former's wedding. One was to become King, the other Tsar. They bore a great family resemblance. Until the hour of his death, Nicholas believed George would save him from the Bolsheviks.

ABOVE: A fantasy come true. Wedding portrait—Prince George, second heir to the Throne, with his bride, Princess May of Teck, recently bereaved fiancée of his elder brother.

BELOW: York Cottage, the newly married royal couple's first home—so small "the servants must sleep in the trees," Prince George once commented. Circa 1892.

Sandringham, home of the Prince and Princess of Wales and visible from Princess May's bedroom window at York Cottage.

Princess May and her father-in-law Edward, Prince of Wales, at Mar Lodge, 1892.

Queen Victoria with the infant Edward, Prince of York. Behind them, Princess May and Alexandra, Princess of Wales.

Queen Victoria and her family at Balmoral, 1895. Princess May holds
Edward of York ("David" to his family), her first child. Others in photo-
graph—standing L to R—Princess Helena (Queen Victoria's daughter);
Prince Henry of Battenberg (the Queen's son-in-law); Count Arthur
Mensdorff-Pouelly; Princess Beatrice (daughter); and George, Duke of
York (grandson). Seated—Princess Ena of Battenberg (future Queen of
Spain, granddaughter), Prince Arthur of Connaught (grandson), and
Prince Alexander of Battenberg (grandson).

Princess May and the two
sons who would be King. "I
think they like me a little
more," she said when they
were small. Maturity did
not diminish the distance
between them.

ABOVE: Two future Kings of England, left—George VI—and right—Edward VIII—photographed in their prams by Downey, the Court photographer, 1896.

RIGHT: The two youngest York children—the retarded, epileptic Prince John who died at 13; and Prince George, the future Duke of Kent, the brother who cared the most.

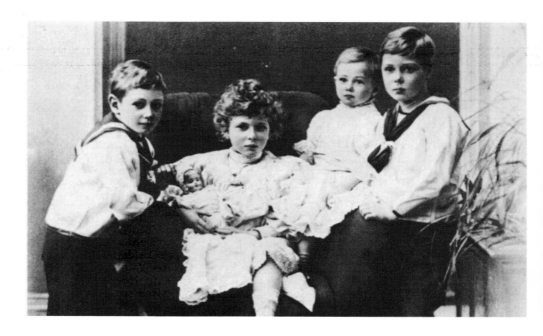

ABOVE: The four oldest York children (L to R), Prince Albert (King George VI), Princess Mary, Prince Henry, and Prince Edward (King Edward VIII).

LEFT: Princess May when she was Duchess of York. She is wearing the famous diamond stomacher suspended from bow at bodice of gown. The pearl-and-diamond choker was one of her favourite pieces of jewelry.

RIGHT: Alexandra, Princess of Wales, a difficult mother-in-law, a doting grandmother.

RIGHT: The Duke and Duchess of York (Princess May) at home at York House, St. James's Palace, 1896.

BELOW: Queen Alexandra's memorabilia-filled sitting-room in Sandringham. Her desk is far left. "All the rooms are more airey now and less full of those odds & ends which beloved Mama wld poke into every corner of the house which was such a pity," her daughter-in-law later wrote.

LEFT: King Edward VII with Caesar who wore a Fabergé collar inscribed in jewels with the legend "I am Caesar the King's dog."

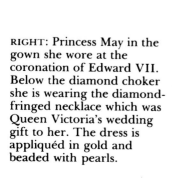

RIGHT: Princess May in the gown she wore at the coronation of Edward VII. Below the diamond choker she is wearing the diamond-fringed necklace which was Queen Victoria's wedding gift to her. The dress is appliquéd in gold and beaded with pearls.

RIGHT: "The most fascinating woman in England," Mrs. Alice Keppel, the King's mistress, 1906. The King's ministers all trusted her.

ABOVE: King Edward VII and Queen Alexandra at Cowes, 1909. The Queen was more tolerant of King Edward's sixteen-year liaison with Mrs. Alice Keppel than Princess May.

RIGHT: The Honourable Mr. George Keppel, Alice Keppel's complaisant husband, "a giant of a man—six foot four inches tall."

ABOVE: Nine Kings at Buckingham Palace for the funeral of Edward VII, May 1910: Back row L to R—Haakon VII of Norway, Ferdinand I of Bulgaria, Manoel II of Portugal, Wilhelm II of Germany, Gustav V of Sweden, Albert I of Belgium. Seated L to R—Alfonso XIII of Spain, George V of England, and Frederick VIII of Denmark.

ABOVE: Funeral of King Edward VII, transferring the body of the late King to Westminster Hall. King George V with his two elder sons following the gun carriage along the Mall. Prince of Wales on right.

RIGHT: The new Prince of Wales riding to his investiture, July 13, 1911.

ABOVE: The coronation procession, Queen Mary inside coach.

BELOW: The first photograph ever taken inside Westminster Abbey during a coronation. King George and Queen Mary in their Chairs of State during the ceremony. The Royal Box is behind them. Princess Mary; Prince Edward; Prince Albert; Prince Henry; Queen Maud of Sweden; Princess Beatrice; Princess Victoria ("Toria"); and Louise, Duchess of Fife, form front row.

Queen Mary in her coronation splendour.

ble gambler. Frank's gambling became more and more a vice with each year." And much as she lectured and warned that she would no longer come to Frank's aid, Princess May kept on doing so, fearing that if she did not, public knowledge of his way of life would discredit the Teck name. In the spring of 1904, thirty-five and still unmarried, Frank lost ten thousand pounds to a professional gambler who threatened scandal if the loss was not made good. At this time, Princess May also learned that Frank had become entangled with an older married woman and had given her some of Princess Mary Adelaide's jewels, which, in fact, had been bequeathed to Princess May.*

Horrified by the commonness of all this, yet aware that she must act, Princess May went to the King. The payment of the gambling debt was arranged, and to guard against further embarrassments of this kind, King Edward decreed Frank should return to India to rejoin the regiment in which he had served during the Boer War. To Princess May's further consternation, Frank sent in his resignation to the Army and refused to leave England. The awful dilemma of the Princess of Wales's brother was to hang over her head for some time to come.

In April 1904, the Prince and Princess of Wales made a glowing state visit to the Emperor Franz Joseph of Austria and were received at Vienna with a rigid protocol long abandoned in England. Dinner at the Hapsburgs' Court was formal, beginning at five in the afternoon. A Court ball, nothing like those held at Buckingham Palace or at Windsor Castle, followed at 8:30 P.M. "My goodness! This Court is stiff!" Prince George wrote in his diary that night.

In the same months, Prince George and Princess May travelled to Stuttgart to invest Princess May's cousin, William II, King of Württemberg, with the Order of the Garter. *Onkle* Willie and *Tante* Charlotte, as Princess May called the King and Queen of Württemberg, were sympathetic and easygoing people. "Their ample figures betrayed the justice they did to their four

---

*These consisted of a magnificent set of matched emeralds—tiara, earrings, necklace, stomacher, brooch, bracelets, and ring—originally owned by Princess Mary Adelaide's mother, the Duchess of Cambridge.

full meals a day." After an enormous lunch, *Onkle* Willie and *Tante* Charlotte took their visitors on a leisurely drive through the suburbs of Stuttgart in an open victoria, and *Onkle* Willie quickly fell asleep, only to receive "a swift jab of the Queen's elbow to acknowledge the salute of one of his soldiers and to straighten his hat that kept sliding rakishly to one side of his head."

Württemberg received the Prince and Princess of Wales with much enthusiasm. Princess May's family connections might have added to the general excitement. Yet everywhere she and Prince George went, they were popular. Even at home, and despite Queen Alexandra's great beauty and the love and devotion she claimed from the people, it was Princess May who always received the greatest ovation at the opera or during a public appearance. Her bearing was a combination of the military and the regal, and her appearance had a startling effect and left a deep and lasting impression. Never bowing to current fashion (she still wore her hair in a "poodle fringe"), she was as dependable as Big Ben and seldom cancelled an engagement. Before the public or in private, she had the talent to say the right thing, no matter how difficult the occasion.

A certain uneasiness in her manner could occasionally be seen —a flicker of nervousness in her eyes at odd moments, an uncontrollable little twitch at the side of her mouth in times of stress, and the flutter of her hand to her throat when unsure. These small indications of her human frailty endeared her more strongly to the public and to the Court. Her "shyness" was often discussed in the press in a flattering way, and it greatly mitigated the austere posture she could and did affect.

Away from England, she was at her most confident. At home there were always worrisome things—Frank, of course, and the older children. David was such a "jumpy" child, Bertie was both shy and moody, and she simply could not find a way to win over her one small daughter.

Princess May had a strong distaste for all the processes of childbirth. Pregnancy depressed her. "Of course it is a great bore to me & requires a great deal of patience to bear it, but this is alas the penalty of being a woman!" she wrote her husband

162

during the soggy, rainy summer of 1905. Her mental outlook was not eased when her Aunt Augusta wrote, upon hearing she was soon to have a sixth child, "The pleasure I always have in receiving your dear letters was rather marred by the secret imparted to me!" Aunt Augusta thought the bearing of six children disgustingly common. Due to give birth in July, Princess May was forced to remain at York Cottage during May and June. Prince George went there whenever he could steal time from his public duties representing the Crown at various functions—but his wife felt resentful that she could not attend with him the festivities of the King of Spain's official visit, which culminated in a gala performance at the opera. Nor could she be at the wedding in June at Windsor of her husband's first cousin, Princess Margaret of Connaught,* to Crown Prince Gustav Adolf of Sweden, which was to be the Royal Family's most festive gathering of the year.

On July 6, Prince George joined his wife at York Cottage to await the birth of their newest child. On the twelfth, after an unduly difficult labour, a fifth son, Prince John Charles Francis, was born. Princess May was indeed supplying her husband with a regiment. For eight days after the birth, Sir John Williams, the doctor in attendance, remained at the cottage. "A charming man. I shall miss him very much," Prince George recorded of the doctor's departure. Princess May had made her usual rapid recovery, but the tiny Prince had had respiratory problems.

The new Prince had been named for Prince George's second brother, a child who had lived only long enough to be christened. (He was buried at Sandringham a short distance from York Cottage in a grave marked with a white cross inscribed: "Suffer little children to come unto Me.") For Lala Bill the name was a bad omen. Lala Bill had become a fixture in the Wales nursery since Mary Peters's departure. She had been head nurse to each child born since Mary. David, who was most attached to

---

*Princess Margaret (1862–1920), daughter of Queen Victoria's son Arthur, Duke of Connaught, and Louise, Princess of Prussia. Prince George had attended the wedding of the Duke and Duchess of Connaught in 1879 (when he was only fourteen), which had also taken place at Windsor.

her, resented the time she had to devote to each newborn in the household.

Except for the three months of the year that their parents spent at Sandringham, the children saw little of them. York Cottage was considered to be *home*, where life fell into a more domestic pattern. Mother and children seldom met until four in the afternoon, when the youngsters would appear in the drawing room for tea, "freshly scrubbed and with hair combed." Tea was their last meal in the day and usually consisted of muffins, jam, and milk. Comfortable enough for three or four people, with five noisy children and their nannies, the room was crowded. As soon as tea was served, Prince George would stride off alone to the library, "where he would remain occupied with his stamp collection, already becoming quite famous, or his correspondence, or entering into his book which game and how many he had shot, or reading The Times," while Princess May, with one of her ladies-in-waiting at the piano, would sing folk songs, among them such American favourites as "Old Black Joe," "Swanee River," "The Camptown Races," and "Oh, My Darling Clementine."

The children would then return to their rooms until an hour before their bedtime, when they would be marched single-file into their mother's boudoir to sit in their own special small chairs around the sofa upon which she would be reclining in her negligee before getting dressed for dinner. Standing a discreet distance away were the nursery staff, poised to remove from their mother's presence any one of the five who misbehaved. Princess May read and talked to the children in her soft, clipped voice that never sluffed a vowel or dropped a consonant. She liked to discuss with them some of her cultural interests in literature, art, and opera, and share with them her prodigious knowledge of Royal history.

Princess May, who had long admired Shakespeare and knew the Histories exceptionally well, would recite long, complicated passages from memory.* In time, the children were terrified of

*A misconception about Princess May's literary interest arose because James Pope-Hennessy mentioned in a passing reference in his book, *Queen Mary*, that Princess May had not read Tolstoy or Dostoevski until late in life and was over reciting Shakespeare to her because she would always catch them out on any mistakes, no matter how small. She was remarkably well read in English, French, and German literature, both classic and contemporary, and had a prejudice against reading a book in a language other than its original. She reread Flaubert and Hugo in French, and Goethe and Schiller in German. When she read the Maud translations of Tolstoy's works in the 1920s, they made a deep impression upon her. To the children, she read not only Dickens and Kipling, Shakespeare and Tennyson, but also foreign works, even though the children could not understand them.

Her boudoir was a cozy place overflowing with personal treasures; to the children she would identify all the people in the photographs and miniatures she kept around her, and she would also explain the background of her various momentoes, gifts given to her on her tours and by family members—a jewelled Fabergé Easter egg from Nicholas II and an antique inlaid ebony-and-mother-of-pearl fan from Queen Ena of Spain among them. Being of a practical nature, she insisted that small hands should never be idle. Each child was given a wooden ring with upright brass pegs, and while she entertained her children, they would loop wool yarn around each peg to form, by means of a succession of crochet stitches, a comforter five feet in length earmarked for one of their mother's many charities. David was the most agile crocheter in the group.*

If Princess May was distant with her children, teaching, explaining, and sermonising instead of sharing, she was most con-

---

fifty when she saw her first production of Shakespeare's *Hamlet.* This last seems to have been a matter of oversight on her part, for it was a work she knew. And since she did not read Russian, she waited until the Dostoevski and Tolstoy novels were translated into English by Maud.

*The Duke of Windsor was to become so proficient with a crochet needle that at the beginning of World War II, when attached to a British mission with the French Army and obliged to make long motor trips through the zone of operations, he crocheted to kill time. He was "understandably discreet" about the products of his hobby (which were sent to a charity for the French Army when complete), for, as he wrote later, "It would hardly have done for the story to get around that a Major General in the British Army had been seen bowling along the roads behind the Maginot Line crocheting."

scious of her own position and of her children's futures as Royalty. She did not share Prince George's fondness for sport (from partridge shooting to deer stalking to fishing), and she was a bad sailor where boats were his special passion. For his part, he lacked enthusiasm for the arts or any history other than Great Britain's. Still, they did forbear with exceptional grace each other's hobbies and interests, and were inveterate creatures of habit.

Christmas at Sandringham was "Dickens in a Cartier setting." Each year *A Christmas Carol* was reread in the sonorous voice of the boys' tutor, Mr. Hansell. On Christmas Eve, Princess May conducted the children in carol singing as everyone crowded about the piano in the sitting room. Directly after, the Prince and Princess of Wales escorted their family to the coach house at the stables to watch the distribution of bounty to the employees at Sandringham. On long tables covered with white tablecloths were laid "scores of bloody joints of beef, one for each family, and each tagged with the name of the recipient. Outside in the stable yard, waiting their turn, were the gamekeepers, gardeners, foresters and stable hands, or their wives—in all some three hundred people." The King and Queen with the Wales family sat just inside, near the door of the coach house, "and as the employees walked out with their meat, the men touching their caps and the women making a quick bob of a curtsy, the King wished each a Happy Christmas."

The children were forced to wait many agonising hours before they were able to exchange and open their gifts, for at Sandringham procedures moved along prescribed lines. Once the estate workers were presented with their Christmas tokens, the children piled into Prince George's horse-drawn omnibus—usually used for transporting the servants—and rode up to the Big House, where the household and the guests for the Christmas holidays were gathered and waiting in the saloon. Not long after, a gong sounded, heralding the approach of Santa Claus himself. An instant later a tall, hooded figure in full regalia—flowing white beard, red coat, black patent-leather boots, a bulging bag over his shoulder, appeared. The fact that they knew this resplendent impersonator to be one of the upper servants in no way diminished the children's joy over his arrival. After bowing to the King and Queen, "who would greet him jovially, Santa Claus led the company out of the Saloon toward the Ballroom. The double doors flew open before his advance, revealing in the centre of the room a fir tree from the woods, tall enough to touch the ceiling, festooned with tinsel, tinted glass balls, patches of cotton in imitation of snow, and ablaze with candles."

The children were always the last to receive their gifts from their grandparents and then permitted to be the first to open all their other packages. The wait was endless, as the hour was already later than they stayed up to on other nights of the year. Still, they managed, as most children would, to honk and pedal their way on their new toy motors through the sea of wrapping paper that covered the ballroom floor.

For months the children looked forward to Christmas at Sandringham. During the rest of the year their parents were either busy or surrounded by private secretaries, equerries, and Ladies-in-Waiting. The nursery and tutoring staff formed a solid wall between the children and their parents. And with David, Princess May had less time than with her other children, as his teaching schedule was more arduous. In the rare moments that they had alone, they discussed English history and visited galleries that specialised in English artists.

When her older son was only two years old, Princess May wrote to her husband, "I really believe he begins to like me, at least he is most civil to me." Civil best describes Princess May's attitude toward her children and theirs to her. She had been blind to David's great need for maternal affection, unaware during the first three years of his life that Mary Peters had so abused him. Bertie's severe emotional problems irritated rather than alarmed her. Mary's desperately poor school record simply brought recriminations to the child and her teachers that they did not recognise the responsibility of being a Royal Princess.

Therefore, with mixed emotions, the children accepted the news that their parents would be leaving in October for India, and would be gone for Christmas and Easter as well (they would be away for a total of eight months). During that period their grandparents would once again be in charge. Bertie felt the least sad over the news of their planned absence, for his fondest memories were of the time his parents had been gone during the equally long tour on the *Ophir*. Now, of course, his dear grand-papa was King. Bertie understood what that meant, but with the hope that only childhood fantasy can nurture, he was confident —as he wished his parents an awkward farewell—that his life would become whole again, that he would stop stuttering and being so frightened of always doing the wrong thing.

For Princess May, the trip to India promised a grateful sur-cease from nursery problems and unpleasant confrontations with her mother-in-law. More than that, it presented an opportunity to shine alone in a country where she believed majesty was viewed with awe by its people, and she prepared for the long journey with enthusiasm that India would be a great and wondrous adventure.

TWELVE

"Fancy you 'Miss May' on an Elephant! I can hardly see you perched up there!" Queen Alexandra replied to a letter written from India by her daughter-in-law in December 1905. During a visit she had made to Egypt in 1869 with her husband, the Queen had not only ridden camels and been photographed on one's humpy back, but had smoked a *huqqah* and had eaten with her fingers among the ladies of Khedive Ismael's harem, an exotic experience she had mentioned many times to Princess May.

The Queen was still smouldering under the hurt of not being chosen to go to India, and, pointed though the thrust might have been, there were many in the Court who would have agreed with the Queen that riding on an elephant's back was an unlikely occupation for the Princess of Wales. The younger woman was now more stately and imposing than her years suggested. Her bearing was so marvellously regal that she could wear a startling quantity of superb jewels. Her demeanor was stiff, often intimidating. However, in India, Princess May's deeper romantic fantasies caught her unawares. "Lovely India, beautiful India," she was heard to murmur like some incantation, and those in her Household who travelled with her noticed that she was "quite different in India."

The land of the British Raj stirred Princess May's emotions as nothing else in her life had done. She was dazzled and more than a little in love with the mystery and adventure of this exotic and strange world. Princess May, despite the fact that it was unpleasantly hot and very little sea breeze blew, was intoxicated with India's charm from the first moment that the battleship H.M.S. *Renown* entered the sullen green waters of the Bay of Bombay. She was to see India mainly from an English viewpoint, and therefore the romantic illusion was to remain throughout the tour and for many years to come. The more realistic side of India was seen by Prince George, and with growing concern over the Indian image of the British as conquerors. The trip, therefore, worked miracles in tearing Prince George out of his political complacency. He was shocked to learn in Bombay that Indians were not allowed as members of British clubs in any of the larger cities, and disturbed that there was so little social exchange between the British and the Indians. With much more maturity than he exercised on the tour of the *Ophir,* Prince George now observed India as a conquered country ruled by England, but separated by two social worlds.

A curious dichotomy did exist. The English were "coddled by dark servants in flaring turbans," their children in swaddling clothes cared for by ayahs. But English women avidly devoured their late issues of the *Lady's Pictorial* and copied the newest English and French patterns, while the Indian women wore their gossamer sarees. And whereas the better-educated Indian men discussed the rise of Gandhi and the Congress Party, Englishmen followed Parliament's disputes in month-old, dog-eared copies of the *Times* or the *Illustrated London News* and argued about happenings thousands of miles away. Except for the odd occasion, the British dined on the cuisine and foods of their distant homeland, and the men were never to be found without a coat and tie even in the most torrid weather, or the women without their feathered and flowered hats and lacy parasols. They frequently attended lavish parties and receptions because, as one *grande dame* of the period claimed: "Everyone with *any* standing had a ballroom at least 80 feet long." At smaller dinner parties of forty or fifty people, there was a servant for each guest. But at most gatherings both small or grand, few Indians were to be counted, and these few were either government officials or representatives of the British Raj. An attitude of racial superiority abounded. A state visit by the Heir Apparent and his wife would, it was hoped, help bridge that chasm, for the British knew how great was the Indians' respect for the Monarchy.

Princess May had read all the relevant books she could in the few months preceding their departure, learning a good deal about the Hindu, Mohammedan, and Buddhist religions and memorising several greetings in Indian dialects. She had also spent an extravagant amount on clothes. "In all the papers I see accounts of your dresses," her husband commented a few weeks before they sailed. And Aunt Augusta, in her usual caustic tone, chided as she wished the Princess bon voyage: "Your Dresses amuse me to read about, so many too! and *who* is to *pay?* The one for the tiger hunt gave me the shivers!"

They arrived in Bombay on November 9, 1905, and were received by the outgoing Viceroy, Lord Curzon, and by Lord Lamington, Governor of Bombay, whose guests they had been in Australia five years earlier. In an historic quarrel, Curzon had clashed with Kitchener over the degree to which the civil government should control the Indian Army. Having lost, Curzon was obliged to resign, but welcoming the Prince and Princess of Wales to India was one of his last official duties.*

According to one historian, Curzon had been "out of his time —in some ways too soon, in others too late." He had "dared" to approach the civilisation of India with its 400 million people (one-fifth of the world's population at that time) "with a respect rare among the pig-stickers and box wallahs, and tried to convince the Indians themselves that they should not simply wish to be brown Britons." He championed Indian crafts: woodworks, enamels, carpets, potteries, and lovely silks. He devoted himself to Indian archaeology, restored the Taj Mahal to its original perfection, cherished the half-buried glories of Fetehpur Sekri and the exquisite Pearl Mosque in the fort at Lahore.

---

*The Royal itinerary which Curzon had supervised was as follows: Bombay, Indore, Jaipur, Lahore, Peshawar, Delhi, Agra, Gwalior, Lucknow, Calcutta, Rangoon, Mandalay, Madras, Bangalore, Mysore, Hyderabad, Bengares, Gwalior again, Quetta, and Karachi. A full account of the journey is given in *The Royal Tour of India,* by Sir Stanley Reed.

171

He also revived the moribund Department of Antiquities and gave to the British Raj in India—"just in time"—a scholarly distinction.

Curzon, who had impressed Princess May at the coronation, was a man of conflicting emotions. On the one hand, he was a forthright imperialist; on the other, a man who deplored the fact that the vast majority—even of educated Englishmen in India—"regarded the Indians as less than fully human."

From the time of their arrival in India, the Royal couple were protected from the true plight of the Indian people. After Bombay, they were to visit Ajmere, but because famine and plague had taken the lives of thousands there, the Royal party was redirected to Indore, which they reached on November 16. They were greeted by a youthful maharajah, splendid in scarlet and gold, and the maharani, who looked like "a little bundle of lilac silk crowned with diamonds, the position of her eyes indicated by two holes veiled with gauze." Princess May managed a simple conversation in Indian dialect with the tiny maharani, a feat that won her the instant approval of the maharaja's court at Indore. She also quickly discovered that the Indian woman was regarded as little more than a chattel by the Indian man. This so dismayed and disturbed her that she frequently brought the subject to Prince George's attention, and when, toward the end of the Royal tour, Prince George was to have a conversation with the President of the Indian Congress Party about it, her strong influence is in evidence.

"I have been reading your speech at Benares," Prince George began, "in which you said it would be better for India if the Indians had a much larger part in the administration. I have now been travelling for some months in India, seeing vast crowds of Indians in many parts of the continent, and I have never seen a happier-looking people, and I understand the look in the eyes of the Indians. Would the people of India be happier if you ran the country?"

"No, sir," President Gokhale replied, "I do not say they would be happier, but they would have more self-respect."

"That may be," Prince George snapped back, "but I cannot see how there can be real self-respect while the Indians treat their women as they do now," and he was caught glancing over at Princess May for her approval.

When home in England, Prince George was in daily contact with both his mother and his sister Toria. This habit was continued in India, where he would write the women in his family a running account of his and Princess May's daily experiences.

Queen Alexandra's special affection was for Bertie and for the baby John, but she wrote Prince George, "Dear David, grown and such a sturdy, manly-looking little fellow, and little Mary also grown a good deal and sweet Bertie my particular friend." Five-year-old Henry (whom his family called Harry) she had nicknamed "little Bobs" because he had a noticeable lisp that caused him to transpose "w's" for "r's" so that he pronounced his family name "Hawee," and because his godfather was Lord Roberts. The Queen usually spoiled the children to excess, playing games with them, romping with the younger ones, acting out charades, giving them full run of Windsor Castle or Buckingham Palace, but this time they were left with their tutors and nurses for long periods. Through it all, however, she never forgot her pique at not having been allowed to go to India. "I do envy you dreadfully and *never* shall cease regretting having been left behind," she wrote her son. And to her daughter-in-law she added, "I am glad you sometimes think of old me and *how* I would have enjoyed it all!" The Queen also reminded Prince George and Princess May that "darling Eddy" had loved India so. Not that they had to be reminded, for whenever possible Prince George took Princess May to places in India where Eddy had been before.

"I must say that although we had very hard work, our stay in Calcutta was a great success politically," he informed the King. "Our visit too was most opportune, as the feeling was very strong against the government owing to the partition of Bengal and it made them think of something else and the Bengalis certainly showed their loyalty to the Throne in a most unmistakeable manner."

Prince George was as sensitive to the problem of caste as he was to the plight of the Indian women. "No doubt," he wrote in his diary, "the Natives are better treated by us than in the past, but I could not help being struck by the way in which all salutations by the Natives were disregarded by the persons to whom they were given. Evidently we are too much inclined to look upon them as a conquered and down-trodden race and the Native, who is becoming more and more educated, realises this. I could not help noticing that the general bearing of the European towards the Native was to say the least unsympathetic. In fact not the same as that of superiors to inferiors at home."

Sir Walter Lawrence, formerly a member of Lord Curzon's staff, wrote that the Prince and Princess of Wales both found the use of the word "Natives" offensive to them and that the Prince was "convinced that the Ruling Chiefs should no longer be treated as schoolboys." Still, Prince George did use the word in his diary, whereas, if it had disturbed him so greatly, he might easily have substituted the words "the Indian people."

In each city they visited, the Royal couple were entertained in a lavish style unequaled in their own Court or in any other they had visited. When Sir Walter Lawrence had agreed to join the tour as Chief of Staff, he did so with the condition that the Prince and Princess of Wales accept no gifts from the Indian princes, an act that he felt sure could be misread by the Indian politicians. Perhaps because of this, each maharajah attempted to outdo the last. Princess May was at her elegant best at these gala receptions and garden parties, but Prince George was always happier setting aside ceremonial formality and talking to people individually. His personality was better suited to tiger hunts and yacht trips and small dinners than to ceremony. Men understood his frankness and were not offended as women were by his loud laugh and occasional explosive comments. Men also appreciated his talent as a crack shot and his endurance on a hunt.

Perhaps with a twinge of disappointment, women were surprised at the great dissimilarity between Prince George and his father. He did not have the roving eye and ate little, being fussy where food was concerned. He was a strong churchman. Whether in the train or on the road, on Sunday he would always pull up at eleven o'clock when a service, sometimes in a tent, sometimes in a convenient house near the railway, was held. On board ship, church services were conducted daily.

174

The Royal party went from Jaipur to Gryna, to Peshawar, through the Khyber Pass as far as Lundi Kotal, then on to the slopes of the Himalayas to Jammu, then to Delhi and Agra and into Gwalior for Christmas, sometimes sleeping on their special luxurious train, at other times enjoying the hospitality of some Indian prince or English governor. And all through it, Princess May moved as though "in a dream." On a few occasions, she walked incognito about the side streets of some big city, looking at the mud dwellings of the poor and making purchases in the shops. The people might not have known she was the Princess of Wales, yet with her jewels and fine clothes and her large entourage, they were certainly aware that she was of a high social caste.

She wrote a running travelogue of the journey to her Aunt Augusta. "The Maharani with native chiefs met us at the station on Saty & we drove her thro' rows of fine looking retainers, some in old armour, a wonderful scene," she wrote from Udaipur. "We are now staying with the nice Maharaja of Bikanir," she informed her Aunt from Gujner, "we especially admired his fine camel corps." At Lundi Kotal, "48 massed bands played" and the Maharaja of Gwalior "showed us his jewels which are really magnificent." From Karachi, where they were finally to depart India, after 9,000 miles of railway travel, she wrote Aunt Augusta, "We steamed away about 6 our band playing 'for Auld Lang Syne' which was most upsetting. We went on to the bridge & watched dear beautiful India vanish from our sight."

What is glaringly apparent in Princess May's correspondence during her trip to India was the loosening of most of her maternal ties (however slight) to her children. She sent them romantic picture postcards but surprisingly few letters, and even in correspondence to the Queen she did not reveal any great emotion in being separated from her six children—one a baby of only a few months—for over half a year. Shortly after Christmas, she received a letter written on copybook paper in her third son's six-year-old studied hand. "I thank you very much for the Indian toys, Auntie Toria gave me a drum and a trumpet, Granny gave me a motor torpedo boat and a basket full of chocolate, Aunt Louise sent a box of pencils. Lord Farquhar sent a nice box of soldiers with tents, both red and green. Did you like the snow

175

drops that Georgie and I sent you. I worked very well on my lessons yesterday. With much love from Harry," he concluded, allocating six circular kisses labelled "P" for Papa and six more labelled "M" for Mama.

"Darling Harry," his mother wrote back on a postcard, "Papa & I thank you for your 2 long letters which were very nicely written, also for the little snowdrops you & Georgie sent. There are no flowers like them in this country. Love from Mama." No special kisses, no anecdotes told for the little boy's pleasure were included in her notes to her children. Nor did she admit missing her children, or comment on being parted from them at Christmas.

Princess May was looked upon by those close to her as "very cold and stiff and *very* unmaternal." She dealt with her children almost as if they belonged to someone else. Both David and Harry were to claim that they could not recall ever being alone with their mother during any part of their childhood or adolescence. A Lady-in-Waiting or a servant or a private secretary was always present. The King, on the other hand, often spent time alone with his grandchildren.

One story told is that a tailor's assistant called at York House with a suit to be fitted for David, but upon hearing voices in the nursery where she had been directed, waited outside the room. The little Prince, who was fond of the woman, rushed out to her. "Come in," he said, "there's nobody here. Nobody that matters, only Grandpa!" The children had as a comparison reprimands in their father's study with no outsider present. Perverse as it might seem, the young Princes recalled these lone moments with their father with a certain warmth.

Prince George was unable to relax the bonds of discipline even when in India. Strict rules had been left that each of the four older children was to write the parents individually on *alternate* weeks. David and Bertie, however, got their schedules confused, and their father wrote in reproof to Bertie from Delhi, "David ought to have written last week and you ought to have written to me this week. I don't know how the confusion has come." And to Mr. Hansell he added, "The two boys ought to write the Princess and I each week alternately so that they both write each week." It never occurred to him that such inflexibility might take the spontaneity out of his children's correspondence.

Toward the middle of the tour, a British political upheaval meant that the children saw less and less of their grandparents. Following a split in the Conservative Party over tariff protection, the Prime Minister, Arthur Balfour, was forced to resign.*

The Prince and Princess of Wales arrived home the first of May, only to learn that Ena, Prince George's cousin, his Aunt Beatrice's daughter (the same Ena whom Princess May had entertained as a child at Balmoral when she had gone to see the Queen about marrying Prince Eddy), was to be married on May 21 to Alfonso XIII, King of Spain. ("So Ena is to become Spanish Queen! A Battenberg, good gracious!" Aunt Augusta had written, never having thought very highly of Queen Victoria's youngest daughter's deceased husband, Henry of Battenberg.) Queen Alexandra was in mourning for the death of her father. Therefore, Princess May and Prince George were to represent the Crown at the wedding in Madrid as the King's personal representatives. Princess May had only three weeks to refurbish her wardrobe and "swot up," as the children called it, on Spanish history. Her activities left very little time to give to six small children whom she had not seen since the previous October.

The demands for her maternal attention nearly overwhelmed Princess May. Bertie's stuttering was worse than ever, and he was thin and pale. He still wore the braces on his legs at night, slept fitfully, and was not doing well in his studies. Princess Mary had had to be removed from her brothers' classrooms because she was a "disturbing influence." David had just been found to suffer some deafness in one ear, a condition that was feared could be related to Queen Alexandra's hearing disability.† Harry had unaccountable fits of crying, as well as spates of nervous giggling. Georgie cried whenever he was brought into the presence of his mother, and the baby John, though eleven months old, was not sitting up as his nursemaids thought he should. Dealing with these problems could be postponed until after Madrid was Princess May's attitude, and in the

*Arthur Balfour (created Earl of Balfour, 1922) was replaced by Sir Henry Campbell-Bannerman.

†He was to have some deafness in his ear thereafter.

weeks before her departure she saw her children sparingly.

However, on May 26, 1906, she celebrated her thirty-ninth birthday. Birthdays were important events in the family calendar, but their parents' birthdays invariably confronted the children "with an agonising problem." They were expected, according to family custom, to render happy-birthday greetings with a poem each had committed to memory. Under Mr. Hansell, they had to memorise and practise reciting excerpts from Shakespeare or Tennyson until word-perfect, and then they were further obliged to copy them out "with painful care on long sheets of white paper, which were then tied together with bright-coloured ribbons. Directly after breakfast on these birthdays we would bear the compositions to the person celebrating. Mary, Bertie and I [David] would advance in turn, each nervously recite his or her poem, and then, with a bow, present the copy."

On this day, the children, all impeccably groomed, filed into the sitting room. Mary recited some verses from Tennyson's *Idylls of the King* and acquitted herself well. Then came Bertie, who had been given Goethe's stirring ballad *Der Sänger* to say in German. English was difficult enough for Bertie to manage in public, and after he stuttered unmercifully for a few minutes, David stepped forward to recite Thomas Wolsey's farewell from Shakespeare's *Henry the Eighth.* A bit of tittering was heard when he spoke the line, "Like little wanton boys that swim on bladders," but there was not a sound in the crowded room at York Cottage when, in a voice far more mature than that of a boy of twelve, he recited,

O how wretched
Is that poor man that hangs on princes' favours;
There is betwixt that smile we would aspire to,
That sweet aspect of princes, and their ruin
More pangs and fears than wars or women have;
And when he falls, he falls like Lucifer
Never to hope again.

Lala Bill, who was holding Prince John, stifled a small shuddery sigh as the boy who would be king ended,

Had I but serv'd my God with half the Zeal
I serv'd my King, he would not in mine age
Have left me naked to mine enemies.

That same evening, Princess May and Prince George left for London on the first leg of their journey to Spain for the wedding of Princess Ena to King Alfonso XIII.

Prince George had met the young King of Spain when he had made a Royal tour of Great Britain, intent on selecting a suitable bride from the numerous British Royal Princesses. That had been the previous June, and at a Buckingham Palace gala where Nellie Melba and Enrico Caruso had sung. The youthful Spanish ruler had been overwhelmed by the grandeur of the occasion. But seeing King Alfonso in his own land where he was greatly revered was another matter.

Ena had grown into a fine young woman, and Princess May, who had known her since she was a small child, had a special fondness for her. A good-natured girl with beautiful dark eyes and a lovely fair complexion, she laughed easily but had a bit too much of "the common touch" for Aunt Augusta. "Did you see that ridiculous Photo of them all, *laughing,* Beatrice leaning down over the young lovers spreading her arms out like an Eagle," she wrote her niece shortly after Ena's engagement had been announced, "too funny & not Royal!"

King Alfonso XIII was twenty years old, his bride only a year his junior. Because his father had died six months before his birth,* he had grown up under the guardianship of his mother, Queen Maria Christina. A slight young man with a pompous stiff posture and a head that was too small for his neck and body, nonetheless he had a military air and a protective attitude toward women that was quite attractive. A great deal of speculation was offered as to what Queen Victoria would have said about her granddaughter's alliance with a Catholic whose background was always being questioned in Royal circles. His grandmother, Queen Isobella II, had said after her unsuccessful wedding night with her King Consort (and cousin, François de Asis), "What can I say about a man who wore more lace than I

*King Alfonso XII (1857–1885) died at the age of twenty-eight.

179

did?" Still, Isobella had had eight children, though it was rumoured "not necessarily by the King Consort."

The "train de luxe" that Princess May and Prince George took from Paris to the Spanish frontier town of Irún was one of two carrying most of the European Royal families to the wedding in Madrid. The weather had been unseasonably hot and dry, and the dust and dirt inside the carriages were intolerable. Late at night at the unlit wayside station in Irún, everyone had to get out to change trains. The Prince and Princess of Wales disembarked with their entourage, which included Prince Dolly of Teck and his wife, as well as numerous chamberlains, equerries, ladies-in-waiting, dressers, and footmen. All stood about in the dark, not quite knowing what to do, for no arrangements had been made for the hour's wait between connections. The Grand Duke Vladimir of Russia and his suite were most vociferous about this inconvenience, and Princess Marie of Erbach-Schönberg bustled from one group of Royalties to the other, considerably distressed.*

Finally, they were all packed into one long Spanish train with a great deal of confusion, as rank and precedence had not been taken into account. The new accommodations were crowded and "insufferably hot. At midnight all the visiting Royals met in the dining car," recorded Princess Marie of Erbach-Schönberg, "to refresh ourselves with cooling drinks."

At 3:00 P.M. the next day, the train at last reached its destination, and the fatigued passengers were transferred to carriages to form a long procession through the factory section of Madrid, uphill "through ornamental gardens and, by way of splendid wrought-iron gates, into the great courtyard" of the Palacio Real, which dominated the town "like a colossus." Troops of soldiers lined the drive, and the trumpets and drums of the massed bands played the appropriate national anthem so loudly as each carriageload of Royalties was discharged that it was almost impossible to hear the greetings of the Spanish officials.

Unlike many of the Royal guests who were accommodated in other palaces and in the palatial homes of grandees, Princess May and Prince George were lodged in cathedral-high apart-

*Born Princess Marie of Battenberg, an aunt of the bride.

ments in the Palacio Real itself. Their quarters were guarded by halberdiers with pikes, who, as the Royal couple approached, would present arms and pass from one to another the cry, *"Arriba Princessa! Arriba Principe!"*

The morning of the wedding, May 31, 1906, was stifling hot. At 9:15, the royal visitors gathered in the great courtyard of the Palacio Real where nineteen state coaches waited, each drawn by six white or six black horses wearing flaring pink and orange ostrich plumes.* This procession then wound its way slowly through narrow streets made almost impassable by the crowds and the troops that tried to keep order. The wedding was at the ancient Gothic Church of San Jeronimo.

"The service in the church was very fine, the music and singing splendid," Prince George wrote in his diary that day, "it lasted from 11 to 1. Alfonso and Ena were married at 12. She looked very well [although she was overdressed, in Princess May's opinion, her gown too covered in ruffles and lace] and went through a trying ordeal with a great dignity."

The Prince and Princess of Wales left the church in procession to return to the Palace for a bridal luncheon. They rode in the third coach from the rear. Immediately behind them came the coach bearing Princess Beatrice and Queen Maria Christina. This was followed by the empty *coche de respeto* (the spare coach that tradition dictated), and finally, the golden-crowned coach in which King Alfonso and the new Queen Ena rode alone. "Just before our carriage reached the Palace," Prince George records in his diary, "we heard a loud report & thought it was the first gun salute."

They were on a narrow street, the Calle Mayer, close to the Italian Embassy and only two hundred yards from the palace. The driver of the coach in which the Prince and Princess of Wales were riding continued without altering speed. Not until they were once again in the courtyard of the Palacio Real did

---

*A question remains as to the number of state coaches used in the procession to the wedding. Prince George records in his diary entry of May 31, 1906, that there were nineteen, while Princess Marie Erbach-Schönberg claims the number was forty. Forty carriages had been necessary to take the Royalties and their entourages from the station to the Palacio Real.

they discover what had happened. The bride and groom—clothes blood-streaked and in disarray—stepped from the *coche de respeto* amidst a great deal of shouting and crying and confusion. An anarchist, Mateo Moral, had thrown a bomb from the upstairs window of Number 88 Calle Mayer just as the bridal coach passed below. The bomb burst between the lead horses and the front of the carriage, killing the driver and about twenty spectators, including the Marquesa Torloso and her niece who were standing on the balcony of Number 88 (directly below where the assassin had thrown the bomb). The windows of the bridal coach had been smashed; glass, debris, and fragments of uniforms flew into the coach; and blood was everywhere. It so happened that the British Ambassador, Sir Maurice de Bunsen, was watching the procession with officers of the 16th Lancers from a nearby balcony when the tragedy occurred. Along with his regiment officers, Sir Maurice rushed out of the house; the men positioned themselves as a barricade around the damaged vehicle and helped Queen Ena and King Alfonso descend. Miraculously, neither was seriously hurt. Queen Ena's wedding dress had been slashed by flying glass, but its many layers of whalebone and fabric and its heavily embroidered and jeweled decoration had saved her being cut. Bride and groom had been swiftly transferred into the empty *coche de respeto* and escorted the short remaining distance to the palace by Sir Maurice's British guard.

Queen Ena was safely inside the locked gates of her new home when she was heard to cry, "I saw a man without any legs! I saw a man without any legs!" At which point, she and her husband broke down and sobbed. Princess Beatrice fluttered about in a state of near-hysteria until she was finally assured that her daughter had not been injured, but she was dazed and unable to control her emotion during the bridal luncheon that followed at 3:00 P.M. Prince George proposed a toast—"not easy after the emotions caused by this terrible affair"—to the newlyweds' health. Luncheon was a dreadful ordeal with everyone politely picking at the food and conversation strained.

"We can only thank God that the anarchist did not get into the church," Princess May wrote her Aunt Augusta, "in which case we must all have been blown up! Nothing could have been

braver than the young couple were, but what a beginning for her
. . . I saw the Coach . . . still with blood on the wheels & behind
where the footmen were standing."

Despite the tragedy, the following evening's gala banquet and
reception for five thousand guests went ahead as planned. "Very
hot affair & tiring," wrote Prince George in his diary, "much
talking bowing & clicking of spurs . . . we walked through the
rooms the heat was awful & every window shut. Had some supper & walked back through the rooms, smell even worse."

The Prince and Princess of Wales were still in Madrid on June
3. "My birthday (41). The Palace Madrid," his diary entry reads
for that day. "A man in a village close to Madrid yesterday
evening shot a Garde Civile and then shot himself. He has been
identified as the swine that threw the bomb."

The visit to Spain did not end until June 7, when the Prince
and Princess returned to Marlborough House by way of Paris.
The wedding trip had been a gruelling experience. For the first
time, Princess May realised how vulnerable Royalty was to the
schemes of terrorists, anarchists, and madmen. They arrived
home on June 10 and then, only six days later, sailed on the
Royal Yacht *Victoria & Albert* to Norway for the coronation of
King Haakon and Prince George's sister, Queen Maud.* The
nine-year-old Princess Mary accompanied her parents, although
her two older brothers, as Heirs to the Throne, were not permitted to travel out of the country with their father.

"So Maud is sitting on her very unsafe throne—to say the least
of it," Aunt Augusta wrote Princess May, "he making speeches,
poor fellow, thanking the revolutionary Norwegians for having
elected him . . . no, really, it is all too odd . . . 'Motherdear' will

---

*King Haakon of Norway was formerly Prince Charles of Denmark (also called
Carl), a young man thought singularly without prospects when he married
Princess Maud, the Prince of Wales's sister. But when Norway dissolved its
union with Sweden in 1905, the throne was offered to him after the people of
Norway voted four to one in favor of a monarchy. Prince Charles accepted with
alacrity, renounced his Danish nationality, and assumed the name Haakon,
after the early Norse kings of Norway. Haakon was Norway's first independent
king in 600 years. He ruled for fifty-two years. Haakon proved a brave king,
resisting Hitler and contributing by his courage to the German dictator's final
defeat.

not like it either, besides they have but one *peaky* Boy* . . . A revolutionary Coronation! such a farce, I don't like your being there for it looks like *sanctioning* all that nasty Revolution . . . How can a future K & Q of E go to Witness a Coronation *'par la grace du People et de la Revolution!!!'* Makes me sick & I should say, you, too!" To which Princess May replied, "The whole thing seems curious but we live in *very* modern days."

On July 6, their thirteenth wedding anniversary, Princess May and Prince George arrived home from Norway. They had missed David's twelfth birthday on June 23 and incorporated it, as well as Toria's birthday, into their own celebration. From his grandfather, David received a diamond stickpin of Persimmon, King Edward's Derby winner, complete with jewelled jockey; from his father, a silver watch; and from his mother, a prayer book. The young boy was, thought Lord Esher, beginning to grow more like the *"old* family every day. He has the mouth and expression of Queen Charlotte,"† and would in a few months, like his father before him, be sent away from home to join the Navy.

The decision was unfortunate, for distance and hostility were created between father and son that would always remain to alienate one from the other.

---

*That *peaky* boy, who was two years old at the time, was to become King Olav V and grew to resemble the Norsemen of his father's adopted country.

†Queen Charlotte of Mecklenburg-Strelitz, Queen Consort of George III, mother of George IV and William IV.

THIRTEEN

T he idea of one day becoming King was terrifying to young David. He was always asking Lala Bill not to discuss his future, and Lord Esher also noted his reticence. Esher records a significant incident in 1904, when David was ten and Bertie eight. He was looking after the children, who were at Windsor with their grandparents, and recorded being "walked off my legs and pulled off them by the children. The youngest is the most riotous. The eldest, a sort of head nurse. It is queer looking through a weekly paper and coming to a picture of the eldest with the label 'our future King.' Prince Albert at once drew attention to it—but the elder hastily brushed his brother's finger away and turned the page."

For David to become King meant that his beloved *grandpapa* would have to die, and his father, whose love he was never sure of, would be dead as well—a fairly scary thought for a sensitive boy. At twelve, he was as jumpy as he had been as a toddler, pulling constantly at his tie, smiling nervously at inapt times; and he remained as insecure—holding on overpossessively to childhood treasures, looking to Lala Bill and his grandmother for the love and attention he did not get from Princess May.

Denied mother love as a child, David was to seek it for the rest of his life. But Princess May was only partly responsible for the severe emotional problems suffered by her children, and especially her sons. Prince George was an overbearingly dominating father, and his excessive authority had damaging effects. Whether Princess May or Prince George was more to blame for the children's shortcomings and insecurities is not easy to assess. But the combination was formidable, and there were other difficult aspects of the children's lives. For one thing, they were lonely because of the isolation imposed upon them by virtue of their father's position, and for another because of the absence of the close association with children their own ages. Occasionally Mr. Hansell would escort the Princes to Sandringham's village school, where the local boys would be forced to play a game of football with them. These events were painful for both David and Bertie, the former because the village boys treated him with a kind of uncomfortable awe ("Here, *Sir,* you can have the ball if you. like," was one remembered comment by a ten-year-old village lad), and the latter because he was too terrified to speak at all for fear of revealing his stutter. When David was nine, his mother had organised a dancing class with twenty or thirty children of people she knew. But the enterprise failed, having none of the spontaneity that had been hoped for.

In 1906, the six Royal children, their parents, and the Household were a closed society. Even in this, David's exalted destiny gave him dominance over his siblings. The three oldest formed a triumvirate. With Finch in attendance, they bicycled to the nearby village of Dersingham, where they bought sweets or watched the trains at Wolverton Station. David was always the leader, Bertie and Mary crouched over their handlebars racing along behind him.

Their walled-in life was relieved only during those short periods when they were at York Cottage and their grandparents were in the Big House. November 9 was the King's birthday, and he always celebrated it at Sandringham. Excitement ran high for the children as they watched the small army of servants arrive several days before this, followed by the arrival of the Royal chef, M. Menager. Then came the horses and carts of the royal tradesmen, bringing "two hundred shoulders of mutton or two hundred and fifty joints of beef," along with huge quantities of fruits and vegetables, and delicacies such as prawns, oysters, Italian truffles, and the enormous hot-house grapes grown by the gardeners at Windsor Castle and brought down to Sandringham solely for use as garnishing. Hundreds of sugar loaves (weighing fourteen pounds each) and at least a hundred pounds of a special Turkish coffee were delivered. The King had dispensed with the services of the Indians of his mother's Household staff and taken on an Egyptian coffee-maker, whose only task was to brew and serve coffee for Royal guests after dinner.

The King liked the splendour of "*la Bonne cuisine,*" but at Sandringham, he served a lot of good English cooking. Without fail, Sunday's dinner would be roast beef and Yorkshire pudding with plain roast potatoes and horseradish sauce.

At twilight the evening of the King's birthday, Sandringham would itself spring to life with "a bonfire blaze of lights." The children waited for the sound of the clatter of horses' hoofs on the driveway, which heralded the arrival of their grandparents and their many guests, each with his or her own valet or personal maid. A gala dinner was held the first night, and early the next day the fields and coverts resounded to the fusillades of Sandringham's Royal shooting party. Sometimes David and Bertie were allowed to follow their grandfather as he shot and be a part of all the excitement of the competition to see who could bring down the largest number of birds. By dusk, the day's kill might total two thousand pheasants.

A hamper luncheon for all the guns and their ladies would be laid out in a big tent near the woods. Footmen swept the site clean, then laid down straw. The party, usually no less than forty people, would eat at long wooden tables covered with the finest cloth and plate, and David and Bertie thought there was nothing as grand or wonderful as when they were asked by their grandfather to join the shooting party at these luncheons. Outside the tent would be spread the morning's bag, and if the King had had a good day's shooting, the party would be in high spirits.

In King Edward's household, both guests and staff ate meat three times a day, and whatever was left over after dinner would be given to the poor villagers who (at both Windsor and Sandringham) waited at the kitchen doors. Evening menus in the country were much more elaborate than the luncheons. One dinner menu in 1906 at Sandringham consisted of cold consommé, salmon cutlets, stuffed ortolons (small Egyptian birds

187

which were the King's favourites), lamb in champagne, duck, chicken casserole, salad, asparagus in sauce *mousseline,* and four desserts and a savoury, including *Pêches à la Reine Alexandra* (a slight variation on *Pêches Melba,* using a red currant sauce in place of raspberries).

After tea if Bertie and David had done their homework, they were allowed to run up the hill to the Big House to say good night to their grandparents. It was a memorable time for them; they were being given carte blanche to a different world. But they had to remember their father's rule that they must be back at York Cottage by seven o'clock. The boys kept an "anxious eye" on the ornate clock on the mantelpiece of the saloon. Their grandparents were impervious to the situation and did not hurry their return. These good-night excursions, therefore, which began so happily often would end in the library with their father upbraiding them for disobeying his orders.

David adored his grandfather, and his dearest wish was to grow up to be exactly like him. He never ceased to wonder how his father and grandfather could be such opposites; the one so stiff and the other so warm. King Edward's bellowy voice, his hearty laugh, the arm that swooped about David and clamped him to the big, robust body were reassuring. The skipped generation released all inhibitions in the King, who as a young father had not been loving, gentle, or tolerant with his own two sons. However, since the coronation, the King's relationship to Prince George had been most devoted, and as each year passed the two men became even closer. Mrs. Keppel may have been responsible for some of the King's tolerance of Prince George's stodgy personality, since she never ceased to speak well of the younger man.

When his grandfather left Sandringham at the end of the season, David would sit by the small window in the narrow classroom on the ground floor of York Cottage, straining to hear the departing carriages and fourgons on the gravel drive. He would remain listening until there was no sound at all—and always at that moment he experienced a fear that perhaps the Big House would never again flare up with light and he would never again see his exciting *grandpapa.*

In 1907, the average age for entering the Royal Naval College was thirteen. At the time of his entrance examinations in February, David was twelve and a half, but, unlike the boys he would soon join, he had never attended school. At the possible risk of losing his job, Mr. Hansell had repeatedly warned Prince George that if his elder son were ever to hold his own at the Naval College, he should be sent to a good preparatory school first. Prince George's naive answer had been, "The Navy will teach David all that he needs to know." The five educationally ineffectual years under Mr. Hansell's tutelage, the circumstances of his birth, and the sheltered upbringing in his close-knit household had not prepared the young Prince for the outer world.

Of Mr. Hansell's teaching, his student was later to say, "I am appalled to discover how little I really learned. If Mr. Hansell harboured strong views about anything, he was careful to conceal them. Although I was in his care on and off for more than 12 years, I am today unable to recall anything brilliant or original that he ever said." And then he adds, "The British constitutional monarch must, indeed, stand aloof from and above politics. As a device for preserving the Crown as a symbol of national unity while divesting it from abhorrent forms of absolutism it is a remarkable example of the British genius for accommodation. But one effect of this system, which is perhaps not so well understood by the public, is the handicap imposed upon a British Prince, who, while obliged to live and work within one of the most intensely political societies on earth, is expected to remain not merely above party and faction, but apolitical!"

In view of this, the choice of Mr. Hansell was, perhaps, all for the best. To have placed a Prince in the direct line of succession under the tutelage of a teacher of strong convictions might have created future conflicts for both the Prince and the British constitutional system.* But Mr. Hansell's weak personality and the cloistered atmosphere in which he taught were in total opposition to any necessary preparation David required to become a Naval cadet.

He had never been without the company of his siblings. This

---

*Despite Mr. Hansell's tutelage, David, when Prince of Wales and as Edward VIII, had several of these conflicts.

had helped allay the consuming fear of the dark he had suffered since the days of Mary Peters's nannyship. David leaned strongly toward his mother's love of languages and the arts—subjects not included in the education of a Naval cadet. But his father loved the sea and ships, and would hear of no other training for his elder son than the Royal Navy.

For three days David struggled with test papers at a narrow wood desk in a public examination hall in London, along with a hundred other hopeful applicants (the first time he had ever been in a public situation without members of his family or his own staff). He was one of sixty-seven boys who passed into the Navy. His father personally supervised the fitting of his blue jacket with its brass buttons and cadet's white collar tab and Naval cap, and then—on a May day of unseasonable wind and rain, and to David's surprise—accompanied him on the train from London to Portsmouth to begin his Navy life. Despite all his determined effort to be brave on his departure from Marlborough House, the young boy was unable to control his tears as he said goodbye to Bertie and Mary. He clung to Lala Bill an inordinately long time and burst out crying again when Finch—who had tended his every need for almost thirteen years—handed him his packed dressing case.

Father and son rode in the Royal train along the seacoast, Prince George in splendid good humour as he recounted stories of his own early Naval life. In Portsmouth, they transferred to the Admiralty yacht for the short journey across the Solent to the Isle of Wight, where the Royal Naval College had been established at Osborne. (Shortly after the death of Queen Victoria, King Edward had given his mother's home to the nation.) Ironically, David, for the next two years of his life, was to live in a collection of prefabricated buildings grouped around the old Osborne House stables, which had been converted into a mess hall and classrooms opening into the stable yard. The construction of new buildings had not yet begun. The flimsy structures used for the dormitories in which the cadets slept had in six years so deteriorated that holes could be kicked in the outer walls with very little effort and no injury. The greatest problem in these Spartan, uncomfortable quarters was to keep warm. From the service and luxury of his different homes,

David's orbit of living now shrank "to a hard iron bed and a black-and-white sea chest" at its foot that contained all his possessions. Thirty boys occupied each barren hut. Reveille was at six o'clock in summer and six-thirty in winter, proclaimed on a "blaring bugle." Moments later, the cadet captain would rout the sleepy boys out of their beds "with one peremptory pull of the gong above his bunk." Three minutes were allowed for prayers said on bony knees on a cold, hard floor. Then a gong would peal twice and everyone would run to the long trough at the far end of the hut, where they were expected to brush their teeth in one minute. The boys were then given ten minutes to use one of the two toilets and to return to their beds and make them. The gong sounded three times, the signal that they must strip off their nightclothes and fold them away, and, naked and shivering, be herded to the end of the dormitory, where they had to plunge into icy water for a communal bath in a green-tiled pool.

Rather than helping him, David's princely position made him the instant target for ragging by other cadets, a situation for which he was not prepared. After a week he was given the nickname of *Sardine* because "he's too puny to be a Wale[s]." Not one boy in his quarters befriended him. His Royal parentage, his restrained personality and well-trained manners, and the fact that he had never attended a school branded him a "freak" and placed him—perversely—in a position of contempt, especially where the older boys were concerned. For the first weeks at Osborne, David observed the traditions of ragging that the college set for new boys; he stepped into the gutter when senior cadets passed him on the street and scurried out of common rooms when they appeared at the door. When one day he raised a faint protest and sauntered, not hurried, from the room, one of the boys grabbed him and said, "You are the Prince, are you? Well, learn to respect your seniors." He was then made to stand at attention while one of them poured a bottle of red ink over his head, turning his golden hair scarlet before it dripped down his neck and ruined one of the few white shirts he possessed. "A moment later," he was to recall, "the bugle sounded off quarters, and the seniors dashed away to fall in their ranks leaving me in a terrifying dilemma. I couldn't go to quarters dripping

191

red ink—that would have been telling on the seniors—but, if I missed quarters, I was for the Commander's Report the next morning." He chose the latter, slinking away "under the cover of darkness" to wash the ink from his hair as best he could and to get a clean shirt out of his sea chest. For being late to quarters, he was sentenced to spend his leisure hours for the next three days "alternately going round the stable yard at the double carrying a rod across the back of my shoulders and facing the paint work for an hour at a time in the seamanship room."

Punishment was meted out cruelly at the college. That same term, Mervyn Alexander-Sinclair, the son of one of the two Commanders of the school, was in David's class. Mervyn suffered from chronic tardiness and was sentenced for this misdemeanor by his father to "six official cuts" with a bamboo rod, clearly an extreme and harsh punishment. A Naval doctor was called to be in attendance. But even more inhumane than the severity of the sentence was the fact that the beating was carried out in the presence of all the cadets, fallen into two ranks and made to stand at attention while the boy was strapped to a gymnasium "horse" and the cuts administered by a sturdy physical-training petty officer. The offender was so severely beaten that he spent a fortnight in the school sick bay and his father was relieved of duty shortly after the incident. But the atmosphere of Osborne, which had once meant exciting days at Cowes and marvellous family get-togethers for David, had taken on a Dickensian quality.

David suffered nightmares that he fought desperately to conceal, and he often went hungry, for princely training had made him unable to eat as fast as the rules demanded and leftovers were stealthily commandeered by seniors. Once, he was so ravenous that he took the chance of severe punishment by feigning sickness, hoping he might get some food to eat in sick bay. Luckily for him, the matron—though she admonished him for his deception—took him into her kitchen and "with true Irish sympathy" prepared for him a sumptuous tea of buttered eggs, fresh bread, and jam.

His fears almost reached their limits when one day he saw a group of seniors advancing on him in an empty classroom where he had returned to retrieve a forgotten book. They cornered him by the window and pushed his head through and then, guillotine fashion and with accompanying jeers and realistic sounds, banged the window down on his neck, "a crude reminder of the sad fate of Charles I and the British capacity to deal with Royalty who displeased." His neck bruised and pain searing through his head, he still waited until the seniors' retreating footsteps had died away before crying out, finally attracting a sympathetic passerby who released him, "fortunately" with his head intact.

None of this did he write his parents. Nor did he confide his unhappiness to them when he came home to York Cottage for Christmas of 1907, bringing with him his school report in a sealed envelope. He handed it straightaway to his father, who apparently did not read it that day. But "the next morning Finch appeared with a long face and a chilling summons to the Library." He had received a bad report—which he had not expected. After a harsh lecture, Prince George announced that he had engaged a master from Osborne, one of the boy's most tyrannical teachers, to work with him during the holidays, and as an added punishment, his hours at the Big House were curtailed.

With imponderable logic, Prince George had decided that the Navy was the best education for his elder son, despite his lack of aptitude or love for the sea. He insisted, with equal determination, Bertie should follow that career. Christmas 1907, Bertie was told that in a year he was also to enter the Royal Naval College. Because he was terribly weak in mathematics, a tutor was brought in to prepare him for his examinations. Despair overwhelmed him; the subject was simply too difficult for him, and ultimately he dissolved into tears of frustration.

"You must . . . remember now you are nearly 12 years old and ought no longer to behave like a little child of 6," his father wrote Bertie, at the same time warning his tutor, "you must be very strict and make him stick to it and do many papers."

On November 5, 1908, Bertie took his oral examination, which was a painful experience. He stammered so badly the board agreed that "he was the most shy and nervous candidate ever to come before them." Still, he managed to survive the ordeal without breaking down or backing off. A month later he

193

took the written examination and passed in all subjects most credibly except for geometry, "where he seems to have been below average." January 15, 1909, Bertie followed David to Osborne, but because of school tradition, the brothers were not allowed to associate or talk.

Bertie had an even more difficult time than David adjusting to life at the Naval College. In the beginning, his contemporaries thought he was both a bit strange and a sissy. He twitched when frightened, was so homesick that he cried at nights during almost the entire first year. He also had trouble controlling his bladder in the cold early mornings as he waited to use the facilities. David took the chance of arranging to meet his brother secretly in a small hidden area on the grounds where their great-grandmother and her ladies-in-waiting had once enjoyed picnics. Yet curiously, by the end of the year it was Bertie, not David, who began to make friends. He evoked a great deal of personal sympathy. He began to show a "grit and never-say-I'm-beaten spirit." The splints were off his legs, and though he was not much better at sports than David, he was fast and had great endurance. Unlike David, he made a little circle of intimate friends, and when he relaxed with this small coterie his stammer would virtually disappear. But in class he was as tongue-tied as ever.

On August 2, 1909—the end of the summer term—twenty-four battleships, sixteen armoured cruisers, forty-eight destroyers, and more than fifty other vessels crossed the Solent to welcome the Tsar, the Empress, the four young Grand Duchesses, and the little Tsarevitch as they arrived at Spithead in the Imperial yacht *Standart*. Bertie, who had contracted whooping cough, was confined to sick bay, while David, after a three-day wait, was allowed time off from classes to visit his relatives and nominated to escort them about the Naval College. David told his frail little cousin with the large frightened eyes—who was the Tsarevitch of Russia—stories about his school life and flirted with the pretty Grand Duchesses. Olga, the oldest, was closest to his age, and he had overheard his grandmother say that she might one day be a suitable bride for him. David favoured Tatiana, who was only twelve at the time. The tallest, slenderest, and most elegant of the sisters, she had deep auburn hair and wide grey eyes. The three other Grand Duchesses turned to her as their leader and even jokingly referred to her as "the Governess." When their mother was preoccupied, Tatiana stood by to guard her little brother from any possible danger, for he suffered from haemophilia,* a disease that could cause him to bleed to death with the slightest injury. David, always sensitive, had great sympathy for the small boy and for his mother, the Tsarina, who "wore such a sad expression on her face." But the best moments of all were when the King and Queen arrived on the Royal yacht, the *Victoria & Albert,* and he was allowed to go on board. The King looked dapper and more robust than ever, and he walked David round and round the deck, talking to him as an intimate and not as a grandparent or a King. He wore his sailor's cap and carried a stick, while his small terrier, Caesar, paraded the decks at his heels.

Like Bertie, Harry suffered knock-knees and wore the same loathsome leg splints. He was of an even more nervous disposition than Bertie, and whereas he did not stutter, he had retained his baby lisp. He was also given to alternate fits of crying and giggling, and suffered constantly from some indisposition. On February 2, 1909, Prince George wrote to Mr. Hansell, "You must remember that he is rather fragile and must be treated differently to his two elder brothers who are more robust." In February 1910, at the age of ten, Harry was sent to live at York Gate Cottage, Broadstairs, the seaside home of the Court physician, Sir Francis Laking (who was seldom in residence). There —many miles from home—Harry was placed in the care of a nurse, Sister Edith Ward.

The boy liked Broadstairs well enough, yet after three months, he still cried at the slightest provocation. Neither of his parents visited him during this time, although they kept up a fairly consistent correspondence with him and with Sister Edith. Prince George attributed his son's nervous condition in part to the "thundery weather," but never considered the total rejection by his parents and the sense of lonesomeness the child must

---

*Haemophilia was passed on by Queen Victoria to several of her descendants. Queen Ena, as well as the Empress Alexandra, was a haemophilia carrier, and therefore her sons suffered the consequences.

have experienced. He wrote Harry during this time, "Now, that you are 10 years old I had hoped that you were going to try to be better. You must . . . be obedient and do what she [Sister Edith] tells you and not behave like a little baby, otherwise I shall have to take you away from Broadstairs and send you somewhere else. You must behave like a boy and not a little child."

The letter carried a fearsome threat to the child, who could not imagine what terrible and lonely future he might be forced to endure if sent away from Sister Edith's care. His health began to improve, and though he still wore the splints as well as special heavy orthopedic boots, he suffered no organic problems. A decision was made that for a few hours each day he would attend St. Peter's Court, a preparatory school nearby.

Of the five boys, only Georgie and John remained at home. The extremes between the two youngest of the family could not have been greater. Georgie had always been "something of a handful," much more the "real boy" than any of his brothers, and more personable and charming than all, save perhaps David. He was gifted as they were not "academically, musically, culturally . . . streets ahead of anyone else in the immediate family circle." He was only seven, three years younger than Harry in the spring of 1910, yet he was much farther advanced and even spoke French better than any one of his older brothers. If intelligence, affability, cleverness, and insight were necessary requisites for a monarch, this fourth son, fifth in the succession, was the most qualified to be King.

Prince John celebrated his fourth birthday in July of 1909. He was a winsome child, painfully slow, and he began to suffer the first stages of an incurable epileptic illness. Grave doubts now existed that he would survive to adulthood. Placed entirely in Lala Bill's care, he remained in the nursery at York Cottage, where his brother Georgie treated him in almost parental fashion. John did not often see his parents. His grandmother, the Queen, however, favoured him above all the other Wales children and spent long hours amusing him whenever she was at Sandringham.

Those happy Royal Family portraits notwithstanding, Princess May and her brood of Royal Princes and her single flowering Princess were not in private the ideal family the Royals would have the public believe. Not one among Prince George and his sons lusted for power or knew how to use it to his advantage. In truth, except for young Georgie, not one of them possessed any qualities that would have caused him to stand out in his time had he not been who he was.

One day soon Aunt Augusta was to say of Princess May, "She will indeed be a Queen!" Although her husband was Heir Apparent and her five sons in direct line to the succession, Princess May had been endowed with a quality of majesty denied her Royal husband and princely sons.

FOURTEEN

The years of King Edward's reign had brought Princess May forward and into constant view before the public. She possessed a powerful charisma. There was purpose in her step, strength in her voice, and a rightness in all her appearances. Whenever she and Prince George were on display, it was Princess May who caught the immediate attention of the crowds, Princess May whose photograph appeared almost daily in the press. And since she had made the long tour on the *Ophir* and the trip to India, her image was more recognisable throughout the world than was Queen Alexandra's.

King Edward had no doubts that when the time came, his heir, with Princess May by his side, would have a popular reign. But in 1910, at the age of sixty-seven, King Edward suffered increasingly frequent moods of depression. He had come to believe that the Monarchy was in serious jeopardy and that his very own Ministers were intent upon reducing him to a "mere signing machine" and eroding by degrees those "few prerogatives that still remained to the Crown." His fear was that his heir might not have the power to remain King.

In the nine years of his reign, King Edward had seen his Royal powers slip away with incredible steadiness. The right to cede territory was no longer his but Parliament's. Nor did he have the absolute right to appoint and dismiss Secretaries of State. He did not give way without a struggle that in the end caused ill-feelings with almost every one of his Ministers, and he added to the problem by virtually abandoning the practise of seeing them in audience at Buckingham Palace. Therefore, unless they should meet the King socially, his Ministers were forced to go through a third person—most likely Mrs. Keppel, Admiral Lord Fisher, Sir Charles Hardinge, Sir Francis Knollys, or Sir Frederick Ponsonby—in all their dealings. He was constantly complaining to Mrs. Keppel that his Ministers did not bother to inform him about their policies and kept him "completely left in the dark."

Lloyd George, Chancellor of the Exchequer under the government of Herbert Henry Asquith, later 1st Earl of Oxford, was the King's particular nemesis. He was convinced that Lloyd George was a danger to the Monarchy and that his flaming oratory with its abiding message "that the poor should inherit the earth . . . his wonderful flow of eloquence, his musical cadences, his devastating ridicule, his capacity for identifying himself with 'left-out' millions" was only a clever façade for his true design—"the preaching of class wars." The King read Lloyd George's speeches with horror, instructing Sir Francis Knollys in one case to protest "in the most vigourous terms . . . a speech . . . full of false statements, of socialism in its worst and most insidious form of virulent abuse against one particular class, which can only have the effect of setting class against class and of stirring up the worst passions of his audience."

The King's fury did not arise because he opposed social reform. To the contrary, King Edward shared with his people an awakening conscience, and he did not hesitate to condemn the "perfectly disgraceful conditions" in which so many of the poor were forced to live. Nonetheless, Lloyd George's suspiciously socialistic "implacable warfare against poverty and squalidness" appeared to the King to be "primarily a campaign against property and capital," perhaps even to discredit "the political impartiality of the Crown to the ultimate ruin of its reputation."

The idea that the Monarchy was being threatened with dissolution and that his son might not reign after him preyed heavily upon his mind. He confessed his fears to Princess May, and he spoke gloomily of abdication to Alice Keppel. During the early months of 1910, the King was in a severe state of mental depression, as well as suffering serious breathing problems and violent fits of coughing. Mrs. Keppel consulted Dr. Laking, who informed her that he had begged King Edward to winter abroad for the good of his health, but that the King had refused. Enlisting Prime Minister Asquith's help, Alice Keppel finally was able to convince the King to leave the bitter cold of London; and on March 6, she and King Edward set out for the warmer climate of Biarritz. En route, he insisted on stopping in Paris for three days. No sooner had they arrived than winds in that city reached blizzard velocity, and he caught a chill while driving to and from his engagements. Alarmed at his feverish condition, Alice Keppel suggested they return immediately to London, but King Edward would not hear of it. He grew weaker during the short journey, and upon his arrival in Biarritz, he collapsed.

The Queen, who was in Denmark with her daughter Toria and her sister, the Dowager Empress Maria, received a telegram that the King had been taken ill. Knowing Mrs. Keppel was with him, she decided that it would be "both embarrassing and inopportune" for her to make an appearance. She did telegraph Dr. Laking with a request that the physician be ready to meet her in Biarritz if the King should take a further turn for the worse. However, King Edward slowly improved and within a few weeks was able to take walks and play croquet with Mrs. Keppel. The Queen wrote and begged him to "leave that horrid Biarritz" to join her on a Mediterranean cruise, but he refused, much irritated that she did not understand that a cruise—which would keep him abroad at a time of political crisis in England—would be impossible. Queen Alexandra went on to Corfu with her entourage, and the King and Mrs. Keppel returned to England, arriving on April 27 at Victoria Station, where Prince George met them, much relieved to find his father looking quite well. That evening, the two men and David and Bertie (who were home on school holiday) went to Covent Garden to hear Madame Tetrazzini sing Gilda in *Rigoletto,* one of the King's favourite operas. The King took his usual place in the Royal Box and, according to one observer, "sat sad-eyed throughout the performance." When it was ended, he was seen to sigh deeply, stand, and take a long look around the house. His attitude struck one member of the audience as being "so unlike [the King]."

That Friday, David and Bertie joined their father for lunch with the King at Buckingham Palace. Prince George was alarmed at his father's deep-chested cough, which the King blamed on his smoking. He was, anyway, too pleased to have his grandsons with him to pay much mind to his indisposition. The boys were dressed in Navy cadet uniforms and told their grandfather about all their school experiences. For once, the King was more concerned with David than with Bertie, having on his mind that David would never be King.

The next day, a Saturday, the King and Mrs. Keppel departed London for Sandringham with Caesar, the King's long-haired, white-coated fox terrier. Caesar—on whose jewelled Fabergé collar was engraved the legend, "I am Caesar, the King's dog" —had been deeply attached to his master during King Edward's reign, and they had seldom been parted for even a few days. At night, Caesar slept curled up in an armchair beside the King's bed, and every morning, Wellard, the second footman, washed and combed him. Caesar might be seen wherever the King went, trotting behind him down the Rue de la Paix, or strolling along the beach at Biarritz. Stamper, King Edward's motor mechanic, notes that "Caesar was neither aristocratic nor strictly speaking, handsome, but had what the French call *La beauté du Diable,* and made up for lack of looks by engaging ways." The dog was mischievous and always a bit too curious. Once, when King Edward was taking coffee in the garden of the Café Glatzen,* Stamper heard terrible screams and rushed to see what was happening. He found the King shouting, "Caesar! Come here! Come here, you bad dog!" The terrier was too intent upon chasing a white peacock to answer. In the end, Stamper managed to catch the errant terrier and lock him in the car, while the dog's master stood shaking his stick and repeating over and over, "You naughty, naughty dog." Caesar just barked and wagged his stubby tail.

Despite a high wind the Sunday after his arrival at Sandringham, King Edward walked the grounds with Caesar bounding ahead, stopping from time to time to see if his master was

*In Biarritz.

following. The King's pace was always brisk, but this day Alice Keppel could hardly keep up with him. Speed was "the very essence of his nature . . . he spoke rapidly, ate fast, thought apace. He even smoked hard," Stamper says. Something this day drove him faster than usual. Mrs. Keppel fell back and waved him on. When they met again a short time later in the library of Sandringham, the King was coughing badly and looked feverish, and upon their return to London the next day, he was confined to bed. A decision was made by the King's Ministers to send for the Queen. The communiqué merely said that the King was not well; no hint was given of the seriousness of his illness. In fact, the telegram, signed by the King's Private Secretary, Sir Francis Knollys, was so unalarming that the Queen and Toria considered staying for twenty-four hours in Venice on their way home from Corfu, then changed their minds.

Knollys was in no way trying to deceive the Queen about the severity of the King's illness. Whenever any member of the Royal Family was ill, no matter how slight the indisposition, a "curious air of mystery" prevailed. Osbert Sitwell,* who became a particular friend of the Royal Family some years later, speculated that this arose "because kings and queens must not appear to be in any sense fallible. Though unlike Roman Emperors they now make no pretension to downright divinity. Yet, a faint odour of ex-officio immortality still surrounds them, and the possibility of an illness attacking them always brings a sense of shock, reminds them—and still more those in waiting upon them—of the transitoriness of their human splendour."

Sir Francis Knollys was, therefore, acting according to tradition in playing down the gravity of the King's condition to the Queen. The Queen did not press for more definitive information, despite her knowledge that the King had not been well.

Princess May, Prince George, and David and Bertie met Queen Alexandra and Toria at Victoria Station the evening of May 5. The Queen took the grave news Prince George told her stoically. Toria, however, fell into a state of near-collapse, and

---

*Sir Osbert Sitwell (1892–1969), author and member of one of England's most celebrated literary families. Succeeded his father as 5th Baronet in 1943. Lady Geraldine Somerset was his great-aunt.

Queen Alexandra and Princess May had to calm her. The grief-stricken family then went directly to Buckingham Palace, where King Edward had personally given all directions for the Queen's reception upon her arrival. He was dressed and, though "hunched . . . grey in the face and fighting for breath," told her, in the slow-clipped Germanic voice he always used in speaking to her—an effort made so that she might be able to read his lips,* that he was doing better and that he had a box reserved for her for the evening performance at Covent Garden, a plan that he thought would diminish public speculation on his health. Shocked at his feeble appearance, which suddenly made reality of what her son had told her, the Queen refused to leave the ill man. Perhaps because Queen Alexandra's presence meant Alice Keppel's absence, King Edward was not too pleased.

The next morning, May 6, he claimed he felt better and insisted that his valet dress him in a frock coat before he received Sir Francis Knollys. Sir Francis begged him to rest. King Edward would not hear of it. "I shall work to the end," he said, "or what use is it to be alive?" A short time later, he demanded help to put on formal attire to greet Sir Ernest Cassel,† then rose from his chair and shook hands with Sir Ernest, and even managed to smoke half a cigar before he was seized by a coughing spasm. Moments later, he suffered a "fainting fit" and was put to bed. The Queen, Prince George, Princess May, and David and Bertie rushed to his side and remained in his room throughout the day. The final vigil had begun, and Dr. Laking could not withhold the truth when Queen Alexandra asked him if death was near. She then did a remarkable and magnanimous thing. She sent for Alice Keppel and, when the King's mistress arrived a few moments later, left the room with the rest of the King's intimate family so that her husband could have a few last, lucid moments with the woman he had loved faithfully during his entire reign. Mrs. Keppel remained with him for about an hour and then left. Caesar, who had been curled at the foot of his master's bed,

---

*It was the use of this method of speaking to his wife that caused the rumour that the King spoke with a German accent.

†Sir Ernest Cassel (1832–1921), financier. Grandfather of Edwina Ashley, who married Lord Louis Mountbatten (later 1st Earl Mountbatten of Burma).

followed after her and did not return to the room while his master fought with death.

"At 11:45 beloved Papa passed peacefully away," Prince George wrote in his diary for Friday, May 6, "& I have lost my best friend & the best of fathers. I never had a [cross] word with him in his life. I am heartbroken & overwhelmed with grief, but God will help me in my great responsibilities & darling May will be my comfort as she always has been. May God give me strength & guidance in the heavy task which has fallen on me. I sent telegrams to the Lord Mayor & the Prime Minister. Left Motherdear & Toria & drove back to M[arlborough] H[ouse] with darling May. I am quite stunned by this awful blow. Bed at 1.0."

The old King was dead, and the new King—after a fitful night's sleep—was ready to carry on with "darling May" by his side.

No one awakened the two elder boys at Marlborough House to tell them their grandfather had died the night of May 6. About seven the next morning, Bertie chanced to rise first and from the window of the bedroom he shared with David saw the Royal standard flying at half-mast. When he cried out to his brother, David jumped out of bed and ran to Bertie's side. "Across the Mall, Buckingham Palace stood grey and silent, and on the roof in the bright morning sunlight the Standard hung limply on the mast," he recalled.

Finch then appeared and, after tearfully confirming the truth, conveyed the message that their father wished to see them both downstairs. Bertie was unable to control his shaking, but neither of them cried. Marlborough House was grey and sullen as they made their way down the mansion's magnificent black marble staircase, behind them the grim mural of the Battle of Ramillies.* They could hear the sound of some servant's muffled tears, but neither boy cast a glance back over his shoulder to see who might be crying.

---

*The Battle of Ramillies (1706—one of the Duke of Marlborough's most notable victories over the French) mural on the wall of the staircase at Marlborough House was painted by Louis Laguerre, a Frenchman, and was completed in 1711.

204

Their father sat at his desk, his face "grey with fatigue," and he cried as he told them that their grandfather was dead. David answered sadly that they had already seen the Royal standard at half-mast. Their father went on to describe in exact detail the scene around the deathbed. Then he asked sharply, "What did you say about the standard?"

"It is flying at half-mast over the palace," David answered.

His father frowned and muttered distractedly, "But that's all wrong. The King is dead. Long live the King!" He then sent for his equerry and in "a preemptory naval manner" ordered that a mast be rigged at once on the roof of Marlborough House. Within an hour the Royal standard was flying "close-up" over the house, the order to raise it—the new King's first.

At nine o'clock on Monday morning, May 9, 1910, the Prince of Wales was proclaimed King George V from the balcony of Friary Court, St. James's Palace, a ceremony that "May and I watched from the window of the boys' room." The two boys, dressed in their cadet blues and standing at salute, their small brother George solemn between them,* watched it from a separated part of the courtyard below. Prime Minister Asquith was on a yacht in Gibraltar Harbour when he heard of the King's death.† Lloyd George, Winston Churchill, the hereditary Earl Marshal (the Duke of Norfolk), and the remaining Ministers and Privy Councillors in uniform stood at the back of the balcony as the proclamation was read to a massive, hushed crowd below by Sir Alfred Scott-Gatty, Garter King-of-Arms, supported by seven of the King's Heralds and Pursuivants dressed in their tabards of scarlet, blue, and gold. In a booming voice that echoed through the courtyard, Sir Alfred declared "that the High and Mighty Prince George Frederick Ernest Albert is now, by the death of our late Sovereign of happy memory, become our only lawful right Liege Lord, George the Fifth, by the Grace

---

*Prince Henry was still at Broadstairs.

†Prime Minister Asquith subsequently recorded, "I went up on deck. I felt bewildered and indeed stunned. At a most anxious moment in the fortunes of the State we had lost, without warning or preparation, the Sovereign whose wide experience, trained sagacity, equitable judgement and unvarying consideration counted for so much."

of God, King of the United Kingdom of Great Britain and Ireland and of the British Dominions beyond the Seas, Defender of the Faith, Emperor of India, to whom we acknowledge all faith and constant obedience, with all hearty and humble affection, beseeching God, by whom Kings and Queens do reign, to bless the Royal Prince George the Fifth with long and happy years to reign over us."

The heralding trumpets sounded. Guns in the adjoining park thundered their salute. Then one man in the reverent crowd sang the opening bars of "God Save the King." The hymn was taken up by another voice and then by a third. In a moment, the surge of Britain's national anthem rose majestically from the crowds at St. James's Palace, its rhythm punctuated by the crash of guns.

Princess May had always been known as May, although she still signed all official papers with her two christened names, Victoria Mary. Now she would have to choose a new name as Queen Consort. "George dislikes double names and I could not be Victoria," she explained to Aunt Augusta on May 15, 1910. "But it strikes me as curious to be rechristened at the age of 43." To the world from that time she was Queen Mary, but to her husband she remained "Darling May" or "Angel May."

While Queen Mary was suddenly deluged with the many problems and decisions that came with her new position, the old Queen was desperately trying to make peace with her sudden widowhood. Four days after King Edward's death, Lord Esher wrote poignantly, "The Queen sent for me, and there she was, in a simple black dress with nothing to mark specially her widowhood, and moving gently about his room as if he were a child asleep. And I honestly believe that this is what has been in her mind all these days [that he was asleep—not dead].

"The King was lying on the bed in which he always slept—the curtainless simple bed. His head was inclined gently to one side as if in comfortable sleep and his hands laid on the counterpane, with the pink sleeve of his pink nightdress showing. No appearance of pain or death. There was even a glow on his face, and the usual happy smile of the dead who die peacefully.

"The Queen moved about . . . quietly but perfectly naturally and talked for half an hour . . . with only a slight diminution of

her natural gaiety, but with a tenderness which betrayed the
. . . feeling that she had got him there altogether to herself.

"In a way she seemed, and is, I am convinced, happy. It is the
womanly happiness of complete possession of the man who was
the love of her youth, and—as I fervently believe—of all her life.

"Once she said, 'What is to become of me?' . . . Once or twice
she gripped my arm, as she has so often done before—a favourite gesture—and I kissed both her hands when I left her, and
came back to kiss them again . . . I left her—moved just at the
end to tears—and she sat down in the little chair which had been
placed at the King's bedside. Round the room were all the things
just as he had last used them, with his hats hanging on the pegs
as he loved them to do."

Alexandra sent for all the King's close friends to say "goodbye" privately to him in his bedroom. Sir Frederick Ponsonby
found "the blinds were down and there was a screen round the
bed, so that at first I could see nothing, but when we came round
it I saw the poor King lying apparently asleep. I was very awed
and hardly liked to speak except in a whisper, but the Queen
spoke naturally and said how peaceful he looked and that it was a
comfort to think he had suffered no pain. She added that it was
not Sandringham but 'horrid Biarritz' that had killed him, although no doubt, the political crisis had something to do with it."

After about ten minutes, Ponsonby left the King's bedroom.
In the corridor directly outside were the new King and Queen.
"I debated in my mind," he recalled, "what I should do and
although kissing their hands seemed a tiresome formality, so out
of keeping with the simplicity of Queen Alexandra's grief, and
although I knew that both King George and Queen Mary disliked anything at all theatrical in private, I came to the conclusion that as everyone else had probably gone through this
formality I had better go through it, too. I sank down on one
knee and kissed their hands in turn."

Ponsonby and Pom McDonnell were to be in charge of arrangements for the King's Lying-in-State at Westminster Hall
and his funeral at St. George's Chapel at Windsor.* Before they

---

*Sir Schomberg McDonnell (1861–1915), formerly Lord Salisbury's Private
Secretary.

could set the plans, they had to persuade Queen Alexandra to allow the King's body to be moved. On the twelfth she received McDonnell in the King's bedroom, where he now lay in a military greatcoat. "They want to take him away," she said piteously, "but I can't bear to part with him. Once they hide his face from me, everything is gone forever." McDonnell was "very much broken up by the interview."

Not until Saturday, May 14, were the King's remains placed in an oak coffin and moved to the throne room of Buckingham Palace. The Royal standard was draped over the coffin, Saint Edward's crown at the head, and the sceptre and orb at the roof. Four tall grenadier guardsmen of the King's Company "stood rigidly at each corner, resting on their arms reversed, their bearskin-capped heads inclined in respect." Queen Alexandra could not stay out of the throne room; she returned there constantly to rearrange the flowers or "to show a foreign relative or old friend the scene."

By the sixteenth, the two men, Ponsonby and McDonnell, were able to convince Queen Alexandra that the funeral had to take place as soon as possible. McDonnell met with a hundred journalists at Westminster Hall and told them all was ready. A date, May 20, had been set for the funeral. The procession with the coffin left Buckingham Palace for the hall at 11:30 on the morning of May 17. "A glorious service followed, marred only by the loudness of the band that accompanied the choir, the famous hammer-beam roof being responsible. Then the procession left to the strains of Chopin's *Funeral March,* while McDonnell prepared the Hall for the public." That same day Queen Alexandra's sister, the Empress Maria Fyodorovna (Aunt Minnie), arrived, and after the service the two women left for Sandringham, where they welcomed the next day ex-President Theodore Roosevelt, who had been sent to England as the special envoy of the United States by President William Taft. Roosevelt found Queen Alexandra in a terrible state. "They took him away from me, they took him away from me," she cried, unable to control her emotions. "You see, he was so wonderfully preserved. It must have been the oxygen they gave him before he died. It was most extraordinary—but they took him away from me."

In the midst of all the problems of the funeral arrangements caused by his mother's mental condition, King George had difficulty with Winston Churchill, who took this inappropriate time to challenge the new King on the Constitution, calling for violent changes. Then, to the King and Queen's great distress and shock, Alexandra demanded she have precedence over Queen Mary—an honour that by British Royal covenants was not hers. After a great deal of unpleasantness, Queen Mary gave in to the King's request that she do so, registering her irritation to Aunt Augusta.

"I am now very tired after the strain of the past weeks & now as you know come all the disagreeables, so much to arrange, so much that must be changed, most awkward & unpleasant for both sides, if only things can be managed without having rows, but it is difficult to get a certain person to see things in their right light."

Not only did the old Queen demand precedence at the funeral, she also refused to give up her "lovely little crown,"* and though she had complained about moving into Buckingham Palace in 1902, she could not be persuaded to move out. "The odd part," Queen Mary wrote to her Aunt Augusta, "is that the person causing the delay and trouble remains supremely unconscious to the inconvenience it is causing, such a funny state of things & everyone seems afraid to speak."

Kaiser Wilhelm had travelled to England on his private yacht, the *Hohenzollern,* escorted by four British destroyers. The vessel was anchored in the Thames Estuary and Wilhelm then boarded the Royal train for London, arriving on the stroke of noon at Victoria Station to be met by his cousin, King George, whom he kissed on both cheeks. The uncle he had never been able to win over was dead. Perhaps now he could rely on the British Empire when a need came for Germany to stand against France and Russia.

The two cousins lunched at Marlborough House and then rode together to Westminster, where the Kaiser laid a wreath of purple and white flowers on King Edward's coffin and then knelt

---

*Reference to the crown made especially for Queen Victoria. Part of the Crown Jewels and worn by custom by the Queen to the opening of Parliament.

beside Britain's new King in silent prayer, waiting sympathetically until the dead man's son rose before rising himself. Then
he grasped King George's hand in a warm handshake, a gesture
newsmen reported favourably and the King believed was an
honest show of emotion.

The Kaiser was not the least bit reticent about exposing some
of his hostilities. At King Edward's funeral, he told the King of
Italy, "All the long years of my reign my colleagues, the Monarchs of Europe, have paid no attention to what I have to say.
Soon, with my great Navy to endorse my words, they will be
more respectful." He was envious of the older European nations
and bitterly reported to Theodore Roosevelt that King Edward
had never visited Berlin, but had always gone to Paris. He considered this an unpardonable snub. He added that King George
was "a very nice boy. He is a thorough Englishman and hates all
foreigners but I do not mind that as long as he does not hate
Germans more than other foreigners." Still, no matter what
Wilhelm might personally have felt, Germany's officers of the
Army and Navy were ordered to wear mourning for eight days,
and the German fleet in home waters flew its flags at half-
mast.

The black-clad crowds that lined the path of the funeral procession on the hot, sultry morning of May 20 were hushed and
orderly until that moment when the glorious spectacle passed
them by. No one could blame them for pushing and shoving to
get a front-line view, or their gasps of admiration. Flanking King
George were Kaiser Wilhelm and Arthur, Duke of Connaught,
King Edward's sole surviving brother. Behind them rode seven
sovereigns, making nine kings in all, and each one related to the
dead monarch.* Their jewelled orders and gold-and-silver scab-

---

*The nine sovereigns and their relationship to King Edward were: King
George V (son); Kaiser Wilhelm, German Emperor (nephew); King George I
of Greece (brother-in-law); King Frederick VIII of Denmark (brother-in-law);
King Haakon of Norway (son-in-law); King Manuel II of Portugal (cousin);
King Ferdinand I of Bulgaria (cousin); King Alfonso XIII of Spain (cousin);
King Albert I of the Belgians (cousin). Also in the procession in carriages were
ex-U.S. President Theodore Roosevelt; the French Foreign Minister, M. Stephen Pichon; the Grand Duke Michael of Russia; and the Duke of Aosta (the
former Princess Hélène's husband), representing the King of Italy.

bards and helmets glittered in the harsh sun, and their brilliantly hued uniforms trimmed in gold braid and their crimson sashes were a shocking contrast to the mourning attire of the spectators. After the monarchs came five heir-apparents,* seven queens,† another forty-five Royalties, and several special Ambassadors (Theodore Roosevelt among them) of countries that were not monarchies. Seventy nations were represented in this last and greatest gathering of royalty and rank.

David and Mary, scarcely ever turning their glances toward the crowds, rode stiffly in one of the state coaches with their mother. The children appeared to be concentrating on the mournful sound of the funeral marches of the massed military bands, the musical selections having been chosen by their grandmother,‡ who rode before them in a glass coach with her sister, the Empress Maria.

When the procession arrived at Westminster Hall, from where the coffin was to be removed, Queen Alexandra's carriage was given precedence and was the first to arrive at the entrance. Kaiser Wilhelm reached the door of her coach even before her footman. However, he was on the street side of the coach and had to dash round the rear of the vehicle to help her down. To her irritation, he kissed her affectionately. Alexandra loathed Wilhelm for his arrogance, and, though she had been only eight years old when Germany had seized the duchies from her native Denmark, she had never forgiven him or Germany for this act. In 1890, when her son was made honorary Colonel of a Prussian regiment, she wrote him scathingly: "And so my Georgie boy has become a real live filthy blue-coated *Piekelhaube* German soldier!!! Well, I never thought I'd live to see that!" Determined not to be escorted into Westminster by Wilhelm, Alexandra

*The Crown Princes of Rumania, Montenegro, Serbia, and Greece, and the Archduke Franz Ferdinand of Austria.

†Queen Alexandra, Queen Mother; the Dowager Empress Maria of Russia; the Queen Dowager of the Netherlands; Queen Emma of Waldock-Pyrmont; Queen Mary; Queen Ena of Spain; and Queen Maud of Sweden attended the funeral.

‡The *Dead March* from Saul and Chopin's *Funeral March* were the selections played.

walked away and took hold of her sister's arm and propelled her forward.

The coffin, wrapped in the Royal standard, was borne by blue-jackets in straw hats from Westminster to the sound of muffled drums and wailing bagpipes. Much of the funeral procession was now on foot and included King Edward's sixty-three aides-de-camp, and many officers and peers. Then came Lord Kitchener, Lord Roberts, and Sir Evelyn Wood—England's three field marshals—and detachments from the most famous regiments from England and the Continent.

The procession ended at Paddington Station, where the coffin was lifted onto the Royal train for a half-hour journey to Windsor Station, accompanied by the Royal Family and all the visiting dignitaries. At Windsor, it was placed on a waiting gun carriage. Blue-jackets dragged it slowly uphill to St. George's Chapel, all of the long funeral procession following on foot except for one coach carrying Queen Alexandra and the Empress Maria. Caesar, his lead held securely by a Highlander, trotted behind the coffin; and the King's favourite charger, Kildare, with empty saddle and boots reversed in the stirrups, was led by two grooms. Then came King George, again flanked by Kaiser Wilhelm and the Duke of Connaught, and marching behind them, David and Bertie in their trim Naval cadet uniforms.

Alice Keppel arrived inconspicuously at Windsor for the funeral, almost unrecognisable behind her thick black veil, and was led by McDonnell into the cloister entrance. McDonnell then had to move quickly to restrain the Empress Maria from throwing her wreath onto the coffin where it might have caught and stopped the machinery that was to lower it into the ground. A member of the Royal Household "cast earth upon the coffin, as it slowly sank out of sight."*

The funeral was an overpowering—even a somewhat eerie—experience for the dead King's grandchildren. Not until it was over did the full meaning of King Edward's death register itself on their young minds. That their parents had become King and Queen of England they took for granted. But their own position, especially in David's case, was harder to accept. For now, as

*Master of the Household, Charles Frederick.

Heir-Apparent, nothing save death itself was at all likely to prevent David from one day becoming "by the Grace of God, of Great Britain, Ireland, and the British Dominions beyond the Seas, King, Defender of the Faith, Emperor of India."

Although a few days after the funeral both older boys returned to their schools—David to Dartmouth and Bertie to Osborne—life would no longer be the same for them. On June 4, the King sent for Lord Esher to discuss plans for creating David Prince of Wales on his sixteenth birthday, June 23. With great frankness, he confessed to Esher that David was young for his years, and that because of this, he wanted to postpone the boy's entry into public life as long as possible. Esher—though he privately thought of David as "a mere child," for which he blamed Mr. Hansell—told the King that he did not think David could be sheltered "beyond the time when the boy was 'royally of age.' "*

David was both Heir-Apparent and Prince of Wales, and had become Duke of Cornwall as well and independently wealthy, the entire Duchy of Cornwall now his personal estate, its holdings including thousands of acres in the West Country and valuable London property. From receiving a weekly shilling of pocket money doled out by the Naval College, he was now one of the richest young men in England. His father's financial advisors immediately took over the administrations of the funds and the maintenance of his household and establishment. Still, his final approval had to be sought in most matters.

At school, "subtle respect" for his new position created an unconscious barrier between him and his term mates; and when at home, the responsibilities involved (his signature on papers and reports, portraits to be painted, briefings on his affairs) left much less time for him to be with Bertie.

Until he was back at Osborne, Bertie was unable to grasp the fact that his grandfather was dead. Of all the grandchildren, Bertie would miss King Edward the most. For thirteen years his grandfather's infectious laugh, the warmth of that great bear body as he was held in affectionate greeting, had been Bertie's solace and refuge. Papa and Mama being King and Queen meant

*Eighteen.

he would see them less than ever, Grannie was acting strangely, a terrible row was going on between her and his mother, and David was now at Dartmouth and was the Prince of Wales. The latter was the most unbelievable to him, for, after all, that meant his brother had taken over his father's former position. Not only had he lost all those near and dear to him, but Bertie could no longer be called "of Wales," that name, of course, now belonging solely to David.

Within a few weeks of his return to Osborne, Bertie's work had deteriorated so badly that he occupied one of the lowest positions in his class (seventy-first out of seventy-four). A stern, parental rebuke was immediately forthcoming, along with a warning that he would have to give up his summer holidays to work with a tutor if his grades did not drastically improve. Bertie's stuttering grew worse. His situation looked hopeless. Then the college's assistant medical officer, Louis Greig,* a twenty-nine-year-old Scot, took the boy under his wing and, with confidence, affection, and gaiety, helped him through the difficult time he was to have during his last year at Osborne. Without Greig's interest, Bertie might not have matriculated to Dartmouth the following year because of his grades and the possibility of a complete nervous collapse.

Harry remained at Broadstairs, the King and Queen having decided he was still too frail to attend the funeral of his grandfather. From there, the little boy wrote his father, "I am so awfully sorry that dear Grandpapa is dead, and that you, Mama, Grannie, and Aunt Toria are in such trouble. I shall try to help you by being a good boy."

In the matter of money, the new King was one of the very few English monarchs who had ascended the Throne without a penny of debt. Unlike his father and other Royal antecedents, he was not a gambler, nor did he spend his money on mistresses. Therefore, he had no need to be beholden to men of money. And though the people did not know much about him yet, he was determined, energetic, and held strong Tory views—not the kind of man who would be content to be a mere figurehead

---

*Sir Louis Greig (1880–1953), Comptroller and Equerry to Duke of York (1920–23).

controlled by the politicians. Still, great fear remained in the hearts of the new King's subjects that George did not have the stature to be King.

"I saw Francis Knollys today," Lord Esher recorded on May 31, "and Caesar, the dear King's dog, came to tea in Miss Charlotte's [Knollys] room. He won't go near the Queen—and waits all day for his master, wandering about the house. He sleeps either on the King's bed or on . . . [a bed] in a small room next to the King's room . . ."

Of all creatures large and small who had been devoted to King Edward VII, Queen Alexandra had taken a strong dislike to Caesar. "Horrid little dog!" she exclaimed to Margot Asquith (Prime Minister Asquith's wife) just a few days after the funeral, and she was furious when an enterprising publisher issued a memoir of the late King, with Caesar's picture on the cover, entitled, "Where's Master?" Since no provision was made for the little dog in the King's will, Alice Keppel inquired of Charlotte Knollys if the Queen might not let her care for him. Queen Alexandra, upon being asked, had returned to Mrs. Keppel her gift to King Edward for his sixty-third birthday (a blue enamelled-and-diamond Fabergé cigarette case), and so her refusal to grant this request was surprising.* More unexpectedly, she made a complete about-face and took an immediate interest in Caesar and his welfare. (In fact, two years later she was to confide to a friend that she could not help but spoil Caesar because the King had been so strict!)

Extravagant eulogies filled the world's newspapers. Lord Esher's was, perhaps, the most simply eloquent. "I have known all the great men of my time in this land, of course," he wrote, "and many beyond it. He was the most Kingly of them all."

A fortnight after the funeral, Asquith spoke in the House of Commons of the King's "abiding sense of his regal responsibilities," a tribute that would have greatly pleased his mother, Queen Victoria. Her grandson did not have King Edward's great human qualities. He was without political experience and knew very little about the minds and power drives of men. With Brit-

---

*Alice Keppel in turn gave this cigarette case to Queen Mary in 1935 to include in her famous Royal Fabergé collection.

ain on the verge of a crisis almost without example in its constitutional history, the question on everyone's mind was whether
the new King could deal competently with the matter. Most were
doubtful. Even Queen Mary, whom it was rumoured the King
stood much in awe of, wrote Aunt Augusta, "The whole task
seems so stupendous, so difficult, one can only pray for guidance and courage to be given us."

But the people needed more than a new Queen's frightened
prayers. Edwardians had felt confidence in the dead King's familiar Royal bulk. They believed he could achieve prosperity for
the nation and keep the peace that had been established in his
decade of rule. A charwoman in the popular *Pelissier's Follies of
1909* had sung:

> There'll be no wo'ar
> As long as There's a King like old King Edward
> There'll be no wo'ar
> For 'e 'ates that sort of thing!
> Mothers needn't worry
> As long as we've a King like good King Edward
> Peace with 'onner
> Is 'is motter
> So God Save the King!

Now the rotund Edward with his barrelling laugh and good
nature was dead, and a solemn monarch sat in the place of the
King who, people felt, had "kept things together somehow."
King George had made no great impression as Prince of Wales.
So little was known about him that the people were not aware
of his single-mindedness and insecurity. Equally, they were
uninformed as to the new Prince of Wales's immaturity and his
loathing of the idea of one day becoming their King. To add to
their ignorance, the public had no inkling of Bertie's current
unsuitability to take his elder brother's place, if necessary. They
did have great admiration for the majesty of their new Queen
Consort, a source of much comfort in a transition that appeared
to many to augur trouble.

PART THREE

PAPA
AND MAMA
ARE CROWNED

FIFTEEN

"**L**ife is *too* fatiguing for me, I have *too* much to do, to think of, I am getting worn out & people bother one so, I am sick of the everlasting begging for favours of all kinds!" the new Queen wrote Helene Bricka shortly after her husband's succession. The coronation had been set for June 22 the following year. Even so, this presented overwhelming pressures. The greatly enlarged Household; the planned move and takeovers of the Royal homes of Buckingham, Windsor, and Balmoral; and the difficulties caused by Queen Alexandra's reluctance to let go of these, her Crown Jewels, and her position at Court—all were to be dealt with. King Edward had bequeathed Sandringham to Alexandra for her lifetime. So, though altogether too small and unsuitable for a Monarch's residence, King George still had to make do with York Cottage as his family's country home.

June 1910, momentarily unable to cope with the problems, Queen Mary rested at Balmoral. She had visited Balmoral numerous times over the past nineteen years. Now her return proclaimed the end of one era and the beginning of another. The young woman who had come here years before to seek Queen Victoria's approval to marry the unsound Prince Eddy so that she might one day be Queen had fulfilled her greatest desire and her mother's dream. A bright sun was overhead as she stepped down from the Royal train—a stately, slim, imposing woman of forty-three, dressed in a subtle and elegant mauve travelling suit with a matching toque and parasol, arrayed in a quantity of jewels. Those members of Balmoral's Household who came to greet her claim that she was the most queenly *Queen* they had ever seen—and *that* despite the fact that several of them had been in the Household of Victoria and Alexandra, and had met numerous visiting monarchs.

The trip from the station to the castle was made in a grand-looking "Silent Knight" motor which had replaced the old Royal coach. The staff that curtsied to Queen Mary as she entered the sombre panelled and tartaned entrance were now part of her own Household. She had no hesitation in taking over Queen Victoria's old rooms, which Queen Alexandra had never liked. Her various ladies-in-waiting recorded Queen Mary's straight-forward acceptance of her new position, but she was lonely for the first time in many years, for her husband was now overburdened with the problems of making a smooth transition from one King and Court to another. Curiously, Queen Mary turned for companionship at this time to her brother Frank, to whom she had hardly spoken since their mother's death when he had given Princess Mary Adelaide's jewels to his mistress.

When his sister telegraphed him to join her at Balmoral, Prince Frank was recovering from minor nasal surgery necessitated by an injury suffered some years before. Leaving hospital premature to doctors' orders, he arrived at Balmoral in a weakened condition, having hemorrhaged profusely. His sister was now Queen, and though he was not a man to beg favours, he knew his life, which had been difficult in the last few years, could be considerably easier with her patronage. Frank became Queen Mary's constant companion. They had breakfast, lunch, tea, and dinner together. They walked the grounds of the castle daily, though the Scottish summer had turned suddenly to drizzle and dampness. Frank agreed not to act in a foolish manner ever again, and they reminisced over childhood memories and sat up late at night, talking about their parents and the past.

At the end of the week, Frank suffered severe coughing spasms. Sir James Reid, Queen Victoria's old doctor, insisted he remain in bed under his care while the Queen returned to London. Within days, pleurisy developed, and, accompanied by Sir James, Frank made a long, agonising train trip back to London, where his lungs were immediately operated upon by a specialist. He did not survive the surgery, and Frank's death at thirty-nine was a blow to Queen Mary, "for we were so very intimate in the old days until alas the 'rift' came," she wrote her husband. "I am so thankful I still had that nice week with him at Balmoral when he was quite like his old self . . ."

Displaying emotion she seldom revealed, Queen Mary, as she wrote to her Aunt Augusta, "broke down and wept freely" at Frank's funeral in St. George's Chapel, where his coffin "lies with that of dear Mama." She added that the Royal vault was well lit and that King Edward lay "on the stone in the centre for the present. Ultimately he is to be moved to the Memorial Chapel where Eddy & Uncle Leopold are."*

Less than a week later, Prince Frank's former inamorata, who still had in her possession Princess Mary Adelaide's jewels, was requested by Queen Mary to return them. Princess Alice, Queen Mary's sister-in-law, records a great deal of family discussion about this unusual action by the Queen, for her other brothers —Alge (Princess Alice's husband) and Dolly—feared the woman might refuse and an incident develop. But, in fact, the jewels— all in perfect condition—were delivered to Queen Mary just a few days after the Royal request was made.

The problem of where to live was a pressing one for King George and Queen Mary throughout the summer of 1910. The Queen packed up all her treasured possessions in Marlborough House and turned the premises immediately back to Queen Alexandra, thinking that with her beloved "Marl House" hers again, her mother-in-law might begin to move her things out of Buckingham Palace and Windsor Castle.

Queen Alexandra made no step in that direction, and the Royal Family spent the month of August at Balmoral, which Queen Alexandra had never liked and had given over to her son and daughter-in-law without a struggle.

*Prince Leopold, Duke of Albany (1853–1884), King Edward's youngest brother. But the King's final resting place is his tomb on the right of the sanctuary.

On August 21, Lord Esher was at Balmoral with the King and Queen. "It is altogether different here from former years," he wrote in his journal on that date. "There is no longer the old atmosphere about the house—that curious electric element which pervaded the surroundings of King Edward." Dreary as it was, Balmoral had now become a home and a rather domestic one at that. The children and their parents and the Royal Household all had lunch together. John was six, a small boy, already showing signs of mental retardation, and who, Esher notes, kept "running round the table all the while" they ate.

"I went yesterday with the Queen and the Girl [Princess Mary] and two others to 'Rob Roy's Cave,' a purely fictitious place," Lord Esher writes on August 23. "But they ran over the heather and ate tea spread out on rugs on the hillside. Simplicity itself." And the next day, "We had a drive down the Dee yesterday and tea on the river bank, quite in public . . . Most unsophisticated. Last night the French governess [Princess Mary's tutor] sat on the King's right hand at dinner. Imagine the Courtiers of Berlin or Vienna if they could have seen."

Unsophisticated though their life-style might have appeared, the truth was that the new King and Queen adhered much more strongly to Royal protocol with their Household and family than had King Edward and Queen Alexandra. To David, Queen Mary wrote at this time, "I believe the right way for you to address me is the Queen and to Grannie Queen Alexandra, as she is now the Queen Mother and I am the wife of the King."

York Cottage was unable to accommodate the new, enlarged staff and the vast number of visitors whose business it was to confer with the King.* With no home as yet in London, Queen

---

*The Royal Household was greatly increased in number from the Household of the Prince of Wales. Lady Cynthia Colville has given an extremely good explanation of the heirarchical traditions of the Royal Household in *Crowded Life*, London, 1963. "As far as women were concerned, the principal and unique 'officer' was the Mistress of the Robes, always a Duchess and the head of her department so to speak, the male opposite number on ceremonial occasions being the Lord Chamberlain, by whose side she would walk at State functions such as Courts, and Court Balls. Next in importance came the Ladies of the Bedchamber, four in number, all peeresses who attended the Queen for her bigger and more impressive engagements; their male counterparts were

Mary had combined the life-styles of her country home and of Marlborough House, which had the effect of giving the family a sense of continuity.

Throughout August, the Deeside was cold and grey—"unwinning." Breakfast was at eight, bedtime early. The Queen knitted in the evenings. "Not a sign of 'bridge,' " Esher notes, recalling King Edward's tenure. After dinner, the King allowed people to sit while he was standing. (King Edward had not permitted this, nor had he allowed his guests and Household to leave before both he and Queen Alexandra had gone to bed—usually sometime after midnight.) On one evening of such domesticity, "the King sat on the sofa talking with me until bedtime," Esher writes. "Everything is very 'easy.' That does not imply license—only the perfect ease of English homelife."

What came out of "a week of intimate talk with the King and Queen" was King George's hope "to do for the Empire what King Edward did for the peace of Europe." The King also confided to Esher that he proposed to attend the Indian Durbar in January 1911,* and be crowned as Emperor of India at Delhi as well as to visit every Dominion—bold projects that Lord Esher thought would bring him opposition from his Ministers.

The most difficult task Queen Mary had to face at this time was to define what were the Queen Consort's duties without anything official to fall back on. The position of Queen Consort (which was "no bed of roses," she wrote Aunt Augusta on August 10) was "so to speak, whatever you felt inclined, or had the

---

the Lords-in-Waiting, whose service with the King was on similar lines. The third group consisted of the Women of the Bedchamber, also a quartette, they were daughters of peers, mostly Lady Somebody Something (that is children of dukes, marquesses or earls), but they were of a much humbler variety than these 'Lady' Colleagues. Equerries were their opposite number in the King's Household. There was a fourth group, Maids-of-Honour . . . their male opposites were grooms-in-waiting." They also lived in and were the daughters or sons of viscounts and barons, and were granted the title of "the Honourable." None of the holders of these titles did any domestic job, as their titles might falsely suggest. They did accompany the King and Queen and handle a certain amount of correspondence.

*Esher says January 1911, but that would have been before the coronation; and, in fact, the Durbar was held on December 12, 1911.

ability to make it." Queen Charlotte, Queen Caroline, and Queen Adelaide (all of whom were German) had failed to make much impression upon the consciousness of the people. Queen Alexandra had concentrated on being decorative and generous. These traits had earned her the love of her husband's subjects but had not added any more to the Monarchy than had Queen Charlotte's devotion to her many children. But Queen Mary had one consuming passion that ruled her life, something her predecessors did not possess, and it dictated her interpretation of her role as Queen Consort. As James Pope-Hennessy stresses, "Her passion was for the British Monarch.

"The fact that the new King-Emperor was her husband and cousin—the 'Georgie' she had known since childhood—in no way diminished in her eyes the lofty solitary splendour that invested the person of the Monarch," he adds.

From the moment they had stood side by side in "the boys' room" at Marlborough House and heard George proclaimed King across the Court at St. James's, a change in Queen Mary's attitude toward her husband was noted by just about everyone who attended them. Princess May had never been the least bit afraid of her husband, nor had she been hesitant in speaking her mind to him. But as Queen Mary, "she would no longer contradict him even in the family circle, she would no longer protest save in private or by letter when he was unfair to one or other of his sons . . . She believed that all should defer to the King's slightest wish, and she made herself into a living example of her creed," writes James Pope-Hennessy.

Sublimating herself to her ideal of the British Crown in such an absolute way forced Queen Mary to exert a spectacular amount of self-control. The people close to her were surprised by the dramatic change in her personality. Her nature became at once imperious and benevolent, a combination that filled people with much awe in her presence. "I used to be rather shy," she later wrote beside a passage in the proofs of John Gore's *Personal Memoir of George V,* which she read and annotated thirty years later, "but after the King succeeded & when one shared the central figure with the King this feeling vanished." And she adds, "You all go on as if I had been *stutteringly shy!* but I can assure you I wasn't as bad as that."

In retrospect, Queen Mary had not been really shy at any point in her life. She was, however, a reserved person who was in tremendous control of her public demeanor. She had the wisdom to know when she should and should not set herself forward. Before her engagement to Prince Eddy, she had practised for hours on end before a mirror the small Royal smile that she wore on every state or Royal occasion thereafter. She was never heard to laugh in public. Unlike Queen Alexandra and most other Royal women of her acquaintance who had married men destined to be monarchs, Queen Mary had not been born or raised with any Royal aspiration. Only as a grown woman who had suffered many humiliations had her Royal future been set, and she had studied every proper nuance that would be expected of her so that she would not fail in her duty.

Princess Mary Adelaide had instilled in her daughter not only a love for beautiful clothes and lavish jewels, but the necessity of Royal women to wear them well. Queen Mary, because of her long, graceful neck, her height, her bearing, and her instinctive flair for elegance, had always been able to display an extraordinary quantity of jewels on her person. Now she had "serious jewels to display." Within a year of King George's succession, photographs of Queen Mary proliferated in newspapers and magazines around the world. In all of them, her jewels and gowns were dazzling. In one, she is wearing a blazing diamond crown, a collar of rows of diamonds, another large diamond necklace below that, a diamond stomacher, the Koh-i-noor, the Star of Africa, lesser South African Stars, the Garter, two family orders, and the Crown of India.

The astounding manner in which she could wear *so many* glittering gems at one time and the curious poodle hairstyle that she had never altered gave the new Queen Consort an appearance that made her uniquely recognisable not only to the British public but to the world. King George was supposedly the one who insisted his wife keep her coiffure because he wanted her "to grow old looking exactly as she had looked when they had first become engaged." But, in fact, King George had never been interested in clothes or jewels. Much more probable is the idea that Princess May, who had designed the coiffure, had found a certain security and courage in looking "different," and

225

that she still drew strength from the reliability of her appearance. Though masquerade balls had been tremendously popular for years, and even her mother had adored getting dressed in a costume, Princess May had disliked such affairs intensely, and, in her husband's reign, the *bal masque* suffered a quick demise from which it never recovered.

In the same way that Princess Mary Adelaide's huge figure had made her instantly identifiable in public, so did Queen Mary's poodle hairstyle single her out. The inimitable toque was a natural evolution—for when a hat was required and the hairstyle not on display, she could still be recognised across the vast space of a palace courtyard merely by the uniqueness of her silhouette. The new Queen's ability to take the stage she had been given and her instant popularity did not improve her relationship with the old Queen, who became more quarrelsome with each passing day.

After the funeral and before Kaiser Wilhelm had returned to Germany, he saw the problem his cousin, England's new King, was having in removing his mother from Buckingham Palace, and he took it upon himself to try to persuade Queen Alexandra to move. He stressed the love his aunt had always had for Marlborough House, and how much more comfortable and less lonely she would be if she returned there. As she smiled patiently, her eyes fastened upon his lips when he spoke, Kaiser Wilhelm thought he had convinced her of what she must do. But when he had finished, she remarked sweetly, "Willy dear, you know that you always speak rather indistinctly; I am afraid I have not understood a single word you are saying."

Six months after Edward's death, the situation still had not been resolved. Drastic action was called for, and with Queen Alexandra at Sandringham (as was the King), Queen Mary travelled up to London and moved her family into temporary quarters in Buckingham Palace. "It is rather strange & lonely here without you & the children & I feel rather lost," she wrote her husband. "Oh! how I regret our dear beloved Marl Hse. the most perfect of all houses & so compact. Here everything is so straggly, such distances to go & so fatiguing."

Rather unsympathetically, the King replied, "I am sure the rooms are very comfortable. The distances are great but it is good exercise for you as you never walk a yard in London." Aunt Augusta, however, was more understanding. "I so understand your disliking the change of abode. Your saying 'here one can never find anyone' so well describes the discomfort of a bigger palace."

Buckingham Palace required over three hundred servants. Its innumerable windowless, narrow corridors were hung with a seemingly inexhaustible number of sombre Royal portraits and grim battle scenes. The cavernous Throne Room with its crystal chandeliers now converted to electricity, the ballroom, the state rooms, the many dining rooms ranged from vast to enormous. There were endless picture galleries, reception rooms, sitting rooms, nests of suites, bedrooms—six hundred rooms in all— and an equal number of corridors, landings, and staircases, all strung together with blood-red carpeting and designed to form four sides of an inner courtyard. Her new home was certainly not *gemütlich,* a word Queen Mary often used to describe Marlborough House. After quickly deciding on her decorative schemes, Queen Mary returned to Sandringham to spend Christmas at York Cottage with her family, assured by her husband that his mother had issued orders for her possessions to be moved to Marlborough House.

Christmas at Sandringham was not the gay occasion of former years. No other Royal home contained as much of the dead King's spirit. His absence—the first Christmas in half a century he was not there—gave an eerie quality to the holiday. Each time a door blew open or slammed shut, the Household fully expected King Edward's ghost to appear roaring with laughter, as in life.

Only a few guests had been invited, whereas in King Edward's tenure, the house and grounds were bustling with dancers, bridge players, hunters with their horses and dogs, and many servants. Gottlieb's Viennese Orchestra had not been engaged, but since Queen Mary had struck up a recent friendship with the opera singer, Nellie Melba, the diva arrived and sang for the disconsolate Royal Family and their Household.

The move of Prince John with Lala Bill to Wood Farm, Wolferton, two miles to the west on the Sandringham estate, caused spirits to be lower than ever at York Cottage that Christmas.

227

John's epileptic fits had become more frequent and intense. A decision, therefore, had been made that his presence with his parents and brothers and sister—now that they were the Royal Family—was an undesirable image. Thereafter, John remained segregated from his family. Georgie, who was nine, was the most affected by his brother's absence. He went to see John every day, as did Queen Alexandra and Mr. Hansell. But the other members of the family and Household found it too heart-wrenching a task. Queen Mary's emotion toward John's disablement is hard to assess. No mention of John was made in any of her correspondence—not even to Helene Bricka or her Aunt Augusta, to whom she might have confided her fears, guilts, or unhappiness with considerable intimacy and ease. Nor did she appear to have discussed John with any of her ladies-in-waiting or family members such as her brothers and their wives. Her overt acceptance and avoidance of the situation set the tone for those close to the Royal Family. Lala Bill dedicated her life to the child, and he appeared to those who saw him to be happier than he had been living with his family. But if John's segregation added a further note of unhappiness to the holiday gathering, Bertie's presence created a tense and difficult situation.

On his return to Osborne after the summer holiday at Balmoral, Bertie's schoolwork had not improved, and as the examinations approached in December before the Christmas holiday, "there was considerable perturbation at Osborne, not only as to how Prince Albert would do in them but what the effect would be, if he did badly, upon the King, his father. No uncertain starter on the eve of a great race was watched with greater care and anxiety than that lavished by Mr. Watt [his tutor] on his unpredictable pupil," his biographer, Sir John Wheeler-Bennett, informs us. Mr. Watt worked with Bertie up until the eve of the examinations. The results were still calamitous. Bertie's final position in his last term at Osborne was sixty-eighth out of sixty-eight.

"I am so afraid that P[rince] A[lbert] has gone a mucker," Mr. Watt wrote to Mr. Hansell, to whom he sent frequent reports of his pupil's progress. "He has been quite off his head with the excitement of getting home for the last few days, and unfortunately as these were the days of the examination he had come quite to grief . . . I am afraid Their Majesties will be very disappointed and I can well understand it."

Without Royal intervention, Bertie could not have passed into the Royal Naval College at Dartmouth where he would go after the holidays, for as well as placing last in his class, he had failed mathematics and engineering, the Navy's two most important prerequisites. He spent the Christmas holiday studying practically from sunrise to sunrise. The best that could be said of such long hours and hard work was that they kept him out of the pathway of his parents' fury.

David, on the other hand, had done surprisingly well in his term at Dartmouth. He was quieter, more mature, and during the holiday he and his mother became closer than previously. At the same time, her attitude toward him was more reverential. When he returned to Dartmouth, she wrote him letters that reflected more of an adult exchange than her former maternal notes.

"Well, at last *me voila*," she wrote him on February 26, 1911, from Buckingham Palace, "writing to you from my *new* rooms which we took possession of last Wedy." The same day she confided to her Aunt Augusta, "I feel more at home now, glad that this *great eruption* is at an end and that one can begin to turn one's thoughts to other things, tho' I confess much is left still to do in the Palace as so much has been removed & must be replaced—I am trying to rehang the pictures in the various rooms, according to family date, etc., not an easy task when one has miles of corridors to cover to find anything—however, I hope to do it in time if my legs hold out."

In March, she wrote to Aunt Augusta, "I really am beginning to like our new rooms & to feel more at home in them, they certainly have turned out pretty & are not as full of things as Motherdear had them."

Anticipating trouble with his mother over his wife's decorations, King George wrote placatingly to Queen Alexandra, "I expect you will think May's rooms rather empty, but then you have so many more things than she has." And indeed he was wise to prepare for his mother's displeasure, for a day later from Sandringham, Alexandra wrote her daughter-in-law that she had heard of the alterations to the Royal suite at Buckingham

Palace. *"Our* dear old rooms," she wrote, underscoring the possessive pronoun. "I shall indeed be very curious & anxious to see them & how you have arranged it all. Yes the sitting room with its nice & pretty bow window is certainly very cold & draughty in the winter—particularly where my writing table stood—I wonder where you have put yours—& the lovely bedroom with its pretty arches—which I hear you have *removed,* * how is that arranged—"

With Lady Eva Dugdale and her husband to help her in the final arrangement of her possessions, Queen Mary had been able to make the move in Buckingham Palace from their temporary quarters to their permanent rooms in a matter of three weeks. She had devised a decorating scheme whereby each room was devoted to a particular date and style of furniture. Especially effective had been the final result of the Chinese Chippendale room. To her great satisfaction, the director of the Victoria and Albert Museum, after a tour of the new rooms, decided upon an exhibit that would display the museum's furniture and porcelain collections in the same manner as she had displayed hers.

But Queen Mary was far from pleased with the results of her redecorating. The palace would still require much renovation to bring it up to her standards of good taste and design. Except for the scrubbing of the front façade of the east wing when King Edward took over the palace and the minor redecoration carried out at that time, little had been done either to renovate or to modernise Buckingham Palace since the death of Prince Albert.

Queen Mary's work had taken her into the many storerooms of the palace, where numerous great treasures—silks, brocades, furniture, rugs, and paintings—had been housed since George III and William IV's occupancy, and she resolved that sometime in the future she would renovate the palace and restore some of these family heirlooms.

After the *gemütlich* life-style of Marlborough House and the cramped quarters of York Cottage, Buckingham Palace was like living in an antiquated museum. One man worked a full day, every day, to wind the three hundred clocks in the palace, and six full-time florists arranged and watered the floral bouquets

---

*Italicised words were underscored by Queen Alexandra in the original.

that brightened the rooms. Over two hundred thousand electric light bulbs needed constant replacement, and the palace post office had a dozen postmen who made their rounds along the palace corridors, handling about fifteen hundred letters daily, thousands on special occasions or in the event of an illness in the Royal Family. There was also a telegraph and telegraphers, a telephone switchboard and numerous operators, and a palace police station with a large detail of security men.

Queen Mary was determined that one day she would make this awesome establishment into a comfortable home for her family and a Royal residence of which the nation could be proud. She enjoyed the Opening of Parliament on February 6, 1911 (especially since Queen Alexandra had returned "the little Crown").* Then her attention turned toward the date of the coronation, June 22, 1911, which, she wrote her brother Alge, "will be a great ordeal & we are dreading it as you can imagine."

In a short time, Queen Mary and King George would be officially crowned. The closer that day approached, the more of "a pitiable figure" Alexandra became—"hopeless & helpless." Languishing in her grief with her widowed sister and her spinster daughter at Sandringham, she now turned her painful thoughts back to her dead son, Prince Eddy, who, she reminded her family, should rightfully have been King after his father's death. No one could be quite sure of *how* she would react under the strain of the coronation. A sigh of relief greeted the decision that she would not attend the service. The public was told that she had a persistent cough and that the long service might be a strain on her health. Such an unusual palace announcement was so rare that press and public alike (while sending satchels of reassuring good wishes) speculated morbidly as to the seri-

---

*On this occasion, Queen Alexandra had written her daughter-in-law, "My darling May, My thoughts have never left you today & have followed you step by step to Westminster & the House of Lords & on yr way back from yr first opening of Parliament—Were you both very alarmed & shy & *emotionne* as we were the *first time* particularly! I wished all the time I cld have had a peep at you! What did you wear? & did the cloak of Gd Mama's do? Did you wear the big or small crown? Please [write] me [as] it interests me to hear also what Jewels you wore etc.—I always *heard* & felt my heart beating loud all the time we were seated on that very conspicuous place."

231

ousness of her illness, a situation that placed a small cloud over the excitement of the coming coronation.

"Just as well," Queen Mary wrote her Aunt Augusta when she learned that her mother-in-law was not to attend the coronation. She was disappointed that her dear-Mother-Aunt, "the Grand Duchess Augusta," would not be at the historical event. Eighty-nine and beginning to fail badly, Aunt Augusta wrote in answer to her niece's pleas that she change her mind, "Oh! that wd have been *my fourth* [coronation] but this I dare not think of, unless some Aerobike takes me to fly across!"*

The week before the event was filled with preparations, rehearsals, deputations to receive, foreign royalties to be met, and family luncheons and huge banquets to attend. On the eve of the coronation, the King and Queen dined privately with David and Bertie. Queen Mary had received a huge bouquet of flowers from her brother Dolly just before dinner, and it had moved her to tears. Dolly, after all, had taken that first journey with her to Balmoral to be interviewed by Queen Victoria. Shortly after dinner, a letter arrived for the King from his mother. "May God bless you both," she wrote in a rather shaky hand, "& give a little thought to your poor, sad broken-hearted Motherdear." Although her son and daughter-in-law did not know it, at the time they received the letter she was pacing her rooms at Marlborough House, crying, *"Eddy* should be King, not *Georgie!"*

---

*The Grand Duchess Augusta had attended the coronations of William IV and Queen Adelaide, as well as those of Queen Victoria and King Edward VII.

SIXTEEN

There is a magic to hereditary succession; a sense of continuity, of everlastingness. Apart from the brief seven-year interval of Cromwell's Commonwealth,* King George's direct ancestors had ruled England for 1,100 years, since Egbert had ascended the throne in Wessex in 809 and was recognised as Bretwalda in 829. By 1911, Parliament had secured control of taxation and therefore of government; dynastic conflicts were no longer a menace; Kingship "had ceased to be transcendental and had become one of many alternative institutional forms"; and the doctrine of Divine Right, "profoundly shaken" by the Reformation,† had not survived the execution of Charles I.‡ Since that time, a system of limited or constitutional monarchy had been developed through the growing power of Parliament and historical accident. The executive powers of the present King George were strictly limited. Still, he retained an indefinable—yet very great—*influence.*

Despite King Edward's fears to the contrary, the Monarch

---

*Oliver Cromwell, Lord Protector (self-styled) of Britain's short period of Commonwealth (1653–1660), which followed on the heels of the execution of Charles I.

†The Restoration took place in 1660, upsetting Cromwell's Commonwealth.

‡Charles I (see earlier note).

received *full* information on all matters of state and was able to express, if not enforce, an opinion, which, in the course of a long reign, could have great value. Ministers come and go, and their policies may not be those of the next, and the sovereign must listen to all of them. An intelligent sovereign cannot help but acquire expertise, even wisdom, which can be used to influence subsequent Ministers.

In mid-November, the uncrowned King was faced with the necessity of reaching an immediate decision about his constitutional duty in the crisis left unsolved at the time of King Edward's death. The "Constitutional Crisis" of 1910–1911 was a most complicated matter. The rejection of the 1909 budget by the House of Lords had been its original cause. A general election was held the following January, resulting in an equal number of Conservatives and Liberals, and placing the balance of power in the hands of forty Socialists and eighty-one Irish Nationalists. Prime Minister Asquith, in the hope of winning over these last two groups, introduced a Parliament Bill limiting the power of the House of Lords. Commons duly passed this. The Parliament Bill raised the question: Would the King, to ensure its passage through the House of Lords, guarantee to create a sufficient number of peers?

On Wednesday, November 16, Prime Minister Asquith in audience at Buckingham Palace sought the King's secret pledge to be ready to use the one unquestionable prerogative the King still retained—that of creating new peers. "After a long talk," King George wrote in his diary that evening, "I agreed most reluctantly to give the Cabinet a secret understanding that in the event of the Government being returned with a majority at the General Election, I should use my Prerogative to make Peers if asked for. I disliked having to do this very much, but agreed that this was the only alternative to the Cabinet resigning, which at this moment would be disastrous."

King George was also to regret the fact that he gave *secret* guarantees to the Government *before* that next August, when required. He did so believing he had no alternatives. Still, the pledge he made placed a heavy burden on his heart and took away much of the joy he might have had from the approaching coronation. By June 1911, he had more problems to weigh upon him. A massive transport strike took place that was to open "a new period of deep industrial warfare." Workers now struck not against a particular employer but against a whole industry. The strike involved 77,000 men, spread from London to most of England's major cities and ports, and lasted 72 days.

On July 1, an international crisis threatened for several weeks when the German gunboat *Panther* docked at Agadir in Morocco, in an attempt to force France to remove troops it had sent to the Moorish capital. The crisis coincided with Kaiser Wilhelm's visit to London for the unveiling of the Queen Victoria Memorial.

The German Emperor had always been a thorn in the side of his British relatives. Queen Victoria had been indulgent of his willfulness and arrogance because of his withered arm. King Edward, however, had disliked *Willy* (his nephew) since childhood, and the Kaiser's quick appearance at any time of celebration or grief in the British branch of the family created only more hostility. King Edward greatly resented his nephew's presence at Queen Victoria's deathbed and was quite outspoken about Willy's "takeover" of the funeral ceremonies. He would have been furious but not surprised that Willy had been a pallbearer at his funeral and had received more press coverage than any other visiting royalty.

King George had also never felt kindly toward his cousin's "bossy" nature. Because of Queen Mary, who quite admired the Kaiser and had always been somewhat in awe of him, the King tried to keep relations civil between them. The Kaiser harboured deep and bitter resentments, though he gave no outward indication of his feelings.

At the unveiling of the memorial, another of Wilhelm's first cousins, Princess Marie Louise, daughter of Queen Victoria's third daughter Helena, remarked to him, "It is so funny to think of George as King when one has always regarded him as a very close relation."

The German Emperor replied, "Yes, of course, he is your cousin and nearest relative but, above all, never forget he is your Sovereign and King as well." After the unveiling, the Kaiser and King George met privately. Of that meeting, the Kaiser was later to say that he had warned King George of his intention to send a warship to southern Morocco and the latter had raised no objection. King George, on the other hand—outraged and surprised at Germany's action—claimed he did not recall Kaiser Wilhelm mentioning Agadir and vowed that he "absolutely did not express to him my own, or my Government's consent to any such action." Years later, in his memoirs, the German Emperor changed his version of this meeting with his cousin.

> I asked him if he considered that the French methods were still in accordance with the Algeciras Agreement. The King remarked that the Agreement, to tell the truth, was no longer in force, that the best thing to do was to forget it; that the French fundamentally were doing nothing different in Morocco from what the English had previously done in Egypt; that therefore, England would place no obstacles in the path of the French, and would follow their own course; that the only thing to do was to recognize the *fait accompli* of the occupation of Morocco and make arrangements for commercial protection with France.

The Agadir crisis lasted several months before it was settled in an agreement between France and Germany, by which the former obtained a free hand to establish a Protectorate in Morocco and at a price (a fair area of the Congo to be handed over to Germany) that was not high. The crisis had proved "a fiasco for Germany," Winston Churchill wrote, and that no doubt "deep and violent passions of humiliation and resentment were coursing beneath the glittering uniforms which thronged the palaces through which the Kaiser moved."

The entire incident had made Britain aware of Germany's warlike nature and impelled the British Government to review their defences and the nature of their commitments and general relations with all foreign powers.

King George's uncrowned year had not been easy.

As Prince of Wales, David had precedence over the peers of the realm and would normally have worn the regulation peer's robes at the coronation. But he was under twenty-one, too young to take his seat in the House of Lords. To compensate for this situation, on June 10, 1911, White Rose Day, just twelve days before the coronation, David was invested by King George's order with the Order of the Garter, so that he could wear the robes of a knight for the coronation. The service, revived for the first time since the eighteenth century, took place in the Garter Throne Room at Windsor Castle, its panelled walls hung with innumerable portraits of British Monarchs in their vivid costumes. He wore a cloth-of-silver suit, white stockings, and white satin slippers with red heels; a sword in a red velvet scabbard hung at his side. None of the pageantry of the occasion awed David, who that day recorded in his diary, "After Papa & Mama had gone into the Garter Room, I waited outside the Rubens Room until Uncle Arthur [Duke of Connaught] & Cousin Arthur [the Duke of Connaught's son] had come for me. Then I fell in between the two & we walked in & up the room, bowing three times. Then Papa put the garter, riband & george, & star on me, & then I went round the table shaking hands with each knight in turn. I kissed both Papa & Mama's hands."

Harry arrived home on June 17, just barely recovered from a case of mumps. That same day 40,000 suffragettes marched (to Queen Mary's disapproval) in a great column four miles long from Westminster to Albert Hall, where £103,000 was raised for "the cause." Bertie was not granted a leave from Dartmouth until June 20. The two days before the ceremony were crowded with more excitement than any of the Royal children had ever seen before: dress parades, illuminations, and foreign visitors from exotic lands. Large groups of people came and went in the palace almost round the clock. None of the boys got any sleep. David was terrified that he would not remember all the words of the oath he had to speak or follow the instructions on his participation in the proceedings.

The morning of June 22 was grey and windy. The coronation was to be far grander than any living Englishman might have witnessed. There were to be more troops, a greater gathering of representatives from the Dominions and dependencies abroad, and a longer procession through the streets than there had been at either Queen Victoria's Golden Jubilee or King Edward's coronation. The decision to go "all out" was deliberate on the part of the coronation committee. Their hope was to dispel any private fear that, with King Edward gone, the country might slip back into the depths of Victorianism. Every house, store, and club along the route of the procession was now barricaded with stands jammed with people, some of whom had been waiting since the previous night for the procession to begin.

The trains were splashed with the brilliance of uniformed admirals, generals, and privy councillors incongruously paired with hordes of sightseers with luncheon bags and baskets. By 8:00 A.M., the whole of Victoria Street was one solid mass of motors, peers' coaches, taxicabs, and broughams, "each with its vision of nodding plumes and gleaming jewels and resplendent masculinity within." The stands and tiers before the grey Abbey had been "multitudinously crowded" since dawn. The windows and roofs of nearby buildings were alive with faces, and the usually quiet Dean's Yard that abutted the Abbey was "bustling and brilliant with troops and guests and officials, women in Court dresses with gorgeous trains carried over the arms, [and with] naval and military men, and judges and officers of the Court."

The members of the Royal Family had risen with the dawn as well. John had remained at Wood Farm. He was told and understood that his Papa and Mama were to be crowned King and Queen that day. The other brothers and Mary ate breakfast early and then at 9:00 A.M. briefly saw their parents, who were too distracted to do much more than acknowledge their children's presence. Everyone then dispersed to dress for the awesome occasion, the King and Queen in their coronation splendour, David in his Garter robes, Bertie in his cadet's uniform, Harry and Georgie in Highland costume, and Mary in a coronet and a purple velvet robe of state lined with ermine over a white satin dress with overlayers of lace.

As Prince of Wales, David had his own procession. He left Buckingham Palace at 10:00 A.M. and drove with his brothers and sister in a gold state carriage drawn by eight cream horses. Everywhere he looked he saw the gleam of exotic raiment— turbans and uniforms from India, Africa, and the Orient dispersing the greyness of the day. London was a feast of colour and a panorama of marvellous diversity among the races of mankind. David was as mesmerised by the spectacle as any one of the crowds of people who gaped and pointed and cheered as he drove past their post.

At half-past ten, the young Prince of Wales reached the Abbey, where, to the blare of silver trumpets and preceded by pursuivants in dazzling colours, he was conducted to his chair —a wholesome, unaffected boyish figure carrying a vast, plumed hat and looking almost ludicrously costumed in the mantle of the elaborate Garter that overwhelmed his small frame.* After he was seated in the south transept, just in front of the peers' benches, Bertie, Harry, and Georgie saluted him solemnly in turn as they passed to their appointed places. Then Mary approached and curtsied deeply. David rose and gravely bowed to her. Someone touched him gently on the shoulder and whispered that he was not to rise. From that moment he sat rigidly, jerking his head and shoulders in acknowledgement as princes and princesses of the blood royal, each with an attendant page or officer or Lady-in-Waiting, made his or her obeisance to him on their way to the Royal boxes.

The north transept was occupied by the peeresses of the realm, the galleries that led up the triforium by members of Parliament and their wives. The Royal box, reserved for the King and Queen's personal and untitled friends (Mr. Hansell and Nellie Melba among them), was above and slightly to the side of the glittering cream-and-gold altar laden with its gold-and-jewelled sacred vessels. In the space between the north and south transepts was the "theatre," where the two thrones in crimson damask sat on a dais facing the altar—the King's to the right, the Queen's farther down and to the left.

Every seat in the Abbey was taken, seven thousand in all, each occupant awaiting the entrance of the King and Queen. At eleven o'clock, the booming of the guns and the faint echo of cheering could be heard without. All eyes turned to the West Door. Slowly, the Queen's procession entered: first the Abbey beadle in robes of silken blue, then the ten chaplains-in-ordinary scarlet-hooded, after them the domestic chaplains, the sacrist bearing the Cross of Westminster, followed by more ecclesias-

---

*The Prince of Wales at the time of King George's coronation was 17, 5'4" tall, and weighed 7 stone, 8 pounds (106 pounds).

tics. Then the pursuivants all gold and mulberry; and the officers of the orders of knighthood in mantles of glimmering hues; heralds in blazoned tabards; household officials; great nobles bearing the standards of the British Dominions, India, Ireland, Scotland, England, and the United Kingdom; Lord Lansdowne holding aloft the Royal standard; the four Knights of the Garter appointed to hold the canopy for the King's anointing; great political dignitaries; chancellors; the Lord Chamberlain; the Archbishop of Canterbury; more pursuivants; the bearers of the Queen's Regalia; and then Queen Mary herself, pale and tense but splendidly dignified—her stupendous train borne by eight ladies in snowy white and followed by "double dazzling lines of attendant retinue."

At the sight of the Queen in her brilliant tiara made entirely of diamonds,* an audible murmur was heard. Her deep purple velvet robes, six yards long, were lined with ermine dotted with ermine tails; and her gown of white satin was thickly embroidered with gold, as were her gloves and shoes. What made her magnificent coronation robes even more spectacular was the indescribable majesty with which she wore them. Breaking precedent, she had decided not to wear any order that would detract from the drama of the rich purple and shimmering gold of her costume.

The first thing Queen Mary saw on her entrance was the deep blue Worcester carpet stretching along the vista to the carved platform on which were massed the orchestra and trumpeters led by the scarlet-robed conductor Sir Frederick Bridges. On either side of the carpet a wide border of soft blue grey ran up to the edge of the partitions, three feet in height, that walled off the seats from the Abbey floors. The partitions were hung with silver brocade embossed with patterns in royal blue. Behind them, row upon row, tier upon tier, ascended the seats, their straight pale-blue lines merging exquisitely with the sombre grey of the walls and arches.

Queen Mary kept her eyes trained straight ahead and did not

---

*This was replaced later in the service by the even more splendid Coronation Crown with the Koh-i-noor at its centre and above and below the Stars of Africa.

raise them to the sudden burst of sound from the organ and choir as they began the anthem, "I was glad when they said unto me, we will go into the house of the Lord"; nor did she lower them to exchange glances with her eldest son as she approached his chair. But when the Westminster boys flung out their greeting, "*Vivat Regina Maria! Vivat, vivat, vivat!*" she paused almost imperceptibly before continuing. Moments later, the King's procession entered the Abbey, and even the grandeur of Queen Mary's entrance was surpassed.

The King's procession was even grander and longer than the Queen's. Finally, the King, in his crimson robe of state with an ermine cape over his shoulders and the Cap of Maintenance on his head, appeared, flanked by twenty gentlemen-in-arms, his train borne by eight scarlet-costumed pages. Following the King were the high officers of the Household. The procession was closed by twenty Yeomen of the Guard. A hushed awe fell over the audience. The magnificence of the King and Queen's processions massed together now before the thrones and altar was almost too much for any one pair of eyes to take in. The *Vivats* of the Westminster boys broke the silence, and the service began.

The coronation ceremony—a tissue of medieval mysticism and chivalry, feudalism, ecclesiasticism, and politics—falls into four successive phases, each of which possesses historical symbolism: the Recognition, the Oath, the Anointing and Crowning, and the Homage of the Lords. The King noted later that it was "most beautiful . . . grand, yet simple & most dignified & went without a hitch . . . May looked so lovely." And Queen Mary wrote her Aunt Augusta later, "To me, who love tradition and the past, & who am English from top to toe, the service was a very real solemn thing & appealed to my feelings more than I can express—everything was most perfectly & reverently done—" Yet one reservation was to disturb her greatly. A special phrase had been introduced into the service to cover what the Archbishop considered to be a deficiency in the new Queen Consort's royal heritage, the morganatic status of the Duke of Teck. He prayed that "by the powerful and mild influence of her piety and virtue she may adorn the dignity which she hath *obtained.*" The Archbishop's words intimated that her paternal

241

ancestry was not Royal. Before the day was ended, she was determined to correct this unfair slur, for the King and Queen were second cousins once removed.

David saw the coronation through boyish eyes. "All the relatives & people were most civil & bowed to me as they passed. Then Mama & Papa came in & the ceremony commenced. There was the recognition, the anointing & then the Crowning of Papa & then I put on my coronet with the peers. Then I had to go & do hommage [sic] to Papa at his throne & I was very nervous." With difficulty in keeping his unaccustomed sword carefully to one side, David knelt at his father's feet and swore, "I, Edward, Prince of Wales, do become your liege man of life and limb and of earthly worship, and faith and truth I will bear unto you, to live and die, against all manner of folks. So help me God."

"It reminded me so much of when I did the same thing to beloved Papa," King George wrote in his diary that night, "he did it so well . . . I nearly broke down."

"Then Mama was crowned," David continues in his diary. "We got into our cariage, [sic] & had a long drive back. My Coronet felt very heavy as we had to bow to people as we went along."

The entry in King George's diary concludes, "We left Westminster Abbey at 2.15 (having arrived there before 11.0) with our Crowns on and sceptres in our hands. This time we drove by the Mall, St. James' Street & Piccadilly, crowds enormous & decorations very pretty. On reaching B.P. [Buckingham Palace] just before 3.0 May & I went out on the balcony to show ourselves to the people. Downey photographed us in our robes with Crowns on.* Had some lunch with guests here. Worked all afternoon with Bigge & others answering telegrams & letters of which I have had hundreds.† Such a large crowd collected in front of the Palace that I went out on the balcony again. Our guests dined with us at 8.30.‡ May and I showed ourselves again

*Downey, Royal photographer.

†Sir Arthur Bigge (1849–1931), Lord Stamfordham, Private Secretary to King George from 1901 to 1931. From 1896 to 1901, he had been Queen Victoria's Private and Principal Secretary as well.

‡Visiting Royalty and family members were present at this dinner.

242

to the people. Wrote & read. Rather tired. Bed at 11.45. Beautiful illuminations everywhere."

Despite the happy events of the coronation week, Queen Mary was sufficiently angered by the Archbishop's slur against her father's lineage that she took whatever free time she had to laboriously complete the Teck genealogy and to present a copy to College of Arms.

David's seventeenth birthday was June 23, and the Royal Family celebrated with all their visiting Royal guests, most of whom were related, which meant that David received more presents than he had ever seen in his life. A fortnight later on a sweltering summer day in July, within the vast grey ruin of Carnavon Castle and before some 10,000 people, with Winston Churchill, the Home Secretary, "mellifluously proclaiming" his titles, David was invested as Prince of Wales by his father. A coronet cap as a token of principality was placed on his head, the gold rod of government given to him to hold, and the gold ring of responsibility slipped onto his middle finger. King George then led his son through an archway to one of the towers of the battlements and presented him to the people of Wales. "Half-fainting of heat & nervousness," David repeated a few Welsh sentences that began, "*Mor a gan yw Cymru i gyd,*" "All Wales is a sea of song," taught to him by Lloyd George with the counsel, "All Welshmen will love you for that."

But when the excitement and magnificence of the coronation festivities were over and his investiture complete, David realised that he had made "a painful discovery about myself. It was that, while I was prepared to fulfill my role in all this pomp & ritual, I recoiled from anything that tended to set me up as a person requiring homage. Even if my father was now beginning to remind me of the obligations of my position, had he not been at pains to give me a strict and unaffected upbringing? And if my association with the village boys at Sandringham and the cadets of the Naval Colleges had done anything for me it was to make me desperately anxious to be treated exactly like any other boy of my age!"

However, David was unrealistic to think that he might have been treated as any other boy his age. He was the Prince of Wales, Heir-Apparent to the Throne. Still, the idea that he would one day be King was as terrifying to him now as when he was a child. He desperately wanted to play the common man and not the prince, for he was sure that true happiness was reserved only for the common lot.

King George did not know, or even suspect, that the son he had just invested as Prince of Wales might one day place the Monarchy in much greater jeopardy than the current constitutional crisis and his secret pledge to Asquith placed it. Or that it would be his second son, that knobbly-kneed boy who was the last in his class, who could not speak without stammering painfully and was not being prepared for the role of King, who would be forced to save the Throne for the family.

SEVENTEEN

With Queen Mary as Consort, the ultra-fashionables of King Edward's Court were not often seen in the Royal circle, which was now considerably more select. Their friends were old and tried. Queen Mary's confidantes were women like Lady Airlie, whom she had known from childhood; her brothers and their wives; and as she had a fervent interest in history, architecture, and design, representatives from those fields. She set immediately upon the task of learning as much as she could about the homes she now occupied and was determined from the very beginning of King George's reign to restore them to the time of their apogee. The country had more or less thought of Queen Alexandra as a charming appendage to King Edward. Their Monarch's powerful and charismatic personality had roused the people's sense of allegiance toward the Monarchy, whereby the public seldom thought of King George without Queen Mary.

Together they represented the ideal family. There were press photographs of King George riding through Windsor Park with his eldest four sons, and Queen Mary at Army reviews or garden parties accompanied most often by David and Bertie and Mary, and seldom without King George somewhere in the background. The sight of her with umbrella and huge hat in the daytime and tiara and ropes of pearls and jewels in the evening was etched in the public's memory. In 1910, at the age of forty-three, she already had the distinctive look of a royal matriarch, a quality possessed by Queen Victoria, but not by Queen Alexandra.

In the year since he had become King, George had not yet established between himself and his subjects the same bond of camaraderie that his father had manufactured almost without an effort. Still, the aristocracy felt that under his reign they would once again come into their own and that the Court, while somewhat stiffer than during King Edward's time, was—as one contemporary wrote—"more English, and less under the influence of Germans, Jews, and capitalists and that the King's 'set' is one for which no Englishman had to apologize." One of the great arts of Royalty is to be liked by those who never come—and are never likely to come—into personal contact with the sovereign, those grey, undistinguished masses who watch and judge him from a distance, and whose opinions are swayed or determined by a thousand trivial things. Popularity for a King is much more important among those he does not know than among those he does.

King Edward's strength had been his astonishing gift for attracting the affections of the multitudes who had never heard him speak a single word or had come within twenty yards of his magnetic presence. King George had ascended the Throne with none of his father's *bonhomie,* his air of being at home and enjoying himself wherever he was, his all-around cosmopolitan experience, or his prolonged social training. In fact, King George had a way of looking bored even when a subject or a person interested him. He preferred a quiet life by his own fireplace with his wife to society and ceremony; he was a domesticated man, really, of a straightforward, downright temperament, rather naive and immature, bluff and voluble in speech, with "a boisterously British and liberal sense of humour." Certainly not a man of the world, he was somewhat uncomfortable at finding himself the central figure on public occasions. This is most probably responsible for his encouraging Queen Mary to accompany him whenever possible and his obvious pleasure that she had inadvertently garnered centre stage. A contemporary notes that King George put up with the ceremony "not because he likes it, but because he knows it to be his duty, and with an uneasy feeling that all the time he is not doing himself justice or striking quite the right note of graciousness." Queen Mary, on the other hand, was at her best on ceremonial occasions and struck not only the right note of graciousness but set the standard for the future of the women in the Royal Family.

King George's greatest fear was not that his subjects might find him lacking in the confidence and charm so associated with his father, but that when his pledge to Asquith became public knowledge he might be irreparably humiliated before his people. After David's investiture as Prince of Wales on July 13, 1911, the King travelled to Holyrood, in Scotland, for a holiday. When he returned to London, the moment of truth had arrived. At 11:00 P.M. on the single hottest August 10 in English history (the thermometer had registered 100 degrees), the King's secretary, Arthur Bigge, returned from the House of Lords with the good news. To the King's great relief, the Parliament bill to create new peers had been defeated.

Six days later he wrote to Bigge, "It is impossible to pat the Opposition on the back, but I am indeed grateful for what they have done & saved me from humiliation which I should never have survived. If the creation had taken place, I should not have been the same person again."

In September, Sir Edward Grey remarked to Winston Churchill, "What a remarkable year this has been: the heat, the strikes, and now the foreign situation."

"Why," said Winston, "you've forgotten the Parliament Bill," and a friend who recorded the conversation added, "And so he had and so had everybody."

Queen Mary had kept her silence on the issue of the Parliament Bill but, as soon as the crisis was over, appeared as frequently as possible in public with the King. As always, her presence enhanced his image. Together, they represented everything right and proper and English.

Since his tour of India six years before as the Prince of Wales, King George had been harbouring an idea that the Sovereign should visit that great empire. "I am convinced that were it possible for me, accompanied by the Queen, to go to India &

247

hold a Coronation Durbar at Delhi, where we should meet all the Princes, officials & vast number of the People, the greatest benefits would accrue to the Country at large," he wrote Lord Morley, Secretary of State for India, on September 8, 1910. "I also trust & believe that if the proposed visit could be made known sometime before, it would tend to allay unrest & I am sorry to say, seditious spirit which unfortunately exists in some parts of India."

Lord Esher had been right in suspecting the King would have some trouble with his Ministers in carrying out this scheme, for Lord Morley's reply on September 12, 1910, had been tactful, but not too receptive to the proposal. "The cost of such a proceeding with all the grandeur of it, wd be great, and wd presumably have to be borne by India. Apart from the general body of Indian taxpayers, the Princes and ruling Chiefs wd no doubt be eager to demonstrate their loyalty on the scale of splendour natural for such an occasion and this splendour would be very costly as the last Durbar only too abundantly proved.* Again stress may be laid on embarrassments that might arise to public business at home, from the absence of the Sovereign from home for so long a time and at such immense distance."

The Government was against the outlay of the huge sums that the trip would cost and thought unwise such an extravagant display as a coronation Durbar at a time when so many sections of India were suffering famine. Also, anti-British revolutionary movements in India had grown considerably in the past five years, and security risks were to be considered.

Despite these reservations, two months later the proposal was submitted to the Cabinet. On November 8, 1910, they agreed that the King and Queen should visit India, but they did so "not without a certain amount of criticism, and with a strong expression of opinion that the decision was not to be taken as precluding the discussion at a later stage of how the expenses were to be borne," Prime Minister Asquith's secretary informed the King through Lord Knollys.

*A reference to the 1901 Durbar when Lord Kitchener was in India. It was not attended by the Monarch.

Solutions to the most serious problems of the King's proposal took the entire coronation year. The first was King George's original idea to be crowned at Delhi, which would present an awkward precedent for the King's successors. "To be crowned" implied a second coronation and would necessarily have to include a religious service of consecration "unfitting for a ceremony attended by so many Moslems and Hindus." A decision was finally reached that the King appear "wearing his crown and receive the homage of the Princes and rulers seated upon his throne." Of serious consequence was the resultant problem of the crown itself.

The law prohibited the King's crown being removed from the country. Therefore, an entirely new crown had to be made, and some provision had to be decided upon for its final repository. This issue created a great deal of debate. First thoughts were that the crown should be preserved at Delhi. But the more cautious feared its very *existence* in the centre of India would prove "an irresistible temptation to potential usurpers." This quandary was resolved by deciding the crown should be brought back and housed in the Tower of London directly after the Durbar.

Of equal concern was the problem of the gifts to and from the people and their Indian rulers that, according to immemorial custom, would have to be proportionate to the event. A King-Emperor's visit would be considered of the greatest magnitude. Such boons as the usual remission from taxes and penal sentences would not nearly suffice. A gift of a crore of rupees (then £666,666) from Great Britain to India was proposed by the Viceroy and unanimously rejected by the Cabinet. An alternative proposal was submitted that two boons not involving a gift of money be proclaimed at the Durbar. Lord Curzon's "unintentional but grievous mistake" in partitioning Bengal should be reversed, and the capital should be transferred from Calcutta to Delhi. The Cabinet agreed to those proposals reluctantly, for they were fearful they might not be popular choices in India and could lead to considerable controversy, which would place the King in an awkward situation of giving a gift that was not wanted by the majority of Indians.

*　　*　　*

249

The King and Queen were to travel to India on the *Medina.* *
The latest addition to the Peninsular and Oriental Fleet, the
Medina was built of steel, weighed 13 tons, and could accommodate 750 passengers. The Royal party consisted of twenty-four
Court and family members, which included Queen Mary's
brother Dolly, Duke of Teck since his father's death. David had
hoped he might be allowed to join his parents, but his father
prescribed that he should remain in Great Britain to prepare
himself for his entrance at Oxford. On November 11, 1911—a
black, forbidding day—David, disappointed though he was,
travelled to Portsmouth with his younger brother, Georgie, to
see their father and mother embark.

A luncheon party was given aboard the *Medina* for the large
gathering of relatives, government officials, and foreign diplomats who had accompanied the King and Queen to Portsmouth.
Queen Alexandra's frail appearance was a shock to everyone. At
half-past two, the well-wishers prepared to leave. Queen Mary
supported Motherdear as she led her to the gangway. Almost
the very moment that the *Medina* was eased from the quay by her
three tugs, the storm that had been threatening all day broke
with particular violence. Queen Mary hurried inside for protective cover from the gale-force winds, but the King stood on the
bridge. "I shall never forget that moment," he wrote his mother
almost immediately, "when I saw you waving from the window
of the railway carriage as we slowly steamed away from you into
the wind & rain."

The last sight that Queen Mary had of the British shore was
the bunting that decorated the ships of the home fleet lined up
in the port and a "mushroom bank of shining wet umbrellas."

For five days, Queen Mary was unable to leave her cabin as

---

*On board the *Medina* in the Royal party were Lord Crewe; Lord Stamfordham
(Arthur Bigge); Sir Edward Henry, Chief of the Metropolitan Police; Sir James
Dunlop Smith, political officer; Lord and Lady Shaftesbury; the Duke of Teck;
Lord Durham; Lord Annaly; Sir Derek Keppel; Captain Godfrey Faussett; Sir
Charles Cust; Lord Charles Fitzmaurice; Major Clive Wigram; Sir Havelock
Charles; Mr. John Fortescue, historian; and Mr. Jacomb Hood, official artist.
The *Medina* carried 32 officers, 360 petty officers and ratings, and 210 Marines,
all under the command of Admiral Sir Colin Keppel, with Captain Chatfield
as his flag captain.

the *Medina* lurched and rolled its way through heavy storms. Even King George, who had never been known to be seasick, was ill, as was most of the crew. Finally, once they had left Gibraltar and were in warmer and smoother waters, the journey became more pleasant. A Marine band played at eleven in the morning, after lunch, at dinner, and later in the after-saloon on deck. The men held sports competitions, and Queen Mary reread a good deal of Kipling and a prodigious number of volumes on various Indian subjects.

On December 2, a suffocatingly hot day, the sea like burnished brass, the *Medina* landed at the Apollo Bander, Bombay. The King and Queen stepped onto Indian soil to the sound of 101 guns. The crowds of people waiting for hours in the intense heat of the brightly decorated streets cheered lustily upon seeing the King but were not sure what to make of Queen Mary. For her first public appearance in India she had chosen a gown of yellow-flowered chiffon, slashed by the royal blue of the Garter ribbon, and on top of her tousled hairdo she wore a platelike straw hat heaped with artificial roses to match her dress. Tousle and hat added an alarming eight to ten inches to her height and caused her to tower over King George in his white uniform of the Admiral of the Fleet.

Their reception in Bombay had been impressive. Four days later, en route for Delhi, the Imperial train had taken them past one wayside station after the other bedecked in gay bunting, smothered in brilliant fuchsia bougainvillea, and crowded with dark men in snowy-white turbans and women swathed in gaudy sarees of "vivid pink or turquoise blue or acid green." Yet nothing had prepared them for the grandeur and splendour of their official entry into Delhi through the Gate of the Elephants, its great stone namesakes guarding its arched portals.

"It was a wonderful sight," Queen Mary wrote Aunt Augusta. "George rode and I followed in a carriage with the Mistress of the Robes & Lord Durham—Very grand & I felt proud to take part in so interesting & historical an event, just the kind of thing which appeals to my feelings of tradition—*you* will understand."

However, King George wrote his mother that "there were crowds but they were not particularly demonstrative." The trip's historian, Mr. John Fortescue, attributed the chill of this reception to the King's having entered Delhi on a horse and not an elephant, as was customary for Royal visitors to do. And since his uniform was not much grander than Lord Hardinger's or Lord Crewe's, he was not recognised.

A vast canvas city, covering forty-five square miles and housing a quarter of a million people, had been set up for the Durbar on the wide marshy plains beside the Jumna River. Many of these tents were magnificent and belonged to the majarajas and their suites. But the most luxurious of all accommodations had been constructed for the King-Emperor and his Consort. Six great lavish tents had been raised and connected to form the Royal apartments. Queen Mary's bedroom and boudoir were lined with *vieux-rose* silk, heavy with embroideries and carpeted with priceless Oriental rugs. The King's private rooms glittered with gold cloth and jewelled and gold vessels. The Royal suite also had a drawing room, an anteroom, an office, and a dining room that connected with the state reception tents.

Ceremonies, processions, and tournaments filled the five days immediately preceding the coronation Durbar. Later, Queen Mary commented regretfully to Lord Esher that she saw no Indian women in private audience and that none of the Rajputs she visited admitted her into their intimate interiors. Queen Mary did receive a deputation of Indian ladies headed by the Maharani of Patiala, who presented her with "a large square of emeralds of historic interest, engraved and set in diamonds, and a necklace and pendant of emeralds, set in rosettes of diamonds." The Maharani then read a short message of homage, in which she explained that it would be a mistake "to suppose that simply because the women of India live in *purdah*, that they are strangers to that mighty process of evolution which manifests itself beyond the limits of its four walls."

Much of the emotion toward the inferior position of Indian women that she had felt in her last visit to India welled up in Queen Mary at this time, and she replied that she felt "increasing solicitude for those who live 'within the walls.'" Then she added rather eloquently in words of her own and from an address she had written, "The jewel you have given me will ever be very precious to my eyes and whenever I wear it, though thousands of miles of land and sea separate us, my thoughts will fly to the homes of India, and create again and again this happy meeting and recall the tender love your hearts have yielded me. Your jewel shall pass to future generations as an Imperial heirloom, and always stand as a token of the first meeting of an English Queen with the ladies of India."

Before leaving England, Queen Mary had prevailed upon Lord Esher to speak with the King about her being given the Order of the Star of India, which she desperately wanted to wear on the bodice of her gown at the Durbar. King George was initially opposed to the idea, but a few days before the Durbar, he changed his mind and presented it to her "in a regular little installation," and she was tremendously pleased.

The Durbar took place on December 12 at noon, with a relentless midday sun beating down on the two concentric amphitheatres—the larger one constructed to accommodate a hundred thousand spectators, and the smaller and grander one the princes, rulers, and notables of the Indian Empire. The two amphitheatres were joined by a dais two hundred feet wide. In the very centre of this construction was a series of marble step-like platforms. On the top stood two solid-silver thrones encased in gold, placed upon a cloth-of-gold carpet and beneath a golden cupola sixty-eight feet from the ground, which assured that the Royal couple would be seen by all.

A great crisis arose just before the King and Queen, in their heavy Imperial robes of velvet and ermine, were to leave their camp for the arena, seated side-by-side in an open-top state barouche. Two veteran *chuprassi*, dressed in scarlet and gold, had been chosen to hold the cumbrous Imperial state umbrellas over the heads of the Royal couple to protect them from the murderous sun. However, the umbrellas proved too heavy for the old men to carry. A very rickety awning made of flexible bamboo canes and gold-and-silver cloth was hastily concocted over the carriage and wired on to its sides. As Their Majesties drove into the arena—their arrival heralded by a salute of 101 guns—the whole thing wobbled horribly. The strange beauty of the Durbar ceremony more than made up for this poor beginning.

The following day, King George wrote his mother that the Durbar "was the most wonderful & beautiful sight I have ever seen & one I shall remember all my life. We wore our robes & I the new crown made for the occasion. May had her best tiara on . . . I can only say it was most magnificent, the clothes & colours were marvellous . . . I had six pages & May had four to carry all our robes, they were either young Maharajas or sons of Maharajas & all wore beautiful clothes of white & gold with gold turbans & they did look nice."

Besides her most distinctive and "best tiara" (in the centre of its fifteen interlaced circles of diamonds hung a large cabochon emerald which could be interchanged for fifteen magnificent drop pearls), the badge of the Star of India was suspended from a ribbon across her bodice. She wore the dazzling jewels given her by the ladies of India, as well as the famous emeralds that had once belonged to her grandmother, the Duchess of Cambridge. This suite of jewels consisted of the perfectly matched emeralds in her tiara, a diamond-and-emerald necklace with two drops of uneven lengths—one a large pear-shaped emerald and the other a marquise diamond cut from the Cullinan—emerald-and-diamond earrings, two bracelets, a brooch with an emerald of immense size and superb quality, and an elaborate stomacher also of emeralds and diamonds. "Mama's emeralds appearing *there* amused and pleased me," her Aunt Augusta wrote. "What would she have said to her grandchild's Imperial Glory?"

On December 16, after ten days in Delhi, King George went off for a fortnight to shoot in Nepal, and Queen Mary travelled to Agra and toured Rajputana. They were thus separated for Christmas, a fact that did not disturb the Queen greatly since her schedule was filled with many interesting activities—but did distress the King. On December 22 he wrote her from his shooting camp in Nepal, "Each year I feel we become more & more necessary to one another & our lives become more & more wrapt up in each other's. And I am sure that I love you more each year & am simply devoted to you & loathe being separated from you even for a day." He added that he was "very proud of being your husband & feel that our coming here to India as the first Emperor & Empress has certainly proved itself to be what I always predicted, a great success & one which will have far-reaching effects & I trust lasting effects throughout this great Empire."

On December 29 each of them travelled to Bankepore, where their trains were shunted together. The Queen was then escorted through the cars to meet her husband, and they disembarked together to greet the crowds that had been waiting since the previous night for a glimpse of the Royal couple. From Bankepore they went to Calcutta ("too European for my taste," Queen Mary wrote Aunt Augusta), and then to Bombay, where the *Medina* was waiting to take them on their homeward journey.

As King George read his farewell speech, he broke down and began to cry. "I simply couldn't help it," he wrote his mother. "It flashed across my mind that I would never see India again and the thought was too much for me."

And en route home from Malta, he wrote her: "What joy that there are only 9 more days before we meet! I shall then feel proud that our historical visit to India has been accomplished, successfully, I hope, & that I have done my duty before God & this great Empire & last but not least, that I have gained the approval of my beloved Motherdear."

King George's relationship to his mother remained that of the obedient and adoring son. He never chastised her for her tardiness or other small foibles. She simply refused to address her letters to him, "to the King," which was proper, and still called him "Georgie." "Characteristically feminine," he remarked of this. In church he could be seen interrupting his own concentration to find the correct page for her in the prayer book. Her mother-in-law's lack of reverence for the Monarch was always a source of great irritation to Queen Mary, but she held her silence.

EIGHTEEN

The Great Coal Strike of 1912 that greeted King George and Queen Mary on their return from India brought industry to an alarming standstill. The miners were demanding a minimum wage of five shillings a day for men and two shillings a day for boys. Negotiations broke down four weeks after the start of the strike, and Prime Minister Asquith, using unprecedented dictatorial powers, forced acceptance of the Minimum Wages Bill over the protests of Parliament. The King gave it his Royal Assent a fortnight later.

Queen Mary took the plight of the miners during this period "very much to heart" and wrote Aunt Augusta: "If only one could act, but like this one feels so impotent, & all this time our blessed & beloved country is in a state of stagnation & misery —Most people seem to go on as if everything were in a normal state, but we feel the whole thing too much to take it lightly."

The sudden revolt of factory workers and miners against disgraceful living conditions, long working hours, and low wages gathered momentum. Rapid social changes were occurring, bringing grave danger to the status quo. Politicians were out of touch with the things that really mattered, but the King and Queen were doing what they could to redress the balance by giving the people greater access to the Monarch. Queen Mary took tea with a miner's wife in South Wales, and together the

Royal couple visited the mines of stricken Yorkshire, the railway works at Crewe, and the potteries of the "five towns" nearby. To a public that could recall the grand, open landaus of Queen Alexandra and King Edward, the human touch of King George and Queen Mary was "a revelation."

Fully aware of the discretion required in the Consort of a constitutional monarch, Queen Mary never revealed her political feelings in public. But she did make them known to her husband, and in the coal-strike crisis she adamantly blamed the Government. "I think you are a little hard on the Gov't," he chided her in a letter. "They have really been doing all they can to find a solution to this most serious state of affairs." She answered on a conciliatory note: "You scold me for blaming the Gov't, well, I do think the unrest is due to their extraordinary tactics in encouraging Socialism all these years & in pandering to the Labour Party; but I do quite agree that Gov't has behaved splendidly the past week in averting what might have been a national disaster."

Her husband quickly wrote to assure her: "I quite understand what you mean when you say you blame the Gov't about the strikes, yes no doubt through their very stupid & unwise speeches last year they have done much to put class against class, but now that the strikes [have] begun you admit they have behaved well, that is what I mean to say."

No sooner had the coal strike been settled than the railways struck. And while all this was going on, the London suffragettes had been conducting a relentless campaign of smashing plate-glass and other windows with hammers concealed in their muffs. Despite her intense feeling about women's rights, Queen Mary could not sympathise with the suffragettes. "Those horrid Suffragettes burnt down the little tea house (modern) close to the Pagoda in Kew Gardens," she wrote Aunt Augusta, adding in a later letter, "There seems no end to their iniquities."

"Can these females not be shut up on some island?" Aunt Augusta asked in reply.

When the King and Queen returned from India, Mr. Hansell was still in charge of the Prince of Wales's education. But with his new status and title, and after four years in Naval College and time at sea, David no longer stood for being ordered about "in quite the same way as before."

Bertie and Harry were both away at school and came back only for the Christmas holidays. John was, of course, living in his cottage with Lala Bill. That left David and Georgie at York Cottage. Although Georgie was eight and a half years his brother's junior, he was surprisingly mature, and the two boys were most compatible. They laughed at the same things, and Georgie, only ten years of age at the time, was intelligent and had an understanding nature. David was able to confide many things to his younger brother that he had not been able to say to anyone else, certainly not to Bertie, to whom he felt more protector than confidant. In the six weeks that they were alone at York Cottage, David and Georgie became close friends.

The two brothers would go together in the evenings up to the Big House to see their grandmother and play patience or do jigsaw puzzles with her. David noted that suddenly she seemed "quite an old lady." Queen Alexandra still retained the delicately chiseled features and the grace of manner that had made her such a beauty in her youth. She did not often leave Sandringham and lived there with her daughter, Toria (who was now more subservient to her mother than ever); her old devoted friend and inseparable companion, Charlotte Knollys; and the elderly Sir Dighton Probyn, V.C., who was her Comptroller. To David, Sir Dighton, "with his white beard flowing over his chest," was a heroic personage for having once led a famous Indian cavalry regiment called *Probyn's Horses* during the Indian mutiny. Old now and dedicated with respectful adoration to "the Beloved Lady," as he affectionately referred to Queen Alexandra, he did not have the same bravura in the field of finance as he had had on the battlefield and was unable to control her extravagant gifts to charities and supplicants.

No more did the Big House light up at Christmas. House parties were a part of the past. Queen Alexandra lived a cloistered life with her three companions and two or three members of her small Court, although she was well cared for by a Household staff of about forty-five persons. Occasionally, she motored to London to visit some of her old friends. But Marlborough House, which she had once so loved, had become depressing to her.

On one of these excursions into London, she went to see Lady Geraldine Somerset, who was now an "intimidating old lady, armed with an enormous ear trumpet edged with a black silk fringe, who lived in a small house on Upper Brook Street, each room of which resembled a tent made of faded photographs." Lady Geraldine, in her eighties and thought to be on her death-bed, managed to raise herself up when Queen Alexandra entered and said loudly, "Go way, Ma'am, I am too old and ugly for you to see me." Queen Alexandra, who was even more hard of hearing than her old friend, misunderstood and, turning to Charlotte Knollys, who had accompanied her, said, "That is *too* much! She said I am too old and too ugly!" and marched angrily out of the room. Charlotte Knollys attempted to make amends with Lady Geraldine and then to assure Queen Alexandra that the old woman had not insulted her. Queen Alexandra refused to believe that she had not heard correctly. Lady Geraldine died a few weeks later, but Queen Alexandra remained so angry that she did not attend the funeral.

While his father was in India, David, with Georgie as specta-tor, would go shooting at Sandringham—a sport David had not shared previously with King George. On January 11, 1912, he wrote the King:

> I love shooting more than anything else, & it was very kind of you to allow me to shoot so much here while you were away. I have had some splendid practise, & feel that my shooting has very much improved. It is the small days that give one far more prac-tise than the big ones. One can take one's time & shoot much better . . .*

The King, who was strict in the handling of firearms, an-swered with a piece of doggerel entitled, "A Father's Advice," which he insisted David memorise.

> If a sportsman true you'd be
> Listen carefully to me;

*The phrase "small days" meant shooting privately on the grounds of San-dringham, and the phrase "big ones," the event of shooting parties.

Never, never let your gun
Pointed be at anyone;
That it might unloaded be
Matters not the least to me.

You may hit or you may miss,
But at all times think of this:
All the game birds ever bred
Won't pay for one man dead.

Forty years later, David could still recite the first and last verses. In the sport of shooting, father and son had a shared interest that would bring them—for a short span of time, at least—closer together after the Royal couple returned from India.

In April, the *Titanic* was sunk with great loss of life. That same month, the introduction of the Home Rule Bill in Parliament moved Ireland precariously close to civil war. Ulster had set up a provisional government under Sir Edward Carson,* and the probability of the Army being drawn in was ever present. Ulster was a hotbed of divided passions. The six Protestant counties were "resolved to resist by force any attempt to coerce them into union with Southern Ireland, and they found many stalwart allies in the British Parliament."

The tension of the long months since their return from India was given a short respite when Queen Mary decided to travel to Strelitz to celebrate Aunt Augusta's ninetieth birthday with her. "I should come incognito & want no fuss whatsoever," she wrote the Grand Duchess, "let it be a visit from a very devoted niece to her very dear aunt. I . . . only hope your answer in your next letter will be 'yes.' "

"Yes! Yes! Yes!" Aunt Augusta wrote back.

Queen Mary disembarked at Neu-strelitz railway station with her fifteen-year-old daughter, Princess Mary, early on an August morning. "Aunt is wonderful, looks rather thinner & is rather deaf but otherwise unaltered," Queen Mary wrote King George. Dressed in black, a black poke bonnet ornamented with a tuft of

*Sir Edward Carson. Lord Carson (1854–1935), Lord of the Appeal in Ordinary, 1921–29.

white feathers and secured with velvet strings beneath her chin, the diminutive elderly woman walked out on a strip of red carpet to greet her niece, who bowed her head to kiss her aunt. There were tears in Queen Mary's eyes, and she was far less controlled at this meeting than her aunt. A film camera recorded the emotional meeting, and one is instantly struck by the queenliness of Aunt Augusta's demeanour, and one thinks of a meeting between Princess May and Queen Victoria so many years before.

Her week in Neu-strelitz was a pleasant interlude for Queen Mary. To her amazement, Aunt Augusta dared a motor ride for the first time and regaled her niece with stories of the family. "Queen and yet May," Aunt Augusta pronounced after her departure. Both feared—because of the older woman's age—this might be the last time they would meet, but neither made the departure a sad affair.

"Next year!" Queen Mary waved to her aunt as she boarded her train for Calais.

"God grant this hope may come true," Aunt Augusta called back.

Strelitz was, of course, in Germany, and though King George and Queen Mary did not share King Edward and Queen Alexandra's great animosity to Kaiser Wilhelm, his country now threatened the peace of Europe. The Foreign Secretary, Sir Edward Grey, tried to dissuade the King and Queen from travelling there, fearing that France and Russia could take such a trip as a formal affirmation of Britain's friendship with Germany. The guns of war were already cocked. The Balkans were in bloody combat. The King of Greece—Queen Alexandra's brother—was assassinated at Salonica in March of 1913, and the following month a failed attempt was made on the life of the Kaiser and of the Grand Duke of Baden. But the King and Queen could not be made to refuse an invitation to the wedding of Kaiser Wilhelm's daughter, Victoria Louise, to their cousin, Ernest, Duke of Brunswick-Luneburg, who was Queen Alexandra's nephew.* Aunt Augusta was not well enough to travel to the wedding, even though the distance was not great, so plans were made for King George and Queen Mary to visit with her briefly on their way home.

*King George I of Greece, son of Princess Thyra of Denmark.

Although the trip to Berlin was not a state visit, Kaiser Wilhelm arranged a grand display of pomp and ceremony to greet the King and Queen of England appropriately. Despite their dislike of Wilhelm, Tsar Nicholas and the Empress Alexandra came to the wedding, as did all the other Royal cousins and aunts and uncles then reigning in foreign lands.

The highlight of the wedding was the *Fackeltanz,* an historic dance performed solely at German royal weddings. Only Royal Highnesses could take part in it, while everyone else (1,200 people in this instance) stood watching. The bride began the dance by making a low curtsy to her father, the Kaiser, and then, preceded by pages bearing lighted candles in glowing silver candelabra, they danced in a circle around the entire ballroom. The bride curtsied and danced with King George, then the Tsar, and so on until she had danced with all the visiting Kings and Royal Princes as well.

None of the Royalties gathered for this *Götterdämmerung* of the kings and queens of Europe realised that this was to be the last assemblage of the "royal mob." Within five years, all except the King and Queen of England would be assassinated, deposed, exiled, "or living in impoverished retirement." But for this one week in May, the countryside of Germany never more lavish with bloom, they gorged themselves at "Willy's" colossal banquets and were treated daily to his great military parades.

On the twenty-seventh, the Kaiser and the King motored down to Potsdam to review the garrison. Queen Mary and the Empress Augusta Victoria [Wilhelm's Consort] followed with their suites. Sir Frederick Ponsonby, who had accompanied the King and Queen to Berlin and was included in this parade, was amazed to find that the only two wearing British uniforms on the field were Kaiser Wilhelm, in an English field marshal's uniform, and himself. (King George wore a German uniform for the occasion.)

"I had some talk with the Emperor on the subject of aeroplanes and dirigibles," Ponsonby reports, "which he said would undoubtedly play a great part in future warfare. The King and the Emperor then rode out, followed by [General] Loewenfeldt and myself. We came straight to the parade ground . . . It was a magnificent sight, and of course we saw the pick of the German Army.

"The Emperor left his place with the King and went past the head of the Guards. The way he managed his horse was certainly wonderful. His left arm was a deformity and absolutely powerless. Usually when he rode he held the reins in his right hand. When he rode past, however, it was necessary for him to hold a sword in his right hand and the reins in his left. The horse was therefore practically left to itself . . . He [Kaiser Wilhelm] saluted with a magnificent sweep of the sword and then cantered slowly around to join the King."

Queen Mary, who feared horses, could not but wonder at the courage it took for the Kaiser to trust his life so casually to one. However, the Kaiser's horse had been trained in this manoeuvre every morning for three months. Ponsonby said of the magnificent animal he was given that it was "more like a motor-car than a horse. It was so perfectly trained that by touching the reins you could make it do anything." The Kaiser's horse had to work independently, with no guiding hand whatsoever.

The young woman who once said, "Imagine me in the place of honour beside William," though Queen of England, was still impressed by her husband's cousin and flattered by his lavish gifts and floral offerings. The truth was that Queen Mary found Kaiser Wilhelm an exciting and stimulating man.

Queen Mary's appearance at the wedding service was perhaps the most splendid she had yet achieved. "A lady [in attendance there] told me, she never saw anything like your magnificent Dresses and Diamonds, and your regal appearance, the Wedding toilette surpassing all!" Aunt Augusta wrote. And dazzling she must have been in a gown of India cloth-of-gold, embroidered with a woven design of flowers in gold. On her head was the tiara she had worn to the Durbar—this time exchanging the emerald drops for pearls. For necklaces, she wore a diamond collar and Queen Victoria's diamond necklace beneath this with the Star of Africa as a pendant. Her corsage of white flowers— sent to her by the Kaiser—was decorated with diamond bows, pearl drops, and the "smaller South African pendant," which was approximately thirty-three carats.

By December 1913, rumbles of war had spread across the whole of Europe, but in England they were silenced by the Irish question, which, for the British, completely overshadowed everything else that year. "King George was fully prepared," Harold Nicolson reports, "if such were the desire of the two nations, that Home Rule should be accorded the Irish. He believed that, if the problems were handled with tact and generosity, Ireland would become a friendly and contented Dominion, cooperating with other Dominions in joint allegiance to the Crown. What he dreaded was the tension between the Roman Catholics and the Protestants in Ireland . . . might cause lasting damage to our Parliamentary tradition, involve the Crown in an odious constitutional dilemma and, at a time of serious international disorder, weaken the country by internal dissension and even expose it to the disaster of civil war."

Lengthy memoranda made their way between King George and Prime Minister Asquith. Gravely fearing civil war, the King wrote the Prime Minister in September, ". . . it behooves us all to withhold no efforts to avert those threatening events which would inevitably outrage humanity and lower the British name in the mind of the whole civilised world."

Queen Mary was already suffering great humiliation on the Irish question. She and the King were planning a trip to Paris that next spring, and she confessed to Aunt Augusta, "How I hate having to go there when matters are so unsettled here; especially as one feels so acutely how England has fallen in prestige abroad. I really feel so ashamed I shld prefer to hide— certainly not to have to smile & make oneself agreeable when one's heart is not in it, for then nobody gives one the credit for having a heart or feeling things in these days—It seems to me that '*finesse*' has gone out of the world, that indescribable something which, was *born* in one & which was inherited thro' generations."

The Christmas holidays spent at Sandringham, as always, brought the Royal Family a short surcease from their troubles, although Bertie's absence was sorely felt. Bertie had received his appointment as a midshipman, "the lowest form of Marine life,"* on September 15 and was attached to the 19,250-ton

---

*The midshipman no longer exists in the Navy, having been abolished in the Admiralty education reforms of 1954, when the age entry into the Royal Navy

battleship H.M.S. *Collingwood.* On October 28, H.M.S. *Collingwood,* with the First Battle Squadron, sailed from Devonport to join in manoeuvres in the Mediterranean, and later to cruise in Egyptian and Aegean waters. While at sea, Bertie celebrated his eighteenth birthday.

"My 18th birthday & I'm allowed to smoke," he wrote in his diary. In recognition of this new emancipation, his mother had sent him a cigarette case, which Bertie received when his ship docked at Toulon. On Christmas Day, H.M.S. *Collingwood* rode at anchor in Gibraltar Harbour.

Bertie did not share his father's great love for the sea. He even disliked yachting. Like his mother, he fought "a continual battle against seasickness." Nonetheless, Bertie was certain that he would make a career as a naval officer.* Wheeler-Bennett states that "his ultimate ambition at this stage of his life was to have his own independent command and to rise, as his father had done, to the rank of Captain on the active list."

What Bertie enjoyed most about the Navy was the feeling of camaraderie that existed between his contemporaries and himself. He was known as "Mr. Johnson" for practical reasons (although everyone knew he was Prince Albert), and he was given not even the slightest privilege. He shared the flat outside the gunroom with fifteen other young sailors, stored his clothes in a sea chest and slept in a hammock slung above it, and stowed away in the morning. Nowhere could he be alone. He stood

---

was raised to eighteen years. The term Naval Cadet was also abolished at this time, and students at the Royal Naval College were known as midshipmen.

*Prince Albert held the following Royal Naval ranks:
  Naval Cadet—1909–1913
  Midshipman—September 15, 1913
  Acting Sub-Lieutenant—September 15, 1915
  Sub-Lieutenant—May 15, 1916
  Lieutenant—June 15, 1916
  Commander—December 31, 1920
  Captain—June 30, 1925
  Rear-Admiral—June 3, 1932
  Vice-Admiral—January 1, 1936
  Admiral—January 21, 1936
  Admiral of the Fleet—December 11, 1936

watch, toiled in the coal-black hold of a dirty collier, and ate bread and cheese and onions and beer along with his mates. He was treated with rigid discipline by his superiors; the junior sub-lieutenant whom he trailed after when off duty became "a bloody tyrant" without complaint on his part. This masochistic tendency—which David shared—followed both brothers into their middle years.

Since David had confessed liking shooting to his father, King George had included him that Christmas in what he called "small days" at Sandringham—where they would shoot together in the coverts and heathland and the marshes on the shore of the wash. Each spot had its name—Wain Hill, Cat's Bottom, Folly Hang, Ugly Dale—and these days spent together were to be the fondest memories David had of his father. He was not able to discuss anything of a personal nature with him, but a closeness formed in the sharing of the intricacies of the sport. The invitation to accompany his father to Hall Barn in Buckinghamshire, the home of Lord Burnham (proprietor of the *Daily Telegraph*), on December 18 was the first big shoot that David attended. This was a sumptuous affair with close to a hundred hunters engaged to drive or flush the birds toward the group. A day's bag of two thousand head was not uncommon.

"We were six hours in the field," David was later to recall, "and the show of birds was fantastic. My father was deadly that day and used three guns. He had an individual, stylized way of shooting—left arm extended straight along the barrel, both eyes open. An onlooker reported that at one stand he saw my father bring down thirty-nine pheasants before missing one. Young and unused to firing so many shells, as I was, my left arm ached from lifting my gun, my shoulder from the recoil, and I was deaf and stunned from the banging . . . When in the late afternoon the carnage stopped, almost 4,000 pheasants had been killed. The bright, limp carcasses were laid out in rows of 100; the whole place was littered with feathers and empty shells. My father had shot over 1,000 birds; I had even passed the 300 mark. He was proud of the way he had shot that day, but I think that the scale of the bag troubled even his conscience; for . . . he remarked, 'Perhaps we went a little too far today, David.' "

On a shoot, King George "was in his element." Stimulated by

the bracing air and hard exercise and on the alert for a flushed bird, he would put aside the cares of state. He would also laugh and joke, and David was thus to see a lighter side of his father. Killing on the scale of Lord Burnham's shoot, however, was intensely distasteful to the young man, who deemed it senseless. His father must have sensed his displeasure. He did not include him on many other shoots, and the intimacy shared on "small days" was quickly to become only memory. Too soon father and son would be parted by a war for which neither they nor their country was prepared.

In April 1914, Queen Mary and King George departed London for their long-planned state journey to Paris.* "Of course I wanted to go to Vienna first but Sir Edward Grey will not hear of it!" Queen Mary wrote Aunt Augusta. The Paris trip had been set in motion by Sir Edward Grey shortly after the wedding of the Kaiser's daughter, to assure French President Poincaré and the French people that England's sympathies would not be with Germany in case of a war between the countries. Unless, of course, the neutrality of Belgium was violated by the French.

The King and Queen of England's visit to Paris in April could well have been one of the major events that was propelling Germany, and therefore all of Europe, into a war. It came at the time that England had begun Naval talks with Russia, and Germany feared being encircled by Russia and France. Russia would not be a sophisticated enemy, but she did have overwhelming numbers of men to serve in her Army. Combining that force with England's Navy was a formidable threat. Germany's work on the widening of the Kiel Canal, permitting her new dreadnoughts direct access from the North Sea to the Baltic, was greatly accelerated. By June 1, the Kiel Canal was completed,

---

*Their Majesties' suite consisted of Sir Frederick Ponsonby, Lady Desborough (Lady-in-Waiting), Lord Charles Nairne, Equerry to King George V (killed in action October 1914), the Duchess of Devonshire (Mistress of the Robes), Sir Edward Grey (Minister in Attendance), Lord Shaftesbury (Lord Chamberlain to the Queen), Lord Annaly (Lord-in-Waiting), Lord Stamfordham (Private Secretary), James Reid (Groom-in-Waiting; later Major General, the Hon. Sir William Lambton), Charles Fitzmaurice (Equerry), and the future Lord Tyrell (Private Secretary to Sir Edward Grey).

and German Field Marshal Moltke said to Baron Eckhardstein, "We are ready, and the sooner the better for us."

France and Britain were also sharpening their readiness. Working jointly by the time of the King and Queen's trip to Paris in April, the French and British General Staffs were completed. The number of French railroad cars to be allocated, the assignments of interpreters, the preparation of codes and ciphers, and the forage of horses as well were expected to be completed by July.

As Queen Mary boarded the Royal train from Victoria Station to Paris, the intimidating prospect of a visit to a foreign land with no Court, no relatives, and no Royal protocol was far more worrying to her than the threat and machinations of countries revving up for war. The trip, as Pope-Hennessy says, was "a venture into the unknown . . ." She need not have worried. The Royal couple's arrival in France was greeted with great enthusiasm and as "a reassuring symbol of the Entente Cordiale." The Queen entered Paris in an open carriage, seated beside a decidedly dowdy Mme. Poincaré, and the crowds in the streets went wild at the grand sight of a queen gowned in luxurious pale blue *crepe de soie*, a hat piled up with bluish-white ostrich plumes that made her appear at least a foot taller than the President's wife, and around her throat ropes and ropes of magnificent pearls that gleamed with light in the warm spring sun.

Wherever the King and Queen went, there were crowds "milling round the carriage" . . . "Wonderful reception & crowds of people" . . . "Crowds in the street in spite of late hour" . . . "Crowds in the streets both going & coming," Queen Mary wrote in her diary. And she adds that all this enthusiasm "shows that the French people wish to be on good terms with us."

However much the reports of their grand success in Paris might have delighted Aunt Augusta (who wrote her niece a glowing letter), Kaiser Wilhelm was considerably less pleased.

NINETEEN

I n 1914, at the age of eighty-four, Emperor Franz Joseph had ruled Austria for sixty-six years. His wife, the beautiful Empress Elisabeth, had been struck down by an assassin's knife in Geneva. His only son—the brooding, possibly mad Crown Prince Rudolf—had been a victim of a double-suicide pact at Mayerling. His brother, Maximilian, Emperor of Mexico, had been executed at Juarez's order before a firing squad on a Mexican hillside. And his great-nephew and heir, Archduke Franz Ferdinand, had married a commoner, invalidating their three children's right to succession. The old gentleman had survived these tragedies with great dignity, and Queen Mary felt a warmth and an admiration for him.*

Shortly after their return from Berlin and the wedding of Kaiser Wilhelm's daughter, Princess Victoria Louise, in 1913, King George and Queen Mary were hosts at Windsor to Archduke Franz Ferdinand and his wife, Sophie Chotek, now the Duchess of Hohenberg. On public occasions in Austria, Sophie Chotek's morganatic status placed her in the humiliating posi-

---

*Emperor Franz Joseph (1830–1916); Empress Elisabeth (1837–1898) assassinated in Geneva by an Italian anarchist; Crown Prince Rudolf (1858–1889) committed suicide with his mistress, Maria Vetsera, at Mayerling, near Vienna; Emperor Maximilian (1832–1867).

tion of having "to walk behind the least important ladies of royal blood and to sit at a distant end of the Imperial table." These insults were intolerable to both Sophie and the Archduke, and since nothing could be done about them at his own Court, Franz Ferdinand would generally demand archducal honours for his wife when abroad. To the King and Queen's great relief, this did not occur in England.

Indeed, the five-day visit of the Archduke and his wife was a pleasant and nostalgic one, filled for the two Royal couples with an exchange of memories of the recent wedding, their meeting in Madrid at the wedding of Queen Ena and King Alfonso XIII several years earlier, and the visit King George and Queen Mary had made to the Austrian Court when Prince and Princess of Wales.

Recently, Franz Ferdinand had been intent on transforming the dual Austro-Hungarian Empire into a triple monarchy to include the Austrian, Magyar, and Slavic kingdoms under Croatian leadership. These efforts had gained him the enmity of Serbia and Germany, as well as that of his own Austrian ministers and their Magyar counterparts who did not want to share their power. Franz Ferdinand would not be deterred from his objective. Directly after his stay at Windsor, he became Inspector General of the Austro-Hungarian Armies. One of his first ceremonial visits was to be to the provincial capital of Sarajevo. Aiming toward better relations, he requested that no troops line his and Sophie's path through the city. The streets of Sarajevo were thus manned by only 150 local policemen.

The Archduke was dressed in his green Austrian field marshal's uniform, ostrich feathers attached to his military hat. Sophie rode beside him in the open backseat of the second car of a motorcade. A blazing June sun beat down on them. Sarajevo's streets were brightly decorated with flags and banners and portraits of the Austrian Heir to the Throne. The Archduke was certain his gesture of friendship had been a success. Then, suddenly, as the motorcade approached the city hall, a bomb was hurled from the crowd. The chauffeur saw the object coming toward them, accelerated the car's speed, and the bomb hit the vehicle behind them, wounding two officers. The welcome at Sarajevo's city hall was now filled with tension. A second assassination attempt was feared, and Franz Ferdinand's return route was changed. Ironically, the driver of the lead vehicle became confused and turned into a street on the original route, and the Archduke's chauffeur followed. "Not that way, you fool!" shouted the governor from the front seat of the car. But his warning came too late. Two pistol shots were sounded not five feet from them.* Although mortally wounded in the neck, Franz Ferdinand managed to cry: "Sophie! Sophie! Don't die! Stay alive for our children!" Sophie was already dead. Fifteen minutes later, the Archduke muttered his last words, "It is nothing."

King George and Queen Mary received the tragic news late that same afternoon. "Terrible shock for the dear old Emperor," King George wrote in his diary without any awareness that the dual assassinations might prove to be the "match of fate which would set Europe ablaze." Nor, for that matter, did Queen Mary have any presentiments. "The horrible tragedy to the poor Archduke and his wife came as a great shock to us," she wrote Aunt Augusta on the fifth of July, "particularly as they had been our guests so very recently and we were really quite attached to them both. Poor Emperor, nothing is he spared . . . I think it is a great blessing that husband & wife died together, making the future less complicated with regard to their children . . ."†

The murders at Sarajevo began a rush of events that led tragically toward war. On July 5, Germany offered Austria its support if any punitive action taken against Serbia should bring Russia to the Serbs' defense. Strengthened by the Kaiser's declaration, Austria delivered an ultimatum to Serbia on July 23. In England, for the first time in over a year, the Home Rule crisis was put aside. Europe was on the verge of war. Queen Mary's entry in her diary for July 28 reads: "Austria has declared war against Serbia!" And to Aunt Augusta that same day, she wrote, "God grant we may not have a European War thrust upon us, & for such a stupid reason too, no I don't mean stupid, but to have to go to war on account of tiresome Serbia beggars belief!"

*The shots were fired by a nineteen-year-old assassin, Gavrilo Princip.

†When Emperor Franz Joseph died in 1916, he was succeeded by a grand-nephew, Karl I (1870–1922). Two years later, Austria became a republic.

271

All eyes were on Russia, for unless she moved, the war might still remain a Balkan affair. Apparently with the hope that Germany need not be involved, Kaiser Wilhelm telegraphed the Tsar on July 28:

> It is with the gravest concern that I hear of the impression which the action of Austria against Serbia is creating in your country. The unscrupulous agitation that has been going on in Serbia for years has resulted in the outrageous crime to which Archduke Ferdinand fell victim. You will doubtless agree with me that we both, you and I, have a common interest as well as all Sovereigns, to insist that all the persons morally responsible for this dastardly murder should receive their deserved punishment. In this politics play no part at all.
>
> On the other hand, I fully understand how difficult it is for you and your government to face the cry of public opinion.
>
> Therefore, with regard to the hearty and tender friendship which binds us both from long ago with firm ties, I am exerting my utmost influence to induce the Austrians to deal straightly to arrive at a satisfactory understanding with you. I confidently hope you will help me in my efforts to smooth over difficulties that may still arise. Your very sincere and devoted friend and cousin.
>
> Willy

And in a telegram that crossed the Kaiser's, the Tsar begged his German cousin "to try and avoid such a calamity as a European War. I beg you in the name of our old friendship to do what you can to stop your allies from going too far. Nicky."

On July 29, Austria bombarded Belgrade, and to the Kaiser's fury and the consternation of Serbia's allies, Russia mobilised along her Austrian frontier. King George's entry in his diary for that day reads: "Where will it end? . . . Winston Churchill [First Lord of the Admiralty] came to see me, the Navy is all ready for war, but please God it will not come. These are anxious days for me to live in." And on July 30: "Foreign telegrams coming in all day we are doing all we can for peace and to prevent a European War but things look very black . . . the debate in H[ouse] of C[ommons] on Irish question today has been postponed on account of gravity of European situation."

272

Following his meeting with King George, Churchill ordered the First Fleet to move by night from Portland to its new stations at Scapa and Rosyth. "Everything tends towards catastrophe & collapse," he wrote his wife, Clementine. "I am interested, geared up & happy. Is it not horrible to be built like that? The preparations have a hideous fascination for me. I pray to God to forgive me for such fearful moods of levity. Yet I wd do my best for peace & nothing would induce me wrongfully to strike the blow."

The next day an ultimatum was issued to Russia by Germany to "demobilise within twelve hours and make us a distinct declaration to that effect."

Prime Minister Asquith had a special audience with the King to inform him of the gravity of the situation. Nothing was likely to stop the eventuality of world war. Lloyd George recorded that "the Kaiser, frightened by the thunder clouds, intervened personally with the Czar to avert war, he begged 'Nicky' to cancel his Decree which had already gone forth, for the mobilisation of the Russian army. The Czar was willing to accede to this not unreasonable request, but the army leaders assured him that the 'technical' difficulties of cancellation and even partial mobilisation were insuperable. It was thus that the military chiefs in the leading countries of the Continent thrust the nations into war, whilst their impotent statesmen [and sovereigns] were still fumbling for Peace." In fact, at 12:30 A.M. on July 31, Prime Minister Asquith returned to Buckingham Palace and awakened the King. "I got up and saw him in the Audience Room," the King recorded in his diary later that night, "and he showed me a draft of a telegram he wanted me to send to Nicky as a last resort to try to prevent War, which, of course, I did."

King George also telegraphed the Kaiser a guarded appeal the same day:

I cannot help thinking that some misunderstanding has produced this deadlock. I am most anxious not to miss any possibility of avoiding the terrible calamity which at present threatens the whole world. I, therefore, make a personal appeal to you to remove the misapprehension about Russian mobilisation which I feel must have occurred, and to leave still open grounds for negotiation and possible peace. If you think that I can in any way contribute to that all-important purpose, I will do everything in my power to assist in reopening the interrupted conversations between the Powers concerned. I feel confident that you are as anxious as I am that all that is possible should be done to secure the peace of the world.

George.

And, on the thirtieth of July, M. Jules Cambon, French Ambassador in Berlin, had telegraphed President Poincaré: "Germans are quite hopeful as to successful issue of their fight against France and Russia, if these are unsupported. Nothing but the chance of English intervention affects the Emperor, his Government or German interests."

France had immediately appealed to the King to stand up to the Germans and pledge his support to France and Russia. But the Government had not made up its mind about England's intervention, and King George could do no more than attempt to appeal to his cousin Willy's conscience. The Kaiser's reply was to declare war on Russia the very evening he received King George's plea for peace.

"Saw Sir Edward Grey. Germany declared War on Russia at 7:30 this evening and German Ambassador left Petersburg," King George wrote in his diary later that night. "Whether we shall be dragged into it God only knows, but we shall not send Expeditionary Force of the Army now. France is begging us to come to their assistance. At this moment public opinion here is dead against our joining in the War but I think it will be impossible to keep out of it as we cannot allow France to be smashed." On August 2, he wrote grimly: "We issued orders to mobilise the fleet last night . . . "

A German observer of this period was to say: "We must prove to Russia the superiority of our culture and of our military might. We must force France onto her knees until she chokes . . . but between Russia and Germany there are no insoluble problems. France, too, fights chiefly for honour's sake. It is from England we must wring the uttermost price for this gigantic

274

struggle, however dearly others may have to pay for the help they give her."*

The Kaiser would not have thrown his country into a war against France and Russia for the sole purpose of forcing England's hand. He would have much preferred *both* England and Russia to remain neutral. But once Russia had mobilised, he could not turn back. His deep sense of hostility toward his English relations—that had begun with Edward's cool attitude—came fully to the surface.

Inside Buckingham Palace during the last days of July and the first days of August, the anguish was great. In the event that England would have to go to war—a probability that grew more threatening with the passage of each hour—Bertie, as a Naval officer, would most likely be in the thick of it. All their foreign relations' lives and thrones would be endangered. Three cousins reigned as sovereigns of three warring nations. The war that would take millions of young lives (at this stage) resembled a family feud. Within a shockingly short time, several dozen Royal relatives, who for generations had lived in harmony, would be forced to take sides against each other. In the Royal Family's private rooms at Buckingham Palace, family conferences were many, and these personal concerns brought even more tension to King George and Queen Mary's mounting fears for their country and their people.

Outside the palace, beneath summer showers and in a warm but persistent wind, crowds had begun to gather on July 31 and had stood since then "collecting, dispersing, and reforming, filling the great rooms with their tumultuous sounds." David watched them from his bedroom window. He called them "friendly, patient, hopeful, and patriotic . . . people . . . of good conscience."

Each day the crowds continued to grow, extending from Trafalgar Square, where they formed a dense mass, right along to the House of Commons, where their greatest number gathered about Downing Street, opposite the War Office. Groups of young men passed along in taxicabs singing the "Marseillaise,"

Hamburger Nachricten.

and hundreds of Union Jacks were waved all over London. The greatest throngs gathered at Buckingham Palace.

At half-past ten on the night of August 4, Germany declared war on England. "A Privy Council was at once summoned for Papa to sign our declaration of War," David wrote in his diary for that night, "& as soon as this was known in the crowd outside, excitement became intense. Then amid an unparalleled demonstration of patriotism the parents showed themselves at 11:00 before going to bed. But the people remained singing, cheering, and whistling for another 3 hours & I was lulled to sleep by their fearful shindy at 1:30. The die is cast; may God protect the Fleet!!!"

"I held a Council at 10:45 [P.M.] to declare War with Germany," King George recorded that night. "It is a terrible catastrophe but it is not our fault . . . When they [the crowds outside the palace] heard that War had been declared the [ir] excitement increased & it was a never to be forgotten sight when May & I with David went on the balcony. The cheering was terrific. Please God it may soon be over & that He will protect dear Bertie's life."

One month after England went to war, and H.M.S. *Collingwood,* Bertie's ship, to sea patrolling the coasts of Britain, the young seaman was doubled with pain and suffering extreme nausea. Appendicitis was diagnosed, and Bertie was transferred to the hospital ship *Rohilla,* then to the Northern Nursing Home in Aberdeen. On September 9, surgery was performed by Professor John Marnoch of Aberdeen University in the presence of Sir John Reid. The removal of his appendix did not cure Bertie's severe stomach and gastric problems, however,* and he was to be benched from active duty—to his great sense of guilt—for nearly one year.

"Looking into some magic mirror, a modern Cagliostro might easily be dumbfounded at the highly civilised European nations slaughtering their first-born and trampling on the Ark of their historic Covenant," Esher wrote in his journal on August 11. "Millions of splendid youths, the heirs of European ages, will go

_____

*An ulcer was suspected but never diagnosed.

childless to their graves. Monuments of chivalry, of learning, of religious enthusiasm will be burnt, broken and destroyed. And the yellow races will gather strength . . . "

The news reached Britain on the evening of August 5 that the Germans had begun their assault on Liège, "the portcullis guarding the gateway into Belgium from Germany." The first brutal battle of the war had begun. With this reality greeting them on the front pages of England's newspapers, the grey morning of August 6, Britain's young patriots exchanged their indignation and belligerence over the Irish crisis for their respect for the small country of Belgium—for she had put up a valiant resistance. A Belgian officer had reported that the German infantry had come on "line after line, almost shoulder to shoulder, until as we shot them down, the fallen were heaped on top of each other in an awful barricade of dead and wounded that threatened to mask our guns and cause us trouble. So high did the barricade become that we did not know whether to fire through it or to go out and clear openings with our hands . . . But would you believe it? the veritable wall of dead and dying enabled those wonderful Germans to creep closer, and actually to charge up the glacis. They got no farther than halfway because our machine guns and rifles swept them back. Of course, we had our losses but they were slight compared to the carnage we inflicted on our enemies."

Ponsonby had said on hearing of England's declaration of war that he found it "thrilling." Recruiting stations were mobbed, and twenty-four hours later not enough uniforms remained in the British Army stores to clothe the new enlistees. Since he was in the reserves, Ponsonby reported for duty. He had to wear the same khaki he had worn in the South Africa War, which was much lighter in colour than current order. He was given a company of "200 splendid men and many, too many, officers, and was told to begin training them. It was," he said, "the blind leading the blind . . . "

David's Army commission was signed by his father. He was gazetted to the Grenadier Guards and detailed to the King's Company, a special honour. Since he was seven inches short of the minimum height of six feet that was required for men of this company, he thought of himself as "a pygmy among giants." By

277

mid-September his battalion was sent overseas, and he was left behind to be transferred to the Third Battalion, which was stationed at the same barracks. His pride hurt, he went to see his father, who could tell him only that Lord Kitchener, the new Secretary for War, did not want him to go to France just then. Mustering all his courage, David secured an interview with Lord Kitchener. "What does it matter if I am killed?" David pleaded. "I have four brothers."

The immense, fierce-looking Kitchener looked down his patrician nose at the young man who by birth and law would one day be King. His steely-blue eyes met David's upturned earnest stare and he replied, "If I were sure you would be killed, I do not know if I should be right to restrain you. But I cannot take the chance, which always exists until we have a settled line, of the enemy taking you prisoner."

David was assigned to West End duties and put on King's Guard (the men who take part in the guard-mounting ceremony in the forecourt of Buckingham Palace when the King is in London and in Friary Court, St. James's Palace, when he is away). David's job was to carry the colour, "a good weight!" David noted. Ten years before, he and Bertie had thrilled to this ceremony when they had watched it from the garden wall of Marlborough House. But by this time, "the British Expeditionary Force had been fighting for its life in France and Belgium, the German rush on Paris had been halted at the Battle of the Marne and retreating divisions had turned about and advanced northward across the Aisne and the Somme to Ypres." With such awesome events taking place, the fulfillment of a childhood dream to one day be part of the handsome, glamourous King's Guard had lost its meaning.

Casualty lists began to appear within four weeks of the war's start, and on them were the names of many of David and Bertie's school friends and brother officers. David's equerry, Major William Cadogan, was killed with the 10th Hussars; and their cousin, Queen Ena's youngest brother, Prince Maurice of Battenberg, as well as two of King George's equerries, lost their lives in the first few months of the war. "I shan't have a friend left soon," David wrote in his diary at the end of October.

Yet David, along with millions of Englishmen and -women, felt a certain nobility about the war and a pride in the manner of death of so many idealistic young men who rushed off to battle, believing (as H. G. Wells announced in the press on August 4) that the defeat of Germany might "open the way to disarmament and peace throughout the world."

When the Battle of the Marne ended in a German retreat on the ninth of September, most of England believed the war would end by Christmas, but the tragedy of the Marne was that the Allies had not gained a decisive victory. The war and its death toll ground on. The upper classes still tended to look upon the war "as a sort of picnic, chequered by untoward incident," Lord Esher noted, adding that he thought there would be a "rude awakening" if, as Lord Kitchener believed, the war should go on for at least three years. The general view, especially following the Battle of the Marne, was that it would be short and never fought on home ground.

Queen Mary was now a wartime Queen, and she quickly took on the role expected of her with more than her usual drive and energy. Less than one month after the war's start, the effects upon those at home were evident. Her country's needs were great, and Queen Mary filled her days with visits to hospitals—often as many as three or four in one afternoon—munitions factories, and soup kitchens. Lady Airlie was Lady-in-Waiting to the Queen during much of 1914. "Very few people suspected how great an ordeal her hospital visits were to her," she later wrote. "She had always been so affected at the sight of suffering that even as a child she once fainted when a footman at White Lodge cut his finger badly. But . . . she trained herself to talk calmly to frightfully mutilated and disfigured men. Her habit of self-discipline gave her complete physical control."

During her youth, Queen Mary had learned how to veil fear, grief, or anxiety behind the smile that is always exacted of Royalty. She was terrified of guns, and any loud noise—even a peal of thunder—had an abnormal effect on her. A "Royal salute of 101 guns was sheer misery to her," yet she endured it with a smiling face.

*   *   *

279

By Christmas on the Western Front alone, 95,654 British soldiers had been killed, and the injured list was treble this. The war would not be a short one. In January 1915, the zeppelin raids began and soon became a reality of London life, their victims now added to the injured whom Queen Mary visited at hospitals. A protective wire-mesh net was stretched across the top of Buckingham Palace, and air-raid precaution rules were put into effect. Despite such restrictions and her terror at the crash of falling bombs, the Queen would go out with the King on the balcony at Buckingham Palace during these raids.

With the advent of the war, Alice Keppel had returned to London from her travels with her daughters, while George Keppel, now a captain, was serving with his battalion in France. During the summer of 1915, Alice, still much admired by England's great men, opened her house twice a week at luncheon time to her country's most famous politicians, service chiefs, diplomats, war heroes home on leave, war correspondents, and such of her women friends as were available to amuse them. Prime Minister Asquith, Winston Churchill, and even his mother Jenny found their way to Alice's salon. Queen Mary never approved of Mrs. Keppel's lavish luncheons and grand afternoons at a time when the palace was advocating great austerity. The intellectuals whom Alice gathered at the two tables in her dining room (she always hosted the larger one where the most honoured guests would also be seated) found these luncheons a reassuring continuum of the old order of things.

At Buckingham Palace, however, the King's order, issued in the first weeks of the war, was that there should be strict rationing of all food. Menus were cut to three courses, and nothing was to be cooked with wine or sherry, and no wine was to be served with Royal meals. Alcohol, King George had decided, was not consistent with emergency measures for winning a war. The then-current Royal chef, M. Cerard (M. Menager having returned to France) sent the Queen a note asking what *was* to be served at mealtimes. Her reply, in her own hand, came back promptly: "Serve water boiled with a little sugar in dining-room." Queen Mary also issued an order that meat—which was not scarce in the early stages of the war —was to be served no more than three times a week, both to the Royal Family and to the Household staff of several hundred.

Queen Mary—who had never liked a large breakfast herself and had always been critical of the eight-course breakfasts served in Edward's reign—exercised her greatest economies on that meal. Shortly after the Battle of the Marne, she sent down a message to M. Cerard that under no circumstances was anyone in the Household, guest or servant, to have more than two courses at breakfast. A variety of dishes—eggs, bacon, sausages, kippers, and other fish—was served, but the Queen made sure her two-course rule was observed. Only enough of each to equal two portions a person was to be prepared. Her breakfast order for the seven members of the Royal Family,* Monday, September 4, 1914, was as follows: "Bacon for five, sausage for four, fish for two, eggs for three," making fourteen portions, two each. This arbitrary selection caused much confusion, since it meant someone was bound to be left with a dish he or she did not like. One look from Queen Mary, however, was enough to silence any complaints.

Gabriel Tschumi, M. Cerard's assistant at that time, wrote in his memoir, "Queen Mary was always first down in the mornings, and she knew at a glance whether her orders had been followed. To disregard them, even for the most pitiful plea of hunger, was likely to result in dismissal, so we were pledged to carry them out. Prince Henry, the Duke of Gloucester [Harry], was the only one who ever put up a successful revolt against the two-course rule for breakfast. He claimed that for health reasons it was essential he had two fried eggs and bacon for breakfast even if he was allowed nothing else, and his arguments were so convincing that Queen Mary relented. An extra fried egg was included on the breakfast order from then onwards, but though other members of the family tried to gain the same privilege they did not succeed."

None of Queen Mary's economy measures worked with her mother-in-law, however. Early in the war, Queen Alexandra retired almost entirely to Sandringham. She did not allow this to curb her extravagance. King Edward's widow had been given

---

*At that time, the King and Queen, David, Bertie, Mary, Harry, and Georgie were in residence at Buckingham Palace.

a Parliamentary Annuity, which was in no way commensurate with her spending habits. Both her son and daughter-in-law were alarmed at the "hundreds and thousands of pounds" she was spending on various war charities. By the summer of 1915, her gifts were vastly in excess of her annual income.

Queen Mary suggested to her that she might save money and labour by ordering fewer cut flowers, to which Queen Alexandra curtly replied, "I *like* a lot of lovely flowers about the house and in my rooms."

And, "If I get into debt *they* can pay," she told an old friend of King Edward's, Arthur Davidson.

"*Who* will pay, Ma'am?" he countered. "Certainly not the nation for they won't pay a penny." Queen Alexandra sweetly answered that her deafness had kept her from hearing a word he had said.

In her seventies now, in physical and mental decline, "Motherdear" was more difficult than ever, and Queen Mary—her main efforts directed toward the war—greatly resented having to cope with her mother-in-law's ineptitude.

TWENTY

Among the members of the Royal Family, Queen Alexandra's anti-German feeling was the strongest, and with every new report of German atrocities her hatred grew. Her letters, with abusive epithets toward both Germany and the Kaiser, arrived with alarming frequency at Buckingham Palace and were answered with extraordinary filial patience by her son. Queen Alexandra had relations fighting on both sides. Her sister Thyra had married the Crown Prince of Hanover, Prince Ernst August, and their son was with the German Army. The majority of her close blood relatives were British, Russian, or aligned with the Allied cause. On the other hand, Queen Mary and King George each had many blood relatives on both sides, and their own backgrounds were Germanic. Queen Mary was, after all, Mary of Teck; her grandmother had been Augusta, Princess of Hesse, before she became Duchess of Cambridge; and her great-grandmother (and King George's great-great-grandmother) had been King George III's Consort, Queen Charlotte of Mecklenburg-Strelitz. And, of course, both Queen Victoria *and* Prince Albert, who were cousins, were of the Saxe-Coburg line, and six of their nine children had married Germans.*

*Victoria, Princess Royal: Frederick III, German Emperor and King of Prussia; Alice: Louis IV, Grand Duke of Hesse and by the Rhine; Helena: Christian,

Anti-German hysteria, which gripped Britain immediately following the Kaiser's ruthless burning and sacking of Belgium towns in August and September, reached a head in October. Every day the newspapers bannered stories about the burning of Ardennes; the brutal reprisal at Seilles, where 50 civilians were shot and the houses given over to looting and burning; the senseless herding together of 400 citizens in the main square of Tamenas to be shot and bayoneted to death; and the tragic burning and destruction of the beautiful medieval city of Louvain. In England, sentiment was so strong that German churches were stoned, German shops looted, and German parishioners and shopkeepers attacked. German music was no longer performed. The English are well known for their enduring devotion to dogs, yet dachshunds were abused and kicked in the street, and many owners of German breeds shot their dogs lest they meet a more painful, lingering death at the hands of zealots. Buckingham Palace was not exempt from the fear that such hysteria generates.

Princess Mary, now seventeen, had her own maid, Else, who had been with the Royal Family for over a decade and whom all of them loved for her "devotion and warm-hearted personality." Else was German, and Queen Mary and King George came to the wrenching decision early in August that "the Royal Family could not harbour a German maid" and that Else must return to Germany. David later recalled how his mother, Mary, and all of the brothers wept as they said goodbye to "this fine woman whom war, with its relentless disregard for humanities, was taking" from their midst.

Fear that the public would be outraged at Else's position in the Royal Household was not unfounded. People were certain that spies lurked everywhere. All public officials with German backgrounds were suddenly considered suspect, and the greatest clamour arose over England's First Sea Lord, Admiral Prince Louis of Battenberg.

At the age of fourteen, Prince Louis had become a British

Prince of Schleswig-Holstein; Arthur, Duke of Connaught: Louise Margaret, Princess of Prussia; Leopold, Duke of Albany: Helen, Princess of Waldeck and Pyrmont; and Beatrice: Prince Henry of Battenberg.

subject and entered the Royal Navy. In 1884, he married Princess Alice's daughter, Victoria, and so became the Queen's grandson.* A further bond was established with the English Royal Family when his younger brother Henry married Queen Victoria's daughter Beatrice, most especially since Prince Henry and his wife lived the majority of their married life with the Queen. By his early twenties, Prince Louis was known as one of Britain's "finest and most able Naval officers." When Churchill was made First Lord of the Admiralty, he had brought in Prince Louis (an admiral at this time) as Second Sea Lord under Admiral Sir Francis Bridgeman, whom he quickly replaced.

Attacks upon Prince Louis and his German birth, insinuating that he could be a spy, started first in the *Globe* and other London newspapers, a smear campaign that finally reached the floor of Parliament. Such a furor was raised that by October 29 Prince Louis had no alternative but to resign, and King George was obliged to condone the dismissal of a man whom he not only much admired, but whom he thought the most able man for the job. He felt great mortification, as well as sadness, at having to give in to public clamour. Now sixty, Prince Louis had been a British subject for forty-six years, all of them loyally dedicated to the Royal Navy. Prince Louis's health and mental state after this ignominious end to his brilliant Naval career was a matter of great concern to the Royal Family. His young cousin, the Prince of Wales, visited him at the Admiralty and was shocked to see the pain that showed "in his tired, lined face." The Royal Family was worried about how Prince Louis's ordeal would affect his older son Georgie, who was in the Grand Fleet, and his younger son Dickie, who had just passed out of Osborne and was to go on to Royal Naval College, Dartmouth.† Both of these Battenberg boys were close friends—as well as cousins—to Bertie and David.

Queen Mary worked hard to overcome her "dull despair" at

---

*Since Princess Alice was also the mother of Empress Alexandra (Princess Alix of Hesse), Prince Louis was a brother-in-law to the Tsar and Tsarina.

†Prince Louis relinquished his princely titles in 1917. After his death, his son George (1892–1938) became 2nd Marquess of Milford Haven; Dickie became First Earl Mountbatten of Burma (1900–1979).

the terrible succession of events and at the news from the front. Day after day, week after week, found her encouraging those who had returned from the front blinded, gassed, wounded, or missing limbs. She visited some of the families of the tens of thousands who would never return. She toured munitions plants and appeared at food centres. With zeppelin raids and a guard of 120 Grenadiers as well as two manned Naval guns, York Cottage was no longer a peaceful retreat. Several times while Queen Mary was in residence at the cottage and Queen Alexandra at the Big House, zeppelin raiders dropped bombs in the neighbourhood. Demanding a unique (and nonexistent) instrument of warfare, Queen Alexandra wrote to her son after one of these raids, "Please let me have a lot of *rockets* with spikes or hooks to defend our Norfolk Coast. I am sure you could invent something of the sort which would bring down a few of these rascals."

David believed his life was expendable because he had four brothers at home. One cannot say that he was particularly willing to take chances with his life because his death would bring no threat to the line of succession. Still, he certainly would have preferred that awesome responsibility not ever to become his. The problem was, his family was greatly apprehensive that Bertie could ever emotionally deal with such an eventuality. Harry was perpetually ill. Georgie, the fourth brother, was stable, healthy, and capable, but his position made it highly unlikely that he would ever have to be called upon.

Georgie was twelve when the war began, and his greatest fantasies became realities. An avid reader of Jules Verne and H. G. Wells, he had, through them, envisaged with boyish excitement the advent of the flying machine. His heroes quickly became the air aces who rarely lived long, the average life expectancy of a pilot at the battlefront being three weeks. This extraordinarily heavy rate of casualties did not deter young men from entering this branch of the service. Several reasons were responsible for the grim death toll. Pilots had only ten to fifteen flying hours before being thrust into battle. They hardly knew their aeroplanes, and were faced with conditions and situations with which they could not cope. If a pilot was flying low, at

300–400 feet on dawn patrol, he was directly in the trajectories of the gunfire and was often shot to bits by his own side's shells. And if he was flying at 7,000 or 8,000 feet, he had to dodge the enemy's howitzer shells; still, Georgie viewed the pilot's life with great enthusiasm. Boys were being taken into the Royal Air Force at age sixteen. Georgie made it known that he wanted to be a pilot if the war lasted that long. Portraits of various flying heroes hung on the walls of his room, and whenever his mother visited the hospitals where injured airmen were being cared for, he offered (with unsuccessful results) to accompany her.

At home, Bertie's stammer kept him from taking an active part in the badinage and repartee that are natural aspects of family life. According to Wheeler-Bennett, he "bitterly resented the imitation of his inflection to which, with unthinking and unintentional cruelty of the young [Harry and Georgie], he was subjected." Jubilantly, he rejoined H.M.S. *Collingwood* on February 12, 1915. His mates at sea tended to ignore Bertie's stammering; consequently, his impediment was never as intense when he was away from home.

Bertie was now a senior midshipman, and his job alternated between control of searchlights by night and charge of submarine lookouts by day. In port, he assisted the gunnery and torpedo lieutenants "and ran the steam pinnaces and picketboats under the supervision of the Commander." Only three months after his return to H.M.S. *Collingwood,* Bertie's abdominal attacks occurred again with much frequency, and on July 9 he was transferred to the hospital ship *Drina.* He was not to rejoin his ship until May 5, 1916. On the thirtieth, he encountered his first enemy action.

"We opened fire at 5:37 P.M. on some German light cruisers," he wrote in his journal for that date. "The *Collingwood*'s second salvo hit one of them which set her on fire, and sank after two more salvoes were fired into her. We then shifted on to another light cruiser and helped to sink her as well. Our next target was a battle cruiser. We think the *Deerflinger* [sic] or *Lutzow,* and one of the *Collingwood*'s salvoes hit her abaft the after turret which burst into a fierce flame. After this she turned away and disappeared into the mist. By this time it was too dark to fire and we went to Night Defence stations . . . the German Fleet all turned away from us after dark, followed by our light cruisers and destroyers who attacked them during the night. We were not attacked at all during the night and everything was very quiet."

Three days later, the Germans struck again. "At the commencement," Bertie records, "I was sitting on top of A turret and had a very good view of the proceedings. I was up there during a lull, when a German ship started firing at us, and one salvo 'straddled' us . . . I was distinctly startled and jumped down the hole in the top of the turret like a shot rabbit!!! . . . the ship was in a fine state on the main deck, inches of water sluicing about to prevent fires from getting a hold on the deck. Most of the cabins were also flooded.

"The hands behaved splendidly and all of them in the best of spirits as their hearts' desire had at last been granted, which was to be in action with the Germans."

To his brother David, he wrote: "When I was on top of the turret I never felt any fear of shells or anything else. It seems curious but all sense of danger and everything else goes except the one longing of dealing death in every possible way to the enemy."

No restrictions were taken regarding Bertie's "rendezvous with history." David, however, felt he was "being kept, so to speak, on ice, against the day that death would claim my father. But in the midst of all the slaughter of the Western Front, I found it hard to accept his unique dispensation."

By September 29, 1915, David was a member of the Guards Division and tauntingly close to the combat zone at Noeux-les-Mènes. He had managed to have his driver take him to the spot where—four days before—assaulting parties of the division had engaged the Germans in bloody battle. The dead lay unburied in the pastures and on the spots where they had fallen. The cruel sight of the bloodied, dismembered dead killed within yards of their objective was pathetic and gruesome. "It moved and impressed me most enormously!!!" he wrote in his diary, adding, "We emerged near Vermelles Church, a muddy pair [Lord Cavan accompanied him], for it was one continuous wallow in a foot of mud all the way in the trenches. We found our car all right but had a bad shock when we were told that Green [his driver] had been killed by a burst of shrapnel!!!! We went into No. 4. F.A. dressing sta. close by and saw the poor man's body; he was hit in the heart and death must have been instantaneous . . . I can't yet realize that it has happened!! . . . This push is a failure . . . I have seen & learnt a lot about war today . . ."

He was sent to the Somme in July 1916, where a big offensive had been under way for several weeks. Again, he was expected only to be an observer. "Oh, to be fighting with those grand fellows & not sitting back here doing so little as compared to them who are sacrificing their lives!!" he wrote. "There could be no finer death, & if one was spared how proud one would feel to have been thro' it . . ."

During the opening stages of the war, American public opinion, except for the Southern states, was overwhelmingly in favour of maintaining "firm neutrality toward the European struggle." After all, the warring nations were thousands of miles from America's shores. German zeppelin raids and food blockades were very remote happenings. In American opinion, if the Allies won, Russia would most certainly dominate the continent of Europe; and if Germany won, "unspeakable tyranny of militarism for generations to come" would follow.

Most Americans shuddered at any thought of an alliance with the Tsarist government of Russia. Huge waves of recently arrived immigrants were refugees from brutal pogroms. The country also had a large and politically powerful Irish-American population, "trained to hatred of England as to a religion." Germans living in America were a "highly respected, diligent, and peaceable community." Moreover, they also were a strong political force controlling millions of determining votes.

None of this withstanding, American intellectual sympathies were strongly with the Allies, and because Britain was the most affluent of the belligerents and able to pay cash for large orders of war supplies, the business community was particularly supportive of the Allies. Not until the latter half of 1915, with the prospect of the presidential election of 1916 looming, did America's attitude begin to solidify.

In May 1915, when the Germans sank the *Lusitania*,* many American lives were lost. Vociferous cries that the United States declare war on Germany were raised in both America and Great Britain. The official British view was that the U.S. entry into the war would be a disaster. Duff Cooper,† who was to become Secretary of State for War, commented in his diary:

> The feeling in America is so strong that they may be forced to go to war . . . I cannot help feeling that in the long run neutral nations, and even more the thoughtful of the Germans, could not fail to be impressed by the spectacle of all the most civilised nations of the world joined in alliance against one enemy.

Munitions and manpower were a serious problem to the English. Churchill reminded the House of Commons that "nearly a thousand men—Englishmen, Britishers, men of our own race —are knocked into bundles of bloody rags every twenty-four hours, and carried away to hasty graves or to field ambulances." Late-night consultations were held at Buckingham Palace to discuss the "ever-increasing demand for the imposition of Compulsory Military Service," a subject that was "creating a conflict within the Cabinet." On August 24, 1915, Prime Minister Asquith ("wearing a very light brown overcoat, the collar turned up, his long white hair sticking out behind his red face . . ."), Sir Edward Grey (". . . [looking] ominous with white face and black spectacles . . ."), Mr. Balfour, and Lord Kitchener (". . . [looking] like an officer who got mixed up with a lot of strolling players and is trying to pretend he doesn't know them . . .") met at Buckingham Palace for lunch.‡ From this meeting the Derby scheme was hatched, and on October 23 it was promulgated

*The *Lusitania* was under British registration. It was sunk May 7, 1915, off the Irish Coast by a German submarine; 1,195 persons were lost, of whom 128 were Americans.

†Alfred Duff Cooper (1890–1954), 1st Viscount Norwich; Secretary of State for War 1935–37; 1st Lord of the Admiralty 1938; Minister of Information 1940–41; Ambassador to France 1944–47.

‡In 1916, Lord Kitchener embarked on a mission to encourage Russians to continue their resistance to the Germans. He was drowned when his ship, the H.M.S. *Hampshire*, hit a German mine and sank off the Orkneys.

together with a proclamation issued in the King's name. The scheme called for all men to "attest" their willingness to serve if necessary. The men were then classified into twenty-three groups, married men and men who were the sole support of their family falling into two of the last groups. By Christmas, the politicians knew their scheme had failed—over a million single men had not registered.

A Military Service Bill compelling all single men between the ages of eighteen and forty-one to register was drafted and, on January 27, 1916, became law. The bill still excluded the compulsory conscription of married men. Lloyd George led the move to have Asquith withdraw this bill and introduce another to impose immediate and general conscription. The Prime Minister, recognising the power that opposed him, obliged. This new bill passed with only thirty-seven votes of dissent and received the Royal Assent on May 25.

These early war years were particularly critical and strenuous times for the King and Queen. The most trying crisis came on October 28, 1915. In the heat of the discussions on the passing of the Military Service Bill, King George had decided to pay a visit to the front lines in France. In view of the terrible losses of the British Army and the battering by the Germans, an appearance by the King, who embodied the spirit of Empire, was a good way to bolster the Army's morale.*

The King was accompanied by Sir Frederick Ponsonby, Sir Charles Cust, Derek Keppel, and M. Cerard—the Royal chef ("A most important addition to the retinue," Ponsonby notes). On one of the King's first stops, Aire, a small medieval town with cobblestoned streets dominated by a fifteenth-century church, "the Prince of Wales turned up and stayed for dinner . . . It always seemed to me," Ponsonby ruminates, "that the Prince was at that time very nervous before his father. He remained singularly silent only opening his mouth when he was addressed and then weighing carefully each word he uttered."

Later that day the Royal party, including David, motored to Archeux, where, with President and Mme. Millerand, they were

---

*King George had paid an earlier visit to the Western Front in November 1914, with good results.

to inspect French battalions. The men were blue with cold, and, according to Ponsonby, "the President and Mme. Millerand looked rather ridiculous walking through the mud. After going down the line we stopped under a sort of tent, and here the President presented the Prince of Wales with the Croix de Guerre . . . The Prince had very strange views on foreign decorations and we had the greatest difficulty in getting him to wear the ribbon of the Croix de Guerre. At first he flatly refused as he said he had not earned it; but I pointed out to him that his refusal to wear it would hurt the feelings of the French, so reluctantly he pinned it on."

Accompanied by Ponsonby, David, and Sir Charles Cust, the King motored from Aire to a crossroads near Hesdigneul on October 28, where they met General Sir Douglas Haig and his staff. The King and Ponsonby then mounted horses for the short distance to Hesdigneul, where the 11th and 1st Corps were stationed. Rain fell steadily, and the wet weather made the ground impossible for any march past the corps' three parades. The King and Ponsonby therefore decided they would simply ride down the line. After viewing the third and last parade, the Flying Corps, the King paused in the saddle long enough to exchange a few words with the commanding officer. At that moment another officer, thinking this a good time, called for three cheers to the King from his company. The King's horse, startled by the sudden outburst, quivered in terror and crouched down on its haunches. The King held fast to the reins. Then, suddenly, the animal sprang up and reared straight into the air and—its hind legs slipping in the slush and mud underfoot—fell backward, right on top of the King. Ponsonby jumped off his horse. He was by the King's inert body in brief moments. By the time—within two or three minutes—that the King opened his eyes, David had reached him and was kneeling by his side.

The King turned his head slowly toward the hushed and frightened parade of men still standing in formation and whispered to Ponsonby to fetch him his military cap, which had rolled several feet away. When Ponsonby returned, the King insisted that David and Ponsonby help him to his feet and support him on each side. After an effort to walk proved to be too painful, he allowed his son and Ponsonby to carry him in a sitting position to his motor, where he was propped up in the rear seat. David got in with him and they returned to the Château de la Jusnelle in Aire, where he was lodged.

Because almost everyone at the château had taken the opportunity of the King's absence for a few hours' respite, Ponsonby had to hammer on the kitchen window for some time before one of M. Cerard's assistants appeared. The man ran to fetch a footman. In the meantime, David and Sir Charles Cust were already carrying the King up the stone stairs to his room, where they laid him on a sofa. The King refused to see any of the Army doctors until his own surgeon, Sir Anthony Bowlby, travelling with him, arrived about an hour later (miraculously with a nurse serving on a nearby hospital barge, who had attended King George when he had had typhus twenty years before). At the time, the suspicion that the King had broken his pelvis had been discounted. Ponsonby telephoned Buckingham Palace and relayed to the Queen, through Lord Stamfordham, the news of the King's accident, and David was dispatched to London that very evening to tell his mother the details. He left France reluctantly, knowing that the slightest movement gave his father "untold pain."

Two days later, Sir John French came to see the King and remained for about ten minutes.* When he saw Ponsonby afterwards, he expressed his fear that the whole incident would soon reach the Germans through spies, and that "the enemy's aeroplanes would buzz round and drop bombs on the villa." Therefore, he said it was imperative that the King be moved. Ponsonby repeated this to the King, who replied, "You can tell French from me to go to hell and stay there. I don't intend to move for any bombs."

On October 31, with the pain still totally immobilising him, the King returned to England on a stretcher by train and hospital ship. "You can't think how thankful we shall all be to get you back & every preparation is being made to make all as comfortable as possible under the circumstances," Queen Mary wrote the

*Field Marshal Sir John French (1852–1925), later 1st Earl of Ypres. Commander-in-Chief of Expeditionary Force in France, 1914–15.

King. "Nobody to meet you *anywhere* & I will wait in my room until *you* send for me for I presume you would rather be settled in your bed before you see me."

Upon his return home, X rays established that the first diagnosis had been wrong. The King had sustained a fracture of the pelvis, for which he blamed Ponsonby, who, he claimed, should never have moved him in the first place (although not to have done so would have countermanded the King's own order). His convalescence was lengthy. In fact, he was never to fully recover from this accident. Always thereafter he suffered considerable pain if he was on his feet too long or astride a horse for any length of time. He practised relentlessly to cover the small limp with which he had been left. All in all, he considered himself lucky. On January 2, 1916, he wrote to Lord Stamfordham (Arthur Bigge), who had lost his son John to the war that year: ". . . my boys are still safe and He spared my life the other day in France. The Country is united and determined to win this war whatever the sacrifices are and please God 1916 may bring us victory and peace once more . . ."

This "heartfelt prayer" was not to be answered. The war dragged tragically on, the epicenter in Western Europe. Month after month, trench after trench, gassed, mined, and mutilated, shivering in the penetrating cold and half-starved on alien rations, British soldiers floundered and died in the mud and rain of Flanders and France. The casualty lists grew ever longer. By the summer of 1917, few English families had not lost a close relative. Aunt Augusta had died, and Queen Mary had not been able to attend her funeral.* The worst news came from Russia, where revolutionary forces had taken over the Imperial Government in Petrograd [Saint Petersburg] on March 12, 1917. The Tsar had abdicated and signed away his son's rights to succession. The Royal Family, most especially Queen Alexandra, thought "Nicky must have lost his mind."

A decade later, that grand phrase-maker, Winston Churchill, was to say: "It is the shallow fashion of these times to dismiss

---

*The Grand Duchess Augusta's son later wrote to Queen Mary that his mother had died with the name "May" on her lips.

the Tsarist regime as a purblind, corrupt, incompetent tyranny. But a survey of its thirty months of war with Germany and Austria should correct these loose impressions and expose the dominant facts . . . War or no War? Advance or retreat? Right or left? Democratise or hold firm? Quit or persevere? These are the battlefields of Nicholas II. Why should he reap no honour from them? The devoted onset of the Russian armies which saved Paris in 1914; the mastered agony of the munitionless retreat; the slowly regathered forces; the victories of Bruselov; the Russian entry upon the Campaign of 1917, unconquered stronger than ever; has he no share in these? In spite of errors vast and terrible, the regime he personified, over which he presided, to which his personal character gave the vital spark, had at this moment won the war for Russia."

In their imprisonment at Tsarskoe Selo, Nicholas and his family were in danger of being murdered. The Empress Alexandra—after all, German by birth—had been separated from her family, and an investigation was made by her jailors into her "treasonable, pro-German" sympathies.* What had kept the Russian Royal Family going was the belief that King George would come to their rescue and they would be transferred to England. Had Asquith still been Prime Minister, a good chance exists that Nicky and his family—Queen Victoria's granddaughter, Alix of Hesse, and her great-grandchildren, the four grand duchesses and their small haemophiliac brother—would have been brought to England without delay. But the preceding winter, Asquith's Government had been brought down. Lloyd George was now the Liberal Prime Minister, and the feisty Welshman had little sympathy for the Russian autocracy. Reluctantly and under pressure from his Ministers and the King, Lloyd George had offered the Tsar and his family asylum in England the day of Nicholas's abdication, and Kerenski, head of the Provisional Russian Government, had agreed to personally escort the Imperial family to a British ship. By this time the Soviet and the Provisional Government were at an impasse, and the latter was not sufficiently master of the coun-

---

*The Empress Alexandra was, however, allowed to eat with her family, but she could speak only Russian at the table.

try or of the railroads to engineer the Tsar's departure.

Word had got through to Nicholas and Alexandra at Tsarskoe Selo that King George and Queen Mary were deeply concerned about their plight. Hope stirred in both their hearts. Then, on April 10, a semiofficial British Foreign Office statement was received by the Provisional Government stating that "His Majesty's Government does not insist on its former offer of hospitality to the Imperial family." The plan to transfer the deposed Tsar and his family to England was therefore suspended until early summer, when in June the Russian Government actually approached England on the matter of asylum.

"[We] inquired of Sir George Buchanan [English Ambassador to Russia] as to when a cruiser could be sent to take on board the deposed ruler and his family," Kerenski reported. "Simultaneously, a promise was obtained from the German Government through the medium of the Danish minister, Skavenius, that German submarines would not attack the particular warship which carried the Royal exiles. Sir George Buchanan and ourselves were impatiently awaiting a reply from London. I do not remember exactly whether it was late in June or early in July when the British Ambassador called, greatly distressed . . . With tears in his eyes, scarcely able to control his emotions, Sir George informed . . . [us] of the British Government's final refusal to give refuge to the former Emperor of Russia . . . I can say definitely that this refusal was due exclusively to considerations of internal British Politics."

In England, anti-German hysteria had never abated, and the Empress Alexandra was believed to be German by birth, and, erroneously, pro-German in sentiment. Lloyd George was adamant that England could not offer hospitality to people whose "pro-German sympathies were well-known."

The Royal Family had lived in distress throughout this long debate over their Russian cousins. On the one hand were their fears for the lives of Nicky and his family, and on the other the condemnation of their subjects and the possible charge that they themselves—because of their family ties—might also be pro-German. The King had Lloyd George to contend with as well as Queen Alexandra, whose sister, the Dowager Empress Maria ("Aunt Minnie"), Nicky's mother, was in Russia. Because of the widespread indignation felt in England against the Tsar, the King in the end sanctioned the withdrawal of Britain's offer of asylum.

The strain of all these political and family problems told on Queen Mary. Her hair was now streaked with grey, and hard lines were etched into her face. She was suffering from neuritis in her right arm and shoulder. Still, she fought to keep her posture rigid despite the pain it caused. In a brilliant stroke of public relations the same week England had withdrawn its offer to the Tsar, it had been decided that King George and Queen Mary would travel to France so that the King could visit troops and the Queen see for herself the conditions of the hospitals there. News of the Royal Couple's courageous and patriotic trip instantly replaced the crisis in Russia on the front pages of the press.

They boarded the *Pembroke* at Dover on the third of July and were escorted across the Channel by destroyers and seaplanes. David and Queen Mary's brother, Prince Alge, met them in Calais. Shortly after, the King and Queen separated, he to tour the battlefields, she the hospitals.

"One of the most important visits of the tour was to the Headquarters of the W.A.A.C.'s," Lady Airlie, who accompanied the Queen on this trip, recalls. "As our cars drew up there we were confronted with the sight of 1,500 men just detrained for a rest from the fighting at Sens. Covered with mud, bleary-eyed and haggard from fatigue, they stared blankly at us. The Queen said softly to Colonel Fletcher '. . . I want to speak to those men.'

"There were tremendous cheers as she crossed over to them. The W.A.A.C. Commanders, unwilling to have their thunder stolen, pressed to her side. Seeing cameras being directed towards her she whispered to me, 'I suppose I shall go down to posterity reviewing my troops with two of my women aides-de-camp!'

". . . Everywhere on our tour the Queen had enthusiastic reception from the troops and from the French civilians, especially when she was accompanied by the Prince of Wales who joined us for part of the time. He told me several times how much he liked being with his mother instead of with the King, but he was worried over her health. He did not think she looked well . . . "

During the entire trip to France, Queen Mary could not help but think about the fate of Nicky and Alix, harbouring guilt along with her anxiety. If any tragic fate befell them, she knew she would always feel a measure of the responsibility. At the same time, her dedication to the Monarch disallowed her attempting to apply further pressure on the King. She also knew she must abide by the Prime Minister and the Cabinet's decisions in this matter.

Queen Mary and Lady Airlie were inexhaustible in their visits to hospitals, some of which "were old and grimy *Hôtels Dieu* with layers of dust on the floors and the indescribable stench of death and sickness hanging in the air because there were no disinfectants to dispell it."

The most harrowing sight of their tour was the battlefield, ". . . a vast stretch of land that had once been fertile and smiling, covered with crops, but was now only a tumbled mass of blackened earth fringed by sparse and splintered trees. The ground was strewn with rocks and stones and mounds of soil flung up by mines, and pitted with deep craters that had swallowed up farms and villages." Lady Airlie recalls: "We climbed over a mound composed of German dead, buried by their comrades— all that was left of a whole regiment who had died in wresting this strip of land from our troops, only to lose it again. Over this devil's charnel house nature had thrown a merciful veil of gently creeping plants.

"Scattered everywhere in the ineffable desolation were the pathetic reminders of human life—rifles fallen from dead hands, old water bottles, iron helmets, and in the distance, the guns boomed relentlessly, making new sites of destruction like this one.

"We stood there speechless. It was impossible to find words. The Queen's face was ashen and her lips were tightly compressed. I felt that like me she was afraid of breaking down."

President Wilson had been elected for a second term in November 1916, largely on the slogan, "He kept us out of the war." Earlier that year the President's emissary, Colonel House, had met with King George at Buckingham Palace. His aim had been to "elicit from the Allies a statement of their peace terms such as would appeal to American and neutral opinion as reasonable and just." If the Germans rejected these terms, then "America would enter the war against Germany." Before coming to London, House had met with the Kaiser in Berlin and had been led to believe that the German government was determined to secure what he called "a victory peace."

A series of threats and disputes involving German actions were to pass before America was to enter the war. Finally, when Germany, on the first of February, 1917, announced that it would impose an unrestricted blockade by submarine on Great Britain—an act that the Germans knew would result in the United States entering the war against them—America revved up its war machine. The Kaiser and his generals believed that Germany could win the war by starving Great Britain into submission before "a sufficient number of American troops could be trained, equipped, or transported to Europe."

President Wilson broke off diplomatic relations with Germany on February 3. Not until he had evidence of an "overt act" did he begin the mechanics of joining the Allied cause. A *raison d'état* in the form of a telegram presented itself on February 26. The telegram from Berlin to the German Minister in Mexico City—instructing him to offer the Mexican Government, in return for an alliance against the United States, "the sundered provinces of New Mexico, Texas and Arizona"—had been intercepted and instantly communicated to Washington by British Intelligence. The authenticity of this document, known as the Zimmermann telegram, has never been solidly proven. If Wilson had any doubts about his next move, the German torpedoing of the steamer *Laconia,* with a heavy loss of American lives, negated them.

President Wilson released the contents of the Zimmermann telegram to the press on March 1. A tremendous wave of anti-German feeling spread across America, and on the morning of April 6, the United States declared war against Germany. That afternoon, Lloyd George received the American correspondents in London in the Cabinet Chamber in Downing Street. With the correspondents seated about the Cabinet table, he read to them, in his melodramatic, strident Welsh voice, a message to the American people, which he said he had been asked to deliver on behalf of the Imperial War Cabinet.

"The American people," he declared passionately, "held back until they were fully convinced that the fight was not a sordid scrimmage for power and possessions, but an unselfish struggle to overthrow a sinister conspiracy against human liberty and human rights.

"Once that conviction was reached, the great republic of the West has leaped into the arena, and she stands now side by side with the European democracies who, bruised and bleeding after three years of grim conflict, are still fighting the most savage foe that ever menaced the freedom of the world."

At Buckingham Palace, no great rejoicing greeted the news that the United States had entered the war. King George and Queen Mary were still shaken by the collapse of the Tsarist regime in Russia. Only a fortnight earlier, Nicky had abdicated and been placed under arrest with his family. The previous week, a mass meeting to celebrate the fall of Tsarism had been held in Albert Hall. With great miscalculation, the speeches delivered at the latter had been refused newspaper coverage by the Censor. False rumours and suspicions therefore abounded that there had been threats against the Monarchy. H. G. Wells, in a letter to the *Times,* asserted that "the time has come to rid ourselves of the ancient trappings of throne and sceptre" and urged that Republican societies should immediately be formed. Harold Nicolson claims, "There were some who exploited the occasion [the fall of the Tsar] to deride the monarchial tradition and to advocate an English Revolution upon Russian lines." In another verbal assault, Mr. Wells referred to the Court as "alien and uninspiring."

Incensed by this imputation, King George told Lord Carnock, "I may be uninspiring but I'll be damned if I'm alien!"

Yet despite this protestation, the dark shadow of fear had slithered its way into the private Royal apartments of Buckingham Palace.

TWENTY-ONE

At a small dinner party at Buckingham Palace toward the end of May, Lady Maud Warrender confided to Queen Mary rumours abounding that the Royal Family must be pro-German since their surnames were German. King George overheard this remark, "started and grew pale." Moments later, he left the gathering, quite disturbed; and, shortly after, the Queen made a polite but early departure. Lady Maud had inadvertently propelled the King into an historic decision.

A barrage of ugly letters had been received at 10 Downing Street, alluding to the possibility that a king, whose ancestors came from Hanover, and a queen, whose ancestors came from Teck, could well have pro-German feelings and be responsible in some treasonable manner for the length of the war. Much alarmed, the Prime Minister had come to King George with, what seemed at that moment, an outlandish suggestion that the King and his Family and all their naturalized cousins who bore German names and titles renounce them and be rechristened with names that had an English heritage. In the beginning, the King and Queen had been extremely negative to Lloyd George's scheme and remained so, even in the face of H. G. Wells's public attack on the Monarchy. But the morning after Lady Maud's remark, the King conferred with Lord Stamfordham and decided to agree to the Prime Minister's proposal.

Mr. Farnham Burke of the College of Arms was consulted as to exactly what was the King's name. Mr. Burke's opinion was that it might not be Coburg. Since the Saxe-Coburg family belonged to the House of Wettin in the District of Wipper, *Wettin* or *Wipper* might be more appropriate. Either one could have passed for an English name, but both were considered "unsuitably comic." Prince Louis of Battenberg was called in as the representative for all the Royal relations with German names and titles. The King, Queen Mary, Prince Louis, and Lord Stamfordham, along with the Duke of Connaught ("Uncle Arthur"), Lord Rosebery, and Mr. Asquith spent the next week trying out possible names. The historic names of York, Lancaster, and Plantagenet were rejected by one and all, along with those of Tudor-Stewart, England, D'Este, and Fitzroy (a curious choice, which meant "King's son" and was a name that Charles II had chosen to indicate illegitimate royal descent).

In the end, Lord Stamfordham had the final distinction of christening a dynasty. Edward III, he recalled, had been known as *Edward of Windsor*. * The name "Windsor" greatly appealed to both the King and Queen, who associated it with their distant royal predecessor and the castle that figured so strongly in the youth of both. And certainly, the name *Windsor* was "as English as the earth upon which the castle stood, its smooth solid walls encircling its wards, mound, towers, and chapel." Also, Windsor was unique in that it had never been the title of a royal dukedom, such as Cornwall, Edinburgh, Kent, Lancaster, or York.

Once the King and Queen had settled upon a name, the rest of the Royal Family residing in England and bearing German titles and surnames began to search frantically for names for their own families, not all with good humour. Queen Mary's brother Dolly, the Duke of Teck, was extremely ruffled at the

---

*Edward III (1312–77), King of England (1327–77). Only fifteen when crowned, the real power for his first three years as King was exercised by his mother, Queen Isabella, and her lover, Roger de Mortimer, 1st Earl of March. In 1330, the King executed a coup and seized the reins of government, putting Mortimer to death and forcing his mother into retirement. The French Hundred Years War and the Scottish Wars dominated his reign, as did the emergence of the Commons as a distinct and powerful group within Parliament. Edward III could easily have been the model for Shakespeare's *Hamlet*.

idea of forfeiting his German title, which would cause him to lose his rank since he had no English title. The same situation also existed for Alge, Prince of Teck, and for Queen Victoria's Battenberg grandsons, as well as for Prince Louis and his family. Peerages were thus worked out for those close Royal Family members. Dolly and Alge became, respectively, Marquess of Cambridge and Earl of Athlone with the family name of Cambridge. And Queen Victoria's two Battenberg grandsons, Prince Alexander and Prince Leopold, became, respectively, 1st Marquess of Carisbrooke and Lord Leopold Mountbatten.*

On July 17, 1917, a proclamation by the King was printed declaring that the name of Windsor was to be borne by his Royal House and Family, and that he and his family, as well as all his descendants and the descendants of Queen Victoria who were subjects of Great Britain, relinquished and enjoined the discontinuance of all Germanic titles.

Kaiser Wilhelm was said to have snidely remarked on hearing of his cousin's new family name that he was "going to the theatre to see a performance of *The Merry Wives of Saxe-Coburg-Gotha.*" But for Queen Mary there was a sense of great pride at her new name and in the fact that she was to be the matriarch of a new dynasty—the Royal House of Windsor.

The war ground on and the casualty lists grew "ever longer" as yet more men were poured into the trenches of France and Flanders. Throughout the summer of 1917, London suffered constant raids by squadrons of German aeroplanes and zeppelin airships. Considerable damage was done and many lives lost; still, the people of London seemed only to become more determined to show their grit. When a raid was imminent, they found safety where they could in an orderly fashion and with few visible signs of panic. Lord Hardinge,† who was then Permanent

---

*The third of Queen Victoria's Battenberg grandchildren, Prince Maurice, had been killed in action in France.

†Sir Charles Hardinge (1858–1944). Created Lord Hardinge of Penshurst, 1910. Minister in Tehran, Ambassador at Saint Petersburg and Paris, Viceroy of India, and for many years Permanent Under-Secretary of State at the Foreign Office. During the reign of King Edward VII, he always accompanied the

Under-Secretary of State, recalls that:

> The only person who to my knowledge showed alarm under these [raids] was the Prime Minister, Lloyd George. He had a room in the basement of the Foreign Office, where the walls were so thick as to offer the greatest security, fitted up as a sitting-room and bedroom with sandbagged windows, and whenever a raid was reported he went there. On one occasion when a raid had been signalled . . . I myself from an upper window saw Lloyd George rush from No. 10, hatless, and with hair flying, into the Foreign Office to his sandbagged room.

The Prime Minister held a pessimistic outlook for the Allies and was alarmed for his own safety. As the long, dark winter months of 1917–18 approached, Lloyd George could see that the Allied armies were "exhausted and disillusioned. The war fever had burnt itself out . . . enthusiasms had cooled down. There were no more patriotic demonstrations in the streets . . . The Russian Armies had ceased to exist as a fighting force and were rapidly disintegrating into a mutinous rabble . . . French troops could not be relied upon for any operation that involved sustained attack on a great scale." The likelihood that the Americans would be ready before 1919 with an army of sufficient force to help the Allies make up for these failings was dim. Could the English Army hold out that long? In mid-December, its infantry showed a loss of 116,000 men. An appalling 399,000 men had been killed in the ghastly massacres of the Flanders Campaign, and the infantry had borne the brunt of these casualties.

Lloyd George and the Allies would have taken heart if they had known at the end of 1917 that Germany did not have enough food to feed its armies or its population for more than a few months, or that "the military ardour of Germany's allies was evaporating." The only hope Germany had of obtaining food supplies was in the exploitation of Russia, which could not be accomplished without employing considerable forces in the occupation of Russian farmlands. This meant that Germany had

---

King on his official visits abroad, a duty usually performed by the Secretary of State.

to force the war to a conclusion "at the earliest possible moment." Since the Germans calculated that "only a comparatively small proportion of the American Army could be put into the fighting line during the critical months of 1918," they did not attach much importance to the American Army.

"Not very good news from France. We all feel very anxious," Queen Mary recorded in her diary on March 21, 1918, the day the Germans opened their massive offensive on the Western Front. When German victory seemed possible, King George rushed to France to see if his presence might not help the flagging morale of the British Armies.

In anguish, Queen Mary wrote the King on March 27: ". . . I have never in my life suffered so much *mentally* as I am suffering *now* and I know you are feeling the *same . . .* One must just have faith and believe that God cannot allow those huns to win and that our brave and gallant troops will be able to withstand the onslaughts in spite of the overwhelming numbers of the enemy. God bless and keep you my own beloved husband."

The Queen had had her own personal problems, however small when compared to the great losses of so many of her husband's subjects. Bertie had been seriously ill throughout most of 1917 and was finally—and correctly—diagnosed and operated upon for a duodenal ulcer in November. She had heard all sorts of gossip about David's unrepressed behaviour when he was home on leave—how he attended (against the King's wishes, an unforgivable transgression in Queen Mary's eyes) all the debutante balls, dancing until dawn and arranging assignations with various married women. All of these stories were, in fact, quite true. Lady Cynthia Asquith notes in her diary:* "So far [the Prince of Wales] dances most with Rosemary and also motors with her in the daytime.† No girl is allowed to leave London during the three weeks of his leave and every mother's heart beats high." But it was Lady Rosemary's friend,

---

*Lady Cynthia Asquith (1887–1960), eldest daughter of the 11th Earl of Wemyss. She married Herbert Asquith (1881–1947), second son of Prime Minister Asquith.

†Lady Rosemary Leveson-Gower (d. 1930), eldest daughter of the 4th Duke of Sutherland. She married in 1919 Lord Ednam, later 3rd Earl of Dudley.

Mrs. Freda Dudley Ward,* who was to catch David's eye and heart when they met quite romantically in an air-raid shelter. "Saw the Prince of Wales dancing around with Mrs. Dudley Ward, a pretty little fluff with whom he is said to be rather in love," Lady Cynthia records on March 12, 1918. "He is a dapper little fellow—too small—but really a pretty face. He looked as pleased as Punch and chatted away the whole time. I have never seen a man talk so fluently while dancing. He obviously means to have fun."

That the Prince of Wales should carry on in such a flippant manner in a time of great and serious crisis was reprehensible to Queen Mary, who tried whenever possible to keep such gossip away from the King.

On February 19, the Prince of Wales had taken his seat in the House of Lords. The House was "fairly full," the Ladies' Gallery "thronged," and the ceremony was more "pompous than usual when a peer takes his seat," Lord Esher records. Of the young Prince of whom he had been fond since childhood, he comments, "The boy looked more boyish than ever in such surroundings [he was twenty-three at the time]. A youthful fair figure, smooth as Henry the Fifth. His blush is ready as ever on a fair cheek, but his eyes have lost their dreamy *Weltzschmerz* look. He was composed and modest. Later he took his Grandfather's seat on the Cross Benches." Some of the fear of the war's toll shows in Lord Esher as he adds, "Amid this world-changing turmoil the old traditional ceremony was moving and who knows but that for the last time a Prince of Wales thus takes his seat in this historic House."

A less sentimental view was taken by Lady Cynthia up in the Ladies' Gallery. She described the Prince of Wales as having "a wooden body with bland, meek, milk-and-water countenance— [pretty but] stripped of all character, nothing of the bulldog breed . . ."

---

*Mrs. Freda Dudley Ward (1894–1983), Winifred May, elder daughter of Colonel C. W. Birkin. In 1913, she married William Dudley Ward, divorcing him in 1932. In 1937, she married the Marques de Casa Maury. This marriage was dissolved in 1954, but she remained the Marquesa de Casa Maury until her death.

Queen Mary continued her visits to London's hospitals, talking to the returned injured soldiers and to the victims of bombs and air raids. Something of myth was now being perpetuated about Queen Mary's character. One story being circulated was that while she was "going round a hospital, Queen Mary was struck by a fair-haired mother with a very dark baby. She commented on this and returned to the woman's bedside on completing her round, saying, 'His father must have been very dark—wasn't he?' To which the woman breezily replied, 'Sure, ma'am, I don't know—he never took his hat off.' " A bottomless supply of such Queen Mary stories travelled around the fashionable squares of London. Her stateliness, self-control, unique appearance, along with her aloofness, all contributed to the tone of the "Queen Mary" stories. Young, iconoclastic aristocrats like Lady Cynthia enjoyed stories that characterized the Queen as unworldly. The fact that she had had six children did not enjoin youthful opinion that as for sexual intercourse—"King George, yes, but Queen Mary—*never!*"

Another false precept (for the Queen was anything but naive) was that Queen Mary was a *maitresse femme* who dominated her husband. Cholly Knickerbocker, an American newspaper columnist, nicknamed the British Royal Couple "George and the Dragon," and shortly after the war a cartoon was published in America showing Queen Mary as an enormous woman in an apron with a diminutive King George dangling on one string and the Prince of Wales on another. Lady Airlie reports that someone sent the clipping of this cartoon to the Queen, and the two of them "laughed together over its absurdity." In truth, Queen Mary's obeisance to her husband was almost oriental in its absoluteness. She did speak her mind when the King requested she do so, but never without his approval, and she was not close enough to David to pull the strings in his life (had she been, his future would not have been what it was to be).

London antique dealers were to claim that they hid all the bibelots and precious items that they knew might appeal to the Queen when they expected her to visit their premises, for the Queen was prone to take what she wished and they would go without payment.* If while visiting in some aristocratic home she sighted an object that had once belonged to the Royal Family, she often would request its return, and the current owner could do nothing else but oblige. Queen Mary was determined to restore all former possessions of the various Royal homes to their original places. Her research and memory regarding Royal property were staggering. And if she spied a painting or a vase or a piece of silver that she knew had once been Royal property —though perhaps given to a mistress or a Royal retainer and then sold—she expected (in the name of historic preservation) the dealer or host to contribute the piece to the Crown and the nation.

April 1918 was deceptively warm and reassuring. American troops were pouring into France. England and France were slowly obtaining air supremacy. New inventions for tracing submarines under water were helping to diminish the German submarine menace. By Easter, Germany had made peace with Russia via the Treaty of Brest-Litovsk, and the danger of the Germans manning the Russian Black Sea Fleet and making their way through the Straits into the Mediterranean was present. By July, the German advance toward Amiens on the Western Front had finally been stopped by a concentration of French and British troops, with a high cost in Allied casualties.

The roses at Windsor were in glorious blossom when Queen Mary moved her Household there for the month of July. The King's Aunt Helena (Queen Victoria's daughter), and her two daughters—Marie Louise and Thora—were at nearby Cumberland Lodge. In consequence, the two families spent a good deal of time together, and lunch on Sunday at the castle was an established ritual.

At about 1:00 P.M., Sunday, July 21, Princess Helena and her family were assembled in the corridor of Windsor waiting for the King and Queen who were—for the first time in anyone's memory—a half-hour late. When the King appeared on the landing above them, his face was drained of all colour. Queen Mary stood stiffly behind him. They descended the stairs so slowly and

*This led to a story that still proliferates that Queen Mary was a kleptomaniac, an accusation never substantiated and thoroughly untrue.

308

both looked so grave and distressed that the group gathered there feared news might have come of a German victory.

"Oh, George, is the news very bad?" Princess Helena exclaimed.

He said, "Yes, but it is not what you think. Nicky, Alix, and their five children have all been murdered by the Bolsheviks at Ekaterinburg . . ." All were shaken by the news, and lunch was a grim affair. Details were not learned until a week later.

"It's too horrible and heartless," Queen Mary wrote on that day in her diary.

At midnight on July 16, the entire Russian Imperial Family had been awakened and told to gather downstairs. Jacob Yurovsky, a member of the Bolshevik secret police, explained to them that the regional Soviet had decided that they must be moved. He then led them to a small semibasement room, sixteen by eighteen feet, with a heavy iron grillwork on the window. He told them to wait there until the automobiles arrived.

Nicholas, his sleepy son in his arms, asked for chairs so that Alexandra and the small boy could sit while they waited. "Yurovsky ordered these chairs brought. Alexandra took one," Robert Massie says as he describes the horrifying drama at Ekaterinburg. "Nicholas took another, using his arm and shoulder to support Alexis, who lay back across the third chair. Behind their mother stood the four girls (Anastasia clinging to her spaniel, Jimmy) and Demidova, the Empress's parlourmaid. Demidova carried two pillows, one of which she placed in the chair behind the Empress's back, the other pillow she clutched tightly. Inside, sewed deep into the feathers, was a box containing a collection of the Imperial jewels.

"When all were assembled, Yurovsky reentered the room, followed by his entire Cheka squad carrying revolvers. He stepped forward and declared quickly, '*Your relations have tried to save you. They have failed* and we must now shoot you.'

"Nicholas, his arm still around Alexis, began to rise from his chair to protect his wife and son. He had just time to say 'What . . . ?' before Yurovsky pointed his revolver directly at the Tsar's head and fired. Nicholas died instantly. At this signal, the entire squad of executioners began to shoot. Alexandra had time only to raise her hand and make the sign of the cross before she too was killed by a single bullet. Olga, Tatiana, and Marie, standing behind their mother, were hit and died quickly . . . Demidova, the maid, survived the first volley, and rather than reload, the executioners took rifles from the next room and pursued her, stabbing with bayonets. Screaming, running back and forth along the wall like a trapped animal, she tried to fend them off with the cushion. At last she fell, pierced by bayonets more than thirty times. Jimmy, the spaniel, was killed when his head was crushed by a rifle butt.

"Alexis, lying on the floor still in the arms of the Tsar, feebly moved his hand to clutch his father's coat. Savagely, one of the executioners kicked the Tsarevich in the head with his heavy boot. Yurovsky stepped up and fired two shots into the boy's ear. Just at that moment, Anastasia, who had only fainted, regained consciousness and screamed. With bayonets and rifle butts, the entire band turned on her. In a moment, she too lay still."

The full ruthlessness of the murders was not known for many months, nor was the ghoulish disposal of the bodies—all dismembered, burnt, and then the bone that resisted fire dissolved with sulphuric acid. As each further horror was uncovered, the Russian Imperial Family's relations in Great Britain suffered anew.* Yurovsky's account of the murders told much later contains the tell-tale phrase: *"Your relatives have tried to save you. They have failed."* He could only have been referring to King George and Queen Mary. The tone of the statement implied that forces beyond their control caused them to fail, that a last-ditch effort had been made by England to save the Tsar and his family.† No evidence exists that in the months preceding the murders King George made any further effort to bring the deposed Imperial Family out of Russia. David, for the rest of his life, was to insist

*Besides the Royal Family who were cousins, and the children and grandchildren of Queen Victoria, who were also cousins, Queen Alexandra was Nicholas and Alexandra's aunt; and the Russian Empress's eldest sister, Victoria, was Lord Louis Mountbatten's mother.

†As late as 1970, after the publication of *Nicholas and Alexandra,* the Duke of Windsor was to tell Robert Massie, the author, that he had been unduly harsh on his father and that King George had indeed tried everything possible but failed.

310

that his father did everything he could to effect their freedom. Memories of the Tsar's family at Osborne when he was a cadet could very well have haunted David.

At no time would the Kaiser have barred his Imperial cousins from passing through Germany to freedom. However, once the Bolsheviks were in control, neither the Kaiser, King George, nor the British Government could have saved the Tsar and his family with an offer of free passage and asylum. Ironically, Ekaterinburg fell eight days after the murders to the advancing White Army, at whose hands the lives of the Russian Imperial Family might have been spared.

The vile murders of Nicky and Alicky, little Alexis, and the four young Grand Duchesses were a horrifying family tragedy as well as a loathsome historic event. All the grim sadness and self-recriminations caused by the brutal murders began afresh when the grieving Empress Maria, mother of the murdered Tsar and his family, found safe passage from Russia to England, where she stayed with Queen Alexandra at Sandringham.

The Germans had begun their ultimate offensive only twenty-four hours before the tragic happenings at Ekaterinburg. On the morning of July 15, the Kaiser stood in the soft summer rain on the summit of a specially constructed gazebo in Champagne, watching "the distant drifting smoke of battle." He was a desperate man. Either he was to win this offensive or lose his power and title. For three days, he maintained a pose of "triumphant hilarity." Then, on July 18, as he waited for news of final victory came the blow that he had lost the Battle of Champagne. He walked dejectedly downhill from his gazebo to board the Imperial train, riding all through the night toward Spa, and exile.* The following night he paced the narrow corridor outside his luxurious coach, pausing from time to time to gaze intently at a huge photograph on the wall. The picture showed him seated having tea with his grandmother, Queen Victoria, under a tent on the lawn at Osborne. Wilhelm knew the end was near and that he would never conquer England.

On August 8, King George paid his fifth visit to the French

*Spa is near Liège, in East Belgium, where in 1920 the Allies accepted a German scheme for paying reparations.

front. At dawn the next day the British Army, led by 450 tanks, broke through the German lines and advanced 9 miles. The American army, under General Pershing, heavily defeated the Germans at Saint Mihiel on September 12. With the Kaiser in exile and with a new German government under Prince Max of Baden,* on October 3 an appeal for an immediate armistice was addressed to President Wilson. Within a few weeks Turkey and Austria had capitulated. Prince Max handed over the German government to the Socialist leader, Friedrich Ebert† and the abdication of Emperor Wilhelm was accepted as the establishment of the German Republic was proclaimed from the steps of the Reichstag.

By November 1918, the war was nearing its bloody end. The Prince of Wales—created a major on the staff of the Canadian Corps during the summer—had turned his mind "increasingly to upheavals that seemed to be rapidly sweeping away the world of my youth." On November 5, from the front near Mons where the British Expeditionary Force had had its initial encounter with the Germans, the Prince of Wales had written his father:

> Dearest Papa,
> . . . There seems to be a regular epidemic of revolutions & abdications throughout the enemy countries which certainly makes it a hard & critical time for the remaining monarchies, but of those that remain I have no hesitation in saying that ours is by far the most solid tho of course it must be kept so & I more than anyone realise that this can only be done by keeping in the closest possible touch with the people & I can promise you that this point is always at the back of my mind & that I am & always shall make every effort to carry it out as I know how vitally it will influence the future of the Empire! . . . I'm sure you won't mind when I tell you that I'm out the whole of every day seeing & visiting *the troops* i.e. *the people.*

The world of my youth—his father had been crowned King of Great Britain, Ireland, and the British Dominions beyond the

---

*Max (Maximilian), Prince of Baden (1867–1929), a Liberal who thought he could save the Monarchy in Germany by forcing Wilhelm II to abdicate.

†Friedrich Ebert (1871–1925), President of the German Republic 1919–1925.

Seas, King and Emperor of India, the day before the Prince of Wales's seventeenth birthday. The previous year, the German Emperor and eight reigning kings and emperors, seven crown princes, and two dowager queens had attended the funeral of Edward VII. By 1922 there would be no ruling German Emperor; King Manoel II, fleeing the revolutionary forces in Portugal, would take refuge in Britain; and Emperor Karl I of Austria (the last of the Hapsburgs) would be forced to abdicate. Already the Russian Revolution of 1917 had been responsible for the murders of Tsar Nicholas II and his family, which had ended the monarchy in Russia. A decade later, the young King Farouk of Egypt was to say to the Prince of Wales, "Someday there will be only five kings—the kings of hearts, diamonds, clubs, and spades; and the King of England."*

Everywhere in Germany pictures of the ex-Kaiser were removed from walls, and almost all German Royalties were in general flight, fearing imprisonment or assassination. Wilhelm, his wife, and his eldest son had taken refuge in Arnhem, a port on the lower Rhine in East Netherlands. There were two attempts on the life of Wilhelm's brother, Prince Henry, and two of Prince Henry's daughters were wounded by gunshot.

Peace had come at 11:00 A.M. the morning of November 11. As the news spread throughout London, the feeling of relief was "indescribably intense." By nightfall, in a pouring rain, an ex-

---

*There were nine reigning families in Europe at this time—the Wattins (Belgiums), Oldenburgs (Denmark and Norway), Liechtensteins (Liechtenstein), Nassaus (Luxembourg), Grimaldis (Monaco), Orange-Nassaus (Netherlands), Bourbons (Spain), Bernadottes (Sweden), and Windsors (Great Britain). None of the current ruling monarchies truly wield power. Hypothetically, Queen Elizabeth would have to sign her own death warrant should Parliament and the courts vote *yea* on the issue. But the House of Windsor, of all of Europe's surviving reigning royal families, still embodies the royal mystique and commands more celebrity than any other monarch, president, politician, author, or film actor. To the world, the House of Windsor gives Great Britain a glittering aura that has been extremely prestigious for that country. And the monarchy remains and seems likely to perpetuate itself for generations to come because of this, and because—as Winston Churchill once remarked— "The monarchy is so extraordinarily *useful*. When Britain wins a battle she shouts, 'God save the Queen'; when she loses, she votes down the Prime Minister."

cited, shouting crowd of nearly 100,000 people was stamping
and cheering beneath the brightly lit balcony at Buckingham
Palace, whose own gaslights were gleaming. Every few hours the
King and Queen would appear, and the shouts would reach a
deafening crescendo.

"A day full of emotion and thankfulness—tinged with regret
at the many lives who have fallen in this ghastly war," Queen
Mary wrote in her diary the night of the Armistice.

The war had come to an end, but with an awesome loss
of lives. The British Empire had lost 767,000 men; France,
1,383,000; the United States, 81,000; Italy, 564,000; Germany,
1,686,000; and Russia, 1,700,000. At least 1,000,000 men were
missing in action, and over 12,000,000 had suffered serious
injury; many maimed, blinded, or mentally unbalanced. The
prospect of peace was going to require great courage. Kingdoms
had toppled. Nations were bankrupt. Millions of survivors had
to be fed and rehabilitated. Values had to be closely examined,
and, as Lady Cynthia Asquith wrote poignantly, "One will at last
fully recognise that the dead are not only dead for the duration
of the War."

All of Queen Mary and King George's German relations had
lost their titles and rights. Aunt Augusta's grandson, the young
Grand Duke of Mecklenburg-Strelitz, had shot himself. "Onkle
Willie" Württemberg had abdicated, and the family of Prince
Albert, Queen Victoria's Consort, ruled no longer in Coburg.
The current Duke of Saxe-Coburg-Gotha was, in fact, doubly
related to Queen Mary. He was the brother of her sister-in-law,
Princess Alice, and King George's first cousin, his father having
been King Edward's brother Leopold.

The Duke of Saxe-Coburg-Gotha was a tragic example of the
Royal Family's divided loyalties during the war. As an Eton
schoolboy of fifteen, having inherited the title upon his father's
early death, Queen Victoria had insisted the boy, who had never
been out of Britain, be sent to Germany to prepare to reign in
his duchy. Now he had been stripped of all his British and
German lands and titles, and was *persona non grata* in both countries.

"It has all been very wonderful and gratifying that after all
these 4 years of ghastly warfare the people did crowd here to

us the moment they knew the War was practically over,"* Queen Mary wrote to Harry, who had just entered his first year at Dartmouth.

Still, the Monarchy was not as stable in 1918 as it had been at the beginning of the war. It was imperative (so claimed Lord Cromer) for "no stone to be left unturned in the endeavour to consolidate the position of the Crown. The Crown is the link of Empire and its fate is inseparable from that of all British possessions."

The Prince of Wales's popularity was a great asset. Bertie, although terrified of aeroplanes, had been transferred from his beloved Navy to the Royal Air Force in Cambrai, in the north of France (but at least with the compensating comfort of his good friend, Lieutenant Commander Grieg, being transferred with him); and David was in Mons at the end of the war. The King did not feel that either of his sons should return until the armies were demobilised. Cautiously, Queen Mary wrote the King: "I think David ought to return home before *very* long, as he must help us in these difficult days; he is quite ready to do anything we want, for I had some capital talks with him while he was here and he was most sensible."

Christmas was to pass before the Prince of Wales returned to England. He was greeted everywhere he went as a hero, his popularity at its height. For the rest of the year (1919), he was kept constantly before the public, his speeches always sounding a personal note that brought him more and more admirers. In May, at his admission to the Freedom of the City of London at Guildhall, he confided, "I shall never forget my period of service overseas. In those four years I mixed with men. In those four years I found my manhood." Despite the awful sight of charred battlefields littered with "blood-stained shreds of khaki & tartan, the ground grey with corpses [and] mired horses struggling as they drowned in shellholes," the Prince of Wales's letters and his appearance still bore the smooth cheek of boyhood. Bertie, on the other hand, had matured quite noticeably. The King's next decision, to have Bertie, not David, accompany the Belgian Royal Family into Brussels (a great honour), was to have the

*The final peace was signed June 28, 1919.

unpleasant effect of alienating his older son just that little bit more, and of creating an insidious sense of competition between the two brothers.

The war years and the horror Queen Mary had seen (perhaps more than any other woman who was not in the nursing profession), the murders at Ekaterinburg, the fall of so many empires had marked her. She was fifty-one, resentful of the passage of her youth; her hair was grey, her body more matronly. Yet age and difficult times had not altered her proud carriage. Indeed, her presence had taken on an aura of ultimate queenliness that neither the stolid Victoria nor the vain Alexandra had possessed.

TWENTY-TWO

If ever there was a person ill suited to a decade, it was Queen Mary to the twenties. Yet she sailed through them with Nelsonian perseverance. Now the mother of four marriageable offspring,* she considered it her duty to King and Country to see that they chose their life partners wisely.

Prince John had died in his sleep on Saturday, January 18, 1919. "At 5:30," Queen Mary recorded in her diary, "Lala Bill telephoned me from Wood Farm, Wolferton, that our poor darling little Johnnie had passed away suddenly after one of his [epileptic] attacks. The news gave me a great shock, tho' for the poor little boy's restless soul, death came as a great release. I broke the news to George & we motored down to Wood Farm. Found poor Lala very resigned but heartbroken." And to an old friend,† she wrote, ". . . as his malady was becoming worse as he grew older . . . he has thus been spared much suffering. I cannot say how grateful we feel to God for having taken him in such a peaceful way, he just slipt quietly into his heavenly home, no pain, no struggle, just peace for the poor little troubled spirit

*The Prince of Wales, Prince Albert, Princess Mary, and Prince Henry. Prince George was sixteen in 1920.

†Emily Alcock, a friend of Queen Mary's since their meeting in Vienna in 1884.

which has been a great anxiety to us for many years, ever since he was four years old—"

The cause of death (his final attack had resulted in fatal heart damage) or Prince John's epilepsy and retardation were not reported in his obituaries. Nor was there any explanation of why he should have been at Wood Farm, Wolferton, and not at one of the Royal residences.

For Queen Alexandra, little Prince John's death was another great sadness to survive. She lingered at his small grave after his quiet funeral at Sandringham, heavily veiled and supported by Charlotte Knollys and Sir Dighton Probyn, long after Queen Mary had departed. According to one contemporary observer, Queen Alexandra was now "an old lady of ghostly and tenuous beauty." Another describes her during an audience at Marlborough House as a "mummied thing, the bird-like head cocked on one side, not artfully but by disease, the red-rimmed eyes, the enamelled face, which the famous smile scissored across all angular and heart-rending." "The ghosts of all her lovely airs" remained; "the little graces, the once effective sway and movement of the figure . . ." Still, the image is one of wizened age —("Her bony fingers, clashing in the tunnel of their rings, fiddled with albums, penholders, photographs, toys upon the table . . .")—which becomes more and more terrible, when one recalls how much youth and beauty were prized by Queen Alexandra.

The word "enamelled" was again used in describing her face by author Beverly Nicols, who writes that as a child he asked his mother how Queen Alexandra could smile if she "enamelled" her face. His mother replied gravely, "She does not smile. If she did, she would crack."

"Enamelled" or not, Queen Alexandra appeared at the wedding on April 21, 1920, of Harold Macmillan and Lady Dorothy Cavendish (daughter of the Duke of Devonshire). A guest noted that there were "roses flaming all too brightly on her parched skin."

A rash of marriages between the members of English and Scottish nobility followed the Macmillan wedding. No longer was it considered out of the question for an alliance to take place between a peer's son or daughter and a commoner, as long as the latter came from a well-connected family. This held true for all members of the Royal Family except the Prince of Wales. In the direct aftermath of the war, the British public would have expressed great anger at the idea of the King's children marrying anyone of German origin. Queen Mary could not help but wonder what would have been the result if one of her sons had been married to the Kaiser's daughter, or Princess Mary to one of *his* sons. Family feeling would have been rent asunder, and she and King George would have been powerless to help their children.

Princess Mary celebrated her twenty-fourth birthday on April 25, 1921. She bore a great resemblance to her Aunt Toria, and although she possessed a sense of humour, she had an otherwise colourless personality. Nevertheless, Princess Mary was her father's favourite, and he was not too pleased when Queen Mary introduced the subject of a possible husband for her. Most suggestions ended in his curt dismissal; not so the name of Henry, Viscount Lascelles,* eldest son of the 5th Earl of Harewood. The Court referred to Lord Lascelles as "poor Henry" because a decade earlier he had been hopelessly in love with Vita Sackville-West and had lost her to Harold Nicolson. "Poor Henry" was fifteen years Princess Mary's senior; looked like a "dismal bloodhound"; and, except for his air of the rejected suitor, was an altogether unromantic figure. He did have a personal fortune of over £3 million, owned vast lands, was a connoisseur of fine paintings, and would one day succeed, as the 6th Earl of Harewood, to Harewood House near Leeds. The match was thus encouraged. Lord Lascelles became a frequent guest at Balmoral during the summer of 1921 and in November stayed in one of the small, draughty rooms at York Cottage.

Queen Mary was resting in her room dressed in an embroidered kimono and talking to Prince Alge, who was visiting for the weekend, when during Lord Lascelles's visit in November Princess Mary burst in and said breathlessly, "Mama, I must speak with you," and proceeded to tell her mother and uncle of Lord Lascelles's proposal. "Please ask Papa's permission now," the young woman pleaded.

*Viscount Lascelles (1882–1947) succeeded as 6th Earl of Harewood, 1929.

Queen Mary glanced at her kimono and demurred, "I can't go like this."

Her daughter pressed on, and finally Queen Mary, in kimono and slippers, Mary in close pursuit, marched down the stairs and knocked at the door of King George's study. "I don't know what the pages must have thought of me dressed like that," she confided to the family at dinner. The King confessed that he had been a bit startled as well.

David was twenty-five, the bachelor Prince Charming, and all eyes were on him. At galas and at sporting events, he was always photographed with a different debutante. Gossip had it that beautiful Florence Mills, the black star of *Blackbirds,* was his mistress. But to his parents' distraction, he was privately seeing Freda Dudley Ward to the exclusion of all other young women. With Freda—small, fun-loving, and somewhat domineering—he could relax. He was often referred to by the King's Ministers as "The Little Man." Yet his name evoked the ultimate in glamour. He was thought to be a bit "wild." Lord Stamfordham suggested he be sent abroad as the Empire's Ambassador-at-Large, and in 1919 he began what would be a decade of travelling by touring Newfoundland, Canada, and the United States, where he paid a dutiful call on President Wilson before getting down to the business of enjoying himself.

American women fell instantly in love with him, surprised that he was not arrogant and remote, but a smiling, appealing young man who dissolved the distance Americans believed lay between Royalty and just plain folk. "Hats off," the American magazine *Vanity Fair* said, "to the indestructible Dancing Drinking Tumbling Kissing Walking Talking—but not Marrying—Idol of the British Empire."

He was called back to England by the King, who told him, "The war has made it possible for you to mix with all manner of people . . . But don't think that this means you can now act like other people. You must always remember your position and who you are."

But who exactly was he?

"The idea that my birth and title should somehow or other set me apart from or above other people struck me as wrong," he wrote of his feelings at the time. "If the leveling process of the

320

Royal Naval College, Oxford University, or the democracy of
the battlefield had taught me anything, it was, firstly, that my
desires and interests were much the same as those of other
people, and secondly, that however hard I tried, my capacity was
somehow not appreciably above the standards demanded by the
fiercely competitive world outside the palace walls . . . I wanted
no part of . . . [the] advantages attached to a position that
shelters one from the consequences of one's shortcomings
. . . I was in unconscious rebellion against my position."

"The Monarchy must always retain an element of mystery,"
Sir Frederick Ponsonby, then King George's Keeper of the Privy
Purse, advised him. "A Prince should not show himself too
much. The Monarchy must remain on a pedestal."

The Prince of Wales chose to ignore Ponsonby's advice. His
relationship with Freda Dudley Ward became more indiscreet.
They danced together at social gatherings, attended races, spent
weekends at country houses, and attended private parties. Freda
Dudley Ward was married to Lord Esher's nephew, who was a
Liberal Whip. "Be like Mrs. Keppel," Lord Esher warned her,
"be discreet." But by 1920 the Prince of Wales was "madly,
passionately, *abjectly* in love with [Mrs. Dudley Ward]." He visited her daily at five o'clock when in London, remaining to dine
or to take her out to dinner, if not to a friend's home then to
the Embassy Club, which was his favourite nightclub. Located in
the basement of an elegant Bond Street building, it hardly
earned the title of "Little Buckingham Palace," which he gave
it. The guests who frequented the Embassy were mostly "upper
crust" and knew that the Prince and his lady should be left quite
alone. After a public engagement, he would return to Freda
Dudley Ward's home late in the evening, despite the fact that
Mr. Dudley Ward and their two children remained in residence.

The Prince, with Finch as his majordomo, had recently moved
into York House, St. James's Palace, where he had once lived
with his family as a child. With Mrs. Dudley Ward to help him,
he redecorated the rambling old rooms that Queen Mary had so
loathed, and the place took on a look of masculine domesticity.
Reds and browns were the most frequent colours, and the sitting
room was hung not with the usual family portraits, but with
magnificently framed survey maps, specially rendered so that

321

London appeared in vivid scarlet against a Great Britain or
Europe in tones of sand to dark brown. When the work was
completed, he and Mrs. Dudley Ward (ignoring the lovely formal dining room) dined intimately at a table in front of the fire
in this room.

Within a short time, and upon the Queen's prodding, young
Lord Louis Mountbatten occupied a suite in the numerous
rooms of York House, a move that was obviously meant to
confuse people as to whose mistress Mrs. Dudley Ward might
truly be, but which fooled no one.

The Prince of Wales's favourite song was Noël Coward's "A
Room with a View," especially the second verse, and he would
request it to be sung at clubs and parties.

A room with a view and you
and no one to give advice
that sounds like paradise
few could fail to choose.

With fingers entwined
we'll find
relief from the preachers
who always beseech us
to mind our P's and Q's.
We'll watch
the whole world pass before us
while we are sitting still
leaning on our windersill.

We'll bill and we'll coo
and maybe a stork will bring
this that and t'other thing to
our room with a view.

The lyrics of the song suggest quiet domesticity. David was still
highly visible in the role of Prince of Wales, being present at the
laying of cornerstones and ceremonial tree plantings, opening
new highways and appearing before civic groups, "and assuming the honourary chairmanships of worthy charities and other
institutions"; still, domesticity was much prized by him.

Freda Dudley Ward was fun-loving, but she did not like to share her lover's attention with every eligible young woman or her mother or her aunt, who always besieged him at a party. She also had to contend with a great many married ladies who would have willingly and swiftly traded places with her. A large part of his attraction to Mrs. Dudley Ward had been the maturity that marriage and motherhood had brought to her young years. She knew how to decorate a house for a man's comfort, be a hostess, and tend to his needs. Not beautiful in the accepted sense, she had a charming piquant quality. Small and petite and somewhat gamine, she possessed a unique voice with a high tremor to it.

Not at all the "pretty little fluff" Lady Cynthia Asquith described her to be, Freda was witty, intelligent, and had original opinions that she was not afraid to express. She treated the Prince of Wales as though his title and wealth and notoriety had no effect on her, that it was *David* whom she adored. When a small, intimate group gathered in his sitting room, she sat before the fire at his feet leaning against his leg. He trusted her as he had never trusted another person. She did not laugh at his jokes if she thought them dull, nor accepted his pronouncements if she found them wrong in her opinion. And she never treated him with that aloof awe with which his own mother, despite her frequent censure, gave to the Heir-Apparent to the Throne. The plain truth was that with Mrs. Dudley Ward the Prince of Wales felt he was experiencing the same kind of man-woman relationship that other young men, not Royal, could look forward to.

From the autumn of 1920 until the autumn of 1921, with his constant attendance on Mrs. Dudley Ward, the Prince of Wales and Queen Mary were estranged. In his mother's view, a long separation of vast distance would be the only thing that might break up his slavish devotion to his mistress. She put forth her theory to the King, who without hesitation suggested it might be just the right time for a Prince of Wales again to visit India.

At a party given by Lady Wimborne, at Wimborne House, for his cousin Queen Ena's husband, King Alfonso of Spain, David, in an ill-tempered mood and having imbibed considerable

Champagne, approached Frances Stevenson,* secretary and mistress of Prime Minister Lloyd George (who was married at the time), and petulantly brought up the planned trip to India.

"Don't you want to go?" Miss Stevenson asked.

"Of course I don't want to go," he replied.

"But I thought you had become more or less reconciled to the idea."

"Oh, I suppose I can become reconciled to anything. Does the P.M. think I ought to go?"

"I don't know why he brought the subject up again," Miss Stevenson wrote in her diary the next day, "but I suppose he must have been feeling particularly depressed about it. Apparently he had been having an argument with his father about it for I heard that the Prince said to the King he would ask the P.M. whether he really wanted him to go. Whereupon the King said, 'I don't care whether the P.M. wants you to go or not. *I* want you to go & you are going.' "

And, indeed, on October 26, 1921, David departed on the *Renown* for India after a tearful goodbye to Mrs. Dudley Ward. His year at home had been the gayest in his memory. Full-dress uniforms had been restored to the Household Troops. All society was *en fête* and the Court in a gala mood. True, Britain was in a serious recession and there was a major coal strike. Thousands upon thousands of soldiers who had returned with hopes of beginning their lives anew were unemployed, with no prospects for the future. Yet in London society, a mood of gaiety prevailed. The great houses which had been hospitals during the war had been refurbished and once again thrown their doors open with a flourish of hospitality. For the Prince of Wales the year was joyous. He had found a stimulating mistress who could double as a loving mother. With Freda Dudley Ward he received his first real taste of what the life of the common man—that is, the lucky ones with fortunes—could be. The knowledge ratified his own conviction and reinforced his loathing to be King.

However, Queen Mary need not have been alarmed at Mrs. Dudley Ward's presence in the life of the future King of En-

---

*Frances Stevenson (1888–1972) became Lady Frances Lloyd-George upon her marriage to Lloyd George after the death of his first wife, Margaret.

gland. Freda Dudley Ward was a woman who knew just how far she could and should go. She has said that the Prince of Wales suggested several times they run off and that she always discouraged such ideas. Later historians might leap to the conclusion that the Prince of Wales remained a bachelor for the sixteen years that Mrs. Dudley Ward was to be his mistress because he feared losing her if he married. The truth is far more fundamental. A wife would not have diminished Freda Dudley Ward's devotion any more than Queen Alexandra had turned aside Alice Keppel's.

Princess Mary's wedding to Lord Lascelles took place on February 28, 1922, at Westminster Abbey, while David was still on his Indian tour. His sister's wedding—the first big state pageant since the war—was curiously scheduled for a time when the Prince of Wales could not attend. His absence did, however, keep the press from publicly wondering when and whom the Heir-Apparent might wed.

Bertie wrote his older brother in India, "Mary's wedding is causing a great deal of work to many people, & as far as I can make out the 28th is going to be a day of national rejoicing in every conceivable & unconceivable manner . . . In fact it is now no longer Mary's wedding, but (this from the paper) it is the 'Abbey Wedding' or the 'Royal Wedding' or the 'National Wedding,' or even the 'People's Wedding' (I have heard it called) 'of our beloved Princess.' "

Among Princess Mary's bridesmaids was Lady Elizabeth Bowes-Lyon,* the youngest daughter of Lord and Lady Strathmore. Bertie was quite obviously and hopelessly in love with the lovely young woman, who did not share his feelings. Queen Mary was completely convinced that Elizabeth was "the one girl who could make Bertie happy. But I shall say nothing to either of them."

Both Princess Mary and Bertie had met Elizabeth in late 1920 through the auspices of Lady Airlie, who had a family estate in

*Lady Elizabeth Bowes-Lyon (b. 1900–   ). Fourth daughter and ninth child of the 14th Earl of Strathmore. She became Queen Consort in 1936 on the Duke of York's accession to the Throne, and since his death in February 1952 has been known as Queen Elizabeth, The Queen Mother.

Scotland near the Strathmore home, Glamis Castle. In the spring of 1921, Bertie, after asking his father's permission, proposed and was refused. He was so disconsolate that everyone close felt sorry for him. After his sister's wedding, Elizabeth, feeling responsible, left London almost immediately with another of Princess Mary's bridesmaids, Diamond Hardinge. The two young women went to Paris, where Diamond's father, Lord Hardinge, was now Ambassador.

During the winter of 1921–22, discontent grew among the people, agitators seized their opportunities. Marches were organised, and fear spread that the troops would have to be called out to stop riots. Haunting memories of the Russian Revolution seeped under the draughty thresholds of the Royal Palaces, and even a Conservative like Lord Stamfordham wrote Lloyd George (whose power was slipping) that the King was "daily growing more anxious" and that organised resistance ". . . begets riot and possibly revolution." Even the solving of the Irish Question with an agreement on December 6, 1921, creating "the Irish Free State" as a Dominion within the Commonwealth, did not put an end to the civil war that continued to ravage the Free State and led to daily reports of wounded and dead.

"The wonderful day has come & gone," Queen Mary wrote David on March 2, "& Mary is married & has flown her home leaving a terrible blank behind her as you can well imagine. Papa & I are feeling very low & sad without her especially as Georgie had to return to Malta yesterday while Harry has at last joined the 10th Hussars at Canterbury & Bertie has gone hunting for a few days." She adds, "Nothing could have gone off better than the wedding did, a fine day, a beautiful pageant from start to finish, a fine service in the Abbey, Mary doing her part to perfection (a very great ordeal before so many people)—& everyone happy & pleased . . . Grannie was wonderful & looked very nice in violet velvet wearing the Garter & many fine jewels. Enormous crowds everywhere & a great reception when we stepped on to the Balcony—We gave a large family luncheon (both families) in the state dining room & Mary & Harry L. drove off at 3.45 —Papa & all of us throwing rice & little paper horse shoes & rose leaves after them. Papa & I felt miserable at parting, poor Papa broke down, but I mercifully managed to keep up as I so much

326

feared Mary wld break down. However she was very brave & smiled away as they drove off in triumph to the station."

King George adds in his own diary for the same night, "I went up to Mary's room & took leave of her & quite broke down . . . Felt very down & depressed now that darling Mary has gone."

Queen Mary and King George's daily lives took on a reclusive quality. Their round of Royal duties was always scheduled after they had lunched by themselves. They accepted very few social engagements and "night after night" dined "alone together."

Not that the King and Queen led a simple life. Both enjoyed the best of everything, great comfort perhaps more than anything else. Still, they dressed extravagantly, and, of course, no previous Queen of England had ever worn—or owned, for that matter—more priceless jewels. The King enjoyed shooting more than any other relaxation and, on his part, used only fine hammer guns by Purdey. His cigarette cases were made by Fabergé. Gala dinners at Windsor Castle might have lacked the high spirits of such dinners during King Edward's reign, but they were perhaps even more elegant.

King Edward would never have approved the solemn atmosphere. Later, David was to write that "over the port wine, coffee, and liqueurs the day's racing and current politics would be discussed" by the King and his male guests—the Queen and the women guests having withdrawn. The King "never sat more than twenty minutes," his son continues. "There was barely time to smoke even the shortest cigar. Abruptly, as if controlled by a hidden time clock, he would rise and lead his guests back to the Green Drawing Room to join my mother. At 11 o'clock as if by magic the company would resume the same circle in which he had found them, the ladies on one side, the men on the other. Bidding their guests good night, my parents would withdraw with the members of the Royal Family. The door would close silently behind us. The evening was over."

Queen Mary was never known to behave in the purely spoiled fashion of Queen Alexandra. She was never rude or abrupt, nor did she keep people waiting. Her worst flaw might have been her aloofness, for it tended to add to the image of correctness that surrounded her. Then fifty-six years old, the King was disappointed that the way of life that he had known before the war had not returned. He was as out of step with the twenties as was Queen Mary, although for a while she did try to bridge the gulf between her generation and her children's. They were grown now, and, as Lady Airlie says, "[the Queen] loved them and was proud of them but with the exception of Princess Mary they were strangers to her emotionally—a nest of wild birds already spreading their wings and soaring beyond her horizon."

Lady Airlie remembers the Queen laughing over the jokes in *Punch,* and even in *La Vie Parisienne.* She sent comic postcards (in envelopes) to her ladies-in-waiting; and even learned "Yes, We Have No Bananas," which she would later sing to David's accompaniment on the banjo. Women's hemlines had risen, and she tentatively suggested to Lady Airlie that they both might shorten their skirts by a modest two or three inches. She was concerned that King George might find even this unseemly. Lady Airlie volunteered to test his reactions and appeared at Windsor one day in a dress shorter than usual. Later, the King commented to the Queen that he had not liked Lady Airlie's dress, it was too short. Lady Airlie had her hem let down "with all speed," and Queen Mary remained faithful to her long, full skirts.

While Queen Mary was occupied with the romantic alliances of her Royal brood, Britain's economic condition became perilous. The glory of Empire was being threatened. As an epilogue to the war, a wave of antinationalist protest had swept India. It had picked up winds in 1919 with the tragedy of Amritsar, where riots and demonstrations had ended with five Englishmen killed and an Englishwoman missionary, innocently peddling her bicycle through the narrow, mud-paved, foetid streets of the city, brutally assaulted. British retaliation had followed less than a week later, when many hundreds of people jammed into a public enclosure called the Jalianwala Bagh in the centre of Amritsar for a political meeting. Surrounded by high walls and sunk below the level of the streets on which it bordered, the Bagh had only three entrances—and they were hardly wide enough for more than one man to pass.

As soon as the political speaker began his address, the approach of heavy vehicles was announced by a sudden loud rumble. In moments, armed men led by English officers pushed their way into the square and onto the higher ground behind the speaker. They turned and kneeled, facing the crowd with loaded rifles. The speaker, in an effort to calm the rising panic around him, continued his speech. To his horror and shock, a shouted command from one of the officers was followed instantly by the rapid report of many guns. Armed soldiers shot at point-blank range into the crowd. Terrified people trampled one another as they frantically tried to climb the high walls and crush through the narrow exits which soon became impassable with wounded and dead. The shooting lasted for 6 minutes; 379 people had been killed, another 1,500 wounded. The Indians now had their Bastille, as well as the saviour who would free India from Imperialist England.

A little emaciated man, barely 5 foot 4 inches, clothed in saintly white robes of common hopsacking, with vivid black eyes that peered through round spectacles above a broad nose and a toothless smile, Mahatma Gandhi had risen to form "a radical movement of incalculable power." To the people, he was semidivine, and after Amritsar he became the unrivalled leader in the Indian struggle for independence. It could be said that the horror of Amritsar was a seminal moment; the beginning of the end of the British Empire.

The British had been shaken and remorseful after Amritsar, and fearful as well that world condemnation of the massacre would severely affect their foreign relations. Blame was placed on General Dyer, who had given the order (called by the press a "tragic miscalculation") to fire. Obviously, a form of distraction, something that would place England in a more sympathetic light, had to be found. With the great enthusiasm given to the Prince of Wales on his travels, a quasi-solution was achieved.

A short lull in hostilities took place just before the advent of his tour of India. Nevertheless, for Queen Mary and King George not to realise the risks was naive. Fortunately, the Prince of Wales departed India just before Gandhi was arrested and charged with sedition because of articles he had written in his political journal *Young India*. Gandhi, appearing more humble and saintly than ever to his followers, immediately admitted his guilt and was sentenced to prison in Poona for six years. (He was released less than two years later, giving Indians not a saint but a martyr.)

At home, the political situation had been changing rapidly. By October 1922, the Liberals under Lloyd George had been defeated, and Bonar Law,* leader of the Conservative Party, became Prime Minister. Churchill still stood "as a Liberal and a Free Trader," but he also asked the electors to authorise him "to cooperate freely with sober-minded and progressive Conservatives." Six months later, Bonar Law was forced to resign as Prime Minister. He had cancer of the throat and died soon afterwards. After consulting with leading members of the Conservative Party, the King chose Stanley Baldwin as Law's successor.† Baldwin had entered the Cabinet only two years earlier, an inexperienced and curious choice. However, aside from Lord Curzon, who had the disadvantage of being a member of the House of Lords, there was no other serious contender.

In the same year, a book was published purporting to be a biography of Queen Mary. On the margin of a page that asserted she was easily bored, she had written in her distinctive flowing script: "As a matter of fact, the Queen is never bored." Though not social-minded, Queen Mary was deeply and emotionally involved in so many areas that boredom was not possible. Books still formed a major part of her life, and she was as politically knowledgeable as she had been when King Edward had suggested she be allowed to read the contents of the King's boxes. The problems abroad and the political anxieties at home greatly distressed her. During one crisis in late 1922, one of her Ladies-in-Waiting wrote: "The Queen stayed in bed all day & could not come to dinner, as she had lost her voice & she worried over the troublous times."‡

In May 1923, Princess Nicholas of Greece (the daughter-in-law of Queen Alexandra's brother, George I of Greece) was a guest at Windsor with her daughter, Princess Marina, one of the

*Andrew Bonar Law (1858–1923).

†Stanley Baldwin, 1st Earl of Baldwin Bewdley (1867–1947).

‡Lady Bertha Dawkins.

few remaining princesses who would qualify as a bride for the Prince of Wales. Princess Marina was extraordinarily striking; dark hair and eyes and marvellous fair skin, a lithe figure, and naturally elegant taste. She was also young (seventeen at the time), intelligent, and charming. David had returned from his eight-month tour and resumed his relationship with Freda Dudley Ward. Queen Mary arranged that he meet Princess Marina. The Prince of Wales could not have been less impressed. Prince George, however, was quite taken with the lovely Princess Marina, who departed with her mother before anything could come of it. For weeks, Georgie, only twenty-one at the time, was inconsolable, and Queen Mary was never again to attempt to play matchmaker in her son David's life.

TWENTY-THREE

Of his four surviving sons, only Bertie had the basic qualities of character the King respected: sticktoedness and a strong sense of duty. David remained an insoluble enigma to him. Harry's frequent illness had separated rather than drawn father and son together. Georgie's interests in aviation and the social scene were of little consequence to the King. Nonetheless, the King treated Bertie in a tutorial manner that never gave credit to his years. In truth, though Bertie had suffered many physical vicissitudes and had seen active duty, his emotional maturity *was* far behind that of other young men of his age. Not as smooth-faced as David and considerably more masculine in physique; still, an air of pubescence marked his personality.

On June 5, 1920, King George had created Bertie Duke of York, Earl of Inverness, and Baron Killarney. "I must write and thank you again ever so very much for having made me Duke of York," Bertie had written to his father. "I am very proud to bear the name that you did for many years, and I hope I shall live up to it in every way."

The King had replied:

Dearest Bertie,
I was delighted to get your letter this morning, & to know that you appreciate that I have given you that fine old title of Duke of

York which I bore for more than 9 years & is the oldest Dukedom in this country. I know that you have behaved very well in a difficult situation for a young man & that you have done what I asked you to do. I feel that this splendid old title will be safe in your hands & that you will never do anything which could tarnish it. I hope you will always look upon me as yr. best friend & always tell me everything & you will find me ever ready to help you & give you good advice.

Ever my dear boy.

Yr. very devoted Papa
GRI

This approving letter notwithstanding, King George was not a father easy to please, and Bertie's attempts to do so frequently failed and sent him into a state of melancholia. Those close to him were alarmed at these times at how much whisky he drank. His stuttering was worse than ever. In view of these obstacles and his painful shyness, his pursuit of Lady Elizabeth Bowes-Lyon was a stressful affair.

With Mary married, David so often abroad and living at York House when he was not, Harry in the Army, and Georgie at sea, it was Bertie who had to spend the most time at home with his parents. His mother's aloofness and his father's stern criticisms were not easy to endure. He had been his father's representative in October 1922 at the coronation of King Ferdinand and Queen Marie of Rumania. For reasons not altogether clear, the King was not wholly appreciative of Bertie's diplomatic achievements, even though Lord Stamfordham, who had accompanied him, spoke with high praise of his actions. Bertie fell into an acute state of depression, and his drinking intensified. Lord Stamfordham, much concerned and feeling empathy for the Duke of York, wrote a letter to Queen Mary with the hope that her understanding might somehow redress the balance of injustice.

"I venture to trouble Your Majesty," he wrote, "in case you may not quite realise what an unqualified success the Duke of York was in Rumania.

"I happened to be in the King's room when His Majesty was talking on this subject to Your Majesty . . . and I felt that His Majesty's praise was quite inadequate. For Colonel Waterhouse

[Private Secretary and Equerry to the Duke of York] said he could not exaggerate how admirably in every way [the Duke of York] had done—and that once he got away 'on his own' he was a different being and never failing to 'rise to the occasion,' and proved himself to be far away the most important foreign visitor at the Coronation."

Queen Mary did not respond to this letter. Despite Lord Stamfordham's praise, observers had noted Bertie's despondency and excessive drinking at the Rumanian coronation. The Queen was strong in her conviction that personal disappointment must necessarily be a private and concealed emotion in Royal emissaries. The problem was felt to be Bertie's great dilemma over Lady Bowes-Lyon and her elusive affections. He had visited her at Glamis Castle just before his trip to Rumania and once again proposed—to be gently but nonetheless rejected.

Bertie was deeply in love, and Queen Mary, ordinarily not a meddler in her children's lives to the extent that her mother had been, did enlist Lady Airlie's assistance. Lady Airlie spoke to her friend and neighbor, Lady Strathmore, Elizabeth's mother. The two older women applied some small pressure on the young woman, discussing Bertie's good qualities and her opportunities should she agree to marry him. Lady Strathmore was aware of her daughter's "perturbed and abstracted air" and later wrote, "that winter was the first time I have ever known Elizabeth really worried. I think she was torn between her longing to make Bertie happy and her reluctance to take on the big responsibilities this marriage must bring."

Previous Royal historians have also attributed Lady Elizabeth Bowes-Lyon's early rejection and later hesitancy in accepting the Duke of York's proposal to her fear of the heavy duties a Royal marriage would bring. However, the Duke of York was not the Heir-Apparent, and at the time there was no reason not to believe the Prince of Wales would marry and supply numerous heirs who would supplant Bertie from the direct line of succession. Also, Lady Elizabeth doted on responsibility. She was next to the youngest of eleven children; still, she was the one to nurse her father when he was ill and to understudy her mother as hostess at Glamis. She also loved London society, and her greatest friends were among the young members of these families. Her resistance to Bertie had much more to do with the young man himself. Apart from his extreme moodiness, Bertie was not of a strong constitution, and he was disconcertingly nervous. He had a serious speech impediment and numerous twitches, sometimes blinking his eyes with too much frequency and unable to control the muscles around his mouth. In addition, his drinking problem, though thought to be kept secret, had grown worse and had been observed by members of the Court, who talked about it among themselves. Nonetheless, the Duke of York's position and wealth were to be considered. And he was a sensitive young man with considerable disarming vulnerability and a strong need for the kind of warmth and affection his mother had never given him.

The desperate suitor was in a shocking state of depression over the 1922 Christmas holidays. He kept much to himself, whether walking the dismal winter paths of Sandringham or going shooting alone—the latter to his mother's consternation. Lady Airlie was consulted again, and shortly after New Year's Day 1923, she had Lady Bowes-Lyon to tea and regaled her with stories of her own marriage, how she had not known for sure in the beginning if she had loved her future husband, how she had hated the idea of an Army life and only tolerated it after her marriage for her husband's sake, and how she had grown to love him deeply and Army life as well.

Bertie arrived at Glamis Castle a few days later. Often accompanied by her brothers, Michael and David,* Lady Bowes-Lyon walked the hills and bogs of Glamis with Bertie. She was a good shot with a gun and rifle, and her keen enthusiasm and sense of adventure quickly buoyed the Duke of York's spirits. Evenings were spent in the romantic atmosphere of a candlelit drawing room, with the young people gathered about the piano singing. The Strathmores were an affectionate, closely knit family with an easy badinage, and Bertie, at ease with them, was able to allow his own personality to surface.

Queen Mary, who supported Bertie's determination to marry

---

*Michael Claud Bowes-Lyon (1893–1954) married Margaret Cator. David Bowes-Lyon (1902–1961) married Rachel Pauline Spender-Clay.

Lady Bowes-Lyon, remained at Sandringham, anxious for word. On Saturday, January 13, it finally came in the form of a terse telegram, "ALL RIGHT BERTIE."

To Lady Airlie, the Duke of York wrote of his gratitude to her and confided that his ". . . dream has at last been realised. It seems so marvellous to me to know that my darling Elizabeth will one day be my wife . . ."

The King's consent to the marriage was given on February 12. Bertie was to be the first English Prince to marry a commoner with consent since James, Duke of York, married Anne Hyde in 1660. He was also the first King's son to be married in Westminster Abbey since 1382, when Richard II exchanged vows with Anne of Bohemia.

The sun broke through the rain clouds when Lady Elizabeth, in elegant bridal dress, entered the Abbey the morning of April 26. She was attended by six bridesmaids, the bridegroom by his brothers David and Harry. There was even more of a display of public enthusiasm over this Royal Wedding than had been exercised at Princess Mary's marriage to Lord Lascelles. Still, the *Times* pointed out editorially, there was "one wedding to which the people look forward with still deeper interest—the wedding which will give a wife to the Heir to the Throne and in the course of nature, a future Queen of England to the British peoples." The article ended sympathetically that "whilst the Princes of Wales have almost invariably been compelled to accept the brides that State policy selected, the Dukes of York have nearly always obeyed the dictates of their hearts."

Bertie looked radiantly happy, and the two of them were enormously appealing to the public. They spent the first part of their honeymoon at Polesden Lacy, near Dorking, in Surrey, the home of Mrs. Ronald Greville,* and then went to Glamis, where the new Duchess of York came down with whooping cough. "So unromantic . . . on your honeymoon," Bertie wrote Queen Mary, adding, "I do hope you will not miss me very much though I

---

*The Honourable Mrs. Ronald Greville, "Maggie" to her friends, was the daughter of a whisky magnate and extremely rich. She had only recently been instrumental in the match between Lord Louis Mountbatten and Edwina Ashley.

believe you will as I have stayed with you so much longer really than the brothers.''

To Bertie's surprise, his father was the one who replied to this. "I miss you very much," he wrote. "You have always been so sensible & easy to work with & you have always been ready to listen to any advice & to agree with my opinion about people & things, that I feel that we have always got on very well together (very different to dear David)."

The newly married Yorks were given White Lodge, Richmond, as their first home and moved into it with great delight. For the first time, that old house had a jaunty, youthful air. Bright floral chintzes and pastel paints replaced its former heavy Victorian decoration, a change that Queen Mary approved and helped to accomplish.

Queen Mary and her first daughter-in-law had a rapport that the older woman would have wished to have had with her own mother-in-law. But then, Queen Mary never had the need to substitute the affections of a son for a husband's neglect, as had Queen Alexandra.

The Duchess of York had great warmth and charm. An incident that occurred while the Yorks were on an Empire tour a few years after their marriage illustrates her charisma. A local Communist leader in Canada was so bewitched by the "little Duchess" that he said in a press interview, "I've done with Communism! She *looked* at me—and waved—and smiled!"

The Duchess of York had no desire to compete with Queen Mary and never pushed herself or her opinions forward with her Royal in-laws. After all, she had not married the son who would one day make his wife Queen.

"It is hard to see that beautiful woman Queen Alexandra come to this," Queen Mary told Lady Airlie in the winter of 1924. Nine months had elapsed since the Queen had seen her mother-in-law, who had just celebrated her eightieth birthday. By now not only was she deaf, her eyesight was failing as well, and the combination had so upset her nerves that her will to live had been greatly impaired. In March 1925, she wrote to Queen Mary, "I feel *completely* collapsed—I shall soon go."

Month after month, Queen Alexandra, with Charlotte Knollys

and Toria as her lone companions, remained cloistered at Sandringham.* The gay ambiance that had once pervaded Sandringham had long ago disappeared. The footmen and door-keepers were now all white-haired, the halls hushed. With Charlotte Knollys almost ninety, wasted and sallow, and Toria an old maid nearing sixty, the atmosphere was aromatic of illness and age, and the fustiness so disturbed Queen Mary that she could hardly bear it. Seven more months were to pass before she ventured up to see Motherdear again. "Went to tea with Mama whom I had not seen since Feb.," she wrote in her diary in October 1925; "she looked well in the face but it is difficult to understand what she says." Queen Mary's Lady-in-Waiting, Lady Cynthia Colville, recalls that tea much more vividly.

Although she had frequently visited Sandringham with Queen Mary, Lady Colville had never had tea at the Big House. Usually, Queen Mary wore tweed dresses and coats in the country. Still, Lady Colville was in something of a quandary about the correct attire to be worn for tea at Queen Alexandra's home. Assuming that they would walk the couple of hundred yards between York Cottage and the Big House, and taking into consideration her knowledge of Queen Alexandra's love of clothes, Lady Colville compromised on a dark green fur-trimmed mid-calf dress with coat and hat to match, an outfit that she deemed her "country Sunday best."

To Lady Colville's dismay, when she met Queen Mary at the appointed hour in the small downstairs waiting room, the Queen was dressed in a floor-length silver gown, and hatless. The poor Lady-in-Waiting had no time to do more than remove her hat, for a grand old carriage drawn by two of Sandringham's finest horses was waiting outside. Moments later, they were met by Queen Alexandra in a magnificent tea gown, her face perfectly but heavily made up, looking almost waxen. Her emaciated wrenlike hands, overburdened with rings and bracelets, shook the fragile gold-crested cup and saucer she held as she sipped her tea. Lady Colville had not often been in the company of the two Queens together, and she noted that "their attitude to each other . . . was entirely correct but there was no

*Sir Dighton Probyn had recently died.

338

natural sympathy or instinctive understanding between them."

Queen Alexandra no longer even made an effort to read lips. She had suffered a small stroke a year before this meeting, and her speech was somewhat slurred. Nonetheless, an underlying warmth and understanding passed between her and Charlotte Knollys that was most touching to observe. The air of bored distraction on Queen Alexandra's part toward her daughter-in-law created a strong contrast.

In her letters to her son (in a most unsteady hand), Queen Alexandra complained of "everlasting pain & *noises* in my wretched old head," and signed herself "your poor old blind & deaf old Motherdear." She still took a great pride in "precious" David ("May God grant him a perfect wife!") and "beloved" Bertie. Memories of the past were her most frequent visitors. To Bertie, she wrote of the time she and her other "beloved Bertie . . . were walking together in the pretty garden . . . when he suddenly proposed to me! My surprise was great & I accepted him with *greatest* delight!"

In the afternoons, she sometimes was taken for a short ride around the estate. In the evenings, conversation was almost impossible because of her bad hearing.

"Did you know, Ma'am, that His Majesty has a new car?" a member of her dwindling Court asked her one night.

"A new cow?"

"No, Ma'am, a new *car.*"

"Yes, yes," she said emphatically, "I hear you, I understand; the old one has calved."

She spent the last weeks of October and the first half of November paying daily visits to her kennels and stables, amusing herself with jigsaw puzzles and feeding the sea gulls. She remained regular in her attendance at Sandringham Church. She never left the house without being heavily veiled. "Think of me as I used to be, now I am breaking up," she wrote to an old friend in July 1925.*

An early snow arrived on the morning of November 19. At noon, as she was readying her arduous toilette for lunch, Queen Alexandra suffered a heart attack. The King and Queen hurried

---

*Lord Knutsford.

to Sandringham and remained by her bedside all through that night and the next day.

In a room nearby to the one where she had once sat vigil during Prince Eddy's last hours, Queen Mary sat holding Queen Alexandra's pathetically frail hand. Occasionally, the old lady inclined her head in one direction or the other, or almost imperceptibly pressed the hand that held her own. She never spoke or uttered a cry, and the silence in the room—so cluttered with memorabilia that there was hardly a space for chairs for Toria and Charlotte Knollys—was almost unendurable.

David and Bertie—who had been hunting in Leicestershire—arrived at Wolferton Station early on the evening of November 20, too late; their "Grannie" had died only moments before their arrival. The Big House was a great shadow against a darkening sky. The last light of the Edwardian era had flickered out.

A flat was found for Charlotte Knollys in London, and Toria was given rooms in Kensington Palace. The King rang his sister on the telephone every day without fail; still, he did not have the binding attachment to his sister that he had had for his mother. Only one woman remained in his life, his wife, and he turned to her with greater devotion and attendance than ever. The Court instantly noted a new attitude in Queen Mary. She had, of course, always possessed her own unique and powerful personality. With Queen Alexandra's death, she had become a more matriarchal figure, and both her Court and her personal life took on a sharper edge of formality.

Queen Mary was now the only Queen in England. She was looked upon by the public "as a figure of superlative dignity and splendour, kindly and generous, too." But she was never as generous as Queen Alexandra had been. From her youth, she had known the meaning of serious debt and financial worry. Tremendous wealth had not obscured her memory of bailiffs sitting in the hall of her parents' home, or of the Tecks' two-year meagre and humiliating exile abroad to save money simply to repay a portion of Princess Mary Adelaide's hopeless debts. The Queen considered large parties a great extravagance. Because of this and the King's lack of interest in society other than state occasions, there were very few galas.

More time was now spent at Buckingham Palace, where behaviour and dress were formal. King George wore a frock coat in the daytime, and the men of the Household and Ministers and other visitors were expected to do the same. During their private tête-à-tête dinners in London, the King wore a tailcoat, Queen Mary an evening gown and diamond tiara.

At Sandringham, the King and Queen could at last vacate York Cottage and take over the Big House. For a good part of 1926, the Queen was occupied with its redecoration, as well as sifting through the sixty years of accumulation by Queen Alexandra at Marlborough House. "You never saw such a mass of things of all kinds as there are," Queen Mary wrote her sister-in-law Margaret, Marchioness of Cambridge. "A motley collection of good & bad things—A warning to one not to keep too much for nothing was ever thrown away . . ."

She tried desperately hard to convince David to move to Marlborough House, but, content with his home, York House, across the way, he refused, much to his mother's long-range irritation. The Queen took a good part of six months to get Sandringham House into a livable condition. In August, David joined her at York Cottage for two days to help supervise the work being done.

"I am delighted you & David were both pleased with the dear place. In summer it is lovely," King George wrote Queen Mary at Sandringham just after the Prince of Wales had left. ". . . I am glad he took an interest in it, although he certainly didn't stop long, but rushed off to his tiresome golf . . . So you are pleased with the alterations & with the decorations of the rooms at the house, yr rooms, in fact all our rooms will I am sure be most comfortable. Hope you are gradually getting the ballroom cleared, as I do not want it to become a store room or lumber room." A few days later he added, "The pictures want sorting out & arranging, but you must remember that there will be marks on the walls where the paper has faded."

Queen Mary, unable to let go the ghost of her disapproval of Queen Alexandra's household habits, replied, "All the rooms are more airey now and less full of those odds & ends which beloved Mama wld poke into every corner of the house which was such a pity."

Any free day Queen Mary now had would include a trip to an antique shop or museum. She was busily engaged in the work being done at Sandringham and Marlborough House. Her insatiable fascination in rearranging and completing the great Royal collections at Buckingham Palace and Windsor Castle left museum directors no more protection from her obsession than antique dealers. If she saw something that she thought should be placed in a Royal residence, she requested a permanent loan of the piece. Hardly a painting, objet d'art, or piece of furniture in the remotest rooms or back passages of any of the Royal palaces and houses can be found without a label in Queen Mary's fluid script, describing its subject and origin. Unfortunately, she was never a serious Royal collector of art, like Charles I and George IV, for with her thoroughness and diligence, Britain's Royal Art Collection might have been greatly benefited. She was not a great arbiter of taste, nor did she exert any influence through her husband on architecture, interior decorating, or furniture design. Victoria and Edward had both contributed to the styles of their periods. Georgian style clearly referred to another King.

The fashionable world meant nothing to Queen Mary, nor did she have the least desire to be an innovator. Her great passion was preservation and restoration. And, of course, her nature was too conservative to spend fortunes on acquiring new Royal possessions, when for almost no outlay she could reshuffle or request the return of the old.

Queen Mary also had a passion for miniature objets d'art; they were, in fact, some of her few frivolous purchases. The English called it "tiny craft." Glass cases were installed at Sandringham to display her collection of exquisite golden tea sets, the cups the size of a thumbnail; tiny, intricate mother-of-pearl chairs; and gilt and tortoiseshell carriages that could be held in a baby's hand. Princess Marie Louise (King George's cousin) suggested the idea of building Queen Mary's Doll's House to be decorated to scale by the leading craftsmen and artists of the day. When complete, it "would enable future generations to see how a King and Queen of England lived in the twentieth century and what authors [miniature books were to be included], artists, and craftsmen of note there were during their reign." The plan could not help but please the Queen, for, of course, all the contents were to be given in the form of gifts.

Princess Marie Louise did an exhaustive job of supervising the project, along with Sir Edwin Lutyens, who drew the plans.* The façade was Georgian. Inside, the house was to be a replica of the private apartments of the King and Queen, as well as of some of the rooms at Buckingham Palace that were used for ceremonies. In the ceremonial hall, six-inch-high knights in medieval armour stood on a marble-and-lapis lazuli floor guarding the grand marble staircase that had miniature replicas of fifteenth-century tapestries and tiny bronze models of sculpture by the world's greatest sculptors. Every appliance in the house, down to the kitchen scales and vacuum cleaner, worked. Dumb-waiters and elevators were installed, and a fully operational parlour grand piano gilded and hand painted. The wine cellar had a superb collection of spirits, beer, and wine in inch-high bottles, among them Margaux '99, Romanée '04, Yquem '74, and an 1854 brandy.

In the Royal garage were parked a Rolls-Royce, two Daimlers, a Lancaster, a Vauxhall, and a Sunbeam, all with gasoline engines that ran; as well as a 6¾-inch motorcycle, a bicycle, gas pumps, and a fire engine.

The full Royal china service had been copied, as had Queen Mary's simpler white china bearing her cipher crowned. Paintings were reduced to one-twelfth their original size without any loss of detail. The dozens of clocks all ran, the fireplaces worked, and the many exquisite crystal chandeliers were all electrified.

Perhaps the most amazing room was the library; the leather-bound books, like everything else made to the scale, were filled with handwritten entries by Rudyard Kipling, A. A. Milne, Somerset Maugham, Arthur Conan Doyle, Max Beerbohm, and other great contemporary writers.† George Bernard Shaw was, in fact, the only author who refused to contribute—and wrote a reply to the request "in a very rude manner."

---

*Sir Edwin Lutyens (1869–1944). Leading English architect responsible for many famous buildings constructed in England from the 1890s onward. He also was the architect of eight square miles of New Delhi.

†The contents of these books were short excerpts of the authors' works.

The Queen had few intimate friends. King George, however, had many. The closest was perhaps Sir Charles Cust, his equerry and constant companion. Lady Cynthia Colville tells a story about the two men, just before the move from York Cottage to Sandringham, that gives a fine insight into the King's relations to those close to him but not a part of his family. The King had a parrot named Charlotte (after Charlotte Knollys), given to him by his sister Toria. "Charlotte had the freedom of the house," Lady Cynthia wrote, "and one of her less agreeable habits was to walk about the dining room table during breakfast at York Cottage and dig her beak in the boiled egg of some guest or member of the Household. This was too much for Sir Charles Cust and I remember him giving his views on Charlotte in terms which were to say the least an unusual method of addressing one's Sovereign. I don't think the King resented it, but equally I don't think Charlotte mended her ways."

Such a relaxation of Royal regard was unthinkable to Queen Mary, and it kept her back from making very close associations. She may have dressed in tweeds in the country, but she was never the countrywoman. And, in truth, she was more at home now in Windsor Castle or Buckingham Palace, where life had something ceremonial about it. Female members of the Household were expected to carry gloves at meals, even to their private dining room. The Queen never let anyone forget that Windsor Castle had been the home of English kings for hundreds of years and, in a sense, was symbolic of all that the Monarchy stood for. Her Household and contemporaries always looked upon her as the Queen of England, not as the Consort of the King of England. Such an attitude was not meant in any way to diminish the power or lustre of the Monarch himself. Queen Mary, in fact, would have been quite horrified to have found even a hint of truth to that.

England was on the brink of industrial chaos during most of 1926. Longstanding trouble in the coal industry had ended in a general strike. Lady Airlie relates that she ". . . spent a morning in one canteen working with a team of voluntary helpers . . . the great tent was filled with gaunt men eating ravenously . . . It struck me as a terrible indictment against our social system that they should have been labelled 'unemployable' . . . The teams of amateur waitresses serving them were all what were called 'society girls,' looking exactly like working girls; no prettier, in fact rather more untidy. They were very tired—some of them had been on duty fourteen hours a day behind the enormous tea urns—but they were determined to carry on. The whole country had one fixed resolve—to break the 'tyranny' of the strike."

At Buckingham Palace, the sentries at the gate had exchanged their red coats and bearskins for khaki and forage caps. Inside, except for "a great scurrying of messengers," Queen Mary had commanded "business as usual." No one, however, was allowed to use the telephones, which meant that a vast number of letters had to be written and delivered by hand. On May 13, the strike ended in the humiliating defeat of the strikers, who had surrendered unconditionally. A more happy note had been heard when at 2:40 the morning of April 21, the Duchess of York gave birth to her first child, a daughter, who was third in succession to the Throne. Queen Mary motored to London that afternoon to view her first granddaughter,* born at the London home of the Duchess's parents.

"At 2.30 we went to London to 17 Bruton Street," Queen Mary wrote in her diary, "to congratulate Bertie & we found Celia Strathmore there, saw the baby who is a little darling with a lovely complexion & pretty fair hair."

On May 29, in the private chapel at Buckingham Palace, Princess Elizabeth Alexandra Mary of York was christened.†

"Of course poor baby cried," Queen Mary commented with a touch of matriarchal condescension.

---

*Princess Mary and Lord Lascelles had had a son (the present Earl of Harewood) born to them February 7, 1923.

†Queen Elizabeth II (b. 1926).

TWENTY-FOUR

Queen Mary had a growing horror of illness, her own or that of anyone close to her. With great discipline, she had managed to control her fear during the war years so that she could make her weekly rounds of the injured in hospitals. Shortly thereafter, she turned almost completely away from such duties. Members of her Household have variously said that the Queen did not have a stomach for hospitals any more than she had for the sea. The illness of anyone of her immediate family was even more difficult for her to bear.

On November 21, 1928, King George confided to her that he was feeling feverish and not at all well. He went directly to bed. Sir Stanley Hewett, the King's physician, was summoned. Alarmed at what he found, he in turn sent for Lord Dawson of Penn, a specialist in lung diseases. The King had acute septicemia at the base of the right lung, not a typical pleuro-pneumonia "but a case of severe general blood infection and toxemia." His condition became so grave that within a few days he was too weak to deal with matters of state. A warrant was prepared nominating six Councillors of State (the Queen, the Prince of Wales, the Duke of York, the Archbishop of Canterbury, the Lord Chancellor, and the Prime Minister) to act for the King during his illness.

A telegram was sent to the Prince of Wales in East Africa

where he was on tour, and he started back immediately on the long 7,000-mile nine-day journey to England. En route he received word that his father's condition had worsened and that the King's heart had been affected.

On December 6, when the Prince of Wales had finally reached France, Bertie wrote him, "There is a lovely story going around which emanated from the East End of London that the reason of your rushing home is that in the event of anything happening to Papa I am going to bag the Throne in your absence!!!!! Just like the Middle Ages . . . "

The brothers met two days later at Victoria Station. Bertie's face was white and drawn. "You will find Papa greatly changed," he told David as they drove to Buckingham Palace. "And now Dawson says that an operation will be necessary in a day or two. Mama has been amazing. Through all the anxiety she has never once revealed her feelings to any of us. She is really far too reserved. She keeps too much locked up inside of her. I fear a breakdown if anything awful happens . . . "

Queen Mary was standing when her two older sons entered her sitting room. Bertie had been right. Her composure was remarkable. She kissed David perfunctorily on his cheek and then quickly stepped back. Her attitude, if anything, was more restrained than ever toward him.

David, from a lifetime's observation of his mother, knew what Bertie had not been able to discern. Queen Mary was already preparing herself for the possibility of moving down the rung one step to Queen Mother, and she was treating David in the manner not of a woman whose husband might be dying, but as a son who might soon be her King. She led him into his father's dimly lit bedroom and withdrew into the shadows.

The Prince of Wales later wrote that his father recognised him instantly and mumbled feebly about hoping he had had good sport in East Africa. Stanley Baldwin, the Prime Minister, who was also present, tells quite another story:

"[The Prince of Wales] was told that he might not on any account go *near* his father, who was, we all thought, near death, for at least 48 hours [the fear being that the King would know he was dying if his heir had travelled 7,000 miles to see him]. He simply took no notice, damned everybody and marched in.

347

The old King,* who had for nearly a week been practically unconscious, just opened half an eye, looked up at him and said:
"'Damn you, what the devil are you doing here?'"
Baldwin's memory could well have been faulty. In any event, his niece Monica Baldwin, who recorded this incident for him, might have played up the scene. The presence of a Prince of Wales to *any* English King was a constant reminder of his mortality. And to a Prince of Wales, a dying King was the final rung on his ascent to power. One is reminded of the scene in Shakespeare's *Henry IV*, when Prince Henry tries on the crown while his father, the King, lies dying nearby.

The King's will to live never deserted him. On the evening of December 13, the needed operation was performed. The King's chances of surviving it were slim; death, however, was certain without it. For a fortnight thereafter, he wavered on the edge of life and death, the country unaware of the true seriousness of his condition. From the time that King George took ill, Queen Mary had maintained his diary. On January 6, 1929, she was finally able to write, "After tea G. sent for me, he was perfectly clear & we had a talk for 20 minutes which cheered me much after not having spoken to me for practically six weeks. George signed his name just to show me he could do so."

His recuperation was slow. Added to his weak condition was a dramatic loss of hearing. He looked an invalid, an old man, and he was still not strong enough to handle any public business. The Prince of Wales, with the aid of the other five Chancellors, was, in effect, acting-King. The situation did not help the relationship between father and son.

On the ninth of February (the Queen travelling separately in her own motorcar), King George was transported by ambulance from London to Bognor,† where he was to convalesce at Craigwell, a house beside the sea that he loved. Looking haggard and worn, his long face thin, all eyes, he nevertheless "had the blinds up on the drive & waved to the people *en route* . . . " The King and Queen remained at Bognor until mid-May, when they motored to Windsor. Two weeks later, a new and unsuspected

---

*King George was sixty-three at the time.

†Always afterwards to be called Bognor Regis.

abscess broke through the scar left by the King's operation. For months he suffered an open wound that would not drain properly. On July 15, he was operated upon again. The doctors were not confident that he was on the road to full recovery until the end of September.

The King's prolonged illness had not been easy for Queen Mary. He had been a bad patient and an even worse convalescent. Often querulous and languishing frequently in moods of self-pity, he was no longer the man she knew, but irascible, delicate, and older by many years than his true chronological age. A nurse, Sister Catherine Black, remained on after he had recovered and was to stay with the King for the rest of his life. For, in truth, King George was never again to be in anything but failing health.

By 1930, Queen Mary had spent twenty years as Queen of England, giving the majority of her days and all of her energy to creating a façade on which nothing private was revealed. Even to her Household, family, and friends, she was hard to get to know. Small talk had no place in her private life. She refused to discuss even the predictability of the English weather or the unpredictability of young people. Anyone's health, including her own and the King's, was considered a distasteful topic.

Familiarity was not in her nature. Only the King called her May. To all others, she was either "Ma'am" or "Your Majesty." Except in print, she was never addressed as Queen Mary. She did not smile in public either frequently or easily. Graciousness and a priceless stateliness comprised her public style, and nothing pleased onlookers (who would wait hours to see her pass in a glass coach or appear on the balcony of Buckingham Palace) more than for her to bow or to raise her arm in a gesture of greeting.

No matter what the calendar said, Queen Mary was a pure nineteenth-century personality. The people thought of her as being typically English, and since King George's illness, they thought of her often. She was now before the public on a daily basis and thoroughly enjoyed her increased popularity. The country had entered into a time of severe Depression, and she used her position tirelessly as a means to stimulate business.

British industrialists claimed she and the Prince of Wales were England's two best salesmen. In a contemporary profile, one magazine writer said, "This is unfair. The Queen is the *two* best salesmen."

The Queen, indeed, had the best business head in the family. Her shopping expeditions were legend. Crowds followed her; whatever she was seen wearing or buying would swiftly be in such demand that manufacturers would increase production. She attended all industrial fairs and home-furnishing expositions, and photographs were always taken when she made a homely selection for Buckingham Palace—an electric icebox one time, bath mats another. Immediately a sign would go up on a display of the item, "Purchased by Her Majesty the Queen."

She made cheap brown pottery teapots from the quite humble Marks & Spencer stores indispensable in English homes by buying them for the King's morning tea in all the Royal residences. She also bought him "a new design of woollen underclothing" (one-piece with a back-flap but no legs) of all English wool, scratchier, nonetheless, than softer-textured foreign imports. At one fair alone, starting out at 10:00 A.M., she walked seven miles stopping at almost every stall, buying handbags, quince and peach jams, Deeside bilberries, Dundee herrings, paint boxes for her grandchildren, and even an 1887 Jubilee umbrella (copies were instantly made and sold at stores all over England). By 1:30 she reached the last stall having been photographed repeatedly, no signs of weariness in her step or expression and not a wisp of hair out of place. Three rooms at Buckingham Palace were needed to cope with her shopping sprees. But much of what she bought she gave away; at Christmas her list of recipients exceeded even those of King Edward.

In 1931, when the economy was at its worst, the Queen insisted on maintaining the formality of the Courts. The number of young ladies being presented doubled in one year from 1,200 to 2,400 (by 1934, this number had risen to 8,000), and with their curtsies, the commerce of thousands of merchants rose in harmony.

In today's world where so little protocol has been left intact, these Court presentations are difficult to conceive. London correspondent for the *New Yorker*, Janet Flanner, in her coverage of the four given in 1934, wrote perhaps one of the best of all descriptions:

"The King and Queen," she began, "want gowns low and long regardless of fashion. Last year stylish high-fronted numbers appeared. The King didn't like that. The Prince of Wales's three white ostrich feathers plus a twenty-seven-inch white veil, must be placed on the head in the *Ich Dein* motto manner; . . . three black ostrich feathers in the case of a widow. The 1934 trains stretch eighteen inches back from the heel . . . were four and a half yards long before the war, were cut off entirely in post-war 1919, and the following year cut down to the present two and a half yards from the shoulder (the extra long queues of *nouveaux riches*, plus their fourteen-foot trains, were apparently more than the Queen could stand) . . . the train's weight is distributed between shoulder hooks and stocking tops by a special net corselet, with garters to prevent the gown from pulling back, or even off. Rehearsal of gown, shoes, feathers, fan, jewels, and curtsy are held in the shop before the gown is delivered. Jewels are a great problem in Court-dress designing where fine family stones form the front of the frock. Court gowns must be flamboyant to show against the Palace gilt, the Queen's blaze of diamonds, and the Royal Household uniforms; a mere chic Paris frock would stand no chance in Buckingham. Before entry to the Throne Room, trains are settled in place by attendants with long ivory poles. Curtsies have from time immemorial been taught by Miss Vacani; Trufitt or Douglas of Bond Street are still the hieratic hairdressers. A debutante is presented by her mother; after marriage, is re-presented by her mother-in-law. Court begins at 9.30 P.M. and ends around midnight, with supper after, the King's catering and the Queen's choice being done by Lyons, the teashop people, and very good."

Besides the four Courts, there was the annual Royal garden party with a record number of guests, the state balls, and the various state banquets. The King and Queen were expected to receive each guest.* No one ever forgot the superb sight of the

---

*The Queen wore a pair of white kid gloves only once and then disposed of them. During this season she had to cast off so many pairs that she complained to her Ladies-in-Waiting of this waste.

351

stately Queen, a magnificent crown on her tousled greying head, wearing *décolletage* that evidenced a full womanly breast, loaded with priceless jewels, and seated column-straight, hands poised eloquently on her cloth-of-gold or silver or creamy ivory or pale pastel lap. The Queen's Court gowns had no modern connection whatsoever. Elaborate in cut, beaded, gold-and-silver-embroidered, "gusseted, gored, looped, draped, cap-sleeved," they were uniquely anachronistic; part Empire, part Edwardian. No Royal jewel collection in the world remained that could compare to hers. At Courts, she liked to wear alternating sets of gems—diamonds and emeralds, or pearls, or sapphires. At state dinners, she often wore an outer rope of a hundred and fifty enormous pearls that fell to her waist, three inner strands, a nine-strand dog collar, pearl-and-diamond earrings, a diamond-and-pearl tiara, and all her brilliant orders.

She dressed during the day in light colours, favouring blues that complemented her eyes. The year before the war, Nicholas II had given her magnificent sables as a Christmas gift, and she often wore them. Fur trimmed many of her tweed outfits, and she never wore one without one of her inimitable toques "worn high on her head like a crown." Janet Flanner remarked that the Queen "dresses in the height of fashion—for queens," adding that "she looks like herself with the elegant eccentricities . . . of a wealthy white-haired *grande dame* who has grown into the mature style she set for herself too young." The fact was that whether the Queen was shopping at a street stall or bowing from inside a Royal landau, she could not have been mistaken for anyone but the Queen.

When little Princess Elizabeth (back already Royal straight, bow and wave near perfect) accompanied her, cockney kerbside admirers would comment loudly, "She's the spit of her granny!" Lilibet, as Queen Mary called the small girl, bore no resemblance to the Queen, apart from her regal poise and fair hair.

The Queen's public style was a curious mixture of majesty and maternalism, the last probably inspired by her full bosom and kindly manner. She was the quintessential fairy queen, distant and yet approachable at the same time. Entering the kitchen on a tour of a home for crippled boys at Blackheath, the Queen in high toque, pearls, and white fox, said to the cook and the

ABOVE: Queen Mary entering Delhi to begin the Durbar tour.

LEFT: The King Emperor and Queen Empress leaving the train at Salimgarh Bastian; they walked beneath the imperial umbrella. December 30, 1911. The young girl in photograph is the daughter of a British official.

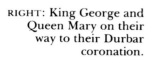

RIGHT: King George and Queen Mary on their way to their Durbar coronation.

ABOVE: King George as big game hunter (seen standing in Howdaw of the third elephant from left), the result of a morning's sport on grass before him. Nepal, 1911.

RIGHT: King George and a pensive Queen Mary at the time of the Durbar.

BELOW: King George V's drawing room in the imperial tent at Delhi during Durbar.

RIGHT: Princess Victoria Louise, Kaiser Wilhelm's daughter, and her bridegroom, Prince Ernest Augustus of Brunswick, Luneburg. Prince Ernest was a descendant of George II, the only surviving son of the Duke of Cumberland, and a British Prince. King George gave his official consent to the marriage.

LEFT: King George (right, in a German uniform) and Kaiser Wilhelm at the wedding festivities in Berlin of the Kaiser's daughter, Princess Victoria Louise, May 1913. In a year they would be enemies.

Queen Mary wearing the emeralds that were among the world's most priceless matched collections. Circa 1912.

RIGHT: King George and Queen Mary welcome President and Mrs. Woodrow Wilson to England after signing of armistice, 1919.

BELOW: King George and the boyish Prince of Wales in France at early stage of World War I, 1915.

ABOVE: Queen Mary visits Woolwich Arsenal (Princess Mary behind her), 1916.

ABOVE: Review of American troops by King George as the troops passed the Royal Party, May 1918.

LEFT: Prince Edward (left) and his brother Prince Albert.

RIGHT: Back in London from a Mediterranean cruise. L to R— Queen Mary; King George; Prince George; and Prince Henry, Duke of Gloucester, 1925.

King George riding in Windsor Park with his four sons, the Prince of Wales; Duke of York; Prince Henry; and, not visible, Prince George.

ABOVE: A royal luncheon at Sandringham, 1922. At Queen Alexandra's round table (R to L) King George, Queen Alexandra, Queen Mary, Sir Arthur Davidson, the Honourable Charlotte Knollys, Sir Dighton Probyn, and Princess Mary.

ABOVE: Royal guests at the Mountbatten wedding—Queen Mary with Queen Alexandra and behind them Princess Victoria ("Toria").

RIGHT: Lord Louis Mountbatten and his bride, Edwina Ashley, 1922.

ABOVE: An early photograph of the Prince of Wales with Mrs. Wallis Simpson. He dared to take her to Ascot on a day when King George and Queen Mary did not attend, 1933.

ABOVE RIGHT: Edward, the Playboy Prince, at the Derby, 1930.

RIGHT: Queen Mary smiling despite her concern over the unmarried Heir to the Throne.

RIGHT: For sixteen years Mrs. Freda Dudley Ward, here with Sir Phillip Sassoon at Wimbledon, 1931, was mistress to the Prince of Wales. Mrs. Simpson made sure she and her friends were banned from the Prince's circle.

LEFT: (L to R) Thelma, Lady Furness, and her twin sister Mrs. Gloria Vanderbilt at the unveiling of a portrait of them painted by Paul Trebilcock. Thelma's affair with the Prince of Wales was a chapter from a romantic novel.

RIGHT: Prince Albert (the future George VI) and his reluctant fiancée, Lady Elizabeth Bowes-Lyon. Here the couple fail to avoid photographers, 1926.

ABOVE: The royal family on the balcony of Buckingham Palace after their return from the Jubilee Thanksgiving service, 1935. (Left to right): Prince Arthur of Connaught, Queen Maud of Norway, the Duke of York, the Princess Royal, King George, Princess Margaret Rose, the Honourable Gerald Lascelles, the Earl of Harewood (at back), Princess Elizabeth, Viscount Lascelles, Queen Mary, the Duchess of Kent, the Duke of Kent, Princess Victoria, the Duchess of York, the Prince of Wales, the Earl of Athlone, and Princess Alice, Countess of Athlone.

ABOVE: Queen Mary and King George at Ilford. The Queen would poke the King with her umbrella if she felt he was going on too long.

RIGHT: Sister Catherine Black; she was in constant nursing attendance to King George for the last seven years of his life.

BELOW: Queen Mary and King George with their granddaughter Princess Elizabeth (Elizabeth II), 1933. The little princess was King George's favourite and he hoped someday she would reign.

The State Funeral Procession of King George V in London: Five kings, the French president, and princes representing foreign nations walking behind the coffin: In the leading row, but not here visible, was Lord Harewood, next to King Haakon of Norway. In order from left to right, in successive rows, the figures seen are: *1st row:* King of Norway (extreme left); Crown Prince of Norway; Earl of Athlone; *2nd row:* King of Rumania (only plumed cap visible above Earl of Athlone); King of Denmark; President Lebrun (France); *3rd row:* King of the Belgians; King of Bulgaria; *4th row:* Prince of Piedmont; Prince Regent of Yugoslavia: Crown Prince of Sweden; *5th row:* Crown Prince of Greece; Prince Zeid; Prince of Said (Prince Faruk of Egypt); *6th row:* Prince

Felix of Luxemburg (right); *7th row:* Grand Duke of Hesse (in top hat); Duke of Saxe-Coburg and Gotha (in German helmet); Prince Axel of Denmark; *8th row:* Prince Nicholas of Greece (behind Duke of Saxe-Coburg); Prince George of Greece; Duc de Nemours (wearing big white cross on cloak). In the next row is seen the Count of Flanders (in khaki). He was between Prince Frederick of Prussia and Prince Ernst August of Brunswick. Next came Prince Alvaro of Orleans-Bourbon, the Infante Alfonso of Spain, and the Duke of Braganza. Then came Prince Salih (representing his uncle, the King of Albania) with the Grand Duke Dimitri of Russia. Not all these last groups are distinguishable. 1936.

LEFT: Queen Mary and King Edward VIII after Armistice ceremony at Cenotaph, November 12, 1936.

BELOW: Sir Osbert Sitwell (3rd from L), Queen Mary's good friend during the war years. Here, at a Poets' Reading at the Aeolian Hall, (L to R) Arthur Waley, Princess Elizabeth, Sir Osbert, Queen Elizabeth, Princess Margaret, and Walter De la Mare, 1943.

King George VI and Queen Elizabeth with Mrs. Eleanor Roosevelt, 1942.

LEFT: Three Queens, future—(Queen Elizabeth II), past—(Queen Mary), and present—(Queen Elizabeth), 1951.

BELOW: The imperturbable Royal Family at home during wartime. London was under constant attack, and Buckingham Palace was bombed, 1943.

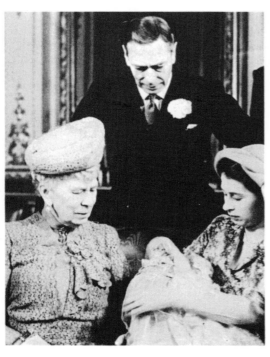

LEFT: Four Generations: Queen Mary, King George VI, and the future Queen Elizabeth II with Princess Anne, 1950.

LEFT: Queen Mary at the Festival of Britain. Age and ill health did not keep her from her duty.

BELOW: The Festival of Britain. A severe case of bursitis confined Queen Mary to a wheelchair.

ABOVE: Queen Mary's last photograph.

RIGHT: A Royal Matriarch's funeral. Walking behind Queen Mary's coffin (L to R), Prince Phillip, Duke of Edinburgh; the Duke of Windsor; Henry, Duke of Gloucester; and the youthful Duke of Kent, March 29, 1953.

scullery maid standing rigidly after their nervous curtsies, "What an airy room! And that stove. I know its kind and how useful it is."

"Oh, yes, Your Majesty, 'is Majesty warmed 'is 'ands by it ten years gone," the cook spoke up.

"Really? Was it so cold as that?" the Queen inquired.

"Oh, yes, Your Majesty!" the woman replied, and then, somewhat embarrassed at her outspokenness, curtsied nervously again.

In the workshop of this same institution, the Queen examined the jacket worn by a fifteen-year-old crippled boy that the youngster had restitched himself. "It really looks as good as new," the Queen said, giving him one of her private smiles and patting his shoulder.

Queen Mary was as clever a manager of money as she was a saleswoman. The twenty or more day dresses and fifteen or so evening gowns she bought yearly cost her twenty-five guineas or less each despite their intricate handwork. For years she bought her clothes from two rival English fashion houses. The top price the Queen would pay was tacitly accepted at these couturiers, and seldom had much to do with the actual cost. The Queen's patronage was worth many thousands of pounds in revenues to both concerns, and it did them no service if she was photographed in an outfit stitched by some seamstress in the back streets of Pimlico (the Queen would have a dress copied if she could not get it for the price she wanted to pay).

Various members of her Household have contributed to a picture of the Queen "at home." She rose at 7:30 A.M. on days when she had morning engagements, 8:00 A.M. otherwise. In either case, she always poured the King his second cup of tea (he rose at 6:00) from the brown earthenware Marks & Spencer teapot, at which time they both glanced at the *Times* (an edition on special paper delivered from Printing House Square).* Lady Cynthia Colville reports that the Queen was an avid reader of social reporter Marianne Mayfayre's column (page 8, the

*This was the Royal edition of the *Times*. As well as copies for Buckingham Palace, this special printing provided copies for bound editions of the *Times* in the Printing House Square archives.

Woman's Page of the *Times*), where every day an item appeared about herself or her family or a member of the Court. Her son Georgie has said that as the Queen passed through the Oriental room on her way back from tea with the King, she would pause in a morning ritual before "a row of tall Buddhas whose heads rest on articulated necks which permit them if touched to nod up and down . . . As she approached each figure, [she would] gently tap its head, sending the row nodding."

She whistled in the morning when alone in her apartments (alone usually meaning just the Queen and a lady-in-waiting or one or two of her three dressers). She enjoyed a glass of sherry before lunch and afterward smoked a Virginia tobacco, straw-tipped cigarette (a fact forbidden to be repeated beyond the palace gates). At Sandringham, she poured the afternoon tea herself and passed it around. (The tea—her special blend—was kept in a locked jade tea caddy that she kept in a glass vitrine with other of her jade collection, also under lock and key.)* Her favourite meal was "a nice cut off the joint, two vegs, a spot of cheese (the Queen likes her cheese) and a bit of a sweet," and she was not in the least bashful about taking a second helping of anything. Knitting, crocheting, and embroidering still kept her hands from being idle in the evening, when she and the King were alone. He liked to listen to the radio; she did not.

"Now, George," she would say, prodding the King inconspicuously with her umbrella when he either swore mildly or spoke too long in public.

Janet Flanner confirms that the Queen had "one of the best memories in the British Empire, certainly the best in the Royal Family, which is high praise since royalty, unlike its subjects, is trained never to forget . . . The Queen can remember in Dresden a miniature she had merely read about twenty years before in Richmond Park . . . She knows every piece, and on what shelf it stands, of her Chinese collections, which involve hundreds of objects; she remembers every chair in the formal furnishing of her castles' hundreds of rooms . . . Her memory is ocular, not

---

*Queen Mary's specially blended tea of the finest Darjeeling and China tea was one of her few Royal extravagances. It cost about six guineas a pound.

aural; by nature she is more interested in looking than in listening." However, the Queen could recall the name and recognise the face of a person she had met years before, only once—and at that in a long queue of men and women who were being presented to her.

The twenties had been dominated by the innocent belief that another world war was unthinkable. Young people were filled with idealism, although the Great War could hardly be packed away along with other souvenirs. Ex-officers retained their titles in civilian life to help bolster their status and careers. Throughout the twenties, most of rural England still had no central heating, electricity, and very few telephones. Almost every middle-class house had a piano or pianola. In most homes, books that were in any small way realistic in their treatment of the brutality of the war or the advent of the sexual revolution were covered in paper to hide the title, and hidden beneath cushions and furniture when not being read. The decade had been strange, frenetic, romantic—almost heroic—and no one was ready to accept a new decade with the fear of another war hanging over everyone's head.

The one constancy the English had—rich, poor, or middle-class—was the imperturbability of their Queen. She was still *démodée* enough to count promptness, manners, and awe of the Crown as vital for England's safe journey through time. No matter how sick the King, despite the rumbles of far-off guns, the economic despair of most of the world, the upheaval in England's own Government with first the Socialist Ramsay Mac-Donald and then the Conservative Stanley Baldwin leading the National Government, and the ever-present threat of Mr. Gandhi's civil-disobedience movement in India, Queen Mary's public self-assuredness never wavered.

She was a reminder of the matriarchal reign of Queen Victoria, and since her personality exuded good sense and strength of character, the people reacted to Queen Mary in kind. When a Government crisis forced an ailing King George back to London from his usual summer holiday at Balmoral in August 1931, the Queen remarked furiously to Lady Cynthia Colville that she proposed joining the King in London to stand by him during the crisis. "I will not be left sitting on a mountain!" she declared. "Pack immediately."

Queen Victoria had chosen wisely. Princess May had become every inch a Queen and one whom Victoria's grandson, the King, could look to for strength. The conundrum was that only the King's strength could secure Queen Mary's crown, and as 1934 dawned, the King's strength was draining slowly and inexorably away.

TWENTY-FIVE

So many things were on Queen Mary's mind at this time—the King's illness, the Government crisis, her own busy schedule—that she was unaware that David was under great strain. Close observers of the Prince of Wales noticed changes in him. He paced a lot, smoked more heavily than usual, and drank more than he could hold on numerous occasions. Several times, he sought an audience with his mother to discuss problems that troubled him. In the end, he had mentioned only superficial matters. He belonged to a family whose members did not easily reveal their true nature to each other. Rationalisation of this failure was not difficult. Royalty was well practised in the art of self-containment.

As early as 1934, the Prince of Wales recognised his desperate need for a strong woman at his side if he were ever to be King. But who was there for him to marry? There were few Royal princesses from whom to choose, and a marriage of the Heir-Apparent to a commoner would not have received Royal consent. His family and Britain wanted nothing more than to see the Prince of Wales married. No effort appears to have been made to help him find an acceptable young woman.

Despite her strong views on her eldest son's duty to his country, Queen Mary neither pressed him into looking for a bride nor herself took an active interest in the matter. By 1934, the Prince of Wales had celebrated his fortieth birthday. Bachelorhood was at least a possibility, and the King and Queen had by now accepted the fact that he might not marry. Their great devotion had turned to Bertie and the two small Princesses—Elizabeth and Margaret Rose. Elizabeth was her grandfather's favourite; he mentions her frequently in his diary. If David should have no heir, the Crown eventually (provided she had no younger brother) would pass to her.

History might regard the Prince of Wales as a superficial person. Nonetheless, he loved intensely and with a slavish devotion. Frances Donaldson, his biographer, says that if Freda Dudley Ward "had loved him more than she did, or if she had been insensately ambitious, history might have been not completely different, but altered, because it seems possible that from the earliest time the Prince regarded his predestined role as not inescapable, and viewed the Duke of York much as one brother might another in the case of a family firm." Mrs. Dudley Ward was a charming but dominating, quasi-maternal woman who, in their later years together, treated the Prince of Wales more as a martinet mother would than like a loving mistress. Angela Dudley Ward recalls the Prince of Wales frequently saying to her mother, whenever she made some proposal to him, "Anything to please, anything to please."*

Until the time of King George's illness, the Prince of Wales was almost unerringly faithful to Freda Dudley Ward. Even during his long periods out of the country, his dedication was observed by his staff. Mrs. Dudley Ward did not return David's love with the same passion with which his was given, and there were quite a few indications that she was not always faithful to him. Having not been born into the English gentry, she was quite comfortable with the role of King's mistress and too steeped in Monarchy ever to consider marriage to the Prince of Wales.

Eventually, a time came when the Prince of Wales realised that

*Clair Angela Louise Ward (1917–) married in 1935 to Major-General Sir Robert Laycock, Chief of Combined Operations in the Second World War. There were (and remain) rumours that Angela was an illegitimate child of the Prince of Wales, but this story, like the ones circulating about Sonia Keppel Cubitt, have never been substantiated.

the King and Queen and all of England expected him to marry. So too did Freda Dudley Ward. The idea was not abhorrent to him; he simply was not prepared to make a loveless marriage. He wanted what he believed his father had had—a strong woman who would dedicate her life to him. He might have had some sexual perversions, some masochistic tendencies that had to be satisfied and that related back to Mary Peters and his shocking nursery experiences. If so, he could not indulge them without believing they were coupled with a great and passionate love.

His good friend, young Lord Louis Mountbatten, had married years before,* at which time the Prince of Wales's younger brother Georgie (now Duke of Kent) had come to live with him. A strong bond had always existed between David and Georgie, and the latter's presence had been much welcomed. Georgie and Princess Marina (now twenty-seven), however, had met again, and this time they both were very much in love. They were married on November 29, 1934, in Westminster Abbey.† The Duke of Kent was thus too taken up with his own affairs to give much time to his brother.

"What could you possibly want that queer old place for?" the King had asked the Prince of Wales with some surprise when David had proposed converting the castellated conglomeration called Fort Belvedere, situated on Crown land bordering the Great Park of Windsor, for a country residence. Then the King had added sharply, "Those damn weekends, I suppose."

Those damn weekends were all that kept the Prince of Wales from feeling "caged." Since 1925, his practise had been to spend his weekends and holidays in small rented country houses "selected because of their proximity to good golf courses." Begun in the eighteenth century by William, Duke of Cumberland, the third

---

*Louis Mountbatten married Edwina Ashley.

†At the wedding of the Duke and Duchess of Kent, Queen Mary, without realising what she had done, received Mrs. Simpson for the first and only time. The Prince of Wales had managed an invitation to the wedding for Mr. and Mrs. Simpson. At the reception he had brought Wallis Simpson up to his mother, exclaiming with a bright smile, "I want to introduce a great friend of mine." The Queen had shaken hands without thinking much about it.

son of George III, Fort Belvedere had been enlarged eighty years later by George IV to house one of his mistresses. An imposing tower, rising high above the surrounding trees, gave it a look of great antiquity. Actually, it was a pseudo-Gothic hodgepodge. A profusion of yew trees kept one side of the house in perpetual shadow, staining the walls with green, acidulous mould. The grounds were beautifully situated, however, and Windsor Castle was only six miles away on the opposite side of the Great Park. But to the Prince of Wales, Fort Belvedere's most endearing attribute was that "from the top of the tower on a clear afternoon one could see London and with a spy glass make out the dome of St. Paul's Cathedral nearly twenty-five miles away."

Freda Dudley Ward helped the Prince of Wales renovate and decorate the interior, and she included "modern comforts" not found in any other Royal residence: a bathroom for nearly every bedroom, showers, a steam bath, built-in wardrobes, and central heating. Once Mrs. Dudley Ward's work was complete on Fort Belvedere, her hold on the Prince of Wales had loosened. While the work was being carried out, David had met the young American bride of Viscount Furness. The beautiful Thelma Furness was the first American woman to whom he had been strongly attracted.

American women were dazzled by the idea of Royalty. The sense of reverence or of servitude that an Englishwoman instinctively exhibited was missing. Friendship with the Prince of Wales was, of course, the ultimate rung on the social ladder. When she met the Prince of Wales, Thelma Furness had learned only recently of her husband's numerous infidelities. Faced with a despairing wife, Lord Furness informed her that her ideas were too American, and that in England husbands and wives went their separate ways. A chance to avenge herself and at the same time live out a classic American fantasy was presented to Lady Furness when the Prince of Wales invited her to dine with him.

"I arrived at York House, St. James's Palace," she later wrote, "at eight o'clock sharp. To my surprise, there were no other guests. I looked around me. The room I found myself in [the sitting room] was big, an enormous map of the world covered the entire far wall. A large and beautiful Empire desk dominated

360

the corner of the room by the windows. Comfortable quilted chintz sofas had been placed on each side of the fireplace, over which hung a portrait of Queen Mary in a white evening gown wearing the Order of the Garter, a magnificent tiara on her head, and a fabulous diamond necklace around her neck.

". . . We sat by the fireplace and had cocktails, while the Prince chatted pleasantly about the small things one can discuss without strain or effort. In time he asked me where I would like to go to dinner. We decided on the Hotel Splendide which was famous for its cuisine and its Viennese orchestra. It was a happy choice; we both loved to waltz . . . We talked of many things . . . just little things . . . the admiration in his eyes as we danced, the frank, disarming way in which he spoke as if there had never been a time when we did not know one another, quickened my heart. It all seemed so natural, so right . . ."

She describes David as ". . . a little shy. His hand went often to his white tie. He held his head a little to one side when spoken to. He looked younger than his years . . . and very handsome.

"The Prince," his new inamorata wrote, "was shy, gracious, meticulously considerate . . ." Almost like a loving son, she could have easily added.

Thelma Furness's relationship to the Prince was bizarre enough to make her suffer tremendous guilt. Her husband condoned the liaison and often joined them in a party of six or eight at the Embassy, the Kit Kat, or some other nightclub. Lord Furness was even host at parties at his own home at which the Prince would be one of the guests. After one of these gatherings, Lord Furness would withdraw and leave his wife and the Prince alone. To an Englishman, honour existed in his wife being chosen as the Prince of Wales's favourite. To an American girl, she became a scarlet woman, and to assuage her own misgivings the affair had to be wrapped in romantic gauze.

When the Prince of Wales went to Africa in 1933, Lady Furness flew to Nairobi with her husband, left him there, and continued on the journey with the Prince, the Governor and his wife, and about forty native guides and servants. Nothing in her and the Prince's comfort was overlooked. Their equipment included portable bathtubs, dining tables, wine coolers, toilet facilities, the finest mosquito-proofed tents, and a private plane

361

to scout for lions. "It was our enchanted time to be together," Lady Furness wrote. "As we sat by our own fire, now little more than glowing embers, the tropic African night would come closer and closer . . . the air was like a caress, silken soft. No one could remain insensitive to the vastness of the starry sky, the teaming fecund sense of nature at its most prodigal . . . We instinctively drew closer . . . this was our Eden . . . His arms around me were the only reality; his words of love my only bridge to life. Borne along on the morning tide of his ardour I felt myself being inexorably swept from the accustomed moorings of caution. Each night I felt more possessed by his love . . ."

No romance novel could have exceeded the impassioned narrative given here. Lady Furness thought herself the incarnate heroine of every American girl's youthful fantasies. As with all enchanted stories, the magic could not survive reality. Once back in London, David still maintained a relationship with Mrs. Dudley Ward. To his consternation, she had no objection to the presence of Lady Furness in his life and even teased him about the lady's American insouciance and romantic illusions.

Lady Furness often came to Fort Belvedere at the weekends when Mrs. Dudley Ward was engaged elsewhere. As a token of love, Thelma made a petit-point fire screen for the Prince. He was pleased with it and asked her if she would help him make one for his mother. For many months to follow, the two of them (seated beneath the portrait of Queen Mary), worked hard on a petit-point paperweight with a royal crown, below which were the initials M.R. in gold.

Lady Furness brought into the Prince of Wales's life other Americans of her acquaintance, among them Wallis Warfield Simpson, who was also married to an Englishman (albeit one who had had an American mother). Wallis was in her late thirties. Born into an old and respected Baltimore family, nonetheless she had not had an easy childhood. After her father's death, she and her mother had had to live on the charity of his family, which was not always graciously given. Wallis's first husband, Earl Winfield Spencer, though from an old family, was a ne'er-do-well with neither money nor a grand future. He was also violent and an alcoholic. Wallis divorced him in 1927 and married Ernest Simpson the following year. Gossip spread about her own divorce, and there were rumours that she had set out to break up Mr. Simpson's first marriage. Simpson's father transferred his son from the New York to the London office of the family firm. For the first time in Wallis's life, she was well off, and she wanted more than anything else to move up in society and to have fun.

Before long she met other American expatriates, including Benjamin Thaw and his wife, the former Consuelo Morgan, who was Lady Furness's sister. In the autumn of 1930, Thelma introduced Wallis to the Prince of Wales. If he was attracted to her at that time, he put all thoughts aside. His life was complicated enough with two women and his additional responsibilities resulting from his father's ill health. Six months later, prodded by Lady Furness, who simply enjoyed Wallis Simpson's high good spirits, the Prince of Wales invited the Simpsons to the fort for the weekend. Lady Furness was hostess. Everyone had a lively time, and so the Simpsons were then included in numerous other weekend gatherings. In June 1933, the Prince of Wales gave a birthday party for Wallis (he often made such gestures to acquaintances) at Quaglino's with Thelma present. A month later, he dined for the first time with the Simpsons at their Bryanston Square flat. The following January, Thelma was called back to the States for family reasons. To leave the Prince for five or six weeks could easily have given Mrs. Dudley Ward the upper hand. A few days before she sailed, she had lunch with Wallis at the Ritz Hotel.

"Oh, Thelma, the little man is going to be so lonely," Wallis said.

"Well, dear," Thelma answered, "you look after him for me while I'm away. See that he does not get into any mischief."

On the surface, Wallis Simpson did not appear to be an extraordinary woman. At the age of thirty-eight, youth was not in her favour, nor was she a woman of great beauty. She gave an illusion of height, yet was only 5 feet, 2 inches tall. She was, however, attractive, possessing distinctive looks: the well-poised forehead, the dark hair coiffed in a nineteenth-century manner to emphasise height, the long face, dark eyes heavily browed, the wide mouth (invariably perfectly drawn in bright red lipstick),

363

and the large mole that looked almost like a beauty spot stuck on her chin at a perfect distance from her lower lip.

She dressed simply and elegantly (usually in Mainbocher), and always looked as though at least three personal maids had helped her to achieve her flawless tidiness (she had, in fact, none). She was self-conscious only about her hands, which were broad, with stubby fingers; because of them she seldom wore rings. Besides her habitual neatness and her dark attractiveness, her feet were her best feature; with "classically separated toes and rouged nails," they were small (size three) by English standards. She swaggered slightly in her walk and had a brisk step that made it difficult for others, including the Prince of Wales, to remain abreast of her. She was fond of ankle bracelets (perhaps she even inspired the fashion in these that continued into the forties) and once startled a group on the Côte d'Azur by wearing an exquisite emerald-and-diamond ring on one of her small toes. Her voice was fairly strident, with an exaggerated Southern drawl that some people thought must be affected because she used a broad "a": "caawn't" and "caaw" (for car). In fact, she had spoken this way all her life.

Bessie Wallis Warfield Simpson was born in Baltimore, Maryland, which—though it considered itself the northernmost point of the South—did not secede from the Union during the Civil War; an historic choice that divided the sympathies of the population. The Warfields were with the Confederate cause, and Wallis's grandfather spent a year and two months as a Union prisoner. Civil War divisions did not die swiftly in the South, and forty years later, when Bessie Wallis was born, people still bitterly remembered that Grandfather Warfield had refused to take the oath of allegiance to the Union. In addition to the Confederate history, Wallis (Bessie she claimed sounded too much like a cow) grew up fatherless (he had died when she was a small child) and as poor gentility, reliant upon the charity of relatives; these painful roots formed her character.

Her four years in London had been remarkable only for the excellence of her parties. She was a connoisseur of wine and had a gastronome's gift for the preparation of good food. When dining out, she could identify the ingredients of a good sauce by taste alone and then reproduce it in her small kitchen, usually improving the recipe in so doing. Her flat and her dinner table had a very special look, distinguished by the unique Eastern style of floral arrangement she had learned in Peking when married to her first husband, Earl Winfield Spencer.

In some respects, Mrs. Simpson was atypical of her generation. She was a "wisecracker" and could tell a ribald story as well as any man, and never looked abashed or injured if one was told to her. Her laugh was easy, her memory exceptional. She did not gossip and was not a snob. In America she would have been called "a good sport" or "a man's woman."

Lady Furness returned six weeks later, after her meeting with Wallis Simpson, to a cool and distant Prince. In America, Aly Khan had been attentive to her, but, according to Thelma, nothing had happened between them. Still, she thought the Prince might have heard about the flirtation and been jealous. She asked him if this was the case. He refused to answer. The following weekend at the Fort, he did his best to avoid her while still being a polite host.

Deeply troubled when she got back to London that Monday, she telephoned her friend Wallis and made a date at the Simpsons' for tea. Wallis, after all, was her good friend and one person with whom she felt she could discuss her problem openly.

As Wallis escorted the distressed Lady Furness into her sitting room, she told her maid, Kane, "We don't want to be disturbed for any reason. Please answer the phone." After listening sympathetically to Thelma, she assured her, "Darling, you know the little man loves you very much. The little man was just lost without you."

"Wallis," Thelma replied, "the Prince has asked me to come to the Fort next weekend. It's Easter weekend, you know. Would you and Ernest care to come down? It might help."

"Of course," Wallis replied warmly. "We'd love to."

Lady Furness later wrote that at that moment Kane entered the room to tell Wallis that she was wanted on the telephone. "I told you," she replied with fierce irritation, "I did not want to be disturbed."

"But Madam," Kane said hesitantly, half in a whisper, "it's His Royal Highness."

"Wallis looked at me strangely," Lady Furness wrote. " 'Excuse me,' she said and left the room. The door was left open. I heard Wallis in the next room saying to the Prince, 'Thelma is here,' and I half rose from my chair, expecting to be called to the telephone. There was no summons, however, and when Wallis returned, she made no reference to the conversation."

Lady Furness left in a quandary almost immediately. She had not been able to ask Wallis the question that had come instantly to her thoughts: Was it Wallis, not Mrs. Dudley Ward, she had to fear?

That weekend she knew. The Prince and Wallis had their private jokes. Once he picked up a piece of salad with his fingers; Wallis playfully slapped his hand. Later that night, the Prince came up to Thelma's bedroom.

"Darling," [she] asked bluntly, "is it Wallis?"

The Prince's features froze. "Don't be silly!" he said crisply and then left the room, closing the door quietly behind him.

Lady Furness knew better. She left the Fort the following morning before the weekend had officially ended.

Queen Mary was never known to have discussed her son's liaison with anyone, but members of her Household were conscious of a disruptive element in her life. She was unusually short-tempered, seldom was amused, and often was seen looking off, distracted, her forehead furrowed, her lips tight. For a woman who was an expert at masking her emotions, such behaviour was enough to give cause for alarm. Her Ladies-in-Waiting were more inclined to believe that the Queen was distressed because the Prince of Wales was causing the King grief than because of any threat to the country. Queen Mary always hated gossip, and for the son she had raised to be King to encourage such scandal was a hard cross for her to bear. Neither she nor the King ever spoke directly to him of this matter.

No one had feared Freda Dudley Ward's influence on the Prince of Wales. With the years, Freda had developed more in the tradition of Alice Keppel, content to remain out of the public eye. Not so Mrs. Simpson, whose photograph with the Prince of Wales at various outings was frequently published and whose possessive attitude toward him at parties and sports events encouraged much talk. Still, as long as Freda Dudley Ward remained a presence in his life, there was no reason to think he might do anything as untoward as making Mrs. Simpson his established and only mistress. The idea that he might consider marrying Mrs. Simpson was never an option. Mrs. Simpson as a future King's mistress was enough to cause concern. She was American and divorced, a woman with no sense of propriety or the order of things.

Members of the Queen's Household spoke together about the situation. Discussions usually ended in the decision that Mrs. Simpson would soon be discarded by the Prince of Wales, as had been Lady Furness, and that he would return once again to Freda Dudley Ward's safe companionship. Queen Mary herself believed this would be the case.

If Queen Mary had sought out the Prince of Wales and addressed herself directly to the problem of Wallis Simpson early in 1934, would history have been altered? All that we know of modern psychiatry substantiates at least the possibility that the Prince of Wales would have welcomed and followed his mother's directive. His entire childhood and youth had been marked by her inattention to him as an individual and his desire to obtain it. What ability Queen Mary had to give love to her children had now been turned to Bertie, his complacent wife, and the two little Princesses. With unerring inevitability, the Prince of Wales became attracted to a woman who filled his mother's place in his life. Such a replacement could not have been a soft, compliant woman like his brother Bertie's wife, for Queen Mary had been her complete antithesis—as was Mrs. Simpson.

One day in June 1934, as had been her almost daily habit for years, Freda Dudley Ward put a call through to St. James's Palace to speak to the Prince of Wales. The telephonist on the palace switchboard answered in tones of the greatest distress. "I have something so terrible to tell you that I don't know how to say it." When pressed by Mrs. Dudley Ward, she added in a shaking voice, "I have orders not to put you through."

For seventeen years, Angela Dudley Ward had regarded her mother's lover, the Prince of Wales, as a father image. He had showered her with loving and extravagant gifts, and she had always had immediate access to him and had been able to discuss with him any problem she had, no matter how inconsequential. About the same time as the conversation between her mother and the telephonist, Angela had received a summons for driving without a license. Fearful that she might have to appear in court, she put a call in to the Prince of Wales at the Fort. His butler, who had known her since childhood, told her that His Royal Highness was out. She left an urgent message for him to return her call. When she did not hear from him, she wrote him a plea for help and then tried calling again, unsuccessfully. Puzzled and hurt, she turned to her mother for answers.

"Haven't you noticed that he hasn't been here for weeks?" her mother replied.

In fact, Freda Dudley Ward would never again either see or speak to the Prince of Wales. So sharply did he sever his alliance with her that he also cruelly cut from his life the one young woman who had been a daughter figure to him. Wallis Simpson had insisted on his sole loyalty to her. The fatal mistake that Queen Mary made at this time was not to recognise that Mrs. Dudley Ward's ignominious exit from his life signalled the end for the Prince of Wales of any bond that would bind him to England and—in the future—to the Throne.

TWENTY-SIX

T he Silver Jubilee was Queen Mary's idea. Tradition had
been to fete only golden anniversaries. Twelve previous
monarchs had reigned twenty-five years without com-
memorating the occasion.* As she had shrewdly insisted on
maintaining the dressiness of the Court during the Depression,
so Queen Mary now instigated plans for a jubilee of such pomp
and magnificence that it would overshadow the King's illness
and at the same time give Britain an opportunity for "the biggest
money-spending festival since the war." Only fourteen years
had passed since the Allies had won, and rumbles of a new war
were being heard. Hopefully, a jubilee would reassure the people of the strength of the Monarchy.

Many in and out of government held a pessimistic view of
Germany's military revival and the rise of Adolf Hitler. In Octo-
ber 1933, Herr Hitler had ordered his delegation to leave the
Disarmament Conference in Geneva. Still, men like Sir John

---

*The twelve English monarchs who reigned more than twenty-five years were:
Henry I (1100–1135); Henry II (1154–1189); Henry III (1216–1272); Edward
I (1272–1307); Edward III (1327–1377); Henry VI (1422–1461); Henry VIII
(1509–1547); Elizabeth I (1558–1603); Charles II (1660–1685); George II
(1727–1760; George III (1760–1820; Victoria (1837–1901). Of these, only
Henry III, Edward III, George III, and Victoria reigned for more than fifty
years.

Simon, the British Foreign Secretary, did not take this too seriously. ". . . time must be given to see how this works out," he wrote King George on October 23. "Fortunately, time is available for Germany is at present quite incapable of undertaking aggression . . ." Winston Churchill did not agree. On February 7, 1934, he vehemently warned against the danger of a powerful German Air Force, adding on March 8 that he "dreaded the day when the means of threatening the heart of the British Empire should pass into the hands of the present rulers of Germany."

On April 24, 1934, the King met Leopold von Hoesch, the German Ambassador, and asked outspokenly why Germany was arming when no one wanted to attack her, and why she was forcing all the other countries to prepare for an attack on her part. Von Hoesch replied that French fortification was impregnable and that Germany had no fortifications on her side. The King refused to accept this answer and reminded the Ambassador that in the last war "fortifications were useless and would be even more so in the next."

A few months later, through Sir John Simon, he wrote to Sir Horace Rumbold, British Ambassador in Berlin, "We must not be blinded by the apparent sweet reasonableness of the Germans, but be wary and not be taken unawares."

Early in February 1935, Hitler introduced military conscription, created an overt Air Force, and increased the German Army to thirty-six divisions. Winston Churchill warned an uneasy Parliament that Britain was entering "a corridor of deepening and darkening danger along which [she] should be forced to move, perhaps for months, perhaps for years."

This gloomy outlook was at least temporarily displaced by the increasing excitement over the Jubilee, set now for May 6, 1935. The King and Queen remained at Windsor for the month of April. King George was looking old and bent, and he had taken to dining alone in his room because the effort of dressing for dinner was too much. His intimate friends were concerned that he might not be strong enough to endure the strain of the Jubilee. Clearly, he was a man too tired and ill for parades, but the Queen did not back down. To delay or cancel the celebrations at this late stage would instantly have given rise to rumours that the King was dying. The Queen saw her dressmakers and

went over the plans for the many functions comprising the celebration. Jubilee plans took over her schedule, and her diary for
this period contains hectic, almost frantic notes.

Queen Mary knew her husband was dying and that her days
as Queen Consort were numbered. Would the King have lived
longer without the physical exhaustion the Jubilee was to cost
him? Perhaps, but the nation's enthusiasm did give him great
happiness. For Queen Mary, the Jubilee was a last chance for the
applause and adulation that came with being Queen Consort.

On April 24, David had tea at Windsor with his mother and
his brother Harry, who had just returned from a visit to Australia. Harry had been away when his brother George had married Princess Marina, and the Queen had written him at the time,
"Now you will have to follow suit, for marriage is in the air."
Unlike her attitude of silence where marriage and David were
concerned, she had even appended the names of two princesses
in order of priority for consideration and added, "I hope now
my darling boy will think about marrying on your return."

Harry had not responded favourably to his mother's suggestions, and the King had considered this issue of enough importance to write to his son, "Of course, Mama & I have always been
anxious that you should marry & settle down & I am sure you
could find someone who would make you a good wife & be a
help to you in yr duties." David and Bertie met his ship on March
28 and rode with him on the Royal train to Victoria Station,
where they were met by their parents. The King's appearance
greatly shocked Harry. He looked emaciated in his full-dress
field marshal's uniform; his chest—albeit covered with medals
and ribbons—had become concave. The question of a bride for
Harry was once more the subject of discussion with the family.
More names were mentioned. Harry felt under pressure. His
parents' hope was that the high spirits generated by the Jubilee
would be extended by an announcement of another Royal Wedding.

Everyone knew, but did not say, that it was David whom the
nation was anxious to marry off. Yet no member of the family
felt like pressing him. Both the King and Queen were aware of
his devotion to Wallis Simpson, for the Duke and Duchess of
Kent had reported to them their many occasions in David and

371

Mrs. Simpson's company. The King and Queen sensed that unlike his relationships with Lady Furness and Mrs. Dudley Ward, this was different and that the wrong approach could end in a disastrous rebellion on David's part. They still hoped that he would tire of Mrs. Simpson, who was, they had been told, pushy, but also extremely clever.

The Prince of Wales at this time was attempting to launch his new love socially. Chips Channon,* who was to become a close friend of Wallis Simpson, wrote in his diary for April 5, 1935, "Mrs. Simpson . . . has already the air of a personage who walks into a room as though she almost expected to be curtsied to. At least she wouldn't be too surprised. She has complete power over the Prince of Wales."

Queen Mary was at Windsor Castle, with David nearby at Fort Belvedere, throughout April. They did not meet, except for the night Harry returned and for tea nearly four weeks later. Possessing neither the knack nor the language of intimacy with her sons, especially David, she was unable to encourage him to talk to her freely about his situation.

The week of the Jubilee was one of ceaseless activity for the King and Queen. The day itself, May 6, was unseasonably warm, with the temperature reaching 79 degrees by ten o'clock when the first of the day's carriage processions began to form in the courtyard of Buckingham Palace. The King and Queen left for St. Paul's Cathedral for a Thanksgiving Service at 10:55 in an open carriage with six grey horses.

Chips Channon saw the procession from the front of Sir Frederick Ponsonby's house near St. James's Palace.† "The Yorks in a large landau with the two tiny pink children," he writes. "The Duchess of York was charming and gracious, the baby princesses much interested in the proceedings, and waving. The next landau carried the Kents, that dazzling pair; Princess Marina wore an enormous platter hat, chic but slightly unsuitable.‡ She was much cheered . . . Finally the Prince of Wales smiling his dentist

*Sir Henry ("Chips") Channon (1897–1958) was born in Chicago, Illinois. He moved to England in 1918 and married Lady Honor Guinness.

†Sir Frederick Ponsonby died three months later.

‡Marina, Duchess of Kent, was pregnant at this time.

smile and waving to his friends, but he still has his old spell for the crowd. The Norway aunt [Queen Maud] who was with him looked comic, and then more troops, and suddenly, the coach with Their Majesties. All eyes were on the Queen in her white and silvery splendour. Never has she looked so serene, so regally majestic, even so attractive. She completely eclipsed the King. Suddenly, she has become the best dressed woman in the world."

Inside St. Paul's Cathedral, sunlight gleamed down from the clerestory windows through the tranquil spaces and touched the uniforms and the bright clothes of the assembled congregation, evoking patches of brilliant colour. The King's plumed hat rested at his feet; his shoulders were slumped, and his head bent slightly on his chest as he and the Queen listened to the Archbishop of Canterbury from their throne chairs directly below his podium. Queen Mary sat column-straight, her spine not touching the back of her throne chair. She wore a silver-and-white gown, a cape with a large white fox collar, and a white toque with a tall aigrette that was visible from almost any position in the cathedral. Princess Elizabeth and Princess Margaret sat on cushioned stools directly behind their grandparents, and beside them their parents, their Uncle David, Aunt Mary, and great-uncle Arthur of Connaught. Uncle George Kent, his wife, and Uncle Harry Gloucester sat behind them with their Aunts Maud and Toria. They were a solemn family group as they heard the words of the Archbishop's Silver Jubilee Thanksgiving Service:

"Twenty-five years have passed since the reign of our beloved Sovereign began. Looking back upon them we realise . . . they have been years of almost unbroken anxiety and strain. They began in an atmosphere of embittered party strife. Into the midst of them came suddenly the fiercest ordeal which the nation has ever been summoned to face. Since then have followed years of toilsome effort in the midst of a world restless, bewildered, broken by the shock of war, to revive the trade and industry on which the lives of multitudes depend and to find the basis of a settled peace. Yet, beneath the troubled surface there has been in the life of our nation the deep overflow of a spirit of unity, confidence, and steadfast strength. That spirit has found a centre in the Throne. Elsewhere ancient monarchies have been swept

373

away by the storms of revolution. Here the Throne has been established in ever stronger security . . . As we lift our hearts in Thanksgiving, so let us bow them in humble prayer for our King and Queen that God may continue to bestow His blessing upon them . . . Pray for this dear land and for the Empire which has grown around it, that by God's help they may uphold before the world the cause of peace among all nations, the principles of liberty and justice, and a community wherein all the citizens are the willing servants of the common weal."

A difficult moment occurred at the end of the service when the King, having retrieved his hat, was unable to rise. Bertie, being the closest, placed his hand beneath his father's arm. David also stepped forward to assist. The King, though unsteady, was already on his feet.

The Royal Family rode back to Buckingham Palace amidst the tumultuous cheering of the crowds and made several appearances on the balcony during the afternoon. At eight that evening, King George broadcast a message of thanks to his people.* "How can I express what is in my heart . . . I can only say to you, my very, very dear people that the Queen and I thank you from the depth of our hearts for all the loyalty and—may I say?—the love with which this day and always you have surrounded us. I dedicate myself anew to your service for the years that may still be given to me. I am speaking to the children above all. Remember Children, the King is speaking to *you.*" His voice was strong, clipped, emphatic, vibrant, devoid of all condescension, and its effect was intense.

"Most moving," Queen Mary wrote in her diary after listening to the King's short message.

His nurse, Sister Catherine Black, immediately helped him to his room after his radio speech. Despite his exhaustion, he took time for the ritual of writing in his diary, "A never-to-be-forgotten day."

The weeks that followed Jubilee Day were filled with activities. There were two state balls at Buckingham Palace, the first on May 14. To the King and Queen's shock, David brought Ernest

---

*King George broadcast his first radio message at Christmas Day 1932, and had been issuing yearly messages since that time.

and Wallis Simpson as his personal guests. Mrs. Simpson recalls in rather purple prose that "after the King and Queen had made their entrance and taken their seats on the dais at the end of the room, the dancing began. As David and I danced past, I thought I felt the King's eyes rest searchingly on me. Something in his look made me feel that all this graciousness and pageantry were but the glittering tip of an iceberg that extended down into unseen depths I could never plumb, depths filled with an icy menace for such as me. Also through the panoply of pomp I discerned that here was a frail old man. The King was then only a few days away from his seventieth birthday, and David had told me more than once of his concern over his father's failing strength. A premonitory shiver ran through me at the thought of what his passing might bring, the startling and immeasurable changes that of necessity would come to all of us. In spite of David's gaiety and the lively strains of a foxtrot, the sense of foreboding refused to lift; in that moment I knew that between David's world and mine lay an abyss that I could never cross, one he could never bridge for me."

The Queen made no comment in her diary about seeing Mrs. Simpson. The Simpsons, however, were not at the second state ball on June 13. By this time, King George was noticeably fatigued. He had carried through as planned four ceremonial drives through North, South, East, and West London. Queen Mary had suggested that these be made on Saturday afternoons so that a larger number of people could see them. They travelled by motorcar to a suburban point, where they transferred to an open landau with an escort of Life Guards. At selected points, Mayors and local Councillors assembled to present addresses. For their procession through North London, Constitution Hill and the Mall were reserved for 70,000 London schoolchildren. After their much-cheered drive through the poorer sections of East London, King George, very tired but radiantly happy, said to Catherine Black, "I'd no idea they felt that about me. I am beginning to think they must really like me for myself."

Queen Mary had been right about the Jubilee. It increased the people's pride in their monarchy and its survival, "unimpaired in dignity" for more than a thousand years. Observers believed that the Jubilee had reinforced the Crown as "a symbol of patriotism, a focus of unison, and an emblem of continuity in a rapidly dissolving world." King George appeared to his people now as a "strong benevolent patriarch."

Queen Mary celebrated her sixty-eighth birthday on May 26, 1935. The Grenadier Guards Band played at a family luncheon, and in the afternoon she and the King drove round North London with Lilibet to look at the decorations that were still up. Age did not perturb her now. She had grown into her persona. Her appearance was formidable, her manner—"Well," as one witness of her reign says, "it was like talking to St. Paul's Cathedral . . ." adding, "she was magnificent, humourous, worldly, in fact nearly sublime, though cold and hard."

A family celebration on June 3, the King's birthday, was held at Buckingham Palace. The King was not at all well. The Jubilee decorations were finally taken down on June 12, and the King, suffering a hacking cough and difficulty in breathing, went to Sandringham to rest, while the Queen moved to Windsor Castle with Harry, where the guests included Lady Alice Montagu-Douglas-Scott. And on June 21, Harry wrote his father that he "saw Alice Scott several times & met her out riding each morning. I think Mama liked her." *Mama* obviously did, for she had arranged the meeting.

The Jubilee had been an unqualified success, and the new romance in the Royal Family added to the sense of well-being. The Jubilee, however, had one irreversible result. The Royal Family and the Ministers had been so distracted by the added responsibilities demanded by the Jubilee that no attention had been paid to the happenings in the life of the heir to the Throne, a terrible oversight, for King George was a dying monarch.

During the Jubilee weeks, the Prince of Wales and Mrs. Simpson became a formidable pair. She was madly anxious to storm society, and he, never having been so in love, was madly anxious that she succeed. During those six weeks, they became bolder and more public in their relationship. Mrs. Simpson's influence grew so powerful that she banned all those who were friends of Mrs. Dudley Ward from both York House and the Fort. She was taking no chance that the Prince of Wales might be persuaded to return to Freda Dudley Ward's arms, which, in view of his obvious infatuation, was most unlikely.

While the King and Queen were visiting the East End of London on May 18, Wallis Simpson gave a cocktail party in her home. "The Prince was charm itself," a guest reports. "He is boisterous, wrinkled and gay . . . He shook and passed the cocktails very much the *'Jeune homme de la maison.'* "

To those close to him, David's voice had become "more American than ever." His speech had always veered away from the high-toned cadences of the upper classes and from the Germanic quality of the voices of most members of his family, and he had never made an effort to lose the slight Cockney twang he had picked up in Lala Bill's care.

On the evening of May 31, the Prince of Wales, with Wallis and her husband, attended Covent Garden to hear Lily Pons in the *Barber of Seville,* watching the opera from Emerald Cunard's box.* Those in the party were somewhat taken aback when, during the interval, Mrs. Simpson told the Prince (in a slightly scolding voice) that he must hurry or he would be late in joining the Queen at the ball. (The King had been too indisposed to attend.) Then she had removed a cigar from his breast pocket. "It doesn't look very pretty," she said. He went, escorted his mother to the ball, made a few polite stabs at conversation, danced with no one, looked distracted, and then disappeared within an hour and returned to the opera, slipping in quietly beside Wallis.

He retained his interest in politics and made an extraordinary speech to the British Legion on June 11, advocating friendship with Germany, a gesture that many thought could be taken seriously. The King and Queen were much discomfited by the speech and by the gossip going around the Court of David's "alleged Nazi leanings." He was thought to be influenced in this matter by Wallis. His father requested he attend the Court Ball on June 13 alone, and he did, but in a very bad temper. It was noticed that he did not have more than a few polite words with

---

*Chips Channon writes in his diary for May 18, 1935, "London Society is now divided between the old gang, who support Freda Dudley Ward, whom the Prince now ignores, and Emerald Cunard, who is rallying to the new regime."

his mother and left early, as did the King. A moving moment occurred at this point when Queen Mary sent for the aging Begum Aga Khan and motioned her to the King's Throne to sit beside her during the remainder of the evening.

For Royal Ascot the following week, the Prince of Wales gave a party at the fort, inviting Emerald Cunard to act as hostess for him. (This was merely a façade, as Wallis Simpson —invited with her husband—supervised the arrangements.) Emerald Cunard was a friend of the German Ambassador to London, Leopold von Hoesch, and no matter how mindless the friendship might have been, the King and Queen were not pleased that the Prince of Wales might have sanctioned it. True, the British were not yet aware of the full evil of Naziism, but Hitler and Germany were considered distinct threats, and von Hoesch was being called "the arch-Hitler spy of Europe." The Royal Family had purged themselves of all Germanic names and titles, but the fear persisted that their German ties would be used against them. For this reason, if for no other, the Prince of Wales's speech and his continued friendship with Emerald Cunard was irresponsible.*

At Ascot, the Prince of Wales made his boldest move. The Duke and Duchess of Kent had frequently been in Mrs. Simpson's company, but he introduced her to all the members of his family in the Royal Enclosure. It should be added that the King (because of his continuing ill-health) and the Queen were not present.

The question that was most posed during this stage of Wallis Simpson's affair with the Prince of Wales was why he would choose as his mistress a twice-married American, verging on forty, who was no outstanding beauty when he could have had almost any woman in Britain, perhaps in the world. Mrs. Simpson had a sense of authority about her and a kind of reckless

---

*Emerald Cunard was most certainly being used by Leopold von Hoesch. She was not generally a silly woman, but she was attracted to von Hoesch and his rather courtly manners and good looks. It is highly unlikely that Emerald Cunard owed any allegiance to either von Hoesch or the Nazi Party.

fearlessness that the Prince of Wales found especially exciting. His prestige and power did not stop her from speaking her mind to him. She stood up for what (and in whom) she believed and never changed her views or her friends according to fashion. Intelligent people and good conversation triggered her, and she was not a slave to convention or to the status quo.

With Mrs. Simpson, the Prince of Wales felt he was being accepted and loved for himself and not for the external trappings of royalty. She had the American woman's tendency to reform her man in small ways. Her treatment of Lady Furness and her determination to banish Freda Dudley Ward and every member of her "group" notwithstanding, she was never known to say an evil word—or speak a rude one—about or to either woman. Her style was far more peremptory, even regal.

Would Wallis Simpson have loved the Prince of Wales as indefatigably if he had not been the Prince of Wales? Probably yes, given his money and a certain social position. She had gone after her first two husbands in the same determined fashion. Her marriage to Ernest Simpson had not been happy for some years. Simpson was a weak man controlled by a domineering father who had never wanted her as a daughter-in-law. They had been married for seven years and had no children. Simpson had a mistress about whom she knew. Little bound them except their social life. In the circumstances, Wallis's infidelity was inevitable. However, it is doubtful that Simpson would have encouraged his wife in a liaison with any man but the Prince of Wales, for he was perhaps even more dazzled by the Royal presence than his wife.

By the end of the Jubilee, Wallis Simpson and the Prince of Wales had the look of a couple mutually in love. He was completely at ease by her side, entertaining *their* guests. And if he was not mixing drinks at her flat or at the Fort, then she did the chore herself, using a small, low table and several shakers. There was not a cocktail asked for that she could not make, and without fuss, measuring the proportions with her eye and handing over a glassful that was the equal of any barman's. She herself drank whisky and soda and smoked Turkish cigarettes, as did the Prince of Wales. They elicited a sense of tremendous togetherness, of domesticity, of mutual response.

She had a love of antiques; "snuff boxes, eighteenth-century *étuis* with portraits on them, and the like;" and hated modern decor. He shared her tastes, and their need for each other was strong. If David was madly in love for the first time, Wallis was happier than any of her friends had ever known her to be. Unlike Mrs. Dudley Ward or Lady Furness, she was devotedly faithful to him, as he was to her. And their relationship appeared so unshakable that young women no longer threw themselves at him, nor did their mothers try to engineer meetings. Only one other woman was important to David—Queen Mary—for he still had unresolved feelings toward his mother.

During Jubilee summer, Wallis Simpson made a few decorative changes at the Fort, an effort to erase Freda Dudley Ward's mark. Many of the reds and dark colours in the rooms she replaced with yellows and creams and touches of mandarin orange, giving the house a brighter, more country look. Next, she removed the portrait of Queen Mary from the wall of the sitting room. The plan was that it should be returned to its original place in York House, St. James's, but somehow it was never rehung.

Harry became engaged to Lady Alice Montagu-Douglas-Scott, the third daughter of the Duke of Buccleuch, on August 30. "Don't buy a lot of jewellry in a hurry," Queen Mary wrote him, "because Cousin Frederica of Hanover left you some nice diamond things which can be converted & I have various ornaments which I have long ago selected for yr wife from my collection."

Three days earlier, the Queen's sister-in-law, Princess Alice, Countess of Athlone, wrote her, "This is indeed good news & I congratulate you on settling another son & upon getting what I know to be a really splendid daughter-in-law. If only David would follow suit. He seems to have missed his best chances. But never mind, one must look on the blessings one has & be thankful for them."

The last months of 1935 were taken with preparations for the Royal Wedding on November 6. His sister Toria's death on December 3 was a shock that King George was not physically able to endure. For the first time he cancelled the state opening of Parliament, due that same afternoon, and remained in his bed at Sandringham just a few doors down the dark corridor from the bedroom in which his brother, Prince Eddy, had died forty-four years before.

As New Year's 1936 approached, Queen Mary walked in the gardens of Sandringham, light snow covering the bare garden beds and dusting the giant dark evergreens. Her husband had suffered irreparable damage to his lungs and heart; his life was ebbing away, her days as Queen dwindling, too. Added to her husband's grave illness was the shadow of war that darkened everything. She was less concerned about David than she had been earlier in the year. Perhaps his father's impending death (and in December 1935, those close to the King knew his time was short) would save him from the unhappy years as an aging Prince of Wales that his grandfather had suffered. It would have to end such unsuitable relationships as the one he now had with this American woman, Mrs. Simpson. The responsibilities of the Throne, especially during what looked like difficult times ahead, would work as no prodding from her could. David was her son, born to the Blood Royal, fated to be King. He would do as she had always done—carry out with integrity and honour any duty expected of him.

TWENTY-SEVEN

The general election in November 1935 returned to power the Conservative Party, led by Stanley Baldwin and with Anthony Eden as Foreign Secretary, just one week after Harry's marriage to Lady Alice Scott in the private chapel of Buckingham Palace. Plans for a wedding on a grander scale in Westminster Abbey had been cancelled because of the recent death of the bride's father. The King attended the wedding and afterward wrote in his diary, "Now all the children are married but David." It was to be his last appearance at any occasion, either social or governmental.

As the King's health declined and Queen Mary remained with him at Sandringham to prepare for a family gathering at Christmas, the country was absorbed in the growing world crisis. Italian legions had pressed forward into Abyssinia, and the problems of sanctions had soured relations between Italy and Britain. At the end of November, Mr. Baldwin had an audience with the King at Sandringham. After discussing Abyssinia, the King expressed his concern about the Prince of Wales and Mrs. Simpson, and asked the Prime Minister for his advice. Mr. Baldwin had nothing specific to offer; the King's face clouded with emotion and his hand trembled dramatically as he said, "After I am dead the boy will ruin himself in twelve months."

The King's anxiety over his eldest son must be attributed to something more than the Prince of Wales's slavish devotion to Mrs. Simpson. After all, Wallis Simpson *was* married, and his son, though reckless in his open admiration of her, could not expect Parliamentary approval of a marriage should she divorce Mr. Simpson. Nor could the King suspect that David might forfeit all his rights to the succession. During the autumn of 1935, his feelings toward the Prince of Wales had grown quite bitter. A week after Baldwin's visit, he exclaimed to a close friend,* "I pray to God that my eldest son will never marry and have children and that nothing will come between Bertie and Lilibet and the Throne."

This shocking statement discounts Mrs. Simpson as the basis of the King's fears, for at this time neither he—nor the Queen nor any member of the Government—seriously thought the Prince of Wales would marry Wallis Simpson. In December 1935, with Germany rearming and stronger by the month, King George's greatest anxiety was that the son who had been born to be King might not have the wisdom and judgement to reign. His statement, which shows a strong preference for the accession of his second son, can only be interpreted as an indication that he did not want the Prince of Wales to succeed him.

Taken on the surface, the King's antipathy to the Heir-Apparent at this time was inordinate. Certainly, the Prince of Wales had idiosyncrasies and was obstinate in his refusal to follow the accepted conventions set down by his parents. But he was extraordinarily popular and well loved throughout the Empire. His frequent and demanding foreign tours and his accessibility to the people had added much devotion to the Crown. His charm and personableness had contributed greatly to the magic of monarchy. King George was an exception in the line of Britain's male monarchs who had had controversial mistresses. But not one King could be said to have had a disastrous reign because of a Royal favourite, or because of a shrewish or demanding wife.

A month before the Jubilee, the Prince of Wales met with Leopold von Hoesch, the German Ambassador, and discussed

*Lady Algernon Gordon-Lennox (1864–1945), born Hon Blanche Maynard. She and her husband were good friends of King George V and often at Sandringham.

with him in great detail Anglo-German relations. Von Hoesch reported to the Reich Chancellery that the Prince of Wales had shown his "complete understanding of Germany's position and aspirations," adding that he was also critical of the "too one-sided attitude of the [British] Foreign Office."

The Prince of Wales's firsthand wartime experience had convinced him that wars, quite apart from their destruction, were no longer a means of solving political problems. Also, he had never believed in the right of a victorious state to subjugate a vanquished nation and was of the strong opinion that such a situation could only bring about new causes for future conflicts. All this he told von Hoesch, who at the end of his report to his superior stated:

"He fully understood that Germany wished to face the other nations squarely, her head high, relying on her strength and conscious that Germany's word counted as much in the world as that of other nations.

"I told the Prince in reply that what he had just said corresponded as it were, word for word, with the opinion of our Führer and Chancellor, such as I had heard it myself from his lips."

Then in June 1935, the Prince of Wales made his much-criticised pro-German speech at the annual conference of the British Legion. In it, he suggested that "a deputation or a visit might be paid by representative members of the Legion to Germany at some future time."

Father and son had their first and perhaps only confrontation immediately following this "indiscretion." The King crossly reminded the Prince of Wales that he was never again to speak on controversial matters such as politics and foreign affairs without consulting the Government.

In direct defiance of his father's orders, a fortnight later the Prince of Wales made a speech at Berkhamsted School, decrying a ban by the London County Council on the use of guns by boys in the cadet corps of schools within their jurisdiction.

The Prince of Wales was now under the constant surveillance of the security service. Wallis Simpson had a few German acquaintances within her social circle, and Mrs. Simpson and the Prince of Wales were together so frequently, any investigation of the former had to extend to the latter. Soon it became obvious that Mrs. Simpson was no security risk and had no German links. Beyond her need to be informed and to be a good conversationalist, Mrs. Simpson showed little interest in politics and was never associated with any cause. She did endorse the Prince of Wales's idealistic and pacifistic ideas much in the way millions of women support their men's opinions, simply by not contradicting these views when spoken.

In all fairness to the Prince of Wales, his desire to avoid a war was greater than his "warm sympathy for Germany," which, von Hoesch reported to his superiors, was "deep-rooted and strong enough to withstand the contrary influences to which they are seldom exposed." The Prince of Wales saw himself as a rebel in both his private and his public life. He was striking out for those rights that other Englishmen took for granted: freedom of opinion and speech. For a private citizen to advocate pacifistic views, even to stand up at Hyde Park Corner and shout them, would not have been considered untoward. The Prince of Wales never gave any evidence of approving the Nazi regime (nor of disapproving it). What he was against was any interference that would bring Britain and Germany into another war; and what he refused to accept was that in a constitutional monarchy he could not publicly express views that were not in accordance with government policies.

King George was given and read these security reports on his Heir-Apparent's pro-German sentiments, freely expressed, often in public and generally with disregard for his own position and his father's demand that he "must never speak on controversial matters without consulting the government." As Christmas at Sandringham approached, the King's condition grew worse and his anxiety about his successor grew stronger. By this time, King George no longer considered David simply as a defiant son, but as a future King who could place the Monarchy and the country in grave danger.

Queen Mary gathered together the entire family for Christmas. A shared sense of foreboding that this might be the King's last Christmas overshadowed the festivities. A concerted effort was made to make it an especially happy holiday. A twenty-foot tree dominated the spacious white ballroom, scene of so many gay Christmases during the reign of Edward VII. The King, who had seldom played with his own children, instigated games and sat lovingly watching as Bertie's two daughters and Mary's two sons romped around the tree. The Duke and Duchess of Kent now had an infant son, Edward (a name that had been chosen to please the King), and the cries and sounds of children's voices filled the room. The Prince of Wales was the last to arrive. He was unable to enter into the spirit of the holiday, even for his father's sake. "My brothers were secure in their private lives," he remarked, "whereas I was caught up in an inner conflict and would have no peace of mind until I had resolved it." One wonders in retrospect if he meant a decision to ask Wallis Simpson to divorce her husband and marry him, or whether he had begun to think about the possibility of abdicating all his rights to the Throne.

His parents' wish was to avoid marring the holidays by any unpleasant discussion. The Queen had heard through a Lady-in-Waiting that for Christmas he had given Mrs. Simpson jewels valued at over £50,000, including several pieces that had been in the Royal Family for generations. Her son's mistress now had a magnificent collection of rubies, as well as emeralds and diamonds.* The Queen was not pleased with the Prince of Wales's extravagant gift-giving, and she was distant and cool to him; he left on Boxing Day, having spent only a day and a half with his family.

On Thursday afternoon, January 16, Lord Dawson, the King's physician, warned the Queen that the end was in sight. She took the news calmly and went back to her sitting room to do what she must. "I think you ought to know that Papa is not very well," she wrote her eldest son. "And although I do not consider the danger immediate, Lord Dawson is not too pleased with Papa's state at the present moment. I therefore suggest that you propose yourself for the coming weekend at Sandringham, but do so in a manner that will not lead Papa to suspect that I have warned you of his condition."

---

*The day after New Year's, the Prince of Wales was said to have presented Mrs. Simpson with another £50,000 gift of jewellry of matched sapphires.

The Prince of Wales, who was at the Fort at the time, flew to Sandringham the next morning. His sister Mary was already there, and the two of them went into their father's bedroom together. King George sat slumped half-asleep in his favourite chair in front of a fire. He was dressed in an old Tibetan dressing gown, a faded relic of one of his Indian tours, and had a lap blanket about the lower half of his body. His bed, placed in one corner, was the same simple brass one in which Edward VII had slept. From the bay window across the sunken garden could be seen the square church tower from which the Royal standard flew.

The King roused himself when his children entered. For a moment a flicker of recognition came into his eyes, but he said nothing. A few minutes later, his mind trailing back in time, he asked Mary if she had been skating. He dozed off again, and Mary and David left the room.

Bertie arrived shortly after, and George was on his way. Harry, unfortunately, was ill with a bad throat and could not travel in such cold weather. The freezing temperature did not disturb the Queen. "It will do us good to get out of doors for a little while," she told the three children who were with her. Then, as they walked briskly around the grounds four abreast, their mother, surefooted on the icy paths, deftly put into words the grave thoughts none of them had previously verbalised. The King would soon be dead. David would be King, and as soon as possible she would vacate Buckingham Palace, Windsor Castle, and Sandringham and move back once more to Marlborough House. They returned to the house. David could have asked for a few private moments with her. He let the opportunity pass.

The Queen now stood almost constant vigil at the King's bedside, Bertie and David relieving her at night so that she could get some sleep. On Sunday, David motored to London to meet with Prime Minister Stanley Baldwin. He left Sandringham in a state of desolation, dark circles under his eyes, his face white and drawn. He had not slept much during the time there, always expecting a summons to his father's deathbed. He had a great deal on his mind. For one thing, the King had not acknowledged his presence. For another, now that the moment had arrived when a decision had to be made to accept the oath or not, he was unable to do so. Bertie was with him on the trip to London and in a terrible emotional state, the old tics and stammering having returned.

News of the King's imminent death brought press and reporters and photographers to keep watch outside the fading red-brick walls of Sandringham estate. Many members of the Royal Family beyond the intimate circle had arrived, along with the Privy Councillors.* The latter required the King's consent to appoint the Councillors of State. The red dispatch boxes had piled up during the previous fortnight, and the King's business had to be transacted.

"G. about the same," the Queen wrote in her diary on Sunday, "sat with him from time to time—Did not go to Church as the place was surrounded by reporters & photographers, too heartless—Walked with Mary morning & afternoon . . . Georgie arrived at 7—also Archbishop of Canterbury—David & Bertie left but will return tomorrow—"

The next morning, the King was propped up in a chair before the open door of his room, just visible to the Privy Councillors. The scene was macabre. Nurse Catherine Black stood nearby, and beside her, the Queen. The King's doctor, Lord Dawson, leaned over his cadaverous figure and with great effort got him to understand the necessity for him to try to form the word "approved," so that the appointment of the Councillors of State —who were to be the Queen; the Prince of Wales; and the Dukes of York, Gloucester, and Kent—could be made. After about ten minutes, a faint whisper was heard and accepted as Royal consent. Then the King was handed a paper, and Lord Dawson, visibly exhausted, managed to get the King, by holding his hand with the pen in it, to make two little crosses. Tears filled King George's eyes. He understood that his effort would be his last act as King.

At 2:30 in the afternoon, David and Bertie returned by aeroplane to Sandringham. They were both silent during the jour-

---

*The Privy Councillors present were: the Lord President, Mr. Ramsay MacDonald; the Archbishop of Canterbury, Dr. Lang; the Lord Chancellor, Lord Hailsham; the Home Secretary, Sir John Simon; the King's doctors, Lord Dawson and Lord Wigram; with Sir Maurice Hankey as Clerk to the Council.

ney, quite unable to communicate. While outside the Big House the crowds stood their death watch, inside, "a sad quiet" came over the family circle. At this point, an incident occurred that Dr. Dawson and others present interpreted as bizarre and insensitive on the part of the Prince of Wales.

As the end approached, the Queen and four of her children stood by the King's bedside. Lord Dawson slipped in and out of the room to examine his patient and to compose the latest bulletin, each time inquiring as to the correct hour—for the clocks inside Sandringham were set, as always, a half-hour ahead, while the waiting journalists had their watches set at Greenwich time. Dawson's constant interruption so unnerved the Prince of Wales that he left his father's bedside in a state of near-hysteria and peremptorily ordered Sandringham's chief clockmaker, Mr. David Burlingham, to immediately correct the time on all of the estate's clocks. Unlike Dr. Dawson, Queen Mary had not seen any evil intent on the heir's part to take over the King's command prematurely. Of King George's last few hours, she wrote in her diary: "My children were all angels."

An explanation for the Prince of Wales's behaviour can be found in his lifelong fear of becoming King. The clocks at Sandringham, set a half-hour forward, were accelerating the eventuality. He was emotionally spent and so nervous that he burned his finger on a cigarette he was smoking. He was anxiously waiting for the father from whom he had always felt estranged to acknowledge him with some personal last bequest of love or understanding. In a matter of minutes he would be King, and the confusion of Sandringham time and real time only magnified the terror he felt. His uncontrollable impulse, therefore, was to keep the clocks from ticking away too fast, to forestall the time of his father's death.

The King's life was extinguished at five minutes before midnight with no signs of pain or suffering. His breathing had simply ceased. Queen Mary glanced over his still form to Lord Dawson to confirm her fears. The doctor nodded. The King's death had been so peaceful that no one else gathered round the bed had yet comprehended what had just taken place. Instantly, the Queen turned to her eldest son and, bowing, took his hand in hers and kissed it.

"God save the King," she said in a strong, unwavering voice, and looked him squarely in the eye. She then stepped back with a slight curtsy, and Georgie, who was standing next to her, stepped forward, bowed, and followed her example. The new King appeared startled, then noticeably embarrassed. "I could not bring myself to believe that the members of my own family or indeed anyone else, should be expected to humble themselves before me in this way," he was to write later.

A half-hour after King George's death, a bareheaded youth carrying the message to the waiting journalists rode his bicycle, a dim oil lamp flickering in front of him, down Sandringham's darkened drive. In one hand he carried an old brown leather case containing the announcement of the death of the Sovereign, while with the other he gripped a handlebar. He reached the lodge gate just as the chimes of the Sandringham Church clock struck half-past twelve and, without dismounting, delivered the case to the gatekeeper, who removed the bulletin and slowly walked across the drive and posted the notice between the lights of two great lanterns. A small crowd of villagers and journalists read the announcement. When the reporters left to telephone the news, a small, silent, bareheaded crowd remained.

By five o'clock the following day, the new King had flown back to London with Bertie. Black-bordered placards announcing their father's death lined their route. But at Buckingham Palace, the sentry still marched up and down as sentries had done for hundreds of years. One King had died, but another was on the Throne and Great Britain had not changed. Still, the new King spent the first night of his reign in London at York House, St. James's.

Shortly after he had left Sandringham, the lid of the late King's coffin was screwed down and the coffin placed upon a small bier and carried by towering grenadiers from the King's Company through the dark and rainy late afternoon to the little church at Sandringham. Queen Mary, heavily veiled in black, followed directly behind the grenadiers. She was flanked by her family and some members of the Household (in all, twelve persons). She appeared to be the tallest mourner, setting a pace that her daughter, who was much shaken, and the elderly members of the Household found difficult to match.

"Such a sad day," Queen Mary wrote that night. "It is curious my having been present in this house at the death beds of 2 brothers Eddy & George."

What was perhaps more curious was the fact that she had been so composed during her husband's death and the immediate attendant ceremony that no one had seen her shed a tear. And the next day, when the new King returned to discuss the funeral arrangements with her, she seemed relieved. David, King Edward VIII, as he had been styled, was safely on the Throne.

The most memorable impression of the funeral week was the Queen's awesome dignity and incredible stoicism. The Royal women, darkly veiled and all in black, were constantly being photographed in a group with Queen Mary the pivotal figure, erect, a shrouded statue of majesty. Around her huddled her despondent daughter, unable to control her emotions, to her mother's frequent irritation; her three daughters-in-law—Elizabeth, visibly weak after a recent bout of flu; Marina, infinitely more elegant than the others, fresh violets tucked under her veil and wearing sheer black stockings that called attention to her shapely legs; and Alice, so unsure of what she must do that she was always just one too-close step behind the others—the aged Princess Beatrice shivering with the cold that was unrelenting throughout the protocol; and the old King's only surviving sister, Queen Maud, so thickly veiled she was unrecognisable.*

The King had died on January 20. The next day, the Privy Council announced the accession of King Edward VIII. A few moments later, the new King was sent for. He entered the Council Chamber ". . . solemn, grave, sad and dignified in Admiral's uniform. Everyone was most impressed by his seeming youth, and his dignity. Much bowing and he in turn swore his Oath." The next day, King Edward's accession was proclaimed in "a fleeting, brilliant ceremony." He had arranged for a few personal friends, including Mrs. Simpson, to watch the ceremony

---

*Princess Louise had died in 1931, at which time King George's only daughter, Princess Mary, had been named Princess Royal.

391

from his boyhood room at St. James's overlooking Friary Court. During the ceremony, he was "swept by conflicting emotions," he admitted. "There was a flash of pride in becoming King Emperor . . . At the same time these words seemed to tell me that my relations with Wallis had suddenly entered a more significant stage."

Chips Channon reports seeing "a large black car (the King's) drive away [from St. James's] with the blinds pulled half down. The crowd bowed thinking it contained the Duchess of Kent, but I saw Mrs. Simpson . . ."

When Queen Mary arrived in London on the Royal train on January 23 with King George's coffin, a sharp wind blew off the North Sea and the temperature was biting cold. Upon her request to King Edward, the Lying-in-State and the funeral would be over in a week's time. She had never much approved of the panoply of Royal deaths and intensely disliked the wearing of mourning for long periods. The new King had agreed to issue a decree that mourning be restrained to a period of only six months. Her four sons walked behind the gun carriage carrying the coffin to Westminster Hall. Harry had not yet recuperated from his bad throat and was swathed in wool beneath his uniform to ward off the cold.

During the procession, the cross on top of the Imperial Crown fell to the pavement. Immediately, a company sergeant major of the grenadier escort retrieved it. King Edward had seen the incident and deemed it "a most terrible omen."

Of that day, Anne Morrow Lindbergh,* who watched the procession from a window of her suite at the Ritz Hotel, recalls, "The sound of pipers—unmistakable and rather eerie—in the distance and then, with a startling suddenness below us around the corner those even lines of sailors, white collars all in line and the white ropes, taut like a woven pattern . . . They pulled evenly that little gun carriage—the coffin, terribly small, covered in the rich gold of the flag. On top, those familiar unbelievable signs

---

*Anne Morrow Lindbergh (1906–). Author and wife of Charles Lindbergh. Her first book, *North to the Orient* (1935), an account of a flight she had made with her husband, had just been published.

of the Throne: the orb, the crown, the sceptre, and a crown of roses. The tiny and yet terrifically powerful sight of the coffin, wrapped in the Standard, fastened your attention, your emotions in a strange way . . . The Standard flapping down, the King in Naval uniform walking jerkily (. . . alone, small, pathetic) . . ."

Behind the four Royal brothers, Lord Harewood led the heads of state, the Kings of Norway, Denmark, Belgium, and Bulgaria among them. The pathetic Duke of Saxe-Coburg and Gotha,* in a German helmet, hunched and arthritic, had trouble keeping up.†

As Big Ben began to strike four, the gun carriage drew up before Westminster Hall. The coffin was carried by six huge guardsmen with bared heads, who placed it upon a catafalque draped in purple velvet and occupying the centre of the Great Hall. A moment of panic arose as the Royal standard caught

---

*When Queen Victoria married Prince Albert, he was heir-apparent to his elder childless brother, Ernest II, reigning Duke of Saxe-Coburg and Gotha. As Prince Albert predeceased Ernest II in 1861, Albert's eldest son, the Prince of Wales (later Edward VII), became heir-apparent to the dukedom. When Prince Ernest II died in 1893, the Prince of Wales waived his right to succession to the dukedom of Saxe-Coburg and Gotha in favour of his younger brother, Alfred, Duke of Edinburgh, who reigned until 1900. Alfred had no surviving heirs. Queen Victoria was responsible for the decision that the next in line, her third son, Duke of Connaught (who was her favourite), should not leave England, nor should his young son, Prince Arthur. The next in succession was Prince Charles, son of Queen Victoria's deceased son, Prince Leopold, and brother of Princess Alice (married to Princess May's brother, Prince Alexander, later Lord Athlone).

†Foreign royalties in the procession were King Haakon of Norway; Crown Prince Olav of Norway; Leopold III, King of the Belgians; Boris III, King of Bulgaria; Prince of Piedmont; Paul, Prince Regent of Yugoslavia; Gustav, Crown Prince of Sweden; Paul, Crown Prince of Greece; Prince Zeid; Prince Farouk of Egypt; Prince Felix of Luxembourg; Grand Duke of Hesse; Charles, Duke of Saxe-Coburg and Gotha; Prince Axel of Denmark; Prince Nicholas of Greece; Prince George of Greece; Duke de Nemours; the Count of Flanders; Prince Frederick of Prussia; Prince Ernest August of Brunswick; Prince Alvaro of Orleans-Bourbon; the Infante of Spain; the Duke of Braganza; Prince Salik of Albania; and the Grand Duke Dimitri of Russia. Eight of these men had been deposed.

393

beneath the catafalque. The officer in command managed to free it without too much difficulty.

King Edward had followed the coffin, "boyish, sad and tired," Chips Channon noted, "and the Queen, erect and more magnificent than ever."

Shortly after midnight, in an act without precedent, the King and his three brothers, dressed in full uniform, descended into the Hall and stationed themselves around the catafalque between the officers already on vigil. For twenty minutes in the dim candlelight, the King's four sons stood motionless and unrecognised by the parade of people shuffling past with bowed heads.

King George's coffin remained in Westminster Hall for four days. On January 28, a damp miserable day, the Queen prepared herself for the funeral. "First we fetched him from Westminster Hall, he was drawn by blue-jackets on the gun carriage, then a long drive, the men walking, to Paddington through wonderful crowds of sorrowing people mourning their dead King," the Queen wrote in her diary. She sat at the window of the Royal funeral coach with its red trappings and black chassis, Chips Channon noted, looking "incredibly magnificent and composed." The footmen wore gold-and-red cloaks, and her attendants wore plumed hats. Ahead was the distant sound of the band, the echoing sound of the minute gun punctuating the music. Rain fell and umbrellas "popped up like hundreds of mushrooms."

Then suddenly the procession had passed and the "silence" in the streets was impressive. "Men jumped out of taxis and stood with bared heads at attention . . . and the gun going off and then no noise or movement at all. Only natural things, like birds wheeling in the sky and papers blowing in the street."

The procession stopped at Paddington Station, and the coffin was transferred once again into the Royal train, this time for Windsor. The day was a tremendous ordeal but one of great meaning for the Royal Family, Britain's statesmen, and for all the visiting royalties. Feeling for the dead King was strong and "much, much more . . . the continuity of all kinds of traditional beliefs, ideals, standards, characteristics—a strong pride and sense of them and their permanence."

The Queen sat in majestic forebearance by the window of the Royal coach as the train rumbled sonorously through the western outskirts of London to Windsor. Sombre dark figures sharing the nation's grief were waiting to pay homage at each station that the train passed, and the Queen would acknowledge them with a slight bow of her head, the graceful flutter of a white cambric handkerchief; then there was "another drive, the men walking thro' Windsor & the gates into the grounds, to St. George's Chapel." The Dean of Windsor, in his robes as Register of the Order of the Garter, stood on the steps of St. George's Chapel, awaiting the dead Sovereign. As the choir began to sing, "I am the Resurrection and the Life," their voices blended with the sad lament of the bagpipes outside the chapel. The Queen, King Edward beside her, walked evenly behind the coffin. Fully two feet separated mother and son as they mounted the long, steep stairs. Never once did the Queen's step falter or her hand reach out for support.

Before the coffin was lowered through the floor to the Royal vaults below, King Edward tossed a handful of earth onto it. "We left him [King George] sadly," the Queen wrote in her diary, "lying for the present with his ancestors in the vaults."

The harrowing, exhausting week finally ended in Queen Mary's return to London. The next day, Dr. Lang, the Archbishop of Canterbury, went to Buckingham Palace to speak with her and found her already preparing to move back to Marlborough House. "I had a long talk with her," he wrote, "her [the Queen's] fortitude still unbroken . . . I was told afterwards that the sons . . . were painfully upset—I suppose they had seldom if ever seen death—and that it was the Queen, still marvellously self-controlled, who supported and strengthened them."

The King transferred his office to Buckingham Palace, occupying on the ground floor a small waiting room, decorated and furnished in oriental style and looking out on the courtyard. For the first time in over twenty years, Queen Mary was resident in a home to which her son came daily, motoring from nearby St. James's (though he would have much preferred to have walked) in King George's immense and sombre Daimler.

"How glad I am to be a Queen Mother and not only a Queen

395

Dowager," Queen Mary said to Lady Airlie. She then explained to her old friend that at the time of King Edward VII's accession, the two positions had been investigated, and it had been established that a Queen Mother had certain rights, whereas a Queen Dowager had no particular privileges except those voluntarily accorded to her by the reigning Sovereign. The distinction was an important one to Queen Mary, for her status had been clearly defined.

PART FOUR

MAMA—
MATRIARCH AND
QUEEN MOTHER

TWENTY-EIGHT

One afternoon in February 1935, Queen Mary suddenly interrupted Lady Airlie while she was reading aloud. "Your sons are about the age of mine, Mabell, and you have had to bring them up without a father. Tell me, have they ever disappointed you?"

Lady Airlie, sensing the direction of this conversation and hoping to avoid any unpleasantness, commented lightly that most children disappointed their parents at some time or other.

"Yes," the Queen replied, "one can apply that to individuals, but not to a Sovereign. He is not responsible to himself alone." She picked up her embroidery and stitched in silence for a moment. Then she added, "I have not liked to talk to David about this affair with Mrs. Simpson, in the first place because I don't want to give the impression of interfering in his private life, and also because he is the most obstinate of all my sons. To oppose him over doing anything is only to make him more determined to do it. At present he is utterly infatuated. But my great hope is that violent infatuations usually wear off."

She was thoughtful for a long time. The conversation went on to other matters but quickly returned to the subject of Wallis Simpson. "He gives Mrs. Simpson the most beautiful jewels." Her eyes clouded. "I am so afraid that he may ask me to receive her and I have promised King George I shall never do so...."

Not long after this, Queen Mary asked her old friend, "Has there been a great deal of gossip, Mabell—I mean here in London?" Lady Airlie replied truthfully that there had been. A few moments later, the Queen said passionately, ". . . it's too late. He's very, very much in love with her. Poor boy!"

In the first months after the King's death, Queen Mary concentrated on the task of sorting out all his letters and possessions, and then on preparations for her own move to Marlborough House. "It was a terrible wrench to her to leave Buckingham Palace with all its associations," Lady Airlie commented, "but as always her own feelings were sublimated in her sense of duty. The King who had been her husband was dead but the Sovereign lived; the Palace which had been her home for over a quarter of a century now belonged to him. She deliberately filled her disciplined mind with trivial things—with the packing of her objets d'art, and the redecorating of the rooms at Marlborough House—to shut out her loneliness and her anxiety."

"I took leave of my lovely rooms with a sad heart," Queen Mary confessed on July 30, when she left Buckingham Palace forever, to spend the summer at Sandringham before making the move into Marlborough House, which was being redecorated. "David kindly came to see me off . . . I am so glad to be here but miss my G. too dreadfully, his rooms look so empty & deserted . . ." To the King she wrote, "I fear I was very quiet today when you came to see me but I feel sure you realised that I felt very sad at leaving those lovely comfortable rooms which have been my happy Home for 25 years & that I was terribly afraid of breaking down—It was dear of you to come & see me off & I thank you with all my heart . . ."

Queen Mary was enduring a wrenching change in her life. She was a widow, and all her children had left home and had fulfilling and demanding lives of their own. Unlike Queen Alexandra, she had not been possessive of any of her offspring. The result was that she was left very much on her own, even further removed from her family than she had been during her husband's lifetime. King George had been a magnetic force in the lives of his family, drawing all those close to him by monarchial awe and paternal respect, and Queen Mary had shared with him the polarising results. The power had now shifted and been split. David was King and earned his family's wholehearted support, but he did not hold them together as a unit.

For over twenty-five years, Queen Mary had played the role of the Sovereign's closest devoted subject. Because of King George's great respect for her intelligence and ability, this had never squashed her independent spirit. Not being of a maternal or a frivolous nature, her days had always been filled with the gathering of new information. Mindless chatter echoed chillingly in her presence. She had little in common with any of her daughters-in-law, and perhaps even less with her own daughter. Marina was the brightest of the lot, but she was a bit too socially oriented for her mother-in-law's taste. Elizabeth—the most attentive and kind—lacked any spark of original thinking, and Alice remained timidly withdrawn. Queen Mary and her daughter had never had a great rapport, and widowhood did not alter this situation. Nor did having grandchildren warm her undemonstrative temperament.

She thought very little of her daughter-in-law Elizabeth's intellectual or artistic capacities and took on a programme of educational visits with her two young granddaughters (Lilibet, then ten, and Margaret Rose, seven) to various museums and exhibitions about London. These excursions were seldom organised by mutual consent and were usually undertaken on extremely short notice, most often to fill in a gap in Queen Mary's day. With one girl grasped firmly by each hand, she would troop through the British Museum or the Wallace Collection acting as guide, reeling off a prodigious list of names, dates, and historic references, infallibly correct. Lilibet could manage only to "keep walking with every expression of great interest on her face when her feet were hurting her and it was getting towards tea-time." But little Margaret Rose proved an eager listener. And whereas Lilibet had been her grandfather's favourite, Queen Mary's was the younger sister, who was quicker as well as more eager to learn.

Bertie's wife did not take education for women too seriously. Privately educated herself, the Duchess of York believed there were other attainments "just as important as academic excellence. To spend as long as possible in the open air, to enjoy to the full the pleasures of the country, to be able to dance and draw and appreciate music, to acquire good manners and perfect deportment, and to cultivate all the distinctively feminine graces." Her mother's priorities made a great impression on Lilibet, who had been unable to progress beyond the basic principles of mathematics and who confided to her governess, Marian Crawford, that when she grew up she wanted only to be "a lady living in the country with lots of horses and dogs."

Horses and dogs, indeed! Queen Mary cared little for either. She and Lilibet did share a kind of personal strength that made each the dominating personality in her family, Queen Mary with her sons and daughter, and Lilibet with her parents and sister.

Members of Queen Mary's Household were careful to avoid using the term "the Queen Mother." Publicly, she was thought of as the shrewd matriarch of the Royal Family. As the first months of Edward VIII's reign passed and his family's angst became a national crisis, many people wished a widowed Queen Consort might inherit her husband's monarchial powers. For by the summer of 1936, her mourning abandoned, Queen Mary was quite the most inspiring Royal figure in the Monarchy.

What had been common gossip in the United States within a few months of King Edward's reign had hardly been guessed at by the British people. The King was besotted by Mrs. Simpson, and his open flaunting of his feelings was at the very least an indication that his passion now controlled his reason. Queen Mary had only to look at the photographs of the King and Mrs. Simpson taken on the cruise of the *Nahlin* in July and August 1936 to recognise the truth—and she was no fool. American and French photographers and journalists had followed the yacht en masse from port to port, and their newspapers had carried daily front-page banner stories that revealed a bare-chested King Edward staring moon-eyed at his smugly smiling American mistress.

Queen Mary was informed of the day-to-day developments in her son's affair by friends and relations abroad who enclosed press cuttings in their letters. As always in her life, Queen Mary refused to succumb to gossip, although occasionally she displayed displeasure to Lady Airlie at the King's lack of discretion.

His mother, members of the Cabinet, and those few with contacts abroad knew of the King's romantic activities, but his subjects did not, for there was a voluntary suppression of all news about the King and his affair in the British press. Mrs. Simpson's name—always coupled with her husband's—had appeared only a few times in the Court Circular. And only group pictures had been printed in which she was to be seen—true, most often beside the King, but never in a pose that revealed personal attachment.

Originally, the cruise of the *Nahlin* had been planned by the King as a holiday. The Foreign Office, perhaps fearing what was the eventuality anyway—international press coverage of the King's companion and their affair—attempted to distract the public by turning the vacation into a diplomatic tour. Thus, the King met with Prime Minister Metaxas in Athens; Cabinet ministers in Istanbul; King Boris in Bulgaria; the Prince Regent, Prince Paul in Yugoslavia; and in Vienna called upon President Nicklas and received the Chancellor, Dr. Schuschnigg, in a half-hour audience at the British Legation. These meetings were duly reported in the world press, but the photographs that were given front-page attention were intimate ones of the King and Wallis Simpson bathing in the sea or sitting close together in a small boat, "her hand on his arm, and he looking down at her." Every line of his face and body told ". . . of his unalterable devotion." These last were the clippings received by Queen Mary.

Within one hour of the King's return to London on September 14, he dined privately with his mother at Buckingham Palace. He was well tanned and had gained a few much-needed pounds. As he greeted Queen Mary in his study, he appeared more nervous than usual and lacking his former boyishness. To his irritation, she curtsied slightly in greeting, and when she straightened and glanced down—for with the shoes she wore, she was several inches taller than her son—he claimed that he "wondered how much she knew about the stories appearing in the American press."

Her conversation told him nothing.

"Did you enjoy the cruise?" she asked.

He assured her that he had had a wonderful time.

"Didn't you find it terribly warm in the Adriatic?" she inquired.

The King flushed. Conversation was difficult. His mother's superficial questions reminded him of similar confrontations when he had returned home from school bursting with emotions to share, fears to have explained away, experiences to relate. He did not understand then or at this time why she could not treat him in a maternal or at least familial fashion, even though he had been the Heir-Apparent and was now the King. Georgie was the only member of the family with whom he really had the kind of relationship he saw in other families like the Mountbattens and the Churchills.

"I read in the *Times* of your meeting with King George [of Greece] at Corfu," she said. "How is he getting along?"

"He's lost weight and [he's] quite homesick for his friends in London, I'm afraid," he replied.

"Poor George," she commented, "I don't envy the rulers of those Balkan countries."

They then went in to dinner, their conversation remaining casual. She was pleased to hear that he intended to spend the last two weeks of September at Balmoral, an indication that he was aware how important it was to maintain the habits and customs of the family.

What the King did not know was how much Queen Mary still hoped he would give up Mrs. Simpson and her "crowd" and return more to the ways of his father. She had begun to receive a volume of letters from friends and members of the government, urging her to act. The London and the provincial press kept their voluntary silence on the subject. On October 1, the day that marked David's official move to Buckingham Palace, that solemn pact was near its end.

After lunching together at Buckingham Palace, David drove with his mother to Marlborough House. They had tea and wandered from room to room, altering small things together—the position of some of the objets d'art, removing a firescreen—these homely exchanges constituting more intimacy than the two had previously shared. David was eager to please his mother, and interest in and enthusiasm over her most cherished possessions was the one way he knew to do so. The subject of Court presentation of divorced people arose when they were joined by his sister, the Princess Royal, and Lady Colville, prompted perhaps by the knowledge that Mrs. Simpson's divorce case was known to be coming up for hearing. Conversation was immediately turned elsewhere, and a few moments later the King wished his mother well and departed.

Members of the government had a sense of impending disaster. No story illustrates this better than one told by Harold Nicolson. Nicolson was talking with James H. Thomas, then Secretary of State for the Colonies and formerly the Lord Privy Seal.* "J.H." had come up from cockney roots, and King George had always been amused by him.

" 'J.H.,' 'e says to me one day," J.H. repeated to Harold Nicolson, " 'did I ever tell you that my grandmother asked me not to call myself George but Albert? I found a letter on my dressing table at Windsor saying that it was her dearest wish that I should change my name. But I said I wouldn't. I had been christened George, and George I would remain.' 'E was like that, you know, 'arold, not afraid of people, if you know what I mean. And now 'ere we 'ave this little obstinate man with 'is Mrs. Simpson. H'it won't do, 'arold, I tell you straight. I know the people of this country. I *know* them. They 'ate 'aving no family life at Court."

A divorce decree *nisi* was granted to Mrs. Simpson on October 27, and on November 16 the King saw the Prime Minister, Stanley Baldwin, and announced that he intended to marry Wallis Simpson and to do so would, if necessary, abdicate the Throne. On the evening of this day, he went to dine in white tie and tailcoat with his mother and sister at Marlborough House. Queen Mary, the Princess Royal, and his brother Harry's wife, Alice, waited to greet him in his mother's boudoir. He was surprised at Alice's presence but was reassured when Queen Mary announced that Alice would leave soon after dinner. It became obvious to the King that a discussion was planned for

---

*James H. Thomas was later found guilty by a tribunal appointed by Parliament of revealing Budget secrets to Sir Alfred Butt, M.P., who was also found guilty for profiting by this information.

that time and that Alice had been included in the dinner to keep the tone of the meal light.

For the troubled King, the meal, for which he had little appetite, "seemed endless. I was preoccupied with what I was going to say afterward," he later confessed; "no matter how gracefully I proceeded, the evening was bound to be difficult for all of us. I tried to ease the tension by keeping the conversation on a light plane. I congratulated my mother upon the record contribution of garments to her favourite charity, the London Needlework Guild. She was glad to hear that I had arranged to have the outside of Buckingham Palace painted before the coronation next year. 'It's high time,' she said. I asked Mary whether she and her husband had bought any yearlings at the Newmarket sales. But I felt especially sorry for poor Alice. Shy and retiring by nature, she had all unwittingly sat down at my mother's table only to find herself caught up in the opening scene of one of the most poignant episodes in the annals of the British Royal Family. Never loquacious, this evening she uttered not a word. And, when at last we got up to leave the table, she eagerly seized upon the interruption to protest that she was extremely tired and to ask that she be excused. After making her curtsy she almost fled from the room. My mother, Mary, and I retired to the boudoir. We were alone.

"Settling down in a chair, I told them of my love for Wallis and my determination to marry her and of the opposition of the Prime Minister and the Government to the marriage. The telling was all the harder because until that evening the subject had not been discussed between us."

What the King did not know was that only a few days before Mrs. Simpson's divorce case came up for hearing, Queen Mary, in an unprecedented show of maternal concern, had in private urged members of the Cabinet to take some kind of action (presumably to block the divorce). Considering Queen Mary's strict views on divorce, for her to sanction her eldest son marrying a woman with "two husbands living" would have been out of the question.

The more the King talked, the clearer his intention was made that he would abdicate rather than give up Wallis Simpson. Queen Mary became even more rigid and withdrawn, and he was to say, "My mother had been schooled to put duty in the stoic Victorian sense before everything else in life. From her invincible virtue and correctness she looked out as from a fortress upon the rest of humanity with all its tremulous uncertainties and distractions."

To Queen Mary, the Monarchy was, indeed, "something sacred and the Sovereign a personage apart." The steel gate of the word *duty* fell between mother and son. Desperation and the feeling that, if he could but win over his mother, she could then plead his case to the Prime Minister and Cabinet caused the King to press on: "Please, won't you let me bring Wallis Simpson to see you?" he asked.

Her answer was a strong and deliberate, "That is quite out of the question."

David rose to leave, and she walked him to the door of her boudoir. "I hope, sir, that you will make a wise decision for your future," she said, adding, "I fear your visit to South Wales [the King was leaving for a short tour the next morning] will be trying in more ways than one."

The King felt that what separated him and his mother "was not a question of duty but a different concept of Kingship." Shockingly, either he did not understand or did not accept the fact that Britain was a *constitutional* monarchy and he did not have the inalienable right to do as he pleased. At this stage, he truly believed he could make Wallis Simpson his Queen without the consent of the Cabinet. In a man raised to be King, such a limited knowledge of English history is hard to believe. Most teen-aged British schoolchildren knew what their King did not —that the Sovereign was bound by the Constitutional Rule of 1688 and ultimately subject to the advice of Parliament through his Ministers. If he acted in direct opposition to Parliament and the Cabinet, like James II, he would have to forfeit his Crown.

But if he did not realise this, Queen Mary did. Therefore, when he returned from Wales, having decided, apparently, that he would marry Wallis Simpson *and* make her his Queen Consort, he pressed the issue with Baldwin. For though the Crown held no fascination for him and he had already seriously considered abdication, he thought it did have meaning to Mrs. Simpson and—if she could be Queen—would rectify the humiliation to which he believed she had been subjected. Queen Mary was patently exasperated at her "difficult" son. When the Prime Minister came to talk with her about the situation, she swept her hands before her in a gesture of despair and exclaimed, "Well, Mr. Baldwin! This is a pretty kettle of fish!" For two hours Queen Mary and the Prime Minister debated the question at hand. In the end, she agreed to speak with her son in what can only be termed "a last-ditch effort" to make him see where his duty lay. On November 24, at her request he came to tea at Marlborough House. At this meeting the King did indeed see his "duty," but not from the same vantage point as his mother. *Poor Bertie* was Queen Mary's argument. How could he do this to Bertie, for surely if he persisted on his present course he would have to abdicate, and Bertie was weak and not well and had never been trained to be King. The responsibilities of the Sovereign would kill Bertie. To remind her that his own father had not been raised to be King was hopeless, or that his brother and his wife were still young enough to parent a male heir.

The unfairness that Bertie should be expected to be free from the kind of responsibility the King had struck deep. Additionally, Bertie's drinking habit, which often robbed him of lucidity, was not censured. His brother's nervous nature was always an excuse for this weakness. David had neither the rights of the common man, nor those of any other member of the Royal family. And his mother neither saw nor empathised with his sense of injustice. He left Queen Mary determined to marry Mrs. Simpson and retreated to the security of Fort Belvedere, Wallis and her aunt, Mrs. Bessie Merriman, as "chaperone," taking refuge there with him.

On December 3, the press, which had been "hypnotised by long habit into seeing not only no evil but no idiosyncrasy in the Royal Family, hearing none and reporting none," broke the story of the constitutional crisis. The country was catapulted into immediate chaos. With no real warning, the public suddenly and in a matter of days had to reexamine their views on the Monarchy. What was at stake was the power of the people, through Parliament, against the power of the Monarchy.

Unlike the American Constitution, the British Constitution is mostly unwritten and is not much more than a "rhetorical abstraction." Precedents have been set through the centuries that have become *unwritten* laws; no Sovereign in more than a century had dared to flout them. It is certainly correct that the King had the legal right to marry whomever he wished. Constitutional precedent had also been established in any crisis where there was a conflict of power. At such times, Parliament is above the King and he must accept the advice of Parliament through his Ministers on everything that affects public policy and the public interest.

A marriage that made Mrs. Simpson Queen Consort was simply not considered by Parliament to be in the public interest.

"Really! This might be Rumania!" Queen Mary remarked bitterly over the hysterical debates in Parliament and the ugly press coverage.

The day before the story broke, Queen Mary sent the King a note asking to see him as soon as possible. Though exhausted physically and emotionally at this point, he drove, late at night, from Fort Belvedere to Marlborough House. He found his mother, Bertie, and Bertie's wife (who had accompanied her husband despite a case of the flu). The meeting was a dismal failure. If Queen Mary thought she could change her eldest son's mind by creating a sudden sense of guilty duty in him, a silent plea that he must somehow save Bertie, she had calculated wrongly. He assured her that he did not wish to bring any of them pain, but that he had to handle this situation alone and in his own way.

The hour was too late when he left Marlborough House to return to the Fort, and so he ordered the car to Buckingham Palace.* As the immense walls of the palace loomed, he had great forebodings. A crowd was gathered, silent and ominous, at the gates, and he claimed that there came over him at that moment, "like a wave, a powerful resurgence of the intense dislike for the building" he had always felt. He was now questioning if he belonged there at all. And the answer came swiftly

---

*King Edward VIII had recently vacated St. James's Palace. His apartments there were now occupied by the Duke and Duchess of Gloucester.

—"certainly not alone." Within an hour, he set out again for Fort Belvedere. As he drove out of the gate, a cheer went up in the crowd, and he did not know if it was given in his support or at his departure.

The Cabinet refused to sanction a marriage where Mrs. Simpson became Queen and therefore entitled to all the status, rights, and privileges that the law and constitutional custom granted a Queen Consort. The King's wishes were further doomed by the Statute of Westminster, which had been incorporated in the Constitution in 1931. This rule declared that "any alteration in the law touching the succession of the Throne or the Royal Style and titles shall hereafter require the assent as well of the Parliament *of all the Dominions* as of the Parliament of the United Kingdom." Australia, Canada, and South Africa were resolved that they would not accept as Queen an American woman, twice divorced and with two living husbands. Nor would they approve a morganatic marriage. Clearly, the King could not "both remain on the Throne and marry Mrs. Simpson."

Although the suggestion has often been made that the Government was using Mrs. Simpson as a means to remove the King from the Throne, this is unlikely. Edward VIII's German sympathies were hardly suspected by a public that idolised him. To the youth he had become "an ideal figure which had captured their imagination and affection." A fear of civil unrest that could follow in the footsteps of the King's abdication existed among some members of Parliament. Youth was often unwilling to believe that their gods had any clay in their composition. The sticking point was that if the King married Mrs. Simpson and did not abdicate, he would be doing so without Parliamentary approval and would therefore be acting unconstitutionally, and he might well act independently in other matters. This possibility brought to the mind of the Cabinet the King's views toward Germany and toward war. What was proved in the early days of December 1936 was that "the Sovereign is free to choose his own Consort providing his choice is approved by the Prime Minister and government of the day. If, on the other hand, he chooses someone generally regarded as unsuitable to be Queen, it in fact becomes a Constitutional matter."

At a Cabinet meeting on December 2, only Duff Cooper

pleaded that the issue be tabled until after the coronation and that the King be asked to delay any decision for a year. The rest of the Cabinet had been unanimous in rejecting all other alternatives to abdication, even postponement. The King had either to abdicate or renounce any plan to marry Mrs. Simpson. On December 3, Wallis Simpson took things in her own hands. She claims she was certain that there was only one solution, to remove herself from the King's life. Her effort, however, was only a half-hearted one. On the day the King went to Marlborough House to see Queen Mary and Bertie, she left Fort Belvedere but retreated only as far as Newhaven, the home of Lord Brownlow, the King's Lord-in-Waiting, reasoning that if she left the country the King would follow and a worse crisis would develop.

On December 7, with Mrs. Simpson tantalisingly near, yet removed, the King's mood was one of confusion and desperation. A friend records in her diary for that day, ". . . the King's one idea is Mrs. Simpson. Nothing that stands between him and her will meet his approval. The Crown is only valuable if it would interest *her*. He must have marriage because then she can be with him always."*

From the night of the confrontation between the King and Queen Mary and the Duke of York, Bertie had been in a state of extreme agitation. Clearly, he would be the one most affected by his brother's proposed abdication, and unlike the majority of heirs to the Throne before him, he had no taste or ambition for the position of King. The idea, in fact, was terrifying and abhorrent to him. The King knew this, and also that it was their mother's fervent wish and his sister-in-law Elizabeth's prayer that Bertie would never have to wear the Crown. Bertie's dilemma is shown in his own chronicle of the crisis.

"[On December 3] I saw my brother (together with Walter Monckton) who was in a great state of excitement,† who said he

---

*Blanche E. Dugdale; this diary was published as *Baffy, the Diaries of Blanche Dugdale, 1936–37.*

†Sir Walter Monckton's name is incorrectly spelled here. Walter Turner (1891–1965). First Viscount Monckton of Brenchley, Attorney General to the Prince of Wales 1932–1936, Minister of Labour 1951–1955, Minister of Defence 1955–1956, and Postmaster General 1956–1957.

would leave the country as King after making a broadcast to his subjects & leave it to them to decide what should be done.* The Prime Minister went to see him at 9.0 P.M. that evening & later (in Mary's & my presence) David said to Queen Mary that he could not live alone as King & must marry Mrs.————. When David left after making this dreadful announcement to his mother he told me to come & see him at the Fort the next morning [Friday, December 4]. I rang him up but he would not see me & put me off till Saturday. I told him I would be at Royal Lodge [Windsor] on Saturday by 12:30 P.M. I rang him up Saturday. 'Come & see me Sunday' was his answer. 'I will see you & tell you my decision when I have made up my mind.' Sunday evening I rang up. 'The King has a conference & will speak to you later' was the answer. But he did not ring up. Monday morning [December 7] came. I rang up at 1.0 P.M. & my brother told me he might be able to see me that evening. I told him I must go to London but would come to the Fort when he wanted me! I did not go to London but waited. I sent a telephone message to the Fort to say that if I was wanted I would be at Royal Lodge. My brother rang me up at 10 minutes to 7.0 P.M. to say 'Come & see me after dinner.' I said 'No, I will come & see you at once.' I was with him at 7.0 P.M. the awful & ghastly suspense of waiting was over. I found him pacing up & down the room, & he told me his decision that he would go. I went back to Royal Lodge for dinner & returned to the Fort later. I felt having once got there I was not going to leave. As he is my eldest brother I had to be there to try & help him in his hour of need.

"I went back to London that night with my wife.

"I saw Queen Mary on Tuesday morning [the following day, December 8]."

What is interesting throughout this paper is the Duke of York's reference to his mother as "Queen Mary," and to his brother—who, after all, was still King—as "David" or "my brother." His own frustrations and anger toward the King's disregard of the duty of his birth intensified with each Royal snub and disregard for his own position in the crisis. Never in

*This was the suggestion by the King of a morganatic marriage that was rejected in a special Cabinet meeting December 4, 1936.

his lifetime would he forget his older brother's actions during the abdication crisis, a fact that coloured their relationship from then on with a strong undercurrent of revenge on Bertie's part.

Queen Mary did what she could to help Bertie regain his composure, for he was in a shocking state when she saw him on December 8. With his mother's encouragement, Bertie forced a meeting that same afternoon with Walter Monckton, who was then closest to the King. Monckton spoke frankly to him and told him that there was no chance of the King changing his mind. He would indeed abdicate in Bertie's favour. Bertie returned immediately to his mother at Marlborough House and told her what Monckton had said. Queen Mary as much as replied that in that case the duty was now his, and that he had to pull himself together and shoulder it with pride. He was stuttering badly and visibly upset, and the meeting ended without any of his anxieties being calmed.

That evening he was summoned by the King to dine at the Fort with the Prime Minister; Walter Monckton; Sir Edward Peacock (Receiver-General of the Duchy of Cornwall); Sir George Allen (private solicitor to the King); Major Thomas Dugdale (the Prime Minister's Parliamentary Private Secretary); and his younger brother, George, Duke of Kent. "A dinner I am never likely to forget," Bertie recorded. "While the rest of us (8 in all) . . . were very sad (we knew the final & irrevocable decision he had made) my brother was the life & soul of the party, telling the P.M. things I am sure he had never heard before about unemployed centres etc. [referring to King Edward's visit in South Wales]. I whispered to W.M. '& this is the man we are going to lose.' One couldn't, nobody could, believe it."

The next day, after meeting again with Queen Mary, Bertie had his first long talk with the King. "I could see that nothing I said would alter his decision. His mind was made up," he noted. "I went to see Queen Mary & when I told her what had happened I broke down & sobbed like a child." (The latter to Queen Mary's embarrassment, for Walter Monckton was in the room with them.)

In her account, Queen Mary adds: "Bertie arrived very late from Fort Belvedere & Mr. W. Monckton brought him & me the paper drawn up for David's abdication of the Throne of this

Empire because he wishes to marry Mrs. Simpson!!!!!! . . . It is a terrible blow to us all & particularly to poor Bertie."

The dark, gloomy day following [December 10, 1936], with his three brothers as witnesses, King Edward VIII signed the Instrument of Abdication and announced that he would tell the people of his action in a radio address. Queen Mary, upon hearing from her other sons of this decision, dispatched a hurried letter addressed to the son who was now once again HRH *Prince* Edward of Windsor, exactly in that fashion. "Don't you think that as [the Prime Minister] has said everything that could be said, it will not be necessary for *you* to broadcast this evening . . . surely you might spare yourself this extra strain & emotion —Do please take my advice—Bertie tells me you wish us to meet you at dinner at Royal Lodge this evening, I hope there will not be any fog."

But fog shrouded the route from London to Royal Lodge, where after his broadcast the ex-King met with his family. Some of the tension between them was eased by the indecision at least being over. Queen Mary and the Princess Royal, after a "dreadful goodbye," left first for the ride back to London. "The whole thing," Queen Mary wrote, "was too pathetic for words." At midnight, the new King and the old King kissed and parted, and David bowed to Bertie as his King. Then, alone in the rear seat of the car (that was no longer rightly his), David rode at a creeping pace through the dark, dense fog to Portsmouth, where he boarded the destroyer H.M.S. *Fury,* which in less than half an hour was moving through the choppy waters of the Channel. He was on the first lap of a journey to Boulogne, then to Austria, and six months later to France again and to the side of the woman for whom he had forfeited the Crown.*

At 11:00 A.M. on December 12, his elder brother now safely in Boulogne, King George VI, shy, hesitant—upon his pale, haggard face the strain of his recent ordeal—slowly and stam-

---

*In an article written for the *Daily Express* on June 3, 1957, the former King Edward VIII stated, "But make no mistake, it is the circumstances, not the decision itself, that I regret. If twenty years were to be erased and I were to be presented with the same choice again under the same circumstances, I would act precisely as I did then."

414

mering humiliatingly, addressed his Accession Council at St. James's Palace. At the end of his short speech accepting all the responsibilities of a Sovereign, he read a declaration written in his own hand.* "Furthermore, my first act on succeeding my brother will be to confer on him a Dukedom and he will henceforth be known as H.R.H. the Duke of Windsor." The title had been agreed upon after lengthy discussion with the King's Ministers, but the exact status and rights accorded the title would not be settled for several more weeks. A few hours later, the King received a telegram that came through the Admiralty: "Glad to hear this morning's ceremony went off so well. Hope Elizabeth better [she still had the flu]. Best love and best of luck to you both. David."

When Lady Airlie's son-in-law spoke sympathetically about the Duke of Windsor three days after the abdication, Queen Mary replied indignantly, "The person who needs most sympathy is my second son. He is the one who is making the sacrifice."

She used much the same words to Lady Airlie when they were alone. Her old friend "recognised beneath them her unspoken condemnation of a Sovereign who had allowed his personal feelings to take precedence over his kingdom." There was no feeling evoked of a mother toward a troubled son. Queen Mary's nature had a definite side of steel. She had recently defended Catherine the Great: "She loved her Kingdom. She was prepared to make any sacrifices for it, to go to any lengths—even to commit terrible crimes for it." With no second thoughts, Queen Mary had transferred her loyalty and allegiance from the son who had abandoned his country and duty to the son who had been forced to take on that burden.

*This document with the paragraph naming Prince Edward, HRH the Duke of Windsor, written in the King's own hand, turned up at a Sotheby's auction in 1979. It had somehow become part of the estate of Sir Eric Leadbetter, who had been clerk to the Privy Council at the time. A great furor was raised over this, and the paper is now held in the Royal Archives at Windsor.

TWENTY-NINE

New Yorker correspondent Janet Flanner reported that on December 11, 1936—the tense day of the Abdication itself—she was lunching at the Ritz. At a table near her was seated, among others, "the venerable Mrs. Keppel," who she could not help overhear making the devastating observation: "Things were done better in *my* day."

Popular reaction was one of grief, as though the Monarch had died. Before the ex-King's radio address announcing that he had given up the Throne, people had stood hushed and bareheaded around the Houses of Parliament and Buckingham Palace, as they had done at Sandringham during King George's last hours. Tears were shed when the radio announcer introduced the former King as Prince Edward. Later, there had been signs of bitterness on the part of the people and great disappointment that the King (who had been called the *roi des humbles,* and won their hearts with his charm and his emotional attachment to the poor) had let them down. Nasty limericks made the rounds. But when the crisis was over and "God Save the King" was played in theatres, cinemas, and concert halls, the audiences rose staunchly and sang their allegiance to the new King.

As an indication of the public's mood, at Mme. Tussaud's Waxworks the morning after the Abdication, the effigy of ex-King Edward VIII in its gold-frogged scarlet tunic was moved and placed on a dais considerably below that of the one where King George VI and Queen Elizabeth were posed beneath a red velvet canopy. A fortnight later, a model of Mrs. Simpson was hurriedly completed and placed a short distance from Prince Edward. At first, some visitors stood before her wax image and said rude and obscene things. This soon stopped. The events that led up to the Abdication were nearly forgotten, "except," as Janet Flanner wrote, "by worldly, political minds that still wonder what effect it must eventually have on succeeding generations in the House of Windsor."*

The masses thought of King George VI as a less lovable man than his elder brother. The *Times,* which was harshly anti-King and pro-Parliament (and had been hard on King Edward VIII), called King George "dry and not very human." True, he lacked his brother's charm and contemporary manner and his father's quarterdeck style, but he had inherited his mother's appreciation of "obedience, duty, rank and work." And somehow the stammer which often caused him to pause painfully in a public address, the fact that though fragile in physique he was a good athlete, and that as a naval officer he had once taken part in the Battle of Jutland were enough to endear him to his subjects. At best, he was only moderately intelligent. According to one source, the country did not want "an inventive, brilliant monarch" and was relieved that it wasn't getting one. What was both wanted and needed was a King who would be constitutionally useful, and King George neatly fit that requirement.

The decision had been to continue with the plans and date that had already been set for King Edward VIII's coronation. For centuries, Hebrew elements based on the ritual used by Samuel in anointing Saul, King of Israel, have formed the basis of all coronation ceremonies in Christian countries, and in theory the English coronation is a religious rite. King Edward VIII had wanted a modification of these rituals which were supposed to pass to him a "spiritual jurisdiction and an inalienable sanc-

---

*Ironically, the Abdication brought the people closer to the Monarchy, and perhaps because of World War II and King George VI's high visibility to his subjects during it, the House of Windsor became even more popular and secure.

tity," an idea that he found disturbing. On the other hand, King George was certain to retain the more pious elements of the service.

To date, no British Queen Dowager had attended the new Monarch's coronation. Queen Victoria had been crowned in 1838 while Queen Adelaide had remained sequestered in Marlborough House, and at King George V's coronation Queen Alexandra had withdrawn to Sandringham.* The tradition was said to date back to the Plantagenet Sovereigns, although its origin was unknown. But to add a sense of solidarity to this particular coronation and to help in the smooth transference of power, Queen Mary proposed to the King a constitutional innovation: that she be in the Abbey when he was to be crowned and that she be a part of the coronation procession.

Her suggestions were quickly agreed to, perhaps because, in Wheeler-Bennett's words, "as the Coronation approached . . . there swept through London a wave of idle and malicious gossip which embraced not only the general health of the King and the Royal Family but also his ability to discharge his functions as a Sovereign . . . [There was] a whispering campaign that the King was in such frail health that he might not be able to support the fatigue and strain of the Coronation ceremony itself." The King's health had been questioned by an announcement that the Indian Durbar would be postponed, and by the King's low visibility since the Abdication. A rumour also spread that the King would not be able to get through the ordeal of the coronation, and that he "would never be able to undertake all the arduous duties which would fall to him, that he would never be able to speak in public, and that he would be a recluse or at best, a 'rubber stamp.' "

As late as May 6, at a luncheon of the Industrial Co-Partnership Association, the Reverend Robert Hyde, a close friend of the King's, made a public statement (that obviously had official approval) defending the King's physical stamina, mental capacity, and forcefulness. "Never have I found any evidence of these shortcomings which notorious gossip has attached to him," Rev-

*Queen Dowagers did enter into other coronation activities. However, at the time of King George V's coronation, Queen Alexandra did not.

418

erend Hyde declared. "Those of us who have watched him for the past twenty years conquering the hesitation in his speech which filled him with real anguish have only been filled with admiration. Those of you who hear this gossip, do not heed it; it is unkind, unworthy and untrue."

Some of the people's concern had been fueled by another speech made by the Archbishop of Canterbury on December 13, 1936, in which he had said, "In manner and speech he [King George] is more quiet and reserved than his brother. (And here I may add a parenthesis which may not be unhelpful. When his people listen to him they will note an occasional and momentary hesitation in his speech. But he has brought it into full control, and to those who hear it need cause no sort of embarrassment, for it causes none to him who speaks.)" This last was wishful thinking. King George bravely shouldered "the unexpected and unwanted burden of Sovereignty" and also managed to endure the tortuous task of frequent speech-giving. His stammer—or his terror at having to expose it to the public—was never to vanish, however.

Intermittent rain fell on Coronation Day, May 12, 1937. Queen Mary left Marlborough House with Queen Maud of Norway in a glass coach escorted by a troop of mounted Horse Guards at ten minutes past ten in the morning. Hers was the first Royal coach in the procession. Enthusiastic crowds along the Mall almost immobilised the vehicle as it inched its way toward the Abbey. To Queen Mary's disapproval, extra police had to be called to hold back the crowds that surged forward to get a look at her as the glass coach passed them by. A special apparatus had been installed at Whitehall to monitor the crowds' enthusiasm during the procession. As proof of Queen Mary's great popularity, it recorded eighty-five decibels of public cheering on sight of her, while the new King and Queen Consort received eighty-three. The emblazoned splendours of Vienna, Madrid, Saint Petersburg, Berlin, and Constantinople had given way to shirt-sleeve or hobnailed bureaucracy. But the sight of Queen Mary, splendid in her dress and magnificent in her majesty, reinforced the belief that at least while she lived, people could still believe in the grandeur of Monarchy.

Ironically, London's 26,000 bus drivers persisted in their

strike for a shorter day. This had not kept away the estimated 2 million visitors from every part of the globe or repressed the spirit of tremendous gaiety in the streets. Britain had stood fast through near-chaos and scandal. Silk-turbaned Indian princes, ordinarily imperturbable, smiled genially. Soldiers on temporary leave locked arms with Chinese from Malaya and black troops from Africa. Liners were anchored in the Thames along with warships of the Home Fleet, and Americans (supposedly 20,000 had arrived for the coronation) were shouting, "Long live King George," as though there had never been an American Revolution.

The Royal visitors had been arriving all week. They came as individuals, since no King officially attends another's coronation. Foreign rulers present were Christian X of Denmark (who marked the twenty-fifth anniversary of his accession that same week), Prince Chichibu of Japan, George II of Greece, King Haakon VII of Norway, Prince Regent Paul of Yugoslavia, and Crown Princess Juliana of the Netherlands and her Consort Bernhard. King Yeta III of Barotseland arrived late "because he and the Royal Canoe's 40 man crew took malaria coming down the Zambesi River." He wore an admiral's uniform that King Edward VII had given his father in 1902 and carried a big feather flyswatter. He also "asked the government to sell him a submarine for torpedoing crocodiles."

General John J. Pershing, one of the three representatives of the United States,* wore a fore-and-aft hat with gold braid and ostrich feathers; blue knee-length coat, high-collared with four stars and gold oak leaves on the collar, cuffs, and belt; and blue trousers with a gold stripe and a buff sash draped over his right shoulder. Quite a storm had arisen in the United States over this outfit that the aged soldier himself had designed. The controversy swept across the Atlantic with his arrival for the coronation, the English press (and, indeed, the American press as well) finding it incomprehensible that an army officer could wear a uniform of his own design.

When Big Ben boomed out 11:00 A.M., a restlessness was

---

*The three United States representatives were Ambassador Robert Worth Bingham, General John Joseph Pershing, and Admiral Hugh Rodman.

evident among the audience in the Abbey. The King's procession was already twenty-five minutes late. Queen Mary had entered five minutes earlier, advancing slowly to her place in the Royal box, "an erect and royal figure in her silver gown crossed with the blue ribbon of the Garter," Lady Airlie noted. "I saw her as the very symbol of the solidity of the British Monarchy in which she so passionately believed." Queen Mary wrote that she was seated "between Maud & Lilibet & Margaret came next, they looked too sweet in their lace dresses & robes, especially when they put on their coronets." The Royal Family sat on a level with and directly behind the Recognition Thrones. The rest of the guests were seated in their allocated chairs—nineteen inches wide for the brightly attired, coroneted peers and peeresses (an unprecedented twenty-seven of them American), eighteen inches for the commoners—the men in tailcoats and knee breeches,* the women in evening dresses. Bewigged justices, vestmented bishops, and gold-braided princes and diplomats had taken their places in the choir stalls.

On the last stroke of eleven the great West Door slowly swung open and the people rose. Following their long and brilliant procession, the King and Queen walked up the 300-foot blue carpet without looking left or right. Passing through the theatre, they knelt before the Recognition Chairs, while the procession members took up their appointed places. As the King rose, he "bowed to Mama & the Family"; then, in his own words:

"After the Introduction I removed my Parliamentary Robes & Cap of Maintainance & moved to the Coronation Chair. Here various vestments were placed upon me, the white Cologium Sindonis, a surplice which the Dean of Westminster insisted I should put on inside out, had not my Groom of the Robes come to the rescue. Before this I knelt at the Altar to take the Coronation Oath. I had two Bishops . . . one on either side to support me & to hold the form of Service for me to follow. When this great moment came neither Bishop could find the words, so the Archbishop held his book down for me to read, but horror of horrors his thumb covered the words of Oath.

---

*Except for dispensations, as in the case of Communist and Socialist M.P.s who could wear ordinary evening dress.

"My Lord Great Chamberlain was supposed to dress me but I found his hands fumbled & shook so I had to fix the hilt of the sword myself. As it was he nearly put the hilt of the sword under my chin trying to attach it to the belt. At last all the various vestments were put on me & the Archbishop had given me the two sceptres. The supreme moment came when the Archbishop placed the Saint Edward's Crown on my head. I had taken every precaution as I thought to see that the Crown was right way round, but the Dean & the Archbishop had been juggling with it so much that I never did know if I had it right or not . . .* then I rose to my feet & walked to the throne in the centre of the amphitheatre. As I turned after leaving the Coronation Chair I was brought up all standing owing to one of the Bishops treading on my robe. I had to tell him off pretty sharply as I nearly fell down."

The Archbishop gave the King to hold "the most valuable thing that this world affords"—the Bible—and quickly snatched it away in token of the Church's independence. Kneeling gingerly, the seventy-three-year-old Archbishop rendered his homage to the King. "I Cosmo Gordon Lang . . . will be faithful and true . . ." The other clergymen in the Abbey repeated the Oath.

Harry next knelt before his elder brother. "I, Henry, Duke of Gloucester . . . do become your liege man of life and limb . . . to live and die against all manner of folks. So help me God." George, Duke of Kent, and all the peers then followed suit. Drums rolled. Trumpets sounded. "God save King George!" the people shouted. "Long live King George! May the King live forever!"

At last, the Archbishop turned to the new Queen Consort and, in a brief ceremony significantly devoid of oaths of allegiance,

---

*The explanation the Archbishop (Cosmo Gordon Lang) had for this incident was as follows: "The King was very anxious that the Crown should be placed on his head with the right side to the front. Accordingly it was arranged that a small thin line of red cotton should be inserted under one of the principal jewels on the front. It was there when I saw the Crown in the Annexe before the ceremony. But when the Dean brought the Crown to me on its cushion from the Altar and I looked for my little red line it was not there. So I had to turn the Crown round to see if it was on the other side; but it was not. Some officious person must have removed it."

bade her "receive the Crown of glory, honour, and joy," and placed on her head the Crown with the Koh-i-noor diamond, which twenty-six years before had been placed on the head of Queen Mary.

The time was now 2:40 P.M. King George was often inaudible despite intensive rehearsals and a microphone attached to his Throne. Queen Mary watched him "like a mother eagle. With a 6-inch diadem, five diamond neckbands, other jewels, and a [silver] lame gown (total value $2,000,000) the firm-chinned widow of George the Good dominated the scene," the American press reported. In Italy, however, obedient to Mussolini's order to boycott the coronation, the official Stefani News Agency's full text read: "The Coronation of King George VI took place this morning."

Queen Mary celebrated her seventieth birthday on May 26—fourteen days after the coronation—"with a luncheon party at Marlborough House where the table was pretty with silver and pink carnations." The occasion was not a happy one, for she had just learned that David would marry Wallis Simpson on June 3. On May 28, the King finally made legal his brother's status as Duke of Windsor. However, in an act that shocked many, he decreed that the Duke was entitled "to hold and enjoy for *himself only* the title style or attribute of Royal Highness." This meant that he and his descendants, if there were any, would be Royal Highnesses, but Wallis was never to be more than the Duchess of Windsor. When in a personal letter from King George David first learned of this, he exclaimed indignantly to Walter Monckton, "This is a nice wedding present. I know Bertie—I know he could not have written this letter on his own." But he wasn't really convinced of this and could not let go of his anger throughout the final preparations for the wedding.

He was, in fact, still so outraged on his wedding day that he "had an outburst to Fruity [Metcalfe, a close friend and his best man] while dressing for dinner," Lady Alexandra Metcalfe wrote in her diary on that day. "The family he is through with, the friends, staff . . . have also been awful. He intends to fight the HRH business as legally the King has no right to stop the courtesy title being assumed by his wife." His first reaction had been to give up his own title if Wallis had none. But then he wrote the King stating that he simply would not *admit* the fact of Wallis not being Her Royal Highness.*

Lady Metcalfe gives a good description of the wedding at the Château de Cande.† "The Civil Ceremony took place first, at which only Fruity & Herman R[ogers] were present.‡ During that time we [the remaining guests] sat & waited talking ordinarily as tho nothing unusual was happening . . .§ [The Reverend] Jardine came in first followed shortly by the Duke & Fruity who stood two yards from my chair.‖ Throughout the ceremony Fruity held for him the prayer book Queen Mary gave him when he was 10 with 'to my darling David from his loving Mother'

---

*Publicly, of course, Wallis Simpson upon her marriage to the Duke of Windsor became the Duchess of Windsor. Socially, it was always to be a problem. English people did not call her HRH, but Americans did. Privately, the Duke of Windsor insisted their staff refer to her as HRH, as he always did in formal situations. And he instructed her to sign the wedding register as royalty always did—with her Christian name. This document is signed by the Duchess of Windsor, simply *Wallis*. However, her true Christian name was *Bessie Wallis*.

†Château de Cande was owned by Charles Bedeaux, who had not even met the Duke of Windsor before his generous offer to the trouble-beset lovers of the château as a place of refuge was accepted.

‡Katherine and Herman Rogers were close American friends of the Duchess of Windsor. Years before she had been their guest in Peking.

§Lady Alexandra Metcalfe claims there were only seven English people present, but in fact there were eight: Lady Alexandra and Major Metcalfe; Walter Monckton; Sir George Allen; Randolph Churchill; Hugh Thomas; Lady Selby; and Dudley Forwood, HRH's Equerry. The owner of the Château de Cande, Mr. Charles Bedeaux and his wife, were also present, as were the Americans, Mrs. Bessie Merryman and Katherine and Herman Rogers.

‖The Church of England did not recognise divorce, and its clergy did not usually officiate at a remarriage of a divorced person. At first it appeared that the bridal couple would have to be married only in a French civil ceremony. Then an offer came from Reverend R. A. Jardine of Darlington, England, and was immediately accepted. Although Jardine could not have remarried a divorced person in England, there was no religious law prohibiting him from officiating at such a wedding on the Continent. Jardine and his wife were later (to the Windsors' distress) to tour the United States as the clergy who had married the Windsors.

written in it. Wallis on Herman's arm came in the other door. She was in a long blue dress short tight-fitting coat blue straw hat with feathers & tulle, the loveliest diamond & sapphire bracelet which was his wedding present.

"Jardine read the service simply & well . . . [The Duke's] responses were clear & very well said . . . Her voice . . . lower but clear . . . He had tears running down his face when he came down into the salon after the ceremony. She also could not have done it better. We shook hands with them in the salon . . . If she occasionally showed a glimmer of softness, took his arm, looked at him as though she loved him one would warm toward her, but her attitude is so correct. The effect is of a woman unmoved by the infatuated love of a younger man. Let's hope that she lets up in private with him otherwise it must be grim."

"Alas the wedding day in France of David & Mrs. Warfield," Queen Mary wrote in her diary on June 3. "We all telegraphed him," she added. The telegram from his mother wishing him and his bride happiness meant so much to the Duke of Windsor that he showed it to almost everyone present at the Château de Cande.

The unthinkable had taken place. David had not only renounced the Throne, he had married "Mrs. Warfield."* But despite the gesture of the telegram, Queen Mary remained unreconciled to her eldest son. Unfortunately, the press covered David's every move: his inappropriate rush to his fiancée's side in France as soon as the divorce *nisi* had been granted, the constant barrage of posed press photographs, his playing in a golf match the day of his brother's coronation. These things only deepened the tension between mother and son. Then his choice of June 3, his father's birthday, as a date for a marriage whose incipient stages had caused King George V such great heartache was, for Queen Mary, the most unpardonable of all his transgressions since the Abdication. Lady Bertha Dawkins, one of her Ladies-in-Waiting, thought her continued fury at David "help[ed] her to bear what she called 'the humiliation of it all.' " The Royal Family felt that much of the smooth transition from

---

*Upon her divorce from Ernest Simpson, the new Duchess of Windsor had taken back the name Warfield.

425

one Monarch to another was due to Queen Mary's strength and popularity. "Thank God," the Princess Royal wrote her mother during the crisis, "we all have got you as a central point, because without it [the family] might easily disintegrate."

There were Court functions and festivities throughout the entire coronation summer, and Queen Mary took part in most of them. She was "ablaze, regal and overpowering" at the Duke and Duchess of Sutherland's ball on May 18, according to Chips Channon; "looking like the Jungfrau, white and sparkling in the sun" on June 22 at the Buckingham Palace garden party. She attended the Derby and the Garter Service, viewed the Aldershot tattoo, watched the International Lawn Tennis Championships at Wimbledon, and in academic robes laid the foundation stone of the new Bodleian Library Annexe at Oxford.

Wherever she appeared, she was greeted with tremendous demonstrations by waiting crowds on both her arrival and departure. One time the cry "Thank God we've still got Queen Mary" was taken up by a whole street of enthusiastic admirers. Her overwhelming popularity did not make it easy for her to retire into the background as tradition demanded of a Queen Consort who had become Queen Mother.

One late August morning, tears welled up into her eyes as she confessed to Lady Airlie, "Oh, Mabell, if you only knew how hard it has been; how I have struggled with myself. All through the years the King always told me everything *first*. I do so miss that."

Lady Diana Cooper, after having "dined and slept" at Windsor as a guest of the King and Queen, commented on how different the atmosphere was from King Edward's late regime. "That was an operetta," she said. "This is an institution." For Lady Airlie and Queen Mary, the new reign also brought changes. "It seemed strange," Lady Airlie wrote, "when Ascot week came round not to be driving down to Windsor for the party; stranger still sometimes to overhear Queen Mary's Household referred to as 'the Old Court.' But it was true; the line of demarcation between past and present is nowhere more apparent than with Monarchy."

Queen Mary's Court adhered more rigidly to protocol than

426

the new Court did. Lady Airlie tells us, "Knee breeches were compulsory for men who dined at Marlborough House, but not at Buckingham Palace," and that Queen Mary refused to make any concessions even to the new American Ambassador, Joseph Kennedy, who told Lady Airlie that if he were to take to wearing English knee breeches, he would "offend folks in America." Lady Airlie reported this to Queen Mary, who understood it perfectly but would not relax her own rule. Mr. Kennedy, therefore, was never invited to dine at Marlborough House.

War clouds peppered the skies toward the end of the summer. Everyone was fearful that all that was needed was "a match to spark off a bigger war than the last one." With Hitler "moulding the German people to *his* aspirations," war, if it came again, would be different from the last, not between nations but "between the forces of evil and everything that Christianity has stood for."

By summer 1938, sixty-nine-year-old Neville Chamberlain had replaced Baldwin as Prime Minister, and Chamberlain was set on obtaining peace at all costs. Hitler had staked his claims to the Sudeten areas of Czechoslovakia. The Czechs refused to give in to the Germans, and France threatened to fight if an inch of Czechoslovakian territory were violated. On September 15, 1938, Neville Chamberlain met Adolf Hitler at Berchtesgäden. He returned with the ominous news that Germany was demanding and would not be satisfied with anything less than secession and incorporation of the Sudetenland into the Reich.

On September 25, after Chamberlain met with the King, Queen Mary, the Royal Family, and most of London were fitted with gas masks. Alarm spread through the country as the newspapers headlined stories that the Fleet had mobilised and that trenches had been dug in Hyde Park. The Prime Minister, it was said, had sent "SOS messages, in a last attempt to save the world, to both Mussolini and to Hitler" on the morning of September 28, the day the House of Commons convened for a special session.

When her daughter-in-law Marina informed her that she was going to the House of Commons to be there when a decision of sorts was made, Queen Mary, in an unprecedented decision, said she would come along.

The House was solemn and every seat filled. There had been no reply from Hitler and Mussolini, and when Prime Minister Chamberlain spoke, he told the story of his negotiations with Hitler calmly. Queen Mary ("a dark black figure"), seated behind the Duchess of Kent in Mrs. Fitzroy's gallery, never moved during the hour speech, which ended with the announcement that Hitler had agreed to postpone negotiations for another twenty-four hours—and that the Führer had invited Chamberlain to Munich the next day, along with M. Daladier of France.

Queen Mary commented in her diary, "The PM's speech was clear and explained everything . . . & the relief felt round the house was remarkable & all the members of the Conservative & National Govt cheered wildly—I was myself so much moved I could not speak to any of the ladies in the Gallery, several of them, even those unknown to me seized my hand, it was very touching. Let us pray now that a lasting Peace may follow." She went directly from the House of Commons to take tea "with Bertie but he had no news from Munich so far."

Not everyone looked upon Chamberlain as a saviour of peace. In fact, a good segment of the government and the public were violently against his "peace negotiations" and his pro-Munich pact, which delineated Czechoslovakia's new frontiers decidedly in Germany's favour. By the majority of his countrymen, Chamberlain was still regarded as a great peacemaker.

Queen Mary, as always, remained above the politics of the day, but personal situations made that a difficult task. In the autumn of 1937, the Duke and Duchess of Windsor had chosen to visit Germany and to meet with Hitler, obviously not recognising the worldwide impression that this visit might somehow have been authorised by the British government. Paul Schmidt, Hitler's interpreter, says the Duke "did not discuss political questions," but he was "frank and friendly" and "displayed the social charm for which he is known throughout the world." The Duchess "joined only occasionally in the conversation, and then with great reserve, when any question of special interest to women arose. She was simply and appropriately dressed and made a lasting impression on Hitler. 'She would have made a good Queen,' he said when they had gone."

The American press duly reported of this trip that indeed "the

Abdication did rob Germany of a firm friend." The Duke of Windsor, in fact, had been very critical of English politics and British Ministers, and these comments had made their way into the German and English press. Queen Mary's anger intensified at the son who would continue to speak his mind on controversial issues, while at the same time, David kept writing to ask his mother to see him and his wife. In July 1938, Queen Mary wrote a strong letter of refusal, closing it with:

". . . I do not think you have realised the shock, which the attitude you took up [referring to his Abdication] caused your family & the whole nation. It seemed inconceivable to those who had made much greater sacrifices during the war that you, as their King, refused a lesser sacrifice . . . My feelings for you as your Mother remain the same, and our being parted and the cause of it, grieve me beyond words. After all, all my life I have put my country before everything else and I simply cannot change now."

Not long after this, Queen Mary was visited by ex-Kaiser Wilhelm's grandson Fritzi, who came directly from a stay with his grandfather in Doorn. Queen Mary was extremely fond of Fritzi, and the visit led to an exchange of letters with Wilhelm and his cousin, King George's widow. After Chamberlain's trip to Munich, he wrote her: "I have not the slightest doubt that Mr. N. Chamberlain was inspired by Heaven & guided by God who took pity on his children on Earth by crowning his mission with such relieving success. God bless him. I kiss your hand in respectful devotion as ever."

"Poor William," Queen Mary wrote Bertie, enclosing the letter with the suggestion that it be consigned to the archives at Windsor,* "he must have been horrified at the thought of another war between our 2 countries."

Wilhelm's grandson had reported to Chips Channon that in Queen Mary's meeting with him she had "been sorely conscience stricken" about King George and her failure to help the Russian Royal Family escape, and that the Kaiser had told Fritzi only the week before that he was "still haunted by the fate which befell the Czar and his family."

*The paper now resides there.

429

In case of a second world war, the Royal Family would not have to fight cousin against cousin as they had in the 1914–1918 war. Unlike Russia then, Queen Mary knew that if war came and if Britain went under, there would be no powerful relation for Britain's Royal Family even to look to for refuge.

THIRTY

From September 1938—when the Prime Minister had sacrificed Czechoslovakia at Munich—until August 23, 1939, when Germany and Russia signed a ten-year nonaggression pact binding each other not to aid opponents in war acts, Britain was in a state of suspended anxiety. A photograph was sent across the world of Leopold von Hoesch driving in a car flying a huge swastika as it passed beneath the red flag at the Kremlin. The treaty had been signed by von Hoesch for the German Government and Vyacheslav Molotov for the Government of the U.S.S.R.

Adolf Hitler had his boot set to march on Poland when warned by the British Ambassador that Britain would fight if such an act of aggression occurred. The Führer announced he would move into Poland at 6:00 P.M. on August 23 but, at the last moment, postponed the date to August 26. Britain was stunned. ". . . it means that we are humbled to dust," Harold Nicolson wrote in his diary. Mobilisation was ordered in France as well as in Britain, giving every indication that France was ready to go to war with Germany upon a call for help from Poland.

Warning notices went out to reservists in all the armed and civilian services; Londoners were ordered to black out their windows at night until further notice; the Royal Air Force was posed for instant action; British warships were reported in the Skagerrak, between the Norwegian and Danish coasts; an immediate embargo was placed on unlicensed exports of essential war materials; and King George was returning from Balmoral to London for an emergency session the following day of both Houses of Parliament, which was expected to give the Government sweeping powers (for any purpose that the national interest might require) of a sort unknown in Britain since the last war.

London was suffocatingly hot and still on August 24. The Prime Minister looked older, drawn, dignified, and solemn. The fire had died in him, and his words were shocking only in their lack of any inspiration. "He was exactly like a coroner summing up a case for murder," Harold Nicolson noted. And Chips Channon adds: ". . . Winston [Churchill] held his face in his hands and occasionally nodded his head in agreement with the P.M. . . . the whole House expects war."

By nightfall, London and all coastal areas were in darkness. Throughout the land there was a frightening calm. The people prepared for war, but they simply could not believe it would come. Then on Sunday morning, September 3, after Hitler had refused an ultimatum to halt his attack on Poland, Britain and France reluctantly declared war. At 11:15 A.M., Prime Minister Chamberlain, speaking over the radio from the Cabinet Room at 10 Downing Street, informed the British people that "this country is at War against Germany." At 11:32 A.M., air-raid sirens rang throughout London, sending its inhabitants to shelters. The calm was gone. But the fear remained. Seventeen minutes later, the all-clear signals were sounded. The alarm had been only a test, but the sirens were a harbinger of things to come.

During the first week of the war, under government order, three million children, invalids, and elderly were evacuated from London and twenty-eight other cities in Britain's greatest ever mass movement of population. To Queen Mary's great irritation, the Government and the King agreed she should be in this first evacuation group.

Her popularity had never waned. In fact, she was held in higher state in 1939 than ever. Several factors contributed to this. First, perhaps, was the visit King George and Queen Elizabeth made to Canada and the United States in May of that year, despite the likelihood of war.* Queen Mary was photographed on the jetty waving goodbye with her handkerchief to the King and Queen, dwarfing Lilibet and Margaret who stood at her side. "I have my handkerchief," Margaret was overheard to say, and Queen Mary warned, "To wave, not to cry into." This kind of "no nonsense" courage which Queen Mary expected and received of her family was also given to her by the country. "If it's good enough for Queen Mary . . ." became a standard, whether it was the earthen teapots she still used or acceptance of the Prime Minister's appeasement policies. (Not that she would ever publicly voice approval of anything political, but she *was* photographed smiling at the dour Chamberlain, which was approval enough.)

The country did not know that while the King and Queen were on this tour the red dispatch boxes were sent to Queen Mary, but if they had, no doubt they would have approved—for whatever she did was a step toward order and correctness. She had become a symbol of an enduring England and a proud reminder of the glory of Empire and of the matriarchal Victorian years.

Almost every large social gathering was livened by a new Queen Mary anecdote. One favourite, while the King and Queen had been on the Canadian tour, involved a serious accident in which a heavy lorry collided head-on with her maroon Daimler, which overturned trapping her inside. It was a wonder that none of the five occupants of the car was killed.† Ladders were swiftly brought to help extricate them. One witness wrote that "Queen Mary climbed up and down these ladders as if she might have been walking down the steps at the Coronation. She had not her hat or one curl out of place . . . The only outward sign of disorder was . . . her umbrella broken in half." In fact,

---

*King George wrote Queen Mary, "I hate leaving here with the situation as it is, but one must carry on with one's plans as they are all settled, & Canada will be so disappointed."

†The five occupants were Queen Mary; Lord Claud Hamilton, her Comptroller; Lady Constance Milnes Gaskell, her Woman of the Bedchamber; the chauffeur, and a security officer.

433

a piece of glass had grazed and injured Queen Mary's eye in the accident; and besides being bruised and shaken, she had hurt her back "abominably" and was confined to bed for ten days, but this information was not given to the public.

Queen Mary's popular appeal owed something to the bland personality of the King. Britain had a loving family on the Throne, and the little princesses had charmed the nation. But Bertie, albeit well-meaning and duty-bound, was uninteresting and certainly no intellectual. Chips Channon, who knew him fairly well, thought "he had no wit, no learning, no humour, except of a rather schoolboy brand." Channon also found him "nervous, ill-at-ease, though slightly better after some champagne" (he was actually making a concerted effort to control his drinking), and possessing "no vices and few interests other than shooting." He had a small Court, few friends, and was "almost entirely dependent on the Queen whom he worshipped." To his credit, he was also "an affectionate father and a loyal friend to the very few people he liked . . ." What he lacked was the ability to stir people. No one was moved to shout or to sing patriotic songs after hearing him speak.

Queen Elizabeth was infinitely more appealing, and what charm her husband lacked she amply supplied. However, her charm was best suited to garden parties and receptions and galas, where she could flash her spellbinding smile and speak to people on an individual basis. She had a lilting voice; dressed in an utterly feminine, unspectacular fashion; "rustled greatly and gracefully" when she walked; and looked somehow very Victorian, short, almost plump. She had a pretty but oddly "old-fashioned face." Anne Morrow Lindbergh describes her after a meeting at a ball as being like "an old-fashioned rose, the small full ones, not brilliant in colouring but very fragrant . . . she really looks at you, too, when she shakes hands. A real person looks out at you. How *can* she do it, when she must go through it so often?"

Queen Elizabeth was the quintessential Royal Consort. In everyday life, her counterpart would have made the perfect wife for a business executive or politician, able to ease most awkward social situations for her husband and charm his associates or constituents, while at the same time gaining the admiration of all their wives. But she did not have the sweep of majesty or the bold appearance of the independent woman of strength that Queen Mary possessed. And her particular style called for a man of strong personality; the King—who had found his task as difficult and as painful as he had feared it might be—was not such a man. Had there not been a war, his reign might well have been ineffective. Yet his every frailty worked in his behalf as London steeled itself against the enemy. Perhaps the King did not display strength or shrewd thinking, but he had remained in London and before the people, when he could easily have chosen the safer position of Balmoral. Bertie had shown the same kind of doggedness on the sporting field as a young man. Britain had a King who—no matter what the odds—was no quitter. For a nation facing a long, harrowing ordeal, that was a matter of great pride and gave rise to an even greater confidence that England would prevail.

Queen Mary would spend the duration of the war in Gloucestershire at Badminton House. The Duke and Duchess of Beaufort, whose home it was, greatly revered and were fond of their Royal guest. Indeed, Henry, Duke of Beaufort, was none other than a great-nephew of Lady Geraldine Somerset, and the Duchess of Beaufort was Queen Mary's niece, Prince Dolly's daughter. Badminton was one of the great mansion homes of Britain and had been in the Beaufort family since the seventeenth century. Queen Mary had visited the house for a long stay in the 1880s with her mother, the Duchess of Teck, and again only the previous year when the government and the King first suggested she be evacuated from London should there be a war. The Beauforts had been quite enthusiastic in their invitation to their aunt to spend "the duration" of the war (a time no one could project) as their guest. They had not foreseen that they would end up with only their bedrooms and a small sitting room for themselves, and although they dined with Queen Mary at their own table, they were, in effect, "the guests" in their own home.

Pandemonium erupted upon Queen Mary's arrival with over seventy pieces of personal luggage and fifty-five servants. The

Duchess of Beaufort reported to her husband's cousin, Osbert Sitwell:*

"The servants [the Beauforts'] revolted . . . They refused to use the excellent rooms assigned to them. Fearful rows and battles royal [were] fought over my body—but I won in the end and reduced them to tears and to pulp . . . I can laugh now, but I have never been so angry! . . . The Queen, quite unconscious of the stir, has settled in well, and is busy cutting down trees and tearing down ivy.† Tremendous activity."

There was also the problem of the Duke of Beaufort's mother, the Dowager Duchess Louisa, a fading beauty Queen Mary's age, who lived in a cottage on the grounds and had immensely enjoyed her senior position at Badminton. The two women did not become boon companions and, at best, might have been said to have tolerated each other. Standing at her cottage window watching Queen Mary and her "Ivy Squad" battling against the green vines that clung tenaciously to stonework, brickwork, and trees, the Dowager Duchess would grimace and make deprecating remarks to whomever was in her company—servant or guest —about the unsuitability of a Queen Mother being engaged in such a task.

Queen Mary was certainly obsessed by her enmity toward ivy. She felt it was a destructive element and dealt with it in a manner that suggested how aggressive she could be, if necessary, to the enemy. The activity gave her days direction, however, and an outlet for her still-great energy.

"Lovely morning which we spent clearing ivy off the trees in the grounds," she wrote in her diary on September 25. "The gardeners began to clear a wall of ivy near Mary B's bedroom."

And on September 26: "Lovely morning which we spent clearing ivy off trees—We watched a whole wall of ivy of 50 years standing at the back of Mary B's bedroom being removed—most of it came down like a blanket."

*Sir Osbert Sitwell (1892–1969), author of poems, short stories, novels, and memoirs, including five volumes about British society during the Edwardian era.

†A reference to the campaign Queen Mary waged against scrubby trees and climbing ivy, two things she abhorred in nature.

Queen Mary's Equerry, her current Lady-in-Waiting, her Private Secretary, and anyone who was staying in the house were quickly enlisted to the "Ivy Squad." To save petrol, Queen Mary rode to the more distant "blighted areas" in a farm cart, drawn by two horses and containing a couple of basket chairs for herself and her Lady-in-Waiting. "Aunt May," remarked her niece, "you look as if you were in a tumbril!"

"Well, it may come to that yet, one never knows," Queen Mary retorted back as the cart jolted off.

She was not cut off from London or from the war news despite her country life. Foreign Office news summaries were sent daily to her in an official leather dispatch box of which she kept the key.* She travelled to London one day a week, although the train ride there and back, due to wartime interruptions, was often over five hours and meant she had to leave Badminton at 6:15 in the morning. "I long to be at Home," she wrote to Lady Bertha Dawkins on September 20. "I feel rather useless here but I can visit Evacuees & Work depots, they seem to like to see one which is a mercy!"

But London looked very warlike, "sand bags, ARP men with tin helmets & gas masks, police ditto—windows boarded up . . . It was curious to see all the precautions on the railway for the blackout," she observed. "From 7.–til 8.15 we could not read as we had only a faint blue light—" Air-raid warnings and planes overhead were a daily occurrence. Under such circumstances and with the pressure for her to remain safely in the country so strong, by the summer of 1940 Queen Mary stopped going to London because it was "simply a waste of time."

Queen Mary was much affected by the air raids in her immediate district and on her beloved London. Lost in the destruction were many City churches with their irreplaceable contents and in particular the Guildhall, which contained among its many other treasures the collection that she had spent so many hours tracing, classifying, and obtaining. Gone was the piece of tapestry mentioned in inventories of Queen Elizabeth I and a matching silver vase of a pair made for King George IV. Every

*In one dispatch box being returned to London, Queen Mary wrote, "From Mary R. the lock of this box is very stiff."

Londoner was now, in actual fact, a soldier at the ready. As one survivor of the summer of 1940 wrote, ". . . sounds became an integral part of life; the bombers circling . . . like dogs trying to pick up a scent . . . the aching empty silence after a bomb fell, broken only by small sounds, the rustle of water from fractured pipes, the little cries of the trapped and wounded, the stealthy shifting of debris. Dawn brought the most welcome sound of all: the notes of the All Clear, like a liner nearing safe haven, crying over the city."

The smells were soon to become as familiar. "The harsh acrid smell of cordite from high explosive bombs, leaking gas and blue London clay, charred wood and pulverised plaster."

By summer's end, 177,000 Londoners were spending the nights underground in damp shelters and tube stations, bedding down on floors made gritty by leaking sandbags. They queued for nighttime shelter as early as 10:30 A.M., and by 4:00 P.M., the permitted hour of descent, there would be more people than designated space. Yet no one was forbidden entry. Sanitation was primitive, confined to bucket latrines behind makeshift screens. At dawn the crowds emerged to scenes now commonplace: huge mounds of fallen brick and timber, clouds of dust, and "the fine glitter of powdered glass that covered the pavements like hoar frost."

London's plight was heart-wrenching, and Queen Mary, through the newspapers and the King, her London friends and her dispatch boxes, kept up with every indignity. She was always the first at Badminton to hear of the destruction of any famous building, or the loss of an acquaintance or friend. She rigidly observed all the war regulations concerning food, dress, coal, and motoring. Without sufficient petrol to drive to the places of historic or artistic interest in the country, Queen Mary was left with considerable time on her hands. The duties of her "Ivy Squad" were thus extended to include clearing away fallen branches and twigs of trees, and she spent several hours every day supervising the stripping of ivy and the tidying of a wooded strip, some ten miles in length, that circles the park at Badminton.

Day after day during London's grim fight, the King and Queen would appear without formality among the debris from the enemy's most concentrated bombardment. On September 9, the Luftwaffe attacked central London. All the windows at Buckingham Palace were shattered, but the structure was otherwise unharmed. Three days later, the Germans scored a direct hit.

"We were both upstairs [the King wrote in his diary] . . . talking in my little sitting room overlooking the quadrangle (I cannot use my ordinary one owing to the broken windows). All of a sudden we heard an aircraft making a zooming noise above us, saw 2 bombs falling past the opposite side of the Palace, & then heard 2 resounding crashes as the bombs fell in the quadrangle about 30 yds. away. We [the Queen was with the King] looked at each other & then we were out into the passage as fast as we could get there. The whole thing happened in a matter of seconds. We . . . wondered why we weren't dead. Two great craters had appeared in the courtyard. The one nearest the Palace had burst a fire hydrant & water was pouring through the broken windows in the passage. 6 bombs had been dropped. The aircraft was seen coming straight down the Mall below the clouds having dived through the clouds & had dropped 2 bombs in the forecourt, 2 in the quadrangle, 1 in the Chapel and the other in the garden. The Chapel is wrecked, & the bomb also wrecked the plumber's workshop below in which 4 men were working. 3 of them were injured & the fourth shocked. Looking at the wreckage how they escaped death is a wonder to me. E & I went all round the basement talking to the servants who were all safe; & quite calm through it all. None of the windows on our side of the Palace were broken. We were told that the bomb in the forecourt was a delay action (DA) bomb so we gave orders for all the east windows to be opened in case it exploded & we remained in our shelter & had lunch there. There is no doubt that it was a direct attack on Buckingham Palace. Luckily the Palace is very narrow, & the bombs fell in the open spaces . . ."

A few days later he noted further, ". . . It was a ghastly experience & I don't want it to be repeated. It certainly teaches one to 'take cover' on all future occasions, but one must be careful not to become 'dugout minded.' "

"This war has drawn the Throne and the people more closely

439

together than was ever before recorded," Winston Churchill wrote the King, "and Your Majesties are more beloved by all classes and conditions than any of the princes of the past."

The fact that the Sovereign's home had been bombed as well as their homes, and that the King and Queen were not immune from the same dangers they suffered, awakened a greater loyalty, devotion, and determination in the people. The attack on Buckingham Palace was a major error in enemy psychological warfare. As Lord Louis Mountbatten wrote to his cousin, the King, "If Goering could have realised the depths of feeling which his bombing of Buckingham Palace has aroused throughout the Empire & America, he would have been well advised to instruct his assassins to keep off."

Although he had remained as Lord President of the Council in Prime Minister Churchill's Cabinet, Neville Chamberlain was a sick and failing man. At the end of September 1940, he sent his resignation to the King, who replied that "as I told you once before your efforts to preserve peace were not in vain, for they established, in the eyes of the civilised world, our entire innocence of the crime which Hitler has determined to commit."*

Be that as it may, Britain remained under siege. Hitler severed their supply lines, hoping to starve the British people into surrender.

"The Battle of France is over," Churchill had warned the nation on June 18. "I expect the Battle of Britain is about to begin."

Myopic, bull-headed, his memorable voice like a beacon of hope, Winston Churchill gave the British courage, while the King shared their lot. The combination was powerful, for when the Prime Minister told the British people ". . . we shall not flag or fail. We shall go on to the end . . . we shall fight in the seas and oceans . . . we shall defend our Island whatever the cost may be," they looked to the King and the Queen who walked so often

---

*Neville Chamberlain died on Saturday, November 9, 1940, and was buried in Westminster Abbey on November 14, with the War Cabinet as his pallbearers and Henry, Duke of Gloucester, as the King's personal representative.

among them—and somehow felt confident that Mr. Churchill spoke the truth.

In April 1939, Chips Channon reported that when Queen Mary was asked when the Duke of Windsor would return to England, she had replied, "Not until he comes to my funeral." However, the war changed that. Within a few hours after Britain had declared war on Germany, Walter Monckton, with the King's permission, arranged for a plane to be sent that very week to bring the Windsors and their party "home" from Cap d'Antibes, France. To Major Fruity Metcalfe's disbelief (he was the person in charge), the Windsors refused to go unless they were invited to stay at Windsor Castle and the invitation and the plane were sent personally by the King.

Major Metcalfe wrote to his wife, "I just sat still, held my head & listened for about 20 minutes & then I started. I said 'I'm going to talk now. First of all I'll say whatever I say is speaking as your *best friend,* I speak only for your good & for W[allis]'s, *understand that.* After what I've said you can ask me to leave if you like but you're going to listen now. You *only* think of yourselves. You don't realise that there is at this moment a war going on that women & children are being bombed & killed while you talk of your *Pride.* What you've now said to Walter has just bitched up everything. You talk of one of H.M.'s Government planes being sent out for Miss Arnold [the secretary] and me!! You are just nuts. Do you really think for one instant they would send a plane out for me & Miss Arnold? It's too absurd even to discuss . . . It was 3.15 A.M. Well at 7.30 I was wakened by *her maid* telling me to get up! to arrange for a car to go to the flying field . . ."

An aircraft was never sent, and the Prime Minister directed that the Duke of Windsor could return only under one condition —if he were prepared to take on either the post of Deputy Regional Commissioner to Sir Syndham Portal in Wales or Liaison Officer with the British Military Mission to General Gamelin under General Howard Vyse. He chose the former. Finally the Windsors and Major Metcalfe and three cairn terriers—Pookie, Prisie, and Detto—motored to Cherbourg under "cloak and dagger" circumstances, where they were met by Lord Louis

Mountbatten, who, on Churchill's instructions, had brought the destroyer H.M.S. *Kelly* to carry them to Britain.

No member of the Royal Family waited to welcome them at Portsmouth, "no messenger, no message." A large red-plush hotel bedroom had been booked for them. But Churchill had asked Admiral James to invite them to stay the night at his home, and the Metcalfes took the hotel room. The next day, the party motored to South Hartfield House.

The King had one short casual meeting with his brother, but apart from this, the family did not acknowledge the ex-King's presence. Wallis was heard to say that there was no place for the Duke in Britain and that she saw no reason ever to return.

Not long after the Windsors arrived, pressure was put on the Duke by the War Minister to take an alternate appointment as a liaison officer in Paris without delay. A brief discussion of money was held. The Duke of Windsor asked if his brother Harry was being paid for his services, quickly explaining that he wanted it known he did not wish to be paid. The Military Secretary replied that the Duke of Gloucester was not being paid, and that, in fact, "no member of the Royal Family ever accepted payment for services in the Army."

The Windsors and Major Metcalfe returned to France at the end of September. When France fell, rumours circulated that a German plot was *en force* to acquire the services of the Duke. Clearly, something had to be done about removing him from the Continent, where his presence was causing talk. According to Lord Halifax, "although his Loyalties are unimpeachable there is always a backwash of Nazi intrigue which seeks, now that the greater part of the continent is in enemy hands, to make trouble about him." Because of all the personal and family difficulties his return to Britain would create, Churchill, with King George's approval, offered the Duke of Windsor the Governorship of the Bahamas. After a dramatic exit from Paris and much more "cloak-and-dagger" en route, the Windsors landed at Nassau on August 17, 1940, where they would remain throughout the war. Ten days before, the Duke's brother Harry had been appointed Chief Liaison Officer, GHO Home Forces, the position the Duke of Windsor had originally been offered.

George, Duke of Kent, as charming and as animated as ever,

remained his mother's favourite. At the outbreak of the war, he was Governor-General designate of the Commonwealth of Australia, but he at once requested a more active position. He was given the rank of Air Commodore. During the summer of 1941, the Duke of Kent revisited the United States (he had been there in 1935). After a tour of inspection of the Empire training scene in Canada, he renewed his relationship with President Roosevelt, who had "a great affection" for him. In fact, when the Duchess of Kent gave birth to a second son on July 4, 1942, Franklin D. Roosevelt was a godfather, and his parents named the child Michael George Charles Franklin.

One of the few excursions Queen Mary took to London was on August 4 for the christening of her new grandson. She saw old friends and servants, as well as many of her royal relations who had been driven out of their own countries by the Nazi invaders. On August 13, she motored to Coppins, the Kents' country home, to visit with her youngest son and his family. "Had luncheon & tea there—walked in the garden—Georgie showed me some of his interesting things—he looked so happy with his lovely wife & the dear baby," she wrote in her diary.

After the visit, Georgie had driven back to Badminton to spend a few days with his mother before returning once again to active service. He took her on a tour of an important Air Force Centre close by, at her request. They also visited some antique shops. His departure on August 16 was sorely felt, since his presence had lifted everyone's spirits. He had gone to Scotland, where he was due to depart on August 25 to fly to Iceland for an inspection tour of RAF establishments. Shortly after 10:00 P.M. the evening of the twenty-fifth, a page interrupted Lady Cynthia Colville as she was reading to Queen Mary. The King's Private Secretary, Sir Eric Melville, the young boy announced, wished to speak to Lady Colville. "You had better go," the Queen said.

Lady Corville went to her room to receive the call and was told that the Duke of Kent had been killed in an air crash soon after starting on his journey to Iceland. The plane had failed to clear a range of Scottish hills. When Lady Corville, much shaken, returned to tell the Queen, Queen Mary half rose from her chair. "What is it? Is it the King?" she asked.

"No, Ma'am, I am afraid it is the Duke of Kent; there was an air crash. He was killed instantaneously."

Queen Mary's face went white and she lowered herself slowly back into her chair. "I must go to Marina tomorrow," she said in a quiet voice. Lady Corville saw her shed no tears, either then or at the funeral in St. George's Chapel on August 29. On her return to Badminton—a journey made in a violent thunderstorm—Queen Mary gave a lift in her limousine to "a charming young American parachutist, most friendly," and to "a nice Sergeant Observer (Air Force) who had taken part in the raid on Dieppe last week." The Princess Royal came to spend the next few days with her mother, and before she departed, Queen Mary was once again going out with her "Ivy Squad."

On September 3, three years to the day from the declaration of war, she wrote in her diary: "I am so glad I can take up my occupations again—Georgie wld have wished me to do so."

Sympathy for the Royal Family was considerable. Their terrible loss brought them even closer to the people. This first period of the war was considered by many to have been Britain's "decisive struggle" and for the people of Britain, "their finest hour," when Britain stood alone. Monarch and subject had shared danger, suffered the threat of death and the loss of someone dear. Throughout much of this time, Britain had been under the shadow of military defeat, following the evacuation of the British Expeditionary Force from the Continent of Europe. But the absolute refusal of the British people to recognise defeat and their ability to overcome disaster with the kind of pride that swept through the land after Dunkirk gave them the power to stand alone in the fight, "stripped and girt for battle, and unimpeded by less determined friends."*

At 4:00 A.M. on June 22, 1941, Germany invaded the U.S.S.R. Britain no longer stood alone. On December 7 of that same year, the Japanese attacked Pearl Harbor, bringing the United States into the war as an increasingly dominant force of the Allied alliance. Nevertheless, for the Allies, the first seven months of 1942 were a record of almost unrelieved disaster. Singapore fell to the Japanese on February 15; Corregidor on April 9; and by

*A reference to France.

444

the end of May the British and Netherlands possessions in the East Indies were overrun, and British and Chinese forces had been driven from Burma.

"We're going through a bad phase at the moment," King George wrote to Queen Mary. This kind of refusal to accept the series of disastrous Allied setbacks as anything more than a "bad phase" endeared King George VI to his subjects. And the stoicism that was so much a part of Queen Mary's makeup caused the people to look to her with pride.

THIRTY-ONE

Dinner at Badminton (a fairly bizarre occasion) was at 8:30 every night. In a note of wartime austerity, Queen Mary had requested that in place of fresh table linen (which would require daily laundering) oilcloth be substituted. All those living in the house were expected to use their napkins for three meals. Queen Mary had her own heavy silver napkin ring with the crown and her monogram engraved on it; the rest had rings of coloured celluloid or plastic. Despite these economies, Queen Mary was always fully gowned, often in sequins, with an ostrich-feather cape and her famous ropes of pearls, thereby imposing a dress code for the rest of her Household and guests.

Sir Osbert Sitwell had become a frequent and favoured guest at Badminton, and his presence filled the void left by the Duke of Kent's tragic death. Though the two men were very different and Sir Osbert a decade older, Queen Mary did share with the latter some of the same pleasures she had had with her youngest son. They walked together, discussed literature, and went in search of antiques. Sir Osbert was a brilliant conversationalist, witty and with the writer's talent for finding good stories and the uncommon ability to tell them exceptionally well. He was also an ardent Royalist, the perfect companion for Queen Mary's long Badminton stay.

Tall, fair, beardless, with a prominent nose, heavy features, and penetrating blue eyes, Sir Osbert bore an uncanny resemblance to George III, and he occasionally acknowledged that he was illicitly descended from George IV.* Queen Mary had no other intimates in the arts. She had once enjoyed a friendship with Nellie Melba, but the diva had not had the intellectual and artistic passion of Sir Osbert. He and the Queen would walk in the park at Badminton, she occasionally pausing to flick a stick or twig from the path with one of the two canes she was forced to use because of some discomfort from bursitis. She liked to talk to him about his work and about her own early life.

After dinner, Queen Mary would take out her knitting while the Household and guests listened to the news on the radio; but never—whether the news was good or bad—would she show "by the flicker of an eyelash" that she was disturbed. "Only once," Sir Osbert recalls, "did I see Her Majesty's expression change during the news . . . Hungary or Roumania was under discussion and the word 'Transylvania' occurred. At this Queen Mary smiled rather archly, and caught the eye of her niece, nodded to her, and repeated softly, in her rather deep voice, 'Transylvania, Transylvania.' And then seeing I had observed this, explained, 'The joke is that some of us came from there.' "†

Sir Osbert was not in the least surprised, for he found many Rumanian traits in Queen Mary—"her manner in which she smoked cigarettes; her love of jewels, and the way she wore them; and the particular sort of film-star glamour that in advanced age overtook her appearance, and made her, with the stylisation of her clothes, such an attractive as well as imposing figure."

Sometime early in 1943, Queen Mary enthusiastically began a campaign to collect scrap for the war effort, an activity that suited her sense of domestic economy and her desire for order and tidiness. If she found a fragment of old iron, she would pick it up and hand it to a somewhat reluctant lady-in-waiting. Sir Osbert recalls that on one occasion he had to carry back to the

*A suggestion by Sir Osbert Sitwell that one of his forebears had been a mistress to George IV.

†Queen Mary's paternal grandmother came from Transylvania.

house "a really filthy dirty old glass bottle." And that "one fine spring noon Her Majesty returned to the house in a triumph after a walk, dragging behind her a large piece of rusty old iron to add to the royal dump. A few minutes later, however, one of her pages brought an urgent message from a neighbouring farmer. 'Please, Your Majesty, a Mr. Hodge has arrived, and he says Your Majesty has taken his plough and will Your Majesty graciously give it back to him, please, at once, as he can't get on without it!' "

One afternoon, Sir Osbert, the Princess Royal, and Queen Mary set off in the vast Daimler to visit some antique shops. Humphries, Queen Mary's elderly chauffeur (who had a penchant for getting lost, and lumbering and bumping over unpaved country roads), was at the wheel, and next to him in the front a portly security detective. At the start of the excursion (and perhaps to compensate for the additional petrol necessary), Queen Mary remarked that if she saw any man in the forces at the side of the road needing a lift, Humphries must stop and take him. An aircraftsman was eventually sighted. Queen Mary tapped with her umbrella on the window behind Humphries's head. The motor pulled up, and the detective got down and ushered the young man into the motorcar, seating him on a jump seat that faced the three occupants in the back without telling him whose car it was.

"He entered in a jaunty manner," Sir Osbert recorded later, "and then saw the Princess Royal. A frantic look of fright came into his eyes, and . . . he cast them round wildly—and beheld Queen Mary . . . his eyes darted here and there in search of escape. But by now . . . the motor had started. Queen Mary . . . talked to him so charmingly that she soon reassured him . . . she asked him what his profession had been before the war [and] he replied, 'I worked in a hospital—in the maternity ward.' "

Silence followed and during it Humphries managed to get lost once more, and the poor aircraftsman was finally released further from his destination than when he had been picked up.

" 'How very odd!' Queen Mary murmured. 'He said he was working in the *maternity ward!* What can he have been doing? It seems very strange! We ought to have asked him. In the *maternity ward!*' "

Queen Mary confided to Sir Osbert that she was terrified of being kidnapped by the Germans, and she had made arrangements for an aeroplane to transport her from Badminton to a secret destination should the Nazis land in England. Three suitcases were kept packed in case of such an occurrence. One, Queen Mary kept herself, and the other two were kept by her two dressers. When an air-raid alert sounded, their duty was to pack a fourth suitcase, filling it with tiaras and other jewels. The Lady-in-Waiting would be responsible for this case.

Princess Elizabeth, who had spent most of the war with her younger sister at Windsor and in Scotland, celebrated her eighteenth birthday on April 21, 1944, an event that raised several issues of importance. She would not reach her legal majority until the age of twenty-one, but still, there were the problems of her debut into public life and the matter of her title. On February 8, 1944, the King noted in his diary: "I talked to W[inston] about the question of my putting out a statement to say that I did not intend to give Lilibet any title on her 18th birthday. The Press & other people, especially in Wales, are agitating for her to become 'Princess of Wales.' W[inston] thought he shld. put it out, but I argued it was a family matter . . ." Twelve days later he wrote Queen Mary: "How could I create Lilibet Princess of Wales when it is the recognised title of the wife of the Prince of Wales? Her own name is so nice and what name would she be called by when she marries, I want to know."

The previous autumn, the King had requested Parliament to amend the Regency Act of 1937 so that Princess Elizabeth could be included among the Councillors of State. The bill met with no opposition in either House. Her constitutional status was therefore established, but the King's final decision was to not make any change in her title at this time.

On the day of Lilibet's eighteenth birthday, Queen Mary journeyed to Windsor for the first time since the war. A family lunch was held, and as the afternoon was unusually warm, later they all sat out in the garden. The next day, Queen Mary remarked

449

to Lady Airlie how very much Lilibet resembled paintings of Queen Victoria at the age of eighteen.

In January 1941, Chips Channon had been sent to Greece on government business. On the evening of his arrival, he had attended a cocktail party also attended by Philip of Greece. "He is to be our Prince Consort," he wrote in his diary (mere speculation on his part at this time). "I deplore such a marriage; he and Princess Elizabeth are too inter-related."* In 1943, Chips once again declared after a visit to Buckingham Palace: ". . . a marriage may well be arranged one day between Princess Elizabeth and Prince Philip of Greece."

One cannot be sure whether this was simply good guessing on Chips Channon's part or if it had been decided when Lilibet was fourteen that she would eventually marry Philip of Greece. The idea of Royal cousins marrying was not an unacceptable idea to Queen Mary, who had herself married a cousin of almost the same relationship after being engaged to his brother.†

Prince Philip had the look of a young Viking with much of the Mountbatten charm. He was five years older than his Royal cousin and more worldly than any of the men in her circle. The teen-age Princess Elizabeth quickly became infatuated. When Prince Philip visited Windsor at Christmas 1943, Marian Crawford (her former governess) had commented, "I have never known Lilibet more animated. There was a sparkle about her none of us had ever seen before. Many people commented on it." During the spring of 1944, numerous mutually timed visits of the couple were arranged by the Duchess of Kent at Coppins. In such troubled and grim days, a Royal romance was a grand respite, and Queen Mary and the Court quite enjoyed its titillation.

*   *   *

*Prince Philip (b. June 10, 1921), later Duke of Edinburgh, was the son of Lord Louis Mountbatten's sister, Alice. His grandmother was Princess Victoria of Hesse, daughter of Queen Victoria's daughter, Alice. On his father's, Prince Andrew of Greece's side, he was related to the Windsors through Queen Alexandra.

†Queen Mary defined Prince Philip's relationship to Princess Elizabeth (later Queen Elizabeth) as being a third cousin on his father's side, and a second cousin on his mother's side.

Operation Overlord—D-Day—a combined British and American enterprise that the Allies were certain would end in the liberation of Europe had been scheduled for dawn on June 5. Gale-force winds prevailed, and it was delayed twenty-four hours. The King and his Prime Minister were so certain of victory that their main concern was whether either of them should cross the Channel with the men and lead the forces on the beaches to victory. Finally, on June 2, the King wrote to Churchill:

"I want to make one more appeal to you not to go to sea on D Day. Please consider my own position. I am a younger man than you, I am a sailor, & as King I am the head of all three Services. There is nothing I would like better than to go to sea but I have agreed to stop at home; is it fair that you should then do exactly what I should have liked to do myself? You said yesterday afternoon that it would be a fine thing for the King to lead his troops into battle, as in old days; if the King cannot do this, it does not seem to me right that his Prime Minister should take his place . . . I ask you most earnestly to consider the whole question again & not let your personal wishes, which I very well understand, lead you to depart from your own high standard of duty to the State . . ."

Although in the end he agreed to remain in England, the next day Churchill replied:

"Sir . . . there is absolutely no comparison in the British Constitution between a Sovereign & a subject. If Your Majesty had gone, as you desired, on board one of your ships in this bombarding action, it would have required the Cabinet approval beforehand & I am very much inclined to think as I told you, that the Cabinet would have advised most strongly against Your Majesty going. On the other hand, as Prime Minister & Minister of Defence, I ought to be allowed to go where I consider it necessary to the discharges of my duty . . . I must most earnestly ask Your Majesty that no principle shall be laid down which inhibits my freedom of movement when I judge it necessary to acquaint myself with conditions in the various theatres of war. Since Your Majesty does me the honour to be so concerned about my personal safety on this occasion, I must defer to Your Majesty's wishes & indeed commands . . ."

This was perhaps the only occasion when Churchill was over-

451

ruled by the Monarch whom he served. The incident reveals in King George the same kind of obdurate behaviour that he exhibited in his confrontation with his brother at the time of the Abdication.

D-Day, the Allied landing in the North of France on June 6, 1944, was a combined operation, brilliantly ordered and carried out. The supreme commander, General Dwight Eisenhower, was American, his deputy, British. The air and naval commanders were British. Land forces were commanded by General Montgomery, British Commander of the invasion forces, and General Eisenhower himself. Nearly 200,000 men were engaged that day in naval operations (two-thirds of them British). By nightfall, 156,000 men had been put ashore. D-Day was a success. Ten days later, King George got his wish and crossed a choppy Channel in cold and gusty weather to visit his troops. He arrived at 12:30 and was back on the cruiser, H.M.S. *Arethusa,* by 4:00 P.M. for his return trip to Portsmouth and then Windsor. That same night Hitler's secret weapon, the V-1—pilotless planes filled with explosives—made their first harrowing and destructive descent on England.

The day following, in his characteristically low-keyed manner, the King wrote in his diary: "A change in our daily routine will be needed."

Christmas 1944 at Badminton was an attempt to recreate the old traditional and gay rituals at Sandringham. Besides Sir Osbert, the Princess Royal, Lord Harewood, the Beauforts, Lady Constance Milnes-Gaskell who was in waiting, and the elderly deaf courier Sir Richard Molyneaux, two American officers were present. ("Perhaps we should still be one country," Queen Mary told the gentlemen, "if my great-grandfather hadn't been so obstinate.") An enormous table was placed in the hallway, and gifts were laid out on it as they had always been at Sandringham, although the contents of the boxes reflected the parsimony of war—with guests giving possessions of their own to each other: books, cigarette cases, small pieces of jewelry.

At dinner Christmas Eve, Queen Mary looked superb. She wore a silver gown, enormous sapphires, a pearl collar, and huge diamond-and-pearl brooches and pendants. "As this magnificent figure, blazing and sparkling, led the way from the room," Sir Osbert writes, "Dick Molyneaux turned to me and said in his loud, deaf voice, like that of a man shouting from a cave into a strong wind, 'I wonder if you realise it, after that old lady has gone, you'll never see anything like this, or like her, again!' "*

At midnight, May 8, 1945, Germany's unconditional surrender was officially announced. As the news had leaked out twenty-four hours earlier, V-E Day lacked an element of surprise. Vast crowds gathered before Buckingham Palace. The Royal Family was given a triumphant ovation when they appeared on the palace balcony, and they were called back again and again. But the struggle was not yet over. Many sacrifices in lives still lay ahead as war continued in the Pacific.

At Badminton, Queen Mary listened with great pride to the victory broadcast by the King. Bertie had endured with constancy and courage. The cheers of the crowds assured her that he had survived this crisis in his reign undaunted and triumphant, and as he spoke she was conscious of the lessening of his stutter.

To the Household's admiration and surprise, Queen Mary accompanied the members of her Court to the Portcullis Club in the local public house "where the village was celebrating," and she cheerfully and lustily joined in as everyone sang songs, many of them the same she had sung in the sitting room at York Cottage to the amusement of her family.

Pandemonium once again prevailed when Queen Mary prepared to leave Badminton to take up residence at Marlborough House on June 11. The endeavor was almost as overwhelming as D-Day. Over seventy crates, boxes, and cases had to be repacked, and Marlborough House had to be readied.

Marlborough House was in a terrible state of disrepair, and it hardly seemed possible that it could be made habitable in time for Queen Mary's arrival. The great ground-floor reception rooms had been damaged by blasts; ceilings were down, doors

*Major the Hon. Sir Richard Molyneaux KCVO (1873–1954) was Groom-in-Waiting to King George V from 1919–1936 and served as Extra Equerry to Queen Mary from 1936 until her death.

blown from their hinges, and glassless windows boarded up. Yet by May 31, "Mahogany, satinwood and lacquered furniture, Chinese and European porcelains, 'treasures' of agate and lapis and gold were now emerging from what Queen Mary termed their 'hide-outs.' "

On May 18—with M[oving] Day still three weeks away, Mary, the Duchess of Beaufort, wrote to Sir Osbert Sitwell: "Vans of boxes and hampers and trunks all marked with the royal cypher continually leave the house. Today I saw such a van leaving with royal crowns and M.R.s bursting from every side, but at the very back and perched on the top of these dignified boxes sat, very cheerily and cheekily a common enamel slop pail—very plebeian, and showing no sign of its royal ownership."

When the day came for her to take her final leave of the Beauforts' hospitality, Marlborough House still did not have windows in its drawing rooms, the library, or the dining room. Many weeks would be required before they could be replaced, since window glass, like all other building materials (and food and clothing), was difficult to obtain. But Queen Mary refused to let this delay her plans.

Tears streamed down Queen Mary's face—a very rare occurrence, indeed—the morning of her departure from Badminton. "Oh, I *have* been so happy here," she said as she handed to each one of Badminton's nine heads of departments a valuable and personally selected gift. To one she added, "Here I've been anybody to everybody, and back in London I shall have to begin being Queen Mary all over again." But to all those with whom she had sat out a war, she had never *ceased* being Queen Mary.

With President Harry Truman's decision to drop an atomic bomb on Hiroshima on August 6, and on August 9 on Nagasaki, the war was ended.* "The great host of the living" who would now return from foreign shores to try to pick up their lives where they had left them found a new England upon their return. Winston Churchill had been voted out of power, and Clement Attlee and the Labour Party, in a landslide victory on July 26, had begun the great task of reorganising postwar Brit-

---

*President Franklin Delano Roosevelt had died on April 12, 1945.

ain.* The King found it difficult to deal with the socialism of the aggressive Labour Ministers. He now realised how greatly he had depended upon Winston Churchill and how sorely he would miss the gruff old man. "I regret what has happened more than perhaps anyone else," he wrote the ex-Prime Minister directly after the election. "I shall miss your counsel to me more than I can say. But please remember that as a friend I hope we shall be able to meet at intervals. Believe me. I am, Yours very sincerely & gratefully, G.R.1."

Queen Mary and Lady Airlie spent January 1946 at Sandringham while the final decorations were completed at Marlborough House. They found the ambiance at Sandringham changed. It had lost much of its Edwardian look and feel. A new informality prevailed. Jigsaw puzzles were set out on a large beige-covered table in the entrance hall, and Princess Elizabeth, who loved the radio, had it blaring all day long. Youth predominated with the two young Princesses and their guests; a cousin, Lady Mary Cambridge; and several young Guardsmen. The atmosphere was relaxed. No orders or medals were worn, the dress code was much more casual, and the Royal Family addressed each other in the manner of an ordinary family. When one of his daughters wanted something, the King would say, "You must ask Mummy."

Margaret, now a lovely young girl of fifteen, displayed a great deal of sibling rivalry toward her older sister and would sulk if not allowed to do the things that Lilibet could. Of the two sisters, she was the greater tease and flirt with the young Guardsmen.

The first evening at Sandringham, Lady Airlie sat next to the King. "His face was tired and strained and he ate practically nothing," she recalls. "I knew that he was forcing himself to talk and entertain me. When I told him how much I had liked his Christmas broadcast, and how well written I thought the script had been, he looked across at the Queen. 'She helps me,' he said proudly. Looking at him and realising how hard he was driving himself I felt a cold fear of the probability of another short reign . . ."

*Clement Richard Attlee (1883–1967), British statesman; Prime Minister 1945–1951. Earl Attlee in 1955.

Queen Mary had not enjoyed herself for a long time as thoroughly as she did at Sandringham that first night. The war was over, and the son she had worried about during those difficult days had acquitted himself admirably. There would be no male heir to the Throne, but Lilibet had all the qualities necessary in a good Sovereign. At about 11:30 that evening dancing began, with Queen Mary on the arm of her son and Lady Airlie escorted by a young Guardsman. And as the country band played "Hickey Hoo," an old favourite, the music brought back the past to the two elderly ladies who were seventy-nine and eighty, respectively, and they outshone the two young Princesses and their guests. At the end of an hour, Lady Airlie stopped after a strenuous "Sir Roger de Coverly," but Queen Mary kept on until nearly 1:00 A.M.

No two sisters could have been less alike than Lilibet and Margaret, the elder with her quiet dignity and rather prim nature, the younger with her ebullient spirits, her puckish expression, and her love of mimicry. Queen Mary described her as "so outrageously amusing that one can't help but encouraging her."

"The King was a devoted father to both his daughters," Lady Airlie wrote. "He spoiled Princess Margaret and still continued to treat her as an enfant terrible, but Princess Elizabeth was his constant companion in shooting, walking, reading—in fact everything. His affection for her was touching. I wondered sometimes whether he was secretly dreading the prospect of an early marriage for her . . ."

Prince Philip was not at Sandringham in January, yet constant rumours circulated that an announcement would soon be made of his engagement to Princess Elizabeth. The ties between the Royal Family and Greece had always been strong. When Prince Philip's father, Prince Andrew, had been arrested after the Abdication of King Constantine of Greece,* and tried by a Revolutionary Committee, he had escaped the death penalty only through the prompt intervention of King George V. Still, since British troops were now actively involved in the Greek Civil War, the timing was delicate. The possibility of Philip taking on British citizenship was discussed. But fear pervaded the Court

---

*King Constantine abdicated in 1917.

456

that such an act might be interpreted as an indication of British support for the Greek royalists. With the Greek general election being held in March, it was hoped that the results would make an announcement of Princess Elizabeth's engagement to a Greek prince less embarrassing. Finally, the King, after consulting the Prime Minister and Queen Mary, decided that his elder daughter's marriage plans would have to wait upon political events in Greece.

Princess Elizabeth celebrated her twenty-first birthday on April 21, 1947, in South Africa, where she was on tour with her parents and sister, the first time the Royal Family had ever undertaken together a tour of one of the Dominions. India was scheduled to gain her independence within the year. Now that so many British territories were on the verge of slipping away, "the hope was to reinforce the Crown as a common symbol." With that in mind, Princess Elizabeth, her voice "still piping and a little child-like," made a broadcast from South Africa, declaring to her future subjects that her whole life, "whether it be long or short, shall be devoted to your service and the service of our great Imperial Commonwealth to which we all belong. But I shall not have strength to carry out this resolution unless you join in it with me, as I now invite you to do . . ."

When she returned from South Africa, progress was under way to make a Greek prince acceptable to the British public. After much deliberation, Prince Philip's name (which was Schleswig-Holstein-Sonderburg-Glucksburg) was changed to Mountbatten, the name his mother's family had chosen in 1917.* He was henceforth to be called plain Lieutenant Mountbatten. On July 10, 1947, Buckingham Palace reported: "It is with the greatest pleasure that the King and Queen announce the betrothal of their dearly beloved daughter The Princess Elizabeth to Lieutenant Philip Mountbatten RN, son of the late Prince Andrew of Greece and Princess Andrew (Princess Alice of Battenberg) to which union the King has gladly given his consent."†

*Princess Alice had never anglicised her name, Battenberg.

†Ten years later it was realised that Prince Philip need not have bothered about naturalisation, due to the Act of Settlement of 1701. This measure gave

The public was not too thrilled with the match; 40 percent in one opinion poll were decidedly against the marriage on the grounds that Philip was foreign. No one was sure what his nationality was—Greek, German, or Danish—but his mother's act of becoming a Greek Orthodox nun, and wearing religious robes and veil, and his father's impecunious life and death in exile did not contribute to a good public image.*

"They both came to see me after luncheon looking radiant," Queen Mary wrote on July 10, just after being told of the engagement. She gave "darling Lilibet" the jewellry that, in July 1893, fifty-four years past, had comprised her own chief wedding present from Queen Victoria (the diamond necklace and stomacher). "Nearly all the members of our family who were present on that occasion are no more," she noted sadly.

The Royal Wedding was held on November 20, 1947. Still recovering from the aftermath of the war, London was dingy and bomb-scarred. To Queen Mary, as to millions of others, the pageantry of a Royal marriage represented "an escape from reality; a cut back to the past."

"It was a week of gaiety such as the Court had not seen for years," Lady Airlie wrote. "[There was] an evening party at Buckingham Palace which seemed after the years of austerity like a scene out of a fairy tale . . . Old friends scattered far and wide by the war were reunited; old feuds and jealousies were swept away. Most of us were sadly shabby—anyone fortunate enough to have a new dress drew all eyes—but all the famous diamonds came out again, even though most of them had not been cleaned since 1939.

"Queen Mary looked supremely happy . . . For the first time in many years I saw the old radiance in her smile. When Winston

---

British nationality and royal status to the Electress Sophia of Hanover and all her descendants. Prince Philip numbered among these and therefore technically had been a British Royal Highness since birth.

*Prince Andrew of Greece was the youngest son of King George I of Greece (Queen Alexandra's brother) and the Princess Olga, granddaughter of Tsar Nicholas I. He died in Monte Carlo in 1944 in poverty, his Spartan funeral expenses finally paid for by the Greek government. When he had been arrested in Greece, his wife, Princess Alice, Prince Philip's mother, had joined a religious order.

458

Churchill went up to greet her she held out both hands to him, a thing I never knew her to do before."

The pleasure she took in the occasion was marked in her diary entry for the day of the grand party: "Saw many old friends, I stood from 9.10 till 12.15 A.M.!!!! not bad for 80."

THIRTY-TWO

Toward the end of their stay in Nassau, the Duchess of Windsor had written Queen Mary a letter:

Madam,

I hope you will forgive my intrusion upon your time as well as my boldness in addressing Your Majesty. My motive for the letter is a simple one. It has always been a source of sorrow and regret to me that I have been the cause of any separation that exists between Mother and Son and I can't help feeling that there must be moments perhaps, however fleeting they may be, when you wonder how David is . . .

The letter was composed to soften a mother's heart and open the way for reconciliation, and was sent, according to *Wallis Windsor* (as the Duchess signed the note) without the Duke of Windsor's knowledge. It contained a plea that Queen Mary permit an audience with the Right Reverend John Dauglish, the Bishop of Nassau, who was a close friend of the Windsors, because "I thought if you wished to hear news of David . . . He can tell you if all the things David gave up are replaced to him in another way and the little details of his life, his job, etc. . . ."

Queen Mary did, indeed, have an audience with Bishop Dauglish, and she showed keen interest in her son's work in the colony and had asked many questions. Above everything else, the Duke of Windsor hoped to return one day to Britain with Wallis to make a new home and to be given some worthwhile job in Government. Little by little, he had accepted the fact that he could never resume his place in the family circle. In Queen Mary's eyes, her eldest son had altered "the natural order of monarchy . . . put aside what he had been born to fulfill until he died . . . he had become something different and apart . . . ."

By the autumn of 1946, Queen Mary was approaching her eightieth birthday. David had never ceased writing to her and she always replied, although her letters were cool and contained no private family news or feelings. She had not seen her son when he had come to England at the start of the war. The decision then had been most difficult, for David had pressed desperately for an audience. Those close to her—Lady Airlie, Lady Colville, Osbert Sitwell—all sincerely believed that she still loved David as a son, but that her sense of rightness and duty to the Monarchy disallowed any other course but the one she had taken.

On his part, the ex-King never gave up hoping his mother would see him. He believed such a meeting would change everything within the family, except, perhaps, his sister-in-law Queen Elizabeth's extreme enmity toward him, her bitter feeling that his actions were responsible for the King's illness, and her fears that her husband did not have long to live. He also knew that the Queen Consort would stand in the way of his ever returning to England to live. But he was determined "to take one more hard try at drumming up interest in the Palace and Whitehall for putting me to work somewhere in the British Diplomatic Service, in the absence of making a place for me in Britain."

After a long and involved correspondence with both Queen Mary and the King, arrangements were made for the Duke of Windsor to fly from Paris to London to spend a week with his mother at Marlborough House.

He arrived in London on October 5, alone. There was no member of the King's household to meet him. His mother had sent her car and chauffeur. The slights cut deeply. A look of tremendous pain is evident in his expression in the news photos of his arrival. As he went to step into the limousine, "A cheering throng of spectators broke through the police cordon and surged around him, with cries of 'Good old Edward!' and 'You must come back, Teddy! We want you back.' Several people were thrown to the ground and trampled on as the besieging mob milled around the automobile."

He met his mother for the first time since the Abdication in her sitting room at Marlborough House. Over a decade had passed. Lady Airlie was in waiting, but, though her habit was to record such events, she made no record of the meeting or of any discussion with Queen Mary about the Duke of Windsor's visit. Neither is there any mention of her son's stay in Queen Mary's diary. In some ways these omissions indicate her feeling that he was now a nonperson; in others that perhaps the confrontation was so painful she could not bring herself to record any part of it or even to acknowledge that it had occurred.

He was given the largest guest room and one of Queen Mary's staff to serve as his valet. From the Court record, it appears they had tea but never dined together. Their meeting must have been a tremendous ordeal for both of them, but piteously humiliating for the Duke of Windsor.

His second day in London he called on Ernest Bevin,* the Foreign Secretary in Clement Attlee's Cabinet, with a proposal that he be created Ambassador-at-Large to the United States. He visualised himself as a public-relations "front man." "Such a job," he later said in an interview, "would require my bringing Americans and visiting Britons together, providing a good table and a comfortable library for informal talk, and helping along what Winston Churchill called 'the mixing up process.' " Ernest Bevin was not impressed by the idea and sent a memorandum to the Prime Minister to that effect. Even had the Foreign Secretary felt more inclined toward the proposition, Clement Attlee would most probably not have agreed to back it.

The Duke of Windsor visited bomb sites in the East End of London with Queen Mary on October 7. The following morning, a Sunday, he accompanied his mother to church. After-

*Ernest Bevin (1881–1951), English trade union leader and statesman; member of Parliament 1940–51; Foreign Minister 1945–51.

wards, he went to an unsatisfactory meeting with the King. On Monday, October 9, two days before he was originally scheduled to do so, he returned to Paris, having not yet been given an answer to his request.

The Windsors were living at the Ritz Hotel at the time. Lady Diana Cooper saw the Duke in France and later remarked, "He had such an awful life in Paris. He couldn't speak French, he didn't enjoy night clubs and he had very few friends he could talk with." Another friend wrote to a mutual acquaintance:*

"He is so pitiful . . . I never saw a man so bored. He said to me, 'How do you manage to remain so cheerful in this ghastly place? . . . You know what my day was today? . . . I got up late and then I went with the Duchess and watched her buy a hat, and then on the way home I had the car drop me off in the Bois to watch some of your [American] soldiers playing football and then I planned to take a walk, but it was so cold I could hardly bear it. In fact I was afraid that I would be struck with cold in the way people are struck with heat so I came straight home . . . When I got home the Duchess was having her French lesson so I had no one to talk to . . .' "

Such a daily schedule reveals a great lack of inner drive and incentive, and is especially pitiable for a man who was once King. Paris was a cosmopolitan city of much culture even after the vicissitudes it had suffered during the war. There were, as well, a monumental amount of restoration and rehabilitation projects in which he could have been involved.

On January 7, 1947, just three months later, he returned to London alone, staying again with Queen Mary. He dined with Winston Churchill on January 8, had an audience with the King on January 9, and on the following day with the King and Mr. Attlee. He flew back to Paris on January 12, still without a final reply. It came at last on January 27, when the Prime Minister stated in the House of Commons that there was to be no diplomatic or official position given the Duke of Windsor. The answer was a serious blow to him. After that, he was to return to England on several occasions, but he brought Wallis and they stayed with

*Susan Mary Alsop to Marietta Tree.

friends, and during these visits Queen Mary would not receive him.*

At the outset of 1948, those close to the King knew he was not well. The war years had depleted the little strength he did have. He had lost nearly twenty pounds in the course of the South African tour and never regained them. In January 1947, he suffered frequent crippling cramps in both legs. They became increasingly worse. By October, deterioration was perceptible; his left foot was numb most of the time, and the pain kept him awake. Then his right foot became affected. During the entire time, the King had kept a daily record of his health but had not consulted the Royal medical advisers. On October 20, he summoned Sir Morton Smart,† who was gravely alarmed and called in two other consulting physicians,‡ and finally Professor James Learmouth,§ of Edinburgh, one of the greatest authorities on vascular disease in Great Britain.

The King's condition was diagnosed as early arteriosclerosis; there was grave fear that his right leg might have to be amputated because of the danger of gangrene. He was confined to bed but was able to conduct most of his duties. All danger of amputation had disappeared by the beginning of December. "I am getting tired and bored with bed," he wrote Queen Mary on December 1. On December 15, he was sufficiently improved to attend the christening of Princess Elizabeth's first child, Prince Charles Philip Arthur George, born on November 14.¶ Still, his

---

*On one of these visits over $3 million of jewels, including Queen Alexandra's bequest to the Duke of Windsor, was burgled. Against all advice, the Duchess of Windsor had brought the jewelry with her and kept it under her bed—refusing to allowed it to be stored in a safe.

†Commander Sir Morton Smart G.C.V.O., D.S.O., M.D., C.H.M. (1878–1956).

‡The two consulting doctors were Sir Thomas Peel Dunhill (1876–1957) and Sir Maurice Cassidy (1880–1949).

§Sir James Learmouth, K.C.V.O., C.B.E., M.B., C.H.M. F.R.C.S. (1895–1965).

¶"I am delighted at being a great-grandmother!" Queen Mary wrote in her diary. "I gave the baby a silver gilt cup & cover which George III had given to a godson in 1780 . . ."

life had become that of semi-invalidisim. A right lumbar sympathectomy operation was recommended. The operation was successfully performed on the morning of March 12, 1949, at Buckingham Palace, where a complete surgical theatre had been established in rooms overlooking the Mall.*

He was able to undertake a good many official duties by May and on June 9 drove in an open carriage to watch his Brigade of Guards troop the Colour, at which ceremony Princess Elizabeth rode at the head of the parade. Lady Airlie's dire prediction loomed as too close to reality. Chances were slim that the King would survive a long reign, and his family daily saw the signs. He had greatly aged in the last two years and was ashen-coloured, thin, and had great saucers about his eyes. More and more, Princess Elizabeth was placed "at the head of the parade," a diversionary tactic that worked well with the public, now ardently enthusiastic about the young woman.

That same winter, Queen Mary had a return attack of bursitis which did not relinquish its grip for a year, and she had to resign herself during that time to the intermittent use of a wheelchair. By May 1951, her old vitality had returned, and she attended the opening of the Festival of Britain held to commemorate the centenary of Queen Victoria's Great Exhibition. The main exhibition in London was arranged on a site on the South Bank of the River Thames, and Queen Mary toured it the following day, declaring it "really extraordinary & very ugly."

The King, jaundiced, shockingly thin, and a bit shaky, spoke on the steps of Saint Paul's for the opening of the Festival of Britain. A cancer had developed on his left lung, and possible liver damage was feared. He was asked to stop drinking. On September 23, he underwent surgery to remove the cancerous portion of his lung. Queen Mary saw him before the operation and found him "very thin but very plucky & reasonable." Three weeks afterwards, she thought he looked "wonderful after his

---

*The King had not rejected the idea of the operation being performed in a hospital but did comment when asked his opinion, "I never heard of a King going to hospital." For the period of time that the King was in surgery and in the early days of his recuperation, Queen Elizabeth, Princess Elizabeth, Princess Margaret, and the Duke of Gloucester were named Councillors of State.

465

long ordeal . . . we had a nice talk." He was believed to have cirrhosis of the liver, not cancer.

Bulletins were issued on the King's progress and, to discount any adverse rumours, a five-month tour of Africa was planned for Princess Elizabeth and the Duke of Edinburgh. The "Edinburghs" lived "across the road" from Queen Mary at Clarence House, and they came over the night before departure to bid her goodbye. Queen Mary did not go out to London Airport to see them off, but the King—gaunt, hatless—stood in a high wind, his hair blowing across his forehead, and watched his daughter regally mount the stairs to the Royal plane as he waved to her. He then drove directly to Sandringham to go shooting. "Suicidal," one observer called his decision.

Lady Cynthia Colville was in waiting at Marlborough House the morning of February 7 and having her breakfast with two other members of the Household,* when Major Edward Ford was ushered in.† He informed her that the King was dead. For the third time, Lady Cynthia had to convey terrible news to Queen Mary, who was in her bedroom having her breakfast in bed. As soon as she saw Lady Cynthia, she guessed the grim news. "The King?" she asked, her hand shaking as she moved the tray aside.

"During the night," Lady Cynthia replied.‡

The new Queen, Elizabeth II, reached London from Nairobi at 4:00 P.M. the day following the King's death. At 4:30, Queen Mary drove from Marlborough House to Clarence House. "Her old Grannie and subject," she told Lady Cynthia, "must be the first to kiss her hand." She wore her mourning clothes and carried a black umbrella. She was thinner now than ever before, and her strong jaw, high forehead, and high-bridged nose had

---

*Lord Claud Hamilton and Major Wickham.

†Major Edward Ford (b. 1910), assistant Private Secretary to George VI 1946–1952, and also to Elizabeth 1952–1967.

‡The King had suffered a coronary thrombosis the night of February 6, 1952. His death was not known until his butler came to bring him tea early the next morning. There was then a lapse of several hours before the new Queen, in Nyeri, could be reached. Queen Elizabeth II was the first sovereign in English history not to have known the time that she became a Monarch.

466

the look of cast stone behind her black veil. She sat rigidly in the rear seat of the Daimler and turned and waved at the crowds gathered on the street as she passed through the gates of Marlborough House. She refused assistance as she walked the few steps from the car to the residence of the new Sovereign, using her umbrella as a cane. She was still dry-eyed and would remain so.

Her elder granddaughter, now Queen Elizabeth II, waited to receive her. For the first time in the young woman's life (she was twenty-five), she had not been the one to make the approach. Despite her grief, the shock, the newness of it all, she reacted as Queen Regnant. She wore a slim black dress and the single row of pearls that had been given to her by her father, a brooch, and pearl-and-diamond earrings. Though small in stature and rather dwarfed by the tall, craggy Prince Philip, who stood slightly behind her, Queen Elizabeth II held herself in such a manner and with such great control that her attitude commanded the room.

Queen Mary walked to her. Queen Elizabeth extended her hand, and her grandmother and subject took it and kissed it lightly. "God save the Queen," she said in a strong voice that had the ring of a declaration.

The Lying-in-State was on February 11 at Westminster Hall. Chips Channon records that "the Great Hall was cold, splendid and impressive . . . a few paces behind [the King's coffin] the Royal Family followed, walking in measured paces like figures in a Greek tragedy. First walked the young Queen, all in black but wearing flesh-coloured stockings; behind her, to the right, was the Queen Mother—unmistakable with her curious side-ways lilting walk. On her left, was Queen Mary, frail and fragile, I thought with her veil and her black umbrella and steel-coloured stockings. I was very sorry for her as she must have known and realised that she is next."

Queen Mary decided not to go to the interment at Windsor on February 15 and asked her old friend, Lady Airlie, to come down from her home in Scotland to be with her. The two old women—both in their eighties, both the very symbol of the *grand dame*—greeted each other warmly in Queen Mary's sitting room at Marlborough House, where they were to watch the funeral procession pass directly before the huge bay window. They sat alone together at the window, looking out into the grey gloom of the cold winter day.

"As the cortege wound slowly along," Lady Airlie recalled vividly, "the Queen whispered in a broken voice, 'Here *he* is,' and I knew that her dry eyes were seeing beyond the coffin a little boy in a sailor suit. She was past weeping wrapped in the ineffable solitude of grief. I could not speak to comfort her. My tears choked me. The words I wanted to say would not come. We held each other's hands in silence."

All of Queen Mary's energies were directed toward the plans for the coronation. She made an expedition to Kensington Palace the first week of May to study the details of Queen Victoria's coronation robes, which she felt should form a precedent for those of Queen Elizabeth II. Now, as in her childhood and youth, Great Britain was ruled by a Queen, and the idea thrilled her.

Her eighty-fifth birthday was May 26, 1952. "Nice fine day, not so hot," she wrote in her diary. "My 85th birthday! spent a hectic morning with endless presents arriving & lots of flowers —Mary kindly came at 12 & helped me, we had lunch & tea together—Between 2.30 & 4.30 a number of my family came to see me, very nice of them—hundreds of letters, cards etc. arrived—we tried to deal with them—I felt very much spoilt & had a nice day in spite of my great age."

The date of the coronation was set for June 2, 1953. Queen Mary was failing and she knew it. She let it be known at Buckingham Palace that if she died in the interim of the year, the coronation must not be postponed. But her spirit remained vital. "I am beginning to lose my memory," she told Osbert Sitwell, "but I mean to get it back." She accepted an occasional invitation to dinner and kept up her style—the toques, the jewels, the hair fringe. She drew up a new will and reorganised the catalogues of what she called "my interesting things" to ensure that all should be in proper order for the new Sovereign.

February 1953 was "horrid and cold," but Queen Mary still managed to take a drive through London. She was suffering high blood pressure and hardening of the arteries, and spells of dizziness began that kept her more safely indoors. She was seldom alone. Some member of the family always paid a daily visit. In the early weeks in March, the young Queen visited twice, despite the pressures of her position and the work of the coronation. Lady Airlie had been warned not to make Queen Mary talk on account of the cough that was troubling her, so she chatted away about trivial things. The day Lady Airlie was to return to Scotland, she sat by her dear old friend's bed, conscious of the perfection of everything around her: ". . . the exquisitely embroidered soft lawn night gown—the same as those she had worn in her youth—the nails delicately shaped and polished a pale pink; the immaculately arranged grey hair. Her face had still a gentle beauty of expression; no trace of hardness as so many faces have in old age, only resignation. As I kissed her hand before leaving her I noticed the extreme softness of her skin." The parting was difficult. The two women had shared more than forty-eight years; they shared a philosophy. "I must go on '*à fin,*' as your father would have said," Lady Airlie wrote her daughter; and Queen Mary had said to her lifelong friend, Lady Shaftesbury, the day following the death of King George VI, ". . . one must force oneself to go on until the end."

On March 18, Queen Mary wrote to the Duke of Baena, who had sent her a catalogue of a recent Goya Exhibition in Basel. Amongst its illustrations was a portrait of Goya's small grandson. "I feel weary and unwell," she admitted, "but your charming catalogue of the Goya pictures has given me great pleasure. I particularly like the portrait of Marianito Goya with the silk hat —as one sees it was painted with great love."

On the morning of March 24, Queen Mary slipped into a coma. Parliament was in a state of inaction all day while the men in Government waited, as Chips Channon phrases it, "for the glorious old girl to die . . . the rumour flew round that she had at 4.02; there was an atmosphere of hushed excitement. Winston came into the chamber . . . the dreaded announcement was expected any moment." An hour later, Clement Attlee, leader of the opposition, came out of the Prime Minister's room and announced that Queen Mary was unconscious, but still alive.

At eleven o'clock, Prime Minister Winston Churchill rose and, moving the adjournment of the House, announced the death of

Queen Mary at 10:35. "There were cries of dismay from the Gallery," Channon continues, "and indeed on all sides there seemed to be grief . . . particularly from the Socialists. She had long captured their imagination, and they rightly thought her above politics, a kind of Olympian Goddess. I drove sadly home, passing Marlborough House . . . It was plunged in darkness and there was a large crowd outside; women were weeping."

With Queen Mary's death, a civilisation had ended, too. The eulogies came tumbling fast, one upon the other. "She was magnificent, humorous, worldly, in fact nearly sublime, though cold and hard. But what a grand Queen," Chips Channon wrote in his diary.

The Duke of Windsor arrived on March 29, in time for the Lying-in-State in dimly lit Westminster Hall. He was nervous and fidgety and stood apart, obviously very unhappy. Lady Airlie walked in with immense dignity. Winston Churchill waved away a chair that someone had brought him and stood throughout the service, although he was known not to be well. The Royal ladies wore short veils, steel-coloured stockings, ropes of pearls, and jewels. The coffin had on it a single wreath from Queen Elizabeth. When the service ended, the whole family, except the young Queen, curtsied and bowed to the coffin. Then they slowly filed out.

Londoners thronged the streets, silent and bareheaded, on March 31 as the coffin was borne from Westminster to Paddington Station, from which Queen Mary would travel for the last time to Windsor to be buried beside King George V in the family vault in St. George's Chapel, Windsor. After the funeral at Windsor, twenty-eight members of the Royal Family met for dinner. The Duke of Windsor was not among the invited guests. Quite extraordinary, perhaps, but an omission that Queen Mary, with her unflagging devotion to the Monarchy and its Monarch, would have understood and forgiven as she was never able to forgive her eldest son. As she had written him not long after the Abdication, ". . . all my life I have put my country before everything else and I simply cannot change now."

Queen Mary had lived her life with dedication to the principle of Monarchy, and she had died as she had lived, as her Sovereign's most devoted subject.

ACKNOWLEDGEMENTS

Both the writing and editing of this book have been a unique and unforgettable experience. So many people came forward and gave unstintingly of their time, wisdom, and talent. To my good fortune I had access to the great talents of *two* editors, Ion Trewin at Hodder and Stoughton, London, and Harvey Ginsberg of William Morrow, New York, both artists in their field. I shall be ever grateful for their incisive editorial criticism and for their staunch belief in this book and in its author.

Additionally I owe a great debt to Hugh Montgomery-Massingberd, Editorial Director of Burke's Peerage, Ltd, for the endless hours he devoted to this book as *Royal Expert Supreme* and for his detailed and lively notations which helped me to understand the complicated relationships of the Royal Family.

At Hodder and Stoughton I want also to thank Mary Lou Nesbitt, Ion Trewin's able assistant and a young woman who gave graciously of her time and energy. My gratitude as well to Fiona Lindsey and to Hugh Vickers for their kind help.

Scores of historians, royal observers, librarians, and archivists assisted me in my research and I owe them my deepest gratitude. My many thanks as well to those members of Queen Mary's Household who shared their memories with me.

This book would never have seen life without the loving care my two marvellous agents lavished upon it. Mitch Douglas, my

American agent, has always been there when I needed him. For ten years his belief in me has never flagged and his encouragement has seen me through some mighty rough patches. Hilary Rubinstein, my English agent, has represented me since I wrote my first book, nineteen years ago. If I have never told him how much his help and enthusiasm have meant to me, I do so now.

During the three long years it has taken to write this book, my husband, Stephen Citron, has been my constant companion. His perceptive editorial eye, his unfailing support, and his cheerful forbearance make me realize what an extraordinary gentleman I have married.

Last, but certainly not least, I owe a debt of thanks for the great assistance given me by my secretary, Barbara Howland.

—ANNE EDWARDS

Blandings Way
Christmas, 1983

NOTES

Authors and/or titles are given in the most convenient abbreviated form; full details can be found in the Bibliography, alphabetically according to the author's last name, with the following exceptions: ML refers to *Marie Louise*, RA to *Royal Archives at Windsor*, PH to *Pope-Hennessy*, PA to *Princess Alice*, and PB to *paperback edition*. Titles are used when multiple references have been made to one author's works.

Page
Preface
12 "It isn't": Wheeler-Bennett, p. 286.
12 "Goodbye": Ibid., p. 287.

Chapter 1
17 "I always have to be": ML, p. 201.
18 "Only a line": RA, Z 152 32 (footnote).
20 "puny & pigeon-chested": Queen Victoria's Journal, June 21, 1867.
20 "the densely crowded": Ibid.
20 "a very fine": Ibid.
20 "had dipped": St. Aubyn, *Edward VII*, p. 41.
21 "under conditions": Ibid.
22 "We are neither": Dalton Papers, March 11, 1883.
22 "Eddy is a very good": RA, Z 162/7.
23 "something that dawns": T. Heald and M. Mohs, H.R.H. *The Man Who Will be King* (New York: Arbor House, 1979), p. 142.

25 "a dissolute nature": Harold Nicolson, *George V*, p. 17.
25 "My dear George": Ibid., p. 35
25 "with cultivated taste": Rumbelow.
25 "It's a real sorrow": Kronberg Archives, May 7, 1890.
26 "What I do not understand": Harold Nicolson, Princess of Wales to Prince George, November 21, 1886.
26 "Don't call him Uncle Eddy": Rumbelow.
28 "I thought it was impossible": Prince Albert Victor to Lady Sybil, June 21, 1891, Westmoreland Papers.
29 "I wonder if you": Prince Albert Victor to Lady Sybil, June 28, 1891, Westmoreland Papers.
29 "Don't be surprised": Prince Albert Victor to Lady Sybil, November 29, 1891, Westmoreland Papers.
29 "I told her": RA, A:M: A/12 1797, Sir Francis Knollys to Sir Henry Ponsonby.

Notes

NOTES

Chapter 2

31 "Reached Aberdeen": Princess May to Princess Mary Adelaide.

34 "a smell of wood": Princess Marie Louise, *Reminiscences of Six Reigns*, p. 15.

35 "the children would squabble": Ibid.

35 "Mind you curtsy": Ibid.

35 "Kiss Aunt Queen's": Ibid.

36 "Your dear children": PH, p. 207.

36 "Most dear & kind": RA, Duchess of Teck to Princess May, November 5, 1891.

37 "You speak": Queen Victoria to Empress Frederick, Kronberg Archives, November 17, 1891.

38 "Presently the rest": Lady Geraldine Somerset, RA, November 12, 1891.

38 "You may, I think": RA/Z 475 No. 23.

39 ". . . the heat was so": RA, Princess May to Grand Duchess of Mecklenburg-Strelitz, November 16, 1886.

40 ". . . over 40 pounds". Lady Geraldine Somerset's Journal, RA, January 12, 1886.

40 "To my surprise": PH, p. 214.

40 "waltzed round and round": Ibid.

41 "The newspapers are twaddling": Lady Geraldine Somerset's Journal, RA, December 7, 1891.

Chapter 3

45 "how much confidence": Queen Victoria to Princess May, RA, December 13, 1891.

45 "Marriage is the": Ibid.

45 "dear, good boy": Ibid.

45 "Keep Eddy up to his mark": PH, p. 222.

45 "Do you think I can": Ibid.

45 "Mary is indeed a lucky person": Cooke, Vol. I, p. 142.

45 "It is an immense position": RA, Grand Duchess of Mecklenburg-Strelitz to Duchess of Teck, December 7, 1891.

46 "long engagements": PH, p. 218.

46 "We danced": Princess May to Grand Duchess of Mecklenburg-Strelitz, December 26, 1891.

46 "Goodbye to": Princess May's Diary, RA, January 4, 1892.

46 "at Windsor": Ibid.

47 "positively rude": PH, p. 216.

47 "I am glad to say": Queen Victoria to Princess Mary Adelaide, December 30, 1891.

50 "a dangerous old": Queen Victoria.

51 "Beauty, wit": The Duke of Windsor, *A King's Story*, p. 50.

51 "the lake and island": RA, Cresswell, *Eighteen Years on the Sandringham Estate*, p. 180.

52 "odious chaffing moods": PH, p. 221.

54 "Poor Eddy": RA/Z 475, 137.

55 "with great difficulty": Princess A. to her parents, Rigsarkivet, Copenhagen.

56 "Something too awful": Battiscombe, p. 190.

56 "Can you do anything": RA/Z 95–9.

56 "Who is that?": Battiscombe, p. 190.

57 "I clung to hope": Duchess of Teck to Queen Victoria, January 14, 1892, PH, p. 225

58 "I shall hide": RA/Z 475/200.

58 ". . . the picture of grief": Battiscombe, p. 192

59 "It is so difficult": Princess May to Miss Emily Alcock, February 13, 1892, Kronberg Archives.

Chapter 4

61 "It must be a Tsarevich": PH, p. 230.

62 "I must say": RA Princess May to Mlle. Bricka, January 24, 1892.

62 "Mama is quite happy": RA Princess May to Mlle. Bricka, April 27, 1892.

63 "May has become": RA, Duke of Teck to his sister Amelie, February 29, 1892.

64 "preferred recognition": Harold Nicolson, p. 157.

66 "Papa and I are coming": RA George V, cc 12.

67 "The reason why we are": Duke of Teck to his sister Amelie, May 15, 1892.

68 "The bond of love": Princess Alexandra to Prince George, RA George V, AA 31 22.

68 "You know my Georgie": Princess Alexandra to Prince George V, AA 31 30.

Chapter 5

69 "unseemly and unfeeling": PH, p. 242.

69 "Well you know": Ibid.

69 "The Prince of Wales must not": PH, p. 253.

70 "Since it seems the tradespeople": PH, p. 244.

70 "the cruel battle": Princess Mary Adelaide to the Grand Duchess of Mecklenburg-Strelitz, January 14, 1893.

71 ". . . How Beautiful it is": PH, p. 245.

72 "He is quite unfit": Martin, *Jennie*, p. 302.

72 "Now Georgie": PH, p. 259.

72 "We walked together": Ibid.

73 "May engaged to Duke of York": Ibid.

73 "Unless announced": Ibid.

73 "God bless you both": Princess Alexandra to Princess May, Kronberg Archives, May 13, 1893

74 "*so* obstinate": PH, p. 262.

74 "like a little devil": Ibid.

74 "forgiven her yet": Ibid.

74 "This is a simply": Ibid.

74 "contribution": PH, p. 264.

74 "dear Aunt Augusta": Ibid.

74 "some beautiful flounces": Ibid.

74 "I am determined": Cooke, Vol II., p. 184.

75 "I must say": Prince George to Princess May, RA, George V, CC 1 10.

75 "it is clear": RA, Lady Geraldine Somerset's Journal, March 6, 1892.

75 "I am sorry": RA, George V, CC 5 9.

75 "Thank God we both": RA, George V CC 1 20.

76 "I say, May, we": PH, p. 428, footnote.

76 "thunderous, drowsy afternoon": *Daily Telegraph*, July 6, 1893.

76 "Inside the Lodge": Ibid.

77 "There was a quick movement": *Times*, July 5, 1893.

77 "Fairyland": *Daily Telegraph*, July 6, 1893.
78 "more appropriate": Ibid.
78 "In every case": *Times*, July 6, 1893.
79 "Uncle Bertie": Massie, *Nicholas and Alexandra*, p. 24.
80 ". . . the third greatest": *Lady's Pictorial*, April 1893.

Chapter 6
82 "I should much like to": RA, George V, CC 5 21.
82 "ethereal in white satin": *Times*, July 7, 1893.
83 "four of the creams": Ibid.
83 "I am going first": Cooke, Vol. II, p. 247.
83 "some moments later": Ibid.
83 "Scarlet was lent": *Daily Telegraph*, July 7, 1893.
84 "Dear May looked so quiet": RA, Queen Victoria's Journal, July 6, 1893.
84 "May's Wedding Day": RA, Lady Geraldine Somerset's Journal, July 6, 1893.
85 "Rather *unlucky* and": Queen Victoria.
86 "We saw her": RA, Lady Geraldine Somerset's Journal, July 6, 1893.
86 "sobbed bitterly": Kronberg Archives, July 8, 1893.
86 "follow the shooters": Gore, *George V*, pp. 128–129.
87 "the servants must sleep. *For My Grandchildren*, p. 124.
88 "a tiny snuggery": *Lady's Pictorial*, September 1893.
88 "still tinier": Ibid.
88 "This too is": Ibid.
88 "very plainly furnished": Ibid.
89 "if the footmen": *For My Grandchildren*, p. 124.

89 "I sometimes think": RA, George V, CC 1 60.
89 "delicate, hypochrondriacal": Battiscombe, p. 199.
89 "a glorified maid": Ibid.
89 "grumbler": Ibid.
89 "it really is *not* wise": Ibid.
90 "May appears to be educating": Princess Frederick to Queen Victoria, RA/Z 152 61.

Chapter 7
92 "I sat next to William": PH, p. 286.
93 "my white broche": Ibid.
93 "all sort": PH, p. 299.
93 "unhealthy and beastly": PH, p. 294.
94 "Are *you* not beside": Grand Duchess of Mecklenburg-Strelitz to the Duchess of Teck, June 25, 1894.
95 "she was such an": *For My Grandchildren*, p. 128.
95 "the Baby, who is": PH, p. 300.
96 "I know how distressed": PH, p. 296
96 "she might have been killed": Ibid.
96 "There is a very good electric light": Ibid.
97 "Splendid equipage": Tuchman, *The Proud Tower*, p. 21.
98 "Tuesday we had a delightful": Athlone Papers, Duchess of Teck to Prince Alexander of Teck, January 17, 1896.
98 "There have been a good many": PH, p. 313
98 "could not be easy": Duchess of York to the Grand Duchess of Mecklenburg-Strelitz, November 9, 1895.

98 "Before her scandal": Hare, Vol. VI, p. 516.

99 "unspeakable agony": PH, p. 300.

100 "Every day": Ibid.

100 "One day in deepest mourning": Massie, p. 13.

100 "looked too": PH, p. 301.

100 "I must say I never saw": Ibid.

101 "A Boy!!": Athlone Papers, Duchess of Teck to Prince Alexander of Teck, December 20, 1895.

101 "Dear Grandmama": RA/Z 447, Vol. 2, p. 236.

101 "He could hardly": RA/Z 477, Vol. II, p. 235.

101 "George will be": Ibid.

102 "Can't you stop that child": Duke of Windsor, *A Family Album*, p. 23.

Chapter 8

103 "England! What shall men": Oscar Wilde, "Ave Imperatrix."

104 ". . . which prevailed": *Daily Telegraph*, June 23, 1897.

106 "The Princess of Wales came": Battiscombe, p. 211.

106 "You will pray for him": Cooke, Vol. II, p. 298.

106 ". . . everyone plunged": Princess of Wales to Grand Duchess of Mecklenburg-Strelitz, RA AM A/8 55.

107 "The partition": Viscount Esher, Vol. I, p. 207.

108 "I dread to think": Princess May to Grand Duchess of Mecklenburg-Strelitz, November 3, 1897, RA.

108 "She was quite superb": Ibid., p. 229.

108 "towsel and fringe": Ibid.

109 "I drove with Gdmama": PH, p. 346.

109 "At four": Ibid.

110 "The result is that": RA, Princess May's Diary, March 8, 1900.

110 ". . . Her memory . . .": Ponsonby, p. 118.

110 "Go up at once": Wilfred S. Cowen Blunt, *My Diaries* (New York: Knopf, 1921) Vol. I, p. 366.

110 "Every Englishman": George Bernard Shaw, *Times*, November 6, 1899.

112 "Imperial troops": Pakenham, p. 449.

112 ". . . dressing cases": Ibid.

112 "Of the new century": Ibid.

113 "Thank God for": Battiscombe, p. 213.

113 "There was no time": Ibid.

113 "cheated of their Armageddon": Pakenham (Prevost Battasby), p. 452.

113 "the last great flight": Ibid.

116 "The Prince of Wales will": Ponsonby, p. 128.

116 "gained consciousness": Ibid.

116 "passed his arm": Ibid.

117 "His tenderness and Firmness": Ibid.

117 "Now she lies": PH, p. 353.

117 "I don't want to die yet": Viscount Esher, Vol. I, p. 282.

117 "to the doleful sound": Leslie, *The Film of Memory*, p. 162.

118 ". . . a very small coffin": Ibid.

118 "The procession": Ibid.

118 "London was plunged in fog": Ibid.

Chapter 9

123 "We are to be called": PH, p. 354.

123 "I believe this is": Ibid.

124 "The Sanctity of the Throne": Viscount Esher, Vol. I, p. 280.

126 "I was tired": Ibid., p. 288.

126 "a smart difference of opinion": Ibid., p. 285.

126 "in tearing": Ibid., p. 289.

127 "some of them": Hibbert, *The Court at Windsor*, footnote 240.

128 "I do not know": St. Aubyn, *Edward VII*, p. 140.

128 "The King plays bridge": Viscount Esher, Vol. I, p. 291.

128 "The oak dining room": Ibid., p. 291.

129 "I regret": Ibid., p. 292.

130 "I sent a list of queries": Ibid., p. 279.

130 "I know better than all": Battiscombe, p. 219.

130 "The opening of ": Viscount Esher, Vol. I, p. 284.

131 "Saw the King again": Ibid., p. 297.

131 "uncontested arbiter": Duke of Windsor, *A Family Album*, p. 35.

131 "Stiff as a breast-plate": Ibid., p. 38.

132 "Queen Alexandra": Ibid., p. 39.

133 "one could see handkerchiefs": Ibid., p. 40.

133 "I detest the sea": PH, p. 366.

134 "lest she spoil": Duke of Windsor, *A King's Story*, p. 17.

134 "My darling Mama and Papa": Gore, *George V*, p. 164.

134 "My dearest little Bertie": Ibid.

135 "the only thing": Battiscombe, p. 241.

135 "little David caught": Ibid.

135 "You must not kill him": Ibid., p. 240

136 "to assume": PH, p. 368.

136 "the proper Royal": Ibid.

136 "I could never have": PH, p. 369.

137 "the drastically altered": Duke of Windsor, *A King's Story*, p. 18.

137 "surrounded by pleasure": Harry Price, p. 27.

137 "simply deafening": Ibid.

138 "May and I went": RA, George V's Journal, January 16, 1902.

138 "the Windsor climate": Ibid.

139 "The feminine": Duke of Windsor, *A King's Story*, p. 18.

139 "I hope your kilts": Ibid., p. 24.

139 "Well, soon I": Gore, *George V*, p. 184.

140 "comforted by the fact": Ibid.

140 "formally almost coldly": Lady Airlie, p. 102.

140 "Dearest, dearest": Ibid.

141 "Money was the passport": Ibid., p. 194.

Chapter 10

143 "Why": Viscount Esher; Vol. I, p. 330.

143 "I think he": Ibid., p. 331.

143 "I have never felt": Lady Lygon to Lady Ampthill, June 27, 1902.

144 "Oh I do pray": PH, p. 372.

144 "smoking a cigar": Gore, *George V*, p. 180.

144 "One of Prince Edward's": Viscount Esher, Vol. I, p. 345.

144 "I don't think": Ibid.

145 "One source": Ibid., p. 346.

145 "She is a funny": Ibid., p. 346.

145 "He had the Victorian's":
Duke of Windsor, *A King's
Story*, p. 28.
145 "an almost fanatical": Ibid.
145 "railroad precision": Ibid.
146 "His Royal Highness": Ibid.
146 "the seat of paternal": Ibid.
146 "a royal command": Duke of
Windsor, *A Family Album*, p. 24.
146 "had difficulty enough":
Wheeler-Bennett, p. 27.
147 "On this being reported":
Ibid., p. 29 (footnote).
147 "I must always remember":
Lady Airlie, p. 112.
150 "Very good reception": PH,
p. 372.
150 "My Princess May": Lady
Lygon to Lady Ampthill,
August 14, 1902.
150 "all up the front": Ibid.

Chapter 11
152 "Monarchy": Harold
Nicolson, *George VI*, p. 62.
153 "A family on the throne":
Burke's Peerage, p. 5455.
153 "the home is revered": Ibid.
153 "pool without a ripple": Ibid.
154 "had found the": Brent, p.
233.
154 "let down": Ibid.
155 "kind, deep": Keppel, p. 23.
155 "a fascinating game": Ibid.
155 "Then, bets": Ibid.
155 "embossed with": Ibid.
155 "In my life": Ibid.
156 "quite unmoved": Princess
Marie Louise, p. 173.
156 "that to wear it": Ibid.
156 "absolutely unruffled": Ibid.,
p. 174.
156 "I was horrified hearing":
Battiscombe, p. 253.
157 "It is queer": Viscount Esher,
Vol. I, p. 373.

157 "The house looked lovely":
RA, Queen Mary's Diary, May
10, 1903.
157 "Motherdear": Ibid.
158 "rang through the": Lady
Airlie, p. 107.
158 "Her Majesty says": Ibid.
158 "How can I tell the King":
Ibid.
158 "used to talk": Ibid.
158 "But Mama doesn't": Ibid., p.
109.
159 "for an Imperial": Morris, p.
146.
160 "Much as I love him": PA, p.
124.
160 "Don't worry about that":
Ibid.
160 "from boyhood": Ibid., p.
128.
161 "My goodness!": Gore, *George
V*, p. 82.
161 "Their ample figures": PH, p.
382.
162 "a swift jab": Ibid.
162 "jumpy": Ibid., p. 392.
162 "Of course it is a": RA,
George V, CC 51 39.
163 "The pleasure I": RA, Grand
Duchess of
Mecklenburg-Strelitz to
Princess of Wales, January 12,
1905.
163 "A charming man": Gore,
George V, p. 194.
164 "freshly scrubbed": Duke of
Windsor, *A King's Story*, p. 26.
164 "where he would remain":
Ibid.
164 "Old Black Joe": Ibid.
166 "was Dickens in a": Ibid., p.
52.
166 "scores of": Ibid.
166 "and as the": Ibid.
167 "who would": Ibid., p. 54.
167 "I really believe": PH, p. 390.

479

Chapter 12

169 "Fancy you 'Miss May' ": RA, QA to Princess of Wales, December 29, 1905.

169 "Lovely India,": PH, p. 396.

170 "coddled by": Collins and Lapierre, p. 26.

170 "Everyone with": Ibid.

171 "In all the papers": PH, p. 396

171 "Your dresses": Ibid.

171 "out of his time": Morris, p. 114.

171 "with a respect": Ibid.

172 "regarded the Indians": Ibid., p. 112.

172 "a little bundle": Arthur, George V, p. 87.

172 "I have been reading": Harold Nicolson, George V, pp. 86–87.

173 "Dear David": Battiscombe, p. 24.

173 "I do envy you": Ibid., p. 260.

173 "I am glad": Ibid., p. 261.

173 "I must say": Harold Nicolson, George V, p. 88.

173 "No doubt": Ibid.

174 "convinced that": Ibid.

175 "in a dream": PH, p. 398.

175 "The Maharani": Ibid.

175 "We are now staying": Ibid.

175 "48 massed bands": Ibid.

175 "We steamed away": Ibid.

175 "I thank you": Frankland, p. 9.

176 "Darling Harry": Ibid.

176 "very cold and stiff": Donaldson, p. 27.

176 "Come in": Saunders, p. 18.

176 "David ought to have": Harold Nicolson, George V, p. 31.

176 "The two boys": Ibid.

177 "So Ena": PH, p. 401.

177 "swot up": Ibid.

177 "disturbing influence": Duke of Windsor, A King's Story, p. 42.

178 "with an agonising problem": Ibid.

178 "with painful care": Ibid.

178 "Like little wantan": Shakespeare, Henry VIII.

179 "the common touch": PH, p. 402.

179 "Did you see": Ibid.

179 "What can I say": Debrett's Foreign Royalties, p. 88.

180 "to refresh ourselves": PH, p. 404.

180 "through ornamental gardens": Ibid.

180 "like a collossus": Ibid.

181 "The service in the church": Gore, p. 211.

181 "Just before our carriage": Ibid.

182 "I saw a man": Ibid., p. 212.

182 "not easy after the": Harold Nicolson, George V, p. 95.

182 "We can only thank": PH, p. 406.

183 "Very hot affair", Harold Nicolson, George V, p. 96.

183 "My birthday": Gore, p. 213.

183 "So Maud is sitting": PH, p. 407.

184 "old family": Viscount Esher, Vol. II, p. 139.

Chapter 13

185 "walked off": Ibid., p. 53.

186 "Here Sir": Duke of Windsor, A King's Story, p. 51.

186 "two hundred shoulders": Tschumi, p. 45.

187 "la Bonne cuisine": Ibid.

187 "a bonfire blaze": Duke of Windsor, A King's Story, p. 48.

188 "an anxious eye": Ibid.

189 "The Navy will": Ibid.
189 "I am appalled": Ibid.
189 "The British constitutional": Ibid.
191 "to a hard iron bed": Ibid.
191 "blaring bugle": Ibid.
191 "he's too puny": Ibid.
191 "You are the Prince": Ibid., p. 63.
191 "A moment later": Ibid.
192 "alternately going round": Ibid.
192 "six official cuts": Ibid.
192 "with true Irish sympathy": Ibid.
193 "a crude reminder of": Ibid.
193 "fortunately": Ibid.
193 "the next morning Finch": Ibid.
193 "You must": Wheeler-Bennett, p. 32.
193 "he was the most shy": Ibid., p. 33.
194 "where he seems to have": Ibid.
194 "grit and never-say-I'm": Ibid.
195 "wore such a sad": Duke of Windsor, *A King's Story*, p. 69.
195 "You must remember": Frankland, p. 10.
195 "thundery weather": Ibid.
196 "Now that you are": Ibid.
196 "something of a handful": Ibid.
196 "academically, musically": Ibid.
197 "She will indeed": PH, p. 417.

Chapter 14
198 "mere signing machine": Hibbert, *The Court of St. James's*, p. 54.
198 "few prerogatives": Ibid.
199 "completely left in the dark": Ibid.
199 "that the poor": St. Aubyn, *Edward VII*, p. 415.
199 "the preaching of": Ibid.
199 "in the most vigourous": Ibid.
199 "perfectly disgraceful": Ibid.
199 "implacable warfare": *Times*, April 30, 1909.
199 "primarily a campaign": St. Aubyn, *Edward VII*, p. 417.
200 "both embarrassing": Battiscombe, p. 268.
200 "leave that horrid": Ibid.
200 "sat sad-eyed": St. Aubyn, *Edward VII*, p. 419.
201 "so unlike [the King]": Ibid.
201 "I am Caesar": Stamper, p. 72.
201 "Caesar was neither": Ibid.
201 "Caesar! Come here!": Ibid.
201 "You naughty": Ibid.
202 "the very essence": St. Aubyn, *Edward VII*, pp. 380–381.
202 "curious air": Sitwell, p. 43.
202 "because kings and queens": Ibid.
203 "hunched . . . grey": St. Aubyn, *Edward VII*, p. 473.
203 "I shall work to the end": Ibid.
204 "At 11:45": Harold Nicolson, *George V*, p. 105.
204 "darling May": Ibid.
204 "Across the Mall": Duke of Windsor, *A King's Story*, p. 73.
205 "grew with fatigue": Ibid.
205 "What did you say?": Ibid.
205 "May and I watched": Harold Nicolson, *George V*, p. 125.
205 "I went up" (footnote): J. A. Spender and Cyril Asquith, *The Life of H. H. Asquith*, p. 296.
205 "that the High": *Times*, May 10, 1910.

206 "George dislikes": RA, Queen Mary to Grand Duchess Augusta.

206 "The Queen sent for me": Viscount Esher, Vol. III, May 10, 1910, p. 1.

207 "the blinds were down": Ponsonby, p. 380.

207 "I debated": Ibid.

208 "They want to take him": Battiscombe, p. 273.

208 "stood rigidly": Ibid.

208 "to show a foreign relative": Ibid.

208 "A glorious service": Ibid.

208 "They took him": Ibid.

209 "I am now very tired": PH, p. 422.

209 "The odd part": Ibid., p. 423.

210 "All the long": Tuchman, *Guns of August*, p. 21.

210 "a very nice boy": Ibid., p. 16.

211 "And so my Georgie": Harold Nicolson, *George V*, p. 42.

212 "cast earth upon the coffin": Battiscombe, p. 273.

213 "by the Grace of": Ibid.

213 "a mere child": Viscount Esher, Vol. III, June 4, 1910, p. 7.

213 "beyond the time": Ibid.

213 "subtle respect": Duke of Windsor, *A King's Story*, p. 75.

214 "I am so awfully sorry": Frankland, p. 18.

215 "I saw Francis Knollys": Viscount Esher, Vol. III, May 31, 1910, p. 5.

215 "I have known all": Viscount Esher, Vol II, p. 461.

215 "abiding sense of his regal": *Times*, May 24, 1910.

216 "The whole task": PH, p. 423.

216 "There'll be no wo'ar": *Pelissier's Follies of 1909.*

216 "kept things together": *Times*, May 24, 1910.

Chapter 15

219 "Life is too fatiguing": PH, p. 424.

221 "for we were so very": Ibid.

221 "broke down and wept": Ibid.

221 "lies with that of": Ibid.

222 "It is altogether": Viscount Esher, Vol. III, August 21, 1910, p. 15.

222 "running round": Ibid.

222 "I went yesterday": Ibid., p. 16.

222 "We had a drive": Ibid., p. 17.

222 "As far as": Colville, p. 108 (footnote).

222 "I believe the right": Duke of Windsor's papers, Queen Mary to Edward Prince of Wales, June 11, 1910.

223 "unwinning": Ibid.

223 "Not a sign of": Ibid.

223 "the King sat": Ibid.

223 "a week of intimate talk": Ibid.

223 "no bed of roses": RA, Queen Mary to Grand Duchess Augusta, August 10, 1910.

223 "so to speak": PH, p. 423.

224 "Her passion": Ibid.

224 "The fact": Ibid.

224 "she would no longer": Ibid., p. 424.

224 "I used to be rather": Ibid.

225 "serious jewels to display": PH, p. 425.

225 "to grow old": PH, p. 431.

226 "Willy dear": Battiscombe, p. 274.

226 "It is rather strange": RA, George V, CC 8121.

226 "I am sure": RA, George V, CC 466.

227 "I so understand": RA, Grand Duchess Augusta to Queen Mary, December 15, 1910.

228 "there was considerable": Wheeler-Bennett, p. 46.

228 "I am so afraid": Ibid.

229 "Well at last": PH, p. 433.

229 "I feel more": Ibid.

229 "I really am beginning": Ibid., March 5, 1911.

229 "I expect you will": RA, George V, AA 3726, February 26, 1911.

230 "Our dear old rooms": RA, Queen Alexandra to Queen Mary, February 27, 1911.

231 "Will be a great ordeal": PH, p. 433.

231 "a pitiable figure": Battiscombe, p. 274.

231 "hopeless & helpless": Ibid.

231 "My Darling May": RA, Queen Alexandra to Queen Mary, February 27, 1911 (footnote).

232 "Just as well": Battiscombe, p. 274

232 "Oh! That we have been": PH, p. 438.

232 "May God bless": PH, p. 441.

232 "Eddy should be King": Ibid.

Chapter 16

233 "had ceased to be": Harold Nicolson, *George V*, p. 108.

233 "profoundly shaken": Ibid.

234 "After a long talk": Ibid., p. 138.

235 "a new period: Tuchman, *The Proud Tower*, p. 461.

235 "It is so funny": Princess Marie Louise, p. 177.

235 "Yes, of course": Ibid.

236 "absolutely did not": Harold Nicolson, *George V*, p. 186.

236 "I asked him": Ibid., p. 185.

236 "a fiasco for": Winston Churchill, *The World Crisis*, Vol. I, p. 114.

236 "deep and violent passions": Ibid.

237 "After Papa & Mama": Duke of Windsor, *A King's Story*, p. 79.

238 "each with its vision": *Independent*, Vol. 71, July 13, 1911.

238 "multitudinously crowded": Ibid.

238 "bustling and brilliant": Ibid.

240 "double dazzling": Ibid.

241 "most beautiful": RA, George V, Diary, June 22, 1911.

241 "To me, who": Ibid.

241 "by the powerful and mild": *Times*, June 22, 1911.

242 "All the relatives": Ibid.

242 "I, Edward, Prince of Wales": Ibid.

242 "It reminded me so much": RA, Queen Mary to Grand Duchess Augusta, June 25, 1911.

242 "Then Mama was crowned": Duke of Windsor, *A King's Story*, p. 258a.

242 "We left Westminster Abbey": Ibid., 263a.

243 "mellifluously proclaiming": Ibid., p. 81.

243 "Half-fainting": Ibid.

243 "a painful discovery": Ibid.

Chapter 17

246 "more English, and less": *Harper's Magazine*, July 1911.

246 "a boisterously British": Ibid.

246 "not because he likes it": Ponsonby, p. 392.
247 "It is impossible": Harold Nicolson, *George V*, p. 155.
247 "What a remarkable year": Tuchman, *The Proud Tower*, p. 47.
247 "I am convinced": Harold Nicolson, *George V*, p. 167.
248 "The cost of such a proceeding": Ibid.
248 "not without a certain amount": Ibid., p. 168.
249 "unfitting for a ceremony": Ibid.
249 "wearing his crown": Ibid.
249 "an irresistible temptation": Ibid., p. 169.
250 "I shall never": PH, p. 452.
250 "mushroom bank": Ibid.
251 "vivid pink": Ibid., p. 457.
251 "It was a": Queen Mary to Grand Duchess Augusta, September 8, 1911.
251 "there were crowds": Harold Nicolson, *George V*, p. 170.
252 "a large square": *Our King and Queen*, Vol. II, p. 504.
252 "to suppose that": Ibid., p. 505.
252 "increasing solicitude": PH, p. 458.
252 "The jewel": Ibid.
253 "in a regular": Viscount Esher, Vol. III, p. 81.
253 "was the most wonderful": PH, p. 459.
254 "Mama's emeralds": Ibid., p. 460.
254 "Each year": RA, George V, CC 4–86.
254 "very proud": Ibid.
255 "too European": PH, p. 461.
255 "I simply couldn't help": Ibid., p. 462.
255 "What joy that there": Ibid.

255 "Characteristically feminine": Colville, p. 111.

Chapter 18
256 "very much to heart": PH, p. 466.
256 "If only one": RA, Queen Mary to Grand Duchess Augusta, March 20, 1912.
257 "a revelation": PH, p. 472.
257 "I think you": Ibid.
257 "You scold me": RA, George V, CC 8, 129.
257 "I quite understand": RA, George V, CC 474.
257 "Those horrid": RA, Queen Mary to Grand Duchess Augusta, February 21, 1913.
257 "There seems no end": Ibid., March 13, 1913.
257 "Can these females": PH, p. 468.
258 "in quite the": Duke of Windsor, *A King's Story*, p. 82.
258 "quite an old lady": Ibid., p. 84.
258 "with his white beard": Ibid., p. 86.
259 "intimidating old lady": Sitwell, p. 42.
259 "Go way": Ibid.
259 "That is too": Ibid.
259 "I love shooting": Duke of Windsor, *A King's Story*, p. 87.
259 "A Father's Advice": Ibid.
260 "resolved to resist": Gore, *George V*, p. 270.
260 "I should come": PH, p. 476.
260 "Yes!": RA, Grand Duchess Augusta to Queen Mary, July 10, 1912.
260 "Aunt is wonderful": RA, George V, CC 8, 151, 152.
261 "Queen and yet May": PH, p. 478.
261 "Next year!": Ibid.

261 "God grant": Ibid.
262 "royal mob": Ibid., p. 480.
262 "or living": Ibid.
262 "I had some talk": Ponsonby, p. 416.
263 "The Emperor": Ibid.
263 "more like a motor-car": Ibid.
263 "A lady": PH, p. 481.
264 "King George": Harold Nicolson, *George V*, p. 209.
264 ". . . it behooves us": Ibid., p. 228.
264 "How I hate": PH, p. 483.
264 "the lowest": Wheeler-Bennett, p. 70.
265 "My 18th birthday": Ibid.
265 "a continual battle": Ibid., p. 66.
265 "his ultimate": Ibid.
266 "a bloody tyrant": Ibid., p. 67.
266 "We were six": Duke of Windsor, *A King's Story*, p. 88.
266 "was in his element": Ibid.
267 "Of course I wanted": PH, p. 483.
268 "We are ready", Tuchman, *Guns of August*, p. 44.
268 "a venture": PH, p. 484.
268 "a reassuring symbol": Ibid.
268 "milling round": Ibid.

Chapter 19
270 "to walk": Massie, p. 242.
271 "Not that way, you fool!": Ibid., p. 243.
271 "Sophie!": Ibid.
271 "It is nothing": Ibid.
271 "Terrible shock": Gore, *George V*, p. 287.
271 "match of fate", Ibid.
271 "The horrible tragedy": PH, p. 486.
271 "Austria has": Ibid.
271 "God grant we may": Ibid.
272 Kaiser Wilhelm's telegram: Massie, p. 255.

272 "to try and avoid": Ibid., p. 256.
272 "Where will it end?", Gore, *George V*, p. 289.
272 "Foreign telegrams": Ibid.
273 "Everything tends": Pelling, PB, p. 177.
273 "demobilise": Tuchman, *Guns of August*, p. 91 (PB).
273 "the Kaiser": Lloyd George, Vol. II, p. 643.
273 "I got up": Gore, *George V*, p. 290.
273 "I cannot help": Arthur, *George V*, p. 295.
274 "Germans are quite hopeful": Ibid.
274 "Saw Sir Edward Grey": Gore, *George V*, p. 290.
274 "We issued orders": Ibid.
274 "We must prove," Arthur, *George V*, p. 296.
275 "collecting, dispersing": Duke of Windsor, *A King's Story*, p. 109.
275 "friendly, patient": Ibid.
276 "A Privy Council": Ibid.
276 "I held a Council": Gore, *George V*, p. 289.
276 "Looking into some": Viscount Esher, Vol. III, p. 176.
277 "the portcullis": Tuchman, *Guns of August*, p. 188 (PB).
277 "line after line": *Times History of the War*, Vol. I, p. 336.
277 "200 splendid men": Ponsonby, p. 431.
277 "a pygmy": Duke of Windsor, *A King's Story*, p. 111.
278 "What does it matter": Ibid.
278 "If I were sure": Ibid.
278 "a good weight!": Ibid., p. 112.
278 "the British Expeditionary": Ibid.

278 "I shan't have a friend": Ibid.
279 "open the way": *New York Times*, August 5, 1914.
279 "as a sort of picnic": Viscount Esher, Vol. III, p. 180.
279 "Very few people": Lady Airlie, p. 132.
279 "Royal salute": Ibid.
281 "Bacon for five": Ibid.
281 "Queen Mary": Ibid.
282 "hundreds and thousands": Battiscombe, p. 293.
282 "I like a lot": Ibid.
282 "If I get into debt": Ibid.

Chapter 20
284 "devotion and warm hearted": Duke of Windsor, *A King's Story*, p. 110.
284 "the Royal Family": Ibid.
284 "this fine woman": Ibid.
285 "finest and most able": Ibid.
285 "in his tired, lined": PH, p. 497.
285 "dull despair": Ibid.
286 "Please let me": Battiscombe, p. 284.
287 "bitterly resented": Ibid.
287 "and ran the steam": Wheeler-Bennett, pp. 94–95.
287 "We opened fire": Ibid.
288 "At the commencement": Ibid.
288 "The hands behaved": Ibid.
288 "When I was on top": Ibid., p. 97.
288 "rendezvous with history": Duke of Windsor, *A King's Story*, p. 119.
288 "being kept": Ibid.
288 "It moved and": Ibid.
289 "Oh to be fighting": Ibid., p. 124.
289 "firm neutrality": Lloyd George, Vol. II, p. 657.

289 "trained to hatred": Ibid., p. 660.
289 "highly respected, diligent": Ibid.
290 "The feeling in America": A. Cooper, p. 51.
290 "nearly a thousand men": Pelling, p. 221 (PB).
290 "ever-increasing demand": Harold Nicolson, *George V*, pp. 269–270.
290 "wearing a very light": A. Cooper, p. 54.
290 "[looking] ominous": Ibid.
290 "[looking] like an officer": Ibid.
291 "A most important": Ponsonby, p. 443.
291 "the Prince of Wales": Ibid.
292 "the President and M. Millirand": Ibid., p. 446.
293 "untold pain": Ibid., p. 447.
293 "the enemy's aeroplanes": Ibid.
293 "You can tell French": Ibid., p. 452.
293 "You can't think": PH, p. 501.
294 ". . . my boys are": Gore, *George V*, p. 298.
294 "Nicky must have": Battiscombe, p. 291.
294 "It is the shallow": Winston Churchill, *World Crisis*, pp. 95–97.
296 "His Majesty's": Massie, p. 439.
296 "[We] inquired": Ibid.
297 "One of the most": Lady Airlie, pp. 136–137.
298 "were old and grimy": Ibid.
298 "a vast stretch": Ibid., pp. 138–139.
298 "We climbed over a mound": Ibid.

298 "He kept us out of the War":
Ibid.

299 "elicit from the allies":
Harold Nicolson, *George V*, p.
296.

299 "America would enter": Ibid.

299 "a sufficient number": Ibid.

299 "the sundered provinces":
Ibid.

300 "The American people":
Times, April 7, 1917.

300 "the time has come": Ibid.,
April 21, 1917.

300 "There are some who":
Harold Nicolson, *George V*, p.
308.

300 "alien and uninspiring": Ibid.

300 "I may be uninspiring": Ibid.

Chapter 21

301 "started and grew pale":
Harold Nicolson, *George V*, p.
309.

302 "unsuitably comic": Longford,
The Royal House of Windsor, p.
21.

302 "as English": Ibid.

303 "going to the theatre": Ibid.,
p. 23.

304 "The only person": Charles
Hardinge, p. 219.

304 "exhausted and": Ibid.

304 "the military ardour": Lloyd
George, Vol. V, p. 2448.

305 "at the earliest": Ibid.

305 "only a comparatively small":
Ibid.

305 "Not very good news": PH, p.
508.

305 ". . . I shall never": Ibid.

305 "So far": Lady Cynthia
Asquith, *Diaries, 1914–18*, p.
416.

306 "Saw the Prince": Ibid., p.
421.

306 "fairly full": Viscount Esher,
Vol. IV, p. 183.

306 "thronged": Ibid.

306 "pompous than usual": Ibid.

306 "The boy looked": Ibid.

306 "Amid this world-changing":
Ibid.

306 "a wooden body": Lady
Cynthia Asquith, *Diaries,
1914–18*, p. 393.

307 "going round a hospital":
Ibid., p. 322.

307 "King George, yes,": Ibid.

307 "laughed together": Lady
Airlie, p. 128.

309 "Oh George": Princess Marie
Louise, p. 186.

309 "Yes; but it": Ibid.

309 "It's too horrible": PH, p.
507.

309 "Yurovsky ordered three":
Massie, p. 49.

311 "the distant drifting": Harold
Nicolson, *George V*, p. 324.

311 "triumphant hilarity": Ibid.

312 "increasingly to": Duke of
Windsor, *A King's Story*, p.
126.

312 "Dearest Papa": Ibid.

313 "Some day there": PI.

313 "indescribably intense":
Charles Hardinge, p. 229.

314 "A day full": PH, p. 509.

314 "One will at last": Lady
Cynthia Asquith, p. 480.

314 "It has all been": PH,
p. 515.

315 "no stone": Wheeler-Bennett,
p. 159.

315 "I think David": PH, p. 515.

315 "I shall never forget": Duke
of Windsor, *A King's Story*, p.
128.

315 "blood-stained shreds": Ibid.

Chapter 22

317 "At 5.30": PH, p. 511.

317 ". . . as his malady was": Ibid.

318 "an old lady": Nichols, p. 235.

318 "mummied thing": Lawrence, *The Mint*, p. 221.

318 "The ghosts of all": Ibid.

318 "the little graces": Ibid.

318 "Her bony fingers": Ibid.

318 "She does not": Nichols, p. 235.

318 "roses flaming": Ibid.

319 "dismal bloodhound": Jenkins, p. 54.

319 "Mama, I must": Lady Airlie, p. 165.

320 "I don't know": Ibid.

320 "Hats off": Jenkins, p. 53.

320 "The war has made it": Duke of Windsor, *A King's Story*, p. 134.

320 "The idea that": Ibid.

321 "The Monarchy must": Ibid.

321 "Be like Mrs. Keppel": Donaldson, p. 73.

321 "madly, passionately": Ibid.

322 "A Room with a View": (verse), Noël Coward.

322 "and assuming the": Duke of Windsor, *A King's Story*, p. 138.

323 "pretty little fluff": Donaldson, p. 75.

324 "Don't you want": Ibid.

324 "I don't know why": Ibid.

325 "Mary's wedding": PH, p. 519.

325 "the one girl": Cathcart, *The Queen Mother Herself*, p. 67.

326 "daily growing more anxious" Lloyd George, Vol I, p. 34.

326 "begets riot": Ibid.

326 "the Irish Free State": Ibid.

326 "The wonderful day": Ibid.

327 "I went up": Harold Nicolson, *George V* p. 366.

327 "night after night": PH, p. 521.

327 "alone together": Ibid.

327 "over the port wine": Ibid.

327 "never sat more than": Duke of Windsor, *A King's Story*, p. 187.

328 "[the Queen] loved them": Ibid.

328 "with all speed": Lady Airlie, p. 129.

329 "a radical movement": Morris, p. 281.

329 "tragic miscalculation": Ibid.

330 "as a Liberal": *Times*, October 17, 1922.

330 "to cooperate freely": Ibid.

330 "As a matter of fact": PH, p. 523.

330 "The Queen stayed in bed": Ibid.

Chapter 23

332 "I must write": Wheeler-Bennett, p. 140.

332 "Dearest Bertie": Ibid.

333 "I venture to trouble": Ibid., p. 147.

334 "Perturbed and abstracted": Cathcart, p. 71.

334 "that winter": Ibid.

336 "All Right Bertie": Wheeler-Bennett, p. 150.

336 ". . . dream which has at last": Lady Airlie, p. 168.

336 "one wedding": *Times*, April 27, 1923.

336 "whilst the Princes of Wales": Ibid.

336 "So unromantic": Wheeler-Bennett, p. 154.

337 "I miss you very much": Ibid.

337 "little Duchess": Jenkins, p. 55.

337 "I've done with Communism!": Ibid.

337 "It is hard to see": PH, p. 537.
337 "I feel completely": Ibid.
338 "Went to tea": Ibid., p. 538.
338 "country Sunday best": Colville, p. 113.
338 "their attitude to each": Ibid.
339 "everlasting pain": Battiscombe, p. 299.
339 "your poor old blind": Ibid.
339 "May God grant him": Ibid.
339 "beloved Bertie . . . were walking": Ibid.
339 "Did you know": Ibid., p. 301.
339 "Think of me": Ibid., p. 302.
339 "as a figure of": Colville, p. 116.
341 "You never saw": PH, p. 540.
341 "I am delighted": Ibid., p. 541.
341 ". . . I am glad": Ibid.
341 "The pictures want": Ibid.
341 "All the rooms": Ibid.
342 "would enable future": Ibid., p. 532.
343 "in a very": Princess Marie Louise, p. 201.
344 "Charlotte had the freedom": Colville, p. 120.
344 ". . . spent a morning": Lady Airlie, p. 178.
345 "a great scurrying": Ibid.
345 "business as usual": Ibid.
345 "At 2.30": Wheeler-Bennett, p. 209.
345 "Of course poor baby": Ibid.

Chapter 24
346 "but a case of": Harold Nicolson, *George V*, p. 431.
347 "There is a": Duke of Windsor, *A King's Story*, p. 225.
347 "You will find": Ibid.
347 "[The Prince of Wales]": Donaldson, p. 148.

348 "After": PH, p. 358.
350 "This is unfair": Flanner, *London Was Yesterday*, p. 22.
350 "a new design of woollen": Ibid.
351 "The King and Queen": Ibid., p. 17.
352 "gusseted, gored": Ibid., p. 28.
352 "worn high on her head": Ibid., p. 32.
352 "dresses in the height": Ibid.
352 "She's the spit": Ibid.
353 "What an airy room": Michael McDonagh, *Illustrated London News*, May 4, 1935, p. 717.
353 "It really looks": Ibid.
354 "a row of tall": Flanner, *London Was Yesterday*, p. 11.
354 "a nice cut off": Ibid., p. 24.
354 "Now George": Ibid.
354 "one of the best": Ibid., p. 22.
356 "I will not be left": PH, p. 550.

Chapter 25
358 "had loved him more": Donaldson, p. 110.
358 "Anything to please": Ibid.
359 "What could you possibly": Duke of Windsor, *A King's Story*, p. 237.
359 "I want to": Lady Airlie, p. 207 (footnote).
359 "selected because of": Duke of Windsor, *A King's Story*, p. 238.
360 "from the top of": Ibid.
360 "I arrived at York House": Vanderbilt, p. 296.
361 "A little shy": Ibid.
362 "It was our enchanted": Ibid.
363 "Oh, Thelma, the little man": Ibid.
364 "classically separated": Flanner, *London Was Yesterday*, p. 33.

365 "We don't want to be":
Vanderbilt, p. 298.
365 "I told you": Ibid.
366 "Darling is it": Ibid.
367 "I have something":
Donaldson, p. 170.
368 "Haven't you noticed": Ibid.,
p. 171.

Chapter 26
369 "the biggest": Flanner, London
Was Yesterday, p. 25.
370 ". . . time must be": Harold
Nicolson, George V, p. 521.
370 "dreaded the day": Ibid.
370 "fortifications were": Ibid.
370 "we must not be": Ibid.
370 "a corridor": Ibid., p. 523.
371 "Now you": Frankland, p.
117.
371 "Of course": Ibid.
372 "Mrs. Simpson": Channon, p.
30.
372 "The Yorks in a": Ibid.
373 "Twenty-five years": Silver
Jubilee Special Edition,
Illustrated London News, May 8,
1935.
374 "How can I express": Harold
Nicolson, George V, p. 525.
374 "Most moving": PH, p. 555.
374 "A never-to-be-": Harold
Nicolson, George V, p. 525.
375 "after the King": Duchess of
Windsor, p. 216.
375 "I'd no idea": Harold
Nicolson, George V, p. 525.
376 "a symbol of": Ibid., p. 526.
376 "strong benevolent": Ibid.
376 "Well, it was": Channon, p.
473.
376 "saw Alice Scott": Frankland,
p. 123.
377 "The Prince": Channon, p.
33.
377 "more American": Ibid.

377 "It doesn't look": Ibid., p. 35.
377 "alleged Nazi": Ibid.
378 "the arch-Hitler": Ibid.
380 "snuff boxes": Flanner,
London Was Yesterday,
p. 25.
380 "Don't buy a lot": Frankland,
p. 123.
380 "This is indeed": Ibid.

Chapter 27
382 "Now all the": Duke of
Windsor, A King's Story, p.
261.
382 "After I am dead": Middlemas
and Barnes, p. 976.
383 "I pray to God": Lady Airlie,
p. 197.
384 "complete understanding":
Donaldson, p. 206.
384 "too one-sided": Ibid.
384 "He fully understood": Ibid.
384 "a deputation": Times, June
12, 1935.
385 "warm sympathy": Ibid., p.
210.
385 "deep-rooted and strong":
Donaldson, p. 207.
385 "must never speak": Ibid.
386 "My brothers": Duke of
Windsor, A King's Story, p.
262.
386 "I think you": Ibid., p. 263.
387 "It will do us": Ibid., p. 264.
388 "G. about the":
Pope-Hennessy, p. 561.
389 "a sad quiet": Ibid.
389 "My children were": Ibid.
390 "God save the King": Duke of
Windsor, A King's Story, p.
265.
390 "I could not": Ibid.
391 "Such a sad day": PH, p. 561.
391 ". . . solemn, grave, sad":
Channon, p. 54.
391 "a fleeting": Ibid.

392 "swept by conflicting": Duke of Windsor, *A King's Story*, p. 267.

392 "a large black car": Channon, p. 54.

392 "a most terrible omen": Harold Nicolson, *Diaries, 1930–1939*, p. 241.

392 "The sound of": Lindbergh, p. 14.

394 "boyish, sad": Channon, p. 55.

394 "First we fetched": PH, p. 562.

394 "incredibly magnificent": Channon, p. 57.

394 "popped up like": Lindbergh, p. 15.

394 "silence": Ibid.

394 "Men jumped": Ibid.

394 "much, much more": Ibid.

395 "another drive": PH, p. 562.

395 "We left him": Ibid., p. 561.

395 "I had a long talk": Ibid., p. 562.

395 "How glad I am": Lady Airlie, p. 207.

Chapter 28

399 "Your sons": Ibid., p. 198.

399 "Yes, one can": Ibid.

399 "He gives Mrs. Simpson": Ibid., p. 200.

400 "Has there been": Ibid.

400 "It was a terrible": Ibid., p. 196.

400 "I took leave": PH, p. 567.

400 "I fear I was": Ibid.

401 "keep walking with": Lacey, p. 121 (PB).

401 "just as important": Ibid.

402 "a lady living": Crawford, p. 109.

403 "her hand on his": Donaldson, p. 227.

403 "wondered how much": Duke of Windsor, *A King's Story*, p. 313.

403 "Did you enjoy": Ibid.

404 "I read in": p. 313.

405 "J.H.": Harold Nicolson, *Diaries, 1930–1939*, p. 246.

406 "seemed endless": Duke of Windsor, *A King's Story*, p. 334.

406 "two husbands living": PH, p. 574.

407 "My mother had": Duke of Windsor, *A King's Story*, p. 334.

407 "something sacred": Ibid.

407 "Please won't you": Ibid.

407 "That is quite": Ibid.

407 "I hope, sir": Ibid.

407 "was not a question": Ibid.

408 "Well, Mr. Baldwin!": PH, p. 557.

408 "hypnotised by": Cooke, p. 75 (PB).

409 "rhetorical abstraction": Ibid.

409 "Really!": PH, p. 557.

409 "like a wave": Duke of Windsor, *A King's Story*, p. 365.

410 "certainly not alone": Ibid.

410 "both remain on the": Donaldson, p. 244.

410 "an ideal figure": Lord Tweedsmuir, Buchan Papers, Queens University Archives.

410 "the Sovereign": Donaldson, p. 263.

411 ". . . the King's one": Dugdale, *Baffy*, p. 34.

411 "[On December 3]": Wheeler-Bennett, p. 285.

413 "A dinner": Ibid., p. 286.

413 "I could see": Ibid.

413 "Bertie arrived": PH, p. 577.

414 "Don't you think": Ibid., p. 580.

414 "dreadful good bye": RA, Queen Mary's Diary, December 12, 1936.

414 "The whole thing": Ibid.
415 "Furthermore": Wheeler-Bennett, p. 288.
415 "Glad to hear": Ibid., pp. 288–289 (footnote).
415 "The person": Duke of Windsor's Papers, Queen Mary to Duke of Windsor, April 3, 1937.
415 "recognised beneath": Lady Airlie, p. 200.
415 "She loved her": Ibid., p. 201.

Chapter 29
416 "the venerable Mrs. Keppel", Flanner, London Was Yesterday, p. 12.
416 "Things were done": Ibid.
417 "except by worldly": Ibid.
417 "dry and not": Times, February 22, 1937.
417 "obedience, duty": Ibid.
417 "an inventive": Ibid.
417 "spiritual jurisdiction": Ibid.
418 "as the Coronation": Wheeler-Bennett, p. 309.
418 "would never be able": Ibid.
418 "Never have I": Sunday Chronicle, March 9, 1937.
419 "In manner and speech": Times, December 14, 1936.
419 "the unexpected": PH, p. 584.
420 "because he and": Newsweek, May 15, 1937.
420 "asked the government": Ibid.
421 "an erect and royal": Lady Airlie, p. 203.
421 "between Maud and": PH, p. 585.
421 "bowed to Mama": Wheeler-Bennett, p. 312.
421 "After the": Ibid.
422 "the most valuable": Times, March 13, 1937.

422 "I, Cosmo": Ibid.
422 "I, Henry": Ibid.
423 "receive the Crown": Ibid.
423 "like a mother": Newsweek, May 22, 1937.
423 "with a luncheon": PH, p. 506.
423 "to hold and enjoy": Wheeler-Bennett, p. 314.
423 "This is a nice": Birkenhead, p. 166.
423 "The family he is": Donaldson, p. 347.
424 "The Civil Ceremony": Ibid.
425 "Alas": PH, p. 586.
425 "help[ed] her": Ibid., p. 582.
426 "Thank God": WB, p. 283.
426 "ablaze, regal": Channon, p. 124.
426 "looking like the": Ibid., p. 133.
426 "Thank God we've still": Lady Airlie, p. 204.
426 "Oh, Mabell": Ibid.
426 "dined and slept": Channon, p. 119.
426 "That was an operetta": Ibid.
426 "It seemed strange": Lady Airlie, p. 207.
427 "Knee breeches": Ibid.
427 "offend folks in America": Ibid.
427 "A match to spark": Ibid., p. 209.
427 "moulding the German": Ibid.
427 "between the forces": Ibid.
427 "SOS messages": Channon, p. 170.
428 "a dark black": Ibid., p. 175.
428 "the PM's speech": PH, p. 591.
428 "did not discuss": Donaldson, p. 354.
428 "the Abdication did": New York Times, October 23, 1937.

429 "... I do not think": PH, p. 575.

429 "I have not": Ibid., p. 592.

429 "Poor William": PH, p. 575.

429 "been sorely conscience": Channon, p. 175.

429 "still haunted": Ibid.

Chapter 30

431 "... it": Harold Nicolson, *Diaries 1930–1939*, p. 411.

432 "He was exactly": Ibid.

433 "I have my handkerchief": PH, p. 594.

433 "I hate leaving here": Ibid. (footnote).

433 "Queen Mary climbed": Ibid., p. 595.

434 "abominably": Ibid.

434 "he had no wit": Channon, p. 463.

434 "nervous, ill-at-ease": Ibid.

434 "no vices": Ibid.

434 "almost entirely": Ibid.

434 "an affectionate": Ibid.

434 "rustled greatly": Lindbergh, p. 275.

434 "old fashioned face": Ibid.

434 "old fashioned rose": Ibid.

436 "The servants revolted": Sitwell, p. 34.

436 "Lovely morning": PH, p. 600.

436 "Lovely morning": Ibid.

437 "Aunt May": Ibid., p. 601.

437 "I long to be": Ibid., p. 599.

437 "I feel rather": Ibid.

437 "sand bags, ARP men": Ibid.

437 "From 7-til": Ibid.

437 "simply a waste": Ibid.

438 "... sounds became": Collier, p. 154.

438 "The harsh acrid": Ibid.

438 "the fine glitter": Ibid.

439 "We were both": Wheeler-Bennett, p. 468.

439 "... It was a ghastly": Ibid., p. 469.

439 "This war has drawn": Ibid., p. 467.

440 "If Goering could": Ibid., p. 469.

440 "as I told you": Ibid., p. 473.

440 "The Battle of France": Collier, p. 154.

440 "... we shall not": Ibid., p. 89.

441 "Not until": Channon, p. 191.

441 "I just sat": Donaldson, p. 370.

442 "no messenger": Ibid.

442 "no member of the": Ibid.

442 "although his": Ibid., p. 385.

443 "a great affection": Wheeler-Bennett, p. 547.

443 "Had luncheon": PH, p. 607.

443 "You had better": Colville, p. 130.

443 "What is it?": Ibid.

444 "I must go": Ibid.

444 "A charming young": PH, p. 608.

444 "I am so glad": Ibid.

444 "stripped and": Wheeler-Bennett, p. 461.

445 "We're going through": Ibid., p. 536.

Chapter 31

447 "by the flicker": Sitwell, p. 40.

447 "Only once": Ibid.

447 "her manner": Ibid.

448 "a really filthy": Ibid., p. 44.

448 "He entered": Ibid., p. 48.

448 "How very odd!": Ibid.

449 "I talked to": Wheeler-Bennett, p. 591.

449 "How could I": Ibid., p. 591–92.

449 "... a marriage may": Ibid.

450 "He is to be our": Channon, p. 286.

450 "I have never": Lacey, p. 148 (PB).

451 "I want to make":
Wheeler-Bennett, p. 605.

451 "Sir . . .": Ibid., p. 606.

452 "A change": Ibid., p. 610.

452 "Perhaps we should": Sitwell,
p. 58.

452 "As this magnificent": Ibid.,
p. 60.

453 "where the village": PH, p.
609.

454 "Mahogany": Ibid., p. 610.

454 "Vans of boxes": Sitwell, p.
61.

454 "Oh, I have": PH, p. 609.

454 "The great host":
Wheeler-Bennett, p. 626.

455 "I regret": Ibid., p. 637.

455 "You must ask": Lady Airlie,
p. 224.

455 "His face was": Ibid.

456 "so outrageously": Ibid., p.
225.

456 "The King was": Ibid.

457 "the hope was": Lacey, p. 159
(PB).

457 "still piping": Ibid.

457 "whether it be":
Wheeler-Bennett, p. 687.

457 "It is with": Times, July 10,
1947.

458 "They both came": PH, p.
615.

458 "an escape": Lady Airlie, p.
229.

458 "It was a": Ibid.

458 "Queen Mary looked": Ibid.

458 "Saw many": PH, p. 616.

Chapter 32

460 "Madam": Duchess of
Windsor, p. 356.

460 "I thought": Ibid.

461 "the natural order": Ibid., p.
288.

461 "to take one": New York Daily
News, October 8, 1966,
interview.

462 "A cheering throng": Ibid.

462 "front man": Ibid.

462 "Such a job": Ibid.

463 "He is so": Inglis, p. 55.

464 "I am getting":
Wheeler-Bennett, p. 765.

464 "I am delighted": PH, p. 616
(footnote).

465 "I never heard":
Wheeler-Bennett, p. 766
(footnote).

465 "really extraordinary": PH, p.
617.

465 "very thin": Ibid.

466 "The King?": PH, p. 619.

466 "Her old Grannie": Ibid.

467 "the Great Hall": Channon,
p. 464.

468 "As the cortege": Lady Airlie,
p. 235.

468 "Nice fine day": PH, p. 620.

468 "I am beginning": Lacey, p.
183 (PB).

468 "my interesting things": Ibid.

469 ". . . the exquisitely": Lady
Airlie, p. 237.

469 "I must go": Ibid., p. 238.

469 ". . . one must force": Ibid.

469 "I feel weary": PH, p. 622.

469 "for the glorious": Channon,
p. 472.

470 "There were cries": Ibid., p.
473.

470 "She was": Ibid.

470 ". . . all my life": PH, p. 575.

BIBLIOGRAPHY

Airlie, Mabell, Countess of, *Thatched with Gold, the Memoirs of Mabell, Countess of Airlie*. Edited and arranged by Jennifer Ellis. Hutchinson, 1962.

Alice, Princess of Great Britain, *For My Grandchildren: Some Reminiscences of Her Royal Highness Princess Alice, Countess of Athlone*. Evans Bros., 1966.

Allen, Frederick Lewis, *Since Yesterday, The Nineteen-Thirties in America September 3, 1929–September 3, 1939*. Blue Ribbon Books, 1943.

Antrim, Lady Louisa Jane Grey, *Recollections of Louisa, Countess of Antrim*. The King's Stone Press, 1937.

Aronson, Theo, *A Family of Kings: The Descendants of Christian IX of Denmark*. Cassell, 1976.

Arthur, Sir George Compton Archiband, *Queen Alexandra*. Chapman & Hall, 1934.

Arthur, Sir George, *King George V*. Jonathan Cape, 1939.

Asquith, Lady Cynthia, *The Family Life of Her Majesty Queen Elizabeth*. 1937.

Asquith, Lady Cynthia, *The Duchess of York*. Hutchinson, 1937.

Asquith, Lady Cynthia, *Diaries 1915–18*. Hutchinson, 1968.

Asquith, Herbert Henry, 1st Earl of Oxford and Asquith, *Fifty Years of British Parliament*. Cassell, 1926.

Asquith, Herbert Henry, 1st Earl of Oxford and Asquith, *Memories and Reflections, 1852–1927*. Cassell, 1928.

BIBLIOGRAPHY

Asquith, Margot, Countess of Oxford and Asquith, *An Autobiography.* T. Butterworth, 1920–22.

Asquith, Margot, Countess of Oxford and Asquith, *More Memories.* Cassell, 1933.

Asquith, Margot, Countess of Oxford and Asquith, *More or Less About Myself.* E. P. Dutton & Co., 1934.

Avon, Earl of, *Full Circle, The Memoirs of Sir Anthony Eden.* Cassell & Company Ltd., 1960.

Avon, Earl of, *The Eden Memoirs.* Cassell, 1962.

Avon, Earl of, *The Reckoning.* Cassell, 1965.

Baedeker, Karl, *London and its Environs, Handbook for Travellers.* 1923.

Bagehot, Walter, *The English Constitution.* 1949.

Baldwin, A. W., *My Father, the True Story.* Allen, 1955.

Baldwin, Monica, *An Unpublished Page of History.* 1937.

Balfour, Arthur James, 1st Earl of Balfour. *Chapters of Autobiography.* Edited by Mrs. Edgar Dugdale. Cassell, 1930.

Barrymaine, Norman, *Peter Townsend.* Peter Davies, 1958.

Battiscombe, Georgina, *Queen Alexandra.* Constable, 1969.

Beal, Erica, *Royal Cavalcade.* S. Paul & Co., 1939.

Beaton, Cecil, *Photobiography.* Odhams, 1951.

Beaton, Cecil, *The Wandering Years.* Weidenfeld & Nicolson, 1961.

Beaton, Cecil, *Memoirs of the 40's.* McGraw-Hill Book Company, 1972.

Beavan, Arthur Henry, *Marlborough House and its Occupants, Present and Past.* F. V. White & Co., 1896.

Beaverbrook, Lord, *The Abdication of King Edward VIII.* Hamish Hamilton, 1966.

Benson, Frederic Edward, *The Kaiser and the English Relations.* Longmans, Green & Co., 1936.

Berton, Pierre, *The Royal Family.* Alfred Knopf, 1954.

Bigelow, Poultney, "The Crown of King George." *The Independent,* 71: 17 August 1911.

Birkenhead, Lord, *Walter Monckton.* Weidenfeld & Nicolson, 1969.

Black, Percy, *The Mystique of Modern Monarchy.* Watts, 1953.

496

BIBLIOGRAPHY

Blunt, Wilfred Scawen, *My Diaries. Being a Personal Narrative of Events, 1888–1914.* M. Secker, 1919.

Bolitho, Hector, *Edward VIII, His Life and Reign.* Eyre and Spottiswoode, 1937.

Bolitho, Hector, *King George VI.* J. B. Lippincott Company, 1938.

Boothroyd, J. Basil, *Philip, an informal biography.* Longman, 1971.

Brent, Peter, *The Edwardians.* British Broadcasting Corporation, 1972.

Broadley, Alexander Meyrick, *The Boyhood of a Great King.* Harper & Bros., 1906.

Brook-Shepherd, Gordon, *Uncle of Europe: The Social and Diplomatic Life of Edward VII.* Collins, 1975.

Brough, James, *The Prince and the Lily.* Hodder & Stoughton, 1974.

Brough, James, *Margaret, The Tragic Princess.* G. P. Putnam's Sons, 1978.

Brown, Ivor, *Balmoral Castle, the History of a Home.* Collins, 1955.

Brust, Detective Inspector Harold, *I Guarded Kings.* Stanley Paul, 1935.

Bryan, J. III, and Murphy, Charles J. V., *The Windsor Story.* William Morrow and Company, Inc., 1979.

Bryant, Arthur, *George V.* Peter Davies Limited, 1936.

Bryant, Arthur, *A Thousand Years of British Monarchy.* Collins, 1975.

Caesar, the King's Dog, *Where's Master.* Hodder & Stoughton, 1910.

Caffrey, Kate, *Edwardian Lady, Edwardian High Society: 1910–1914.* Gorden & Cremonesi, 1979.

Cameron, James, *Yesterday's Witness.* British Broadcasting Corporation, 1979.

Cathcart, Helen, *Her Majesty.* W. H. Allen, 1962.

Cathcart, Helen, *The Queen Mother Herself.* W. H. Allen, 1979.

Chance, Michael, *Our Princesses and Their Dogs.* John Murray, 1936.

Chandes, Lord, *From Peace to War.* The Bodley Head, 1968.

Channon, Sir Henry. *Chips, The Diaries of Sir Henry Channon.* Edited by Roberts Rhodes James. Weidenfeld and Nicolson, 1967.

Churchill, Randolph S., *They Serve the Queen.* Hutchinson, 1953.

Churchill, Randolph S., *Winston S. Churchill.* Heinemann, 1966–7.

Churchill, Sir Winston Leonard Spencer, *The World Crisis.* T. Butterworth, 1923–29.

Churchill, Sir Winston Leonard Spencer, *My Early Life, A Roving Commission.* Butterworth, 1930.

BIBLIOGRAPHY

Churchill, Sir Winston S., *The Second World War*. 6 vols. T. Allen, 1948–54.

Clark, Brigadier Stanley, O.B.E., *Palace Diary*. George G. Harrap & Co. Ltd., 1958.

Collier, Richard, *1940, The World in Flames*. Hamish Hamilton Ltd., 1979.

Collins, L. and S. Lapierre, *Freedom at Midnight*. Simon and Schuster, 1975.

Colville, Lady Cynthia, *Crowded Life*. Evans Bros., 1963.

Cooke, Alistair, *Six Men*. Penguin Books Ltd., 1978.

Cooke, Kinloch, *Pss. Mary Adelaide, Dss. of Teck*. Vol. I and Vol. II. John Murray, 1980.

Cooper, A. Duff, *Old Men Forget*. Rupert Hart-Davis, 1953.

Cooper, Lady Diana, *Diana Cooper, Autobiography: The Rainbow Comes and Goes*, 1958; *The Light of Common Day*, 1959; *Trumpets from the Steep*, 1960. Rupert-Hart Davis, 1958–60.

Cordet, Helene, *Born Bewildered*. Peter Davies, 1961.

Cornwallis-West, George Frederick Myddleton, *Edwardian Hey-Days: or A Little About a Lot of Things*. Putnam, 1930.

Corwallis, Mrs. George, *The Reminiscences of Lady Randolph Churchill* (Lady Randolph [Jenny Jerome] Churchill). Edward Arnold, 1908.

Cowles, Virginia, *Edward VII and His Circle*. Hamish Hamilton, 1956.

Cowles, Virginia, *The Kaiser*. Harper & Row, 1964.

Crawford, Marion, *The Little Princesses*. Cassell, 1950.

Cresswell, Mrs. George, *Eighteen Years on the Sandringham Estate*. Temple, 1888.

Curzon, The Marchioness of Kedleston, G.B.E., *Reminiscences*. Coward-McCann, Inc., 1955.

Cust, Sir Lionel Henry, *King Edward VII and His Court: Some Reminiscences*. J. Murray, 1930.

Daisy, Princess of Pless, *Private Diaries*.

Dalton, Dr. Hugh, *The Fateful Years, 1931–45*. Frederick Muller Ltd., 1957.

Dean, John, *H.R.H. Prince Philip, Duke of Edinburgh*. Robert Hale Limited, 1968.

de Castries, Duc, *The Lives of Kings and Queens of France*. Translated by Anne Dobell. Alfred A. Knopf, 1979.

Delderfield, Eric R., ed. *Kings and Queens of England and Great Britain*. David & Charles [Holdings] Ltd., 1970.

BIBLIOGRAPHY

Dempster, Nigel, *H.R.H. The Princess Margaret, A Life Unfulfilled.* Quartet Books Limited, 1981.

Dennis, Geoffrey, *Coronation Commentary.* Heinemann, 1937.

Donaldson, Frances, *Edward VIII, The Road to Abdication.* J. B. Lippincott Company, 1974.

Drabble, Margaret, *A Writer's Britain, Landscape in Literature.* Thames and Hudson Ltd., 1979.

Driberg, Tom, *Beaverbrook, A Story in Power and Frustration.* Weidenfeld and Nicolson, 1956.

Dugdale, Blanche E., *Arthur James Balfour, First Earl of Balfour.* Hutchinson, 1936.

Dugdale, Blanche, *Baffy, The Diaries of Blanche Dugdale, 1936–37.* Vallentine, Mitchell, 1973.

Edgar, Donald, *Prince Andrew.* Arthur Barker Limited, 1980.

Edwards, William Hayden, *The Tragedy of Edward VII: a Psychological Study.* V. Gollancz Ltd., 1928.

Emden, Paul H., *Behind the Throne.* Hodder & Stoughton, 1937.

Esher, Reginald Baliol Brett, 2nd Viscount, *The Influence of King Edward and Essays on Other Subjects.* J. Murray, 1915.

Esher, Reginald Baliol Brett, 2nd Viscount, *Cloud-capp'd Towers.* J. Murray, 1927.

Esher, Reginald Viscount, *Journals and Letters.* Edited by Maurice V. Brett. 4 vols. Ivor Nicholson & Watson, 1934–8.

Falls, Cyril, *The Second World War.* Methuen, 1948.

Fastnedge, Ralph, *English Furniture Styles 1500–1830.* Penguin Books Ltd., 1955.

Fisher, H. A. L., *A History of Europe.* Vols. I and II. Eyre & Spottiswoode, 1935.

Flanner, Janet, *Paris Was Yesterday, 1925–1939.* Edited by Irving Drutman. Popular Library, 1972.

Flanner, Janet (Genet), *Paris Journal, 1965–1971.* Vol. Two. Harcourt Brace Jovanovich, 1971.

Flanner, Janet, *London Was Yesterday.* Edited by Irving Drutman. Michael Joseph, 1975.

Flanner, Janet, *Janet Flanner's World, Uncollected Writings 1932–1975.* Edited by Irving Drutman. Martin Secker & Warburg, 1980.

BIBLIOGRAPHY

Fleming, Peter, *Invasion 1940*. Hart-Davis, 1957.

Fletcher, I. H., *The British Court: Its Traditions and Ceremonial*. Cassell & Co. Ltd., 1953.

Forbes, Lady Angela Selina Bianca (St. Clair-Erskine), *Memories and Base Details*. Hutchinson & Co., 1921.

Forde-Johnston, J., *Castles & Fortifications of Britain & Ireland*. J. M. Dent & Sons Ltd., 1977.

Fortescue, J. W., *Narrative of the Visit to India, of Their Majesties King George V and Queen Mary*. Macmillan, 1912.

Frankland, Noble, *Prince Henry, Duke of Gloucester*. Weidenfeld and Nicolson, 1980.

Fraser, Antonia, *Royal Charles, Charles II and the Restoration*. Alfred A. Knopf, 1979.

Gascoigne, Christina, *Castles of Britain*. Thames and Hudson, 1975.

Gibbs-Smith, Charles H., *The Fashionable Lady in the 19th Century*. Her Majesty's Stationery Office, Victoria and Albert Museum, 1960.

Girouard, Mark, *Historical Houses of Britain*. Artus Publishing Company Ltd., 1979.

Gore, John, *King George V, a Personal Memoir*. Murray, 1941.

Gore, John, *Edwardian Scrapbook*. Evans Bros., 1951.

Gore, John, "Mary (Victoria Mary Augusta Louise Olga Pauline Claudine Agnes) (1867–1953)."

Greville, Frances Evelyn (Maynard), Countess of Warwick, *Life's Ebb and Flow*. Hutchinson & Co., 1929.

Greville, Frances Evelyn (Maynard), Countess of Warwick, *Afterthoughts*. Cassell & Co., 1931.

Halls, Zillah, *Women's Costume 1600–1750*. Her Majesty's Stationery Office, 1969.

Hardinge, Charles, *Old Diplomacy; the Reminiscences of Lord Hardinge of Penshurst*. J. Murray, 1947.

Hardinge, Lady Helen, of Penhurst, *The Path of Kings*. Blandford Press, 1952.

Hardinge, Lady Helen, *Loyal to Three Kings*. William Kimber, 1967.

Hare, Augustus, *The Story of My Life*. Vol. VI. November 1895.

Harriman, Margaret Case, "The King and the Girl from Baltimore." *The Aspirin Age 1919–1941*. Edited by Isabel Leighton. Simon and Schuster, 1963.

500

BIBLIOGRAPHY

Harrison, Michael, *Painful Details: Twelve Victorian Scandals*. M. Parrish, 1962.

Harrison, Michael, *Clarence: The Life of HRH The Duke of Clarence and Avondale, 1864–92*. W. H. Allen, 1972.

Hartnell, Norman, *Silver and Gold*. Odhams, 1958.

Hartnell, Norman, *Royal Courts of Fashion*. Cassell, 1971.

Hastings, Sir Patrick, *Famous and Infamous Cases*. Heinemann, 1950.

Heese, Fitz, *Hitler and the English*. Edited and translated by F. A. Voight. Allen Wingate, 1954.

Hibbert, Chrisopher, *The Court at Windsor, a Domestic History*. Longman, 1964.

Hibbert, Christopher, *Edward VII: A Portrait*. A. Lane, 1976.

Hibbert, Christopher, *The Court of St. James's, The Monarch at Work from Victoria to Elizabeth II*. Weidenfeld and Nicolson, 1979.

Hogart, A. M., *Kingship*. Oxford, 1927.

Holden, Anthony, *Charles Prince of Wales*. Weidenfeld and Nicolson, 1979.

Holden, Edith, *The Country Diary of an Edwardian Lady*. Webb & Bower Ltd., 1977.

Hood, Diana, *Working for the Windsors*. Allan Wingate, 1957.

Hyde, H. Montgomery, *Baldwin, the Unexpected Prime Minister*. Hart-Davis McGibbon, 1973.

Inglis, Brian St. John, *Abdication*. Hodder and Stoughton, 1965.

James, Robert Rhodes, *Lord Randolph Churchill*. Weidenfeld and Nicolson, 1959.

James, Robert Rhodes, *Rosebery, a Biography of Archibald Philip, Fifth Earl of Rosebery*. Weidenfeld and Nicolson, 1963.

Jenkins, Alan, *The Twenties*. Heinemann, 1974.

Jones, H. T., *Recollections of a Court Painter*.

Judd, Denis, *Edward VII: A Pictorial Biography*. Macdonald & Jane's, 1975.

Judd, Denis, *Eclipse of Kings*. Stein and Day, 1976.

Keith, A. B., *The King, the Constitution, the Empire and Foreign Affairs*. 1938.

Keith, A.B., *The British Cabinet System*. 1939.

Keith, A.B., *The Constitution of England from Victoria to George VI*. 1940.

Keppel, Sonia, *Edwardian Daughter*. H. Hamilton, 1958.

BIBLIOGRAPHY

Kroll, Maria, and Lindsey, Jason, *Europe's Royal Families.* Burke's Peerage Limited, 1979.

Lacey, Robert, *Majesty, Elizabeth II and the House of Windsor.* Hutchinson & Co., 1977.

Langtry, Lillie, *The Days That I Knew.* Futura Publications Limited, 1978.

Laski, Harold, "The King's Secretary." *Fortnight Review* July–December 1942.

Lawrence, T. E., *The Mint.* Doubleday & Company, Inc., 1935.

Legge, Edward, *King Edward, the Kaiser and the War.* G. Richards Ltd., 1917.

Legge, Edward, *King George and the Royal Family.* G. Richards Ltd., 1918.

Leslie, Anita, *Jennie: The Life of Lady Randolph Churchill.* Hutchinson, 1969.

Leslie, Anita, *Lady Randolph Churchill: The Story of Jennie Jerome.* Scribner, 1969.

Leslie, Sir Shane Bart, *The End of a Chapter.* Constable, 1916.

Leslie, Sir Shane Bart, *Men Were Different: Five Studies in Late Victorian Biography.* M. Joseph, 1937.

Leslie, Shane, *The Film of Memory.* Michael Joseph Ltd., 1938.

Lindbergh, Anne Morrow, *The Flower and the Nettle.* Harcourt Brace Jovanovich, Inc., 1976.

Liversidge, Douglas, *Prince Philip, First Gentleman of the Realm.* Arthur Barker Ltd., 1976.

Lloyd George, David, *War Memoirs.* 5 vols. Ivor Nicholson & Watson, 1936.

Longford, Elizabeth, Countess of, *The Royal House of Windsor.* Weidenfeld and Nicolson, 1974.

Longford, Elizabeth, Countess of, *Louisa Lady in Waiting.* Edited. Jonathan Cape Limited, 1979.

Lowndes, Marie Belloc, *Diaries and Letters.* Chatto and Windus, 1971.

Mackenzie, Compton, *The Windsor Tapestry.* Rich and Cowan, 1938.

Mackenzie, Sir Compton, *The Queen's House, a History of Buckingham Palace.* Hutchinson, 1953.

Macleod, Iain, *Neville Chamberlain.* Frederick Muller, 1961.

Macmillan, Harold, *Tides of Fortune.* Macmillan, 1969.

Macmillan, Harold, *Riding the Storm, 1956–1959.* Macmillan, 1971.

Macmillan, Harold, *Pointing the Way, 1959–1961.* Macmillan, 1972.

BIBLIOGRAPHY

Macmillan, Harold, *At the End of the Day, 1961–1963.* Macmillan, 1973.

Madol, Hans Roger, *The Private Life of Queen Alexandra as Viewed by Her Friends.* Hutchinson, 1940.

Magnus, Sir Philip Montefiore Bart, *Kitchener: Portrait of an Imperialist.* J. Murray, 1958.

Magnus, Sir Philip Montefiore Bart, *Gladstone: A Biography.* J. Murray, 1960.

Magnus, Sir Philip Montefiore Bart, *King Edward the Seventh.* J. Murray, 1964.

Mallet, Victor, *Life with Queen Victoria: Marie Mallet's Letters from Court, 1887–1901.* Edited. J. Murray, 1968.

Marie, Consort of Ferdinand I, King of Rumania, *The Story of My Life.* Cassell & Co., 1934.

Marie Louise, Princess, *My Memories of Six Reigns.* Evans Bros., 1956.

Marlborough, Laura, Duchess of, *Laughter from a Cloud.* Weidenfeld & Nicolson Limited, 1980.

Marlow, Joyce, *Kings and Queens of Britain.* Artus Publishing Company Limited, 1977.

Martin, Ralph G., *Jennie, The Life of Lady Randolph Churchill, The Romantic Years 1854–1895.* Prentice-Hall Signet paperback, 1969.

Martin, Ralph G., *Lady Randolph Churchill: A Biography.* Cassell, 1969–71.

Martin, Ralph G., *The Woman He Loved.* W. H. Allen, 1974.

Massie, Robert K. *Nicholas and Alexandra.* Victor Gollancz Ltd., 1968.

Michie, Allan A., *The Crown and the People.* 1952.

Middlemass, Keith and Barnes, John, *Stanley Baldwin.* Weidenfeld and Nicolson, 1969.

Moffat, Leading Seaman James, *King George Was My Shipmate.* Stanley Paul, 1940.

Morris, James, *Farewell the Trumpets.* Harcourt Brace Jovanovich, 1978.

Mountbatten, Earl, *Mountbatten, Eighty years in pictures.* Macmillan London Limited, 1979.

Mowat, Charles Lock, *Britain Between the Wars, 1918–1940.* 1955.

Nares, Gordon, *Royal Homes. Country Life,* 1953.

Nevill, Lady Dorothy Fanny (Walpole), *The Reminiscences of Lady Dorothy Nevill.* Edited by her son, Ralph Nevill. Edward Arnold, 1906.

Nevill, Lady Dorothy Fanny (Walpole), *Under Five Reigns.* Methuen, 1910.

BIBLIOGRAPHY

Nicholas II, Emperor of Russia, *The Letters of Tsar Nicholas II and Empress Maria: Being the Confidential Correspondence between Nicholas II, Last of the Tsars, and his Mother, Dowager Empress Maria Feodorovna.* Edited by Edward J. Bing. I. Nicholson & Watson Ltd., 1937.

Nichols, J. Beverly, *The Sweet and Twenties.* Weidenfeld and Nicolson, 1958.

Nicolson, Harold, *King George V, His Life and Reign.* Constable, 1952.

Nicolson, Harold, *Diaries and Letters, 1930–1939.* Edited by Nigel Nicolson. Collins, 1966.

Nicolson, Harold, *Diaries and Letters, 1945–1962.* Edited by Nigel Nicolson. Collins, 1968.

Nicolson, Nigel, *Portrait of a Marriage.* Weidenfeld and Nicolson, 1973.

Nicolson, Nigel, *Mary Curzon.* Harper & Row, 1977.

Nicolson, Nigel, *Great Houses of Britain.* David R. Godine, 1978.

Ormathwaite, Lord, GCVO, Master of Ceremonies to King Edward VII and King George V. Baron Arthur Henry John Walsh Ormathwaite, *When I Was at Court.* Hutchinson & Co., 1937.

Packe, Michael, *King Edward III.* Routledge & Kegan Paul, 1983.

Pakenham, Thomas, *The Boer War.* Random House, Inc., 1979.

Parker, Eileen, *Step Aside for Royalty.* Bachman & Turner Publications, 1982.

Pearson, John, *The Sitwells, A Family's Biography.* Harcourt Brace Jovanovich, 1978.

Pelling, Henry, *Winston Churchill.* Macmillan London Ltd., 1974.

Perkins, Jocelyn, *The Crowning of the Sovereign, of Great Britain and the dominions overseas; a handbook to the coronation.* Methuen, 1953.

Petrie, Sir Charles, *Monarchy in the Twentieth Century.* 1952.

Petrie, Sir Charles, *The Modern British Monarchy.* Eyre and Spottiswoode, 1961.

Pless, Princess of, *What I Left Unsaid.*

Plumb, J. H. and Wheldon, Huw, *Royal Heritage, The Treasures of the British Crown.* Harcourt Brace Jovanovich, 1977.

Ponsonby, Sir Frederick, *Recollections of Three Reigns.* Eyre and Spottiswoode, 1951.

Pope-Hennessy, James, *Queen Mary, 1867–1953.* G. Allen & Unwin, 1959.

Price, G. Ward, *Through South Africa with the Prince.* Gill Publishing Co.

Price, Harry, Petty Officer, *The Royal Tour, 1901.* Webb & Bower, 1980.

Priestley, J. B., *The Edwardians.* Heinemann, 1970.

BIBLIOGRAPHY

Priestley, Dr. H. E., *Book of the Year 1873*. Kenneth Mason, 1972.

Priestley, Dr. H. E., *Book of the Year 1874*. Kenneth Mason, 1973.

Pudney, John, *His Majesty King George VI*. Hutchinson, 1952.

Raleigh, Sir Walter and Jones, H. A., *The War in the Air*.

Regan, Simon, *Margaret, A Love Story*. Everest Books Limited, 1977.

Roosevelt, Eleanor, *This I Remember*. Harper, 1949.

Roosevelt, Theodore, *Cowboys and Kings, Three Great Letters*. Harvard University Press, 1938.

Rose, Kenneth, *Superior Person: A Portrait of Curzon and His Circle in Late Victorian England*. Weidenfeld and Nicolson, 1969.

Rothenstein, William, *Twenty-four Portraits*. George Allen & Unwin Ltd., 1920.

Rothschild, Mrs. James (Dorothy) de, *The Rothschilds at Waddesdon Manor*. The Vendome Press, 1979.

Rumbelow, D., *The Complete Jack the Ripper*. New York Graphic Society, 1975.

Saunders, G. Ivy, *Edward, Prince of Wales*. Nisbet, 1921.

Sewell, Lieut.-Col, *Personal Letters of King Edward VII, together with Extracts from the Correspondence of Queen Alexandra, the Duke of Albany and General Sir Arthur and Lady Paget*. Edited. Hutchinson & Co., 1931.

Shew, Betty Spencer, *Royal Wedding*. MacDonald & Co. Ltd., 1947.

Simon, Viscount, *The Crown and the Commonwealth*. 1953.

Sitwell, Osbert, *Queen Mary and Others*. Michael Joseph, 1974.

Smith, A. C. H., *Edward and Mrs. Simpson*. Weidenfeld & Nicolson, 1978.

Soames, Mary, *Clementine Churchill*. Cassell Ltd., 1979.

Somervell, D. C., *British Politics since 1900*. Oxford, 1953.

Spencer, J. A. and Cyril Asquith, *The Life of H. H. Asquith*.

St. Aubyn, Giles, *The Royal George, 1819–1904: The Life of HRH Prince George, Duke of Cambridge*. Constable, 1963.

St. Aubyn, Giles, *Edward VII Prince and King*. William Collins Sons and Co. Ltd., 1979.

Stamper, Charles William, *What I Know: Reminiscences of Five Years' Personal Attendance Upon His Late Majesty King Edward the Seventh*. Mills & Boon Ltd., 1913.

Steed, Henry Wickham, *Through Thirty Years, 1892–1914*. W. Heinemann Ltd., 1924.

BIBLIOGRAPHY

Stevenson, Frances, *Lloyd George: A Diary.* Edited by A. J. P. Taylor. Hutchinson, 1971.

Sullivan, Mark, *Our Times, 1900–1925.* Charles Scribner's Sons, 1936.

Sykes, Christopher, "The Uncrownable King." *Books and Bookmen* 21: 3 (December 1974) and 4 (January 1975).

Taylor, A. J. P., *English History, 1914–1945.* Penguin Books Ltd., 1970.

Thompson, George Malcolm, *The Life and Times of King George VI.* 1953.

Townsend, Peter, *The Last Emperor, Decline and Fall of the British Empire.* Weidenfeld and Nicolson, 1975.

Townsend, Peter, *Time and Change.* William Collins Sons & Co. Ltd., 1978.

Toynbee, Arnold, *Survey of International Affairs.* 6 vols. Oxford, 1938–1950.

Trevelyan, G. M., *Illustrated English Social History: 2.* Penguin Books Ltd., 1964.

Truman, Harry S. *Year of Decisions.* Doubleday, 1955.

Truman, Harry S., *Years of Trial and Hope.* Doubleday, 1956.

Tschumi, Gabriel, *Royal Chef: Recollections of a Life in Royal Households from Queen Victoria to Queen Mary.* W. Kimber, 1954.

Tuchman, Barbara W., *The Guns of August.* Macmillan Publishing Co., Inc., 1962.

Tuchman, Barbara (Wertheim), *The Proud Tower.* Macmillan, 1966.

Vanderbilt, Gloria and Furness, Lady Thelma, *Double Exposure.* Frederick Muller, 1959.

Victoria, Queen, *The Letters of Queen Victoria, a Selection from Her Majesty's Correspondence and Journal between the Years 1886 and 1878.* 3rd series, 3 vols. Published by authority of His Majesty the King. Edited by George Earle Buckle. J. Murray, 1930–32.

Victoria, Queen, *Further Letters of Queen Victoria, from the Archives of Brandenburg-Prussia.* Translated by Mrs. J. Pudney and Lord Sudley. Edited by Hector Bolitho. T. Butterworth, 1938.

Victoria, Queen, *Dearest Child: Letters between Queen Victoria and the Princess Royal, 1858–61.* Edited by Roger Fulford. Evans Bros., 1964.

Victoria, Queen, *Dearest Mama: Letters between Queen Victoria and the Crown Princess of Prussia.* Edited by Roger Fulford. Evans Bros., 1968.

Victoria, Queen, *Dear and Honoured Lady: The Correspondence between Queen Victoria and Alfred Tennyson.* Edited by Hope Dyson and Charles Tennyson. Macmillan, 1969.

506

Bibliography

Victoria, Queen, *Darling Child: Private Correspondence of Queen Victoria and the Crown Princess of Prussia, 1871–78.* Edited by Roger Fulford. Evans Bros., 1976.

von Bulow, Furst, Bernhard Heinrich Martin Karl, *Memoirs.* 4 vols. Putnam, 1931–32.

von Ribbentrop, Joachim, *The Ribbentrop Memoirs.* Translated by Oliver Watson. Weidenfeld and Nicolson, 1954.

Wakeford, Geoffrey, *Three Consort Queens.* Robert Hale & Company, 1971.

Waterson, Merlin, *The Servants' Hall.* Pantheon Books, 1980.

Weintraub, Stanley, *The London Yankees.* W. H. Allen, 1979.

Wheeler-Bennett, John W., *King George VI—His Life and Reign.* Macmillan & Co. Ltd., 1958.

Williams, Neville, *Chronology of the Modern World 1763–1965.* Barrie & Rockliff, 1966.

Wilson, Mary, et al., *The Queen.* Penguin Books Ltd., 1977.

Windsor, Duchess of, *The Heart Has Its Reasons.* Michael Joseph Ltd., 1956.

Windsor, HRH, the Duke of, *The Crown and the People, 1902–1953.* Cassell, 1953.

Windsor, HRH, the Duke of, *A Family Album.* Cassell & Company Ltd., 1960.

Windsor, HRH, the Duke of, *A King's Story, the Memoirs of H.R.H. the Duke of Windsor.* Cassell, 1951.

Wint, Guy, *The British in India.* 1947.

Woodward, *The Lady of Marlborough House.*

Young, Sheila, *The Queen's Jewellery.* Ebury Press, 1968.

Marie, Princess, zu Erbach-Schonberg, *Reminiscences.*

Architectural Design Magazine, "Britain in the Thirties."

Burke's Guide to the Royal Family. Burke's Peerage Limited, 1973.

The Crown Jewels and Coronation Ritual. Pitkin Pictorials Ltd., 1970.

Encyclopedia of World War II. The Hamlyn Publishing Group Limited, 1977.

Fabergé 1846–1920, foreword by Roy Strong. Debrett's Peerage Ltd., for the Victoria and Albert Museum, 1977.

Familiar Quotations. 12th ed. Little, Brown and Company, 1948.

507

Bibliography

Guide to the Exhibition of Queen Mary's Art Treasures. Her Majesty's Stationery Office.

The Illustrated London News, "Silver Jubillee Record Number, King George V and Queen Mary, 1910–1935." Illustrated London News and Sketch, Ltd., 1935.

The Illustrated London News, "Silver Jubilee Number," No. 511, Vol. 186. *Illustrated London News,* 4 May 1935.

The Illustrated London News, "Silver Jubilee Celebrations Number," No. 5012. Vol. 186. *Illustrated London News,* 11 May 1935.

The Illustrated London News, "Record of the Lying-in-State and Funeral of His Late Majesty King George V." No. 5050, Vol. 188, 1 February 1936. *Illustrated London News.*

The Illustrated London News, "Coronation 1953." Illustrated London News, 1953.

London Street Atlas and Index. Geographers' A–Z Map Company Ltd.

Page One, Major Events 1920–1982 as Presented in the New York Times. Arno Press, 1982.

A Pictorial and Descriptive Guide to London. Word, Lock & Co. Limited, 1901.

Queen Alexandra's Christmas Gift Book, "Photographs from my Camera." *The Daily Telegraph,* 1908.

Queen Mary's Doll's House. Pitkin Pictorials, 1978.

The St. James's Gazette, 14 January 1892.

Shakespeare, Seven Plays, The Songs, The Sonnets, Selections from the Other Plays. Penguin Books Ltd., 1956.

Stalin's Correspondence with Churchill, Attlee, Roosevelt and Truman, 1941–1945. Dutton, 1958.

The Fabulous Century. Vol. V (1940–1950), Vol. VI (1950–1960). Time-Life Books, 1969–1970.

Treasures of Britain. Edited by Drive Publications Limited. Drive Publications Limited, 1968.

House & Garden, "The Prince Regent." Vol. 155, No. 2, February 1983. Condé Nast Publications, Inc.

National Geographic, "Windsor Castle," "Queen Mary's Doll's House." Vol. 158, No. 5, November 1980.

INDEX